AMERICA'S LOST PLAYS

XIX
THE WHITE SLAVE
and Other Plays

XX
MAN AND WIFE
and Other Plays

The White Slave

& Other Plays

BY BARTLEY CAMPBELL

EDITED BY NAPIER WILT

INDIANA UNIVERSITY PRESS
BLOOMINGTON

Requests for authorization of the use of any of the plays
in this volume on the stage, on the screen, or for radio
or television broadcasting, or for any purpose of reproduction, should be addressed to Robert Campbell, in care
of the Actors' Fund of America, 1619 Broadway, New
York City.

ACKNOWLEDGMENTS

THROUGHOUT the preparation of this volume Mr. Robert Campbell, secretary of the Actors' Fund of America and the son of Bartley Campbell, has given me constant and invaluable aid. This formal recognition of his help is but a poor indication of the gratitude I owe him.

I wish to express my thanks to Mrs. Abbott Graves (Montie Aldrich) for answering vexing questions about her manuscript of *My Partner;* to George and Portia Kernodle for searching the Cleveland, Ohio, newspapers for reviews of Campbell's plays and for securing some London reviews of *My Partner;* to Mr. William Coder for giving me, from his unpublished *History of the Philadelphia Theatre, 1855-1878,* the dates of the Campbell performances in Philadelphia; to Miss Henriette Naeseth for information about the Deadwood, S.D., performances; to Mr. John Gerber and Mr. Merwin A. Meyers for searching the Pittsburgh and Boston newspapers respectively; and to Miss Catherine Sturtevant for valuable aid given throughout the editing of the volume. Gratitude is also due to Mr. George Freedley of the New York Public Library, to Miss Beatrice Winser of the Public Library of Newark, N.J., to Miss Irene Stewart of the Carnegie Library of Pittsburgh, to Mr. Richard G. Hensley of the Boston Public Library, and to Mr. Henry House of Springfield, Ill.

CONTENTS

BIOGRAPHICAL SKETCH

BARTLEY CAMPBELL was seen to be an extremely tall and slender, young-ish, light complexioned man, with curly auburn hair; the perfect double for Artemus Ward. Mr. Campbell has been, like him and Mark Twain, and Mr. Howells, a western journalist, and is evidently a genuine product of the soil, with all his Americanisms still flagrant upon him from the cut of his necktie to the cut of his boots." The man so described by the *Boston Evening Transcript* on December 6, 1879, the day after he had made a curtain speech at the opening of his play *Fairfax* at the Park Theatre, had suddenly, after years of comparative failure, become the most popular of American play-wrights. The recent and great success of *My Partner* at the Union Square Theatre, New York, and of *The Galley Slave* at the Chestnut Street Theatre, Philadelphia, had made the opening of *Fairfax* in Boston a highly important theatrical event.

Bartley Thomas Campbell,[1] the son of Bartley and Mary (Eckles) Campbell, both of whom had emigrated from Ireland in 1840, was born on August 12, 1843, in Allegheny City (now a part of Pittsburgh), Pa. His father was the proprietor of a brickyard, in which Bartley worked as a boy. Of his education one obituary notice said, "Bartley, they say, never went to school a year in his life. He never saw the inside of a grammar."[2] While this statement may be somewhat exaggerated, it is certain that he received little schooling except that given him at home by his much older brother Robert. At a very early age[3] Campbell began to work on the *Pittsburgh Post* and until 1868 was engaged mainly in various kinds of journalistic work in Pittsburgh. On the *Pittsburgh Leader,* which he helped to found in 1865, he became dramatic critic. According to the *New York Herald,*[4] he "was regarded as a faithful critic, so faithful in fact as to warrant the chastisement of an actor and endanger the publication of the paper with libel suits. It is

---

[1] For the facts of this biographical sketch not otherwise accounted for, the author is indebted to Mr. Robert Campbell. For other studies of Bartley Campbell, see A. H. Quinn's article in the *Dictionary of American Biography* and his book, *A History of the American Drama from the Civil War to the Present Day,* I, pp. 118-24 and II, pp. 272-3.

[2] *Pittsburgh Chronicle Telegraph,* August 1, 1888.

[3] Harrison Grey Fiske in *The New York Dramatic Mirror* of August 4, 1888, places this in 1858.

[4] July 31, 1888.

remembered that the entire staff of the *Leader* breathed easier when Mr. Campbell left the office and commenced to publish the *Mail*."

In Pittsburgh on March 26, 1868, Campbell married Miss Elizabeth Woodhouse. Throughout Campbell's career his wife was his constant companion and helper. She survived him many years. To Mr. and Mrs. Campbell were born three children: a girl who died in infancy, and two sons, Robert and John, both of whom have been connected with the American theater.

The *Pittsburgh Mail* which Campbell founded in 1868 was very short lived, and upon its failure he left Pittsburgh. After a short stay in Philadelphia, where he worked on the *Press* and where he was arrested because of something he wrote for that paper, he started for New Orleans, in which city his oldest brother was engaged in business. On the way there he stopped in Louisville, Ky., and for a short time was employed by Henry Watterson on the *Louisville Courier Journal*. In New Orleans Campbell founded the *Southern Monthly Magazine*. Although only two issues appeared, August and September 1869, Campbell wrote for it articles, poems, criticism, and one novel. After the failure of the magazine Campbell's brother secured for him the position of official reporter of the Louisiana legislature, a position he held until the spring of 1870 when he started back to Pittsburgh. On his way he stopped in Cincinnati, where he worked for a short time on the *Cincinnati Enquirer*. In Pittsburgh he founded another short-lived newspaper called simply *The Paper*.

Before Campbell began writing plays, he had achieved some little reputation not only as a reporter, dramatic critic, and magazine editor, but as a writer of "popular" tales and verse. From about 1860 to 1872 he wrote tales and sketches which were published, usually anonymously, in such popular magazines as *The Waverly Magazine, The Sunday Mercury, The New York Ledger,* and *Leslie's Weekly*. At least two novels, *Almost Lost*[5] and *Who Killed Her?*[6] were published under his own name. After Campbell began writing plays, he seldom mentioned these works, and when he did, it was with great contempt. But he was very proud of his verse, and continued to write it until the end of his career. Dramatic critics often referred with great respect to Campbell's poetry. This consisted of lyrics, sometimes used as songs in his plays, narrative poems, and all sorts of occasional poems. Campbell's most ambitious poetic effort was his drama *Clio*. It is unfortunate that the manuscript of this play has been lost. A few of Campbell's poems were published in magazines, but most of them appeared in newspapers. Among

[5] *Pittsburgh Leader,* 1868.
[6] *Southern Monthly Magazine,* 1869.

his better known poems were "Grant,"[7] "Victor Hugo,"[8] "The Legend of Eddystone,"[9] and "That Baby of Tuscaroo."[10] The last named, a dialect poem in the manner of Will Carleton's *Farm Ballads,* was frequently recited by Campbell at benefits and first nights, and had the honor of being included in at least one "elocution book."[11] Typical examples of Campbell's prose narratives, essays, dramatic criticism, and verse are to be found in the two issues of *The Southern Monthly Magazine.*

Campbell seems to have begun his career as a dramatist sometime early in 1871. In May of that year his first dramatic work, *America an Historical Allegory,* was published in Pittsburgh. *Peril* was copyrighted November 1, 1871, and *Through Fire* two days later. The latter was first performed at the Pittsburgh Opera House at the Christmas matinée, 1871, and the former at the Chestnut Street Theatre, Philadelphia, February 12, 1872. After the Philadelphia production of *Peril* he superintended a production of it at the Academy of Music in Chicago where it had but little success.

Of the next period in his life Campbell told a reporter: "After that I went east. 'What did I do?' I led a regular Bohemian life for a time, and had some strange experiences. I wrote stories, poems, edited cookbooks, made speeches for political aspirants with more money than brains. I recollect I was employed by a very poetical brewer to bolster up his business in verse. Parnassus and vats don't hitch. 'How was it I fell in with Hooley?' Well," said Bartley, "about a year after the Chicago production of *Peril* I heard Hooley had opened a comedy theater here. Padgett was associated in the management, and when Hooley signified a desire to secure a resident author, Padgett, who had seen *Peril,* recommended me. I was eager for the post, and put my salary at $25 a week and $10 a night for my plays. A bargain was struck. I recollect the day of my arrival distinctly. The city was decked in robes of ermine," Bartley poetically remarked. "Hooley and I went into a neighboring saloon, then called the Marble Pillar—the Sherman house wasn't built—and over Scotch, Hooley unbosomed himself. He began with the solemn statement that the whole thing was a failure and a fraud—meaning the new theater. He had been advised to start a comedy theater here by one of the leading newspaper proprietors. He had been running six weeks, and he [Hooley] had lost $1800. 'I know this,' he said, 'what they want is a nigger

---

[7] *New York Dramatic Mirror,* August 1, 1885.
[8] *New York Herald,* 1884.
[9] *XIX Century Magazine,* Charleston, S.C., January 1869.
[10] The first version has not been located.
[11] *One Hundred Choice Selections,* Vol. xi. Philadelphia [1875].

band. Unless comedy looms up in a couple of weeks, we've got to get right longside of 'em.' "[12]

The Hooley Theatre did finally prosper, and Campbell probably had much to do with bringing this about. From December 1872 until the end of the season of 1875-76, Campbell was connected with the theatrical activities of R. M. Hooley, both as "literary attaché" and general assistant. As "literary attaché" he revised old plays, and wrote *Fate, Risks, On the Rhine, The Virginian, Hearts,* and *Bulls and Bears.* Tradition also ascribes to him the motto of Hooley's Chicago theater, "The Parlor Home of Comedy." As general assistant he aided in the selection of the company,[13] which, incidentally, was one of the best in the West, helped direct it, and assisted in the staging of the plays. Campbell went with the Hooley Company to San Francisco in the summer of 1874 and there met Mark Twain, with whom he formed a lasting friendship. When, in September 1875, Hooley temporarily lost control of the Chicago theater, Campbell went with him to Hooley's Brooklyn theater where he aided the manager in his attempt to change it from a minstrel house to another "parlor home of comedy." Campbell produced there a number of the plays he had brought out for Hooley elsewhere, but evidently without success, for the theater soon returned to minstrelsy.

In addition to the work done for Hooley, between 1872 and 1875 Campbell wrote *Little Sunshine* for Ettie Henderson from whom he received $1600, *Gran Uale* for Con Murphy, *The Orphans* for R. M. Carroll, and *The New World* for W. H. Ellis. He also revised *Through Fire* for Frank Aiken, which piece Aiken copyrighted as *The Argonauts of '49* but played as *Bert; or, Ocean to Ocean.* In the autumn of 1876 Campbell went to London where he supervised a moderately successful production of *The Virginian.* Returning home early in 1876, he sold the rights of *A Heroine in Rags,* which he had written in London, to Effie Ellsler and directed its production in Cleveland and Philadelphia.

In the summer of 1876 Campbell organized a theatrical combination for the production of his own plays, and with it toured the country during the seasons of 1876-77 and 1877-78. The company at various times contained such popular actors and actresses as Harold Forsberg, J. W. Morris, W. H. Leake, Rosa Rand, Estelle Mortimer, and Josie Batchelder. The repertoire consisted of various old favorites and at least three new plays: *How Women Love, My Foolish Wife,* and *Clio.*

[12] *Chicago Tribune,* February 1, 1880.
[13] In 1874 the Hooley Company contained such famous actors and actresses as W. H. Crane, James O'Neill, ohn Dillon, J. W. Blaisdell, Kate Meek, Nate Salisbury, Louise Hawthorne, and Clara Maeder.

During these two seasons Campbell had little success, so little that he seriously considered abandoning the theater. As he later told an interviewer: "I struggled hard against fate—sometimes elated and sometimes depressed. I failed to get a New York opening, and my failure to do that so discouraged me that at the end of the last season I began to look at the footlights as a chimera. I had made up my mind to burn all of my plays, and return to journalism."[14] Campbell then told the reporter of the marvelous change in luck which came to him in the autumn of 1879. "I wrote *My Partner* in about four months. You know its success. Then I produced *The Galley Slave,* a drama written some time ago; *Fairfax* followed at the Park in Boston. It proved another hit. Mr. Longfellow has just written me a letter in which he says: 'I have rarely been so entertained, and I see in it the promise of an American dramatic literature.'"

The great period of Campbell's career which began in the autumn of 1879 continued through 1885. In addition to the three successful plays already mentioned, he wrote during this time *The White Slave, My Geraldine, Siberia, Separation,* and *Paquita.* Not only did he write these plays, but he directed the production of all of them. He also organized and directed a number of road companies—there were at least six in 1884—which produced his plays throughout the country. From 1879 to 1885 Bartley Campbell was not only the most popular American dramatist, but he was regarded by most critics as one of the best. At least two of his plays, *My Partner* and *The Galley Slave,* were popular successes in Germany, and almost all of his later pieces, as well as some of the earlier ones, were presented in England, Australia, and Canada. On April 30, 1885, Campbell took over the lease of the Fourteenth Street Theatre, New York, renamed it Bartley Campbell's Fourteenth Street Theatre, and produced in it *Paquita,* his last play. During this period of success Campbell's income was enormous. The investment of his money, to which he attended himself, further strained an already overburdened mind. By the end of 1885 his mental condition began to cause worry, and in November of 1886 he was committed to the State Hospital for the Insane in Middletown, New York. He remained there until his death on July 30, 1888.

A. M. Palmer and various other friends arranged and announced a funeral service in the Little Church Around the Corner, but because Campbell was a Roman Catholic, his family made other arrangements. The funeral was held in St. Paul's Cathedral, Pittsburgh, and the body was buried in the adjoining St. Mary's Cemetery.

[14] *Chicago Tribune,* February 1, 1880.

Shortly after Campbell's death "Nym Crinkle" (Andrew C. Wheeler) wrote of him: "He never quite reached the level of literary greatness, but he overshot the level of generous impulse—if impulse can have a level. It would be a perfectly truthful epitaph to put on his grave: 'Killed by his own sensibilities.' And if there is anything in this world painful to see, it is a man who is the victim of his own sensibilities. Bartley never wrote a play that the hard sense of the public did not have to correct some of his emotional effusiveness. He said to me once: 'If I could regulate my heart as I do my head, I'd have no trouble with plays. But I fall in love with my heroine; I want to redeem my villain; I want to forgive my erring children. I'd end everything in the traditional pot of grease, if I didn't watch myself continually.'

"The turn in Bartley's intellectual career was coincident with the development in him of the spiritualistic mania. When he first gave attention to this thing, he was quite rational about it. I have seen him at Charley Foster's sweating and plowing over the occultism of raps and pellets, but sensible and good humored. Long afterward I saw him when he was in daily communication with Aristophanes, and had Sappho herself behind his chair. I have a curious little wandering poem that Sappho herself wrote for him.

"In his best estate Bartley was apt to remind me of a literary Abe Lincoln. He had the same rough honesty; the same uncouth humor; the same rusticity and homeliness of method all in a smaller way. He was unschooled, untrained, undisciplined. He went into the fiercest of all arenas with an intellectual fight before him.

"When he got in up to his ears, he began to have new views of the enormous horizon, and he took to books with a new haste. This sudden demand made upon a brain that is no longer elastic is always dangerous. It killed John McCullough.

"One of our most eminent neurologists watched both these men, and predicted cerebral breakdown. No one knows about the stress of theatrical work who has not been through the ordeal.

"I confess that I read of Bartley's death with something like a feeling of satisfaction. It was freedom from the most dreadful of all imprisonments."
—*New York Dramatic Mirror*, August 4, 1888.

ALPHABETICAL LIST OF THE PLAYS OF BARTLEY CAMPBELL

In this list of plays, each entry is followed by a brief description or classification, the date of copyright, when such exists, the date of first performance, and a brief stage history of the play. Following this information excerpts from reviews of the plays are quoted.

Campbell was rather irregular in the matter of copyrighting his plays. Some were copyrighted before they were performed, some shortly after the first performance, some years later, and some not at all. In one case it is strongly suspected he entered for copyright a title for which no play ever existed. When a play was copyrighted, Campbell classified, or rather described, it in a word or two in the entry, and this description is used in the following list. When no such description by Campbell exists, the play is classified according to the terms most frequently used to advertise it.

The date given as that of the first performance is, of course, merely that of the first performance the editor has located. While in most cases it is reasonably, but by no means absolutely, certain that the date listed is actually that of the first performance, in a few cases it is also reasonably certain that the date given is not. No attempt has been made to list all of the casts and all of the performances of any play, but only such as indicate the spread, popularity, and life history of the play in this country and abroad.

A great many, possibly too many, excerpts are quoted from reviews of Campbell's plays. It is hoped, however, these reviews will show how Campbell's contemporaries regarded his plays. When possible, reviews of first performances are given, and these are followed by reviews of New York, Chicago, and foreign performances. A review outlining the plot has been included, whenever one was available, for each of the plays not published in this volume.

AMERICA. Grand historical allegory in three parts. Copyrighted by Samuel Barr, Pittsburgh, May 22, 1871. Published by Samuel Barr, Pittsburgh, 1871.

Although I find no record of any performance of this, Bartley Campbell's first dramatic work, it may have been presented by societies of amateurs on patriotic occasions. A list of properties and costumes indicates that it was written for presentation. *America* contains three parts: I. The Past, the Temple of Liberty; II. 1860; III. The Future, 1971. In the last part there is much talk about air travel—by balloon. Among the characters are Columbia, Peace, War, Progress, Art, Science, Agriculture, etc., also Pat and Jacob (representing immigrant types). Each state of the Union is represented by a "beautiful young lady." The dialogue is mainly in verse.

ARDENDALE. Irish character comedy.

Played in Chicago at Hooley's Theatre during the week of April 13, 1884, it was billed as a "romantic play by Bartley Campbell." The reviews stated (*Tribune,* April 14, 1884, and *Times,* April 14, 1884) that *Ardendale* was but a revision of *My Geraldine* (*q.v.*) with the part of Teddy Cregan enlarged for the star, W. J. Scanlan.

THE ARGONAUTS OF '49. *See* BERT.

BERT; OR, OCEAN TO OCEAN. Sensational play.

The play given under this title was copyrighted December 3, 1875, by Frank Aiken as *The Argonauts of '49; or, Ocean to Ocean,* a title which seemingly was never used when the play was produced. *Bert* was presented in St. Louis during the week of May 1, 1876, and its playbill stated that it was "expressly adapted for him [Frank Aiken] by Bartley Campbell from his great drama, *Through Fire.*" When Aiken gave it at Wood's Theatre in Chicago during the week of May 22, 1876, he chose to be mysterious about its origin; and not only did he suppress Campbell's name, but he intimated that the play was written by some Chicago politician. Oddly enough none of the reviewers recognized the play as a revision of *Through Fire* (*q.v.*). Cast at St. Louis, 1876:

BERT BRISTOW ⎫ WILD NAT ⎭	FRANK AIKEN
GRACE JOSSLYN	GENEVIEVE WARD
JENNIE	ANNIE EVERHAM
MRS. BRISTOW	MARY WREN
PATTY BABBINGTON	ELLA WREN
SAM BAGETT	J. B. EVERHAM
JARVIS JOSSLYN	C. C. JORDEN
ADAM JOSSLYN	DION DE MERBELL
GUS TIVIS	J. H. BROWN
COLONEL BABBINGTON	FRED KENT
LAHEMAN	L. REYNOLDS
TYLER	J. DAMON
M. P. No. 1006	C. ALEXANDER
TICKET AGENT	W. A. STOUT

BRAVE MAN. Comedy. Copyrighted by Bartley Campbell, October 7, 1882. I find no record of this play except the copyright entry. Mr. Robert Campbell thinks that no play of this name was written, but that the title occurred to his father as a good one for a play and hence was copyrighted.

BULLS AND BEARS. A comedy founded on Von Moser's *Ultimo*. Copyrighted by Bartley Campbell, November 15, 1883.

When this play, Campbell's only adaptation, was produced in San Francisco at Maguire's Opera House, June 7-July 3, 1875, the title *Ultimo* was used. When it was played in Chicago at the Academy of Music, September 13-19, 1875, the name had been changed to *Bulls and Bears*. The members of Hooley's company who played in *Ultimo* were: Mr. Crane, Mr. O'Neill, Mr. Jack, Mr. Kennedy, Mr. Buckley, Miss Mayhew, Miss Firmin, Miss Meslayer, Miss Baker, Miss Terry. The Chicago performance of *Bulls and Bears* was given by the "Marion Taylor Combination" in which were George McManus and W. J. Scanlan. Campbell himself directed *Bulls and Bears* at Hooley's Brooklyn Theatre, September 20-26, 1875, with a cast which included M. C. Daly and Minnie Doyle.

The Hooley troupe have found their strong piece in *Ultimo*. It is a kind of high-pressure comedy, full of action and the most absurd vicissitudes. Bartley Campbell has apparently imbibed the atmosphere of this city to some purpose, as his adaptation is full of local bits and phrases of the street. This comedy troupe have their best opportunity since coming to this city, and each member makes the most of his or her part.—*San Francisco Evening Bulletin*, June 8, 1875.

Ultimo—Daly's *Big Bonanza*, so-called—made a decided hit last evening. It is full of rollicking fun from the beginning to the close, and we advise some of the habitués of California Street, and some of the brand-new members of the Pacific Board on Sansome Street, to drop in and see the manner in which the mirror is held up to their nature. The Sir Mulberry Hawks and the Lord Verisophts of the pave and the Board room, may find here an answer to Burns' prayer,

> "O wad some Pow'r the giftie gie us,
> To see oursels as ithers see us,"

and while they laugh at the fun of the situation, learn a useful lesson or two that may stand them in good case.—*San Francisco Morning Call*, June 8, 1875.

CLIO. Romantic play in four acts. Copyrighted by Bartley Campbell, March 12, 1878.

First produced at Haverly's Theatre, Chicago, March 4, 1878, it ran until March 9. I have been unable to find the cast for this first production of *Clio*, and only a few of the actors were mentioned by name in the review.

Rosa Rand played the model; Amy Gordon, the "soubrette"; Josephine Craig, "the countess"; and the dancers were Mlle. Elise and Mlle. Gertie. "The Quaker City quartette," "a dozen beautiful coryphées," and "a group of finely formed females who represent statutes" were also mentioned. A week before the play opened an advertisement appeared in the Chicago newspapers calling for "25 children, 100 ballet girls, and 50 supers" for the production.

A much revised version of *Clio,* with music by G. Operti, was produced at Niblo's Garden, New York, August 17, 1885, and ran until September 12, with the following cast:

Lucia	ADELE BELGARDE
Didi	MARION ELMORE
Countess Ellice	MAY NEWMAN
Duchess de Montmaitre	MRS. CHARLES POOLE
Fabian	FRANK LOSEE
Pietro	T. H. BURNS
Paulo	HARRY RICH
Marquis Mattre	HAROLD FOSBURG
Prince Zellah	HARRY CARTER
King of France	EDGAR DAVENPORT
Phillapaux	JAY HUNT
Sancho	JAMES BECKWITH
Alsozage	F. W. STRONG
Spring	TOMMY RUSSELL
Dancer	MLLE. CORNALBA

A road company, containing most of the members of this cast, played *Clio* in Chicago at Hooley's, March 14-27, 1886, and at the Academy of Music during the week of March 1. In 1887 another road company, headed by Sybil Johnstone, gave *Clio* at the Academy of Music during the week of January 10 and at the People's during the week of February 14. *Clio* was presented at the Elephant and Castle Theatre, London, during the week of August 14, 1885.

To epitomize the story in a paragraph: A sculptor named Fabian picks up a little girl in the streets of Rome, whom he finds begging for a witless father, and gives them both a shelter. When the girl ripens into womanhood she serves him for a model of Clio, which he hopes to bring to the notice of the Medici, and secure lasting fame thereby. Unconsciously the sculptor and his model have conceived an attachment for each other, which is interrupted by the machinations of an adopted daughter of a French Duchess, then resident in Italy, who offers him a position in the Court of France, if he will go there. He refuses at first; but the wicked woman convinces him, through an accomplice, that his model is a wanton, and so he casts her off, and declares for France and fame.

In the next act Fabian has attained to his ambition. He has all the rewards of fame, but finds glory does not mean happiness. To add to his cup of bitterness, his model, who has been a sort of modern Penelope, appears at court as a woman of the world, scorning his work, and weaving her meshes around the King. Stung to frenzy he insults the court, and stigmatizes the King, and, but that the palace is almost immediately destroyed by an earthquake shock, would have worked his ruin. In the next act, his court experiences prove to have been only a dream, the guilty are brought to justice, the lovers united, and Clio proves to be the real countess instead of the wicked Ellice.—*Chicago Tribune, March* 3, 1878.

If Mr. Bartley Campbell had any clearly defined purpose in view when he sat down to build his new drama, *Clio,* it was probably that of bringing poetic language into practical use as an elevator of the modern spectacular drama. Being an experienced and intelligent playwright, as well as something of a poet, he saw with sorrow that the tendency of the great mass of playgoers was in the direction of a foolish fondness for the cheap displays, produced by the scenic artist, that are known as spectacular effects; for an exhibit of feminine legs with the aid of calcium lights; for dancers, for acrobats, and for pose plastiques. A laudable wish was created, undoubtedly, by the contemplation of these things, to evolve harmony out of the mass of apparently discordant elements—to insinuate poetry into it, just as well-disposed persons will shove a religious tract into your hand as you are going into a beer-hall. . . . Mr. Campbell's genius (for sonorous, glittering sentimentalisms) has found free vent, and it would not be surprising to find that he bases his hopes of success on the felicity of expression to be detected throughout the dialogue. . . . The literary excellence of the production hardly plays a figure in such a case. . . . The effort . . . was an honest one, but we think the author has not succeeded in accomplishing his purpose.—*Chicago Tribune,* March 10, 1878.

But *Clio* is positively the least meritorious thing which has emerged from this playwright's workshop. It has neither coherency nor dramatic interests. Plotless, soulless and devoid of dramatic reason and common sense, the singular jumble of detached ideas and improbable incidents reasonably excited mirth when they did not create interest.—*New York Dramatic Mirror,* August 22, 1885.

It is a jumble, but it is a success, and it is not a jumble of tricks, like the coarse comedy play of the day—*The Tin Soldier* and things of that sort—but a jumble of situations and ideas really dramatic. It is hard to say a good word for *Clio* as a whole, yet it deserves many good words for its parts. It is, like its author, striking and strong, but uneven.—*Chicago Tribune,* February 16, 1886.

FAIRFAX. Sensational drama in five acts.

This drama was written for Lester Wallack, but some trouble between him and the author led to Campbell's producing it in Boston, at the Park Theatre, December 8-20, 1879, with the following cast:

EDWIN FAIRFAX	JOSEPH E. WHITING
DR. GAYLORD	JOSEPH WHEELOCK
JAMES MARRIGOLD	W. F. OWEN
WEBSTER WINNE	W. J. FERGUSON
WILLIE WAGSTAFF	ALFRED SELWYN
UNCLE BEN	T. G. RIGGS
MOSES	W. CULLINGHAM
SHERIFF	FRED BOND
MRS. MARRIGOLD	AGNES BOOTH
DIANA DORSIE	SIDNEY COWELL
MRS. DORSIE	MRS. G. H. GILBERT
TIBBETTS	MARIE CHESTER
VIRGIE	LITTLE BELLE WHARTON

Fairfax played at the Park Theatre in New York from December 29, 1879, until January 31, 1880, and at McVicker's Theatre in Chicago May 3-8, 1880. In the New York performances Fred Robinson played Fairfax; Louis F. Barrett, James Marrigold; W. F. Owen, Uncle Ben; and Effie Barrett, Virgie; otherwise the cast was the same as in Boston. When *Fairfax* was taken on tour other changes were made, the main ones being in the rôles of Fairfax, Dr. Gaylord, and Tibbetts, played by Edwin Knowles, Joseph Whiting, and Nellie Whiting, respectively. With an entirely new cast, *Fairfax* was given in Chicago May 2-8, 1881. While this would seem to indicate some popularity for the play, I find records of few performances after this date, nor does Odell[15] record many New York performances after the first engagement.

His play *Fairfax* is not by any means so bad as might be expected from any previous acquaintance with the American drama. As a play of plot, mystery, and dénouement, *Fairfax,* it will be seen, is ingenious, but not of the finest or best possible structure; as a literary production, it has about the same qualified claim to admiration. It has some thrilling bits of naturalism in the dialogue—oftenest in places where the movement of incident is rapid.

The dialogue intended to represent great emotion, on the other hand, falls into the pathos of the *New York Weekly,* and the stilted rhetoric habitually employed by the heroes and heroines of the stories of the Waverly magazines. . . . It is clear

---

[15] George C. D. Odell, *Annals of the New York Stage.* New York, 1927-40. Vol. I-XII.

Mr. Campbell's American drama is a thing to be considered; an institution that promises much, either of weal or of woe, for American art.—*Boston Evening Transcript,* December 9, 1879.

[The] action [is] strongly suggestive of *Lady Audley's Secret* but with a wide difference. . . . The chief merit of the piece, it seems to us, lies in the ingenious way in which the author has worked together so many apparently borrowed bits of dramatic composition into a story of much interest.—*Boston Advertiser,* December 8, 1879.

There is little that is new in Mr. Campbell's plot, the story having been told, with slight variations, in countless novels and plays. . . . He invests the old-time tale with some freshness by clever handling of some of its details.—*New York Herald,* December 30, 1879.

The reader will sufficiently perceive that it is one of the many plays which, starting from a confused basis, strain after startling situations through the medium of illogical mechanism, and that the wish "to see how it will turn out" is the sole motive any spectator can have for following its course.

No attempt has been made to impress by the characters themselves, aside from what they suffer and ail. Mr. Bartley Campbell always means well. It is a splendid basis, this same sincerity of purpose, steadfast pluck and frank willingness to dash pell-mell into dramatic effort—on which to build up the structure of a mind that shall be ripe in the knowledge of the world, fresh in invention, and clear in its perception and strong in its exercise of the methods in which to use a fine and firm artistic faculty.—*New York Tribune,* December 30, 1879.

Fairfax is in many respects the best piece of work Mr. Campbell has thus far offered us. In it he has departed from the methods employed in his other most successful dramas—*The Galley Slave* and *My Partner*—and has produced a piece which possesses the intrinsic merits of brilliancy, strong dramatic interest and broad bold reaches of thought and poetic imagination. The author has given too much scope to this latter quality, and occasionally, by the introduction of an extravagant metaphor in a commonplace situation, an incongruous effect is the result. But this fault is perhaps pardonable, as the originality and beauty of many of the speeches show that the playwright possesses the unusual faculty of blending tints of graceful imagery with the deeper and more lurid hues of melodrama, without detracting from the effectiveness of either. The comedy element is especially praiseworthy. The dialogue contains a degree of finesse and sparkle that eclipses in this respect his previous efforts. There are numerous little subtleties and exquisite passages occurring frequently during the progress of the drama, that appeal to the appreciation of a refined and intelligent audience. . . . Bartley Campbell was right when he said the other day to a *Herald* man that *Fairfax* is the best work he has thus far produced.—*The New York Dramatic Mirror,* January 3, 1880.

Mr. Bartley Campbell's *Fairfax* at the Park Theatre, is a genuine success, though in some respects it is an absurd play. The scene is laid in what Mr. Campbell likes to call the "sunny South," and very sunny it is to judge by the view of the "Fairfax" estate displayed in the first act. This estate is one of those fine old properties once so common in Florida, where Southern gentlemen of ancient family used to be found living before the war, surrounded by their loving slaves and lapped in luxury. At the head of this establishment is Mr. Fairfax himself, a widower in the prime of life and in love with Miss Clarke, who is really Mrs. Marrigold. In the prologue Mrs. Marrigold has very properly refused to surrender to her drunken husband (who has reduced her and her dying child to extreme misery) a bank note given her for her child's benefit by the benevolent (though in manner cynical) Dr. Gaylord. In the struggle which ensues, her husband's pistol goes off and kills him. A tramp has witnessed the act and resolves to profit by it. Fairfax, of course, falls in love with Miss Clarke, who has come into his family as his child's governess, and wishes to marry her; but she is afraid to confess her deception and her past history, though why she is ashamed of it or remorseful about it is not so apparent as a clever dramatist like Mr. Campbell ought to have made it. The situation is made worse by the reappearance of the tramp, who, for purposes of his own, denounces her as a murderess. In the end, of course, true love is triumphant, the tramp meets his deserts, and all ends happily.— *Nation*, January 8, 1880.

Bartley Campbell has become the fashion, and everything he produces must, while his popularity lasts—and let us hope it last forever—be taken as at least worthy of consideration. . . . While *Fairfax* does not compare with *My Partner* in plot and character, it is better than *The Galley Slave*. However, charming comedy saved that play. . . . Many of the scenes are finely contrived and finely written. . . . It may be said Mr. Campbell has managed cleverly to reach his climaxes.—*Chicago Tribune*, May 4, 1880.

[*Fairfax*] won popular approval at once. It has not the bold outline of *My Partner* nor the sensational surprises of *The Galley Slave*, but it possesses the charm of a sustained interest throughout more thoroughly than either of those dramas.— *Chicago Times*, May 5, 1880.

FATE. Drama in five acts. Copyrighted by Charlotte Le Clerq, May 21, 1873.
Fate was written for Hooley's Theatre in Chicago and was presented there January 13-25 and March 31-April 12, 1873, with the following cast:

FRANK FARADAY	J. W. BLAISDELL
PAULDING	J. C. PADGETT
M. T. BLAIZE	JOHN DILLON
LOOMIS LUCKY	W. H. WOODFIELD
DR. LITTLEJOHN	C. H. WILSON

JOE PLUMMER	S. R. REED
POLICEMAN	W. KELLY
HELEN FARADAY	KATE MEEK
JUNO TEMPLE	MRS. WALLACE BRITTON
MISS DYCER	MRS. HOWARD ROGERS
SALLY TODDLE	EMMA CLINE

In May 1873 Campbell sold the play to Charlotte Le Clerq, a popular English actress who specialized in "emotional" rôles. Miss Le Clerq played *Fate* throughout the country during the seasons of 1873-74 and 1874-75, giving it in Chicago at the Academy of Music, October 27-30, 1873, and in New York at Wallack's, June 1-20, 1874. When Miss Le Clerq returned to England in 1876, she kept *Fate* in her repertoire and for a number of years presented it at the principal theaters in the provinces. It was chosen for a special benefit given for Miss Le Clerq at the Olympic in London on August 6, 1885. In September of 1879, Miss Agnes Herndon presented *Fate* in Brooklyn (Odell, XI, p. 202) and in January 1880 gave it in Peoria, Ill., under the title of *A True Woman*. During the week of August 20, 1888, *Fate* was revived at the Windsor Theatre, New York, by Rose Osborn and Russell Bassett, and by them taken on tour during the 1888-89 season. Other revivals of it occurred in Chicago, at the Hopkins Theatre in 1895 and 1898, and at the People's Theatre in 1901. A manuscript of a "revised version" of *Fate* is in the Morton Collection at the University of Chicago.

The moving springs of *Fate* are jealousy and an intriguing woman, and over the incidents growing out of the union of these the baneful doctrine of free love casts a phosphorescent glow. There is a husband, who has come into the possession of boundless wealth; a wife of devoted love; an adventuress who comes like an evil angel between the happy pair; and a half crazy person, husband to the adventuress, but kept out of the way until the dénouement, in order that her ambitious plans may not be thwarted. The subordinate parts are an old uncle of the hapless wife; a returned showman; a lady of free love tendencies and a few other characters of use as convenient padding. The action passes principally in Brooklyn, where the rich but unhappy couple reside. By her intrigues the adventuress brings about a separation between the husband and wife. He gives the divorced lady a rich portion and to the adventuress, for whom he professes nothing more than a simple Platonic regard, the cottage in which they live, and an exceedingly handsome douceur. After a lapse of several years he loses his property and returns to his old home. His divorced wife comes to the same place at the same time, desirous of purchasing the old homestead where so many happy hours had been spent. By a series of events, the guilty woman is exposed by the energies of her misused husband and a happy result is arrived at. The troubles are numerous but the issue out of them more than repays for their bitterness.—*Chicago Tribune,* January 4, 1873.

The piece has many pleasant qualities. The dialogue is sometimes inane and diluted to the thinness of tinfoil, but it sometimes sparkles with bright thoughts, and good, although not pregnant sayings.—*Chicago Tribune,* January 14, 1873.

The dialogue of the play is always lively, generally containing the truthfulness of real life, with occasional passages of the serio-dramatic sort.—*Chicago Times,* January 14, 1873.

It is, of course, one of that class of plays intended to bring out the virtues of a particular star, but still there can be no question that in both plot, dialogue and situation, it is much superior to the run of such plays. . . . The plot into which these several persons are drawn is artistically woven, and while Mr. Campbell has not done his work perfectly, he has written a piece which pleases the audience and draws down rounds of applause at each moment. There is much also that is comic without being burlesque.—*New York Herald,* June 2, 1874.

It is a play of slender merit—whether on the score of invention or that of intellectual treatment of character, emotion, and significance of thought—but it is commended by the domestic sentiment and by the interest of the domestic story.—*New York Tribune,* June 8, 1874.

FRIEND AND FOE. Irish comedy-drama in five acts. A revised version of *On the Rhine* (*q.v.*).

Campbell, pleased with the work W. J. Scanlan had done in *My Geraldine,* reworked his earlier *On the Rhine* (*q.v.*), adapting the part of Carrol Moore to Scanlan's special abilities. The first performance of *Friend and Foe,* of which I have any record, occurred at the Academy of Music in Chicago on September 25, 1882. Scanlan later played it at the Windsor Theatre in New York during the week of October 16, 1882, and he kept it in his repertoire during the seasons of 1883, 1884, and 1885. The cast in Chicago and in New York in 1882 was as follows:

CARROL MOORE	W. J. SCANLAN
QUINTIN LA FONT	R. C. WHITE
AMBROSE	C. B. HAWKINS
PIERRE FONTAINE	G. R. MC CANN
CAPTAIN ROLFMAN	P. SHELLY
BIRKMAN	A. L. MC CRANY
GOUNOD	A. I. SPELLMAN
MAHIEM	C. A. FOSTER

Andrea Fontaine	Florine Arnold
Annette	Annie Franklin
Madame Bullville	Sadie Radcliffe
Cecile	Blanche Whitney

Mr. William J. Scanlan is an Irish comedian who has graduated from the variety stage, and he is to Irish-dialect comedy what Joe Emmet is to the German. He was with the soubrette Minnie Palmer for a time and last season he traveled with Bartley Campbell's *My Geraldine* company. Mr. Campbell was impressed by his neat and genteel style, and he conceived the idea of writing for him a play in which the Irishman should be seen without the traditional red-coats and wicked landlords, so *Friend and Foe* was the result of his labors. It is a play in five acts, picturing an intelligent Irishman in France at the time of the Franco-Prussian war. He is in the family of a music-loving Frenchman, who loves him like a son, and the Irish hero falls in love with the daughter of his French benefactor. An unscrupulous French landowner desires the love of the girl and threatens to turn the family out of the house. Just at that time war is declared and the villain is conscripted. He offers 15,000 francs for a substitute, and, to save the family, the Irish hero accepts it and goes to the front. He is arrested by the Germans as a spy and sentenced to be shot, but his French sweetheart assists him to escape from prison, and finally all ends well with the prospective wedding of the two. The dialogue is very pretty, and in Mr. Campbell's best vein, appealing to the lower part of the house as well as the gallery. The situations are strong at the end of each act, and the play is received nightly with laughter and applause.

Mr. Scanlan as Carrol Moore is in his element. He is graceful and handsome, and introduces a number of original songs which are highly appreciated. The company supporting is a good one.—*Chicago Tribune*, September 27, 1882.

The piece played through the country, but this is the first performance in New York. It is "a great go on the bowery."—*New York Herald*, October 12, 1882.

Friend and Foe, a play that has met with instantaneous success out-of-town, with W. J. Scanlan in the star part, was seen at the Windsor Monday night. A large crowd of people filled the immense auditorium. . . .

The play is deserving of the success it has attained, for it furnishes a very delightful evening's amusement.—*New York Mirror*, October 21, 1882.

THE GALLEY SLAVE. Drama in five acts. Copyrighted by Bartley Campbell, September 4, 1880.

This play was produced at the Chestnut Street Theatre, Philadelphia, September 29, 1879, with the following cast (in part):

Francesca Remini	Emily Rigl
Cicely Blaine	Katherine Rogers
Sidney Norcott	James M. Hardie

PSYCHE	DORA GOLDTHWAITE
MRS. PHOEBE GAY	MRS. J. J. PRIOR
OLIPHANT	GEORGE H. GRIFFITH
FRANKLIN FITTS	CHARLES STANLEY
NICHETTE	ALICE MANSFIELD

Other members of the cast were Henry Lee, Frank B. Wilson, George Hoey, and Mr. Bartram.

The Galley Slave was first given in New York, December 1, 1879, at Haverly's Theatre with the following cast:

CICELY BLAINE	MAUDE GRANGER
PSYCHE	ESTELLE MORTIMER
SIDNEY NORCOTT	FRANK EVANS
NICHETTE	CHARLOTTE NEVILLE
CAROT	CHARLES WEBSTER
FRANKLIN FITTS	T. H. BURNS
BARON LE BOIS	J. J. SULLIVAN
FRANCESCA	SIGNORA MAJERONI
PHOEBE GAY	MRS. M. B. SNYDER
OLIVER OLIPHANT	C. A. MC MANUS
SENTINEL	MR. DENNY
PHILLIPPE	EUGENE ELBERTS
DOLORES, *a child*	LITTLE GEORGIE
WELLESLEY NAPIER	G. HENDERSON

It ran at Haverly's (New York) until January 3, 1880, and was then (January 5) moved to Niblo's Garden, where it was played by the original company until January 23, 1880. A second company continued the play at Niblo's until February 14. The first New York company presented *The Galley Slave* at Haverly's in Chicago, January 25-February 1 and March 25-28, 1880. The play had several years of great popularity in the major theaters, and in the minor theaters it retained its drawing power until the end of the century. The last production of which I have record was at the Thirty-First Street Theatre, Chicago, in 1903. *The Galley Slave* was first given in England at the Theatre Royal in Hull during the week of November 22, 1880. Following these performances, a company organized by Wilson Barrett toured the provincial theaters of the British Isles, playing it under the title of *No Escape; or, The Galley Slave*. It was never performed in London. In the British performances the principal rôles were distributed as follows: Sidney Norcott was played by T. Bolton, Cicely Blaine by Maud

Brennan, Francesca by Agnes Templeton, and Baron Le Bois by Dennis Coyne. *The Galley Slave* was translated into German by Dr. Carlotta under the title *Der Galeerensklaven*. Gettke's *Buhnen-Almanach* (1883, 1884) records the following performances: Berlin at the Wilhelm Theatre during the week of April 30, 1882, Hamburg during the week of April 22, 1883, and St. Gallen during the week of December 2, 1883. A motion picture version of *The Galley Slave,* in which Theda Bara was the star, was made about 1910.

The Galley Slave is a play whose merits are somewhat above the average of those with which Bartley Campbell favored us before he made his hit with *My Partner,* but has some of the bad as well as most of the good qualities of his work. The theme is well chosen; the story is interesting, the development of the plot is consecutive. . . . On the other hand, there is a tendency to give us sentimentality instead of sentiment; the dialogue is frequently sloppy and now and then positively indelicate, and the redundancy of passages explanatory of the most obvious situations is at times very tedious. Luckily these flaws are not so much a part of the texture of the play that they cannot be eradicated by a diligent and unsparing use of a blue pencil and a pair of scissors in competent hands. . . .

Mr. Campbell should begin by modifying the closing scene of the first act, in which a charge is made that were better suggested, and by cutting the coarse passage in the dialogue between the serving people in their courting scene.—*Philadelphia Times,* September 30, 1879.

Of Bartley Campbell's *The Galley Slave* we can say without hesitation that it is one of the best, if not the very best, of plays ever written by an American. . . . It would of course be possible to pick flaws in the work, but mere fault finding is not criticism and as the author has closely followed all the recognized laws of dramatic construction and has treated good materials with rare skillfulness, we see no reason why he should not be accorded in print all the praise which he last evening received from an immense throng of delighted auditors. True, he occasionally defies probability, now and then strains a point for stage effect, and not unfrequently permits the lines of his comedy scenes to sink into double entendres, but he never exceeds the bounds of possibility, never resorts to old-time claptrap, and never allows his humor to become actually vulgar. In a work of such merit the double entendres could well be spared, and should be expunged, but their presence, while demanding notice, cannot be regarded as offensive, for all are witty, none particularly obtrusive. The very worst that could be said of the drama would be that it has the poorest name that a good play was ever burdened with. . . . From the opening lines to the final consummation, *The Galley Slave* bears every evidence of being the work of an experienced dramatist and nothing could exceed the cleverness with which the pathos and humor are at once contrasted and intertwined. . . . Every character is clearly outlined and individually interesting, while the language, though never unnatural, often attains a high plane of rhetorical beauty. . . .—*Philadelphia Press,* September 30, 1879.

It contains materials that should make any play succeed, but the author has not used all of them to the best advantage. There is too much talk that amounts to nothing, and the opportunities to explain the misunderstanding upon which the whole plot hangs are so numerous that the audience can hardly help wondering that the dénoument escaped the second or third acts.—*New York Herald,* December 2, 1879.

Mr. Bartley Campbell has the happy faculty of enlisting and retaining the attention of everyone who is present at the beginning of dramatic stories.—*New York Tribune,* January 5, 1880.

After the first scenes. . . it was evident it was an unusually strong acting play. There is a genuine pathos in the play which is touching and at times powerful, and it was evident that the great audience which witnessed the initial performance was highly delighted with it.—*Chicago Times,* January 26, 1881.

The following quotation, attributed to the *Birmingham Gazette,* appeared on the Edinburgh playbill for May 30, 1881.

The play is one of the best combinations of comedy and drama that has been seen on the stage in years, the comedy element in the first two acts predominating almost to the exclusion of the other, while the drama, although strong and powerful, is distinctly of a modern school and bears very little resemblance, beyond containing powerful situations and somewhat sensational incidents, to the flesh-creeping monstrosities with which we used to be regaled some years ago. A thoroughly well written, interesting, and well constructed play.

GOVERNMENT BONDS. Domestic drama. Copyrighted by Bartley Campbell, September 4, 1880.

Cast at the Grand Theatre, Chicago, February 7-13, 1881:

LEOPOLD LANDERS	GEORGE KNIGHT
LENA	MRS. KNIGHT
FRED FENWICK	HARRY PIERSON
BOB BROWNING	WALTER BROWNSON
MARY BLAKE	N. WORRELL
ARCHIBALD COYNE	A. LINDSAY
BOARDING HOUSE KEEPER	MRS. D. B. VAN DEREN
MR. MODEL	FRANK DREW
SLY SANDFORD	W. H. COLLINS
STATES ATTORNEY, COLONEL MONTOOTH	ROBERT BOWER

Mr. Robert Campbell states that this play was written for the English comedian, John Toole, but that he never played in it. A news item in the *Pittsburgh Telegraph* of August 4, 1877, states, "Bartley Campbell's latest play, *A Government Bond,* was bought for $2,500. The owner is J. Williamson, the actor." Whether Williamson actually bought the play and, if he did, whether he played in it, I do not know. The only performances of it I have found were those at the Grand Theatre, Chicago, February 7-13, 1881, where George Knight played the lead. Inasmuch, however, as the Chicago reviews indicate that Knight was successful in the play, it seems unlikely these performances were the only ones he gave.

The story hinges upon the loss and ultimate discovery of 2000 dollars worth of government bonds. Leopold Lander, an ex-revolutionist of 1848, is the central figure. Lander is engaged in a bank. He, in a fit of absentmindedness, takes a roll of government bonds, the property of the bank, and stuffs them into the lining of a hat that happens to be too large for him. He cannot account for the loss of the bonds. He is arrested, tried, and sentenced, and just as they are removing him from the court, the bonds are discovered in the interior of the hat and everything ends happily. This, in brief, is the plot of the play, out of which naturally grow a number of incidents of more or less interest.—*Chicago Tribune,* February 8, 1881.

The play is short, concise and to the point. The whole secret of the play is disclosed in the first act, and the people look for nothing else than the ultimate discovery of the lost bonds in the lining of Leopold's hat.

Mr. Knight's representation of the Yankeefied Teuton is a most natural piece of acting. Leopold Lander is to be met with any day. He waits on us in stores; he jostles us in the street car; we see him on the street. . . . The character should be a favorite with him for a long time. . . . The various lights and shades of character in the hot-headed German were portrayed with great fidelity. The mental anguish which is caused by the struggle for his daughter and his sense of duty comes out with striking force, while the naturally ludicrous mistakes made, even during the struggle, make the picture only more complete.

The play abounds in catchy humor, the first act especially creating great merriment.—*Chicago Times,* February 8, 1881.

It is a crude piece of dramatic work in its present shape, but Mr. Campbell, we understand, contemplates making alterations which will materially improve it. . . . The out-of-place third act was stupid. Court room scenes usually are.—*Chicago Tribune,* February 13, 1881.

GRANA UAILE.   Irish drama in four acts.

Grana Uaile was given at the Academy of Music in Chicago from February 1 through the matinée of February 13, 1875, with the following cast:

Ryman O'Reilly	CON MURPHY
Conner Kennedy	HARRY MURDOCK
Mary Clare	RACHEL NOAH
Kitty Clare	MRS. FRED WILLIAMS
Ann Murray	HATTIE ROCHE
Dan Kelley	J. W. WALLACK
Mike Mullen	W. J. JOHNSON
Felix Clare	G. B. EVERHAM
Dandy Dunn	FLINT KENNICOTT
Mr. Duggan	J. L. HAY
Judge Glenn	J. B. BIRRELL
Jack Dowler	FRANK HEARTWELL
Mr. Burr	H. C. CURLEY
Priest	MR. CHAMBERLAIN
Guard	MR. WINTERS
Clerk	MR. CHAMBERLAIN
Mrs. O'Reilly	MRS. KEASES
Maggie Murphy	MISS FRANKIE EASTON

This play has usually been referred to as *Gran Uale,* but in the Chicago performances the name always appeared as *Grana Uaile.* The name refers to a celebrated Irish rebel heroine of the time of Queen Elizabeth, but the play's only connection with this person is that its heroine is imprisoned in the ruined tower of her castle. Actually, of course, the Irish name was used because of the popularity of Boucicault's romantic Irish dramas, *Arrah-na-Pogue, The Colleen Bawn,* and *The Shaughraun.* These plays, titles and all, were much imitated in the 1870's and '80's by American dramatists. Fred Marsden's *Kerry Gow* and *Shawn Rhue,* played by Joseph Murphy for many years, were among the most popular.

Although *Grana Uaile* was not a success, Con Murphy, who played its lead, evidently saw that it had some possibilities. In 1884 he copyrighted under his own name a piece called *The Ivy Leaf* in which he acted for many years. This play, as I discovered by a chance reading of a manuscript copy of it, followed exactly the outline of *Grana Uaile.* In answer to my queries about this, Mr. Robert Campbell wrote: "After *The Ivy Leaf* had been played for several years, M. C. Daly, a prominent actor, went to see *The Ivy Leaf* at Niblo's Garden, New York, and reported to Mr. A. M. Palmer, who was Trustee of Bartley Campbell's estate, in 1887, that *The Ivy Leaf* was nothing at all except Bartley Campbell's Irish play, *Grana*

Uaile. . . . A substantial financial settlement would indicate that the claim was well founded."

When Campbell went to Brooklyn with Hooley, he produced *Grana Uaile* at Hooley's Brooklyn Theatre, October 23-27, 1875, under the title of *O'Reilly's Risks.*

Both the *Chicago Tribune* and the *Chicago Times* attacked *Grana Uaile* rather savagely. The *Tribune* said it was nothing but a bad combination of *The Colleen Bawn* and *Arrah-na-Pogue* with bits of *The Shaughraun* thrown in for good measure. It noted the likeness of Mike Mullen to Danny Mann, of Conner Kennedy to Kyrl Daly, of Ryman O'Reilly to Shawn the Post and Myles-na-Coppaleen, and noticed how much the tower-climbing scene was like a scene in *The Shaughraun.* Of the language of the play, the *Tribune* wrote, "Mr. Campbell has discovered an Irish vocabulary which, if he continues to use it in future productions, will damn him to everlasting ridicule." The *Times* said, "Whoever accords to this rising young dramatist the credit of writing an original play on the strength of *Grana Uaile* will extend to him a poetic license at which even Boucicault would not cavil, and which would send Charles Reade mad."

The *Chicago Inter-Ocean,* however, liked the play and said of it, "in plot, construction, in nearly everything except dialogue, *Grana Uaile* is superior to most of Boucicault's Irish dramas."

The scene is laid on the northwest coast of Ireland; Conner Kennedy, the heir of Tullyrush, arrives home from France, where he has spent the last four years of his minority, his estate having meanwhile been managed by a land steward called Dan Kelley. Prior to Conner's going abroad, he has conceived a passion for Mary Clare, the niece of a pedantic pedagogue, who is likewise beloved by Kelley, and, the latter finding his suit spurned, casts about him for some means to outwit his rival. A certain unpleasant character named Ann Murray, who is the foster sister of the young magistrate and deeply in love with him, joins hands with Kelley and between them they hatch up a conspiracy to ruin the reputation of the interesting heroine. By means of a forgery Mary is brought to a lonely spot on the cliffs on the expectation of meeting Conner. She is however confronted by Kelley, who urges his suit with every art he is capable of wielding, but to all his appeals the girl turns a deaf ear. At this point Kelley, looking up, sees Conner, who has been sent there by Ann, standing on a ledge of rocks in the moonlight, and the sudden thought of destroying the girl's character comes to him. At once his pleadings give way to reproaches, and the declaration that he could never marry a girl who could under any circumstances sully her honor. Not understanding the import of words that are to her incomprehensible Mary attempts to force an explanation but is frustrated by Kelley bidding her a hasty adieu and rushing off. Then follows the meeting of the lovers. Conner, believing

Mary is guilty, addresses her in language excessively bitter, and, at length, covering her with reproaches, leaves her. Desperate now, the girl's first thought is suicide but she is saved by the return of Kelley who, finding all argument useless, makes a prisoner of her, taking her to an old ruin where he places her under the care of a villain named Mike Mullen. Conner repenting of his harshness, returns to the cliffs. Finding that she has disappeared leaving her shawl on the edge of the precipice, he comes to the conclusion that she has leaped in the sea, and breaks out into self-reproach and self-accusations which finally lead to his arrest for her murder. At the trial, Mullen, at the insistence of Kelley, swears he saw the squire throw Mary into the sea, and this leads to his conviction.

At this juncture Ryman O'Reilly, a ballad singer, one of that numerous class in Ireland, having faith in the innocence of the accused, finds Mary Clare's place of concealment, and with much strategy succeeds in saving the life of Conner, and reuniting the lovers. Indeed throughout the play, which is in five acts, Ryman is the good angel, turning up very opportunely on almost every occasion. —*Chicago Tribune,* February 14, 1875.

HEARTS. Domestic drama in four acts.

The only performances of this play that I have found occurred in Chicago at Hooley's Theatre, October 20-29, 1873, and in Deadwood, S.D., on September 8, 1879. The Deadwood performance suggests that the piece was played elsewhere on the road. Cast at Hooley's Theatre, Chicago, October 20-29, 1873:

GEORGE GARTNEY	J. W. BLAISDELL
PHIL KIRBY	J. J. SULLIVAN
GREGORY KIRK	C. B. BISHOP
PROFESSOR TWICKS	GEORGE GIDDENS
DR. THORNE	NATE SALSBURY
MARTIN	W. E. EYTINGE
CRAWFORD	HARRY LITTLE
PETER	GUS DUNBAR
AGNES GARTNEY	ELIZA O'CONNOR
FANNY LARRABEE	SIDNEY COWELL
AUNT LARRABEE	MRS. MADER
MADGE MAYBIRD	EMMA CLINE
LILY	ANNIE HAMILTON

The scene opens in a quiet little sea-side village in the vicinity of New York, where an old maid named Larrabee—of genealogical tendencies—lives in rural simplicity with her two nieces, Agnes Chester and Fanny Larrabee. It is Agnes' bridal eve, and Fernleigh is busy with preparations for the coming nuptials.

Among those who are to pay their respects is one Dr. Thorne, who goes with Agnes for a stroll in the garden. While they are absent George Gartney, the prospective bridegroom, arrives in company with a gay, volatile fellow named Phillip Kirby, who engages in a screed against matrimony, when Fanny's arrival puts an end to his badinage and peace of mind at the same time, for Phil falls over head and ears in love with her at first sight. Dr. Thorne, coming in with Agnes, sees Phillip who straightway conceives a dislike for the physician. The latter is deeply in love with Fanny, but being a bashful fellow had not the courage to face her raillery. After a clever scene between Gregory, an amateur detective, and Madge, a housemaid, Dr. Thorne seizes upon the opportunity of finding Agnes alone to inform her of his passion for her lovely cousin. While he is doing so, George enters, and overhearing his avowal, believes the passionate words intended for Agnes, whereupon he steps between Agnes and Thorne and the curtain descends upon a strong picture. Three years are supposed to have intervened between the first and second acts, during which Agnes has become the wife of Gartney and the mother of a little child. She has just returned for a few week's visit to Fernleigh where she again encounters Thorne and is again discovered by her husband tête-à-tête with him. The smouldering fires of jealousy are again fanned into a fresh flame and a scene takes place between husband and wife, which terminates by the wife's promising to forbid Thorne the house. George Gartney goes on an errand to the village. Dr. Thorne returns to seek the cooperation of Agnes in his suit with Fanny. Agnes frankly tells him of her husband's suspicions and he, seeing the trouble he has unwittingly caused, consents to withdraw. Ere doing so he kisses the hand of Agnes in token of friendship merely and as he does so George Gartney appears at the window bathed in the white moonlight. Agnes screams in terror and calls on her husband to come in. He refuses and rushes madly by. The scream arouses the household, who rush in demanding the cause of the outcry. Agnes laughs, says she was frightened at a ghost and sits down in a tremor of terror which is deftly concealed from those about. Jest, songs, and laughter fill up the next few minutes, when a servant, pallid with terror enters and announces the murder of Dr. Thorne. Of course Agnes believes her husband guilty and when he comes in, which he does almost immediately, she in a whisper charges him with the crime, and the curtain descends on a powerful situation. The third act is exceedingly dramatic, giving Agnes splendid opportunities for powerful acting. It is the night of the murder; Agnes attired in her robe-de-chambre, awaits her husband's coming. When at last he does arrive, a stormy scene ensues. Agnes demands his immediate flight to save himself from arrest, but he, protesting his innocence, at first declines to go, but finally consents. A parting scene, very tender and touching between husband, wife and child, follows and just as Gartney disappears Fanny enters. She, too, has suspected George, and moved by a tender memory of the dead doctor, declares her intention of having him immediately apprehended. The wife seizes her frantically and begs, entreats and threatens in vain, when at the

xxxiv ALPHABETICAL LIST OF THE PLAYS

supreme moment, Lily, the daughter of Agnes, rushes into the apartment. The mother catching her up exclaims, "For her sake!" The pleading innocent face of the child conquers and the curtain falls again on a strong situation. In the fourth and last act Agnes is insane, the result of a fever. And Fanny, who by this time has learned to love Phil Kirby, is nursing her tenderly back to reason. After some clever maneuvering on the part of George, the real murderer is discovered in a common tramp, and the dénouement, of course, is a happy one.—*Chicago Tribune,* October 21, 1873.

The *Chicago Tribune* on October 19, 1873, in giving an advance notice of *Hearts* said, "So far as can be judged by reading, this is the best effort of Bartley Campbell's prolific pen." In its review of the play on October 21, it was of the opinion that "Each of the four acts closes with a strong dramatic situation" and that "the leading characters are strongly drawn," but that "the foundation of the plot is the threadbare one of causeless jealousy and it reminds one strongly of the chief features in the groundwork of *Divorce.*"

The *Chicago Times* on October 21 reported the play had "vivacious dialogue" and "situations of real power," but there was a "lack of freshness to the material." It was also of the opinion there was "an access of breath, here and there, in the jokes."

A HEROINE IN RAGS. Drama in five acts. Copyrighted by Bartley Campbell, Cleveland, Ohio, April 4, 1877.

Produced "for the first time in any city" at the Euclid Avenue Opera House, Cleveland, Ohio, March 28, 1877, it ran until April 2. Miss Effie Ellsler, for whom the play was written, played Jeanette Brashear, with Mr. Whiting playing opposite her. Later Miss Ellsler presented *A Heroine in Rags* at the Arch Street Theatre, Philadelphia, May 7-19, 1877, and at Hooley's Theatre in Chicago, December 9-12, 1878. Neither Brown nor Odell record any New York performance. The play was revived in Chicago at the Academy of Music during the week of March 14, 1887, and during the week of January 1, 1893, at the Clark Street Theatre. Cast at Hooley's Theatre, Chicago, December 9-12, 1878:

JEANETTE BRASHEAR	EFFIE ELLSLER
JEAN LA CROSSE	FRANK WESTON
LOUISE CARMON	F. C. MOSLEY
MARTIN BRASHEAR	G. B. CURRAN
VICTOR PRADI	A. T. TRAVENER
M. MARTEL	R. C. HUDSON
M. CAZARAN	A. H. CANBY

Louis   JOHN OGDEN
Fidele La Crosse   ETTIE BAKER
Marrienne Martel   LISETTE LOWEIS

The first representation of Mr. Bartley Campbell's new play entitled a *Heroine in Rags* took place last evening at the Euclid Avenue Opera House. The audience was large, particularly in the upper part of the house. The story of the drama is of intense interest, and the drama is constructed with but very few faults. Indeed, the few blemishes to be found were evidently unperceived to the audience last evening, a fact which was evinced by the intense interest with which the performance was followed. The rich variety of incidents, the frequent thrilling situations, the close commingling of the fresh artlessness of nature with pathos and grief, the vivacious dialogue, frequently very Frenchy, invariably entertaining and often sparkling with wit, form an unfailing source of interest. The new play won an emphatic approval of the large audience last evening, and if an expression of opinion could have been taken, it would have been exceedingly agreeable to the author, the actors and the manager.—*Cleveland Leader,* March 29, 1877.

As a bit of curious information in connection with the production of Miss Effie Ellsler's new play, *A Heroine in Rags,* is the following account of the conception of its plot in the mind of its author. Having long since recognized Miss Ellsler's ability, the author of *Fate, Peril,* and *The Virginian* proposed writing her a play which would give her not only an opportunity to act but also to make use of her magnificent vocal power. "It was no easy matter," said Mr. Campbell, "to concoct a story in which Miss Ellsler could be piquant, playful, tender and tragic and withal, preserve an individuality throughout. For two years I racked my brain for the needed plot but nothing answering the want was forthcoming. Once I thought I had mastered the situation and, full of enthusiasm, sat down to write it out, but before the second act had been finished I realized that it was not what I wanted at all and so, in despair, I set the work aside. Six months ago, while walking along Fleet Street in the city of London, my eye fell upon a picture of a street singer in a shop window. The face was eloquent with feeling and the artist had wrought in the depths of the human eyes the shadow of a deep sorrow. My attention was at once arrested and I began at once to weave about her an imaginary story. The bustle and noise of Fleet Street is not conducive to mental exertion and I determined on reaching some quiet spot, where I could get a chance to think. Finding myself in the neighborhood of old St. Paul's, I entered. The afternoon service was just beginning and the choral service was being chanted, as I turned up the well worn stone stairs to the right, that led to the great dome. Fainter and fainter the strains of the sacred song came to my ear, until finally nothing but the hush of the huge pile and the warm rays of the sinking September sun filled the vaulted corridors; up, up, up, until the whispering gallery was reached and the worshipers among the monumental piles in the aisle below looked like black blotches in the stone flooring. Here, over two hundred feet from the ground, in that wonderful circle Christopher Wren has hung in the sky like a liberty cap on the head of London, the first faint outline of *A Heroine in Rags* was sketched on the back of an old envelope." That same night, at a table in the Savage Club, under the picture of an old Cleveland reporter—Artemus Ward—the story was completed and a Cleveland favorite became possessed of a material out of which her genius will create a character entirely new to our stage.—*Cleveland Plain Dealer,* March 27, 1877.

Being curious to know the opinion of Mr. Bartley Campbell on the interpretation of the character of "Jeanette" in the new play, *A Heroine in Rags,* a *Plain Dealer* reporter called on him at his rooms in the Weddell house yesterday afternoon. We will not tell how we found him; that is no one's business and it shall ever remain a secret. He was not robed in a soft merino gown, however, and his eye was not a frenzy roaming, and he—well, there was a skeleton lying before him on the table. At least he called it a skeleton and said he had been working hard, trying to get it to hang together.

"You see," he said, pushing the loose pile of papers from him, "the skeleton is the hardest thing to arrange. Once the skeleton is built, I have little trouble in hanging on the flesh."

Not exactly catching his meaning we asked him to leave the region of anatomy and invade that of fact, realizing, however, how hard a task we were setting before a man who had a newspaper training. Facts are ugly obstacles to the average editorial mind—they are puzzling and depressing.

"Well, I call my plots skeletons and the dialogue the flesh." We heaved a sigh of relief. "It is a coinage of my own but to me it is full of meaning and very appropriate. If the skeleton is imperfect no flesh tint can make the being fair. Therefore my plots are of the first importance. Once I have action perfected I feel the hardest part of my task has been attained. Remember, there is no one who has a keener appreciation of the value of good dialogue: only that I attach more importance to the fabric—the warp and woof, as it were—than to the conceits and pretty fancies that may be embroidered thereon."

He was talking now at the rate of one hundred and forty words to the minute and we felt the importance of putting a stop to him and coming to the object of our visit at once and so broke in with: "What do you think of *A Heroine in Rags.*"

His face lit up; his eye beamed. "I think it an excellent acting play!" he exclaimed: "in fact, very much better than anything I have hitherto done and since I have seen it played I am enthusiastic on the question of its merit."

"Then you think it well played?"

"Capitally! Indeed there are few companies outside of those organized for comedy who, on the whole, could give it a better illustration. Several of the parts are in excellent hands and—"

He was getting up steam again and distancing an excellent Eagle with a rapidity that filled us with alarm.

"But Miss Ellsler—what do you think of Effie's performance of 'Jeanette'?"
Again there was a glow in his eye and an air of triumph in his mien.

"I have seen all the good actresses that are now on the English speaking stage including Marie Wilton, of the Prince of Wales theatre, London, the Terry girls, of the Court and Haymarket as well as Mrs. John Wood, of the St. James, and, of course, all our American women, but there is not one among them who combines the excellencies Miss Ellsler displays in *A Heroine in Rags*."

"What are these?"

"Piquancy, playfulness, pathos and tenderness, backed up and supplemented by a voice of remarkable vocal expression and power of execution. Indeed I don't know of anyone else who can sing 'Arline' in Balfe's 'Bohemian Girl,' to the satisfaction of a critical audience, play 'Rosalind' and 'Juliet' splendidly and win the public's plaudits in 'Fanchon'—do you?"

He had now reached one hundred and fifty-eight words a minute, and we could only give our head a negative shake. "As for 'Jeanette,' her performance of the part is an inspiration, absolutely faultless. There is one chief charm about her comedy in the first and second acts, and that is not veneer of the actress, but rather the outflowing of the sunshine of the girl's inner consciousness, and her laugh has a bubbling, rippling music, altogether indescribable. It is in fact suggestive of the music of a mountain brook, only a good deal more so."

"You seem to think her first acts the best?" we mildly ventured.

"They would be if her pathos was not so genuine; but, as you can see by the tears on the cheeks of her audience, it goes right home to the heart."

"Then you think you have fitted her?"

"She has a fit in which there is a fortune for her. 'Jeanette' is 'Ophelia,' 'Fanchon' and 'Louise' in the *Two Orphans* all rolled into one, with an opportunity to sing which gives it a musical flavor."

"But," we said, "don't you think that she might—"

"No; I think not. She could not improve the part and any change could not fail to mar the symmetry of her" (one hundred and eighty-nine words a minute; we struggled manfully to catch every word) "performance in its entirety—the perfection of detail—general excellence—"

It was no use. We gave it up and escaped out into the open air and paused for breath.—*Cleveland Plain Dealer*, April 2, 1877.

Her [Miss Ellsler's] simulated madness in order to save her lover, entitles her to respect as a heroine, and affords an opportunity for some pretty performances of a character known in technical phrase as "the soubrette" kind. She has a hard task of breathing the breath of life into a play, the incidents in which would hardly interest anyone who does not intend to go and see it. Some of these incidents might strike one as being amusing, but the most amusing things are unfortunately those that are not intended to be so. The story is not very clearly told and when it is told one is compelled to admit there was not much to tell. Miss Ellsler plays the part of a pretty flower girl—who seems to have extraordinary privileges, such as breaking into courts of justice and singing songs—and she presents the character so prettily as to make us forgive and forget some of the surroundings of her situation. The play is copiously supplied with the usual amount of stock sentiments, such as are supposed to "bring down the house" and they did not fail to carry out their purpose last evening.—*Chicago Tribune,* December 10, 1878.

HOW WOMEN LOVE; OR, THE HEART OF THE SIERRAS. Sensational drama in five acts.

This play was produced at the Arch Street Theatre, Philadelphia, May 21-26, 1877; at the New Chicago Theatre, Chicago, October 15-27, 29-31, and November 16-17, 1877, by the "Bartley Campbell Company." On the programs for the Chicago performances of *How Women Love,* Campbell acknowledged "his indebtedness to Bret Harte's *Outcasts of Poker Flat* for a suggestion which he has embodied in the climax of the fifth act." A later version of this play was called *The Vigilantes* (*q.v.*).

A partial listing of the cast in Philadelphia in 1877:

CLAIRE LE MOYNE	GERALDINE MAY
REUBEN CRAIG	JOSEPH WHEELOCK
JOE COMSTOCK	W. H. LEAKE
BRADY	HAROLD FORSBERG

The cast for the performances in Chicago in 1877 was as follows:

CLAIRE LE MOYNE	ROSA RAND
MABEL MORGAN	ESTELLE MORTIMER
ROXY CRAIG	JOSIE BATCHELDER
MRS. LYON	LOUISA MORSE
LETITIA LAMB	LOUISA ALMEDA
REUBEN CRAIG	J. W. NORRIS
JOE COMSTOCK	W. H. LEAKE
GENERAL LYON	WILLIE MAURICE
BRADY	HAROLD FORSBERG
GEORGE SILSBY	L. R. WILLARD
SILAS CRAIG	H. C. STORY
JIM KENTON	W. F. WALLIS
MAJOR GREEN	N. B. HONEY
JOHN LATIMER	H. WILSON

It is a very poor affair, so poor as to be beneath serious criticism. It is surprising to us that Mr. Campbell should have put his name to so pitiful a production. Of plot or dramatic construction there is no vestige. Throughout the piece the characters wander on and off the stage at their own sweet will. They come like shadows, so depart, and nobody cares a straw for their movements. . . .

As for the incidents, they are fearfully and wonderfully compounded. It is as though the author, having surfeited himself with some of Bret Harte's latest effusions, say with *Gabriel Conroy,* had fallen asleep and been visited by a nightmare, and that upon awaking, he had written out his dream and had then divided it promiscuously into acts and scenes. As a general thing the acting was about on a par with the authorship.—*Philadelphia Inquirer,* May 22, 1877.

In the present effort the dramatist has not been so successful as in his former plays. . . . The dramatist has slighted, to a certain extent, his own ideas and has paid more attention to those of other authors. . . . It is also poorly constructed; the various situations and climaxes being worked up in a very clumsy manner, while the first two acts have nothing to do in reality with the piece, and are too tedious to sit through. Until the fourth act the play does not rise above mediocrity but in this act there is a splendidly effective piece of dramatic writing which calls forth the warmest praise. . . . The dialogue is rather wordy, but is remarkably well written—bright gems of thought every now and then sparkling forth and falling very pleasantly upon the ear. . . . Miss Geraldine May, the clever young actress, essayed the rôle of the heroine—a beautiful creation—and played it with girlish tenderness, rare grace, and an earnestness which was truly impressive.—*Philadelphia Evening Bulletin,* May 22, 1877.

There is much that is natural and forcible in theatrical effect, with occasional lapses into what will be generally condemned as weak and purposeless. As a whole the story is full of action, and the personages introduced clearly drawn, some of them being a real addition to the current stage characterization. Yet, in order to get at a climax the author permits himself to drop into certain wild vagaries and adopt in at least one incident some attenuated trick which would be worthy of a writer of the *New York Weekly Romance.*

The drama relates how Reuben Craig (Mr. Norris) loved Mabel Morgan (Estelle Mortimer), a pretty but thoughtless girl of fashion, who was incapable of any abiding love for anyone. They get married, and soon begin to appreciate that they have made a mistake. Meanwhile Claire Le Moyne (Rosa Rand), an orphan, and a pure-hearted, high-minded, self-sacrificing creature, has become secretly enamoured of Reuben, who fails to see it in that light, much to the distress of Claire. The latter at the same time has won the undying love of an honest miner, Joe Comstock (W. H. Leake), who is ready to make all sorts of sacrifices for her sake. A highly-effective scene occurs between these two in the second act, where Joe blurts out his long-pent-up passion for the girl, and she tells him that she cannot return his love. There are some bickerings between the married pair, and the insidious foe of domestic peace makes his appearance in the shape of one Silsby (L. R. Willard). Reuben goes off one day to escort Claire on some pious mission and Mabel listens to the insinuations of Silsby and elopes with him. The husband comes back and finds himself abandoned and disgraced. He goes to the dogs, and in the fourth act we find him in prison, condemned to death for having shot Silsby. Through the efforts of the brave Claire, however, he is saved, and eventually united to her, after the knowledge that the faithless Mabel is dead. Joe is sacrificed, of course, to the desires of the two selfish lovers, and a faint compensation is dealt out in marrying him off at the end to Roxy Craig (Josie Batchelder), one of your rough diamonds, who plays a conspicuous part in the early scenes of the play.

The weak point in the plot is the cause assigned for the elopement, which is not made very clear nor very strong. The same incident is better defined in the play of *East Lynne*. Here, one cannot help saying this is rather a thin excuse, since the simple incident on which the catastrophe hinges could be so easily explained to all parties interested. The prison scene may be historical, but it certainly looks like an exaggeration, almost a burlesque. . . .—*Chicago Tribune,* Oct. 16, 1877.

KIDNAPPED. *See* THE ORPHANS.

LITTLE SUNSHINE. "Soubrette drama."

This play, a dramatization of a novel which had appeared in the *New York Weekly,* was written expressly for Mrs. Ettie Henderson, who paid $1600 for it. Published (*Lacy,* vol. 110 or *French Acting Drama,* no. 1461) without the author's permission, it was, until the appearance of the present volume, the only one of Campbell's dramatic works available in print with the exception of the allegory *America.* The first performance of which I have found record was at the Bowery Theatre, New York, September 22-27, 1873. It was also given at Conway's Theatre, Brooklyn, during the week of January 5, 1874, and the same year at the Academy of Music, Chicago, during the week of April 6. In the published version of the play performances of it are recorded at Providence, R.I., on November 21, 1873, and at Columbus, Ohio, on April 13, 1874. The cast at the Bowery Theatre, New York, follows:

LILLY DAVIS, "LITTLE SUNSHINE"	ETTIE HENDERSON
COUNT GAROWSKI	J. P. WINTER
LORD MORTIMER	J. FERRIS
ERNEST HARTLEY	P. CONNELLY
MR. FLINT	J. MASON
LUKE DAVIS	CHARLES FOSTER
TONY	E. W. MARSTON

Mr. Moreland	J. Sambrook
Diggs	E. Howard
Imp	G. Semflar
Pinkey	J. Coates
Trillman	W. B. Murray
The Judge	George Hamilton
Sam Brown	Thomas Graham
Jenny	Polly Booth
Mrs. Flint	Mrs. P. Connelly
Mrs. Sutton	Nelly Meeker
Mrs. Moreland	Mrs. R. G. France
Ruth	Tilly Malvern
Miss Rice	Phoebe Malvern
Miss Finkle	E. Glenwood

The drama is far above the average sensational productions of the present day, and achieved a pronounced success. The story of the plot is told in excellent language; the incidents are effectively grouped; the tableaux which terminate the several acts are so skillfully arranged as to elicit liberal applause and to incite the spectators to demand their repetition.—*New York Clipper,* October 4, 1873.

It would appear almost as though Miss Ettie Henderson had appealed to Bartley Campbell and asked him for a play as one would go into a drug store and ask for a box of pills, and received an answer like this from the great writer of Society pieces: "Sorry I haven't any made up. What kind do you want? Oh, yes; I'll have it ready for you in a few minutes if you'll be kind enough to sit down." And the lady, not being in any particular hurry, sits down. "Nice day," says Mr. Campbell. "Very nice, indeed," remarks the lady. "Not so gloomy as usual," says Mr. Campbell, slicing a scene from "Caste" and four or five situations from other plays in pigeonholes round his dramatic pill-shop. . . . "Want something pretty strong, I suppose," puts in Bartley, with the manuscript of another ancient Society drama of the more peppery description. "Yes, just a trifle to move an audience," she replies, and the scissors run through three more papers. "I'd like a goodly part, of course, for the sympathizers," puts in the lady. "Certainly," says Campbell, with a pleasant smile; "I have a heavy stock of that on hand," and he scribbles down a few stock platitudes. "I won't keep you much longer," he adds, shaking up and piecing the scraps. "Here you are, *'Little Sunshine,'*" says he, labelling the mixture "By Bartley Campbell"—"thank you, yes; seeing it's you, I won't charge much for it. Good day. Call again. We've an excellent assortment here of dramatic literature, ready-made or made to order at a few moments' notice." . . . It is a mixture of claptrap sentiment, exaggerated incident, pointless dialogue, washy plot, and mediocre acting.—*Chicago Tribune,* April 8, 1874.

THE LOWER MILLION. In the account of Campbell's work which appeared in the *New York Herald,* July 31, 1888, mention was made of *Through Fire,* "which was repeated in Philadelphia under the name of *The Lower Million* just after the Pittsburgh riots, and was believed at that time to lean pretty heavily towards socialistic principles." Mr. Robert Campbell, in substantial agreement, says the piece was "a capital and labor play, dealing with the Pittsburgh riots in 1877." He, however, locates the production in Pittsburgh. Unfortunately, a careful search of the Pittsburgh and the Philadelphia newspapers for 1877 and 1878 fails to reveal any reference to *The Lower Million.*

MATRIMONY. American comedy. Copyrighted by Bartley Campbell, September 4, 1880.

This play, a "modernized" version of *Peril* (*q.v.*), was produced in New York at the Standard Theatre, December 6-19, 1880, with the following cast:

DICK SEABRIGHT	EDWIN F. THORNE
RALPH VANNOTTE	J. NEWTON GOTTHOLD
COLONEL PLAYFORD	CHARLES MC MANUS
M. LA TOUR	EDWIN F. KNOWLES
LITTLETON DYKE	WILLIAM M. MAURICE
ST. JOHN	CLARENCE GIBSON
LAURA VANNOTTE	LOUISE MULDENER
ALICE PLAYFORD	MRS. EDWIN F. THORNE
MADELAINE	EMILY BAKER
NORA	SARAH GOODRICH
MAUDE	LILLIAN B. CORNWAY
SOPHIA	CHARLOTTE NEVILLE
MRS. DORCAS DORAN	EMMA SKERRETT

These New York City performances are usually given as the first, but *Matrimony* had been produced a week earlier, November 29, 1880, at Haverly's Brooklyn Theatre by the "Bartley Campbell Matrimony Combination." And, as the program for this production reads, "First production in Brooklyn of Bartley Campbell's Highly Successful and Brilliantly Humorous Comedy," the play may well have been tried out elsewhere before coming to Brooklyn.

Miss Dickinson has tried this species of playwriting and failed. This has not deterred the undaunted Mr. Campbell from having his little fling at it, too. We hope he's satisfied that it can't be done—at least by him. The best use he can make of *Matrimony* is to sell it for gun-wadding or food for the Central Park goats. Mr. Campbell's success in turning out two such plays as *The Galley Slave* and *My Partner*—pieces which have justly won for him reputation as a rising American dramatist—should not lead him into the error of giving stage room to his earlier productions, which are crude, rough-edged, and wholly unfit for practical performance, and which require an apologetic note of explanation on the bills. They can only put down and destroy the good foundation he has made on which to build future works of credit. He is now at work on the concluding act of an Irish drama entitled Geraldine, which will be put on at the Standard as soon as it can be got ready, and which, it is said, will rival in merit his two best known plays. Let us hope he will be industrious in giving it speedy production.—*New York Dramatic Mirror*, December 11, 1880.

MY FOOLISH WIFE; OR, A NIGHT AT NIAGARA. Farcical comedy.

This play was presented at the Chestnut Street Theatre, Philadelphia, October 15-20, 1877, and at the New Chicago Theatre, Chicago, November 1-8, 1877. Although I have found records of no other performances, Campbell probably gave the play during his 1877-78 tour of the country with his "Bartley Campbell Combination." Partial cast at Philadelphia:

BRAWLER	MR. BRADSHAW
DIANA	MISS KATE NEWTON
FENIMORE FRIEND	MR. SHERIDAN

The cast at Chicago was "The Bartley Campbell Combination":

FENIMORE FRIEND	J. W. NORRIS
LIONEL LIVINGSTON	W. H. LEAKE
BURTON BRAWLER	WILLIE MAURICE
PARTON PARNELL	W. LOYDS
DIX	HAROLD FORSBERG
FELIX	H. C. STRONG
LETTY LIVINGSTON	ROSA RAND
MAUDE MARBLE	ESTELLE MORTIMER
DIANA DELMAY	JOSIE BATCHELDER
MRS. KENTON	MRS. MORSE
TABBY	LOUISA ALMEDA
SHOP GIRL	ANN BROWNING

[*My Foolish Wife*] is at the most an amusing trifle. Its construction has evidently been based upon the doubtful maxim that the end justifies the means. The author has said to himself "Go to; let us write something amusing; let us raise a laugh; honestly, if we can, dishonestly, if we must, but raise a laugh anyhow," and in the undertaking he has achieved a partial success. If he had only held fast to this original design the effect would have been far better, but reminiscences of the various melodramas he has perpetrated crowded upon him, and like Uncle Dick with the head of Charles the First, he could not keep them out. They crept into his "farcical comedy" and made of it a composite affair, neither óne thing nor the other. . . . The maudlin sentimentality, the forced situations, the pitiful attempts at pathos which the author thrust into the third act, they [the audience] could not away with, and after having once bidden fair to make a hit, the piece fell flat. *My Foolish Wife* has absolutely no plot. It is a bundle of incidents without connection or logical sequence. The "foolish wife" is a stage-struck woman and her eccentricity is the only motif the' play has. Dramatic interest—there is none, while the probabilities are flagrantly violated throughout. In a piece having no pretensions to art, all that might have been pardoned had its burlesque qualities made compensation, but they did not. Some of the dialogue was bright, though much of it was in the most questionable taste, and some of the situations were laughable, though none of them were brilliantly original. . . .—*Philadelphia Inquirer,* October 16, 1877.

[*My Foolish Wife*] is styled a farcical comedy, but is an almost unadulterated farce. The motive of the work seems to be that everybody shall be at cross purposes with everybody else, and this end is cleverly compassed by making the heroine a stage-struck young woman, who gives up most of her time to surreptitious rehearsals—surreptitious because her husband will not permit her to go upon the stage. Naturally these performances lead to endless confusion, continually being regarded by one or another of the characters as the deadliest earnest and fraught with the most horrible consequences. . . . Things are in a good deal of a whirl pretty much all the time; and this fact combined with the confusing effect of the rehearsals, tends to make the play—especially in the second act—rather incoherent. . . .

. . . It does not profess to have any aim higher than to raise a laugh, and this it most certainly accomplishes. To berate it for falling short of compliance with higher canons of dramatic art would be equivalent to hunting butterflies with a shotgun. The author really has shown a great deal of ingenuity in contriving comical situations, and in the majority of cases has shown a very considerable amount of originality. . . .—*Philadelphia Evening Bulletin,* October 16, 1877.

Pink Domino and *My Foolish Wife* may be classed together as extravaganzas of the rough and ready order which are enjoying their day upon the stage. They are situation plays which might be described as "four door" farces. The recipe for the construction of these pieces is a very simple one. Take a room with four doors leading into so many bedrooms, bring in two young married couples, the males bent on mischief, females suspicious, mix the couples and put them into the wrong rooms, then introduce a jocose old party, an innocent young man; get a hired girl in disguise and an eccentric old lady, tumble them all around the stage, overset the furniture, smash a kerosene lamp or so—and you have a play that will pass current. Mr. Campbell has introduced into his play a man whose principal business it is to get in a situation where he can be sat down upon, or pounded with dumbbells, or kicked in the stomach or smashed on the head. There is always someone coming in whose presence involves the necessity of this man concealing himself. Sometimes he gets under the seat of the parlor lounge, and immediately someone comes in and throws a heavy pair of dumbbells on him. Of course, he yells, and sticks his head out in view of the audience, but nobody on the stage notices him. Then he is put in a sandbag and suspended from the ceiling and two young men come in and thump him with their fists. These are specimen situations, and it must be said that while they do provoke laughter at the moment, they reflect small credit on the ingenuity of the author. . . . There are here and there some sprightly bits of dialogue, but it degenerates into senseless frivolity and, what is more objectionable, into something that borders very closely upon indecency.—*Chicago Tribune,* November 2, 1877.

MY GERALDINE. Copyrighted by Bartley Campbell, December 17, 1880.

My Geraldine was first produced at the Park Theatre in New York where it ran from December 21, 1880, to January 15, 1881, with the following cast:

GERALDINE	LOUISE MULDERER
MARY CARROLL	EMILY BAKER
MAURICE ARDEN	EDWIN F. THORNE
SQUIRE ARDEN	JOHN JACK
PHIL CARROLL	J. NEWTON GOTTHOLD
TEDDY CREGAN	W. J. SCANLAN
MIKE MCSHANE	FRANK LAWLOR
LARRY LORNE	W. W. MAURICE
TERRANCE CREGAN	C. A. MC MANUS
NORA BROPHY	MRS. EDWIN F. THORNE
MRS. BEBEE	MRS. EMMA SKERRETT
LITTLE GERALDINE	LITTLE ELKO

In Chicago the original company of *My Geraldine* played three engagements at Hooley's Theatre in 1881: January 31-February 13, April 25-May 1, and October 16-22. In 1882 during the week of April 10 the play was given at the Academy of Music with Emily Rigl playing Mary Carroll; in 1884, May 11-16, a revised version called *Ardendale* (*q.v.*), with the part of Teddy Cregan enlarged for the star, W. J. Scanlan, was given at the Standard Theatre. In 1887 Agnes Robertson played engagements of *My Geraldine* in Chicago at the Academy of Music, August 29; at the College, September 12; and at the Criterion, December 11. The "New York Company" with Marie Brainard and I. O'Hara presented the play in Chicago during the week of June 25, 1888, at the Waverly, and during the week of February 3, 1889, at the Baker Theatre.

The *New York Herald* thought the story "strong but somewhat familiar" and that it was "told too slowly through three acts, but moved rapidly and powerfully in the two acts which followed." The *New York Tribune* considered the play but another imitation of Boucicault and said, "It is called Irish because the scene is laid in Ireland and for no other reason."

The piece is unlike the bulk of Irish plays. Its motive is not the enmity of the Hibernian race for their British oppressors; it has no smugglers, red-coated soldiers, constabulary or conspirators. . . . On the contrary *My Geraldine* is purely domestic. In many respects Mr. Campbell's play is worthy of commendation; in many others it deserves severe criticism. The story is interesting though improbable; the language is less didactic than that to which this particular author has accustomed us. On the other hand the story is tedious and the story is spread out. The scene in the ruined abbey, in which Geraldine goes into hysterics over some imaginary rats, might very properly be curtailed. Many of the incidents are too lurid to coincide with the intense interest of the quiet portions of the play. These rugged faults may assume the guise of virtues to the gallery, but they form no bid to the favor of the downstairs people.—*New York Dramatic Mirror,* December 25, 1880.

Mr. Bartley Campbell's new Irish drama, *My Geraldine,* has now been played for some weeks at the Standard Theatre by a strong company, attracting large and appreciative audiences. The play has a skillfully constructed plot, and contains several very strong situations. It has been produced with new scenery, several of the sets being very handsome and elaborate, notably that of the ruined abbey by moonlight, in the fourth act, which is the subject of our illustration. Mr. Campbell is certainly among the most prolific and enterprising of American dramatists. Four companies are playing his *Galley Slave*—one in England, two in America, and still another in Germany.[16] *My Partner* is now being played in Australia; *Fairfax* has been running in San Francisco; *Van, the Virginian* is being played in the Southern States. The English and Australian press speak in the highest terms of Mr. Campbell's ability, one of them saying: "For the first time in the history of Australia an American play has delighted a refined and cultivated audience." The success that the subject of our sketch has achieved is chiefly due to his ability to develop strong situations, and to mingle with his story broad humor and powerful pathos.—*New York Graphic,* January 12, 1881.

The story hinges on a disputed marriage and the illegal possession of an estate. There is a villain of the very conventional land agent type, who has a drudge

[16] I find no record in Gettke's *Buhnen-Almanach* of any performance of *Der Galeerensklaven* before that of April 30, 1882. This reference is to be explained, I think, in the following fashion: The information given in this quotation was probably told to the *Graphic* reporter by Campbell himself, and Campbell had been consulted about a German translation of *The Galley Slave* and assumed performances of it were being given. It is, of course, possible that performances of it were given but not recorded in Gettke. This, however, does not seem likely.

in the shape of a species of converted Michael Feeney,—that is to say, he has the body of Michael, "the heart of a weak woman and the soul of a poet." The villain gets his just deserts at the end of the play and suffering Virtue, represented by Geraldine and her mother, is rewarded by gazing upon a scene of perfect happiness as the curtain descends.—*Chicago Tribune,* February 1, 1881.

The story is one of strong romantic interest, and, although there can be found throughout the same faults—though not so strongly marked here—which the critics have found in his other works, excepting *My Partner,* the public, we dare say, overlooks those technical blemishes, and only sympathizes with the sorrows of its principal characters, and finds mirth in its excellent comedy.—*Chicago Tribune,* February 6, 1881.

MY PARTNER. Original American play in four acts. Copyrighted by Bartley Campbell, September 4, 1880.

My Partner was presented at the Union Square Theatre, New York, September 16-October 18, 1879, with the following cast:

JOE SAUNDERS	LOUIS ALDRICH
NED SINGLETON	HENRY CRISP
WING LEE	CHARLES T. PARSLOE
MAJOR HENRY CLAY BRITT	FRANK MORDAUNT
MATHEW BRANDON	HARRY EDWARDS
JOSIAH SCRAGGS	J. W. HAGUE
SAM BOWLER	I. H. BURNETT
WELLINGTON WIDGERY	CHARLES WEBSTER
JIM JOHNSON	JOHN DAILY
MARY BRANDON	MAUDE GRANGER
GRACE BRANDON	MINNIE PALMER
MISS POSIE PENTLAND	ALICE GREY

After the New York engagement, when *My Partner* was taken on tour, some changes were made in the cast. The following changes appeared during the Chicago engagement of the company at Hooley's Theatre, February 9-22, 1880:

MATHEW BRANDON	A. D. BILLINGS
SAM BOWLER	WALTER LENNOX JR.
WELLINGTON WIDGERY	G. T. ULMAR
MARY BRANDON	DORA GOLDWAITE
GRACE BRANDON	LAURA THORPE
POSIE PENTLAND	JOSEPHINE LAURENS

The part of Joe Saunders was probably created for Aldrich, who, since the first performance in 1877 of Joaquin Miller's *The Danites,* had played the part of Charles Godfrey, "the parson," and who had also recently played in Campbell's *The Vigilantes* (*q.v.*). Shortly after the opening performance Campbell sold the rights of *My Partner* to Aldrich for the sum of ten dollars a performance—a fact Campbell bitterly regretted later. Aldrich then sold a small interest in the play to Parsloe, and from 1880 to 1884 Aldrich and Parsloe played in *My Partner* throughout the country. In 1884 the partnership was dissolved and Parsloe sold his interest back to Aldrich. After trying another play in which he failed, Aldrich returned to *My Partner,* playing in it until 1887 with various people in Parsloe's old part. After 1887 Aldrich leased the rights to other actors, and the play was frequently given until the end of the century. The last professional performance of which I have any record was at the People's Theatre in Chicago, May 8-14, 1904.

My Partner was performed at the Olympic Theatre, London, April 10-May 8, 1884; in the cast were George Ringold, Phil Beck, Howard Russell, Harry Curtain, Rosina Power, and Alma Murray. A German version was made by Dr. Carlotta with the title of *Mein Kumpan.* This was given at the Residenztheater in Berlin, September 15, 1883, and at Bomberg during the week of June 22, 1884.

A moving picture version of *My Partner* was made in 1909.

While *My Partner* has been less often performed than *The White Slave,* it has received much higher praise than any other of Campbell's plays and has always been regarded as his masterpiece. That suggestions for material used in *My Partner* came from the tales of Bret Harte and from the tales and plays of Joaquin Miller there can be no doubt, but, within its limits, the play remains an original and a good piece of dramatic writing.

It should be noted that many people found *My Partner* a distinctly immoral play. In it Campbell certainly violated one of the dearest principles of the contemporary "satisfactory" play—the principle which demanded death at the end of the play for any "lost" woman, regardless of how sympathetically she may have been treated earlier in the play. Mary Brandon is one of the very few heroines of the drama of the second half of the nineteenth century who "sinned" and later achieved a happy marriage. The following letter published in the *Lewiston* (Maine) *Journal* represents a not uncommon attitude towards the play.

Lewiston, Me., Oct. 2, 1880.

To the Editors of the Lewiston Journal:—

Hon. Wm. P. Frye, in his eloquent dedicatory address at Music Hall as reported in the *Journal,* said: "We have built this hall, and allow me to say that while we own it we pledge you it shall be pure. We shall devote it to pure art and pure drama if such a thing can be."

The play entitled *My Partner* is announced by elaborate pictures upon our bulletin boards to be produced in Music Hall, Oct. 6th. Have the gentlemen for whom Mr. Frye assumed to speak, transferred the hall to other hands? I find upon consulting my scrap book that in an article published in your paper last season, I quoted from the dramatic column of the *Boston Journal* as follows:

"The Boston Theatre is giving every night this week, a play entitled *My Partner.* The *Journal* says: 'Two miners love the same woman. She loves the least worthy of the two, who ruins her. The other avows his love and she confesses her unworthiness. The false lover is slain in a brawl. She returns to her father's house a mother. He demands an explanation. Her true lover opportunely appears and claims to be her husband. To satisfy all doubt, and to hide her shame, he marries her in the presence of her father.' "

Is this a sample of the pure drama the honorable proprietors of Music Hall have promised may occupy their hall?

It would be impertinent to assume that a single Christian will attend this performance; but I appeal to that other large class of our citizens, who possess self-respect and a love for decency, to see to it that plays of such infamous character shall be performed to empty seats. Is there a parent in our community so lost to shame as to encourage by his patronage, the presentation to our young people of such vile lessons in depravity? It is to be hoped not. If the theatre is to cease to be the hot-house of vice and wickedness, as its patrons fondly believe, they must see to it that shamelessness and crime shall not be the central features of the plays that are produced.

Yours Respectfully,

J. Benson Hamilton.

It is almost certain to be a popular success because it is full of local color—or rather of the color which is popularly supposed to be local—thanks to the imagination of Bret Harte and his school, and abounds in interesting situations, some of which are exceedingly dramatic. The piece can be greatly improved by the excisions of some of the sentimental passages, especially those which assert that Heaven looks with especial favor on the frailty of woman. It is one of the weaknesses of the border drama that very ordinary sinners are made to pose as saints and martyrs. The author would do well to restrict the use of the name of the Deity and to cut out the religious opinions of Miss Posie Pentland, which are mere claptrap, and likely to give offense to conscientious persons. It is not work of the highest order, but good of its kind.—*New York Evening Post,* September 17, 1879.

It is a very strong piece. The effort has been made to deal with elemental passions and real persons, and to paint a picture of tragedy and heroism upon the tumultuous background of a turbulent semi-civilization; and the object has been accomplished with startling force and unusual if not even skill.

It makes a very valuable addition to dramatic literature—and one strictly American.

It is a better piece of its class than has hitherto been produced in America.—*New York Tribune,* September 17, 1879.

Bartley Campbell has written several excellent plays—none better, however, than *My Partner.* . . . In the creation of his plot, and development of the story—keeping, as he does, the tide of interest always at the flood, in happily commingling rough humor and homely pathos—the author appears to have succeeded in giving us a purely American drama, based on incidents that are possible and presented by characters not extravagant.—*New York Herald,* September 17, 1879.

The play—*My Partner*—which he has produced is a more natural, a more logical and a more interesting drama of California life than *The Danites.* A good authority once said that Bartley Campbell displays more poetry in his writings than all other living dramatists combined. It is true. There are in *My Partner* lines of the tenderest and most unspeakable pathos, poetry as deep and full and genuine as the sounds wooed and wafted through a forest of pines, and as redolent of the atmosphere of California as the streams which love its valleys, or the snows which crown its heights. There is humor and sentiment, there is sense and sequence, there is chivalry and feeling, and there is poetry throughout. Everyone has imagined that the author or dramatist who has lived within the shadow of a California canyon is brought closer to nature in its grandeur and sublimity than is possible in any other place. It might seem as if nature had selected the forest garden of the Pacific as the last place where man would penetrate, hence the repository of her best gifts in profusion. Mr. Campbell has caught the spirit of this and framed a pretty domestic story in the pure gold of a rough mining habitation. There are no pistols, dirks or shotguns in *My Partner.* There is but one murder.—*New York Dramatic Mirror,* September 20, 1879.

In every respect *My Partner* may be justly said to be the greatest play ever written by Bartley Campbell, and it is a play which should, as it has, make him rank among our foremost dramatists.

It is a purely American play. Unlike some others laid in the Far West, it is less idyllic than realistic.—*Chicago Tribune,* February 10, 1880.

It is not an exaggeration to say that *My Partner* is Campbell's best play, and not only that but the best American drama by an American author ever written and put upon the stage. Its success of last Summer and Fall was a justly merited one, and signalized a marked spot in the history of our own drama. It is as far above *The Danites* in the scale of literary merit and dramatic construction as *The Danites* is below it. Dealing with a subject at once rude and yet with great possibilities of crude beauty, Campbell seized on the very kernel of the rich nut that laid within his grasp, cracked the hard shell that encompassed it, and exposed to view the hidden and dormant attributes of true genius. *My Partner* is a wonderful play. It touches the heart, it stimulates laughter, it arouses the better feelings in man's nature. The frailties, the sacrifices of the kind that makes the whole world kin are brought out with a faithfulness and a truthfulness as rare as it is admirable. About the character of the rough but tender-hearted Joe Saunders there hangs an interest most intense. The nobility of the man raises him above the humble station in which he is placed to a height that fills a sort of ideal niche in the mind of the observer. The play has been noticed at length already in *The Mirror,* and there is little or nothing new to add now in criticism of the play. All the beauties of its dialogue remain intact like diamonds undimmed by usage and wear and tear. *My Partner* is a dramatic work that benefits and betters everybody that sees it, and it is one of a class that should be oftener given to the stage.—*New York Dramatic Mirror,* April 17, 1880.

At the Union Square Mr. Bartley Campbell has made a hit with his new Californian play called *My Partner.* We trust, for the sake of the great future which we still believe lies before the Pacific slope, that there are no such people as Joe Saunders and Mary Brandon inhabiting it. In Major Henry Clay Britt, vulgar and offensive as he is, it is possible to trace some semblance of humanity; we are able, by remembering the lowest politicians in public life, to imagine the sort of man Mr. Campbell may have had in mind; Josiah Scraggs, the pitiless villain who hunts his best friend down behind a smiling mask of hypocrisy, we have met with in other plays, if not in real life; Mathew Brandon is not out of nature; and Ned, during his short life, behaves as we can without difficulty imagine a young man of his education and surroundings behaving. But Joe (Mr. Aldrich) and Mary (Miss Maude Granger) are characters which it required a powerful imagination or else much reading to invent. Were it not that the suggestion would seem to challenge Mr. Campbell's claim of originality, we should say that Joe belonged to a period considerably antedating the present, when it was the delight of novelists and dramatists to clothe virtue in the habiliments of extremely low life, and to attribute to coal-heavers in London or gold-diggers in California a delicacy of sentiment and elevation of spirit which would have done credit to a knight-errant. But Joe is all this, and something more. Mary Brandon is a part of a kind always unpleasant in any form, but particularly so in that in which Mr. Campbell has chosen to present it. The betrayal of a woman may be made use of in tragedy, because it is a peculiarly tragical thing; but a play turning first on betrayal and utter social ruin, and subsequently on rehabilitation through marriage with a sentimental miner, is neither tragical nor comic. We will not say that such a subject cannot be used in a play successfully, but that Mr. Bartley Campbell has not used it successfully. When we say successfully we refer to success in the eyes of the judicious, for there is no doubt that to the average audience *My Partner* seems just what a play ought to be.—*Nation,* October 16, 1879.

. . . This time we looked for salvation to England and America who had thus far shown little distinction in any extraordinary productivity. But the two plays exhibit very little originality. There are the same situations, the same characters, the same discourse which we all know from countless works, and which might well have been spared the trip across the Channel and the Atlantic.

The Residenztheater tried its hand at *Mein Kumpan (My Partner),* a character play in four acts by Bartley Campbell. Many successful performances in the United States are attached to the name of this author. Transatlantic papers assured us that in this author America had produced her playwright. He became known to us by a crass, sensational play, *Der Galeerensklaven (The Galley Slave),* which had delighted our audiences in the suburban theaters.

One need not consider the question whether we are faced by a new dramatic talent. Campbell is simply a man of crafty, theatrical tricks, and his capacity lies merely in being able to convert available poetic motives to fit the demands of the stage. External theatrical effects are his only concern; one finds in his plays neither emotions, dramatically developed passions arising from the depth of the soul, nor close observations of characters. Some sensational situation will create a contrast, in which people will be jerked mechanically to and fro; the author wants to excite our nervous system, he does not care to fill our soul with lasting impressions of the truths of life. This is not merely accidental and has a symbolical significance. The play begins with a coarse kick and ends with a view of the gallows. Here and there are, however, some calmer and more humorous moments, but the background consists of only gruesome and glaring motives: seduction, murder, and false suspicion. The action takes us to California, the land of gold diggers which has been described to us by Bret Harte's novels and sketches. Campbell has also busily studied the author of *Gabriel Conroy,* and has borrowed many characters from him, such as the drunkenly happy Major Britt, a direct descendant of Bret Harte's Colonel Starbottle.

Concerning the fable in *My Partner,* the love story and the inquiry connected with the crime run parallel in it. Two gold miners, Joe Saunders and Ned Singleton, have both fallen in love with the same girl who, in her weak moment, yielded to the latter and is now anxiously awaiting the moment which will make her his legal wife. When Joe hears this, he forces his "partners" to vow to marry her. This done, the two men divide their gold and separate. Now the inevitable frowning villain enters the scene. He tries to persuade Ned to consider himself free from his recent pledge and attempts to arouse his suspicions against the girl. The reader must remember that we are now in California where the vagabonding scoundrel is entitled to play the part of Providence. During the ensuing strife, Ned is fatally wounded, while the murderer, having filled his pockets with gold, calmly goes on his way, after craftily turning public suspicion on Joe who just returned.

While the jury withdraws to decide the sentence on the latter, the love story of the young girl continues. The unhappy creature is being overwhelmed with reproaches and curses by her father, so that Joe affirms his intention to marry the girl, in order to save her from complete misery. A marriage then, while the executioner waits outside for the bridegroom! It is too bad that this situation of a man marrying with his neck in the rope is neither a new one nor a good one. Of course, the author is only making fun. When the situation becomes desperate, the truth comes to light. The murderer had been so inane as to throw his bloody shirt cuff into some corner where it is found by some Chinaman. The whole play rests on this cuff, a play in which the whole relation of cause and effect is turned upside down. Whether the situations develop in this or the exactly opposite direction, this is merely decided by the stage effect, in the lowest sense of the word. The scenes sometimes are flung like firecrackers on the stage. In the dainty little Residenztheater where there exists such an intimate relation between audience and actors, such a smeared wall painting has a quaint effect indeed. One must forget much, if one is to be satisfied with that which is presented on the stage in the Blumenstrasse. One descends from an aristocratic well-furnished *bel etage* to a basement apartment.—Translated from *Die Gegenwart,* vol. 24, p. 206.

At the Olympic, on Thursday, the tenth, was produced, for the first time in England, a rough-and-ready, vigorous melodrama, called "My Partner," written by Mr. Bartley Campbell. The playbill states that "My Partner" is at present being "played with phenomenal success thruout the Australian Colonies, the United States, and Canada." Five-and-twenty years ago, in London, Mr. Bartley Campbell's "powerful emotional drama" would have been accounted one of a purely transpontine type; but now that the bridges have been made toll-free, the transpontine drama has crossed into Middlesex, and seems to be as welcome there as it formerly was in Surrey. . . . —*Illustrated London News,* vol. 84, p. 370.

There is a flavour of Bret Harte and his backwoods about this play of Mr. Bartley Campbell's, and in it there are many of the faults we found eight years ago in *The Virginians* [*sic*], of which the chief are crudeness of method, a sort of spluttering fashion of introducing characters who have little to do with the plot, and a rather rough and brusque fashion of treating moments of passion, coupled curiously enough with very tall talk. The eternal heathen Chinee with his "me washee-washee," and the electioneering stump orator, have been introduced to us by Mr. Edouin and Mr. Florence in other transatlantic plays, and Joaquin Miller gave us dramatic glimpses of mining life in *The Danites.* Still, there is distinct strength and very honest pathos in this play, and it is worth seeing, if only for the sake of the strong central scene. . . .—*Vanity Fair* (London), April 19, 1884.

My Partner, the play by Mr. Bartley Campbell, presented at the Olympic on Thursday, proves to be a fairly satisfactory specimen of the backwoods drama, with something of the rude force as well as most of the crude weaknesses characteristic of such productions. In spite of the fact that its prominent comic characters—a carpet-bagging politician and a heathen Chinee—rather miss fire with English playgoers, Mr. Campbell's play seems likely to gain a good deal more popularity than was achieved by his previous London production, *The Virginian,* at the St. James's in 1876. This it will accomplish mainly through the agency of an effective episode of life in a mining camp as it is delineated in the powerful sketches of Bret Harte. The love of two rough "partners" for the same girl, and the tragedy which brings their rivalry to an end, produce a deep impression, such as will remain long after the foolish and tedious dramatic accessories of the piece are forgotten. The best scene of *My Partner,* which occurs at the close of its second act, gains much from the well-contrived earnestness and sincerity of Mr. George Ringold's interpretation. . . .—*London Observer,* April 13, 1884.

. . . Like most American dramas hitherto introduced to London, it depends for its success to a large extent upon "local colour," a quality that is not likely to help "My Partner" very greatly, for the reason that at subsequent representations Mrs. Conover may deem it expedient to considerably curtail what last night retarded rather than aided the progress of a fairly interesting domestic story. . . . Eccentricities of dialogue and of manner that are doubtless fully understood on the other side of the Atlantic, and perhaps in Australia, are not so plain to metropolitan playgoers.—*London Morning Post,* April 11, 1884.

Local colour is provided by a Chinaman and by a rough "orating," whisky-drinking candidate for the State Legislature. The drama, properly so-called, is a good deal overlaid with tall talk and extraneous matter, much of which is wearisome and even meaningless, but there is one effective situation that will go far to ensure the popularity of the piece.—*London Times,* April 15, 1884.

[*My Partner* is] a play that may very well please the taste of its patrons. Indeed, with certain modifications, Mr. Bartley Campbell's *My Partner* would be quite sure to renew here "the phenomenal success" which is said to have attended its representation in America, Germany, and the Colonies, though in any case it would probably be found better fitted for the provinces than the metropolis. Its scene is laid in Siskiori [*sic*] County, California, a remote mining district, where one naturally expects to meet Bret Harte's typical heroes, including his famous heathen Chinee. What one does not expect is to be bored with an elaborate study of the professional politician of the West, a tiresome personage, who, doubtless in the most life-like manner, wearies his hearers with stump orations, which naturally have no bearing upon the action of the play. This gentleman, a Major Henry Clay Britt, we may dismiss at once, with the remark that, conscientiously though he is portrayed by Mr. Henry Courtaine (who has had over five hundred nights' practice with the part), his excision would, from the English point of view, greatly benefit the drama. . . . A curious incident in these two latter acts is the sheriff's permission to the prisoner during his trial to leave the court and see his friends— a visit during which he goes through an impromptu ceremony of marriage with

Mary, much, apparently, to the relief of that erring damsel's father, although the bridegroom is every moment expected to be condemned to death. For the most part *My Partner* is, it must be confessed, a crude piece of work, and its dialogue is often ridiculous when it is meant to be most impressive. But it is saved by its great situation, which honestly deserves the loud applause that it gains by sheer dramatic force and interest.—*London Illustrated Sporting and Dramatic News,* vol. 21, p. 126.

THE NEW WORLD. Comic opera in three acts. Copyrighted by H. W. Ellis, Cleveland, Ohio, August 21, 1873.

The Cleveland, Ohio, newspapers on September 2, 3, and 4, 1873, carried the announcement that "Sappho and her comic opera company" would present on September 6 at the Academy of Music Bartley Campbell's new comic opera, entitled *The New World*. The advertisement did not appear September 5, nor was the work given on September 6. Sappho and her company left Cleveland after the performance of the sixth, and whether or not *The New World* was ever presented by that organization, I do not know.

NO ESCAPE. *See* THE GALLEY SLAVE.

ON THE RHINE. Military comedy in four acts. Copyrighted by Bartley Campbell, June 17, 1875.

On the Rhine was announced as "in preparation" at Hooley's Theatre in Chicago in November 1874, but it was not produced there. The only performances of which I have any record are those given at Maguire's Opera House, San Francisco, May 31-June 5, 1875, by the company from Hooley's Chicago Theatre. The play was later revised and given as *Friend and Foe* (*q.v.*). The cast (in part) was as follows:

CARROLL MOORE	JAMES O'NEILL
ANDRIA FONTAIN	LOUISE HAWTHORNE
PERRIE FONTAIN	JOHN JACK
QUENTIN LA FOU	MR. HASTINGS
AMBROSE DE CROU	W. H. CRANE
SEXTON	MR. SEFTON

Hooley's Comedy Troupe will produce a new comedy called *On the Rhine*, the scene of which is located in Alsace during the first few months of the late Franco-Prussian war. Carroll Moore, an Irish exile, has fallen in love with Andria Fontain, the pretty daughter of a musical enthusiast named Perrie Fontain. The latter becomes involved and is indebted in a large amount to one Quentin La Fou, who, too, is smitten with the charms of his debtor's daughter, and desires to cancel the obligation by making her his wife. The young girl asks for time to consider the proposition, and consults with Carroll, who makes an avowal of his own love and is accepted. At this moment Quentin returns for his answer and gets a refusal, which closes the first act. In the next act, he institutes proceedings against Fontain and threatens foreclosure of a mortgage. Carroll now regrets his selfishness and recommends Andria to wed La Fou, in order that her father's home may be spared him. To her query, "And where will you go?" he replies, "Where bayonets reap glory; where the foes of France contend against her for the Rhine." Quentin is subsequently drawn as a conscript, and offers 1,500 francs for a substitute. The young exile accepts the money, places it in Perrie's hand, and, having thus saved the old man from ruin, leaves for the seat of war. Three months after, and the Prussians are in possession of the village, and have converted the home of the heroine into a hospital for the wounded. Here Carroll comes in disguise having penetrated the enemy's lines and obtained valuable papers belonging to the Prussian commander. He is hotly pursued, however, and fearful of capture, he places the papers in the hands of Andria, who sends Ambrose De Crou to Chalons with one, and gives the other to her father to hide. Before he can do so a guard enters, searches his person and finds the papers. The old man is about to be taken away, when Carroll rushes in, gives himself up, and is placed under arrest. He is tried, found guilty and condemned to die at the last stroke of the Angelus bell. Andria petitions the old sexton of St. Roque not to ring the Angelus, but in vain. Meanwhile La Fou, who buries his feelings against Carroll in his patriotism, arranges through the aid of Ambrose a surprise, and just as the young soldier is led out to die the town is attacked, Carroll rescued, and all ends happily. —*San Francisco Chronicle*, May 30, 1875.

A new comedy by Bartley Campbell, *On the Rhine*, was produced by the Hooley Company last evening, and received with decided approbation by a well-filled house. The plot of the play is a slight variation from a score of others of the same class, of recent origin, embodying several interesting if not thrilling situations; and but for the interpolation of a few positive vulgarities in the dialogue, and the annoyance of watching supers watching the progress of the play from the wings in full view of the audience, the entertainment was one of the best of the Hooley season. The transmogrification presented in *On the Rhine* is slightly relieved by the introduction of the incident of a popular poem entitled "Curfew Shall Not Ring Tonight," which is doubtless familiar to most readers.— *San Francisco Evening Bulletin*, June 1, 1875.

O'REILLY'S RISKS. *See* GRANA UAILE.

THE ORPHANS. Domestic drama by Bartley Campbell. Copyrighted by R. M. Carroll, July 1, 1874.

The only performances of Bartley Campbell's *The Orphans* I find record of occurred at the Park Theatre, Brooklyn, December 14-15, 1874, but the *New York Herald,* on December 16, 1874, in a brief notice of the play, said it had "made a success in the provinces." Odell[17] gives the following partial cast:

LANTY LANIGAN	R. M. CARROLL
ORREN MORGAN	MASTER EDDIE CARROLL
NELLIE MORGAN	MASTER DICK CARROLL
SLAVE OF THE HARP	"GENERAL" CARLO

Later during the same season, March 1-6, 1875, a play called *Kidnapped* "by Bartley Campbell" was given at Wood's Theatre, New York, by "R. M. Carroll and Sons." For this play Odell[18] gives the following cast:

LANTY LANIGAN	R. M. CARROLL
ORREN MORGAN	EDDIE CARROLL
NELLIE MORGAN	DICK CARROLL
CARLO	"THE GENERAL"
PAUL MASSETTE	T. L. CONNOR
CROSBIE ROWE	E. L. MORTIMER
ROBERT GRAY	H. CLIFTON
LUKE	R. J. LEWIS
MABEL MORGAN	MARION SACKETT
DORA MORGAN	FLORENCE STRATTON
LETTY	THERESA WOOD
MRS. PRIMLEY	MRS. D. B. VAN DEREN
BETTY	NELLIE SANFORD

Obviously, *The Orphans* and *Kidnapped* are the same play.

The *Dramatic Copyright Catalogue* contains no entry of a play called *Kidnapped* by Bartley Campbell, but it does contain, "*Kidnapped,* an original, sensational and emotional play in 4 acts . . . by E. L. Walton, copyrighted by E. L. Walton and R. M. Carroll, 1874, June 10." *The Orphans* by B. Campbell was also copyrighted by R. M. Carroll. Perhaps Campbell's *The Orphans* is merely Walton's *Kidnapped* revised for Carroll by Campbell. The return to the original title might well have been made because of the interest at that time in the Charley Ross kidnapping case.

[17] *Annals of the New York Stage,* IX, 626.
[18] *Ibid.* IX, 562

PAQUITA. Emotional drama in five acts.

First produced at Bartley Campbell's Fourteenth Street Theatre, New York, August 31, 1885, it ran until October 3, with the following cast:

HORTENSE	KATE FORSYTHE
PAQUITA	MARY MILLS
SEÑORA MARIA	IDA VERNON
LUCETTE	ELOISE WILLIS
SINARI	GERNVILLE
LA PETITE HORTENSE	BIJOU FERNANDES
DR. MANUEL DEL REY	FRED DE BELLVILLE
JOSE BOROSCO	H. M. PITT
DR. DELPONTE	C. P. FLOCKTON
STEPHANO	RUSSELL BASSETT
VICTOR	IVAN SHIRLEY
PHILLIPPE	JEROME STEVENS
PADRE	D. VANDEREN

Campbell's company played *Paquita* in Chicago in 1886 at the Criterion Theatre during the week of January 11 and at the People's Theatre during the week of February 8. A second company, headed by Frederick De Bellville, gave the play in San Francisco in 1886. A manuscript of *Paquita* is in the Morton collection at the University of Chicago.

The *New York Herald* was, in general, unsympathetic to *Paquita,* saying of it, "The play is in five acts. Four of them are weak; one of them strong." In Chicago the play was given at minor theaters and was not reviewed. But the *Chicago Tribune,* while commenting on *Clio,* which was playing at Hooley's at the same time, said *Paquita* was a definite failure.

There is much that is wild, fantastic, and absurd in this latest production of Mr. Campbell's restless brain, but there are some genuinely effective situations— his power of melodramatic effect has not weakened. The most distressing parts of the play are the solemn stretches of arid and parched humor. There is enough of action and incident, of strong words and telling points, to enlist the public attention and applause in a generous measure. The first act is biographical and therefore dull. It closes with the entry of the wolf into the sheepfold, the arrival of the gorgeous Mexican cavalier, Don Jose Borosco, with whom the unhappy heroine Hortense proceeds to fall in love. She sets about this self-imposed task with boundless energy and self-determination. In the second act, the husband refuses to take the life of the self-confessed repentant Mexican Don Giovanni, freely offered in expiation of his guilt. In the third act, the inevitable duel occurs in a park near Havana, all the characters having been transported to Cuba in the twinkling of an eye. Don Jose, the Mexican Lothario, falls before the avenging bullet of the brother of Hortense, while Paquita, a wild slip of a girl transplanted from the chaparral and sunk fathoms deep in love with Hortense's husband, takes a shot at Don Jose on her own account. He sinks under the weight of both bullets, but by a most brilliant and daring surgical operation he is saved in the next act by the husband whom he has wronged. In the next act, Hortense is effusively forgiven by her husband, and is dying with her child in her arms, while significant glances are exchanged by Paquita and the bereaved husband.—*New York Tribune,* September 1, 1885.

There is much that pleases and a good deal that produces the opposite result in Bartley Campbell's new romantic drama, *Paquita,* produced at the 14th Street Theatre on Monday night. The dramatist's best and poorest qualities are both illustrated in the progress of its five acts. But Campbell oftener than not wins his victories by appealing irresistibly to the public heart, and the public heart—it is generally admitted—often pulsates responsively to appeals which do not altogether commend themselves to the critical mind. . . . The second and fourth acts are replete with vigor. Nothing in any of Mr. Campbell's plays is better than the situations which precede the close of these acts. The dialogue is dramatic and to the point here, but there are other places where the action is retarded by verbosity, and some incongruous and inartistic comedy scenes are introduced, excision of which would vastly benefit the piece and quicken its action. The audience found much to applaud, and several times during the evening they were carried along to a high pitch of enthusiasm. In spite of its several weak passages, *Paquita* is, we believe, destined to win popular approval.—*New York Dramatic Mirror,* September 5, 1885.

PERIL. Comedy in three acts. Copyrighted by Bartley Campbell, November 1, 1871.

This, the first successful comedy of Bartley Campbell, was presented at the Chestnut Street Theatre, Philadelphia, February 12-23, 1872, as *Peril; or, Love at Long Branch,* with the following cast (in part):

DICK ROTHLEY	MR. P. THORNE
MRS. RALPH HAYDEN	MISS PHILLIS GLOVER
RALPH HAYDEN	MR. HART CONWAY
G. W. BAILEY	MR. HARRY JOSEPHS
MRS. TINSEL	MRS. LOUISA MORSE
PRICE	MR. WILKES

In Chicago *Peril* was first presented at the Academy of Music where it played April 24-27, with Phillis Glover from the Philadelphia cast playing Laura Hayden. After Campbell became "literary attaché" at Hooley's Theatre in Chicago, he directed performances of *Peril* there March 11-22, 24-29, 1873,

September 18-27, 1873, and November 20-21, 1874. The casts at Hooley's were:

	March 1873	September 1873	November 1874
LAURA HAYDEN	PHILLIS GLOVER	KATE MEEK	MRS. FRED WILLIAMS
ALICE PLAYFORD	SIDNEY COWELL	SIDNEY COWELL	MINNIE DOYLE
MRS. TINSEL	CLARA MAEDER	CLARA MAEDER	CLARA MAEDER
NAOMI PORTER	IDA MASON	MISS JACKSON	MISS BERSFORD
MARRAH LIVINGSTON	HATTIE ROCHE	MISS HILTON	MISS GALLAGHER
RALPH HAYDEN	J. W. MORRIS	J. J. SULLIVAN	H. S. MURDOCK
DICK ROTHLEY	J. W. BLAISDELL	J. W. BLAISDELL	JAMES O'NEILL
LORD HAGAR	J. C. PADGETT	NATE SALSBURY	NATE SALSBURY
COLONEL PLAYFORD	RUSSELL SOGGS	RUSSELL SOGGS	GEORGE RYER
G. W. BAILEY	JOHN DILLON	WM. BISHOP	WM. CRANE
PRICE	S. R. REED	S. R. REED	J. DUNBAR
CLOVER	WALTER KELLY	WALTER KELLY	WALTER KELLY
MR. PITTY PAT	HINDMAN BARNEY	MR. OTIS	WM. DADE

New York first saw *Peril* at the Union Square Theatre June 22-July 4, 1874, with McKie Rankin as Dick Rothley, Bevil Ryan as G. W. Bailey, Maude Granger as Laura Hayden, Ada Gilman as Alice Playford, and Mrs. Wilkins as Mrs. Tinsel. Campbell directed this production as he did one at Hooley's Brooklyn Theatre, October 4-13, 1875.

A somewhat shortened version of *Peril,* sometimes played as *Peril* and sometimes as *Flirtation* was popular on the road for many years. Later Campbell completely rewrote *Peril* giving it the name *Matrimony* (*q.v.*).

There is much evidence to the effect that Campbell was constantly re-writing *Peril*. When copyrighted, it was in three acts; when presented in Chicago it was in four; and at the Union Square it was in five. In the first performance was a long scene in the first act between Price and Clover, and this was later dropped. In the early performances Naomi Porter not only flirted with Ralph Hayden offstage, but had one scene with him. And Mr. Pitty Pat, "a society swell," appeared and disappeared from time to time. The Chicago newspapers reported in 1873 and in 1874 that Campbell was making many changes in the text. However, the various accounts of the plot of *Peril* show that the essentials of the story remained the same from the Philadelphia performances in 1872 to the versions used on the road after 1875.

[*Peril*] cannot be regarded as an exceedingly valuable contribution to American drama. It is the work of a playwright who has secured some tolerably fresh and good material, to which he has added a great deal that is very stale and threadbare and then has joined the parts together in a manner which betrays the presence of an inexperienced hand. An almost fatal mistake is made in the very first act, where the current of the plot is stopped when it has hardly obtained headway, to introduce two utterly insipid negroes who have little to do with the story. . . . Faults of construction and the fashion of compelling the characters to do the most desperately wicked and foolish things without any apparent motive, are conspicuous throughout the play. . . .

. . . Much of the dialogue is good; and some of it, notably the gossip of the tale-bearing women, is considerably better than the average. Several of the characters also are capital. Mrs. Tinsel, a professional scandal monger is about the best, as Mrs. Morse's performance of it was the most satisfactory personation of the evening. G. W. Bailey is also original and excellent, and the figure was presented in the happiest manner by Mr. Josephs whose capacity for low comedy is considerable. The other characters are not new nor are they especially interesting.—*Philadelphia Evening Bulletin,* February 13, 1872.

The idea upon which it is based is a good one, but the manner of development is scarcely equal thereto. There are many excellent points but as a whole it is deficient in strength and finish. The language especially is full of inequalities; at times quite felicitous and humorous, it often falls far below the situation. . . .

The first act is better written than some other portions, but the action is rather slow. A considerable improvement in the latter respect is noticeable in the second act which moves forward briskly and concludes with quite a strong situation. The third act shows a falling off but contains one highly amusing episode, a declaration of love from a pettifogging lawyer to a scheming widow, with an altogether unexpected termination. The fourth act gathers up the thread in a fairly satisfactory manner, and the whole winds up with a diverting "tag" in which each person on the stage points what appears to him or her the moral of the whole. . . . There is much humor running through the whole and some of the hits at modern foibles and abuses are very telling. . . .—*Philadelphia Inquirer,* February 13, 1872.

Peril is firmly established as one of the most attractive and popular of modern plays.—*Chicago Tribune,* April 28, 1872.

To construct a successful drama in an age when histrionics have descended from stilts to walk on the terra firma of nature and common sense requires a rare and peculiar combination of power and experience. By the term drama we mean such congeries of delineations and scenes as are co-ordinated with a vivid and harmonious picture of the genuine features of life. The diarrhea of trash and stupidity which a certain class of writers have discharged themselves of, to meet the requirements of hybrid strollers, the bastard fruit of the unholy embrace of negro minstrelsy and legitimate drama, we do not include under this head.

It is therefore a matter of some congratulation when we find a young dramatist, who has enough consciousness of power to devote himself seriously to this branch of literature, sufficiently true to the voice of his intellectual conscience to say *retro sattianas* to such selfish seductions and give his mind up to the writing of legitimate drama. . . . The play is in some respects weak and inconsequent. . . . It is given to but few men to display the ripe genius of Congreve, Sheridan, or Robertson in early years.

But it is only just to ascribe to Mr. Campbell's play a considerable merit as to character and plot. It would be gross flattery to say that his turn of dramatic kaleidoscope reveals an ensemble perfectly harmonious either in structure or coloring; but with all his crudeness we detect some fine sense of effect and situation. It is with much pleasure we feel ourselves justified in assigning to the dialogue a high degree of merit.

The dramatic student will find much in *Peril* which echoes other plays. In several of the characters and passages we were forcibly reminded of Olive Logan's *Surf.—Chicago Times*, April 25, 1872.

Peril is one of the very best of modern society plays—skillfully devised as to dramatic movement and incidents, unexceptionable in its moral tone; its sentiments healthy and unforced; the dialogue crisp and sparkling. . . . Besides it affords the opportunity for the fullest gratification of the popular taste for elaborate scenic appointments and rich costumes.—*Chicago Tribune*, March 12, 1873.

There is some good dialogue, and the situations are sufficiently inspiring to draw applause from the audience; but there is a want of motive, or rather a lack of dignity of motive in the working out of the plot which prevents any active exercise of sympathy.—*New York Graphic*, June 22, 1874.

THE RISING MAN. Farcical comedy in four acts. Copyrighted by Harrigan and Hart, July 26, 1876.

I find no record of the production of a play by this name by Harrigan and Hart, and if the play was given by them under another title, I have been unable to identify it.

RISKS. A comedy in five acts. Copyrighted by Bartley Campbell, May 21, 1873.

Risks, the second play Campbell wrote for the company of Hooley's Theatre in Chicago, was first performed by that organization May 5, 1873. It ran until May 17, and was given again on May 20 and 22. It was revived March 30, 31, April 1, 2, 1874. Cast at Hooley's Theatre, Chicago, 1873:

FRANK MAYBERRY	J. S. GASTON
DEXTER	WALTER KELLY
STANTON	MR. WAITE
PORT BOY	MR. SWISSHELM
BELLA NEWTON	ELIZA O'CONNOR
DOROTHY DORA	JOSIE BATCHELDER
KATIE CARTER	MOLLIE MAEDER
HESTER KENDALL	ALICE SHERWOOD
BERTHA NEWTON	CLARA MAEDER

AUNT MABEL VARNEY	HATTIE ROCHE
LITTLE HESTER VARNEY	DOLLIE HUNTER
PEMBERTON PEMBROKE	JOHN DILLON
PAUL VARNEY	J. W. BLAISDELL
FARMER DUGLYN	RUSSELL SOGGS
DICK PRIGG	J. W. NORRIS

In 1877 John T. Raymond secured the acting rights to *Risks,* and immediately rewrote the play, pushing the main plot into the background and bringing forward the part of P. Pemberton, the comic insurance agent, originally played by John Dillon. Raymond played his version of *Risks* at the Pittsburgh Opera House, September 20-22, 1877, and in Chicago at Hooley's, October 15-24, 1877, where the reviewers recognized the great changes made in the play and realized that Raymond was responsible for them. But when *Risks* was given in New York at the Park, January 14-February 2, 1878, the New York critics who had not seen the earlier version of the play noted that the star rôle had little, if any, relation to the plot, and quite naturally, though wrongly, blamed Campbell for this situation. When Raymond played *Risks* in Chicago he was supported by Harry Pearson, Laura Don, Cora Tanner, and Clara Stoneall; in New York, by W. J. Le Moyne, Minnie Palmer and Sidney Cowell. I find no record of performances of *Risks* after 1879.

The plot is quite Robertsonian in its simplicity. It hinges on the clandestine marriage of Paul Varney, an aristocratic young swell, to Bella Newton, a poor farmer's daughter. Paul is depending on the purse of Aunt Mabel, whom he fears to offend, lest she in a fit of pique, should disinherit him. His passion for Bella, whom he met while she was at boarding school, makes him forget both caste and prudence and a secret marriage is arranged. This takes place in the country where Varney and a number of "friends" are spending the summer. Paul starts for the city to break the news to his aunt and if possible to secure her forgiveness, but before doing so, he receives a letter from his little niece in which she signs herself his "little wife." This epistle he carelessly tears up for the purpose of lighting his cigar, and carelessly casts the unburned portion at his wife's feet. After he leaves, she sees the paper and reads, "I am dying to see you. Your little wife, Hester." Believing now that she has been deceived and that the marriage was made a secret one only for the purpose of ruining her, she resolves to leave home forever. Thereupon she writes a letter to her grandfather and blind mother telling them of her shame, and is about to quit the house, when the entrance of her grandfather forces her to seek refuge. The scene of the next act is in Washington Heights where Paul Varney is entertaining his friends at his aunt's villa. After a great deal of innocent love making, Bella enters, accompanied by an old friend, named Luke Lorring (whom she chanced to meet in the city), and in the grounds encounters Hester Kendall, who, by the way, has designs on Paul's heart, and who, on discovering Bella's secret, informs her that she is the author of the letter, and is Paul's wife. Almost frantic with grief and despair, Bella rushes off, and in a subsequent act, attempts self-destruction by leaping into the East River. From this she is rescued by Luke, and this closes the fourth act with a beautiful panoramic view of New York by twilight. Bella is induced to return to her home, and there meets Paul, who in turn believes she has deserted him for Luke. And then comes the stormy scene followed by an explanation and a happy finale. Through the warp and woof of all runs a vein of comedy supplied by Mr. Dillon, who, in the character of a life insurance agent, insists on taking a risk on everybody, while light and shade is given to the whole by the love affair between Mayberry and Katie Carter.—*Chicago Tribune,* May 4, 1873.

The play is too long, and various of its scenes belong to the drama of sensation rather than to society drama. On the whole *Risks* may be considered a successful play; it resounds with a healthy smack of the simplicity of nature which savors the whole work with the common emotions of mankind.—*Chicago Times,* May 4, 1873.

A full house greeted John T. Raymond at the Opera House last night to see Bartley Campbell's last and best play, *Risks*; or, *Insure Your Life. Risks* has been very well received in Chicago and was a decided hit in St. Louis, and it will prove no less here. . . .—*Pittsburgh Telegraph,* September 21, 1877.

The truth is, P. Pembroke in Raymond's hands, is as far as conceivable from the type of character imagined by the author. The author will be amazed as well as amused with the liberties taken by the actor. He has reduced all the serious elements in the play into merely subordinate episodes, and he injects himself and his comical extravaganzas into each of them in a manner that would appall even an insurance fiend. No audience will object to it. It may not be orthodox, it may not be this or the other, but it is funny.—*Chicago Tribune,* October 21, 1877.

The fun is quite natural. The pathos is not.—*New York Herald,* January 15, 1878.

In developing the comedy rôle, the author has sacrificed both sense and probability as concerning the personages.—*New York Graphic,* January 15, 1878.

The part and the actor are encumbered with a play that is either forced or trivial in situation or silly in language. The comedy does not spring out of its background. Parts of the dialogue are in the vapid and nauseous strain that used to sicken good taste in *Surf* and *Saratoga* and other feeble-minded "society plays" made current in the earlier days of the industrious but not judicious Mr. Daly. . . . He [Bartley Campbell] has been the occasion of a bright comic effort well framed. He might have made it more successful had he used more wit and delved deeper into human nature.—*New York Tribune,* January 15, 1878.

A ROMANCE OF THE ROCKIES.

At the time of Campbell's breakdown he was working on a play to which he had given this title. The scene was to have been Denver, Colo., during its boom days.

SEPARATION. Comedy drama in five acts.

After *Separation* had been rejected by several managers, it was produced with success by Shook and Collier at the Union Square Theatre, January 26-April 5, 1884. After closing at the Union Square, the company played for a week at Haverly's Brooklyn Theatre, and then made a short tour of some eastern cities. A reorganized company presented *Separation* on the Union Square Company's tour of the West during the summer of 1884. During the season of 1884-85 a combination headed by Nelson Wheatcroft, John Dillon and Ellie Wilton presented *Separation* in the East. The Union Square Company cast of *Separation* at the Union Square Theatre, January 28-April 5, 1884, and the cast of the same company on its Western tour during the summer of 1884 follows:

	New York	*Western Tour*
BENTON BLAIR	CHARLES COGHLIN	J. E. WHITING
FELIX FAWN	J. E. WHITING	J. B. MASON
ABNER DAY	J. H. STODDARD	J. H. STODDARD
DUKE WARREN	HENRY CHANFRAU	GOEFFERY HAWLEY
MR. SWIFT	JULIAN MAGNUS	JULIAN MAGNUS
MAJOR MAXWELL	JOHN PARSELLE	JOHN PARSELLE
M. MAIS	FELIX MORRIS	WM. SEYMOUR
MELDRUM	L. THOMPSON	WM. MORSE
MABEL BLAIR	EFFIE ELLSLER	NELLY HOWARD
DORA BLAIR	ELEANOR CAREY	SARA JEWETT
FANNY MAXWELL	MAUD HARRISON	MAUD HARRISON
MAMIE MAXWELL	MRS. E. J. PHILLIPS	MRS. E. J. PHILLIPS
MLLE. FLORINE	GABRIELLE DU SAND	GABRIELLE DU SAND
ABIGAIL DAY	NELLIE WETHERAL	NELLIE WETHERAL
MILLY	ELOISE WILLIS	ELOISE WILLIS

. . . The outline resembles that of *Odette* except the wife, however, becomes an operatic prima donna, instead of going wrong. In several respects *Separation* is the best play the public has seen from the pen of its author. Its literary quality is superior to anything he has ever done. The construction is closer. There is much more play of character, the rôles more balanced, and the movement of the piece is vivacious and free from the spasmodic element which enters into so many of his poorer works.—*New York Herald,* January 29, 1884.

To illustrate this incident of matrimonial infelicity Mr. Campbell has written a large quantity of dialogue, some of which is excellent, and this he has cut off into sections which are called acts, but which in fact are a series of colloquies. A dramatic mechanism—the display of a plot by means of deeds and incidents—has scarcely been attempted. The piece states a case, recites its facts; shows its aspects at different points of time and urges its moral.

Mr. Campbell's play might have been more effective had he thought more of dramatic point and less of moral significance.—*New York Tribune,* January 30, 1884.

Separation was produced at the Union Square Theatre before a crowded house on Monday evening. Its success was emphatic. A greater triumph could not have been wished. Rejected by three leading managers, it proved the judgment of all to have been at fault, justified the author's faith in his work, and rewarded Shook and Collier for their pluck. Indeed it did much more, for it opened the doors of one of our leading stock theatres to the American dramatist, who has never before obtained that recognition which is his due. The depth of significance in this direction cannot be fathomed at the first glance. The success of *Separation* opens vast possibilities by drawing the attention of stock managers to a class of playwrights who have been neglected in first-class quarters, and indicating that profit is not confined to the reproduction of second-hand imported dramas. On the stage, where Sardou, D'Ennery and Belot have held supreme sway, Campbell scores a triumph as brilliant as any of the many identified with the history of this house. . . .

Aside from the ethical aspects of *Separation*—which is likely to arouse some warm discussions, as some people are inclined to think that the conduct of both Blair and his wife is unusual, inconsistent and strained—it is a strong, interesting play. The materials are old but they are handled vigorously, originally. The characters are powerfully drawn; they represent variety of contrast and fidelity to nature, excepting that at the end of the first act, the climaxes are dramatic. The situation where the mother meets the daughter, but refrains from disclosing her identity, is novel and impressive. The comedy is unconventional and effervescent. The parts of Fanny and Felix are quite new to the stage, and that of Maxwell is refreshing and natural. Indeed naturalness pervades the entire play. Mr. Campbell has hit the happy medium between literary excellence and strong human interest. Those wiseacres who predicted that *Separation* would prove unsuitable to a

Union Square audience because Mr. Campbell could not write refined dialogue, were all at sea. The language of this piece is pithy and polished. It abounds with virile ideas, healthy sentiments, and there is a dash of that breezy poetry here and there, that freshens all of this author's work. Furthermore, from beginning to end, in plot and dialogue there is not a suggestion or line that is not pure. Marital infelicity has often been selected by modern playwrights as the basis of their stories, but they have generally used it to construct adulterous dramas which are degrading to the stage and demoralizing in their effects upon the public. Purity, under ordinary circumstances should not be singled out as a merit; it should be expected as a matter of course. But, unhappily, the sins of frail women have been woven so extensively into the woof of society dramas recently, that we may be pardoned for calling attention to the cleanliness of this particular play.

A strong play, fairly acted and exquisitely mounted, invariably attracts a large share of public attention. *Separation,* therefore, will in all probability hold the boards at the Union Square for many weeks to come.—*New York Dramatic Mirror,* February 2, 1884.

The play, like all the plays of Bartley Campbell's, is written down to the level of mediocre taste, but it has a certain vitality that redeems a tone which is always commonplace and is often vulgar. . . . The motive of the drama is trivial; the moral to people of sense is impertinent; nevertheless the story to the multitude must be entertaining, as it illustrates the struggle between two estranged hearts for the possession of a child's love. There is human warmth and vitality in such fiction as this, and supported by the author's instinct in arranging and contrasting characters, perhaps it atones for shallowness of sentiment and cheapness of artistic attire.—*Chicago Tribune,* August 26, 1884.

SIBERIA. Romantic drama in six acts. Copyrighted by Bartley Campbell, July 28, 1882.

Siberia was produced at the California Theatre, San Francisco, November 28-December 23, 1882, with the following cast (in part):

NICOLAI	MR. LEVICK
SARA	MISS CAYVAN
MARIE	MISS SYLVESTER
IVAN	MR. OSBORNE
SPARTA	MR. WESSELS
TROLSKY	MR. LENNOX
THE BANISHED MOTHER	MISS RUSH
THE LANDLORD	W. H. THOMPSON
BALLET LEADER	MLLE. CORNALBA

New York saw *Siberia* at Haverly's 14th Street Theatre, February 26-March 29, 1883, with the following cast (in part):

SARA	GEORGIE CAYVAN
MARIE	BLANCHE MORTIMER
VERA	MARY MILLS
NICOLAI	GUS LEVICK
JARACOFF	GEORGE HOEY
BERTRAND	MAX FREEMAN
IVAN	W. S. HARKINS
PETER	W. H. LYTELL
SPARTA	GEORGE THOMPSON
THE GOVERNOR	FRANK FOSTER

In Chicago *Siberia* was first given at McVicker's Theatre, January 14-26, 1884, with Laurence Atkins, Adele Belgarde, Emma Vaders, and Charles Abbott in its main rôles. By 1886 the play was relegated to the neighborhood theaters where it remained a great favorite until after the end of the century. Its last performance of which I have any record was at the Imperial Theatre in Chicago, December 5-12, 1915. *Siberia* was given at the Princess Theatre, London, December 14-19, 1887.

Campbell was probably moved to write *Siberia* because of the great interest taken by American newspapers in all things Russian following the assassination of Emperor Alexander II in 1881. While it is likely that some of the material for *Siberia* was taken from newspaper and magazine articles, Campbell also received some suggestions from Scribe's *The Jewess* and Von Moser's *Deborah* (*Leah the Forsaken*).

Bartley Campbell's latest play, *Siberia,* was produced last night for the first time on any stage, and was witnessed by an audience that filled the theater from orchestra to gallery. The play deals with the story of two young girls, the daughters of a Jewish father and Christian mother. They wander through seven acts, and are assisted by various characters who help fill in the incidents of which the play is made. Properly speaking, there is little plot and less motive for the melodramatic action and ending of all the acts; but Mr. Campbell's experience as a playwright stood him well in hand in previous plays, and the facility of catching melodramatic effects did not desert him in the construction of his last work. . . . Like all of Mr. Campbell's plays, it is replete with dialogue full of insipid sentimentalisms and old saws worked over into newer and less effective language. The subject gives many opportunities for the display of remarkably fine scenic and melodramatic tableaus, and they have been richly supplied. In fact, the play is crowded with so many incidents and details that the story itself and the real dramatic sequence is less a matter of importance than the smooth working of every particular scene and mechanical contrivance.—*San Francisco Examiner,* November 29, 1882.

A crowded audience waited until the curtain fell on the last scene of *Siberia* last night at the California, and inasmuch as that did not occur until close upon midnight, it may be taken as a sign that the play was acceptable. There is every chance that it will run for some time. It is full of thrilling effects, the scenery is exceptionally fine and a ballet heightens the charm. To take the play to pieces would hardly be generous, since so many melodramas have been accepted for their power to excite. Bartley Campbell has gone in for the unmitigatedly wild and fearful, so much so that it does not seem quite clear to the spectator when he leaves the theater what all the fuss has been about. But there can be no question that it is fuss. The play may be said to open with a massacre of the Jews, although that occurs in the second act. The ballet is the feature of the first.

We would tell the story if we could, but it is too complicated and incoherent. Indeed one only needs to give the ends of the acts to explain it as it stands. . . . There is so much life and action in the piece that it makes a capital evening's amusement, and although the effects are strained and the characters are shifted from Odessa and Siberia and elsewhere in the most extraordinary way, the situations are effective, especially the ends of the acts, which are mainly short.—*San Francisco Chronicle,* November 29, 1882.

There are a number of capital situations in *Siberia.* . . . The scenes are well conceived, the costumes are picturesque and the action is rapid and sustained. The audience overlooked the fact that there was nothing strikingly original, and the action is jerky. There are great spectacular possibilities in the play.— *New York Herald,* February 27, 1883.

The piece is well-calculated to please, for, although it deals with ancient situations and well worn incidents, it casts over them an atmosphere of novelty— obtained by disposing them under fresh conditions. The story is one of love that endures through many trials and of tyranny that is successfully resisted and adroitly baffled.

The expert playwright, however, has handled these materials so as to arouse and maintain an interest in a story that is extravagant and persons who are radically commonplace. The treatment of Russian politics is no less free than easy.—*New York Tribune,* February 27, 1883.

. . . However, melodrama and probability are the opposite of synonymous. So long as the emotions of the audience are sufficiently excited and the eye diverted by rapid and interesting action, the object of the writer is fulfilled. It is not our business to scoff at the class of play to which *Siberia* belongs, but to compare it with other efforts of the same character, and show in what respects it falls short of or excels its rivals. Mr. Campbell's wonderful power of appealing to all kinds of people is shown in this play. He takes a subject that might be made romantic by a less intuitive author and works it up on the realistic principle. So strong and surprising is the climax of each act that the observer forgets the impossibilities, or even absurdities, under the crafty spell of Campbell's subtle dramatic tact. The interest which the story of the piece handled in a less clever way would ordinarily excite is intensified by the author's gift of producing a panorama of situations that can only be described by the word absorbing. Possibly the latter part of the drama would increase in effectiveness were a few of the startling happenings, with which the earlier acts are surcharged, taken out; but it must be admitted that, notwithstanding the presence of such a quantity of sensations near the beginning, the melodrama is thrilling throughout. The dialogue is vigorous in the heroic passages, tender in the love scenes and witty in the comedy portions. Campbell's English, if not always as pure and undefiled as the pro-Jonsonites might desire, is at all times direct, never feeble, and often as melodious as that handed down to us from the literary geniuses who were the contemporaries of his ancestors in the little green isle. With the dual exceptions of *The Ticket-of-Leave Man* and *The Silver King,* no modern British drama will stand comparison with *Siberia.* It is an infinitely better piece from every point of view than any of that dreadful brood to which *Taken From Life* and kindred compositions belong.—*New York Dramatic Mirror,* March 3, 1883.

The story does not possess the interest of intricacy and surprise, but is told straightforwardly, and generally with considerable effect. The incidents are of a sufficiently sensational character to keep the galleries in a state of high excitement, and the uproar in that portion of the house was quite decided in character.—*Chicago Times,* January 15, 1884.

It is a scraggly drama originally intended to be produced with spectacular effects and a ballet. It is little better than a skeleton cheaply padded, and the story is insipid.

Mr. Campbell has picked up nihilism and pogroms as they are popularly supposed to exist in Russia, and following the newspaper reports of wrongs, iniquities, and persecutions, endeavors to show Russia is an exceedingly mismanaged country, and the sooner it is put in a moral strait-jacket the better it will be for the world at large.—*Chicago Inter-Ocean,* January 17, 1884.

Siberia is highly colored and broadly drawn in Bartley Campbell's most characteristic way.

It is hardly necessary to say that the scenery, which is commendable, nor the acting which in the main is acceptable, can lift the drama from the plane of mediocrity or surround it with any clearer atmosphere than that of sensationalism. Mr. Campbell writes for the gallery and presumably should be judged by gallery standards. Such a classification as this, however, virtually puts the play beyond the pale of criticism.—*Chicago Tribune,* January 16, 1884.

It is impossible, however, to assign dramatic vitality to characters so colourless as Mr. Campbell has drawn, and the comic scenes and characters are pitiable.—*Athenaeum* (London), December 17, 1887.

THROUGH FIRE. Sensational play in four acts. Copyrighted by Bartley Campbell, November 3, 1871.

According to tradition, this, the first of Bartley Campbell's plays to be presented, was written at the request of John Ellsler, the manager of the Pittsburgh Opera House, who was seeking a new play for his leading man, J. Newton Gotthold. The play was elaborately mounted, and presented at the Christmas matinée, 1871. It ran until January 6, 1872. The cast (in part):

BERTRAND BRISTOW	
WILD NAT	MR. J. NEWTON GOTTHOLD
ADAM JOCELYN, *banker*	J. F. DEAN
JARVIS JOCELYN	H. S. DUFFIELD
GUS TIVIS	H. J. ROWE
COLONEL BABBINGTON	H. P. WILSON
SAM BADGETT	J. E. IRVING
BROWNING	W. H. CROMPTON
NED LANDSEER	O. STEVENS
GRACE JOCELYN	MISS NELLIE JOHNSON
MRS. BRISTOW	MISS WILLA BRONG
PATTY	MRS. ISABELLA PHILLIPS
JENNY (*with new song*)	GEORGIE DIXON
MRS. MAGUFFIN	LIZZIE IRVING

Through Fire was given in Chicago at the Academy of Music, July 1-5, 1872, by a "combination" directed by Campbell, and containing Frank Evans, W. T. Melville and Miss Bradshaw. After Campbell had become the "literary attaché" at Hooley's Theatre, and had produced *Peril* and *Fate*, *Through Fire* was revived May 26, 27, 28, 1873. At that time the *Chicago Tribune* spoke of its having been "produced all over the country." In the performance at Hooley's, Campbell himself played the part of Tyler; it is the only record I find of him as an actor. The cast at Hooley's, 1873:

BERT BRISTOW	J. W. BLAISDELL
GUS TIVISS	J. W. NORRIS
SAM BADGETT	GEO. GIDDENS
JARVIS JOSSLYN	W. B. ARNOLD
ADAM JOSSLYN	RUSSELL SOGGS
LANDSEER	H. A. WEBBER

COLONEL BABBINGTON	W. H. FLEMING
LAKEMAN	WM. WAITE
POLICE	W. KELLY
TYLER	BARTLEY CAMPBELL
GRACE JOSSLYN	KATE MEEK
JENNY	MISS SIDNEY COWELL
PATTY BABBINGTON	— — —
MRS. BRISTOW	MISS ROCHE
ORANGE WOMAN	EMMA HERNE

Under the title of *Watch and Wait; or, Through Fire*, this play was given at Wood's Theatre in New York, August 11-16, 1873, with the following cast:

BERT BRISTOW	J. W. ALBAUGH
JARVIS JOSSLYN	J. Z. LITTLE
ADAM JOSSLYN	GEORGE O. MORRIS
COLONEL BABBINGTON	L. J. MESTAYER
GUS TIVISS	W. MARDEN
SAM BADGETT	A. H. SHELDON
LAKEMAN	CHARLES STURGES
POLICEMAN	M. PRICE
TYLER	L. R. WILLARD
TICKET AGENT	CHARLES WOODRUFF
TEAMSTER	FRANK LANGLEY
GRACE JOSSLYN	MRS. ALBAUGH
MRS. BRISTOW	LIZZIE EDWARDS
JENNY	THERESA WOOD
MOLLY	HENRIETTA GRANGER
PATTY BABBINGTON	MRS. VAN DEREN

It will be noticed that the dramatis personae for the Pittsburgh, Chicago, and New York performances of this play are slightly different. A revised version of *Through Fire* was given under the title of *Bert; or, From Ocean to Ocean* (*q.v.*), and it is possible that another version may have been given under the title of *The Lower Millions* (*q.v.*).

Modern melodramas as a rule are not the most popular of dramatic productions, at any rate with the thoughtful and educated frequenters of the theater. There are many old dramas of this class which are an exception to the rule, and which are faultless in construction, strong in dialogue and enjoyable in performance. But the melodramas which have been produced during the past ten years cannot be said to possess all, if any, of these desiderata, but on the contrary are constructed with the view to embody so much of the sensational as to sacrifice all the above mentioned qualities thereto. Just at the present time these pieces are being produced with alarming rapidity, and the stage throughout the country is flooded with such material as is found in *Across the Continent, Help, Under the Gaslight,* and a hundred other plays of the same class. It is a sad sign of the times that the theatrical managers of our large cities find it remunerative to provide such questionable pabulum for their patrons.

Bartley T. Campbell's *Through Fire,* if it is anything, is a melodrama, and we are in candor forced to admit, that whatever its excellencies, and it has some, they are more than overshadowed by the evils of that school of drama to which we have referred above. We admit that it has excellencies, and heartily congratulate Mr. Campbell upon some portions of the dialogue, which are really good and far superior to any similar play which we have seen. But that the play is uneven in this respect we must confess, and unwillingly assert that many very weak portions are observable. We do not suppose that Mr. Campbell claims for his production the quality of originality, or that he credits himself with the creation of anything new in the matter of stage effect or business. The piece is a well managed mixture of familiar scenes from other plays cleverly altered, modified and remodelled, with new words put in the mouths of the familiar characters. The first and second acts vividly recall the opening scenes of *Solon Shingle,* the third act brings to our recollection Byron and *Across the Continent,* the first part of the fourth act bears a striking resemblance to portions of the *Streets of New York,* while the latter part reproduces the mountain scene in *No Thoroughfare,* and the last act is a repetition of the closing scenes in the *Lady of Lyons.*

The first act of the play introduces an honest, industrious clerk, Bert Bristow (Mr. Gotthold) and a dissipated, dishonest colleague, Gus. Tivis (Mr. Rowe). The action opens in the counting room of Josslyn & Co., and it is discovered in a conversation between the clerks that Bert is in love with Grace Josslyn (Miss Johnson), the daughter of Adam Josslyn (Mr. Dean), the banker. Jarvis Josslyn (Mr. Duffield), a nephew of the principal of the house, is also in love with Grace. Tivis steals a number of doubloons which form a part of a special deposit with the bank and is caught in the act of opening the safe by Jarvis. The two concoct a plan to accuse Bert of the theft, which is of course done, and as Mr. Josslyn considers the evidence of crime sufficient, Bert is discharged but not prosecuted. In this act Grace enters the office and she and Bert indulge in the wildest love-making, a situation which the surroundings in the scene make very improbable. Another weak point, too, is that Bert, without any opportunity of ascertaining Jarvis's plot, while protesting his innocence, openly accuses that gentleman of having full knowledge of it.

The second act brings Bert home, where he tells his mother of his disgrace, and introduces an extraordinary servant girl, Jenny (Miss Georgie Dickson), who is the sweetheart of Sam Badgett (Mr. Irving), the messenger of Josslyn & Co. Sam, who is scarcely seen in the first act, has, in some way not explained, found out all about the plot against Bert and accuses to him Jarvis and Tivis. Bert visits Tivis and that worthy acknowledges his guilt and agrees with Bert to accuse Jarvis of his crime. Jarvis is introduced preparing to go to Boston, and with him appear two characters which are altogether unnecessary to the action of the piece, to wit, an impossible kind of negro servant and a mercenary faro bank proprietor, who points his pistol in a drawing-room and obtains money by that means from Jarvis. The act concludes with an ineffectual attempt on the part of Bert to effect the arrest of Jarvis in a New York railroad depot where Allegheny Valley tickets are sold.

In the third act a skip of three years is made, and Bert, now Wild Nat, a wagoner, is discovered on the plains with Sam, the reason of their being there and how they came there not being explained. This is an act of mysterious meetings. Grace and Jenny (who is now her maid) both appear in the scene, and Jenny, who is a very talented servant, sings two excellent songs. Bert makes himself known to Grace, and after more love-making, begs her not to sleep in the ranch as he fears something. She sleeps in her wagon, and Jarvis, who has also from some cause turned up in the same place, employs Indians who fire the ranch with the hope of destroying Grace. As she sleeps in the wagon, she with Jenny and two other persons, who accompany, escape uninjured.

The fourth act is the strongest of the piece. Jarvis is a millionaire in California. Tivis turns up, enters his room, and by the muzzle of a pistol obtains from him a confession of the plot against Bert. Jarvis shoots Tivis as he leaves the house. The latter buries the confession, and as he is dying, Bert, who is going over the mountains, falls over him and is told where the confession is. Bert starts to find the paper and meets Jarvis, who is hunting for the dead Tivis, a dreadful encounter takes place and Bert is thrown down a precipice.

The last act brings most of the characters in some way to New York, and Grace is about to marry Jarvis when Claude Melnotte—we beg pardon—Bert enters, produces the confession, and, to use the language of the synopsis, "All went merry as a marriage bell."

With this brief and necessarily somewhat incomplete statement of the material in the piece it will be seen that *Through Fire* belongs to the sensational order, and of the material the company makes the most. Mr. Gotthold throws into his rendering of Bert so much earnestness and force that he makes of the character more than we could believe it possible to make. Some of the speeches which fall to his part are really good, and for these Mr. Campbell deserves much credit. Mr. Duffield, Miss Johnson, Georgie Dickson and Mr. Irving are all that could be desired in their several rôles.

Mr. Campbell has, we think, erred in introducing too many characters into *Through Fire*. The piece is, however, a great improvement on anything he has ever done in the way of the drama, and his friends (and we are among them) would congratulate him upon this improvement. We assure him that our remarks on his production are given in the kindest spirit and for the purpose of pointing

out to him what we consider as mistakes, to the end that in the future he may
be more careful in the preservation of his unities and in the action of his dramas.
—*Pittsburgh Commercial,* December 27, 1871.

On the whole, *Through Fire* would do well to rank with such predecessors as
Across the Continent, The Red Pocket Book and the like. The piece itself is not
wanting in interest by any means. But the situations are so glaringly sensational,
and the evolution of the plot so mazy, and assisted by such a deluge of improbabilities that the piece would readily be recognized as an imperfectly incubated
first effort of a young and ambitious playwright.—*Chicago Tribune,* May 28, 1873.

ULTIMO. *See* BULLS AND BEARS.

VAN, THE VIRGINIAN. *See* THE VIRGINIAN.

THE VIGILANTES; or, THE HEART OF THE SIERRAS. Drama of sensation. Adapted
from Campbell's earlier *How Women Love (q.v.).*

Advertised as a first performance, *The Vigilantes* opened July 1, 1878, at
the Grand Opera House in New York and ran until July 5 with a cast
which included Rosa Rand, Estelle Mortimer, Alice Hastings, Louise Willes,
Louis Aldrich, W. H. Leake, Harry Colton, M. C. Daly, H. S. Duffield. It
was again played in New York, this time at Niblo's Garden, from November
25 to November 30, 1878. In this cast were Annie Tiffany, Blanche Mortimer,
Harry Colton, F. A. Tannehill, and W. H. Lytell. That *The Vigilantes* was
played "on the road" is indicated by the fact that there were performances
of it at Deadwood, S.D., on May 31, 1879, and at Newark, N.J., on December 8, 9, 10, 1879.

The story is one of love, adventure and frontier rudeness, and is now entirely
devoid of the interest with which an intelligent playwright may invest both
dialogue and action, even in this department. . . .
The drama opens in the Sierra Nevadas, where an orphan girl named Violette
Varnett is in love with her foster brother, Frank Ransome. The latter returns
from San Francisco with his heart full of love for another woman, and relates
the story of his passion to Violette. She feigns indifference and wishes him joy,
only to give way to a storm of grief as soon as he quits the room. This is interrupted by the entrance of an old miner named Joe Comstock, who, having saved
the girl's life when she was almost an infant, has long cherished a secret attachment for her. In a graceful love scene, full of pathos, he discloses his secret and
is rejected. Frank finally marries the object of his choice, who is led, through
the machinations of a villain, to desert him after a year of married life. Frank
becomes dissipated, and Violette and Joe, hearing of the organization of the
Vigilance Committee of '56, determine to go to San Francisco to save him. They
arrive just in time to witness his encounter with the seducer of his wife and his
arrest by the vigilantes. In the subsequent act Joe offers to die in Frank's stead,

which the latter refuses, and he is about to be led out to execution when Violette returns from a visit to the committee, now with the pardon of the man she loves. In the remaining act the rescued and rescuers start for their old home in the mountains, are overtaken by a snowstorm and are perishing for food. From another coach, similarly circumstanced, Frank's wife comes only to crave forgiveness and die at the feet of her injured husband. This, of course, is but the vaguest outline of an interesting story.—*New York Herald,* July 2, 1878.

The Vigilantes, a new play of Bartley Campbell, was given at the Newark Opera House. The play has elements of strength; the plot is interesting and the situation somewhat exciting.—*Newark Daily Advertiser,* December 9, 1879.

THE VIRGINIAN. Domestic drama in five acts.

This play was written for and performed at Hooley's Theatre, Chicago, October 26-November 7, 1874, and April 5-7, 1875, with the following cast:

VANDYKE VERNON	JAMES O'NEILL
KATE CALVERT	LOUISE HAWTHORNE
ANANIAS JINGLE	WM. H. CRANE
RICHARD CALVERT	NATE SALSBURY
CROMWELL CALVERT	GEORGE RYDER
JACK PENNINGTON	H. M. BROWN
JEMINAIA JENKINS	MRS. FRED WILLIAMS
LOU MANNING	MISS DOYLE

Campbell directed performances of *The Virginian* at Hooley's Theatre in Brooklyn, September 15-19, 1875, with a cast which included Annie Ward Tiffany, Minnie Doyle, M. V. Lingham, M. C. Daly and Augustus Pitou. A new version of *The Virginian,* one with a "happy ending," was directed by Campbell at St. James's Theatre, London, November 20-December 2, 1876. In this cast were Samuel Piercy, C. Cooper, George Honey, Lydia Foote, and Mrs. John Wood. *The Virginian* was included in the repertoire of the "Bartley Campbell Combination" which toured the country in 1877-78, and under the title of *Van, the Virginian* Frank Mayo and Affie Weaver played it on tour during the season of 1880-81. It was played in Chicago in 1883 and again in 1895. Tradition has it that *The Virginian* was very popular in the South.

The dialogue of the piece is not brilliant, but possesses a quaint, homely, natural quality which is more intelligible to the average audience perhaps than the scintillations of Sheridan, and causes no little merriment to the audience. Mr. Campbell has shown increasing maturity in reaching below the mere surface of events to play upon the feelings which are common to human nature, and in a manner has succeeded in stirring them. But—he fails to stir the audience to any fixed purpose. *The Virginian* is a perfectly pure and wholesome drama, and its story interesting, but we cannot say that the author has exhibited any astonishing power over the sympathies or left any decided impression.—*Chicago Tribune,* October 27, 1874.

The Virginian is a play of strong human passion, and in that sense, of strong human interest; constructed in five acts, every act ends with a powerful situation. With every desire to do justice to Mr. Bartley Campbell's abilities, it may be said that his *Virginian* has the same effect upon the mind as is produced by reading the dialect poems by Bret Harte. *The Virginian* contains the character of a wilful, generous-hearted American girl named Lou Manning, that is an admirable study of character, worthy of Dickens, or even of Sterne. It is essentially a novel theatrical type, and is well worth a visit to see.—*London Sportsman.*

The Virginian is mainly a creditable work. It is, to be sure, over lachrymose, and to be truly artistic, should have a cheerful finale to compensate for the tearful nature of its general story. Mr. Campbell has caught a bit of touching life history, and has compressed it artfully into four acts of rational entertainment. As long as Mr. Campbell can make women in the audience poke handkerchiefs into their eyes, and set men rubbing their coat sleeves across their blurred optic and sniveling noses, he can be forgiven for snubbing the rules of dramatic unity.— *Chicago Times,* October 27, 1874.

It has been stated that the play . . . has enjoyed a large share of popularity in its three year tenure of the American stage, and we feel a great curiosity, to wit: how much of truth this statement may be credited. . . . But not even this excuse can be admitted into any speculations as to the probability of the favor claimed for this play in its own land. It is true that it is called *The Virginian* and that the two principal characters are supposed to have been fighting against the Armies of the North. It is true, moreover, that the sentiments of the characters are occasionally couched in that vernacular and occasionally rendered with that peculiar drawl which is usually accepted as one of the national characteristics. The story might be told of any people, for indeed it has often been told before now. . . . It has been sometimes objected to the comedies of today that the conversation is far brisker and more entertaining than in real life. . . . No such objection can certainly be made to *The Virginian.*—*London Times,* November 22, 1876.

And when on Xmas Day a convenient snow-wreath envelops and suffocates the husband, his wife clasps with ecstacy her second love to her heart, the Xmas bowl is raised aloft in triumph, and the Xmas party overflows with festive raptures. We decline to believe, however, that anywhere in the world the sorrows of a man who returns sick and wounded from fighting his country's battles, to find his wife in the arms of another, and the child of a stranger prattling on her knee, can be regarded with anything but sympathy, and the joy which is raised over the demise of such a one is surely out of place anywhere except in the worship of Moloch. The strong situations which Mr. Campbell has introduced misled the audience for a time, but the closing scenes did not pass without opposition. A drama more unpleasant and more subversive of right feeling has seldom been placed upon the stage. Some dexterity is shown in the treatment, and the comic characters are not without freshness. The serious characters, are, however, altogether unsympathetic, the hero especially displaying a promptitude worthy of Joseph Surface in cloaking with a noble sentiment an indefensible or ignoble action.—*Athenaeum* (London), November 25, 1876.

WATCH AND WAIT. *See* THROUGH FIRE.

WEST POINT. A libretto for a musical comedy written about 1878. The musical score was never added, and the work was not copyrighted. The manuscript of *West Point* is in the possession of Mr. Robert Campbell.

THE WHITE SLAVE. Drama in six acts. Copyrighted by Robert Campbell, 1909.

The most popular of Bartley Campbell's plays, *The White Slave,* had its première at Haverly's Theatre, New York, April 3, 1882, and ran until May 6, with the following cast:

LISA	GEORGIA CAYVAN
DAPHNE	EMMIE WILMONT
NANCE	ETELKA WARDELL
MRS. LEE	MRS. G. C. GERMON
LETTY LEE	FRANCES KEMBLE
MARTHA	MARIE BATES
CLAY BRITTON	GUS LEVICK
WILLIAM LACY	FRANK ROBERTS
JUDGE HARDIN	WELSH EDWARDS
STITCH	M. C. DALY
COUNT STRAIN	JAY HUNT
JOB	W. J. SCANLAN
CLEM	CHAS. WEBSTER
JACK	D. E. VERNON
CAPTAIN STRYKER	G. L. KEAN
BANCROFT	D. E. RALTON
NATCHEZ JIM	SCOTT DAVIS
JAMISON	W. H. SMITH
LITTLE JIM	MASTER LA FORREST

At the close of this run a somewhat changed company then began a coast to coast tour which included a Chicago engagement, at Hooley's Theatre, from October 29 to November 11. For the next several years *The White Slave* was an annual attraction at important theaters throughout the country. After its drawing power at these theaters waned, it began a long career at the minor theaters in New York and throughout the country. Chicago saw at least one week's performance of it every year until 1901. A *White Slave* company, directed by Mr. Robert Campbell, toured the country from 1912 to 1918. Its last official performance was at the Walnut Street Theatre, Philadelphia, February 23, 1918, when Lisa was played by Rita Knight, Nance by Gertrude Perry, Letty Lee by Helen Collier, Clay Britton by Scott Moore, William Lacy by Allen Lee, and Stitch by Harry Sedley.

Now if we should attempt to show how devoid *The White Slave* is of literary merit, we would fall into the trap that caught the critics of all the daily papers, who should not have allowed Bartley Campbell to put salt on their tails. We are wiser birds, and we don't intend to be ensnared by any such patent devices. We will not, therefore, draw and quarter the poor *White Slave* and kick the dismembered pieces in the dust. That is work for Gommys. But Mr. Campbell's play was merely written to please the public, and this by catering to the appetite of the moment. Such a composition must necessarily be utterly innocent of the slightest claim to artistic merit. Dramatists work for money as well as other people. If Wilkie Collins found that trash was craved by the reading public, he would undoubtedly desert the pleasant paths of good literature and write a dime novel— and a reeking one, too. If he did not, he is more conscientious in respect to his profession than nine tenths of his brethren. So it is with the playwright. When Fairfaxes fail, and Geraldines refuse to "catch on" with that tenacity so necessary to their continuance, then the horizon must be carefully scanned, thorough observations taken, and the whereabouts of the ship of "Public Craze" precisely located. This is what Mr. Campbell did; hence *The White Slave,* which, as we have said, shall not fall slaughtered by our hand, because it is a play for the people, and from their standpoint, and not from our own, it shall be regarded. . . .

The White Slave, partaking as it does of the salient virtues of the three—the only three—dramas of the South, has in it all the elements of a popular success. The craze for melodrama has extended far into the East and West, and there is money to be made by feeding it. New Yorkers who can see such magnificent spectacles as *Youth* and *The Lights o' London* will not go wild over the sensations of Mr. Campbell's production; but our country cousins will relish its lurid, thrilling aggregation of incidents amazingly, and a pot o' money will find its way accordingly into the author's capacious pocket.—*New York Dramatic Mirror,* April 8, 1882.

It was all slap-bang on the Fourteenth Street stage Monday night. Fires, villains, knives and sheet lightning mingled in the most startling manner imaginable. When a cannon goes off the snap of the cap is heard a second before the big report. *The White Slave* is the reverse of the cannon. The grand explosion comes first and the puny crack of the percussion afterwards. The first three tableaux rattle off like musketry, the last three drag out with as little effect as the report of a popgun. To be less gunny, Campbell's play needs stiffening up towards the end. If this is done *The White Slave* will take like—like smallpox.

The story is a perfect terror of sensations. They are crowded into every tableau, and as the nervous spectator alternately jumps from his seat or rubs his chin against the big hat of the lady one row ahead, so *The White Slave* is a big success. The people want to exercise their hair—when they've got some—in these days, and the girls all prefer to have their blood chilled than to sip Maillard's creams. At least, that is about the size of it according to Pencil; therefore Campbell's condensed blood-and-thunder will be the favorite diet for the coming fortnight.

The Octoroon is liberally drawn upon all through the play. The same tragic "Touch me not, villain!" "Become your favorite? Never-r-r!" "Royal raiment has not the—" etc., etc., do service again.

In one tableau the villain, hero, heroine, and a quadroon float across the stage, clinging to pieces of burning wreck. This scene is called by Mississippi's other name, "The Father of the Waters." Some irreverent chap said it should have been called the "father of fire and waters." Was this funny?

Kit, the Arkansas Drummer, comes in on the steamboat scene. Campbell has been mean with his bummers—instead of two, there is only one. He should have had 4—count 'em—4. Uncle Tom is brought in as Job. Mr. Scanlan's negro certainly has a wee drop of Irish in his dialect. This is a novelty at any rate.—*New York Dramatic Mirror,* April 8, 1882.

Bartley Campbell is in for another popular success. It is not as well written as *My Partner* and *The Galley Slave* but is full of effects pathetic, melodramatic, and scenic that are sure to please the people who buy theater tickets.—*New York Herald,* April 4, 1882.

There was no call to touch *The Octoroon* unless it could be treated in a better way, and Mr. Campbell is far behind its model.—*New York Tribune,* April 4, 1882.

The play is well worth seeing by all lovers of the drama, and it may be said here that Mr. Campbell has gathered up and put in its construction all that is worth saving of the old Southern society and the conditions of plantation property in the past-and-gone slavery system.—*St. Louis Republican,* quoted by *Chicago Tribune,* October 29, 1882.

The White Slave is an ingenious intaglio or piece of dramatic *marqueterie* with no more originality than a photo engraving. Bits of *Uncle Tom, The Octo-*

roon, *Kit,* and *The World,* and other sensational dramas have been kidnapped, uglified, attenuated, and melted in the Campbellean stewpan, warmed up with the gentle heat of the Bartlean genius. Dispensing with its utter want of originality and evaporating considerable slipshod sentiment in which Campbell cannot help but indulge, the piece will draw. Its rhodomontade of catchpenny sentiments appeal to the half educated, and the cooing of the love-makers charm the fairer sex, so that its popularity will exceed that of many a better play.—*Chicago Daily News,* October 30, 1882.

In the present dearth of original dramatic talent *The White Slave* . . . may pass muster; but Mr. Bartley Campbell had better make the most of it while the public is in the humor for this sort of thing, as the piece is not likely to outlast the season. It is one of those exasperating productions that are beneath serious criticism, and even defy classification. Literary work it is not; dramatic work it assuredly is not, and if in despair one calls it a play, the word must be received in its most liberal acceptance.

Mr. Campbell gages the public taste with great nicety; he is careful to produce nothing that will be caviar to the meanest capacity; he appeals to popular love of claptrap sentiment and cheap virtue; and he recognizes the fact that in a high-pressure age like this, men who have been at business all day do not want to be bothered with too much thought when they visit the theater at night. . . . Yet this thing has been successful. And why? Because it is cunningly put together with an eye to stage effects; because the situations and scenic effects run little risk of failure, having in former and better plays received frequent and public approval, and because to an interesting story is joined that medley of nigger songs and dances, sentimental effects, and transpontine sentiment, defeated villainy and triumphant virtue which seldom fail to appeal to a western audience. "Rags," etc., is one of those sentiments which from the lips of a pretty heroine like Lisa seldom fail to evoke plaudits from the gallery.—*Chicago Tribune,* October 31, 1882.

The White Slave has been found to be greatly to the taste of American audiences. For English sympathies it is a little too heavily weighted with exciting and harrowing incidents. In other words, it is rather ponderously elaborate melodrama. It seemed, however, to give satisfaction to the audience Monday evening, who heartily applauded its negro plantation songs and hymns, and exhibited a creditable amount of compassion for the horrors of slavery in those pre-emancipation days.—*London Graphic,* August 23, 1884.

The following quotations are taken from a playbill of *The White Slave* in New York in 1884.

The moral fibre of Mr. Campbell's plays is always right, and he has an unfailing respect for the dramatic unities. He never goes seriously astray.—*New York Sun.*

It is worth all the "Uncle Toms" and "Octoroons" in the world.—*New York Democrat.*

THE VIRGINIAN

The text of *The Virginian* is based on a processed copy, and undoubtedly a pirated one. The cast of characters is identical with that of the first performance, and the plot follows exactly the rather elaborate outline given in the *Chicago Tribune,* October 21, 1874, and moreover, bits of dialogue in the text correspond with references to the dialogue in the same review. It is, however, improbable that the text is exactly as Campbell wrote it.

CAST OF CHARACTERS

Vandyke Vernon

Richard Calvert

Ananias Jingle

Cromwell Calvert

John Pennington

Jack

Charles Knox

Kate Calvert

Lou Manning

Jeminaia Jessup

Little Hattie

ACT I.

SCENE: *An apartment in Wayside Inn. Boxed in three. Doors, R. and L.2.E. Window, R.C. Old-fashioned sideboard, L.C. Tables R. and L.C. Decanter and glasses on tables, R.C. Cromwell and Ananias discovered seated at table, R.C.*

CROM. [*Singing at rise*] Fill up, fill up the cup and let the golden wine flow free. The blood of the vine we have in the wine and Bacchus is a friend to thee, and Bacchus is a friend to thee.

JING. And Bacchus is a friend to thee, and Bacchus is a friend to thee.

CROM. This is not wine, this is not the purple blood of the grape, but as I can't afford to quaff the royal Rhenish down—why I compromise on beautiful Bourbon.

JING. I think I am too truly a son of the soil to admire Bourbon to the same extent as—

CROM. You compromise in rye?

JING. I really don't know.

CROM. What are you talking about?

JING. I really don't know. Mr. Calvert, I would call your attention to the fact that you are violating the solemn laws of hospitality, and assuming an authoritative attitude, sir, as the master of this house.

CROM. Here, here.

JING. You are, as I have just remarked, the master of this house; you owe—

CROM. I owe nothing, sir. [*Rising and leaning on table*] I pay as I go, sir.

JING. Mr. Calvert!

CROM. And that is more than I can say for you, sir. [*Sitting down*]

JING. I refuse, my dear friend, to reply to your personality. I recognize your right to speak such words as you think fit and proper in your own house, but I reserve to myself, Mr. Calvert, the right to say that the laws of hospitality are as sacred as—are as sacred as—

CROM. Skip it.

JING. Are as sacred as—[*Taps his forehead*]

CROM. You mean Balaam's ass. His was the only sacred ass of which I ever heard.

JING. Sir, I repeat, you are the master of this house; you are, so to speak—

CROM. Take a—little more Bourbon. [*Fills glasses*]

JING. [*Looks at him severely, then relaxes into a smile as he takes glass and drinks*] Thank you. I was discoursing on the sacred laws of hospitality. I was endeavoring in my own feeble way to throw a little light upon the usages that should remain among gentlemen, and I—

CROM. Do you mean to insinuate that I am not a gentleman?

JING. Mr. Calvert!

CROM. Why, sir, I am your social superior, and your presence here is the result of a compromise between my dignity, sir, and my good nature, sir.

JING. Damn your dignity. Damn your good nature, and particularly and positively damn your compromise.

CROM. I am a Calvert. I am a Cromwell. I am a lineal descendent of the Protector.

JING. And must I say, no one needed a protector more.

CROM. And what, on the other hand are you?

JING. [*Rising*] One of nature's noble men, a lineal descendent of the great and good Adam, a son of that beautiful but wayward Eve, a disciple of Blackstone, a column in the temple of American liberty, a corner stone in the fabric of the American independence.

CROM. Then why have you not sent your son into the field as I have done, to fight for the freedom you praise so loudly?

JING. For the very good reason I had no son to send. Had I millions of sons, they all should be there. But yours didn't go because you wished him to—he quitted the paternal roof against your wishes—I may say, in the very face of your earnest expostulations.

CROM. Because I did not believe in the war; I always believe in a compromise.

JING. Exactly. Had you been a Noah you would never have built the ark. You'd have compromised in a raft, and the human family would have perished in the flood. [*Enter Jeminaia, R.2.E., stands by table*]

JEM. Mr. Jingle, what are you shouting about? One can hear every word you utter, all over the house.

CROM. Of course you can.

JING. Is not this a public house, Miss Jessup? And is not every man at home in it as I am?

JEM. Shut up. My poor mistress has been trying to close her eyes for the last half hour, but as long as you keep your mouth open—

CROM. She can't shut her eyes.

JING. May I be permitted to inquire why Mrs. Calvert does not seize upon the quiet calm of night to close her eyes if it be wholly essential to her well-being that her eyes should be closed at all?

CROM. My son's wife is responsible to no one for her acts, Mr. Jingle. On that bright morning when my son left for the front, he placed his wife in my care.

JEM. And you compromised by letting her take care of herself.

CROM. Jeminaia, you are presuming on your connection with the Wayside Inn to wound the feeling of—

JING. Boniface!

CROM. If I were a man of legal attainments, Mr. Jingle, slang would not sully my speech, no, sir, if you—

JEM. [*Coming from sideboard to Cromwell*] Go and see your poor daughter-in-law. She is low-spirited and half dead with fright since the news of the battle came in.

JING. She might keep her spirits up by pouring spirits down.

CROM. [*Severely, rising*] Mr. Jingle! [*Going*]

JEM. [*To Jingle*] Between you two, you do enough of that for the whole town.

JING. For a domestic, Miss Jessup, you do enough exercise on the freedom of speech—

JEM. [*Crossing to him*] Don't dare to call me a domestic, Mr. Jingle. I'm a respectable farmer's daughter, and now what are you?

JING. In a quarrel then?

CROM. Compromise it, Ananias, compromise it. [*Exit, R.1.E.*]

JEM. What do you mean by calling me a domestic? Say.

JING. You receive pay, do you not?

JEM. What of that?

JING. Does not the retaining of labor, especially that of a woman, make her a domestic?

JEM. No such thing. I came here because Mrs. Calvert wanted me, more for a companion than anything else.

JING. There is no companion for a female but a male; Mrs. Calvert should not have permitted her husband to go off to the war before the honeymoon had waned.

JEM. Permit—I'd like to know how a woman is going to prevent a man from doing as he pleases? A man is nine-tenths selfishness, and the other one-tenth is made up of conceit and little petty meanness.

JING. Miss Jessup, I will not remain longer in the room where my sex is publicly assaulted. I may say traduced. [*Putting on hat*] Or to use a word now somewhat obsolete, vilified. [*Going, L.*]

JEM. [*Going to sideboard*] Good afternoon, Mr. Jingle. [*Not looking around*]

JING. [*Pause, aside*] Not a word of regret as symptoms of contrition. [*Aloud*] I am about to depart.

JEM. Very well. [*Not turning*]

JING. Do I understand, Miss Jessup, that we part in anger? [*Approaches her*]

JEM. Yes. [*Turns*] I always thought that a man's shadow followed him.

JING. [*Laughs dry short laugh*] Very good, very good.

JEM. [*Turns on him quickly*] What in the name of sense are you laughing at?

JING. [*Retreating a step*] At your joke, at your joke.

JEM. [*Severely*] It was not a joke.

JING. Excuse me. I thought it was. [*Meekly*] Miss Jessup, permit me to say I think you unnecessarily harsh to me, who would be willing to lay my all at your feet.

JEM. Your all! What's that?

JING. My profession.

JEM. Lawyer's clerk?

JING. My name, my future.

JEM. The poor house, if you don't stop drinking every penny you get.

JING. Jeminaia, my good name is my heritage. That I drink, is my business, and no friend of mine would thus coldly, I may say heartlessly, allude to my only weakness.

JEM. And I wouldn't either, if I thought there was the making of nothing but a sot in you; but Jingle, you are a young man—a talented young man—

JING. [*Bows*] Thank you.

JEM. And if you would only quit rum, you might become an ornament to society, instead of as now, a signpost on the road to ruin—not only pointing the way, but going there yourself.

JING. Is this an admiration or a reproach? Is it actuated by friendship or spurred by malice?

JEM. Why should I bear malice toward you?

JING. [*Sighing*] Ah, why indeed?

JEM. I have none.

JING. Your hand on that.

JEM. [*Giving hand*] There.

JING. [*Holding it in his, looks admiringly in her face*] If I might be permitted to offer you some slight token of forgiveness, some scrap—as it were—if—[*Pause, glances suddenly around*] Miss Jessup, may I kiss you?

JEM. [*Pulls her hand away*] No, sir.

Jing. That settles it. [*Going to L.2.E.*] You might have prevented this fragile bark from going to pieces on the rock of rye; but there is nothing that can save it now. [*Enter Vandyke Vernon, L.2.*]

Van. Better think it over, stranger.

Jing. I refuse, sir, to think it over. I indignantly, persistently, and emphatically refuse to give it a moment's consideration.

Van. [*Crossing, R.*] Oh, well, I only throw out a suggestion which I thought might be of advantage to an individual in your frame of mind; but as you seem determined to die, why—[*Sits at table, R.C. and looking up in his face*] just suit your taste and be—blessed.

Jing. [*Pointing to Jeminaia at sideboard*] There is a lady present, sir. Do you know, sir, you are taking an unwarranted liberty with my affairs?

Van. Your affairs? [*Reaching out and turning him around*] From your present plight, I should judge your affairs were of a very particular notion, and not very interesting to yourself or anyone else.

Jing. [*Indignantly*] Do you mean, sir, to offer me an insult?

Van. Friend, just as you please to take it.

Jing. [*After a pause*] Oh, well, as you seem not to mean it—well, the fact is, I do not regard it as an insult.

Jem. You are a coward, Mr. Jingle. [*Coming down, L., to Jingle*]

Jing. [*Aside to him*] Not at all, only a diplomat. My connection with the law will not permit me to take a hand in assaults.

Van. See here, I'd like to have a drink and something to eat, if it isn't against the rules of the house.

Jing. [*Proudly*] I am not the landlord, sir, I am a lawyer.

Van. Not such a mistake after all. You are connected with the bar?

Jing. Yes, sir, I am.

Van. Anyone can tell that.

Jing. [*Smiling*] Indeed?

Van. [*Touching nose*] You have your sign out.

Jem. [*To Jingle*] Say nothing sharp.

Jing. [*To her*] No use, he is simply eccentric, that's all. Really not worth minding. [*Going up*]

Jem. [*R., to Vandyke*] I think you are very impudent.

Van. And I think you are very pretty. [*Helping himself*]

Jem. [*To Jingle*] Queer man, ain't he?

Jing. Queer in its strongest sense.

Jem. [*To Vandyke*] Anything to eat or drink? [*Goes to back of table*]

Van. Both.

JEM. [*Aside*] Orders like a prince. I'll cultivate him. [*Sits at table*] Beer or spirits?

VAN. A little ale I think would be about the thing.

JEM. You shall have it. [*Exit, R.2.E.*]

JING. Don't you think you had better try the sherry?

VAN. I guess not.

JING. Oh, a little Medford?

VAN. Am I ordering this meal to suit my own taste or yours?

JING. I was only offering a suggestion, nothing more, I can assure you. [*Enter Jeminaia, R.2., with waiter, glass, ale, food, etc.*]

JEM. There.

VAN. Excellent, and I am as hungry as a wolf.

JING. Have you come far?

VAN. Yes, from the other side of the Blue Ridge.

JEM. From Virginia?

VAN. Yes, indeed, all the way from Virginia.

JING. A refugee, eh?

VAN. [*To Jingle*] Help yourself, what'll you have?

JING. Thank you. [*To Jeminaia*] A drop of Bourbon. [*Eating*]

VAN. A refugee, no, not exactly. That means a fellow who runs away, doesn't it?

JING. I cannot say that it always does, but it generally does.

VAN. Then I am not a refugee, generally or otherwise.

JEM. [*Behind table*] Have you been in the army?

VAN. Well, the fact is, I was going into the First Virginian, but my mother died when the bells were ringing out the victory of Manassas, and she was a Northern woman, born somewhere in the hills of Pennsylvania, and she made me promise I wouldn't fight against her kin.

JING. And you kept your promise?

VAN. To a dying mother? Why, man, what do you take me for?

JEM. What brought you into these parts?

VAN. To locate. I couldn't stand it there in Virginia. I was always wanting to go into the fight when I heard of a battle, so I thought it best to get out, and so I did.

JING. Professional man?

VAN. Yes. I propose to turn out the best horseshoe in the state.

JING. Oh, I see. [*Smiles*] Another Tubal Cain.

VAN. [*Rises and beckons Jingle to come C.*] Let me ask, was this Cain a gentleman? [*Meaningly*]

JING. A perfect gentleman.

VAN. [*Relaxes*] Satisfactory. Take another drink.

JING. All your family blacksmiths?

VAN. No, I've a brother a planter, and another a preacher. They wanted to make a lawyer of me, but I found there was no chance to succeed at that unless you were a natural-born liar.

JING. I'm a lawyer.

VAN. You ought to succeed. [*They drink*] But I don't think you will. The fact is, our town was full of a set of those fellows who knew enough to want to make an easy living and didn't know enough to make it. If there is a pitiable sight in this world, it is a young doctor waiting for gray hairs and patients, or a young lawyer starving to death in his own office. [*Enter Cromwell, R.2.E.*]

CROM. Go along, Mr. Jingle?

JING. Where?

CROM. Going to hitch the filly and going to town. Better come along for company.

JING. May I ask what is the object of the expedition?

CROM. Kate has heard of the fight and is anxious about Dick, and wants to get all the particulars. [*To Vandyke*] How do you do, sir?

VAN. At present, tolerably well. Food away head of fun for flesh. [*Sic*]

CROM. Stay all night?

VAN. Can't tell. Depends on how I feel half an hour hence.

JING. [*To Vandyke*] Must excuse me, sir.

VAN. With pleasure, sir, with pleasure, sir.

JING. [*Aside*] There is no occasion for so much jog.

CROM. Back at sunset. Come, let us be off. Come and take fresh air. [*Exit, L.2.*]

JING. I'll go, but I won't take any fresh air. [*Aside*] Wonder if he'll attempt love to Jeminaia. [*Beckons her from window*] Don't encourage him in the slightest degree. He won't stand it.

JEM. Mind your own business, sir.

JING. Thank you. [*Exit, L.2.*]

VAN. Who is that old chap?

JEM. Mr. Calvert, the owner of the inn.

VAN. Looks more like a customer than a landlord. Pretty good judge of his own liquor, eh?

JEM. That's his own affair. [*Going up*]

VAN. Correct. You are what I call a smart girl. Going to marry the chap with the red nose?

JEM. That's my affair.

VAN. Correct again. [*Music. Enter Kate, R.2.E.*]

KATE. Has Mr. Calvert gone yet?

JEM. Not yet. But he's putting the filly into the light wagon.

KATE. I want to see him before he goes. [*Exit, L.2.*]

VAN. [*Looks after her, gives a long low whistle*] Beautiful. [*To Jeminaia*] I say [*Nodding after Kate*], married?

JEM. Yes.

VAN. How long?

JEM. They were married the morning he left for the field.

VAN. Was she very fond of him?

JEM. I think she was when he was going away.

VAN. Ah—many a woman has been won by those little words—good-bye. [*Whistles again*] Pity!

JEM. [*Down L. of Vandyke*] Why is it a pity?

VAN. A woman as beautiful as she ought never to be given to man; but, like the stars in the sky, like the flowers by the roadside, be admired by all, but owned by none.

JEM. But every man wants a flower of his own. I say, you talk real pretty, every pop.

VAN. Why not? Burns was a plowman, and poetry has never been the property of princes.

JEM. Are you married?

VAN. No, but I'd like to be. [*Drinks, enter Kate*]

KATE. [*Looking back*] Don't be too late.

CROM. [*Outside*] All right. [*Crack of whip*]

KATE. [*Going to window and calling*] I'll wait for you. You know how anxious I am.

VAN. [*Aside*] If that woman wasn't another's now—pshaw! It's just my luck.

KATE. [*To Jeminaia*] That man just come from Virginia? Maybe he saw Dick. I'll ask him. [*Coming down, L.*] Are you, sir, from the front?

VAN. If you mean from Virginia, yes.

KATE. Were you there during the battle?

VAN. Do you mean the fight at Fairfax?

KATE. Did you hear any of the names that were killed?

VAN. Lord bless me, no. The names never come in till the smoke clears away.

KATE. Were there any Pennsylvania regiments engaged? [*Earnestly*]

VAN. I heard of two.

KATE. [*Eagerly*] Was the Ninth one of them?

VAN. No. [*Pause*] I think the Ninth was not in the fight.

KATE. [*Sinking into chair*] Thank heaven!

VAN. [*Aside*] If God don't pardon that lie, I'll have to let it go on the old account.

JEM. [*Aside*] That fellow knows more than he tells. [*Exit, R.2.*]

VAN. You seem anxious.

KATE. Yes. My husband is in the Ninth, and when I heard there had been a battle, I felt a nameless terror take possession of me as if I was resting under the shadow of a great cloud that might at any moment break into desolation and end in darkness. No one knows, unless it be those unfortunates who have experienced it, what a painful thing it is to sit day after day and await the arrival of tidings which may come all too soon at last. [*Rising*]

VAN. I sympathize with you, madam, I really feel for you, but I would keep a stout heart. Trouble is always bad enough when it comes. Now if I were you, I would meet it half way.

KATE. You are quite right. I shall try to fight off this presentiment. Do you remain with us over night?

VAN. Might as well, I guess. Ten miles to the next town, ain't it?

KATE. Yes, about ten.

VAN. Then I'll stay. It is sunset now, and the days are growing shorter.

KATE. I will see that you have a pleasant room. [*Exit, R.2.*]

VAN. [*Rising and looking after her*] How that woman seems to love that man. I would give twenty years of my life—yes, pile the years up like faggots—to have a fireplace in a woman's heart as bright for me. But what's the use in me rushing? [*Pause*] Married four months—it's about time. [*Sighing*] But perhaps that accounts for her loving him so much. [*Enter Pennington, L.2.E.*] Good evening, stranger. Walk right in. You look tired. Take a seat.

PENN. Thanks. Are you the landlord? [*Sits at table, L.*]

VAN. Bless your heart, no. Only as the old hymn says—"only a traveler by the way." [*Sits, R. of table*]

PENN. I thought perhaps—

VAN. Exactly. I know what you thought—that I was making myself rather free for a stranger, but Lord bless me, sir, down in old Virginia, the latchstring is always out, and it seems to me that every man ought to have the right to dispense the hospitality of an inn—that is, if he is willing to pay the tip. [*Striking pocket*] Have something hot?

PENN. Not now. You see, I'm wounded, and the doctor does not allow me the use of liquor.

VAN. So you are wounded? [*Sympathizing*] I say, where did you get that?

PENN. At Fairfax.

VAN. Well, I say, that is too bad, isn't it? Pity they couldn't carry on a war without hurting folks.

PENN. Are you a Virginian?

VAN. Well, I should say so, and I love every inch of her soil from Sandy River to the sea.

PENN. Then you sympathize with the South?

VAN. I sympathize with a whole nation that can't find anything better to do with their powder than to slaughter us. But then, what's the use of talking? Fill up and give us a toast. Excuse me, you don't drink. Well, I'll have to go it alone. Here's to the honored dead on both sides.

PENN. On both sides of the line. [*Solemnly*]

VAN. What do you say to a quiet game of Old Sledge, just to pass the evening, you know?

PENN. I cannot. I am here on important business.

VAN. You are right—business before pleasure.

PENN. I wish it was a pleasure. Do you know young Mrs. Calvert?

VAN. The lady who has a husband in the war?

PENN. Yes. Richard Calvert's wife.

VAN. She just left the room as you came in. [*Looking off, R.2.*] Say, you haven't had bad news, have you?

PENN. The very worst she could hear.

VAN. Now stop. It isn't—it isn't death?

PENN. Yes, it is. I saw Dick fall; shot through the head.

VAN. Hush! You haven't got the heart to tell her, have you?

PENN. I promised Dick that very morning, when we went into the fight, to come and tell the folks if he should fall; and you wouldn't have me violate a solemn promise, and that given to one now dead?

VAN. But the woman loves this man.

PENN. But she must hear it sooner or later.

VAN. Then I can't see how it can be kept from her for all time; but say, stranger, you don't know what may follow your story, and—[*Looks off, R.2*] She's coming.

PENN. I'm beginning to regret my promise. [*To Vandyke*] You tell her. Perhaps you can tell her better than—

VAN. Tell her! [*Seizing him by the arm and looking him fiercely in the face*] Why, man, what do you take me for? All the gold in the Sierras wouldn't be an inducement. Now I respect your feelings in the matter, and

I only ask you to break it gently to the poor thing. Break it mild, and in your last hour, Heaven will be as merciful to you.

PENN. I'll do my best. [*Gives hand to Vandyke*]

VAN. Good. [*Enter Kate, R.2.*] A gentleman wishes to see you on very important business. [*Goes up, C.*]

KATE. See me?

PENN. You are Richard Calvert's wife?

KATE. Yes, yes. [*Eagerly*] And you are?

PENN. John Pennington, Ninth Pennsylvania.

KATE. And you bring me news of my husband. Oh, tell me, is he safe? Is he alive? Something in your face, something in your heart, warns me of evil. Speak out, I pray you to speak.

PENN. [*Embarrassed*] We went into the fight together, Dick and I, standing close together, shoulder to shoulder.

KATE. And he, my husband—

VAN. [*Aside*] Poor girl!

PENN. When the enemy charged with their left, our right gave way, and the last I saw of Dick—

KATE. [*Eagerly*] The last you saw of him—

PENN. He was lying close to a fallen tree, bleeding from a wound in the forehead. He fell into the enemy's hands. [*Vandyke crosses, down C., slowly*]

KATE. But not dead. In pity's sake, not dead! [*Music pp. Military march*]

PENN. Dead!

KATE. Dead! Dead! Dead! [*Falls and is caught by Vandyke who holds her head on his knee and looks reproachfully at Pennington*]

VAN. Why didn't you draw it mildly? [*Enter Jeminaia*]

JEM. [*Throws open window, C.*] More troops for the front. [*Music forte. Jeminaia, R., Vandyke and Kate, C., Pennington, L.*]

ACT II.

SCENE: *Lights up. An apartment in Vandyke Vernon's house, comfortably furnished. Time, 1865. Parlor. Doors, R. and L.2.E. Door in flat, L.C. Window, R.C. Music, "Anvil Chorus," at rise. Noise of anvil, L.2.E. Jingle and Jeminaia discovered, looking L.2.E.*

JING. [*At door*] Behold! When the son of mighty Vulcan Van of Virginia swings his sledge and bellows—

JEM. Eh?

JING. His bellows. See, from the forge's fiery flame, he fashions iron miracles, and proudly earns his bread after that peculiar fashion recommended in sacred writ; to wit: Earn thy bread by the perspiration of thy brow—I never say sweat.

JEM. [*Coming down*] Why?

JING. It's vulgar.

JEM. It isn't half so vulgar as to go around with a stomach half full of rum, and a nose so red that it looks like a fire bug at night, doing no good for yourself or anybody else.

JING. Jeminaia, you are harsh! You are even more, you are cruel! And from the way you eye that apprentice there, I may say inclined to be perfidious.

JEM. Don't be a fool! That apprentice is a mere boy.

JING. Boy! Do boys have their suits of clothes? Do boys wear gaiters? Do boys wink slyly at young women? Or do boys do the thousand and one things that I have charged him? And again in that said apprentice, the aforementioned forgo—

JEM. You are a fool, Mr. Jingle!

JING. Thank you. I will go. I will leave you. You have wounded the spirit. [*Going up*]

JEM. [*Down R.*] I wish you would go and never come back, at least until you quit drinking, and become a respectable member of society.

JING. [*Coming down*] Miss Jessup, after what you have just uttered, I will not presume to call you by the more familiar name of Jeminaia. May I ask you who, in your opinion, is an ornament to that vague and indifferent being called—for lack of better appellation—society?

JEM. Why, just Van there. Look at him. Five years ago he came here a stranger, a poor man without a friend in the world, and nothing but his strong arms to depend upon. He went to work like a man.

JING. And married Richard Calvert's widow like a man. Poor fellow! He died in the first year of the struggle. He wasn't such a bad fellow.

JEM. [*C.*] Not half so good as Van: and I knew them both. He would never have made Kate Vernon so happy as Van does. He was too fond of drinking, like yourself, and depending upon his father for support. I say no man is a man that can't hoe his own row! [*Striking her hand under Jingle's nose*]

JING. How can a man hoe a row that has no hoe, and is also without the said row? And besides, I am a professional man. It would be beneath my dignity to work in a forge like Van.

JEM. Rubbish! Better a man had a millstone around his neck, than a lot of learning he can't turn to any use. [*Going*]

JING. Stop! You have said a good thing. You have uttered the one sensible thing of your life. The one sentence necessary to open my eyes to a just appreciation of my position. Jeminaia Jessup, you have made a man of me! From this day henceforth, I'll try to be somebody! [*Going up, enter Vandyke in working clothes, L.2.E.*]

VAN. A pious resolve! Although, my worthy friend, you have a very large contract on your hand. [*Goes C.*]

JING. I know it; but I will triumph as sure as pop. I will turn down a new leaf! What would you advise for a start? [*Down L.*]

VAN. [*Crosses to C.*] A little hard work wouldn't be a bad beginning.

JING. Not manual labor! You don't mean manual labor?

VAN. Yes, I do. Good earnest hard work.

JING. But dignity—

VAN—There is no true dignity without independence; and rough grained hands often make smooth souls. [*To Jeminaia*] Where is Kate?

JEM. Not home. [*Goes up*]

VAN. When shall we see you again, Mr. Jingle?

JING. You shall see me again when I am an altered man. [*Exit, D.F., passes window, kisses Jeminaia and off*]

VAN. Poor fellow! Himself his worst enemy. Where did you say Kate had gone?

JEM. To town. She asked me to tell you she didn't want you to work after four this evening.

VAN. [*R.C.*] What does that mean?

JEM. She said this was your birthday, and she wanted you to give this evening to your wife and child.

VAN. God bless that little woman! She is always thinking of me and my happiness!

JEM. [*Crosses to L. of Vandyke*] You won't tell her if I tell you something?

VAN. [*Rising*] Tell me something! Is it anything about her?

JEM. Lord bless you, sir! How you stare! No, it isn't anything against her. Do you think I could?

VAN. Well—[*Draws a long breath*] I didn't know what you would do. But I know this. I wouldn't hear a word against my little woman for the world. If anything ever could come between us, it would be because I opened my ears to every report. That man who does, like the eavesdropper in the fable, never does any good.

JEM. But you never heard any ill report?

VAN. Against my Kate? No! And it wouldn't be good for any man to utter it. But what is it you're going to tell me?

JEM. She is going to surprise you with something.

VAN. Bless her happy eyes, I have got something in store for her, too.

JEM. You have?

VAN. Yes. I gave out the contract for the new house. It will be ready before Christmas.

JEM. Splendid!

VAN. Well, I should say so. Here's the plan. [*Holding up paper, calls off, R.2.E.*] Hello, there! You Jack? [*Crosses to D.*]

JACK. [*At door, R.2.E.*] Well, sir, what is it?

VAN. You just turn out that set of shoes yourself, and when you get through, go home. I'm going to knock off for the day. [*Going, R.2.E.*]

JACK. All right, sir. [*In whisper*] Jeminaia!

VAN. What did you say? [*Turns quickly*]

JACK. Just coughed, sir!

VAN. You had better take something for that cold, or it might settle around your heart and endanger you. [*Winks at Jeminaia and exit, D.F.*]

JACK. Everybody pokes fun at me. [*Exit, L.2.E. Enter Kate and Hattie, D.F.*]

KATE. Where is Van? [*Taking off shawl*]

JEM. Gone to fix up a bit, I think. [*To Hattie*] Did our little baby come back to us? [*Kisses Hattie*]

KATE. Don't ruffle her, Jeminaia, until her papa has seen her new bonnet.

JEM. Why baby has a new bonnet! Upon my word!

KATE. [*L.C.*] What do you think I bought Van?

JEM. Couldn't guess.

KATE. A new watch. Look! [*Holds it up*] Isn't it a beauty? All out of my chicken money, too.

JEM. It is beautiful! Shall I call him? [*Going, R.*]

KATE. [*L.C.*] No! Not for the world! Sister Lou is coming with a large cake and Charlie Knox with some real port. We are going to have a little spread in honor of Van's birthday.

JEM. A spread? A banquet, you mean. Cake and port, fit for a king!

KATE. And isn't my Van the king of hearts? Now set the table, get the cloth and napkins, and you, baby, sit here. [*Puts Hattie on stool, R.C.*]

JEM. [*Setting table, aside*] Pity my Jingle couldn't have known.

KATE. What can keep Lou? Love makes their journey exceedingly tedious to a third party. [*Crosses to D.R.F.*] Ah! There they come, like a pair of turtle doves, and just as slow. [*Enter Lou and Charles. Lou has large cake, Charles, bottle of port under each arm*]

Lou. Oh, dear, I'm so glad to be here. I really do believe I'm going to drop.

KATE. Not the cake.

Lou. [*Putting cake on table*] No, myself.

KATE. What kept you?

Lou. Nothing, only Charlie was just—

KATE. [*Laughing*] Was he?

Lou. [*L.C.*] Mrs. Vernon, please have some regard for Mr. Knox. [*To Charles*] Shall I tell her, dear?

CHAS. You can if you like, dear.

KATE. I wouldn't. I'll venture to say it wouldn't bear repeating. [*At table*]

Lou. [*Pointing to Charles, C., who looks neither R. nor L.*] Don't you think him perfectly gorgeous?

KATE. I trust you do.

Lou. He's just heavenly! [*To Charles*] Do your arms ache holding those bottles all the time, while I stand chattering like a magpie?

CHAS. No, dear; I could hold them forever.

JEM. [*Taking bottles*] We don't want you to hold them quite so long.

KATE. Mr. Knox, you look very happy.

Lou. You are happy, are you not?

CHAS. Yes, Lou. [*Aside*] I would be if I were alone with you.

Lou. Oh, rapture! [*As about to embrace him*]

KATE. Lou, I'm astonished!

Lou. Well, don't we? Don't we?

CHAS. We do.

KATE. Speak, you what?

Lou. You tell her, Charlie.

CHAS. [*Pause*] Love each other.

Lou. [*Slapping him on back*] Oh, dear me!

CHAS. You hit me.

Lou. Bless me, I thought you were choking.

KATE. Why don't you take off your bonnet?

Lou. Take off my bonnet, and before Van sees it? No, indeed! What are new bonnets made for I'd like to know, if they are to be hid under a bushel; we might as well save our money or wear a queer old headgear such as Hannah Bailey wears in her picture.

CHAS. You are poking fun at my Aunt Hannah.

Lou. And if I am? [*Turning up her nose*]

CHAS. If I were to tell all I know about you—

LOU. Tell! Tell! I insist, you shall tell! You don't know anything.

CHAS. Yes, I do.

JEM. [*Aside*] There's going to be a row.

KATE. There you go again. You two are forever quarreling.

CHAS. It's all your fault.

KATE. I quite agree with you; but I must say, Charlie, your Aunt Hannah's picture is a trifle queer, and—

LOU. I do wish, Kate, you would let Mr. Knox's friends alone. We at least know who they are, which is more than you can say of your husband.

KATE. Why, you just said—

LOU. Well, if I did? I suppose one can say what one likes to one's own. [*Pause*] Because—

KATE. True. [*Speaking earnestly to her*] But don't you think it rather cruel that we should keep all one's hard words for those we love best?

LOU. Everybody does.

KATE. Ah, more is the pity!

LOU. [*Looking at Charles lovingly*] Poor fellow! [*Aloud*] I say, Charlie, do you feel—

CHAS. [*Snappishly and turning his back*] Yes, I do!

LOU. Then go and feel as much as you like.

CHAS. I am going home.

KATE. Mr. Knox, I beg you will—

CHAS. You are always wounding my feelings.

LOU. And you are always picking at me.

KATE. There, there. [*Very gravely*] I see how it is, you were never intended for each other.

LOU. [*Aside*] Oh, dear! How terrible!

KATE. [*Between them*] I think, having discovered this, you had better shake hands and part.

CHAS. [*Aside*] I'm beginning to hate this woman.

KATE. But don't part enemies. There, shake hands for the last time. [*Puts Lou's hand in his*] Now, say farewell forever! [*Goes upstage*]

LOU. [*Aside*] I'm getting weak!

CHAS. My legs are beginning to shake.

KATE. Well, is it separation?

LOU. [*Hesitating*] N-no—no—no.

CHAS. Lou, dear, you will—

LOU. Of course I will.

CHAS. My own you are! [*About to embrace when Jeminaia comes down between with bottle of pickles*]

JEM. [*To Charles*] Pickles. Open the bottle, please.

CHAS. Certainly. [*Takes bottle to table*]

LOU. [*To Hattie*] Take a piece of cake. [*To Charles, pointing to Hattie*] Isn't she lovely!

CHAS. Yes. Now, don't you wish—

LOU. Charlie Knox, are you sane?

KATE. Now everything is ready, and baby must go and tell papa to come. That's the little girl. Tell him mama and Aunt Lou want him right away. [*Exit Hattie, R.2.E.*]

LOU. [*Calling after her*] That's the pretty little toddler toddling. Go for papa and tell him to come here at once, and that Aunt Lou has a thousand—thousand kisses for him.

CHAS. [*In amazement*] Lou!

LOU. Don't be jealous, dear. You know Van is my brother-in-law.

CHAS. I'll go home then.

LOU. If you do I'll never speak to you again.

CHAS. Yes, I will. I don't care for your going on in this way.

LOU. Sit down or I'll—[*Excitedly bursts into tears*] Kate! Kate!

KATE. Why, what on earth is the matter with you two? Lou, I'm astonished. Be reasonable! Talk to Charlie.

LOU. I won't! He's always picking a fight. [*Weeps*]

CHAS. [*Going up*] Lou dear, I'm going.

LOU. Well, I don't care, so I—[*Turns and looks into his face*] O Charlie! How could you!

CHAS. O duckie! [*They embrace*] Don't cry. [*Enter Vandyke, dressed, and Hattie, R.2.E.*]

VAN. Why, what in the name of sense has happened? Here's everybody wearing a holiday dress, and—

KATE. You great big boy, didn't you know this was your birthday? [*Going to him*] See what I have bought you? [*Gives watch*]

VAN. Gold by all that's—well, here now, this is a little bit more than my share. I feel—[*Stops and looks into Kate's face*] You are an angel! [*Kisses her*]

KATE. Don't you see Lou and Charlie?

VAN. So it is. [*Crosses to L.*] Lou, girl, you're looking as fresh as rippling water, and as bright as August sunshine. [*Attempts to kiss her*]

CHAS. Lou!

VAN. Ah!

Lou. You must not kiss me, Van, although I am tremendously glad to see you.

Van. And why not?

Lou. Because—because—[*Pointing to Charles*]

Chas. [*Looking at Vandyke*] We are—

Jem. [*Aside*] I do wish Mr. Jingle was here.

Van. There, I won't kiss you, Lou. I always respect another man's claim.

Lou. But you want to awfully, don't you? [*Goes to him*]

Van. Let us not make Mr. Knox uncomfortable. [*Crossing, L. To Charles*] Straighten up, you don't look cheerful.

Chas. [*Smiling*] Oh, dear, yes, I'm delighted.

Kate. Come, sit down. Jeminaia, open the wine, that's a good girl.

Jem. [*Opening wine*] Everyone look out for their eyes.

Lou. Now isn't that perfectly gorgeous!

Van. What is it?

Kate. Old port, very best.

Lou. [*Sits*] Sit by me, Charlie. This is what I call lovely.

Chas. Don't, Lou.

Lou. Not you, the port.

Van. Jeminaia, why don't you join us? Plenty for all, and to spare.

Jem. No, thank you, I'm full enough. [*Aside*] I do wish Mr. Jingle was here! [*Exit, R.2.E.*]

Van. I think we should have a song. Music is the voice of happiness.

Chas. And Lou sings lovely.

Kate. You are making Lou blush, Charlie.

Chas. I'm always doing that—no, no, I really don't mean—

Lou. Charlie Knox! There are others present.

Chas. I wish there were not.

Van. What!

Lou. He don't mean that. [*Vexed*] I suppose I'll have to sing to keep your mouth closed.

Chas. You needn't sing if you don't want to. I didn't ask you.

Lou. And that is why I am going to do it. [*Song introduced here*]

Chas. I could listen to you forever.

Kate. And so could I.

Van. I think I am the happiest man in the world tonight. Here I sit, with the best little wife in all creation; a regular guardian angel and no mistake; and a child—well, bless her pretty eyes, just look at her.

Lou. Perfectly sublime.

VAN. I feel my house swelling as big as a meetinghouse. I owe no man a grudge or a dollar; and, while I am not rich, I am not too proud to toil for wealth in an honest, manly sort of a fashion.

KATE. And we will be rich some day, won't we, Van?

VAN. [*Pressing her hand*] Leave that to me. You'll ride in your carriage yet.

LOU. Won't that be gorgeous!

VAN. But after all, friends, what is wealth, and all it brings, without knowledge that somewhere in the world there is one pure heart that would sorrow for your fall, or ache when you did?

CHAS. Lou dear, don't you want to take a walk?

VAN. Isn't that rather a sudden notion.

KATE. You won't stay away long?

LOU. Until the moon rises. Charlie likes to walk in the moonlight.

VAN. It is rather romantic for a brace of lovers.

LOU. Heavenly! [*Going to D.F.*]

CHAS. And then there is no harm in it you know.

LOU. Shut up!

VAN. Kate and I had only a year of courting; but while it lasted, we were as big a pair of fools as—

LOU. Don't be a brute, Van. Courting is grand! [*Catches Charles's arm*]

CHAS. You're pinching me!

LOU. Did I pinch you? [*Exit both, D.F.*]

VAN. It is a pretty bad case of spoons and no mistake; but then, it is only the first symptom of a violent fever—matrimonial. When they have been married four or five years, the moon won't have such an effect on them. Now, guess what I have done today.

KATE. I can't. Tell me.

VAN. I gave Sims & Slocum the contract for our new house.

KATE. You did? [*Gleefully*]

VAN. I did that very thing, and we shall be in it by Christmas.

KATE. Oh, dear Van! Tell me all about it.

VAN. Here's the plan. It's a good deal more elegant than I am. [*Spreads paper on table*]

KATE. What is that?

VAN. Ground plan—parlor.

KATE. Goodness! Are we going to have a parlor?

VAN. Parlor? Two of them, one each side the hall.

KATE. [*Claps hands*] And a hall?

VAN. A hall, I should say so; the largest hall you ever saw. There's the dressing room, and Sims says that's the library.

KATE. But you have so little time to read.

VAN. Why, if I couldn't read at all, we should have a library like other folks. [*Enter Jeminaia, R.U.E.*]

JEM. [*Going to Hattie*] Won't baby come to her little bed now? [*Takes Child in arms*]

VAN. Haven't made up my mind about having a porch in the rear. What do you think?

KATE. I don't know, indeed.

VAN. Jeminaia, what do you think of a porch in the rear?

JEM. [*Whispers*] Don't consult your servants.

VAN. [*Pause*] Never mind, Jeminaia, it don't matter what you think.

JEM. [*Aside*] The port has gone to his head, poor fellow. [*Vandyke and Kate kiss Hattie*]

VAN. Good night, little blossom.

JEM. I do wish Mr. Jingle was here [*Exit, R.2.E., with Hattie. Enter Jack, L.2.E.*]

VAN. Well, Jack, are you through?

JACK. All through, sir; but there's a gentleman just came a horseback that would like to have a shoe fixed. The animal is downright lame.

VAN. I'm off for the evening. You do the job, Jack, and put the money in your own pocket.

JACK. Thank you, sir; but the gentleman would like to have a glass of fresh spring water if you please.

VAN. Tell him to come in and he shall have it. [*Exit Jack, L.2.E. To Kate*] Tell Jeminaia to bring a pail, dear, and you bring the poor fellow a glass yourself.

KATE. Of course I will. [*Lights down. Music, exit Kate, R.2.E.*]

VAN. [*Calling, R.2.E.*] Walk right in here, sir. [*Enter Richard Calvert, L.2.E.*] Take a chair. Tired, I suppose?

RICH. Very. [*Sits, L.2.E.*]

VAN. Have you come far?

RICH. From Texas.

VAN. Not on the back of a horse?

RICH. I left the railroad at Chamberlain thirty miles off.

VAN. Sorry you did not come sooner. We could have offered you a drop of something better than water. From Texas, eh? Been there long?

RICH. Yes, since '61. I have been a prisoner of war; was wounded and fell into the hands of the Confederates at Fairfax. Have been in the trans-Mississippi department ever since.

VAN. Precious bad luck you had, my friend. Live hereabouts?

RICH. Eleven miles west on the old national road.

VAN. Better stay all night.

RICH. No, no, I'll rush on the moment the animal is shod. [*Aside*] Moments are hours until I see her!

VAN. Married?

RICH. Yes. [*Aside*] I wish I could say no.

VAN. Then rush on. A regiment couldn't keep me a minute longer than that horse could get over the ground. [*Looks R.*] Ah, here comes Kate. [*Music*] You'll say you never drank such water in your life. [*Enter Kate, R.2.E. Richard rises and Vandyke turns upstage*]

KATE. I am sorry we had nothing better to offer. I—

RICH. Kate Calvert!

KATE. [*Screams*] My husband!

VAN. Husband!

KATE. O Richard! I thought you were dead!

VAN. [*Coming down*] See here—what—what does this all mean?

RICH. It means that this woman is my wife.

VAN. [*To Kate, who has fallen in chair*] And is this man—this man—

KATE. Richard Calvert! O Van, Van! What have I done! What shall we do!

VAN. Do! Do right! That's what we'll do!

RICH. She must come with me.

VAN. And so she shall. [*Quickly*] She is your wife under the written law, and you shall have justice.

RICH. And you will give her up?

VAN. I have never had but one rule in my life—Do unto others as you would have them do unto you.

KATE. But—O Van! What will become of you? [*Weeping*]

VAN. [*Pressing hand to heart*] I don't know! If hearts ever do break, why don't mine? [*Dashes away tears and turns quickly to Calvert*] You will let her remain here tonight? Nay, I will respect her as your wife. She will be as sacred as if she were dead, and in a coffin; for she is dead, sir, now to me! [*Enter Lou and Charles*]

LOU. Richard Calvert! Risen from the dead!

RICH. She must come now.

Van. But see, sir, it is dark, and the way is long, and she is very nervous —and—and I have a few things to say to her. It's natural you know, before we part forever.

Rich. Once for all I refuse.

Van. Do you claim—

Rich. I claim her obedience.

Kate. Richard, hear me.

Rich. Not a word.

Lou. [*Down C.*] Then you shall hear me! You claim a wife's obedience— I claim a sister's love. Before, she slept in my arms; tonight, she shall do so again. [*Draws Kate to her and regards Richard with indifference*]

Rich. Seeing that I have no vehicle, and there is no help for it, she may remain until morning.

Kate. Would to Heaven morning would never come!

Van. Hush! We must not wrong him even by a thought.

ACT III.

Scene: *Same as Act II. Vandyke discovered by window. Lamp on table, light half down. Time, night. Charles sleeping with hand on table by fireplace. Plaintive music at rise.*

Van. How fast the night has slipped away. It is almost light. What will it bring to me? Pshaw! I must not allow this womanish feeling to rob me of self-control. To go out into the tempest, to perish in the thick of battle— that is what the world calls bravery. Stuff! What is either of them to standing by quietly while your heart is being torn out of your body? To be compelled to look down aisles of the future paved only with burning bitter tears.

Chas. [*Waking*] Bless me, it is almost morning. Are you there, Van?

Van. Yes.

Chas. Asleep?

Van. No. Shall I ever sleep again?

Chas. I hope so. I really don't think you'll feel so badly when it is all over.

Van. All over! Ah, Charlie, when will it be all over with me? [*Sighs*]

Chas. Really, I didn't mean—

Van. I want to fix up my affairs before he comes. I would like to consult a lawyer as to the legal points. Would you object to walking over and telling Jingle to come here at once.

Chas. Certainly not. But is Jingle good authority? [*Rising*]

Van. These are simple questions, and probably he is sober now.

CHAS. Which he might not be later in the day. [*Going, D.F.*] Tell Lou I will be back in a moment. [*Aside*] Poor devil. [*Exit*]

VAN. I wonder if this Calvert will be good to her, if she will be happy, and if she will often think of me—of me. [*Enter Lou, L.2.E.*]

LOU. [*Going to him*] You have not slept all night?

VAN. No, but Kate—

LOU. She is sleeping. [*Lights up*]

VAN. [*Aside*] Poor child. After all, the weight of this cruel cross must fall heavily upon her shoulders.

LOU. But in her sleep she murmurs only your name, and said just now, most distinctly, "Van, we shall live in the new house after all."

VAN. Thank God for this most merciful gift of sleep, and such dreams as give the momentary glimpses of a paradise they may never realize.

LOU. [*Aside*] If he goes on that way, he'll start us crying, and when I commence I never know when to stop. [*Aloud*] Van.

VAN. Were you speaking?

LOU. Kate has asked me to say that if you think of remaining here after she has gone, why I will keep house if you prefer it, that is if you—

VAN. [*Takes her hand*] Thank you, Louil. Perhaps I shall avail myself of your kind offer. It is very good of you and Kate, for I—

LOU. O Van, don't talk of our goodness. Kate only regrets that she has not been more thoughtful of your happiness.

VAN. Oh! She has nothing to regret. All the happiness I have ever known has come through her, and now I can't realize that I am about to lose her forever. It don't seem like justice.

LOU. Was Charlie here tonight?

VAN. Yes. He has stepped out and will be back soon.

LOU. [*Aside*] Poor fellow, he isn't used to losing his sleep. [*Enter Charles, D.F.*]

CHAS. Mr. Jingle will be here presently.

VAN. Very good. [*Sits at table*]

CHAS. Oh, is that you, Lou? [*Crosses to her L.*]

LOU. Yes. Where have you been?

CHAS. On business. [*Pointing to Vandyke*]

LOU. What business?

CHAS. [*Whisper*] Come into the shop and I'll tell you.

LOU. O Charlie, dear, is it not appalling? [*Exeunt, L.2.E.*]

VAN. [*Turning out light, lights up*] It is broad daylight at last. [*Enter Jingle, D.F.*]

JING. [*Walks up to Vandyke and extends hand*] I am sorry for you, Van, I am, upon my honor.

VAN. I know you are, Mr. Jingle, and I'm sure I'm grateful. After all a kind word is not air, no, sir. The good feeling that gives it utterance is the alchemist that turns it to gold, and none but the miserable know how deeply it sinks into the heart.

JING. [*Sitting*] But how often do we find, my dear boy, that the world is more niggardly of its kind words than its gold? I have stood in need of a gentle word of admonition, of sympathy—did I receive it? No—save and except from Jeminaia, sir.

VAN. Well, well, to business.

JING. Ah, to business, is it—is it divorce?

VAN. Divorce! Do you think I have sent for you to free myself with the law against her?

JING. [*Meekly*] I really don't know.

VAN. Pity rules my heart, sir. I am not seeking vengeance upon the head of an innocent woman. I hope my anguish will never prompt my selfishness to injure one whom I would gladly shelter in the citadel of my heart.

JING. But under the law she is not your wife.

VAN. I know that, and now let us talk about the legal points of the case. I am worth some money.

JING. Good.

VAN. I own this house.

JING. Yes, so you do.

VAN. Can I give it to her?

JING. You mean without placing it under Calvert's control?

VAN. For herself alone.

JING. No, not in this state.

VAN. But I have money—cash and bank notes.

JING. These you can bestow upon her, your—I mean Mrs. Calvert.

VAN. I would like to make a regular settlement upon her, say five hundred a year.

JING. That you can do, of course, anything but real estate. But I say, I wouldn't advise you to do that. Calvert has always been a—Perhaps I ought not to say it, but I will—a drinking man.

VAN. Well?

JING. Becoming appraised of the fact that his wife has an income, he might demand and squander it in riotous living and—

VAN. Well, well. [*Impatiently*] And what do you propose?

JING. That you place in her hands, without the knowledge of any third party, whatever sum you propose.

VAN. I'll do it. Your fee is? [*Taking out purse*]

JING. Excuse me—a fee from a friend—never.

VAN. But you are a poor man.

JING. Have the rich a prior claim to all the good acts?

VAN. But you may need—

JING. And if I should, I shall have the satisfaction of knowing that in your need, I didn't coin money out of your misery.

VAN. [*Grasping his hand*] God bless you. You're a good, generous, noble-hearted man.

JING. I accept this blessing. No one needs an article of that kind more than I do. [*Going, D.F.*] Later in the day, I'll drop in again. My regards to Jeminaia. Good morning. [*Sighs and exit. Enter Lou, L.2.E.*]

VAN. Lou, tell Kate I want to speak to her a few minutes alone.

LOU. [*L.C.*] I will. O Van. I heard what you said to Mr. Jingle. You are too good. [*Sobs*] You made both of us cry, so you did. [*Exit*]

VAN. I wish I could cry. Perhaps tears might quench the fire that's raging here. [*Strokes heart and crosses, L. Enter Kate*]

KATE. [*Rushing into his arms*] O Van. Must we—must we part? [*Weeps*]

VAN. [*Loosing her hands from his neck*] Let us be calm. We have but a few moments now, and I have so much to say to you.

KATE. I never knew until now how much the human heart could stand and not break.

VAN. Trouble teaches us some queer lessons. Storms, they say, clear the atmosphere, and peoples' sorrow catechises, by reminding us that we still belong to the great legion of poor humanity. This even [*With emotion*] may prove for the best.

KATE. For the best, to tear you from my life! To break up our happy household; to—oh, the very thought of this is enough to drive me mad!

VAN. It does seem like injustice, that he whom you have only known four short months in all your life should have the right to take you from me, in whose heart you have rested for more than as many years, but you are his wife by the right of holy ordinance—let us not forget that.

KATE. I shall miss you so much—your gentle words, your sympathy.

VAN. And shall I not suffer, too? You do not, you cannot know how dear you have grown to me in all those years. You have been so kind, so loyal. But pshaw, I want you to be brave and here I am weakening your sense of right by words which had better be buried in the past, which today we must hide away as something never to be reclaimed in all the coming years.

KATE. Do not expect too much of me, Van. I am nothing but a weak woman, governed more often by impulse than by any sense of right. What would you have me do?

VAN. I would have you be as good a wife to him as you have been to me, even were he a bad man, which, far be it from me to say, he is. Your goodness will find a way to his heart, at least; and who knows but both of you may be happier for this bitter experience.

KATE. But your happiness, what of that?

VAN. My happiness? Well, as to that, I don't think there is much of that kind of thing in store for me, but my burden will be easier to bear if I know you are not crushed with the weight of yours, and I am quite content to stand down in the everlasting gloom if it will only make you happier.

KATE. God help us both to bear this blow. [*Lays head on table and sobs*]

VAN. And so He will. I have here, Kate [*Producing wallet*], our savings. We won't need any new house now, and so we had better make a fair division of it.

KATE. No, no, Van, not a penny.

VAN. But I say you shall receive half. It is your own. You helped to save it, and therefore you must accept it. Besides, it will make me feel easier, and that, I know you desire.

KATE. With all my heart.

VAN. There is $3,250 in all. There is your share. [*Gives notes*] $1,625. You can count it over yourself. As for Hattie—

KATE. Our poor child.

VAN. Aye. Our child. I will not forget her interest, be assured of that. [*Music*] And now [*Going*] I wish to say—to say—a word that I find very hard to say, and that is, farewell.

KATE. [*Rushes into his arms*] O Van. My heart is breaking.

VAN. I only ask that sometimes you will think of me—not to your husband's injury, remember that—but as one whom you have seen in a pleasant dream, that there is no hope of ever dreaming again.

KATE. Your happiness, your welfare, shall be the burden of my every prayer.

VAN. And when the end comes, and you are no longer his nor mine, only Heaven's, why, if I am alive, I'll go to where you lie and kiss your poor dumb lips for the last time, and this I ask of you if I am called first.

KATE. [*Sobbing*] I promise. Is there no hope for us?

VAN. I have put away hope as I would any other temptation. I must go now.

KATE. You'll not leave me until he comes?

VAN. Yes, yes, it is better I should not be here. You will need all your courage then, and I have no wish to see him now.

KATE. [*Clinging to him*] No, no. I cannot let you go.

VAN. Farewell. [*Kissing her*] Farewell, light of my heart. Farewell. [*Rushes off, L.2.E. Music forte*]

KATE. Van! Van! Come back to me! Come back to me! [*Falls. Enter Charles and Lou, L.2.E., bend over her*]

CHAS. She has fainted.

LOU. Poor sister. Is she dead?

CHAS. No, Lou dear, simply shocked.

LOU. Simply heartbroken. [*Sobs*] That's what it is.

KATE. Where is Van? Has he gone?

LOU. Yes, dear, gone.

CHAS. But he will come back, he told me he would.

LOU. [*Aside*] I didn't think he could lie so well.

KATE. [*Rising*] Where is Hattie?

LOU. Sleeping in her crib. Shall I bring her to you?

KATE. No, no. I will go to her. [*Going, R.2.E.*]

CHAS. But when Mr. Calvert comes?

LOU. Yes, when he comes, what shall I say?

KATE. That I am ready. [*Exit*]

LOU. How she does suffer. Van will not be as miserable as she is.

CHAS. Why not?

LOU. Because men forget so easily. [*Snappishly*]

CHAS. But Calvert may be very kind and teach her to forget.

LOU. Dick Calvert is not the man to eclipse Van Vernon's image in a woman's heart. He is selfishness itself, and women are not much given to love men who love themselves, I can tell you that, Mr. Charlie Knox.

CHAS. What are you angry with me for?

LOU. I don't care. It's enough to make a person mad, such scenes as this.

CHAS. Lou, dear, I wouldn't lose my temper.

LOU. Lecturing me again? You do nothing but scold me.

CHAS. Scold you, dear?

LOU. Well, I know you don't scold me in so many words, but you seem to, all the same.

CHAS. Do you want me to lay bare my heart?

LOU. I'd like to catch you. Not before me.

CHAS. I didn't mean—

LOU. I thought you did.

CHAS. You're always thinking.

Lou. And you can't think.

Chas. For heaven's sake, don't let us quarrel again, and we so soon—

Lou. I don't know that we are. I'm going to keep house for Van.

Chas. For a strange man?

Lou. And what were you, only a strange man one year ago?

Chas. But am I a strange man now?

Lou. You act so.

Chas. How?

Lou. At times you are naughty to me.

Chas. At times you are a riddle to me.

Lou. A riddle, indeed. I suppose you feel like giving me up.

Chas. No, no. I would find you out.

Lou. But why do you tantalize me so?

Chas. I don't tantalize you.

Lou. Then I raise all the rows—is that it?

Chas. No, no, I do.

Lou. What do you do it for?

Chas. Well—well—because—I—I—

Lou. Go on.

Chas. Not because I want to, but because I love you.

Lou. Charlie Knox, you are the sweetest creature in all the world. [*Enter Jingle, D.F.*]

Jing. None of that, none of that. I saw it all.

Lou. What did you see?

Jing. Enough to equip half a dozen suits of breach of promise.

Chas. Mr. Jingle, I wouldn't mention it.

Lou. I'd like to catch him.

Jing. Your guilty secret is safe. I only come to inquire after Jeminaia. In the general break-up, what provision, if any, has been made for her?

Lou. She is going to live with sister Kate. She must have somebody, and I am not agreeable to Mr. Calvert, I believe.

Chas. He doesn't understand you, Lou. [*Both go up*]

Jing. Our understanding does not relish. [*Enter Jeminaia, R.2.E.*]

Jem. [*Going quickly to Jingle and staring in his face*] Why bless my life, you are sober and it's almost nine o'clock.

Jing. Miss Jessup, I am an altered man. I will be sober at ten—at eleven —for all the time in the future.

Jem. I hope so, Mr. Jingle, indeed I do.

Jing. You may call me Ananias if you like.

Jem. I would rather call you Jingle.

Lou. [*At window*] Hush, here comes Mr. Calvert.

Chas. Something might happen.

Jem. Oh, dear me.

Chas. Shall we remain?

Lou. No, I don't want to meet him. There might be words between us. [*Exit with Charles, R.2.E.*]

Jem. I guess I won't stay and face the music. I wonder where Van is. [*Enter Richard and Cromwell, D.F.*]

Crom. [*In doorway*] Whoa! Whoa! Them horses are troublesome customers.

Rich. Where is Kate?

Jem. There, sir. [*Pointing, R.2.E.*]

Rich. Is she ready?

Jem. I believe she is.

Rich. Then tell her I am here, and ask her to hurry up, will you?

Jem. Yes, sir, but she is not very well, [*Going, R.*] and perhaps—

Rich. We will have no perhapses. I want her to come now.

Jem. [*Aside*] The brute. [*Exit*]

Crom. I wouldn't have sent that message, my boy, it may lead to ill feeling; ill feeling, sooner or later, ends in a row, and it is always best to compromise.

Rich. You needn't preach to me. I know my right as a man and as a husband.

Crom. And I as a father.

Rich. Do you want to quarrel with me?

Crom. I? Oh, dear no. I never quarreled with anyone in all my life. I always compromise. But Dick, Kate is and always has been a good girl. While she lived under my roof, no daughter could have been better to me than she was and that is why I would have you gentle to her at this time.

Rich. [*Crosses, R.*] One would think I was a barbarian to hear you talk. I suppose I know how to treat a wife.

Crom. No doubt, no doubt, but—

Rich. You can leave us now. She is coming.

Crom. With all my heart. [*Aside*] I have a horrible aversion to scenes. [*Exit, D.F. Enter Kate, holding Hattie by hand, dressed for traveling*]

Rich. I see you are ready.

Kate. Yes, entirely so.

Rich. I am a little early, but I thought it would be more comfortable traveling in the early morning.

Kate. I presume it will.

RICH. Your look is gloomy, as if you were going to an execution. Are you then sorry to leave this man for your husband's roof?

KATE. Let us not discuss that, please. I am ready. Let us go, please.

RICH. So be it, let us go. [*Going, D.F.*]

KATE. Good-bye, dear old home, good-bye.

RICH. Come. [*Open door, enter Vandyke*]

VAN. I thought you had gone.

RICH. Step aside and let my wife pass, please.

VAN. Certainly. [*Sees child*] My child, too. [*Crosses, R.*]

RICH. Come, what do you mean?

VAN. I mean this woman may be your wife, but this little one [*Takes Child*] is my child. [*Child in his arms*] My own. My precious. [*Picture*]

ACT IV.

SCENE: *An apartment in Cromwell Calvert's house. Nicely furnished. Doors, R.2 and L.3. Doors in C., in flat. Windows, R. and L. Enter Jeminaia, R.3.*

JEM. Oh, dear, what a life to lead. Here we have been up all night, bickering and everything else, and all because Kate wanted to go and see her little child. How I do wish Mr. Jingle was here. [*Enter Jingle, C.D.*]

JING. Mr. Jingle is here.

JEM. Oh, dear, so you are. I really didn't expect—

JING. This pleasant suprise. Now don't blush, you know that is what you mean. A blush is more eloquent than a woman's tongue, because it is easily read.

JEM. I hate puns.

JING. A pun! I confess it is the lowest order of wit, but is it not better than no wit at all? How is the family?

JEM. [*C.*] The family? Well, if you had been here since yesterday morning, you would have had such a dose of matrimony as would do you for the rest of your natural life.

JING. You don't mean to say another row?

JEM. Yes, I do.

JING. And the cause?

JEM. Why you see, yesterday was the 4th of August, the first anniversary of Kate's separation from Vandyke Vernon.

JING. Exactly.

JEM. And she promised to go and see her child every 4th of August and every Christmas day.

Jing. And she does so, of course.

Jem. Dick Calvert was furious when she came home last time and said she couldn't repeat that visit again.

Jing. Why this is preposterous. This is inhuman. Did she go yesterday?

Jem. No. He never left the house the whole day—the result—

Jing. Was a quarrel.

Jem. She coaxed, entreated and finally cried the whole livelong day and night.

Jing. Poor thing. I think I'll have to talk with Calvert about it. I'll see what can be accomplished by a little reason.

Jem. [Following him] I wish you would. [Enter Richard, R.2.E.]

Rich. Jeminaia, where is Mrs. Calvert?

Jem. In her room. [Richard, going L.] Please don't disturb her now.

Rich. Why not now?

Jem. She is writing a letter, sir.

Rich. Yes, I understand, to her Virginian. Miss Jessup, my wife, I find, is encouraged by you to disobey my wishes in that matter. I have no desire to retain a spy in my household, and if you can do better, the sooner you do so—

Jem. It is your father's house, not yours.

Rich. I said if you could do better—

Jing. [Confronting him] She can do better, sir. A great deal better. She is not dependent on your miserable service. Here, in your presence, I offer her my heart, which is rich in tenderness, and purse, which, although light at present I can fill with drafts upon my genius. [Taps forehead]

Rich. You're drunk. [Exit, L.3.E.]

Jing. And you lie. [In a very low voice]

Jem. O Jingle dear, I never knew you were so brave.

Jing. What? You don't know me? I am going to surprise you in another direction. I have taken a solemn pledge never to take another drop of liquor during my life.

Jem. And I'll seal your pledge with a kiss.

Jing. Thank you. I only ask three months of study, and I shall be admitted to practice. Shall we marry now or wait?

Jem. Lest you should think I had no faith in your strength of will, I will say—now.

Jing. Amen! [They embrace, enter Cromwell]

Crom. Another compromise, Mr. Jingle?

Jing. No, sir. A legal action without damage.

Jem. I must go and tell Kate. [Aside to Jingle]

Jing. You have my permission. Do just as you please. [Exit Jeminaia, L.]

CROM. Have you seen Richard?

JING. Yes, I heard him, too, and I must say I have not been edified in the least possible degree.

CROM. He has had a heap of trouble, and is mighty crusty, especially with Kate. Poor girl, I pity her, indeed I do. Will you take something?

JING. Thank you, no.

CROM. A little gin and sugar?

JING. No, sir.

CROM. What do you say to a compromise of brandy and water?

JING. No, sir, I don't drink.

CROM. Don't drink—the devil!

JING. I hope not. The devil was never a favorite drink of mine.

CROM. It's a regular pledge, eh?

JING. As regular as the principles of common law.

CROM. I am glad to hear it, Jingle. Perhaps you don't believe it, but I am.

JING. [Shakes hands] Thank you.

CROM. I only wish that you could get Dick to follow your example. I'm afraid he's going to the bad, and no mistake.

JING. I don't think there is any use of talking to Richard Calvert. He is a little harder nut than I would like to attempt to crack. In fact, I'm not certain that I'm fireproof myself, yet.

CROM. Do you think, Jingle, that I could quit drinking at 67?

JING. You can try.

CROM. And so I will. I will take the pledge at once. [Going with Jingle] Remember that this is a matter that don't admit compromise. [Exeunt, C.]

JEM. [Enter, L.] Where on earth did Mr. Jingle go? [Enter Kate, L.]

KATE. You shall not leave, Jeminaia, until I go with you.

JEM. You are then determined to go even against his commands?

KATE. There is a voice in my heart more imperative than his commands —a mother's love for her child. [Crosses, R.]

JEM. But his anger?

KATE. Do you think that the terror of his anger will prevent me from going? I am tired of this dreadful existence; tired of his cruel upbraidings; tired of his unwarranted suspicions.

JEM. But he may not permit you to return.

KATE I care not. I would rather go out into the world as the meanest mendicant that ever solicited alms, than be denied the privilege of seeing my child.

JEM. Then if you will go with me, get your wraps at once before he has a chance to prevent your leaving.

KATE. Yes, yes. I will be ready in an instant. [*Going, R.*]

JEM. This is a serious step.

KATE. And I am prepared to take the consequences. [*Exit, R.*]

JEM. At last he has aroused the tigress in her. I did not think she had the courage. [*Enter Richard, L.*]

RICH. Where is she?

JEM. There. [*Pointing, R.*]

RICH. Not preparing to leave? She would not dare!

JEM. You can ask her for yourself.

RICH. And so I will. [*Exit, R.*]

JEM. Dear me! What if he should attempt violence! Oh, how I do wish Mr. Jingle was here. [*Enter Vandyke and Hattie, C., exit Jeminaia*]

VAN. We are here at last.

HATTIE. And I am so tired.

VAN. Yes, I know you are. The way is long and dusty, and the sun is so hot and parching, but the pilgrimage is over, and now comes your reward.

HATTIE. You said we should see mama here.

VAN. And so we shall, although I fear she is ill or something worse. Had she been alive and well, nothing could prevent her from coming yesterday to see her little girl.

HATTIE. Does mama love me?

VAN. Love you? Why, how often have I told you that she loves you more than all the world besides.

HATTIE. Does she love you?

VAN. Yes, I think she does a little.

HATTIE. Then why don't she come and live with us like other girls' mamas do?

VAN. That is a long story and you wouldn't quite understand it. You are too young yet.

HATTIE. But some day I will be big and then you will tell me why you cried so hard over mama's picture last night, won't you?

VAN. Yes, yes, but there, I must leave you now. [*Goes C.*]

HATTIE. Don't leave me alone in this strange place. [*Going to him*]

VAN. I'll be back presently, after you have seen your mama.

HATTIE. Don't you want to see her, too?

VAN. [*Aside*] Do I want to see her! [*Aloud*] Not now, my child, not now. [*Going, C.*]

RICH. [*Outside*] Once for all, I forbid you.

VAN. That is Calvert's voice. Why, he is angry! They are quarreling. Stop! I must not let him see me. It would only make matters worse. Why,

I always thought they were happy and she contented. Poor child. Ah, he is coming this way. Perhaps going to leave the house. Come, dear, let us go in here. [*Going L.*]

HATTIE. But don't we see mama?

VAN. Yes, yes, we shall see her presently. [*Exeunt, L.*]

RICH. [*Enter, R.*] I will teach her that my word is law, that when I say no, I mean no. [*Enter Kate with shawl and bonnet in hand*] What does this mean? Where are you going?

KATE. I have already answered that question.

RICH. Again I demand a reply. Where are you going?

KATE. To see my child. [*Going C.*]

RICH. That's a subterfuge.

KATE. As your wife, I have reached almost the lowest depths, but I have not fallen so low as to need a subterfuge in this case.

RICH. Can you deny that you are more anxious to see this man than the child?

KATE. To such a question, I have no reply other than my silence. You can contrive as you think proper. [*Crosses, L., and sits*]

RICH. Is that the obedience of a wife?

KATE. What demand have you upon my obedience?

RICH. I am your husband.

KATE. You are in name, nothing more.

RICH. What do you mean by that?

KATE. That you ceased to be my husband when you ceased to love and treat me as one. For a whole year—a long, bitter, dreadful year, I have lived in the dust of your feet, subject to your taunts, your sneers, your malice. I shall do so no longer. [*Crosses, R.*]

RICH. [*Crosses, L.*] Then you have no duty to perform, no responsibility for your acts? If this is your creed, madam, you will learn that I have rights, too, and not only that, but the power to enforce respect from you.

KATE. [*Facing him*] What would you do? [*Goes to him*]

RICH. I will kill you or you will obey me. [*Catches her hand*]

KATE. And do you think I fear to die? [*Goes upstage*] Why should I prolong an existence which is only a long unchanging realization of misery and tears? I have tried to be a patient and ever affectionate wife.

RICH. And you did not try long.

KATE. No, for you met my self-denial with reproaches, my patience with torture, my affection with indifference.

RICH. Why not say cruelty?

KATE. And so I might, for if to spend one's days plotting another's misery is not cruelty, then there is no need for such a term.

RICH. Your indictment is very cleverly drawn; but women like you see but your own wrongs, as you are pleased to term them, forgetting that I, too, have reasons to complain. [*Going to her*] Can you picture to yourself my return, after four years of captivity, to find the woman I had made my wife on the eve of departure the wife of another?

KATE. But I thought you dead.

RICH. I believe you did, at least I will give you credit for as much consideration, but I can never forgive you for forgetting me in one short year as completely as if I never existed.

KATE [*Rises*] But on your return, did I not acknowledge the legality of your rights and leave a home that was a paradise, aye, even the tenderest associations known to a woman, the companionship of her child?

RICH. Only to pine and wail for its or his absence. [*Crosses to her*] Madam, every sign of regret is an injury to me, every tear an insult.

KATE. We cannot lock up our hearts as tombs and lay one's love in them even when duty commands; but you have not tried to kindle the affection I once entertained. You have been the owner, not the lover. The law binds me to you and that the chain clanks unpleasantly in your own ears is not the fault of the slave, but the master.

RICH. You have found your speech at last; but every word you utter is only decreasing your chances of seeing your child. Had you been more choice of your words, had your memory not retained the occurrences of the past years so completely, I might have relented, but now it is too late. [*Locks every door*]

KATE. What will you do?

RICH. Prevent you leaving this house. Kate Calvert, listen to me. You shall not see Vandyke Vernon or his child again. From this day forth, you are a prisoner in this house. When you leave it, it will be in your coffin.

KATE. [*Goes to him*] No, no! You do not mean that! Kill me if you will, in mercy kill me, but let me, oh, let me see my child again! [*On knees*]

RICH. Your prayers and tears are in vain. I am resolved and nothing can shake my purpose.

KATE. [*Rising*] Then do your worst, for I will go.

RICH. [*Pushing her back*] Back I say.

KATE. Your threats have no terror for me. I am desperate now. [*Advances*]

RICH. Back or I will kill you. [*Raises fist*]

VAN. [*Enter, R.2.*] No you won't.

KATE. Van! [*Enter Hattie, L.3.*]

HATTIE. Mama! [*Rushes into Kate's arms*]

RICH. This is my wife, sir. It is her duty to obey.

VAN. She is a woman and therefore it is my duty to protect her.

ACT V.

SCENE: *Richly furnished apartment in Mr. Jingle's house. Lights full up at opening; red for fireplace. Large window, R.C., through which can be seen mountain range, and snow falling at end of Act. Moon rises on mountain and snow ceases. Time, Christmas day, 1867. Jingle discovered at table, R., arranging holly boughs over window.*

JING. That looks like it. There is a suggestion of Christmas in that last sprig. [*Enter Jeminaia, L.3.E.*]

JEM. What on earth are you doing there?

JING. Curb your curiosity, Mrs. Jingle. I know I am asking you to do a very unwomanly thing when I ask you to curb your curiosity, but as your husband, as the partner of your bosom, as the father of your—I mean our child—

JEM. Our child!

JING. Aye! Our child! Excuse a father's emotion.

JEM. You're not crying, Mr. Jingle?

JING. Tears of joy—love!

JEM. We should thank Heaven for sending us such a treasure.

JING. Eh? Oh, yes, certainly, it was Heaven who did it, of course; and the celestial sphere has kindly put its monogram, a bit of blue, in either eye—

JEM. I'm so glad to see you so happy.

JING. Why shouldn't I be? Am I not the owner of this little nest? The husband of one of the best little women?

JEM. Dear Jingle! [*Embraces*]

JING. Besides, there is something about Christmas that mellows the heart, and sets the strings in tune for the merriest airs. By the way, where is the goose?

JEM. The goose? Oh, dear, brown as a berry and the stuffing—

JING. Oh! The stuffing! I do wish Kate would come. I feel as if I would like to turn that stuffing to a particular account.

JEM. She will be here by four o'clock, but Lou and Hattie ought to be here now.

JING. Does Kate expect to see her child here?

JEM. Certainly. It was that she might see her poor baby and spend Christmas with those who love her that I arranged this dinner party.

JING. It's a great pity that Van couldn't be here.

JEM. I don't think he would come. You know that it was only to avoid meeting her that he went to Virginia—to get out of temptation as he called it.

JING. I don't think I would be morally strong enough to do that. But Van, he is made of queer stuff. With him there is only one sentiment—duty. He even felt it his duty to leave his child with Lou, so that the little thing might be near its mother, that she might see it now and then.

JEM. It was a great pity Van ever came here.

JING. It's a great pity the rebel's bullet made a tour round Richard Calvert's cranium instead of going through it as it should have done, and as any sensible bullet would have done. [*Enter Lou, Hattie and Charles, D.F.*]

LOU. Merry Christmas!

JEM. Thank you, thank you.

JING. You did get here at last, and Mr. Knox, too.

LOU. Oh, yes, we couldn't leave Charlie behind, you know. [*Goes to fireplace*]

JEM. And the baby. [*Kisses Hattie*] How nice she does look!

JING. We have been waiting for you rather impatiently, Mr. Knox.

CHAS. Well, you see, we ought to have come sooner, but something happened this morning—shall I tell him, Lou?

JEM. I hope nothing serious.

JING. Nothing of a mortuary character—

CHAS. Not so bad as that.

LOU. Bad! Do you call it bad at all? It isn't bad in any sense. It's the very quintessence of everything that's delicious and delightful.

CHAS. Well, that's what I meant to say.

JING. You pique my curiosity.

JEM. And mine.

CHAS. [*R.C., aside*] I wish I hadn't said anything.

LOU. I won't tell you, Mr. Jingle; but Jeminaia, I don't care so much for you. [*Whispers to her*]

JEM. Why, you don't say so.

LOU. Yes, I do.

JEM. Why, Mr. Knox, how could you?

CHAS. [*To Jingle*] I say, Mr. Jingle, I feel rather uncomfortable. Let us go in. [*Aside*] I wish it was all over.

Jing. And wet our lips—come. [*At door*] She might as well have told me. A secret filters through a woman to her husband like water through charcoal. [*To Hattie*] Come, my little dear. [*Exeunt, R.2.*]

Jem. Tell me how it came about. I didn't think Charlie Knox would muster so much courage.

Lou. He always had courage enough but he was sadly deficient in language. This morning he made a splurge—a desperate leap.

Jem. And he said he loved you.

Lou. Oh, dear no. He told me that long ago; but the thing that stuck in his throat was the all-important question.

Jem. You mean the pop?

Lou. Yes, the asking me to marry him.

Jem. Jingle found no trouble.

Lou. But remember my dear, that Mr. Knox has a keen sense of delicacy.

Jem. Well, how did he bring it about?

Lou. He didn't bring it about.

Jem. Who did?

Lou. I did.

Jem. You!

Lou. Yes. Don't look so.

Jem. How?

Lou. Well, you see when he came in this morning I noticed something wrong with him.

Jem. Wrong!

Lou. Sort of white about his lips, and a general unsteadiness of person. Of course I knew at once the cause.

Jem. You did?

Lou. Certainly. At first I didn't know what to do. It was an awful position to be placed in.

Jem. Terrible.

Lou. I had a notion to run away at first, but I thought better of it. If I run off, says I, the barometer of Mr. Knox's courage may fall to zero and it will take him four or five years to revive. Now you know, my dear, the youngest of us cannot afford to waste so much valuable time.

Jem. No indeed, and you—

Lou. You won't tell Mr. Jingle? You don't tell your husband everything?

Jem. Do you think I am a fool?

Lou. Well, I didn't know. Some women are, you know.

Jem. Go on please.

Lou. I told him he had something on his mind. He admitted he had. I asked him to relieve his—

Jem. Mind.

Lou. Yes, mind, at once. He made several ineffectual attempts, and in time got so far as "How would you like"—when I unfortunately turned my head, and he threw up his hands in despair. Indeed, he looked so forlorn that I really felt for him. The position to a sensitive man must be one full of acute pain, so I said, "Don't attempt it here. Go in the other room and relieve your mind."

Jem. And he did?

Lou. Yes. Through the keyhole he begged me to name the day.

Jem. And you—

Lou. Said February first.

Jem. What followed?

Lou. A heavy fall, as of a limp and helpless body coming in contact with the floor, and then I was away.

Jem. Did he fall?

Lou. I think he did, at least when I came back I found him with a large lump on his forehead.

Jem. And so it is settled?

Lou. Yes, thank heaven. [*Enter Jingle and Charles*]

Jing. Jeminaia, baby is awake. He wants you.

Jem. Mr. Jingle, you must have pinched him; he was sleeping so soundly. I'll be back presently. Yes, I'm coming to his mutty's baby pitsy. [*Exit, R.2.*]

Jing. Ah, it's a glorious thing to be a parent. You should be a father, Mr. Knox.

Chas. I! Oh, dear—no—that is—

Lou. [*Aside*] I do wish he would change the subject.

Chas. How old is he? [*Points off*]

Lou. [*Aside*] Why does he want to know?

Jing. Let me see—nine weeks, thirteen hours and—

Chas. Never mind the minutes, Mr. Jingle.

Jing. Oh, you should hear him crow.

Chas. Does the little rooster crow?

Jing. Crow! Well, I rather think he does—loud as a mountain fowl and always at 2 a.m. We cover our heads with the blankets and kick—

Lou. You don't say so.

Jing. Yes, I do. Why, my dear boy, you never realize you are a father until you have two little dimpling feet in your chest, four or five times before daybreak. Oh, my dear boy, you ought to have a ba—

Chas. Mr. Jingle.

Lou. [*Aside*] I'll faint.

Jing. Eh?

Chas. Let the baby drop.

Jing. I'll do nothing of the kind. Oh, I see—change of subject. [*To Lou*] When did you hear from Van?

Lou. A week ago. He's coming home. He cannot remain away. I thought he would have been here today to spend the Christmas with us, but—

Chas. He may come yet.

Jing. I wish he would. We might cheer him up a bit. [*Enter Jeminaia, R.2.*]

Jem. The dinner is ready; the baby is asleep, and now if Kate would only come.

Jing. Let us go, Charlie, and taste the toddy. We can at least do that.

Jem. Mr. Jingle, be careful.

Lou. My dear, you know your capacity. You are fully aware that a pint won't hold a quart.

Chas. Now don't commence to scold. Remember that Christmas is Christmas.

Lou. Did I say it was New Year's?

Jing. I am waiting for you, Mr. Knox.

Chas. I'm going. [*Crosses, R.*]

Lou. Charlie!

Chas. Eh? [*Lou puts hand to mouth and shakes head*] I understand. [*Exit with Jingle, R.2.E.*]

Lou. Poor fellow. How he does love me.

Jem. And you?

Lou. I? I dote upon him. I always did admire majestic men. Marriage should be the illustration of the fable you know, of the lion and the lamb. Now where would you find a more lion-like man than Charlie? A more—more—lamb-like person than myself?

Jem. Yes, Charlie is very much like a lion. [*Aside*] Heaven forgive me.

Lou. [*Aside*] She don't mean to endorse the lamb. [*Enter Vandyke, D.F.*]

Van. A Merry Christmas to all here.

Lou. Van!

Jem. O Van. I'm so glad. [*Rushes to embrace*]

Van. And I'm glad to be back once more amongst those I love.

Lou. You come as a Christmas gift to us all and none could be more welcome.

VAN. Thank you, Lou dear, you are very good. Words of welcome are strangers to my ears; but they are kindly visitors, and you, Mrs. Jingle? [*Offers hand*]

JEM. [*Cries*] I'm so glad to see you that I can't see you at all. [*Takes hand*]

LOU. How did you know we were here?

VAN. I found the house closed, and Jack told me you and Hattie were here.

JEM. I'll go and send Hattie in and tell Mr. Jingle. I'm so happy.

LOU. You couldn't stay in Virginia—?

VAN. The place was torture to me. I carried a heavy load back to the old homestead—a heart filled with bitter pain and haunting memories. Everything, too, was changed. War had left its desolating signet upon the hearts of the people—tall gaunt chimneys, all that remained of pleasant homes, pointed with spectral fingers to the heavens. A sort of solemn warning against man's dead work and, well, it was—

LOU. No longer home.

VAN. Home! I didn't expect to find a home. There can be no home where there is no heart. But tell me, have you seen—have you seen—

LOU. Kate, do you mean?

VAN. Yes. Is she—is she well?

LOU. She was ill ever since you left, but lately she has improved somewhat.

VAN. And Calvert?

LOU. Has gone from bad to worse, until he is only a drunken sot, a wreck. I do wish to goodness he'd go to pieces some day. Wouldn't you like to see Kate?

VAN. Would I like to see her? Would the prisoner imprisoned in a dungeon for a long, long year like to see the sun-shining landscape? Would a lost soul like a glimpse of Paradise?

LOU. You shall see her. She is coming here today.

VAN. Today! But do you think it would be right?

LOU. Why not?

VAN. I have tried to do what I conceived to be my duty. Heaven knows how hard it has been; but I don't wish to give him any cause to make her any more wretched. Yes, I would give anything to see her once more, to hear her speak, to look into her eyes and try to reach her soul through them as I once did. [*Enter Jeminaia and Hattie, R.*]

HATTIE. Papa! [*Rushes to him*]

VAN. My child! Are you glad to see papa again?

HATTIE. Oh, yes. Aunt Lou said you would come.

LOU. And last night when I asked her what she wanted Santa Claus to bring her, she said, "I want him to bring my papa."

VAN. [*Kisses her*] And so he has. O Lou! Heaven is perfumed with Christmas prayers. [*Enter Jingle and Charles, R.2.E.*]

JING. Welcome back, Van old fellow.

CHAS. This is good luck indeed. This is indeed a merry Christmas. Don't you think so, Lou?

LOU. It's just heavenly!

JEM. It's after four. It's getting dark. I'm afraid Kate will not come now. [*Darken gradually*]

LOU. Perhaps she is ill again.

JING. The dinner is spoiling. Let us sit down ourselves. Come, Van.

VAN. [*Jingle goes R.*] No, no, thank you, not a morsel. I dined at the station.

LOU. I'm weak with hunger.

JEM. Then let us go. Come, Mr. Knox.

CHAS. I feel as empty as a bird's nest in December. [*Exit, R.*]

LOU. Poor Charlie is near starved! [*To Vandyke*] Hattie has had luncheon so I will leave her with you, Van.

VAN. Do; I want to talk with her.

LOU. This is shocking. [*Exit, R.*]

JING. Proceed, Mrs. Jingle.

JEM. You always want me to go before. [*Exit, R.*]

JING. In a social, not a mortuary way, my dear. Van, Van, when the punch bowl is ready, we will bring it in—until then—[*Bows and exit, R.*]

VAN. And so you want to have papa back?

HATTIE. Oh, yes, it is so lonely without you.

VAN. Not more lonely than I was without my little girl. But mama is coming today, and—would you like to see her?

HATTIE. Oh, yes, very much; let us go and meet her.

VAN. It is too cold. But here from the window, we can see the road for miles. [*Puts her in chair at window*]

HATTIE. How it snows!

VAN. Yes, the snow is veiling the mountains, and I can scarcely see to the first turn in the road. But see! There is a sleigh coming out of the darkness, and listen! [*Bells*] To the merry music of the bells. Now I can see a woman in the back seat. It is your mother, darling, I feel it is your mother. We shall have a Merry Christmas after all. A Merry Christmas! What! Can it be possible! They are turning down the crossroad. Oh, my child, they are not coming here, it is not your mother! It is not your mother.

HATTIE. Don't, papa, you make me feel so lonely, too. [*Enter Lou, L.2.E.*]

LOU. Oh, there you are! No sign of her coming yet?

VAN. No.

LOU. I know it; but somehow I cannot give her up. I feel that she will come yet; that she cannot, would not, disappoint her child. Should she do so, I would say, though she is my own sister—

VAN. No! Nothing against her! I would not have my faith shaken in her for a lifetime of happy hours. Why, if I could ever bring myself to doubt, I believe I would lose my belief in Him who is all fondness and fidelity.

LOU. Oh, she will never know how much she was beloved, or how much she has lost in you. Shall I take Hattie with me?

VAN. Yes, if you please. [*Music*]

LOU. Come with auntie. [*Exeunt, R.*]

VAN. How still it is! Even the snow has ceased to fall, and beyond the mountain is the moon struggling with the snow and darkness. I can scarcely believe that I am the same gay, light-hearted fellow I was two short years ago. It don't seem natural that trouble should change a man so much; but it does. A tear makes as deep a furrow as a year does. [*Goes R.*]

KATE. [*Outside*] Open the door! Open! [*Knocks quickly*]

VAN. Kate's voice! [*Rushes to door*]

KATE. [*Staggers in*] At last! At last! [*Drops in chair, C.*]

VAN. Kate, don't you know me?

KATE. Know you? [*Recognizes him*] Van! [*Opens her arms*]

VAN. But you are faint and—

KATE. I ran all the way—and had been ill, so very ill; and I thought I was going to die.

VAN. So bad as that!

KATE. Yes.

VAN. But you would have sent for me?

KATE. I had no one to send; and day after day, night after night, I lay there looking woefully at the large black mountain that seemed to raise its great head between us, and wishing--oh! How I wished for strength to climb over its rugged sides and see your dear kind face once more!

VAN. And He who never turns a deaf ear to a weak woman's prayer, granted yours at last.

KATE. Yes; but it was not until my faith in Him almost died. Heaven, to the stricken, seems a great way off, Van, and to me it seems as if this life was only made up of glimpses of Heaven; little floating islands of emerald upon my ocean of sin and sorrow and heartache.

VAN. I had been looking for you. I had almost given you up.

KATE. I tried to get away earlier this morning, and the horses were harnessed and ready, when Richard came in and ordered me to remain.

VAN. And the pledge he gave his dead father?

KATE. He had forgotten that. Rum steals away the memory as it hardens the heart!

VAN. But how did you get here at last?

KATE. He has been drinking heavily for the past week, and this afternoon he left for the village. With his going, came a craving to see my child which I could not resist.

VAN. I will bring her to you.

KATE. No, no! Don't leave me. It is so lonely here, and it is getting dark and I feel faint!

VAN. What can I do for you?

KATE. Nothing. I only wish to lay my head on your breast and weep out the bitterness that is in my heart. [*Lays head on his shoulder, enter Lou and Hattie*]

HATTIE. Mama! [*Kneels at Kate's feet*]

LOU. Dead! [*Enter Richard*]

RICH. She came here! She is mine! No other has a claim upon her, and she must come home.

VAN. Hush! Heaven has canceled your claim! She is at home! [*Picture*]

CURTAIN

NOTE: It is evident from the *London Athenaeum* review of *The Virginian* (quoted in full in the check list of the plays) that Campbell either rewrote or allowed someone else to rewrite the ending of *The Virginian* for its London production. In this version the husband and not the wife perishes in the "snow wreath," thus allowing for the happy reunion of the lovers. It is as interesting as it is futile to speculate on why this change was made. Did Campbell or his London producer remember that many years before for its London production Dion Boucicault had changed the ending of *The Octoroon* in order to allow Zoe and her white lover to marry? Did they think the "happy ending" more likely to be popular? If the reviewer for the *London Athenaeum* is to be trusted, whoever suggested the change was wrong. Not only did the reviewer find the ending of the play completely shocking, but he noted with pleasure that the audience, although "misled for a time," did not allow the closing scenes to "pass without opposition."

MY PARTNER

The main text of *My Partner* is based on a manuscript owned by Mr. Robert Campbell. The alternate ending of Act II is based on a manuscript in the University of Chicago Library.

CAST OF CHARACTERS

Joe Saunders

Ned Singleton

Wing Lee

Major Henry Clay Britt

Mathew Brandon

Josiah Scraggs

Sam Bowler

Wellington Widgery

Jim Johnson

Mary Brandon

Grace Brandon

Posie Pentland

TIME: ACTS I AND II, MAY 1879. ACTS III AND IV, NOVEMBER 1879.

PLACE: SISKIYOU COUNTY, CALIF.

ACT I.

SCENE: *Exterior of the Golden Gate Hotel, L.1.E. to 3. Northern California. Distant view of Mount Shasta on drop in 5. Pathway over rocks, R. and descent over rocks into valley, L.3. Moon in C. Green medium. Music at rise of curtain. Enter Posie from hotel, L.2., with a broom in hand.*

POSIE. [*Calling*] Wing Lee! Wing Lee! What on earth has become of that Chinaman? It's always the way! The more he's wanted the more he don't show up; talk about Chinese cheap labor, why when it comes to a pinch, they ain't worth a bit a day. Wing Lee! Wing Lee!

WIDG. [*Coming down, R.H., from over the rocks, L.3.E.*] 'Ollerin' agin, eh? Ain't ye afraid ye'll bust yer larynx?

POSIE. [*L. Saucily*] I don't know what that is, and I ain't afeerd of bustin' it if I did.

WIDG. [*R.*] No h'occasion to exhibit h'indignation, Miss Posie—yer larynx is a wittle element connected with yer wind—[*Touching his throat*] 'Ow's the ball a-comin' on?

POSIE. You're a nice party, Mr. Widgery, to ask that question, going off to Frisco and leavin' us up to our eyes in preparin' things, and comin' back the last minit.

WIDG. And I only came back the last minit to go the next. [*Sits on stump, R.C.*]

POSIE. [*In surprise*] Going to leave Mr. Brandon, who helped to bring you all the way from England? [*Sits on rustic bench by hotel, L.*]

WIDG. [*Reflectively*] Yes, 'tis 'ard; but I'm no use 'ere. I can't larn to mix these H'american drinks, and clothes is clothes and wittles is wittles; poor Brandon! Hit's awful to see 'im situated like this—It's a h'awful pity!

POSIE. He's got the best hotel in Siskiyou County.

WIDG. But it's 'orrible to step from the 'ead of a London 'ouse in the dry goods way—Holborn, and a mill in Manchester—[*Sighs*] I've seen coronets in 'is 'ouse—when 'is father gave h'entertainments—genuwine gentlemen; not the sort o' folks h'axed to 'is 'ouse tonight. Ah! [*Sighs*] 'e 'as to do it now, clothes is clothes and wittles is wittles! [*Sighs*]

POSIE. I don't know nothin' 'bout yer titles, but there's just as good gentlemen coming here tonight as ye kin find anywhere.

WIDG. I'm a h'ignorant man, but I doesn't h'admire h'ignorance, an' ye doesn't call these h'unheducated miners like Joe Saunders, gentlemen?

POSIE. If ye measure gentlemen by their manhood, there's enough of Joe to make a dozen of yer coronet fellows, and if ye want education—ther's his partner, Ned Singleton—he's bin to college.

WIDGE. [*Rises. Sagely*] Yes, Ned, 'e's civilized, but still no match for Mary Brandon.

POSIE. [*L.*] How do ye know it isn't Joe she cares most for?

WIDG. Oh! I say! None of that. Might as well think of her fallin' in love with old Scraggs, and her mother turned up her nose at 'im, and nearly caused murder. [*Commence to change, slowly, gradually to moonlight*]

POSIE. [*Amazed, rising and dropping broom*] Did Mr. Scraggs love Mary's mother? [*Widgery closes one eye and nods*] But she wouldn't have him?

WIDG. [*Nods*] H'it was presumption for 'im to think of h'it, but Josiah Scraggs forgot 'imself, and it took a blow of a whip to bring him round to hisself again—I suppose Brandon believes in bleedin' for 'igh fevers; anyhow it cured Scraggs.

POSIE. Do you mean that scar on his cheek?

WIDG. Umph! [*Nods*]

POSIE. I always thought that scar meant something. But they're good friends now?

WIDG. Gammon! He's very oily an' talks h'all right; but Mr. Brandon's friend, oh, no! Take my word for it, Josiah Scraggs is a man wot never forgives or forgets. I tried to 'int it to Mr. Brandon, but 'e is so honest hisself, he never doubts h'others. [*Crosses, L.*]

POSIE. [*Crosses, R.*] I always hated that Scraggs; now I despise him. [*Crosses to R.H.*]

WIDG. [*L.*] Don't say I told ye h'anything; it would hurt me and not 'elp you.

POSIE. [*R.*] Not a word.

WIDG. [*Aside*] That is wery accommodating! [*Aloud*] Don't repeat wot I said, you know, for yer h'own sake! Always remember, clothes is clothes and wittles is wittles. [*Exit into hotel, L.H.*]

POSIE. [*Crossing, L.C., calling*] You're perfectly right, Mr. Widgery! Where is that Chinaman? Wing Lee! Wing Lee!

SCRAG. [*Entering over rocks, L.U.E. Crosses, R.*] Hello, Miss Posie. What are you raisin' the devil for?

POSIE. [*L.H.*] Didn't know as I was, but seein' I raised you—I suppose—

SCRAG. [*R.H.*] Oh, I'm the devil, am I?

POSIE. [*Retreating, L.H.*] Well, if you ain't—you're a pretty good imitation.

SCRAG. You think that smart, don't ye? Ye think that clever, but it ain't; it is simply impudence.

POSIE. Shut up! I hate you!

SCRAG. And who are you, that you should hate me?

POSIE. Your betters, if you want to know!

SCRAG. [*With a grim smile*] Josiah Scraggs has fallen very low, when a kitchen wench is his betters; very low indeed! What next I wonder? [*Music*]

POSIE. [*Advancing angrily*] You want to know what next, do you? I'll tell you, sir—what next.

SCRAG. [*Grinning defiantly in her face*] You will, eh, Miss Posie?

POSIE. That's next, and that, and that! [*Striking at Scraggs with broom, who falls on stage, exit quickly into house, L.1.E., leaving broom on stage. Wing Lee enters over rocks, L.U.E., carrying basket. Comes forward, puts down basket and extends his hand sympathetically to assist Scraggs to rise*]

WING. [*L.*] Melican man fallee downee.

SCRAG. [*R. Rising*] Fall down! No, I was knocked down, kicked, and abused.

WING. [*Business*] Me so sollee.

SCRAG. [*Sitting on stump, R.C.*] What good does your sorrow do? I don't want anyone's pity. I'll make her sorry, which will be more to the purpose, much more.

WING. You go to the ballee tonight?

SCRAG. Idiot! Do you want me to dance on one leg?

WING. Melican man no can dancee on one leggee? [*Business*]

SCRAG. Where is this dance?

WING. Here—hotel—sabee?

SCRAG. A dance, eh? Here at Brandon's?

WING. Humph! [*Nods*] Allee pretty gallee—allee nicee music, allee nicee manee, squeeze allee samee nicee youngee ladee.

POSIE. [*Inside house, calling*] Wing Lee! Wing Lee!

WING. Comee allee timee—Bellee nicee music—nicee dancee. Bellee nicee manee squeeze pretty gallee!

POSIE. [*Inside house, calling*] Wing Lee! Wing Lee!

WING. Allee lightee! Me comee! [*Business and exit into house, L.1.E.*]

SCRAG. A ball at Brandon's, eh? He was always a soft fool, and these young daughters are wrapping him around their fingers. Now that I've returned, he'll invite me, too! And he thinks that I have forgotten and forgiven him, he thinks me an idiot like himself, as if I could forget with that livid scar blazing on my cheek. How I hate him, and his pretty brats! The love I bore their mother has lain in my empty heart all these years until it has turned to poison, for she was the cause of all—she rejected me for him years and years ago—and he was rich then and I was poor. But since he has grown poorer and poorer, and I richer and richer, and when I've broken his heart, and can lie down on his pauper grave and beat upon it with my bag of shining gold, then I'll feel my triumph is complete—complete. [*Is R.C. Rises*]

BRAN. [*L.C. Entering from hotel*] Where can Mary be? [*Sees Scraggs*] Ah, Josiah, is that you?

SCRAG. [*R.H.*] All that's left of me.

BRAN. [*L.H. Shaking hands*] Your arrival is timely.

SCRAG. I'm glad to hear it.

BRAN. We are going to have a bit of a dance tonight, and to have your familiar face among us will revive the memory of the good old days when we were both younger and happier men.

SCRAG. I suppose, from your jolly humor, you have raised the money for me.

BRAN. [*L.H.*] Well, the fact is, not exactly! Business has been rather dull, no water in the mines for months—and knowing you were not pinched—

SCRAG. [*Snappishly*] How did you know that?

BRAN. I read of your successful speculation in Frisco.

SCRAG. Because I have a glimmer of good luck, you imagine I don't want my honest money, eh?

BRAN. [*Proudly*] I imagine nothing of the sort; you shall have your money, every penny, if it costs me the roof over my children's head.

SCRAG. [*L.*] Proud as ever.

BRAN. Do you doubt it?

SCRAG. [*L.*] If I ever did, do you think I would have trusted you?

BRAN. [*R.*] Did you not have good security, and do you not draw your interest regularly?

SCRAG. Of course, it's secure enough; but I loaned it for friendship, not for a beggarly interest, and to have you turn upon me in this way, I'd rather lose it all. [*Meekly*]

BRAN. Perhaps I've been too hasty. I've a bad ugly temper—Josiah.

SCRAG. And a proud spirit, Mathew.

BRAN. Yes, and a proud spirit; and every reverse seems to make me more bitter; but you have been a true friend to me, Josiah, and I ask your pardon. [*Offers hand*]

SCRAG. If it were worth more, it would be yours more readily. [*Shakes hand*]

GRACE. [*Calling inside hotel, L.2.E.*] Papa! Where is papa! [*Entering from hotel, L.2.E.*] Oh, here you are, papa! Say, don't I look real nice! [*Admiring herself, down L.H.*]

BRAN. [*C.*] Yes, a regular wild flower! Grace, don't you see Mr. Scraggs?

GRACE. [*L.*] Why so it is! But I was so busy looking at myself, I couldn't see anyone. [*Shaking out her dress*] Don't you think I look nice, Scraggs?

BRAN. [*C. Reprovingly*] Mr. Scraggs, my child.

GRACE. Well, Mr. Scraggs, then. Don't you think I look lovely?

SCRAG. [*R.H.*] Oh, yes, very pretty. [*Going up, R.H.*]

GRACE. Very pretty! Thank you, is that all you can say? There isn't a bit of gallantry here in California. In the east young girls swim in flattery, they say; here there isn't enough to wet one's shoes.

BRAN. [*C.*] Flattery is the tinsel of society—gallantry the golden warp that makes the whole fabric beautiful; there is a wide margin between them. [*Going up, C. Comes down, L.*]

GRACE. [*L.*] I don't understand you, but it sounds like sense.

SCRAG. [*Down, R.C.*] Your father means to say, flattery is but another name for insincerity.

GRACE. I don't care. I'd rather men were insincere than stupid. [*Going up, C., and looking off for guests*]

BRAN. [*Crossing to L.H.*] Not a bit like her mother, Josiah.

SCRAG. [*R.C.*] Not a bit! Not a bit!

BRAN. [*L.*] Nor like her sister! I sometimes regret having taken my children away from the pleasure of a higher civilization, even for the chance of mending a broken fortune. A mining town is no place for a gentleman's daughter.

SCRAG. They seem to enjoy life.

BRAN. I do what I can to make them forget our altered condition—even this dance is a part of the daily deceit I practice.

SCRAG. [*C.*] Poverty teaches us humility.

BRAN. [*L.*] Don't say that! I hate the word! Humility is a beggarly bit of cant. As long as we are honest, sir, we can afford to be proud. [*Exit into hotel, L.2.E.*]

SCRAG. [*Crossing to and on steps of hotel*] Good evening, Miss Grace.

GRACE. [*Down R.C.*] Good evening, Scraggs. [*Scraggs exit into hotel*] Oh, how I hate that man. [*Seated on stump, R.C.*] I wish he hadn't come! He seems to me like a great black snake, with soft velvet coils full of poison. And sister Mary says he was papa's rival once! Well, if mamma had married that man I never would have forgiven her—never! [*Joe Saunders calls outside, "Hullo-o-o-o." R.U.E. Music. Going, L.H.*] What's that? [*Going up and looking off, R.3.E.*] Why it's Joe Saunders coming down the mountain path—for a wonder he's the first to get here and all fixed up, too. Oh, just dressed to death! Why, Joe! Joe! [*Calling off*]

JOE. [*Enters over rocks, R.3.E. Comes down, C.*] Well, I just got here kind o' early, I reck'n!

GRACE. The first one.

JOE. I ain't too soon, am I? [*Music stops*] Why, hello, Grace, gal! Durn me—if you don't look nice enough to eat.

GRACE. [*L.*] Do I, Joe?

JOE. [*R.*] Why you've got more fine fixings on than I've seen since I left St. Joe in the good State of Missouri.

GRACE. [*L.H.*] Were they stylish in St. Joe?

JOE. Stylish! Well, I should say so! They used to set the fashions for the whole country.

GRACE. [*In wonder*] They did?

JOE. Yes, indeed! Why, I've heard tell that when Sophie Higgins of St. Joe went to Paris, there wasn't a woman there as dressed like her. And Paris ain't no slouch of a place neither.

GRACE. [*Strutting to L.H. corner, delighted*] Do I look like Sophie Higgins, Joe?

JOE. [*R.*] Well no, not exactly—she had a little difficulty with one eye—it always wanted to see what was going on round the corner, there! While your eyes, Miss Grace, are as blue as the skies that bend over Shasta yonder, and as straight as well—

GRACE. [*Eagerly*] Well! Well!

JOE. Never mind—you'll do.

GRACE. [*L.*] Will I, Joe?

JOE. You bet your boots. But where's your sister? Where's Mary?

GRACE. I don't know. Do you want her?

JOE. Not particular! I'd like to see her—that's all.

GRACE. [*Impressively*] Joe Saunders, do you love my sister?

JOE. Oh, go to glory.

GRACE. But do you now, seriously?

JOE. Well, now, who don't love your sister Mary?

GRACE. But do you love her with all your heart?

JOE. Well, now, look here, Grace, gal—love your sister Mary—Don't you think I'd better tell her that?

GRACE. Yes, I do, Joe, and the sooner the better, or it may be too late. [*Enter Sam over the rocks, L.U.E.*]

JOE. Too late! What do you mean! [*Business*] Why there isn't anyone else is there?

SAM. [*C. Coolly coming between, releasing Joe's grasp, puts Grace's arm in his*] Yes, there is someone else, and a very particular person, too. [*Turns to Grace*] I say, Grace, what does it mean? [*Joe goes R., goes upstage, business*]

GRACE. [*L. Going L.*] What do you want to know for?

SAM. [*C. Crossing up. Drops his arm*] I've got some right to know. Didn't I quit the circus for your sake? Didn't I take off the spangles and go to diggin' for your sake?

GRACE. Did I ask you to?

SAM. No, but you looked as if you wanted me to, and that was enough for me. Besides, when I've been tired to death, didn't I come up here and turn cartwheels and handsprings and flip-flaps for you? [*Up, quarrelling with Grace*]

JOE. [*Crossing to hotel, aside*] What's the use of my worrying, it's some of her nonsense, I reckin. [*Ready, voices in laughter, L.U.E.*]

GRACE. [*Upstage. To Joe*] Say, Joe, remember what I said.

JOE. Oh, you git out! [*Aside*] She may be right, though. I'll just have a talk with Mary this very night. [*Exit into hotel*]

GRACE. [*Sits on bench, L. corner, shaking her head sadly*] Poor Joe! It may be too late already.

SAM. [*C.*] Say, look h'yer! What does all this mean?

GRACE. [*Impatiently*] All what?

SAM. This holding your hand, and mysterious remembers. If he's got the inside track, tell me, and I'll leave the mines tomorrow, go back to the circus and break my neck from the trapeze.

GRACE. Don't be a fool. Joe don't care for me; it's sister Mary.

SAM. Where's his partner, Ned Singleton? I thought he was her particular fancy.

GRACE. It is hard to tell which she likes the best; the three are always together. At first I thought it was Joe, then I thought it was Ned, then again I thought it was Joe, and then I gave it up.

SAM. [*Reflectively*] Joe's the best fellow.

GRACE. Yes, indeed.

SAM. But Singleton wears the best clothes, and you women are all alike and fine togs catches you every time. But she knew Joe first, didn't she?

GRACE. Since childhood; he carried her up from the stage office the night we came to the mountains.

SAM. If I get a chance I'm going to put in a good word for Joe. [*Crosses, R.*]

GRACE. [*Rising, crossing to R.*] Hadn't you better attend to your own affairs?

SAM. Oh, I'm all right! I haven't got any partner to steal your heart, and no one else dare. [*Distant voices. Music*]

GRACE. What's that?

SAM. [*Gazing over the precipice, L.3.E., and shading his eyes with his hand*] Major Britt and the rest of the boys coming to the dance.

GRACE. [*Clapping her hands*] Oh, ain't it nice? After all, there isn't any place like California, is there? [*Running up, L.C., and down, R.C.*]

SAM. [*Down, L.H.*] Except Heaven, and California up here in the mountains is so close to it that none of us want to leave it. [*Laughter repeated more forte outside, L.U.E. Enter Joe from hotel followed by Wing Lee, Brandon, Scraggs*]

JOE. [*On platform, L.U.E.*] They're coming—they're coming every one on 'em. Come up, boys, come up everybody.

WING. [*Down by house. R. extreme*] Allee coming! Allee coming! Come lup, boys, come lup, gals, come lup, everybody. Come have dances.

BRAN. [*Crossing to Grace, R.H.*] Where is your sister? Where's Mary?

GRACE. I don't know, papa. [*Sam and Grace meet Miners, R.C., at back*]

JOE. [*Aside. Down L.H.*] Well, it's kinder funny, I don't see Mary no whar, nor my partner Ned neither. [*Music forte until all on. Enter Jim Johnson and six or eight Miners with their Girls, L.3.E. Joe, L.*] Why, whar's the major?

BRITT. [*Enter over rocks, L.3.E., Oratorically*] Here is the major—here! [*Start the moon*]

JOE. [*L. Shaking hands*] Well, major, you got here?

BRITT. [*C.*] Well, I should emphasize! Here we are landed at last on the top of Siskiyou, where the stars drink dew from the daisies and the singing of the Klamath comes mingled with the rustle of the pines.

OMNES. Hurrah! Hurrah! Hurrah!

WING. [*Coming down. Clapping hands*] Hullee! Hullee!

BRITT. [*C.*] Representative of an effete civilization, be quiet—Mongolian, subside. [*All laugh*]

JOE. [*R.C.*] Gentlemen, gentlemen! I move right here that Major Britt, as the representative of this yer district in the legislature, give us a speech.

OMNES. Speech! Speech! [*Enter Posie. Mr. Brandon and Sam assist Major to mount stump*]

BRITT. [*Business of mounting stump*] Gentlemen and ladies! Why, Miss Posie, how—standing here as one might say, among the misty curtains that drape the crystal walls of Heaven. [*To Brandon*] A drop of whiskey, if you please.

BRAN. [*R.C. To Wing Lee*] Wing Lee, bring the gentleman some of the best.

WING. Bestee blandy, for the Melican man dat talkee muchee.

JOE. Go fetch the brandy, yer yellow heathen—[*Points revolver at Wing Lee, who rushes hastily into hotel*]

BRITT. To resume, gentlemen—I—[*Business*] I—where was I?

JOE. Why, you were somewhere about the crystal walls of Heaven, major.

BRITT. Right! As I recently observed in the legislature, we, the people of this glorious commonwealth, blown from the four winds of the universe, are one family—the children of misfortune crowded out of the avenues of trade in the East, and founding a new destiny in the West, leaving behind us the luxuries of civilization, it is only on such occasions as this, when a generous hospitality bids us welcome to the festive board, that we feel—that we feel—[*Drops voice*] I can't get along if I don't get that liquor.

JOE. Whar that Chinaman? [*Looking off into hotel*] Hurry up that thar brandy.

WING. [*Reenters from house with decanter and glass. Handing glass and decanter to Britt*] Goodee landee! Don't drinkee too muchee.

BRITT. [*Pours out glass full*] Ah! [*Bows and drinks*]

WING. Oh, him takee schooner.

BRITT. [*Returning glass to Wing Lee*] Fellow citizens! Gentlemen! I am full—

WING. All leady—[*All laugh. Wing Lee exit into hotel*]

OMNES. [*Laughing and exclaiming*] Oh! Major!

JOE. [*Laughing*] Order! Order, for the major!

BRITT. I am full of admiration of this lovely scene—look about you—the moon like a beacon in motion, afloat upon a sea of azure; the dark pines whispering to each other, the river flashing like liquid silver, and singing as it flows, while the great dome of Shasta, clad in its mantle of eternal snow, shames by its purity and proportion the fabled fabrics of pagan Rome.

SAM. Bully for Shasta!

JIM. Bully for pagan Rome!

JOE. Order! Order! Go on, major!

BRITT. But, I will pass—

JOE. No! No! Major, don't pass—you never pass.

BRITT. It is our proud privilege to live among such scenes. Let us then rejoice and make the most of it. [*Steps down*]

JOE. Three cheers for Major Britt, and the State of California, where the trees are larger, and men's hearts bigger than anywhere else in all creation. [*All cheer*] Look here, gentlemen, I have got a little motion I would like to make—I move—

BRITT. [*With great dignity and crossing to stump*] Order! Order! [*Seats himself on stump*] The chair is ready for the question!

JOE. Well then, I move that we do now all adjourn to the bar of the Golden Gate, and thar liquor up.

BRITT. [*Rising*] As we say in the legislature, if there is no objection, it is carried.

JOE. You bet!

BRITT. Unanimously! [*All exeunt into hotel, followed by Sam and Grace. Business of Joe and Britt arm in arm. Bow to Grace, who exits into hotel*]

JOE. Ah! Ah! Would you, major! Always gallant, eh?

BRITT. [*At hotel steps*] Gallantry! That's my great point—just before an election. [*Exit with Joe into hotel, both laughing heartily*]

SCRAG. A noisy pack.

BRAN. [*Crossing to hotel*] But good-hearted. Won't you come in? [*On steps*]

SCRAG. No! I hate noisy crowds. I'll take a walk in the moonlight.

BRAN. You'll excuse me, Josiah?

SCRAG. Certainly, business is business. [*Brandon exit into hotel*] Yes, he's happy! So wrapt up in his daughters that as long as they are right, he can dine with pleasure on a crust. [*Starts*] But if harm should come to them! Ah! If I could only manage it! If I could only manage it! I must! I will! [*Music. Exit, R.2.E. Noise in hotel. Enter Wing Lee hurriedly. Shouts in house and driven out by the crowd*]

WING. Me get a bouncee! Evlybody busee me, Miss Gracee scoldee me, Miss Posie slapee, cookee hitee, Bossee kickee; me no care, evlybody dancee, me dancee, too, me must have fun, me must have fun. [*This speech can be gagged up. Music, reel inside house. Sam's voice heard calling figures*]

SAM. [*Inside*] 1st. Take your partners. 2nd. For'd two. 3rd. Ladies change. 4th. Swing corners. 5th. Promenade all. [*During which Wing Lee indulges in dance with imaginary partner*]

BRAN. [*Calling inside*] Wing Lee! [*Wing Lee still dancing*]

VOICE. [*Inside, calling*] Wing Lee!

WING. [*Still dancing*] Help yourself.

BRAN. [*Appears at door*] Where is that Chinaman? [*Sees Wing Lee dancing*] Well, what the deuce are you doing now?

WING. [*Stopping suddenly, places hand on stomach*] Oh, me gottee clamps.

BRAN. I'll cramp you. [*Chases Wing Lee off behind house with broom, then exit into hotel. Music of dance inside of house ceases and music in orchestra begins and plays plaintive air until Mary Brandon enters over rocks, L.U.E., and well downstage*]

MARY. [*Impatiently*] Why don't he come? My eyes are weary watching, my heart is sore waiting. I've been down to the river's edge! The dark deep waters have a strange fascination for me, as they glide off in the mist and distance to the great ocean. [*Sits on stump, R.C. Takes off hat*] And I find myself wondering if it is the shortest way to rest after all. But do the guilty ever rest? Are there any waters cold enough to cool a feverish fear, deep enough to hide a wretched, sinful woman! [*Rises excitedly. Paces stage*] No! No! Ned is not so bad! He could not be so cruel, so base, so heartless! Oh! Why have I trusted so much, exacted so little? [*Going up*]

JOE. [*Entering hastily from hotel*] Now, whar is that Chinaman—you bet I'll find him. [*Business. Sees Mary*] Why, it's Mary! Now's my chance. They are all busy in there getting ready for another dance. So you bet, I'll pop right off. [*Aside*] Why—Mary. [*Aloud*] I mean Miss Mary! I've been looking for you everywhere.

MARY. [*Down R. Quietly*] For me, Joe?

JOE. Fact is, I wanted to ask you—[*Business*] to ask you—if—if—

MARY. Well!

JOE. If you'd seen my partner, Ned, anywhere. [*Aside*] That's the darndest lie I ever told.

MARY. No, is he not with you? [*Sits on stump, R.C.*]

JOE. [*Business*] No—you see I left him 'fore the glass making himself pretty, about two hours ago—to come to the ball, but it takes him so cussed long—still there's something to show for it. For I tell you, when that partner of mine gets all them store clothes on, he's a howler! [*Business*]

MARY. You love him dearly, don't you, Joe?

JOE. Love him! My partner—better than a brother; for brothers they quarrel sometimes, but Ned and I have worked together in the same claim, eat out of the same pan, slept under the same blanket. Why, he nursed me through fever, tender as a mother, when there warn't a woman within fifty miles.

MARY. And you saved his life at the risk of your own?

JOE. You mean the time that Jack Walker tried to stab him down in "Dead Man's Gulch"?

MARY. And you received the knife in your own shoulder?

JOE. Ah! That was a big day. [*Business*] Three men killed. Ah! There ain't no such good times in California any more. There were no women in the mines then.

MARY. Were you happier without women?

JOE. Lord bless you, no! Why, there ain't no happiness where there ain't no women. Why the night we heard your father was a-comin' with two gals —you just ought to seen the goings on. If an earthquake had shivered Shasta in splinters the excitement couldn't have been greater. There were more biled shirts around the stage-office that night than ever was seen there before. Every fellow was just smiling his broadest, and a-looking his prettiest, when the stage drove up, and thar war pistols drawn to see who'd open the stage door. Ha, ha, ha! But you should have seen how long their faces got when the two young ladies, as they expected, turned out to be but a pair of babies in pantalettes. [*Business*] I wasn't going to let them see my disappointment, so I just picked you up, little tot as you was, in my arms, and carried you up here to your new home. Do you know I felt better for a month after.

MARY. Indeed?

JOE. Yes, indeed. You see, I'd never had anything to love then, nor nothing to love me, and that's why I suppose my heart went right out to you.

MARY. [*Rises suddenly*] To me, Joe?

JOE. As it never went out to any human being afore. Not even to my partner. Why, I've seen your eyes in the glitter of the bright gold in the wash, in the stars that looked through the branches on the lonely mountain side, and the thought that you might some day be my own sang its song of hope in my heart as ye hear that river now singing to the willows that bend over it.

MARY. [*Retreating, amazed*] Why, Joe—how you talk!

JOE. [*Business*] It isn't me that's talking, it's my heart that's speaking. It's the pent-up flood of years breaking down the bars of silence. I—I—don't know what I'm saying exactly, but if ye can understand that I love ye better than myself—better than my partner—that I would willingly—ay—gladly, die for you, that's all I ask. [*Business*]

MARY. [*In distress, excitedly*] Oh! If I were only worthy of such devotion, I would give all the gold in the Sierras. [*Crosses to L.*]

JOE. [*Taking her hand*] And if all that gold were diamonds, I'd gladly give it all for this little hand I hold. [*Business*]

MARY. [*Turns, looks him steadily in the eye*] Joe Saunders, you have known me ever since I was a little child, have you not?

JOE. Longer than that.

MARY. [*Controlling her excitement*] Do you believe that I am a good, pure woman?

JOE. Do I believe it? Ask me if I believe that there's a God in Heaven!

MARY. [*Losing control of her feelings*] But suppose I should say that I have deceived you? That I have betrayed your blind faith, that I am—

JOE. [*Business*] Stop! I wouldn't believe you.

MARY. [*Turns upstage, covering her face with her hands*] Oh, that I could die! [*Sobbing*]

JOE. [*Business*] You're out of your mind, gal—why ye don't know what you're talking about—Oh, I see how it is, you've got the hysterics, ain't ye? Don't cry—don't cry.

MARY. Oh, let me cry! Tears are signs of penitence, at least, in a wretch like me. Think, if they but knew, if my father—[*Sinks in a faint on rustic bench by hotel. Music, polka*]

JOE. Mary! Mary! Look up, gal! She's fainted. They mustn't see her! What'll I do? Water, water! [*Goes to hotel door, stops*] I can't go in there, they're dancing. I know, there's water at the spring there, down in the canyon. I'll get the water there. [*Runs rapidly down over the rocks, L.U.E. and off. Enter Ned Singleton, slowly down the mountain path, R.2.E. Crosses to hotel door*]

NED. Dancing, eh? Glad to see they are so jolly! [*Turns and sees Mary*] What's this? Mary lying out here in the moonlight! Mary! Mary! [*Arousing her. Music stops*]

MARY. [*Coming to, passing her hand over her eyes*] Yes, I hear, Joe—I—[*Looks up*] Ned! [*Rises, crosses to C.*]

NED. Of course, it's Ned. Your own dear Ned. Why, what has happened? [*Polka inside of house ceases*]

MARY. [*Sinking on stump*] You've come at last. I had almost given you up.

NED. Why, you knew I'd come sometime.

MARY. Sometime is a very long time to those whose hearts carry a secret as heavy as mine. [*Joe returns hurriedly up the mountain path, L.U.E., carrying his hat in his two hands as though it contained water; stops at back as he hears Mary and Ned in conversation; drops hat*]

NED. Why, Mary, what are you saying? The fault is as much mine as yours. Besides, my dear girl, if you are guilty, am I innocent? [*Music*]

JOE. [*Aside, at back*] What's that, guilty! Heaven and earth!

MARY   But if you only knew what I suffer—the fear, the pain, the remorse! Through the long day I live a shameful lie, and gladly welcome the shadows of the coming night. But no night is dark enough to hide me from myself, and its silence only seems to mock the wild unrest that is always here. [*Strikes her breast, paces stage*] Here! Here! [*Crossing to R.H.*]

NED. [*L.*]   Hush, Mary, be calm—they'll hear you in the hotel. For heaven's sake, be calm. [*Crossing to hotel*]

MARY.   Calm! How can I be calm, with the knowledge that you have twice failed to keep your promise to me, that day by day—I am losing faith in your manhood, upon which I have built all my hopes of happiness here and hereafter. [*Scraggs appears at back on rock, R.U.E., listening*]

NED.   You're mad! Out of your senses! Do you think I would betray you! You whom I love so dearly!—Listen, Mary, when the clergyman makes his next monthly visit to Siskiyou, I promise to make you my wife.

JOE. [*C. Coming forward excitedly and placing hand on revolver*]   Swear it! [*Mary, R., and Ned, L.*]

MARY and NED. [*Startled*]   Joe!

JOE. [*C.*]   Swear it! [*About to draw revolver*]

MARY. [*Restraining Joe in terror*]   What would you do? Would you kill your friend, your partner?

JOE. [*Firmly*]   As I would a snake. Swear!

NED. [*L.*]   I give you my word.

JOE. [*C.*]   Your word! You've broken that already. Swear!

NED.   Well, on my honor then—

JOE.   Your honor! O Ned, swear by something purer than that—by the eternal stars that are looking down upon us now, by the memory of your mother. [*Business*] By all that is good and pure and holy. Swear!

NED.   Partner! Take care, you go too far—there is no necessity—

MARY.   No necessity—

JOE.   No necessity! Look at that poor, trembling child standing there, who tells you she hasn't slept for days and nights; whose faith has slipped from her, whose head is bowed, whose heart is crushed. I mean that you shall do her right, that here in the moonlight, on the threshold of that home you have robbed of its purity and peace, you shall solemnly swear to do this poor, motherless child justice. [*Mary sobs through Joe's speech*]

NED. [*Earnestly*]   Any oath you like, Joe. Dictate it!

JOE. [*Dictating*]   Swear then, as sure as there's a God in Heaven—

NED. [*Repeating*]   As sure as there's a God in Heaven—

JOE.   Within three days—

NED.   Within three days—

JOE. I will make this gal—my—my wife.

NED. Within three days, she shall be my wife.

JOE. His wife—his wife! Dead—dead to me forever. [*Business. Picture, quick drop. Music crescendo at end of Act*]

ACT II.

SCENE: *Shasta drop for backing. Interior of Joe and Ned's cabin (not log) in the mountains. Door in F.R.C. Large square window in F.L.C., through which can be seen Mount Shasta. Set door, R.2.E. Large fireplace and hearthstone, L.2.E. Picks and shovels in L.U. corner. Map of California over fireplace and specimens of quartz on mantel. Deer antlers hanging against flat, buffalo robe on floor. Table, L.C., chair on either side. Bottle and glass on table. Cupboard, L.3.E. Scene boxed in 3. The interior of this house or cabin should be clapboard or plaster. Quite plain. Time, afternoon of following day. Plaintive music at rise. Ned Singleton discovered seated, L. of table. Lights all up.*

NED. [*Sadly*] Not home yet! [*Sighs*] Perhaps he has gone, never to return. Curse the luck! I wouldn't for the world lose his good opinion. However, he was unreasonable and it wasn't any of his business particularly. Why, if he had loved the girl—[*Stops short*] Perhaps he did! Nonsense! I wish he'd come. He don't surely mean to go away, and leave all his gold to me. [*Goes up to window*] I hope he hasn't slept out on the mountain all night. Pshaw! I'm a regular old woman! No more grit in me than a baby. [*Leaning in recess of window. Music. Enter Wing Lee, D. in F.R.*]

WING. [*Looking around*] House empty. No bollee in! [*Advances to table*] Bellee bad—leave a bottlee—no corkee. [*Smells of bottle*] Loosee all strengthee. Bellee bad house-keep—[*Takes drink*] Me no let him go to wastee. [*Drinks again*] Him no lose him strengthee now.

NED. [*Coming down, L. of table*] Hello!

WING. [*Concealing bottle under blouse suddenly*] Hello! Hello!

NED. [*L. of table*] What do you want, Wing?

WING. Me gottee lettee—from young lady, sabee?

NED. You have written a letter to a young lady?

WING. No sabee! Wing Lee got a letter—young lady.

NED. What young lady would write a letter to you? Come—no lies now!

WING. Chinaman no tellee lie. [*Putting letter on table*]

NED. [*Searches for bottle, misses it*] There was a bottle here a few minutes ago. [*Still searches*]

WING. [*Affecting surprise*] Bottlee gone?

NED. It cannot have gone very far, in such a short time. [*Glances suspiciously at Wing*] Did you see it?

WING. [*Eyes fixed on ceiling*] Wing Lee can't see bottlee now.

NED. [*Crossing to Wing Lee*] Not as long as your eyes are on the rafters. What's this in your breast? [*Touches his ribs*]

WING. [*Laughs and jumps*] Melican man, Wing Lee—muchee ticklee. Me ticklee! No ticklee! [*Crossing, L.*]

NED. Steady! [*Takes bottle from beneath blouse*] What's this?

WING. [*Affecting innocence*] Looking vellee muchee likee a black bottlee. [*Wonderingly*]

NED. I thought Chinaman didn't see it, and that you didn't tell lies.

WING. Chinaman no tell lies—couldn't see bottlee in a breastee.

NED. Now, what ought I to do to you? [*Putting bottle on table*]

WING. Givee me halfee dollee for lettee—blingee up top side mountain.

NED. [*Threateningly*] What? What ought I to do with you? [*Holding up bottle*]

WING. [*Alarmed*] Ah, no hurtee—don't knock stuffee out poor Chinaman—keep 'im and puttee in glass case.

NED. [*Going for poker*] I'll glass-case you.

WING. No can catchee. [*Exit hurriedly, D. in F.R. Ned returns from fireplace, sees that Wing Lee has disappeared, laughs heartily, throws poker back to fireplace as Wing Lee looks in window from outside*] Ha, ha, ha! Melican man no can strike Wing Lee! [*Hastily closes window as Ned makes start towards him*]

NED. [*At table. Aside. Picks up letter*] Now, what's this? A letter from Mary to Joe! What does this mean? [*Sinks on chair, L. of table*] What can she have to say to him? [*Musingly*] Can it be possible—No! No! The idea is degrading! I'm made of meaner stuff than I thought, to give it a moment's consideration. Come what will, I'll do my duty, and trust Heaven with the rest. [*Knock outside*] Come in. [*Enter Major Britt, D. in F.*]

BRITT. Afternoon! Afternoon!

NED. Come in, major. Come in! Sit down!

BRITT. [*R. of table*] Have only a moment to stay. Middle of a canvass, you know! Make a speech tonight at Lame Man's Lodgings against Billings and the Capitol appropriation. Climbing the mountain takes the wind out of a fellow—whew! [*Sits*]

NED. Perhaps you'd better have a drop of something to steady you? [*Pointing to bottle*]

BRITT. Thank you. [*Starts to drink, then stops*] I'm not touching anything of late. My opponent Billings has been publishing in his infernal newspaper a lot of figures which he calls my bar bill during the last season. It looks like a Chinese puzzle. I'm refuting his figures by an almost total abstinence.

NED. Your bar bill is not calculated to hurt you in this district very much.

BRITT. [*Pursing up his lips*] No—not among the men—but the women.

NED. They have no votes.

BRITT. But their moral influence goes a great way. I tell you once a woman gets her moral influence on a man, he's a goner! Besides they've started a Baptist Church in the lower end of the district, and I'm afraid the canvass will drift on to a high moral plane, and I've got to join the Baptist Church.

NED. You are a Methodist, are you not?

BRITT. Yes, in Sacramento. But a fellow can't maintain his grip on Methodism against a clear majority of two hundred Baptists in the district. [*Looks longingly at bottle*] So, I've flopped.

NED. Politics are not what they were in California, when the longest knives and best shots won.

BRITT. [*In disgust*] Nothing like it! Those were the days when a man was as proud of the hue of his nose as of the color of his meerschaum, when a fellow could throw out a string of adjectives baited with patriotism and haul in enough votes to elect him every time.

NED. [*Turns to Britt*] You had better try a little. [*Offering liquor*] One drink won't hurt you! Just one. Oh, do! [*Persuades him*]

BRITT. [*After persuasion*] Well, I don't care, just a drop. [*Holding glass*]

NED. [*Pouring it out*] Say when you have enough.

BRITT. There! There! There! Why, my dear sir, you don't expect me to drink all that?

NED. It's first rate. I'll get you a cigar. [*Goes to cupboard, L.U.E.*]

BRITT. I wouldn't be able to speak for ten minutes if I were to drink all that. [*Pours out more and drinks hastily, then replenishes the glass, draining the bottle*] There, that's more like it. Ordinarily a little goes a long way with me.

NED. [*Returning to table*] Take a cigar. [*Offers cigar. Business*] What! No!

BRITT. [*Taking cigar*] Ah! Yes!

NED. Have a match. [*Offering match*]

BRITT. I've got a match. [*Produces and lights one, then lights cigar*] As you may suspect, I'm around stirring the boys up a little.

NED. [*Sitting, L.H.*] I hope you will make it hot for Billings.

BRITT. [*Still lighting cigar*] Hot! Hot! [*Burns fingers with match*] Red hot!

NED. He said some hard things about you in his paper.

BRITT. Hard things! He has called me everything. I sent him a challenge but he kicked my friend, Colonel Greene, downstairs, and poured a bottle of ink and mucilage all over him—red ink at that. Then he came out next day with a whole column in his paper shrieking for the freedom of the press. Not that I object to the freedom of the press, if it will only let someone else have a little liberty at the same time. If they call names, why shouldn't I? [*Goes to take another drink. Ned looking straight ahead*] It makes me mad. But I'll have a royal revenge, I'll sweep the district by a clear three hundred majority, if it takes every darned Baptist in it. [*Going to D. in F.*]

NED. That's the proper plan, major.

BRITT. [*Pausing on the threshold*] By the way—we want to draw up some resolutions, requesting me to run again for the legislature. Can we have the use of this room for the purpose during the course of the afternoon?

NED. Certainly! Joe and I are with you heart and soul, major, under any circumstances.

BRITT. [*Shaking hands*] Thanks! Thanks! As we sometimes say in the legislature, *Virtus incendit vires!*

NED. Meaning—

BRITT. Virtue kindles strength. [*Touching his heart*] See you later. [*Exit pompously, D. in F.*]

NED. There are worse men in the world than Britt, [*Taking up bottle*] but few better judges of whiskey. I can't imagine what keeps Joe. I think I'll go down and see Mary. [*Picks up hat*] Perhaps she may have seen him and there is that letter. [*Turns it over on table, biting his lip*] I'd like to know what is in it, but I wouldn't break the seal for a million. [*Seeing Mary, who enters D. in F.*]

MARY. Ned!

NED. Mary!

MARY. Yes, I sent a letter here to Joe, and Wing Lee, failing to find him, and returning somewhat under the influence of liquor, I came myself. Has he received it? Is he in? [*Eagerly*]

NED. [*Coldly*] He has neither received it, nor is he in.

MARY. And the letter?

NED. Is here. [*Handing letter*]

MARY. [*With a sigh of relief*] I feared it had fallen into other hands.

NED. And are its contents such that you dare not have them known? I had no thought [*Bitterly*] that you shared such fearful secrets with him.

MARY. [*Sorrowfully*] That is unkind to me, unjust to him, unworthy of you. How much so you shall judge for yourself. [*Opening letter*]

NED. You need not read it! I know that I am all you say—ungenerous, unkind, unjust—[*Drops in seat at R. of table*] I'm beginning to despise myself!

MARY. [*Placing her hand on his shoulder*] No, Ned, there is enough good in you to save you from that, and in the future let us lead such a life as will win our esteem, the world's regard. Now please let me read the letter. I don't want the shadow of a secret between us—please—please. [*Coaxingly*]

NED. As you will, go on. [*Music*]

MARY. [*Reads*] "Dear Joe: You've been such a good, good friend to me always, that I am sure you will grant me one more favor; please do not blame Ned any more, and for the pain my sin has caused you, forgive us both—[*Her voice trembles with emotion*] And we will try never to wound your dear good heart again"—[*Sinks on her knees beside Ned and places her head upon his knees. Sobs aloud*] O Ned! Ned! [*Music stops*]

NED. [*Places his hand caressingly on her bowed head, and after a long pause*] I'm not worthy of you, Mary, not fit to tie your shoe, and as for Joe, I'm ashamed to look him in the face; ashamed for the first time in my life.

MARY. [*Rising solemnly*] And for the last time, too, with Heaven's good help.

NED. [*Rising*] Yes! We are standing on the threshold of a new future—as man and wife, in a few short days, we will begin a new life, a purer and a better one.

MARY. O Ned, you don't know how happy I am. [*Kisses his hand, they embrace. Enter Britt, Sam and Miners, D.F. Business at door*]

BRITT. [*Turns, looks aside knowingly at Ned*] All right? [*Ned nods, Britt then turns to Miners and resumes*] Come in, boys, what the devil are you doing standing out there for? [*Miners all come in and range themselves on R.H.*] Ahem! Beg pardon! No intrusion, I trust!

NED. [*Taking up hat*] None at all.

BRITT. [*Coming L.C.*] Not driving the lady out? [*Bows politely*]

NED. Oh, no, we are just going down the mountain. Come, Mary! [*Mary takes his arm, they go to the door, Miners standing aside respectfully and bowing*] I will see you home.

BRITT. That's right, gentlemen, respect the ladies always! My dear Miss Brandon, [*Mary stops*] it delights me to see such unaffected chivalry encased in flannel shirts. That's the stuff out of which great states are made. The pioneers of California stand before you; every one of them a knight in courtesy and a king in honor, and what is more important, every one pledged to vote the straight Britt ticket. [*Ned and Mary exeunt, D.F. Britt goes L. of table*]

OMNES. Every time!

NED. [*Through window*] Just make yourselves at home, boys, I'll be back presently. [*Exit, L.H.*]

SAM. Never saw Singleton so agreeable.

BRITT. Gentlemen, are we ready to proceed? [*Using bottle as gavel and rapping on table*]

SAM. [*Back of table*] There is nothing to do but draw up the resolutions, eh, major?

BRITT. Excuse me! [*Drawing paper from pocket*] Everything cut and dried—a regular endorsement of my official course. All we have to do now is to affix the signatures of the committee. [*Gets pen and ink from cupboard*]

SAM. But hadn't they better be read, so as the gentlemen will know what they are signing?

OMNES. Yes! Yes! Read it!

BRITT. Not necessary, a mere formality. I have given hundreds of letters of introduction to men I never saw, vouched for the integrity of others whom I never heard of, recommended men to office whose names I didn't know. Have to do it, they all do it. It's public life! [*Holds up pen*]

OMNES. Sign the paper! Sign the paper! [*General business*]

BRITT. [*Passing pen*] Thanks! Everything regular, I can assure you. [*First and second Men sign their names, third Man makes a cross*] How are you, Mr. Cross? [*They all laugh. A fourth Man approaches, Britt stops him by wave of hand*] Three will do. I will fill in the other 297 names myself. Now, gentlemen, as we have been invited to make ourselves at home, as we sometimes say in the legislature, take a drink with me. [*Coming C.*]

OMNES. [*They all produce cups from cupboard and press around Major Britt*] Three cheers for Britt and the whole ticket. [*Wing Lee enters unobserved during the cheering and passes around to L.H. corner and sits on chair by fireplace. He is much intoxicated*]

BRITT. Before drinking, permit me to make a few remarks.

OMNES. [*Demur*] Oh! Oh!

BRITT. Concerning my career as your representative! To give, as it were, some account of my stewardship.

OMNES. Order! Order!

BRITT. [*Mounting chair, R. of table*] The opposition have opened the sluice gates of vituperation upon us; and for what? [*Pipe business, Wing Lee*] Simply because my opponent says I am not a moral man. [*Wing Lee nods head*] Bah! As if politics and morality had anything in common!

OMNES. Hurrah for Britt!

BRITT. They say I am opposed to immigration, and consequently to the growth of the state—why, gentlemen, I am in favor of every form of increase of population, and I have even gone so far as to draw up a bill furnishing free transportation to one class of immigrants, and nursing bottles to the other.

OMNES. Hurrah for Britt!

BRITT. And if that don't do, I would offer a prize of a new bonnet for every baby born in the state.

OMNES. Hurrah for Major Britt!

WING. [*Down L. Much under influence of liquor*] Hulla for Major Brittee—hulla, hulla, hulla!

BRITT. Gentlemen, I said I favored immigration. I believe in men changing their address at will. Now there is a man whose address should be changed to Hong Kong.

SAM. Chinese must go. Go back to Hong Kong.

WING. Me no go backee Hong Kong.

BRITT. [*Addressing crowd*] I can only add that I am grateful for this spectacle.

WING. Hulla for Major Brittee!

OMNES. Shut up!

BRITT. [*Contemplating Wing Lee in silence a moment*] What is more saddening than to see a fellow man addicted to the soul-destroying influence of rum?

OMNES. [*Holding up cups*] Eh! Major!

BRITT. I mean opium. Rum's all right. [*Taps breast pocket, which contains bottle*]

WING. Melican man talkee muchee allee timee—Chinaman want to talkee allee samee Melican man. [*Staggers from seat to front of table, much under influence of liquor, and falls on stage*]

OMNES. Ha, ha, ha!

BRITT. Order! Order! The gentleman from China has the floor. Pick him up. [*Sam and others carry Wing Lee off, R.2.E., and return*] The last motion having been carried—off—there is nothing more to be done. [*Gets down from chair, all laugh*]

SAM. How about treating, major?

BRITT. [*Coming down, C. Crowd closing up around him, with glasses and cups in hand*] Ah! Yes! Of course! Of course! Excuse me! I quite forgot! Glasses, gentlemen, glasses. [*They gather around*] The bottle is strikingly light. [*Attempts to pour some liquor, all holding up cups and glasses*]

OMNES. [*Disgusted*] Empty! [*Sam whispers into ear of Major Britt*]

BRITT. It would seem, boys, that as much as I dislike to even suggest it, I'm afraid we will have to levy a small—I said a small—assessment to defray the expenses of the campaign. [*Evident disfavor manifested, which Britt is quick to sense*] What! You won't have it?

SAM. As the candidate, I'm afraid you're in for it, major.

BRITT. Well, in that case there is nothing for me to do but throw myself once more upon the hospitality of my friend Brandon, so if there is no objection we will now adjourn to the bar of the Golden Gate.

OMNES. Bully for you, major! Hurrah for Britt! [*Boisterous jolly crowd jams the door to exit*]

BRITT. I've got 'em. I've got 'em, every mother's son of 'em. I've got 'em. [*All go through door, followed by Britt. Ned Singleton enters, D. in F.*]

NED. Not here yet? What's the matter with the man? [*Impatiently*] He can't be such a moralist as all this. If Mary is satisfied, why shouldn't he be? [*Sits, L. of table, with his back to door. Plaintive music. Joe Saunders enters, D.F. Ned, turning to table, sees Joe*] Hello—Joe! Home at last, eh!

JOE. Yes, at last, and for the last time, too.

NED. What do you mean?

JOE. That I'm going away.

NED. Going! Where?

JOE. I don't know where! Anywhere, so it be far enough to bring forgetfulness, and too far to let me ever get back.

NED. Why, Joe, you don't mean to say that you can't forgive me; that after all these years we are [*Dropping his voice*] going to part like this?

JOE. Yes, that's just what I mean.

NED. I can't understand this. I've not wronged you in any way, have I?

JOE. Not much. [*Business*] Only broken my heart—that's all—that's all.

NED. [*Amazed*] Broken your heart?

JOE. Yes, does that surprise you? [*Business*] I'm only a rough, plain, blunt fellow, [*With scorn*] and don't know half as much as you. But, my boy, I—I—loved that gal—Mary Brandon—How well—I never guessed until I knew she was lost to me forever. Why, last night, I felt like a man standing at an open grave, helping to hide under the clay all his hopes of happiness. Can ye understand that the pain was not easier to bear because the blow was struck by my partner?

NED. [*Rises, earnestly*] Joe, had I known you loved her, I would have seen my arm wither, my heart turn to ashes—[*Crosses to R.H. and sits on stool, R.C.*] O Joe! Joe!—

Joe. Pshaw! There's no use in regretting now. All I ask of you is that you'll do her justice, 'cordin' to your oath, and make her life as happy as you can.

Ned. But you—you need not go away.

Joe. I must! Can't you see that you and me must part? The old confidence is gone. I could never trust you again—you see—I'm not angry—only sorry that things happened so. [*Walks to and fro, to R. and then to C.*]

Ned. Pshaw! You've grown morbid over this, by brooding over it all night.

Joe. There you're wrong again. Why I didn't come home last night was 'cause I was too excited to trust myself where you were. 'Twasn't that I lost her—not that. For it's more than likely she wouldn't a had me, under any circumstances, but that you should have caused her to suffer so—you on whose honor I'd have staked my life—you—pshaw! There's no use talking. Come—come, sir—let's settle up and quit. [*Crossing back of table, L. Music*]

Ned. [*With a sigh*] Oh! Very well! [*Goes to table, sits, R.*]

Joe. [*Goes to hearthstone, lifts stone, takes out pan of gold nuggets, brings it to table, pours out gold, etc.*] There's the gold, Ned, thar! Divide it.

Ned. [*Quietly*] No! I would rather you would do that.

Joe. All right! Whar's the scales?

Ned. No need to weigh it. Take what you like, and leave the rest.

Joe. [*L. of table, dividing gold, etc.*] Well, does that seem about right?

Ned. Yes—but how about the claim, and the cabin?

Joe. [*Business of pocketing share of gold, etc.; leaving knife on table*] Well, as you are going to stay here, why, of course, the claim is yours, and as for my share in this house, I give it to Mary, that is, if you don't object.

Ned. No—I would rather pay you for it.

Joe. It won't hurt her to take it, and it'll make me feel better.

Ned. All right. [*With a shrug*] Have it your own way.

Joe. Now, we're square, ain't we? [*Ned nods, with his back to table, still seated, eyes bent upon floor*] Ten years together—[*Goes to door, long and particular business. Gold business*] Ten long years! [*Business. Aside*] I feel something choking me, I must get out of here. [*Aloud*] Good-bye—Ned Singleton—ye can't have more good luck than I wish you both! Good-bye!

Ned. [*Rises and offers hand*] Good-bye, Joe—good-bye!

Joe. No! [*Business*] No need to shake hands now. If when ye've made her your wife—we should ever meet, I'll take the hand ye offer. But I can't now. [*Business*] Ye mustn't think hard of it, but I can't—I can't do it, and I won't. [*Exit hastily, D.F. Passes by window, pauses, looks in, closes window and disappears, L.U.E. Music stops, dim lights*]

NED. [*After pause*]   Gone! [*Walks slowly over to table, sinks on seat, dejected*] Gone! It all seems like an ugly dream! [*As if dazed. Pause. Enter Scraggs, D.F. Aside, speaking as he enters*]

SCRAG.   Quarrelling, eh? So much the better. At last I've got a chance to speak to him. [*Comes forward noiselessly to immediately behind Singleton and coughs to attract attention*]

NED. [*Looking up*]   Well?

SCRAG. [*R.H. Meekly*]   You don't seem to remember?

NED.   Yes, I do—your name is Scraggs—a friend of Mr. Brandon's.

SCRAG.   Correct! [*Crossing behind table*] I will just drop into a chair. [*Sees gold on table. Aside*] Gold! [*Aloud*] You are very careless of your wealth, young man. [*Drops into seat, L. of table*]

NED. [*Moodily*]   It's safe enough.

SCRAG.   You are doubtless astonished that I should make a formal call upon you.

NED. [*Shaking his head*]   No, sir!

SCRAG. [*A trifle disconcerted*]   Ah! [*Pause*] I thought you would be. Fact is, I came into possession of a secret of yours.

NED. [*Suddenly*]   Of mine!

SCRAG.   Yes, of yours! I witnessed that little affair last night between you and Miss Mary Brandon.

NED. [*Angrily*]   You were playing the spy, were you? [*Grasping knife*]

SCRAG. [*Soothingly*]   Not at all! Came across you quite accidentally.

NED. [*Dropping knife*]   As the friend of her father you will feel in duty bound never to speak of this again—as a gentleman, sir, you cannot.

SCRAG. [*With deliberation*]   As far as the outside world is concerned, certainly; but you forget that another knows of it—

NED.   Oh, I'll answer for him.

SCRAG.   You seem to have a great deal of faith in a man who, within twenty-four hours, has threatened your life.

NED. [*Bluntly*]   May I ask what is the object of this visit?

SCRAG.   Nothing but kindness to you, sir. May I speak plainly and without reserve?

NED.   As plain as you wish.

SCRAG.   You, of course, don't mean to be bound by that foolish oath, forced from you in such a manner.

NED.   I don't feel called upon to answer that question.

SCRAG. [*After a pause*]   Oh, you don't seem to appreciate my motive in coming here.

NED. [*Eyeing him closely*] If I could once understand it, perhaps I might. [*Turns away*]

SCRAG. Then to be plain: although a friend of her father—I was a clerk in her grandfather's countinghouse in London, many years ago—I cannot remain silent and witness the success of a scheme to entrap a young man in a disgraceful alliance. [*Music. Agitato*]

NED. [*Fiercely, rising*] Stop, sir, I think you have said quite enough.

SCRAG. [*Rising*] But suppose I should show you that this fellow Joe's work of last night was but a bit of bluster, to cover up his own crime; to force you, my dear young friend, to marry his wretched mistress.

NED. What! What's that you say?

SCRAG. I say Mary Brandon is the mistress of Joe Saunders.

NED. [*Wild with rage*] And I say you lie like a dog!

SCRAG. [*In alarm*] What are you going to do?

NED. Force you to swallow that vile slander upon your knees, or take your worthless life! [*Seizing him by throat and forcing him across table*]

SCRAG. [*As if choking*] Murder! Help! [*Picks up knife from table and plunges it in Ned's side. Ned utters a cry, falls in chair, rises, takes a step towards Scraggs, who stabs him a second time. Ned falls in chair, R. of table, with head on table, his arm resting on gold on table. Plaintive music*] I had to do it! It was self-defense. [*Drops knife*] It was self-defense. [*Goes to window*] No one in sight! Dead! Dead! There's the gold! [*Pauses, looks cautiously around*] If I take it, 'twill divert suspicion! They'll think 'twas robbery. [*Takes gold*] I'm safe! I'm safe! No one need be the wiser. What was that? [*Starts*] No marks! What's this? Blood on my cuff! [*Tears off cuff fiercely, goes to window, looks out, starts back, exclaiming in a fright*] Joe! [*Shrinks back out of sight, R.H., as Joe appears at window*]

JOE. [*Looking in at window at Ned*] There he is! My partner! And he hasn't stirred yit—say—Ned—Ned! [*Leaves window and starts for door; at the same time Scraggs crosses hurriedly from R.H. to window, and disappears through window, dropping cuff in his haste. As Scraggs disappears Joe Saunders enters, D.F. Business, pause*] Well, you see I've come back. [*Business of hat in chair*] I couldn't go away without a feeling that we parted friends—when I got down dar in the canyon—where we worked together, I sat down to take a last look at the old familiar spot. The dry leaves were a-dancin' in the wind, the birds singing in the branches, and the creek laughing among the boulders, as if there were no such thing as pain or parting— Everything came back to me. The days we worked together, the plans we used to lay for the time we had made our pile, and could afford to let the pick grow red and rusty in the mine. All your good acts came a-crowding around me, making me ashamed of myself, that I'd refused a hand I'd often been glad to grasp when I warn't able to help myself—and so—I'm here—here to offer ye my hand, and to ask yer pardon [*Business*] before I go away forever. [*Business. Pause. Extends hand*] What! Ye won't take it—[*Business*] All right—remember I offered it! That's all I can do. [*Business. Goes to door in flat with hat, stops*] Oh! darn it Ned—we mustn't part like this—[*Hat down. Business*] You arn't sick, are you, partner? Say, partner, what's the matter? [*Now takes hand and gets in front*] What's this? Ned! Cold and rigid. [*Business*] Dead. [*Sets him up*] No—No—Ned—Partner—look up! [*Business*] Don't sit staring there like that. Only speak to me once more—only say—say you forgive me—Oh—my God, he's dead—dead—dead. [*Business, very particular. A pause during which there is an utter silence save the plaintive music which continues for 12 bars after Joe speaks last word*]

SCRAG. [*Outside*]   I tell you it's true, they're quarrelling. [*Music changes. Enter Scraggs hurriedly, followed by Sam, Jim, Brandon, Miners and Britt, D. in F. Scraggs, as he enters*] I heard a cry of murder as I passed, and I feared someone had been hurt.

BRAN. [*C., back of table*]   What's this—dead?

OMNES. [*Shrinking back*]   Dead!

JOE. [*Business. Rising*]   Yes, gentlemen! My partner—dead—stone dead, right here!

BRAN. [*Dazed*]   What is to be done?

JOE.   Done! Find the guilty one!

OMNES.   Ay, and hang him.

JOE.   Hang him! No—cut him into pieces.

SCRAG. [*R. corner*]   As you were alone with him, it seems to me you ought to be able to explain.

JOE.   I explain! Why, Mr. Scraggs, you don't dare to suspect, that—[*Appealing to Miners*] Boys! Boys! Look here! If you think for a moment, that I took his—my partner's life—No, no, don't speak, but take me out and—take me out and strangle me without mercy—[*Business*] I don't know that I want to live any longer—Life to me has been a failure every way! Every way! [*Business*]

BRITT. [*Gravely*]   Gentlemen, Saunders has spoken the truth. Is there a man here doubts him?

OMNES.   No! [*Sam picks up knife and hands it to Britt*]

BRAN.   The murderer cannot have escaped—search the premises. [*Sam and one Miner exeunt, R.2.E. Taking Joe's hand*] You don't know how sorry I am.

Joe. You! [*Aside*] Mary's father sorry. [*Aloud*] Ah! He has good cause
—he has good cause. [*Business. Noise of voices in altercation, R.2.E. Sam
and the Miner rush in with Wing Lee, R.2.E.*]

Omnes. [*Rushing at Wing Lee*] Hang him! Hang him!

Joe. Stop! No you don't! He's a poor heathen but the God who made
him made us! He's a stranger in a strange land, and he don't neither understand our language or our laws. But I'll stake my life on his innocence, and
before you take his life—ye'll have to give him a fair square trial. [*Crowd
makes a rush for Wing Lee. Seizing chair, raising it over his head threateningly*] Stand back! [*Sam picks up knife and calls attention of Britt to
blood stains on blade. Wing Lee on knees in front of Joe, Brandon restraining Miners on L.H. Picture, quick curtain*]

In the manuscript of *My Partner* owned by Mrs. Abbott Graves, the
daughter of Louis Aldrich, the end of the second act as given above is followed by a note reading, "When wished to—end at times this way." Then
comes the text printed below. In several of the existing manuscripts of the
play this second ending is used and the first omitted. A discussion of these
two endings follows the text.

Britt. Gentlemen, Saunders has spoken the truth. Is there a man here
who doubts him?

Omnes. No!

Scrag. Indeed! Then what's that? [*Pointing to knife. Sam picks up knife
and hands it to Britt*]

Britt. Joe's knife—and covered with blood?

Sheriff. Joe Saunders, I arrest you, for the murder of Ned Singleton.

Joe. What! My partner? No! No! [*Picture. Curtain*]

Bran. The murderer cannot have escaped—search the premises. [*Sam
and one Miner exeunt, R.2.E. Taking Joe's hand*] You do not know how
sorry I am.

Joe. You. [*Aside*] Mary's father sorry. [*Aloud*] Ah! He has good cause—
good cause. [*Business. Noise of voices in altercation, R.2.E. Sam and the Miner
rush in with Wing Lee, R.2.E.*]

Omnes. [*Rushing at Wing Lee*] Hang him! Hang him!

Joe. Stop! No you don't. He's a poor heathen but the God who made
him made us. He's a stranger in a strange land, but he don't neither understand our language or our laws. But I'll stake my life on his innocence, and
before you take his life—ye'll have to give him a fair square trial. [*Crowd
makes a rush for Wing Lee. Joe seizes chair, raising it over his head threateningly*] Stand back! [*Sam picks up knife, calls attention of Britt to blood*

stains on the blade. Wing Lee on knees in front of Joe, Brandon restraining Miners on L.H. Picture. Curtain]

In discussing the two versions of the ending of the second act of *My Partner,* the ending first given will be referred to as the "first ending" and second one printed, as the "second ending," without any reference to the actual date of composition of either.

In most of the existing manuscripts of *My Partner* the first ending is the only one given. The fact that in the manuscript once belonging to Louis Aldrich the first ending is given as a part of the text and the second ending as a variant which may be used "when wished to" indicates that the first ending was the preferred one. This is corroborated by Mrs. Abbott Graves who writes that the first ending is the "one I consider the most used." Mr. Robert Campbell, who was closely associated with his father and with his father's work, goes even further and says that the first ending was the only official one. He states that it was the ending written by Bartley Campbell, the one used in the first performance, and the one used by Louis Aldrich in all of his performances of *My Partner.*

Unfortunately, the reviewers do not support Mr. Campbell's contention that the first ending was the one used by Louis Aldrich in the first and all subsequent performances. A careful search was made of the reviews of the first New York, Boston, and Chicago performances of *My Partner* with the result that two reviews were found that categorically said Joe was arrested at the end of the second act. The *New York Herald* of September 17, 1879, stated, "Then comes the discovery of the murder and the despair of Joe, while the act closes with Joe's arrest." The *Chicago Tribune* of February 10, 1880, stated that "at the end of the second act Joe Saunders is arrested for the murder of his partner." While none of the other reviews stated positively that Joe was arrested at the end of the second act, none of them said anything which would contradict this. Moreover, none of the reviews made any mention of Joe's plea for Wing Lee. The first reference I have found to this plea is in an 1884 playbill on which there is a picture of the scene.

It seems to me there are three possible interpretations of the facts presented.

1. The first ending was used in the 1879 and 1880 performances, and the *New York Herald's* and *Chicago Tribune's* references to Joe's arrest in the second act were errors.

2. The second version was used in 1879 and 1880, but no reviewers referred to Joe's plea for Wing Lee or even mentioned Wing Lee in connection with the second act.

3. In the 1879 and 1880 performances *neither* the first nor the second ending was used but one in which the act actually ended with Joe's arrest; in which case either or both the first and second endings were written between 1880 and 1884.

At present I am inclined to accept the third possibility and I offer the following defense of my views. Not only do the definite statements of the reviewers that Joe was arrested in the second act make me reject the first ending, but the absence of any reference to Joe's plea for Wing Lee makes it seem improbable that the second was used. Therefore, the act must have ended at the first curtain fall of the second version, that is, with Joe's arrest, and before his plea for Wing Lee. While this ending met all the requirements of the subsequent action and dialogue, it was not a "strong curtain," especially coming after the "big scene" earlier in the act; and so it was rewritten. The "second ending" is then the actual second ending of Act II. This new ending was made simply by adding to the original version another scene, the scene of the mob's attack on Wing Lee and of Joe's defense of him. This new scene was not only a "strong curtain," leaving the hero in a noble attitude, but it had the virtue of bringing together for the first time the two stars, Aldrich as Joe and Parsloe as Wing Lee.

The first ending is, in my opinion, the third version of the ending of the second act of *My Partner*. In it Joe was no longer arrested, but merely made sufficiently the object of suspicion to keep the audience from being too surprised when it found Joe's trial going on at the beginning of the third act. Thus the unpleasantness of the hero's arrest was relegated to offstage and nothing detracted from the big scene.

It may be doubted that Joe's plea for Wing Lee fitted into the logic of the play as a whole as well as did his arrest for murder, but what dramatist of the period ever hesitated for a moment between a "strong" ending to an act and a logical one?

NOTE: While this material was in the process of publication my attention was called to a manuscript written by A. M. Palmer, and now in the Harvard Library. In this Palmer gives an account of his part in the production of *My Partner* at the Union Square Theatre, and although he does not settle the question of the ending of the second act, he does throw some light on the problem. He mentions Aldrich's "predilection for the center of the stage and the ends of acts" and refers to the "interjected part of a Chinaman." As has already been suggested the problematical "original" ending of the second act did not place Aldrich in an especially favorable position, while the "first" and "second" endings gave him the center of the stage. How should the word "interjected" in Palmer's manuscript be interpreted? Does it mean that the part of Wing Lee was added after Campbell had written the play, or, what seems more likely, that the part was not an essential one to the action of the play? Is it not possible that Parsloe, who played Wing Lee, after he bought an interest in the play, asked to

ACT III.

SCENE: *Parlor or general sitting room of the Golden Gate Hotel. Six months after. Room neatly furnished, but not elegantly. Door, R.C. in flat. Window, L.C. in 3. Set practical doors, R.2.E. and L.3.E. Windows look out on wintry landscape. Sofa against flat, R.H. Carpet down. Bunch light behind window, L.C., and behind doors, R. and L. Lights up full. Music.*

GRACE. [*Discovered in armchair by fire*] Do you hear anything, Posie?

POSIE. [*Discovered at window in flat, L.C.*] No! Not one thing.

GRACE. Nor see anything?

POSIE. No! Yes, now I see some men standing at the courtroom door, and shaking their heads solemn like.

GRACE. Poor Joe! Everything seems to go against him.

POSIE. [*Coming down C.*] I suppose they'll hang him. [*Sighs*]

GRACE. [*L.*] If found guilty.

POSIE. [*L.C.*] Somehow, Miss Grace, I can't get it into my head that Joe killed Ned. It don't seem natural.

GRACE. Nothing seems natural any more. Look at Mary's going and disappearing the same night that Ned was killed, and never showing her face again. And now it's six months ago.

POSIE. Well, didn't that Chinaman do the same thing?

GRACE. Yes! But everyone knows he ran away fearful of being arrested for Ned Singleton's murder; while Mary's going is a mystery no one can explain.

POSIE. I wish people didn't try to.

GRACE. [*Rises, crosses, C.*] Has anyone dared—

POSIE. Dared! The last time I was down at the Valley Church I heard one woman say to a lot of other women under the porch, just before service when you and yer father went by, "Ah, there goes Mr. Brandon now," and they all poked out their necks long like [*Stretches her neck*] and looked after ye. An' one freckled-faced thing, with big beau-catchers, turned up her nose like that [*Makes a grimace*] and said, "He don't carry his head so high as he used to before pretty Miss Mary ran away," and then they all giggled.

GRACE. Rejoicing in an old man's misery! A Christian act truly! Did you say nothing?

have his part made more important, and asked to have, not the center of the stage, but a spot near it at the end of the important second act?

Incidently, Palmer states that the part of Posie Pentland was originally that of a young girl, and that at his suggestion Campbell changed it to an old maid.

Posie. I tried to, miss, but I couldn't speak.

Grace. [*Bitterly*] You couldn't say a word for poor Mary, who was always so good to you?

Posie. Not a word! But I flew at them beau-catchers, and tore some of them out by the roots, and then they all rushed into church and sent out the preacher to tell me I was sinful, and needn't come to meetin' any more.

Grace. [*Running over to her*] Posie, you are just the sweetest creature ever lived. [*Embracing her*]

Posie. But I didn't let him off.

Grace. [*Amazed*] You didn't talk back to the preacher!

Posie. Didn't I though! I jist up and told him that if I war sinful, them was the kind of people that the good Lord died for, and if the Bible was true, the Church belonged to God, and wasn't none of his'n and it was his duty to coax people into church, not drive 'em out.

Grace. [*In wonder*] What did he say?

Posie. He got very red at first, as if he was a-going to bust all to pieces; but directly he simmered down, and said he was sorry for me, and axed me to come in and forgive my enemies.

Grace. But you didn't go?

Posie. Yes, I did! When anyone talks soft to me, I always cave right in; but I didn't forgive that freckled-faced thing! I sat close to the organ, and made faces at her all through the meetin'.

Grace. That was dreadful in church.

Posie. One of the deacons got awful mad 'cause he thought I was making faces at him, but when service was over, I axed his pardon, and kind o' explained, and then he said it was all right, and he was a-going to kiss me. [*Quickly*]

Grace. [*Amazed*] And did he?

Posie. [*R.*] Well, no, he didn't; but he wanted to awfully. Oh! some of them deacons are a hard crowd! [*Shakes her head solemnly*]

Grace. Oh, dear me. I do wish we could hear how the trial is going. [*Up to window*] It's a wonder someone don't run over and let us know. Here's Sam Bowler at last.

Sam. [*Enters, R.C.*] I never saw such a crowd in my life! It's almost over! He'll be convicted sure.

Grace. [*L.*] Then the jury must be a very stupid one!

Posie. [*R.*] Reg'lar born fools!

Sam. [*C.*] No, ladies, excuse me! The evidence, while entirely circumstantial, is very strong. Scraggs swears to a quarrel between Joe and Ned, which Joe foolishly admits, and there is Joe's knife covered with blood, and the gold of the firm missing, and found on Joe. It seems as if the chain was complete, and Scraggs's testimony is the rivet that holds it all together.

POSIE. [*R.H.*] But the shirt cuff found in the shed?

GRACE. [*L.H.*] Yes! That ought to be a clue.

SAM. The cuff is of fine linen, and don't seem to belong to any shirt yet found of Joe's, but still that's a mere thread, and won't weigh against the other facts.

GRACE. Why then, did Joe say what the quarrel with his partner was about?

SAM. Why, he wouldn't tell.

POSIE. What did Scraggs say the quarrel between Ned and Joe was about?

SAM. Major Britt was just trying to draw that from him by a clever bit of cross examination when I left.

POSIE. If anyone can get him clear, Major Britt kin! [*Crosses, L.*]

SAM. [*To Grace*] Get rid of Posie for a few minutes. I want to say something to you in private. [*Goes up L.C.*]

GRACE. Posie, you can get the table set now, papa will soon be home. [*Goes up to Sam on his L.*]

POSIE. Say, look here, you won't talk about the trial 'til I come back, will you? [*Going, L.3.E.*]

SAM. [*At door*] Not a word.

POSIE. I won't be long. [*Aside*] Nothin' curdles up the blood so comfortable-like as the particulars of a murder trial, or a hangin'. [*Exit, L.3.E.*]

GRACE. [*L.H.*] Now; what is it?

SAM. [*R.H.*] Haven't you noticed anything in my personal appearance?

GRACE. [*L.*] Nothing but your other clothes.

SAM. [*R.*] You haven't noticed a sort of a desperate resolve, have ye?

GRACE. No!

SAM. Not in the corners of my eyes?

GRACE. Nothing!

SAM. Well, it's there; I've been trying to screw up my courage for some time, but I flatter myself I've got it up at last.

GRACE. For goodness sake, what is it?

SAM. Grace! I am going away.

GRACE. You are not going away now?

SAM. Yes, I am. If Joe is convicted he will be taken across the mountains to Yreka tonight, and I will go with him that far, just to show him that he is not entirely forgotten.

GRACE. And after that?

SAM. I'll rejoin the big show at Marysville and again become "The Peerless Emperor of the Air." [*With a sigh*]

GRACE. What! Join the circus?

SAM. I always loved art!

GRACE. Art! In a circus?

SAM. [*Solemnly*] High art! There is no art half as high as a trapeze fifty feet from the sawdust. Ah, if you could only go with me! We would be so happy!

GRACE. On a trapeze!

SAM. There's no life like it! I've tried burrowing in the ground, but it's low, when compared to tumbling through the air. Grace, may I—[*Business*] may I—speak to your father?

GRACE. Speak to papa with all this trouble! I don't see how you can be so heartless.

SAM. I've waited six months for your sister to come back, and it's getting a trifle monotonous. Suppose she should never come back!

GRACE. [*Starting*] Never come back!

SAM. I don't mean that.

GRACE. If she should not—I will never leave poor papa all alone. I love him too dearly to see him utterly desolate.

SAM. But don't you think of my desolation?

GRACE. Your desolation! Young men's hearts are soon healed; not so, a man of his age. See how changed he is since Mary went away. His spirit seems utterly broken; there are days and days he never breaks the silence with a word, and he appears to have lost interest in everything.

SAM. Except Joe's trial.

GRACE. But if Joe is condemned I fear he will drop into his silent moody way again, that looks so much like despair. [*Crosses to R.H.*]

SAM. Why don't you try and cheer him up?

GRACE. I did try, but every word I spoke seemed a fresh blow, and when I mentioned Mary's name he burst into tears, the first I ever saw him shed. [*Goes to chair, R.H., and sits, crying with handkerchief to eyes. Sam tries to console her*]

POSIE. [*Enters, L.3.E., crossing to C.*] It's all ready now, Miss Grace, and —[*Stops suddenly, sees Grace crying. She bursts into tears, crosses back, L.H., and leans against mantelpiece, sobbing, face to wall, back to audience*]

SAM. Well, if they don't let up soon, I'll blubber myself. [*Goes up C. Enter Major Britt, passing window in L. flat, through door and arch, R.C.; places his hat on sofa and down, L.C.*]

BRITT. Well, it's all over. The judge has summed up, the case has gone to the jury, so I thought I'd just run over and wet my lips.

SAM. [*Down to R.C.*] You made a splendid defense, major.

BRITT. I did my best; ever since my defeat for the legislature, by over nine hundred majority, three hundred of them Baptists at that, I have devoted my entire time to the practice of my profession. I am free to confess that I spread myself in this case, but as they had all the evidence, I fear poor Saunders must make up his mind to die as gracefully as possible. [*Sighs. Sam goes up to window*]

GRACE. [*Rises*] Won't we see him any more?

BRITT. [*C.*] Oh! Yes! He'll get his supper here. No use in locking him up until they take him to Yreka. Besides he has given the sheriff his parole of honor and that settles it. He will come over to supper with your father, I suppose. [*Goes up, C.*]

GRACE. He shall have no reason to complain of his last supper here. [*Crossing to door, R.2.E.*] For I'll get it ready myself. [*Exit, L.3.E.*]

SAM. [*At window*] And while you perform the great culinary act, I will assist. [*Exit, R.2.E.*]

BRITT. [*Coming to R.C.*] Hard heads and soft hearts is becoming a feminine characteristic. [*Posie, still at mantelpiece crying loudly*] Hello! Weeping! [*Turns and sees Posie*] A regular mountain Venus. A rear view hardly does her justice. [*Crosses to Posie, taps her gently on the shoulder, she turns round and blubbers out loudly in his face. They come forward, down C.*] Why surely you're not crying, Miss Posie.

POSIE. [*L.C. Snappishly*] Then I suppose I'm laughing.

BRITT. [*R.C.*] No occasion for losing your temper, Miss Pentland. Anger is rarely becoming in a man, and in a woman it's a positive deformity.

POSIE. [*Tartly*] I don't never lose my temper.

BRITT. [*Shocked*] "Don't never!" Your grammar is even worse than your temper. It actually sets my teeth on edge.

POSIE. [*Crossing to R.H. and upstage*] If you don't like it, take less of it!

BRITT. I shall certainly take as little of it as possible. I have no disposition to lumber my mind with vagrant verbs and broken-backed adjectives.

POSIE. [*Advancing on Britt, who retreats to L.H. corner*] Who's a broken-backed—ad—ad—! Well, what you said.

BRITT. The remark did not apply to you.

POSIE. No!

BRITT. No!

POSIE. Oh! [*Curtsies and goes towards R.C.*]

BRITT. [*Following up*] What! Call you a broken-backed anything, you! A living expression of the primitive innocence and beauty of your sex. [*Posie curtsies*] A lovely type of God's first best gift to man! A fair oasis of femininity in a desert of homely masculinity. [*Business*]

POSIE. [*After a very low curtsy*] Oh! You are always such a comforting man, major!

BRITT. [*C. Bowing*] Thank you! There's nothing so gratifying to a public man as to possess the love and confidence of his constituents—and when said constituents are of the softer sex, the pleasure is doubly distilled.

POSIE. [*R.C. Leaning towards Major and softly*] Major, I'm an orphan.

BRITT. Most women are at your age.

POSIE. [*Sharply*] Eh?

BRITT. I said, it's a great pity at your age.

POSIE. It's awful for a woman to be alone in the world.

BRITT. Yes, I suppose so. [*Turns partly from her*]

POSIE. [*Reclining on Major's shoulder*] O major!

BRITT. [*Aside. Business*] I wonder if she means business. [*Gently disengages himself, aloud*] Yes, I've heard that you were an orphan.

POSIE. But I've a rich uncle in Santa Clara, who's goin' to put me in his will.

BRITT. Will he? For about how much?

POSIE. A good deal! More'n twenty thousand dollars. [*Business*]

BRITT. [*Aside*] Twenty thousand dollars! [*Aloud*] Come into camp. [*Embraces her*] Do you know, Posie, you are a well preserved—

POSIE. [*Indignantly*] Preserved! Major—preserved!

BRITT. [*Business. Aside*] That preserve has got me into a pickle. [*Aloud*] In the sense that preserved is offensive as suggesting ages, I withdraw the remark, [*Business*] but as it also suggests sweets, I refuse to lay it upon the table, and repeat, a very well preserved lady. [*Business*] But, this uncle of yours, does he enjoy health? [*Business*]

POSIE. [*R.C.*] Splendid.

BRITT. [*Seriously. L.C.*] Umph! That's bad!

POSIE. [*Astonished*] Bad!

BRITT. For you.

POSIE. No, it isn't! I'd rather work hard all my life, 'fore Uncle Jack should suffer one day, for he's been very good to me.

BRITT. With twenty thousand dollars, Miss Posie, that sentiment does credit to your heart, even if it does reflect somewhat severely upon your head. [*Contemplating her. Aside*] A good figure—fine eyes—a little ancient! But, that uncle! [*Crosses to her*] Miss Posie, if you and Lindley, Murray,

Webster and Worcester were on better terms, say a sort of speaking acquaintance, your beauty might one day illuminate the galleries of Congress.

Posie. But, I don't want to go to Congress.

'Britt. [*Soothingly*] Oh, don't let that worry you. There's no immediate danger of your being sent there, at least, not against your will. But, by the way, I'm very anxious to wet my lips. Just see how parched they are. [*Puckers up lips*]

Posie. Are they? [*Posie looks at them. Major gradually gets his lips near her face and at last kisses her. Indignantly*] Well, I like that. [*Flounces out, R.3.E.*]

Britt. [*Nonchalantly*] They all do; but few women are frank enough to confess it. [*Going up, C. Gets hat*] That lady is not unattractive, and that uncle—twenty thousand times more so. Twenty thousand dollars would purchase a seat in the Senate—Major Henry Clay Britt, California's a capital state, but hardly large enough for your great genius and usefulness. [*Exit pompously, R.C. Music. Funny music, "Slur." Enter Wing Lee cautiously from R.C., looks around*]

Wing. No bodee homee, me lestee. [*Sits*] Me vellee tired, foot sickee. No can walkee, me sleepee, oh, me allee blokee up. [*Sits in chair by door, R.2., below it. Enter Posie, R.2.E., speaking as she enters and going towards whatnot, L.U. corner*]

Posie. Where is that almanac? If the moon is at its full, I'll know what's the matter with Major Britt. [*Turns and sees Wing Lee*] You back here?

Wing. [*Advancing, R.C.*] Keepee coolee! Keepee coolee!

Posie. Oh, you yellow rascal! To go and run off the same night as poor Miss Mary, and have everyone think she ran away with you.

Wing. No can help what evlybody thinkee—evlybody foolee.

Posie. Hold your tongue. [*Holds tongue. Business Wing Lee*] Don't speak a word! [*Business Wing Lee*] Now tell me where you have been. Speak.

Wing. Me holee tongue. If me dontee speak a wordee how can me tellee where I've been! Sabee?

Posie. Shut up! [*Business Wing Lee*] Where have you been, I say?

Wing. Closs top side mountain.

Posie. Did you see anything of Miss Mary?

Wing. [*Looking up at ceiling*] Me no tellee you! Tellee allee to Missie Gracee. [*Doggedly*]

Posie. Then you do know something!

Wing. Lillie bit! Lillie bit!

POSIE. Just as we all suspected. You've carried her off and killed her. Is that it, eh? [*Business of slapping Wing Lee*]

WING. [*R. Disgusted*] No can tellee! No can tellee! Melican woman all samee likee damee foolee.

POSIE. [*C.*] There's one thing certain, that you better not let Mr. Brandon lay his hands upon you. You'll have to find other lodgings until he forgets your treachery.

WING. Me sleepee anywhere. Up the tree, down the shaftee, top side clothesline. [*Strikes his breast*] Me toughee! Me toughee! All samee like Melican man. [*Business. Spells*] T-u-f-y—toughee.

POSIE. Oh, you rascal, I'd like to pull that pigtail out of you. [*Crosses to him threateningly*]

WING. [*Coiling up and holding pigtail tightly, and in a frightened manner*] Me no can spare pigee tailee. [*Business Posie and Wing Lee*] Chinaman's joss, no like pullee pig tailee. [*Enter Grace and Sam, R.2.E.*]

GRACE. Why, Posie. [*Sees Wing Lee*] Wing Lee at last! [*Crosses to C.*]

POSIE. [*R.C.*] Yes, Miss Grace, and he won't tell anything about Miss Mary except to you.

SAM. [*Eagerly*] Of Mary! What of her?

WING. [*R. corner*] Me no tellee anybody else Miss Gracee. No bolee else! No bolee else!

SAM. Yes, to me. [*Striking breast*]

WING. Him toughee, too. [*Business. Crossing hurriedly to L.H., behind Miss Grace*] To no bolee else! No bolee else. [*Sam makes a break for Wing, but is prevented by Grace*]

GRACE. [*C.*] Leave him alone with me, then. [*Music*]

WING. [*L.*] Yes, go takee walkee, longee walkee. [*Exit Sam and Posie, R.2.E.*]

GRACE. [*C. Turning to him*] Now, what have you got to say? [*Mary enters very slowly, R.C.F., unperceived by Grace, and down R.H.*]

WING. [*L.C.*] Polee Missis Maly wantee to comee velly muchee, sabee?

GRACE. [*Impatiently, with back towards Mary*] Yes! Yes! I understand! But where is she?

WING. [*Pointing to Mary*] There! [*Business and exit, R.C.*]

GRACE. [*Turns and surprised*] Mary!

MARY. [*R.C. Covering her face with her hands*] Yes, Mary.

GRACE. Mary! In heaven's name, what does all this mean?

MARY. [*With emotion*] That I am a sinful wretch.

GRACE. This is terrible. [*Turning away*]

MARY. Don't turn away from me. I know I am unworthy of your love any longer, but oh, I want to feel your arms about me once again and hear you say you forgive me.

GRACE. [*Turning back, coming to Mary*] I have nothing to forgive. You are still my sister. [*About to embrace her*] How pale you are! Have you been ill?

MARY. [*With faltering voice*] Almost unto death, the night the baby died I—

GRACE. [*Aghast*] A mother! [*Mary moans and bows her head in silence*] O Mary! Mary! Our poor father! It will break his heart! [*Turns back to audience*]

MARY. Yes, I know, and I wouldn't have come back, but that Joe, I heard, was to be tried for Ned's murder. He is an innocent man who has suffered much and he must not perish in this way!

GRACE. How do you know?

MARY. Because it is absurd to think that Joe Saunders could do this thing. It's madness to believe he could be guilty of the murder of his friend and partner.

GRACE. But do you know anything that would help him?

MARY. Yes! I know that he has a great good heart, [*Down*] a noble soul, a tender, patient, self-sacrificing nature. I also know that these are not the qualities out of which are made assassins. [*Crosses, L.*]

GRACE. This is faith, not proof. It can do no good.

MARY. [*Passionately*] Perhaps not. But to remain away when he was helpless, friendless, seemed cruel and cowardly, and I could not, and I would not do it. [*Sits in chair, L.*]

GRACE. But what is he to you?

MARY. [*As if dazed*] What is he to me? [*Shakes her head*] Nothing and everything.

GRACE. O Mary, sister, is it possible—

MARY. I don't know! There is in my heart such a mingling of pity, and gratitude and—Oh, [*Wringing her hands*] I don't know what it is—I have never dared to ask my heart.

GRACE. But, father—

MARY. [*In a low voice*] What does he say of me?

GRACE. Nothing! Your name has not crossed his lips for months. Oh, why did you go away at all?

MARY. What could I do? As soon as Ned died, I fled. I feared my father's anger, I could not look upon his misery; oh, what have I done! What have I done!

GRACE. You did not go alone?

MARY. No, I took Wing Lee with me. But for him I would have perished in the mountains. [*Music ceases*]

WING. [*Outside, R.C.F.*] O Missee Malee! [*Appears at C.*] Missie Malee! Bossee comee—me cutee stickee! [*Exit, R.2*]

MARY. [*L. Hopelessly*] What shall I do?

GRACE. [*R. Nervously*] I don't know. It is too late to do anything now, you must meet him.

MARY. Oh, no, I cannot, I cannot. [*Exit hurriedly, L.3.E., followed by Grace. Enter Brandon and Joe arm in arm, followed by Sheriff, through D., with gun*]

JOE. [*C.*] Thank you, sheriff; I won't forget this kindness.

SHERIFF. That's all right, Joe, everybody knows you're square, and your word is as good as your bond. I'll wait outside for you. [*Exit, C.F.*]

BRAN. [*R.C.*] Courage! Courage, man, the jury is sure to be out all night, and that's a good sign. Besides you have the sympathy of everyone, and that is something.

JOE. Yes, but to be accused, that's it—and of this thing—this dreadful thing—of which I am innocent. Oh, it's hard! Hard!

BRAN. Everyone realizes that, Joe, and even with the evidence in view, none of those who knew you both can believe you guilty of this crime.

JOE. Believe! Why, I loved him as dearly as a brother; better than myself— a thousand times better. It's not death I fear—I hope no one here thinks that— but the shame of such an end, the bitter, burning shame. [*Goes up, C.*]

BRAN. [*Down R.H. and in a low voice, aside*] I know what that is—no one better. [*Grace enters slowly, L.3.E.*] Grace, child, is supper ready?

GRACE. Yes, sir. [*Mary enters slowly, L.3.E.*]

BRAN. Why, what's the matter? Your eyes are red and—[*Sees Mary, starts back. Joe Saunders turns quickly and exclaims. Sam and Posie, R.2.E.; Britt enters from R.C. and down, R.H. Scraggs appears at back, C. Joe goes up, L.C.*] Mary! Mary!

MARY. [*L. Starts impulsively forward*] Father!

BRAN. [*R. Puts up his hand and waves her off*] No! No! Not yet!

MARY. [*Sinks on her knees before Brandon*] Mercy! Mercy! [*Music*]

BRAN. Stop! [*Solemnly*] Before you have a right to rest upon my breast, I must first know what you are, where you have been and with whom? [*Sam, Posie, Britt, Scraggs enter here, Mary drops her head*] Why don't you answer? Have you no defense?

MARY. [*L.C.*] Pity! Pity! [*Scraggs at back, gloating, rubbing his hands*]

BRAN. Where was your pity when you left my heart and home empty?

GRACE. [*L., near fireplace. Crossing towards Mary, appealingly*] Father!

BRAN. Don't go near her. She must first answer to me for the spotless name I gave her.

MARY. [*L. of C. Through her tears*] Oh! Father—father, what shall I say?

BRAN. [*L.*] The truth, the whole truth. In heaven's name, girl, don't be dumb—give me some hope—give me the right to look at these people in the face. You see I'm not angry. I don't demand justice, I only ask for pity.

MARY Father, [*Rising*] I cannot speak. Let me go! Let me go! [*Going, L.H.B.*]

BRAN. Go! Where can you go? There is no refuge for such as you. Oh, my child—my heart is breaking. [*Crosses to R.C.*]

SCRAG. [*Coming forward to Mary*] You owe obedience to your father. 'Tis your duty to tell the truth. [*Retires up a little to R. at back*]

MARY. [*Desperately*] Yes—Father, I will speak.

JOE. [*Coming down, L.C., on Mary's R.*] Hush, Mary, not a word.

BRAN. [*R. Pausing, amazed*] Saunders, how dare you interfere; I command her to speak, she is my daughter.

JOE. And I forbid her to utter a word—she is my wife.

OMNES. His wife!

BRAN. [*After a pause, as if dazed*] Wife! Wife! [*Pause*] What does this mean? [*With severity*] When were you married—where? And by whom?

JOE. Why, sir, I—

BRAN. Is this the treatment I had a right to expect at your hands?

JOE. Mr. Brandon—

BRAN. Why your marriage should have been a matter of mystery, why my child should have been subjected to the suspicion of shame, I leave to your conscience, sir! But I demand that you shall go further and make her vindication complete.

JOE. What do you mean?

BRAN. I mean, that I demand you shall give me some proof.

JOE. Proof?

BRAN. Yes, proof so strong that it cannot be gainsaid. Proof strong enough to dispel every vestige of doubt.

JOE. Well, sir, I can prove—

SCRAG. [*To L. of Brandon who is R. corner. Approaching, insinuatingly and to Brandon*] Yes, their marriage certificate. [*Joe and Mary start, look at each other*]

JOE. [*Aside to Mary*] Our marriage certificate—what'll we do?

BRAN. Mr. Scraggs is right—your marriage certificate. [*Holding out his hands for it. Scraggs goes up again, R.*]

JOE. [*L.C. Despairingly*] There was no certificate given.

BRAN. And do you expect me, after what has taken place, to accept your unsupported word?

JOE. Do not ask impossibilities of me. I can give you no further proof.

BRITT. [*Advancing to C.*] Yes, you can. The best proof you can give of your truth, is a repetition of the marriage ceremony. I, as a magistrate, can perform it. [*To Brandon*] There certainly can be no objection to that?

BRAN. [*Pause*] Do you refuse?

JOE. [*Looking at Mary*] No. [*Britt retires, up R.H., with Sam and Posie, Brandon; crosses to C.*]

MARY. [*C. Aside to Joe*] Joe! Joe! Joe! Think, think what you are doing.

BRAN. [*R. Points to door, R.2.E.*] In that room her mother died; it is sacred to her memory. Major Britt, there the ceremony shall take place. [*Britt exit, R.2.E., followed by Posie, Sam and Grace, who goes round by back*] And these friends shall witness it. Come, my child, follow me. [*Crosses and exit, R.2.E.*]

MARY. [*Crossing to R., then returning to him, R.C.*] O Joe, this cannot be; you must not make this sacrifice for me.

JOE. [*Crossing to Mary*] There are others as well—Your poor old father, your sister. Besides, in a few hours I'll leave you forever, and in a few weeks my death will set you free again. Might I but give you my name—it isn't a glorious one—but poor as it is, it will serve as a shield against your enemies. [*Business*]

BRAN. [*Appears at door, R.2.E.*] We are waiting for you. [*Extends hand to Mary, who goes forward with eyes bent on ground and takes her father's hand. Brandon continues*] Well, Saunders? [*Exit Brandon and Mary, R.2.E.*]

JOE. [*L.H. corner*] Yes! Yes! I'm coming! [*Crosses as if towards door. Scraggs, who has been upstage, advances rapidly, grasps Joe by the arm after he has crossed to R.*]

SCRAG. Man, are you mad? Would you cover up that guilty girl with a marriage that to you is but a mockery? [*Joe hastily closes door, R.2.E.*]

JOE. [*Turning fiercely*] How dare you question me, you who have put the halter about my neck?

SCRAG. I had to swear the truth! But did I tell it all? No! I kept her secret! I won't do it again!

JOE. [*Advancing*] Bah! This that I am going to do renders words of yours powerless. As my wife she can defy you.

SCRAG. We shall see. [*Attempts to pass Joe*]

JOE. [*Intercepting him*] Stop! Where are you going?

SCRAG. To tear this gauzy veil in shreds, to show this old fool that his angel daughter is—

JOE. I don't know your motive for such an act, but don't yer do it on yer life!

SCRAG. [*Glaring at him*] What would you do?

JOE. My hands are yet free from the stain of murder, but if you attempt to mar the name of that poor trusting child, I'll fasten my fingers on your false throat and still its cruel work forever! [*Music forte. Picture. Quick curtain. No wait. Move chair down, C., chair, R.H., up R.H., then ring up Act IV*]

ACT IV.

SCENE: *Same as Act III. Music. Time, ten minutes after. Scraggs discovered seated, C., looking off, R.2.E.*

SCRAG. I'm a weak fool! A contemptible coward! I should have told her story to the court! What was I thinking about? Now, none will believe me. His last action is so remarkable, they wouldn't believe the recording angel against it! Ever since that night up there, I am no better than a child in courage. Even the gold I gained seems to have a terror for me. I can't go near it! It seems to be all eyes, yellow, glaring, staring up at me! I'm afraid to take a step, lest it may lead to discovery. Marriage! [*Chuckles*] A wedding and a winding sheet! Odd enough! Odd enough! [*Drops his voice into a whisper. Posie enters, R.2.E., looking back*]

POSIE. [*R.*] Dear me, I never did see such a wedding in all my born days.

SCRAG. [*C. Rising*] It's all over, I suppose.

POSIE. [*Turning*] Oh, you're there, are you, Mr. Scraggs?

SCRAG. You don't like me, do you?

POSIE. Well, I'm not in love with you.

SCRAG. You hate me, don't you?

POSIE. I don't express my private opinion.

SCRAG. Well! What then! Do you think I care! You're a mere worm in my path; not worth my while stepping upon. [*Going towards door, L.3.E.*]

POSIE. If I'm a worm, you're a great big snake. [*Following him up*]

SCRAG. [*At door, L.3.E.*] Take care! I'll have your master teach you better manners. [*Exit, L.3.E.*]

POSIE. [*Calling after him*] Well, he won't learn them of you—you old wretch! [*Alters tone*] Everybody's crying in there. More like a funeral than a wedding. [*Sits by fireplace. Britt enters, R.2.E. Crosses to L.H. and back to C., not seeing Posie*]

BRITT. Well, it's all over. In all my magisterial career, I never met anything like it. A marriage under such circumstances—it's like a dream, a page of unwritten romance. [*Starts to go to C.D.*]

POSIE. [*Rises, to C.*] I don't realize it myself, major.

BRITT. [*Stopping at C.D., turns, replaces his hat on sofa, L., and comes down, R.C., to Posie*] Well, it proves the old adage that "Truth is stranger than fiction." But, after all, you see how easily it is done, once a couple have made up their minds. [*Placing arm around Posie's waist*]

POSIE. Oh, it's easy enough done; but getting out of it, that's the thing. [*Gently disengaging herself and stepping back*]

BRITT. [*R.C.*] But, there need be no thought of that, when Cupid presides at the ceremony.

POSIE. [*L.*] Why, surely you don't call yourself Cupid, major?

BRITT. Hardly! Merely a deputy.

POSIE. Major, why do people always cry when they get married?

BRITT. You mean after marriage—a year or two, say.

POSIE. No, I don't, I mean just at the time.

BRITT. Well, I really can't tell, unless it be that the heart is so full it overflows at the eyes.

POSIE. I don't think I'd cry if I got married.

BRITT. No! I don't think you would.

POSIE. It would just please me so, I believe I'd laugh for a whole week. [*Britt laughs immoderately and ends by a choking cough. Posie hits him on the back*]

BRITT. Thank you! But you forget, my dear woman, the circumstances that surround these nuptials are very remarkable, and not without a very sad aspect.

POSIE. Do you really think they will take Joe away now?

BRITT. I'm sorry to say there is hardly a doubt! Indeed I may say that I regard the verdict as a foregone conclusion. [*Embraces Posie*]

SAM. [*Outside, R.2.E.*] Well, this is a genuine novelty. [*Posie and Britt separate, Posie going towards mantelpiece; Britt, up C. a little. Sam enters, R.2.E., to R.H.*] Never saw anything to excel it under canvas.

BRITT. [*C. Back to Sam*] Don't tell me, Miss Posie. I attribute it all to the sudden rise in the price of butter, and the recent tumble in lard. [*Turns and sees Sam*] Ah! Mr. Bowler! [*Crosses to him*] Let us go over to court and see if we can learn anything new. [*Shakes hands with Sam and goes up, C.*]

SAM. With all my heart! [*Following up Britt, and to Posie*] Posie, I'll be back soon.

BRITT. [*Turning sharply, C., and eyeing first Sam and then Posie*] I'll be back soon. [*Looks daggers at Sam as he exits, C., and off, L.H.*]

POSIE. There's no use talking, this is simply awful. [*Sits in chair R. of C. Wing Lee appears at C.*]

WING. [*Calling*] Missie Posie! Missie Posie!

POSIE. Well? Oh, it's you, eh?

WING. [*Advancing, L.H.*] Yes, Missie Posie, where Mister Blandon? Where im bossee?

POSIE. Oh! You are afraid of meeting him; that shows your good sense.

WING. Me no likee fightee. Me no likee kickee. Kickee hurtee Chinaman samee Melican man! No difflence. No difflence.

POSIE. What's that you've got there? [*Points to Wing Lee's bosom*]

WING. Where? [*Business*]

POSIE. There! [*Touching Wing Lee's breast*]

WING. No got here! No got here!

POSIE. There! There! [*Touching Wing Lee's breast, which appears extended*] Have you broken your breast bone?

WING. No gottee bloke blestie. Me gottee clothsee. See! [*Showing shirt from bosom*] Me washee—washee—

POSIE. Got some clothes, eh? Stole them, I suppose.

WING. Me no stealee, Wing Lee goodee Chinaman, findee clothsee in shaftee, where me sleepee. Me washee im in liber.

POSIE. Found them! Oh! A very likely story.

WING. Vellee likee! Vellee likee!

POSIE. Well, I'd advise you to leave Siskiyou County as soon as possible, for Major Britt will have you arrested as a nuisance.

WING. [*Puts shirt back*] All lightee, me go! Me sollee for Joey—me bellee good to Miss Mally—me good to evlybody—evlybody bad to poor Wing Lee.

POSIE. Poor wretch!

WING. Poor letch! Yes, me poor letch!

POSIE. Well, if you would only learn to keep your place.

WING. Keep place—all lightee—me no takee sackee—me keep place.

POSIE. But you Chinamen are such a precious pack.

WING. Pack! Pack! Me sabee. Me got packee. Chinaman always got packee. You playee. Pokee. Pee Nuckle. Slankee Pleadlee. Seven upee. Me playee all samee Melican man. [*Producing and shuffling cards. Gets R. of table, R.C.*]

POSIE. Well! I like you.

WING. You no likee packee—you likee me!

POSIE. Oh, yes! I'm in love with you. [*Business. Sits, R.C., chair before table*]

WING. Oh! She loves me. Me makee mashee. [*Gets chair and draws it up to Posie. Sits. She moves away, he follows her with chair*] Chinaman no likee Chinawoman. He likee Melican woman—me likee you.

POSIE. [*Startled*] What!

WING. Oh, you no givee bluffee! You lovee me—me lovee you! Me mally you! Me keepee housee, all same Melican man. [*Pokes her in ribs*]

POSIE. [*Rises, screams*] Don't you dare. [*Business of gag*] Oh! Oh! Here comes Mr. Brandon.

WING. [*Hurriedly*] Missee Blandon comee. He catchee me. [*Runs across to C., then up to door, L.C.*] Me catchee kickee. Me skippee. [*Exit quickly, L.3.E.*]

POSIE. Well, I always knew that Chinaman was a fool. [*Crosses to L., up to door. Music. Enter Mary and Grace, R.2.E.*]

GRACE. There! There! Be brave.

MARY. If I only knew what form of bravery would reach this case. [*Sinks into chair, C.*] I might try, but as it is, look which way I may, I see no light—no hope!

POSIE. [*L. Aside*] Poor girl! What a wedding! [*Exit, L.3.E.*]

GRACE. [*R.*] But you owe a duty to Joe; if he sees you suffer so, it will make his lot harder to bear.

MARY. If I could only help him to meet his fate; if I could only aid him in some way.

GRACE. You can, by showing him that you are not hopeless yet.

MARY. [*Earnestly, after a pause*] Grace, I have something to tell you—a secret.

GRACE. A secret! [*Joe appears, R.2.E.; Grace goes up, C.*]

MARY. [*Hesitatingly*] You once thought I—I loved Ned Singleton?

GRACE. I certainly did—but now—

MARY. I thought so, too. He was young, handsome, my ideal! At one time his image filled my heart, and a romantic girl's imagination clothed him in such a garment of goodness and truth that he appeared to me little less than divinity.

GRACE. [*Eagerly*] Yes! Well?

MARY. Since then I have seen with a purer, truer vision; the love of that man in his grave was a shallow stream, lovely to look upon in the sunlight of prosperity, but not deep enough to launch one's barque of life upon.

GRACE. [*In half alarm*] I fear I don't know what you mean.

MARY. I mean that a great love has flooded my life, [*Going R.*] a sweeter, healing tide, with all the power of purification in it.

GRACE. I cannot understand you yet. Do you mean that Joe after all is not—

MARY. I mean to say that to save me—[*Turns and finds herself face to face with Joe. She drops her eyes and stands silently*]

JOE. [*C. Stops Mary, pause, then turns to Grace and speaks*] Grace, just see that we are left alone for a few minutes. I've got something very particular to say to Mary. [*Grace exit, R.2.E.*] Mary—I've heard all—I prefer you should not finish your story—promise you won't. It wouldn't make her happier to know the truth—besides, I want your breast and my—grave alone to hold our secret. Do you promise? [*Pause*]

MARY. [*L.C. In a low voice*] Yes! Yes!

JOE. When I claimed you for my wife, I had no hope of ever gaining anything, but just a tender thought. You kin understand that standing as I am on the edge of my grave, I couldn't have had any plans for the future. 'Twas just an accident—my claiming you—I saw you in tears, I saw your father's agony, I saw your sister's shame—and I did it. The thought that you could love me never crossed my mind. But now, if anything should come to spare my life—

MARY. [*L. Tearfully*] You will be free—don't fear, I will not ask you to sacrifice yourself for me. No—out of my love for you has faded every gleam of selfishness! Let mine be the burden of repentance.

JOE. [*C.*] I was going to say, that if I was spared, and was sure that you did love me—that it wasn't mere gratitude that's filling your heart now, I would give my life to make yours happier.

MARY. Oh, no, Joe. I am not worthy! Think what I've done, think what I am.

JOE. To me, you are his widow, that's all.

MARY. You forgive me then? [*Rising*] You forgive me?

JOE. Forgive you? Why, God bless you, Mary, I've forgotten it long ago! Why, I've forgotten everything but that you was a poor child raised out here in the wilderness, without the same chance as most wimmen, and little as I know about Scripter I feel sartain Heaven will not be too hard on a poor gal as had no mother to guide her.

MARY. But, the world—

JOE. The world of Him who made it; the world of right and marcy and forgiveness has but one law for both sexes, and here where civilization has not built its temples, above the green groves of God—where men live nearer him—wimmen have an equal claim with men to the charity that covers a great mistake.

MARY. [*Solemnly and earnestly*] Joe, I wish, oh, how I wish, that I could die with you. [*Falling on his breast*]

JOE. [*R.C.*] Hush—stop, Mary, don't wish that, [*Business*] for if the worst comes—

MARY. No! No! No! Something must be done.

JOE. Hush! We must be prepared to meet it. So, if the worst comes, and I've got to die—which is likely enough—I want you to go there to Fargo's and git all my gold. It's yourn now! [*Mary sobs*] There, there, gal—don't cry! There's no time for tears now. [*Goes up, C.*]

MARY. [*As if struck with an idea*] Joe, why not escape? Once in the woods—

JOE. No! No! I can't.

MARY. Why not?

JOE. Have you forgotten, gal, that it's owing to the sheriff's kindness, that I'm not in the log coop, up there now; besides, I've given my word of honor, and I'd rather die than break it.

MARY. [*Dropping into chair*] Then all hope is gone!

JOE. [*Coming down to back of chair, L.*] Yes! Yes! It's hard to say farewell forever. But I suppose it might as well be said now, for they'll want me soon, and when they come, both of us must be calm and brave.

MARY. [*Rising, calmly*] Yes, I will be brave. Good-bye.

Joe. Good-bye—and when—it's all—all over and I am dead—[*Mary sobs loudly*] No! No! I mean, when I am gone, forever, I want you to take and bring me up here where I first met you, and lay me out there, 'long side of "My Partner"!

MARY. [*With a wail and falling on Joe's breast*] O Joe! Joe!

JOE. [*Puts her in chair and leans over her*] And when—your own time comes—you can rest beside us both, us partners—And if there's any knowing after death what's going on in this here world of ours, it will make that long eternal sleep sweeter to all of us, I know. [*Enter Brandon with Sheriff. Music stops. Enter Scraggs from L.*]

SCRAG. [*Down, L.H.*] The verdict is in, and—Mr. Saunders, they are coming after you.

JOE. [*Calmly*] And I am ready. [*To Mary*] Remember! [*Grace, R.2.E.*]

BRAN. [*R. To Scraggs*] So the verdict has been reached?

SCRAG. [*L.*] Of course, the verdict is not declared yet, but—[*Enter Sam, C., from L., running*]

JOE. [*C.*] Well!

SAM. [*R.C. To Joe in a low voice*]   The deputy sheriff who had charge of the jury whispered to me there is no hope; it's guilty. [*Music. Grace, Sam and Sheriff go up, R.C.*]

JOE.   Farewell, gal. [*Kisses her, she sobs*] Here—Mr. Brandon, take her away. [*Brandon assists Mary towards door, R.2.E. Joe follows up, kissing her repeatedly, etc. Grace comes down, C. Sam goes to window, L.C.*]

BRAN. [*Leading her off, sobbing, R.2.E.*]   My child.

JOE. [*At door*]   Good-bye—Mary! Forever! Grace, gal, good-bye—and be good to your poor sister, for she has suffered more, ah! more than you can guess. [*Going up, C. Brandon reenters, R.2.E. Comes to R.C., turning boldly to all*] And now gentlemen! I'm ready, ready to hear the verdict that will send me to my death. I am an innocent man, still I've weak moments like others. You'll see now I'm square, for I'm not afraid to die. [*Three loud shouts are heard outside, L.U.E. Posie enters, from L.3.E., and crosses to window in flat*]

SAM. [*At window. With amazement*]   They're cheering.

GRACE. [*Up R.H.*]   Are they cheering at the verdict? [*Coming down, R.*]

SAM.   No! No man in these diggings will cheer at a verdict of guilty against Joe Saunders. What does it mean? [*Coming down to Grace, L. Three more loud cheers are heard outside, L.U.E. Major Britt rushes in, C. from L., excitedly, down C.*]

OMNES.   What does it mean, major?

BRITT.   It means that we've discovered new evidence, that we've got on the trail of the real murderer, and the natural enthusiasm of the boys is such, that they must have an escape valve or bust. [*All the Miners and Girls rush in from C.L. and down, R.H. Britt, C. Authoritatively*] Order! Order! Let us proceed regularly! That we may understand the new find, let me state the case! Circumstances pointed to Joe Saunders very strong, yet, notwithstanding all this, we believe the crime was committed by another.

OMNES.   Another!

SCRAG.   It's growing dark! [*Wipes forehead*]

BRITT. [*C.*]   The man who murdered Singleton had his shirt cuff smeared with the blood of his victim. [*Crossing to Sam, R.C.*]

BRAN. [*R.C.*]   Well, we all know that. [*Britt whispers to Sam, who exits, R.2.E. Scraggs, L., starts to go, but is stopped by Joe*]

JOE. [*C.L.*]   Don't go, Mr. Scraggs, just hear this out, just hear this out.

BRITT. [*Crossing back to C.*]   Exactly! But while we had this cuff, the garment from which it was torn was missing. But a kind of Providence filled a poor wretch with fear and drove him into the black depths of a shaft for safety and sleep, and placed that missing garment, minus the cuff, into the hands of an humble but competent and intelligent witness.

OMNES. A witness?

WING. [*R.C.*] No punchee! No kickee!

BRAN. [*R.*] No!

WING. Then me tellee allee. Me flaid of bossee, me go downe shaftee—me hidee, me sleepee, me findee shirtee!

SCRAG. [*L.*] Pshaw! Is this all?

BRITT. No, it is not all. Wing Lee put me in possession of this new find, and we soon discovered that the cuff in court belonged to the shir—[*Pause*] In view of the ladies present, we will say garment.

WING. You got 'em cuffee—me got'em shirtee. [*Produces it*]

BRITT. And we also made another discovery, more important than any others, and that is that the name of its owner was printed on the band in stencil.

OMNES. What name?

BRITT. Josiah Scraggs. [*General stir*]

BRAN. [*R.*] Mr. Scraggs—impossible!

SCRAG. [*L.*] It's not true! It's not true! [*Sam enters from R.2.E. with handful of gold, and down, R.H.*]

BRITT. Isn't it? We shall soon see. [*To Sam*] Find anything else?

SAM. [*Giving gold to Brandon. On Brandon's R.*] This in Scragg's trunk. [*Goes up, R.H.*]

BRITT. [*C. Looking at gold*] More proof, more proof! [*Waves his handkerchief exultingly*]

WING. [*C., upstage, waving shirt*] More ploof! More ploof!

BRAN. [*R.C.*] I see no reason why this gold should not belong to Mr. Scraggs by right.

SCRAG. [*L.*] Yes, why not?

JOE. What proof is there in that, major?

BRAN. [*Gazing intently at gold, starts, aside*] What's this?

SCRAG. Who says the gold is not mine?

BRAN. [*R.*] I do! You all know, it was the habit of these partners to bury their gold under the hearthstone, and see, these nuggets are filled with ashes. [*Miners come in on each side. All crowd around and look at gold. Joe crosses, Britt, Posie cross to R.*]

JOE. [*Looking at gold*] Boys, he speaks the truth; that is my partner's gold! And here stands the man who killed him. [*Rushes at Scraggs, but is stopped by Britt, who is now L.C. Brandon gives gold to Sheriff*]

SCRAG. It's a lie! He struck me first; he would have killed me; 'twas in self-defense.

OMNES. [*Rushing at Scraggs*] Hang him! Hang him! Lynch him! [*Joe and Britt stop them. Grace exit, R.2.E.*]

JOE. No! Let him live long enough to realize the doom that's waiting for him. Sudden death would be too much mercy to show to such a wretch as him. [*Sheriff gets to L., back of Scraggs. Britt goes up, L.C., to Sam*]

SAM. [*Advancing to L., at back*] All right, Joe! But he swings in one hour. [*Business of Wing Lee with clock, up C. All laugh*]

BRAN. [*Advancing to Scraggs*] And, has it come to this at last, Josiah, I'm sorry—very sorry.

SCRAG. [*L.C.*] I don't want your sorrow! I despise your pity! Besides, you have none to waste! Go to Lady Mary and hear her story, or will I tell it to you here, before all your friends?

JOE. [*Coming to his R. and drawing Brandon away over to R.*] No! No! You must not hear this. [*To Sheriff*] Take him away. [*Exit Scraggs in custody of Sheriff, L.3.E., followed by Miners shouting, "Lynch him! Lynch him!"*]

WING. Lunch him! Lunch him! [*Exit after others. Posie crosses to L.H., to Britt*]

JOE. They've got him now—it's all right, major.

BRITT. [*L.C.*] All we have to do now is to return to court and secure a legal acquittal, so come. [*Crossing to door, R.C.*]

JOE. [*C.*] But, I must see Mary first! [*Calls, R.2.E.*] Mary!

BRAN. [*At door, R.2.E. Calls*] Mary! Mary! [*Mary enters from R.2.E., followed by Grace. They face in front of Brandon, who drops down, R.*]

MARY. [*R.C.*] Is it true? Has the light come at last?

JOE. [*C.*] Yes, dear! The night has been long and dark. But on the heights of happiness, where we are standing now, our love will illuminate our lives forever. [*Music*]

CURTAIN

THE GALLEY SLAVE

The text of *The Galley Slave* is based on a manuscript in the possession of Mr. Robert Campbell.

CAST OF CHARACTERS

Cicely Blaine

Psyche Gay

Francesca Remini

Mrs. Phoebe Gay

Nichette

Sidney Norcott

Baron le Bois

Oliver Oliphant

Franklin Fitts

Wellesley Napier

Carot

Dolores, *child, age 4*

Galley Slaves, Peasants, Sentinels, etc.

ACT I.

SCENE: *Venice. Exterior of an old palazzo on a small island, with a distant view of St. Mark's on drop at back. Palazzo with stone steps leading to doorway, R.2. to R.3., from which an awning of blue and white is swung. Under awning an easel and painting. Heavy stone stairway at back, C., supposed to lead down to water edge, where the gondola lands during progress of the play. Toward close of act, the twilight deepens and the moon rises. Music. Waltz. Franklin Fitts discovered shading his eyes on steps at back and looking off, L. Napier sitting on steps, R., smoking a cigarette indolently.*

NAPIER. Anyone coming?

FITTS. A great many coming and going, but none of our party.

NAPIER. It is too consumedly bad manners to trifle with a painter's time in this way, not to say anything of the bad taste of being late.

FITTS. It is bad taste to keep one's host waiting, but when the host is backed by a substratum of Italian cookery, and a basket of—what's the wine? [*Down L.*]

NAPIER. Red wine—vin rouge of some description, I'll wager a guinea.

FITTS. Wherefore red wine?

NAPIER. Because it's cheap. Your artist fellow may have the loftiest flights of fancy but his wine rarely rises above two shillings. [*Sits*]

FITTS. [*Reflectively*] I hate the old wines. I thought your friend Norcott wealthy.

NAPIER. He will be when an uncle in Edinburgh dies, or he himself gets married. They are an eccentric set, those Norcotts.

FITTS. [*Lighting cigarette*] Does marriage enrich him, then?

NAPIER. The old man don't believe in single life on the Continent. He is a thorough Conservative, votes against Gladstone and believes in marriage.

FITTS. [*Shrugging*] Regular old fogey. As if marriage nowadays had anything to do with morality. I wish my family had put a premium on marriage. [*Sigh*] They never had any regards for my proclivities.

NAPIER. Your remittances are regular and you have a perfect palace in Paris.

FITTS. But do you think my cotton-spinning friends in Massachusetts have any idea of my life here? The old gentleman supposes I am studying sciences abroad.

NAPIER. Have you accomplished much in that direction?

FITTS. Yes, I know every star in the theatrical firmament of Paris. O Paris, Paris!

NAPIER. [*Laughing*] What will you do when you return?

FITTS. Haven't had time to think of that yet. I'm too busy looking after my last love affair.

NAPIER. You and Norcott had better marry the two cousins, Miss Cicely and Miss Psyche, being countrywomen of yours. You ought to get on famously.

FITTS. But Miss Psyche hasn't got a penny, and any mail may cut me off.

NAPIER. But Miss Cicely is consumedly rich, they say. Supports her aunt and her cousin in regal style, and does the magnificent grandly.

FITTS. So if *ever* Cicely and Norcott *do* marry—?

NAPIER. Don't be so wretchedly and absurdly vague, my dear boy—they *must* marry. Poor Norcott has set his heart upon it and is frightfully in earnest.

FITTS. Yes, I know, but women are slippery fish. The wretch who baits his hook with his heart thinks he has them. They are always nibbling but never bite and just when his patience is exhausted and he is about to draw up his line, down goes the cork and he takes new hope and a fresh seat. Ten chances to one, they'll spread their silken fins at last and swim off, taking bait and all.

NAPIER. I hope you haven't lost your heart in that way. No one has fished for you?

FITTS. Fifty times. I bite at anything. I'm a regular soft-mouthed sucker. I can't help it. Women were made to love, and Psyche—[*Rolls eyes heavenward*] Wait till you see her. [*Psyche is heard singing a few bars of a love song. Both Napier and Fitts listen*]

NAPIER. Who's that? [*Goes up, C.*]

FITTS. The woman I worship. [*Goes up to step back*] See, here she comes, like a vision of constancy. [*Stops short, aside*] There's that confounded old Oliphant with her. Decrepit wretch—what chance has he got winning a young girl like Psyche?

NAPIER. [*On steps at back of R.*] Who is the old lady? [*Looking through his glasses*]

FITTS. Our mother—I mean my mother, no, her mother.

NAPIER. And the gentleman?

FITTS. Oliphant, a sort of a Scotch Croesus, who made all his money in Halifax and met us in Switzerland. The curse of Continental travel is that one can never get rid of an English-speaking acquaintance. If you part with them in Paris, you meet them in Rome. If you say adieu in Naples, they embrace you in Venice.

NAPIER. There are but three in the boat. What do you suppose has become of Miss Cicely?

FITTS. [*Gloomily*] Remained behind to tease poor Norcott. That is all women delight in, toasting their victims upon the spit of their caprice. [*L., under trees. A gondola lands during last speech at foot of steps. At back, Phoebe, Oliphant, and Psyche enter down steps laughing*]

PSYCHE. [*C. Laughs*] Don't say another word, Mr. Oliphant—you are so droll you keep my mouth stretched all the time.

OLIPH. [*R.*] But the sequel is funnier still.

PSYCHE. Then don't tell it, for I'll die laughing. I never enjoyed myself so much—in all my life. [*Sees Fitts*] O Franklin, you missed a world of fun.

FITTS. [*L. Gloomily*] I'm glad you didn't.

PSYCHE. [*To Oliphant*] You must tell it to him after dinner.

FITTS. [*Bitterly*] I won't tax our friend, Oliphant. I subscribe for all the comic almanacs and find them awfully stupid.

OLIPH. [*Significantly*] And sometimes they make their readers not only stupid, but ill-natured. [*To Aunt Phoebe*]

FITTS. [*To Psyche*] That's personal.

PSYCHE. And deserved. [*Bowing*] Where is your politeness? Why don't you introduce me to your friend?

FITTS. I beg your pardon. [*Offers her his arm and leading her back to where Napier stands leaning on balustrade and looking off, L.C. Napier turns, bows, she offers hand and they enter into conversation, go R. at back*]

OLIPH. [*Crossing, L.*] There is Norcott's last work, I presume? [*Pointing to easel under awning*]

PHOEBE. I hope it isn't another Madonna.

OLIPH. You forget Norcott is an English painter. The Italians seem to monopolize the maiden mother. [*Lifting curtain from it*]

PHOEBE. What a beautiful picture, but so sad. A young mother. An Italian peasant, too; did you ever see such painted pain before?

OLIPH. There is certainly a great deal of pathos and power. Although I'm in no sense a judge of fine work in art.

PHOEBE. [*R. of Oliphant*] Taste is innate.

OLIPH. [*L.C.*] But needs polish. Miss Psyche, you are fond of painting. Here's something, I suppose, worth looking at.

PSYCHE. I'm sure it is, if you say so. [*Bows to Napier and Fitts and goes L., to picture*]

FITTS. [*To Napier*] A mean little trick to get her away from me. [*Both upstage, R.C.*]

NAPIER. What? Do you really think he meant it? He has a very open, honest face.

FITTS. A mountain of hypocrisy. You'll see how polite he'll be to me. The jailer is never so kind as when he hands you over to the executioner. The hoary-headed old wretch!

PSYCHE. [*With hands on Oliphant's shoulder*] It is very beautiful. What does he call it, Franklin?

FITTS. [*Coming down, R.*] I never asked him. [*Psyche crosses over to Fitts*]

NAPIER. [*C.*] There is a story connected with that picture—not a particularly agreeable one—full of tears and suffering, of man's treachery and woman's wrongs, and all that sort of thing. Quite horrid, I assure you. [*They have all drawn near him*]

PSYCHE. I love the pathetic. Give us the story. [*Moves over to Napier*]

OLIPH. So she loves me when I sing those songs that make her grieve. [*Crosses down, L.1.*]

FITTS. [*Disdainfully*] Coleridge.

OLIPH. [*Bowing*] Exactly.

PHOEBE. [*To Napier*] Now for the romance.

NAPIER. [*C. Languidly*] I hardly think I'm equal to it. You'll have to get Norcott to tell it to you. Romance and this sort of thing is so much in his way and not a bit in mine. [*Crosses to Fitts, R.*]

FITTS. I wonder if Norcott knows we're here.

OLIPH. Perhaps we'd better go in at once.

PSYCHE. [*C.*] No—let us wait on Cicely, and go in together. Her presence will insure us a warmer welcome.

OLIPH. [*Smiling, crosses to Psyche*] Woman's wit again, triumphant. [*Gives arm to Psyche. Both upstage, L.C. Phoebe moves to picture*]

FITTS. [*To Napier*] See, always giving her sugar plums.

NAPIER. For which she seems to have a wonderful relish.

FITTS. Watch me take her from him. [*Crosses, C. Aloud*] Miss Psyche, the view from the other side of the island is simply gorgeous. [*Points to R.1.R.*]

PSYCHE. Indeed! [*Comes down with Oliphant, L.C.*]

FITTS. And while we wait for Miss Blaine, we can enjoy it. [*Offering his arm. Winks at Napier*]

PSYCHE. Thanks. Give mama your arm and lead the way out at once. [*Exit with Oliphant, L.1.E.*]

FITTS. Hoist by my own petard—I'll be only too happy.

PHOEBE. [*Crosses from picture. Taking his arm*] This is rare enjoyment, is it not?

FITTS. [*L. to R. Slowly*] Very rare. [*Aside*] A trifle too rare for a fellow who appreciates things well done. [*Aloud*] Come, Napier, he shall have some of this, too.

NAPIER. [*Comes down to Phoebe. L. of her*] You are enjoying Venice?

PHOEBE. Very much. Our hearts never grow old and I have all a girl's enthusiasms—there is but one Venice after all.

FITTS. Excuse me, there is Venice, Indiana. Not so cold, not so wet, not not so much out of repair, but still a Venice. [*Exeunt Fitts, Phoebe and Napier, R.1.R. Music. A gondola at steps and Le Bois assists Cicely to disembark*]

CICELY. [*R.*] Thanks. Won't you remain?

LE BOIS. [*L.*] You forget, ma'mselle, that I have not the pleasure of Monsieur Norcott's acquaintance nor of his invitation.

CICELY. [*Sitting*] Oh, he never stands on formality. You're quite welcome, I'm sure.

LE BOIS. [*L.C. Significantly*] On your account, eh?

CICELY. Certainly not; on your own.

LE BOIS. I will stay on one condition.

CICELY. Well?

LE BOIS. That you will recognize me as your escort throughout the day, that as we came together, we shall so depart. Is it a bargain?

CICELY. No.

LE BOIS. What am I to understand from this refusal?

CICELY. That I prefer to be free to act as I please, that is all.

LE BOIS. But suppose I say your refusal means more—that it separates us forever?

CICELY. I would say, for so slight a cause, your action was somewhat silly. [*Shrugs shoulders*]

LE BOIS. Does ma'mselle remember she is speaking to the Baron le Bois?

CICELY. [*Laughing*] Bless me, how you scowl. Come, come, I shall cease to admire you if you maintain that visage very long.

LE BOIS. Ma'mselle Blaine is very clever but her gaiety cannot deceive me.

CICELY. [*Seriously*] The occasion is not worthy of deception, Monsieur le Baron.

LE BOIS. I beg your pardon. I had no intention to speak now, but since we have reached this point, I may as well tell you all. I came from Paris especially to see you.

CICELY. It was very kind of you, indeed.

Le Bois. I came to offer you my name—for ma'mselle must know she has won my heart. For a whole year, ever since that first night at Naples I have been your slave. That you did not return 'my love I feared, but that you did not love another I hoped. Have you no reply?

Cicely. I prefer to remain silent.

Le Bois. Then it is true that you love this artist?

Cicely. I do not recognize your right to ask that question. [*Rises*]

Le Bois. Remember, ma'mselle, he is unknown—a mere beggar—

Cicely. [*Turns on him*] Stop, Monsieur Baron. If a beggar, he will never ask you for alms; and if you value my friendship, if you would not have us part enemies, you will never mention Mr. Norcott's name with disrespect again.

Le Bois. [*Coldly bowing, C.*] I will never mention it at all. I will have no rival. If I am not first in ma'mselle's regard, I will not be second. I leave Venice tonight. Adieu. [*Goes up, C.*]

Cicely. [*Offering hand*] We part friends.

Le Bois. [*Comes down to Cicely*] I have lost the battle, and not having philosophy enough to witness the conqueror possess the spoils, I retreat. But though lost, the cause is still dear, and some day ma'mselle may think differently. Adieu. [*Kisses her hand which drops listlessly at her side as she stands with eyes bent on the ground until he exits, L.U.E.*]

Cicely. [*Coming down, L.*] Perhaps I may think differently, and if I should regret, what then? [*Enter Francesca from palazzo; going to steps and shading her eyes, looks after the Baron*]

Fran. Yes, yes, it was Antoine. My Antoine. I could not be mistaken. [*To Cicely*] Pardon, señorita. [*Comes down, C.*]

Cicely. Do you wish to speak to me?

Fran. [*R.C.*] Did I see you speaking to Antoine Brabant a moment since?

Cicely. [*L.C.*] You saw me speaking to the Baron le Bois.

Fran. [*As if dazed*] Baron! O señorita, you are quite sure, quite sure?

Cicely. Quite sure. Why do you ask?

Fran. I have no time to answer now. [*Going to steps*] She is deceiving me, too. [*Exit, off L., calling*] Antoine! Antoine!

Cicely. [*Up C., looks after Francesca*] What a strange girl. She came from the palazzo. [*Looks at house, R.*] She is a friend of Norcott's. [*Turning, sees Picture, L.*] Her picture. [*After a pause*] How beautiful, how sad. Pretty as she is his art has added a new glory. [*Goes L.*] Perhaps he loves—pshaw. [*Enter Norcott, R.2., from palazzo*]

Nor. [*Calling*] Francesca. Francesca. [*Goes to steps*] Gone without a word. Strange that she should act so. I can't understand— [*Sees Cicely*]

Why, Miss Blaine, this is a real pleasure. [*Goes C. Takers her hand*]

CICELY. [*L.C.*] Thanks. I was just admiring the lost Francesca. [*Glances at picture*]

NOR. [*R.C.*] You've seen the original then?

CICELY. A moment since. The work's very fine. Was it a labor of love?

NOR. All artists love their work.

CICELY. And some, their models.

NOR. Nonsense. How long have you been here?

CICELY. A few moments only.

NOR. And the rest?

CICELY. Started half an hour before me. They are not here yet?

NOR. You surely did not come alone?

CICELY. I came with the Baron le Bois.

NOR. [*Suspiciously*] Whom you have been expecting from Paris?

CICELY. Yes.

NOR. Does he remain long in Venice?

CICELY. His stay will be limited to his pleasure, I presume. The baron is a rich man and can go where and when he pleases.

NOR. Wealth is a great blessing.

CICELY. [*Surprised*] Are you selfish enough to wish for wealth?

NOR. There is nothing selfish in my desire. I could be happy in the humblest home, but I would have the woman I worship walk on velvets, live in laces. The world of art I would rob of its treasures to surround her with beauty, not that her own might be eclipsed, but reflected and the world amazed.

CICELY. [*Playfully*] But suppose the woman you love should prefer a lowlier lot, suppose that she was one of those foolish few who still believe that love can exist within a cottage wall and was willing to share the burden of life with you.

NOR. [*Impassioned*] I would repay her with a life's devotion. Cicely, listen to me. My future rests with myself alone. I scorn to play the sycophant for the sake of bounty. I may not inherit a penny but if you are not in jest, give your wealth to those who need it more and let me toil for you. The love I bear for you will make the labor light and—

CICELY. [*Crosses, R.*] This is madness.

NOR. Is that your answer—be it so.

CICELY. Would it make me happier to have you toil for me?

NOR. It would at least prove to you the depths of my devotion.

CICELY. Can it not be proven in any other way?

Nor. [*Earnestly*]   Cicely, since the first I saw you, I felt you were my fate; try as I might, I could not drive you out of my thoughts. It was in the vain hope of doing so I fled from Florence. When I met you here, I wanted to tell you of my love I had tried so hard to strangle; but your wealth was a barrier I could not scale without leaving my self-respect behind, and so—

Cicely.   And so you determined to make yourself and the woman you worshipped wretched; you determined to revenge yourself upon yourself and upon me as well. [*Crosses to L.C.*]

Nor.   On you! I would sooner die, than see you suffer a single pang.

Cicely.   I believe you—it is because I trust in your sincerity that I give you my hand. I give you a more precious gift than all the gold my father gathered—a woman's heart filled with a pure and holy love; and all I ask in return is that the love of the girl and the love of the wife may never be betrayed.

Nor.   A vow I will find very easy to keep.

Cicely.   You have never loved anyone else.

Nor.   No.

Cicely.   Not even the least little bit?

Nor.   Not even the least little bit.

Cicely.   But you have admired others. [*Glancing at picture*]

Nor.   I think I have.

Cicely.   Francesca?

Nor.   Well, yes, I think so.

Cicely.   But only admired?

Nor.   That's all.

Cicely.   Kiss me. [*He kisses her just as Psyche, Napier, Phoebe, Oliphant, and Fitts enter, R.1. and L.1.E.*]

Oliph.   Have we returned too soon?

Nor. [*Pleasantly*]   I rather think you just came in time. [*Psyche and Oliphant down, L.*]

Psyche.   Has anything happened? You needn't speak, mama; it's all over.

Phoebe. [*R., to Norcott*]   I hope you will be very happy.

Fitts. [*Aside to Napier*]   Lucky dog. Thirty thousand dollars a year.

Cicely [*L.C., to Psyche*]   You never liked Englishmen, Psyche, but you must make an exception in this case.

Psyche.   I suppose so. [*Kisses Cicely*]

Nor. [*R.C.*]   Ladies and gentlemen, if you will kindly step into this old palazzo, which has doubtless been the scene of many a betrothal in bygone days, we will endeavor to revive the old time customs.

Oliph. [*L.1.*]   But not the old time romance. The past is past.

Nor. As long as youth and beauty live, love shall reign. As long as love shall live, romance cannot die. [*Enter little Dolores from palazzo; runs to Norcott, C.*] Ah! Dolores, come here.

Cicely. Whose child is that?

Nor. Belongs to the girl Francesca—my model, whom you heard me calling just now.

Cicely. [*Intently*] And its father—where is he?

Nor. Even Francesca cannot answer that. [*About to lift Child when Cicely passes the Child in front of her to Psyche, L.C.*]

Cicely. No, no, not in your arms. Let Psyche take the child. You see, I'm jealous even of a child. [*Leaning on his arm, they walk slowly to palazzo. Psyche kneels and embraces Dolores*]

Fitts. [*To Napier*] Oh, what a mother she'll make!

ACT II.

Scene: *An apartment in the Hotel Britannia in Rome, from the windows of which can be seen the Castle of St. Angelo and the Tiber, on drop L.1. Splendidly furnished. At the rise of curtain, chorus of Monks pass from L. to R., at back, chanting. Time, evening three months later. Music. Enter Napier, R.3.R.*

Napier. What a confounded dull old place Rome is! Not a girl worth looking at except Nichette, Miss Blaine's French maid, and she's as proud as a duchess. Nothing of the grisette I fear. [*Enter Nichette, L.3.E.*] Ah, my pretty Nichette. [*Familiarly*]

Niche. [*Disdainfully*] I beg monsieur's pardon.

Napier. [*R.C., gaily*] There is no necessity for that; but since you ask if you are forgiven, let me give absolution in a kiss. [*Putting his arm around her*]

Niche. [*With spirit*] You must not take such a liberty.

Napier. Come, come, you don't mean it.

Niche. [*Freeing herself*] Would monsieur insult me?

Napier. [*Amazed*] No woman can consider a kiss an insult! Where have you been reared?

Niche. In a Christian home, monsieur, where I was taught that when a rich man kissed a poor girl there is always danger in it.

Napier. I'm astonished, Nichette.

Niche. Astonished that poverty is too proud sometimes to submit to insult?

NAPIER. Why, I've kissed a thousand girls.

NICHE. Which is quite as many as you had a right to.

NAPIER. Now this is carrying the joke a little too far. You're not afraid of a gentleman?

NICHE. A gentleman will never offer a familiarity to one he cannot consider his equal. You offer to kiss me as a favor, a stooping from your exalted position. I refuse the favor. In my own class, I can find not only a lover, but a fireside, a heart and home caressed with respect. [*Going, R.E.*]

NAPIER. [*Whistling*] Well, that's a knockdown. [*Calling after her*] Nichette!

NICHE. [*At door*] Well?

NAPIER. Before you go, let me say I have acted like a jolly cad, and I humbly apologize.

NICHE. [*Feelingly*] Thank you, monsieur, thank you.

NAPIER. Somehow everybody manages to escape me. I hate Rome. I like the antique but one can get enough of that in Westminster and a graveyard to boot. [*Enter Le Bois, L.3.E.*]

LE BOIS. [*Looking behind*] I thought I saw a woman following me.

NAPIER. A woman?

LE BOIS. [*Still looking*] Yes, monsieur, robed in black like a nun. She came to the steps of the hotel.

NAPIER. Doubtless—a beggar, very common in Rome.

LE BOIS. I beg your pardon; but we have met before—at Florence—eh?

NAPIER. [*Surprised*] Why bless me, so it is. [*Offering hand*] Antoine, the artist.

LE BOIS. Antoine no more. Artist no longer. The death of an uncle has made me a baron.

NAPIER. Let me congratulate you. Estate large, any good shooting?

LE BOIS. I can say yes to both, and invite you there next autumn. My address. [*Hands card*] But monsieur must conveniently forget that Baron le Bois was ever a miserable painter. Is it a bargain?

NAPIER. With proper provocation, I can forget almost anything.

LE BOIS. Are you alone?

NAPIER. I came here with some folks from Venice three months ago, an English friend, Norcott, and some American ladies.

LE BOIS. Ma'mselle Blaine?

NAPIER. Yes, did you know her?

LE BOIS. Very well. I have heard Norcott is very attentive in that direction.

NAPIER. Worse than that. They are about to go to Florence, where they first met, to be married.

LE BOIS. [*With a start*] Are you sure?

NAPIER. [*Carelessly*] Positive.

LE BOIS. When do they start?

NAPIER. In the morning. Let us find Miss Blaine. She'll be consumedly glad to see you. Even the most sensible of these Americans are a little weak on you titled chaps—eh? [*Offering his arm*]

LE BOIS. Excuse me. I must go to my apartments first. You see, I'm travel-stained. Later I will be glad to meet you and the ladies. [*Goes, R.E.*] Your servant, monsieur. [*Bows and exit, R.3.E.*]

NAPIER. Good-bye old boy—baron—eh. [*Exit, L.3.E.*]

OLIPH. [*Enter, R.2.E.*] A charming girlish woman that Mrs. Gay—make a good wife for some man. [*Enter Psyche, L.2.E.*]

PSYCHE. Oh, dear, Mr. Oliphant, I'm just exhausted. I've had the awfullest time with that Mr. Fitts. [*Sinks into seat, R.*]

OLIPH. My dear child, I trust nothing serious.

PSYCHE. Serious. He threatened to hang himself from the portico of the Vatican and made himself so ridiculous that I'll never forgive him.

OLIPH. I'm glad you have come to so sensible a determination. Fitts is a good fellow but as a matrimonial candidate, none could be less advisable.

PSYCHE. [*Aghast*] I thought you were Fitts's friend?

OLIPH. So I am. But no man so unfit for the serious battle of his life, as he is, should be permitted to make a young girl miserable.

PSYCHE. But I've promised to marry him.

OLIPH. Not without your mother's consent.

PSYCHE. [*Worried*] He didn't give me time to think of my mother. What will I do?

OLIPH. Come, come, you needn't wring your hands. Fitts is an honorable fellow and will, I'm sure, release you.

PSYCHE. [*Impatiently*] But I don't want to be released.

OLIPH. Oh, you don't, eh? Well, my dear, when a girl without a fortune determines to marry a man without a penny or a profession, any word of advice is a piece of impertinence. [*Sits in chair, R.*]

PSYCHE. [*Pleadingly*] Ah, dear, patient, kind Mr. Oliphant, won't you help me a little with mama?

OLIPH. [*Looking in her face*] Do you think as a friend of the family I can do so conscientiously?

PSYCHE. Fitts is not so bad. [*Shyly*] And Cousin Cicely likes him ever so much.

OLIPH. [*Putting arms around her*] And Cousin Cicely being Lord High Chancellor of the Treasury, that is a very important fact, eh? [*Enter Fitts, L.2.E.*]

FITTS. Stop that! I have had enough of that. [*Threateningly*]

PSYCHE. You'll spoil everything, that's what you'll do. [*Down, L.*]

FITTS. [*Eyeing Oliphant, C.*] I trust I have spoiled it. Oh, you old bunch of deceit and wickedness before my eyes.

OLIPH. [*R.*] Your jealousy is simply ridiculous. As far as I am concerned, she might as well be a baby in arms.

FITTS. Yes, in your arms.

PSYCHE. Fitts!

FITTS. Do you understand, sir, that your antics in Venice will not be tolerated in Rome? That young lady is my promised wife. Can you grasp the sanctity of that title?

OLIPH. Without the consent of her parents she will never marry. The young lady had just secured my hearty cooperation but your bluster has shown me the folly of meddling with other people! I wash my hands of the whole affair. [*Dropping into chair, picks up book*]

PSYCHE. [*Despairingly*] I knew you'd do it.

FITTS. [*Realizing his mistake*] If I have been too hasty, if in assailing an imaginary enemy, I've struck a friend, I'm sorry.

OLIPH. In my country, men think twice before they speak.

FITTS. And in my country they shoot first and then ask for an explanation.

OLIPH. And do you dare to justify such a code?

FITTS. I know it has its disadvantages but it saves time. [*Crosses, L.*]

PSYCHE. Mr. Oliphant, won't you speak to mama—please?

OLIPH. I repeat I wash my hands of the whole affair.

FITTS. [*Scornfully*] The affair isn't so dirty that it needs so much washing.

PSYCHE. Fitts! [*C.*]

FITTS. I won't have my pure love spoken of as if it needed a regular course of starch and blue water.

PSYCHE. [*Determined*] Mr. Franklin Fitts, if you don't want me to positively hate you, go and ask Mr. Oliphant's pardon.

FITTS. Oh, this is too much.

OLIPH. Fitts is quite right, Miss Gay, it is too much. If the gentleman will withdraw his epithet of deceit, it is all I ask.

FITTS. You retract the washing business?

OLIPH. Most heartily.

PSYCHE. And you will speak to mama?

OLIPH. For your sake—hush. Here she comes.

FITTS. Oil her down first.

OLIPH. I don't understand you, sir—

PSYCHE. He means get her in a good humor.

OLIPH. Remember, I'm a bachelor, but I'll do my best.

PSYCHE. [*At door of 2.E.*] We'll wait in the corridor.

FITTS. [*Goes to door, L.2. and returns*] Go it strong, soft side you know. Don't let her have a word. [*Exit, L.2.E. Enter Phoebe, R.2.E.*]

PHOEBE. Wasn't that Mr. Fitts?

OLIPH. Yes, madame, Mr. Franklin Fitts.

PHOEBE. I do wonder where Psyche is. That girl will not remember that what is proper in America is not proper in Rome.

OLIPH. My dear madame, purity is purity all the world over, and when a young girl's honor has to be guarded by an old duenna against its own attack, as seems to be the custom here, it is hardly worth defending.

PHOEBE. But young unmarried women on the Continent are so easily talked about.

OLIPH. Am I to understand then, that wedding rings have displaced the liberty cap as a symbol of freedom; that they are now held up like hoops in a circus through which women vault into a whirling round of pleasure from which modest maidenhood would shrink.

PHOEBE. I hope not. A true woman can be safely left to her own instincts at all times and in all places.

OLIPH. In that I cordially agree with you. [*Brings chair forward from R.*] My dear madame, will you be kind enough to be seated? [*Offers chair*] I have something very important to say to you.

PHOEBE. [*In wonder*] Concerning Psyche?

OLIPH. Concerning you and Psyche and others as well. [*Brings chair from L. Aside*] I hope I'm on her soft side.

PHOEBE. I do wonder what's coming.

OLIPH. To you who have tasted the sweets of matrimonial bliss I need not commend the institution?

PHOEBE. [*Sadly*] Alas, it was too short, Major Gay only survived our bridal three months. [*Sighs*]

OLIPH. But in those three months you knew that sense of safety only found in his sheltering arms.

PHOEBE. To be exact you cannot use the plural. The major had but one arm.

OLIPH. Very embarrassing.

PHOEBE. We found it so on many occasions.

OLIPH. Brief as was your experience, I trust you have no hostility to the marriage state.

PHOEBE. None. Besides it is so easy to love where we respect, and I'll be frank enough to say that from the first I have had for you the most sincere regard.

OLIPH. [*Embarrassed*] You really are too kind. But if I may speak plainly —In fact to correct any misapprehension—Miss Psyche—I—

PHOEBE. She is in no sense a burden to me, nor will she be in the future. Her Cousin Cicely has always provided for us generously since her parent's death and will continue to do so until the dear girl is settled in life.

OLIPH. [*Rising*] But if I may venture to—

PHOEBE. [*Rising*] There, not another word now, please. I am quite exhausted. It was so sudden. In Florence we can arrange the little preliminaries. [*Going, R.2.*]

OLIPH. I am at a loss for words, dear madame. What I wish to say—

PHOEBE. [*Turning to him*] And all I can say is that I will try to make you happy. [*Wipes her eyes*] You see, I am in feelings still a mere girl. Good night, dearest, good night. [*Exit, R.2.*]

OLIPH. I hope I've oiled her down. It's all over. My poor brain is all in a whirl. Well, she's a dear girl and I suppose I ought to rejoice in my good luck. [*Enters Psyche followed by Fitts, L.2.E.*]

PSYCHE. What did she say?

FITTS. [*L.*] Is it all fixed?

OLIPH. I should say it was.

PSYCHE. [*C.*] Did she take it well?

OLIPH. Like sweet oil.

FITTS. Are we to be married right off?

OLIPH. [*Crosses to Fitts, fiercely*] Married! On what, I should like to know? Is the prospect of a disinheritance a fitting dower for a young girl? Is an idle, aimless life a fit offering for the altar of Hymen? If your love for this dear child is sincere, if it is not the outgrowth of a selfish nature, fed on self-indulgence, prove it by taking off your coat and going to work for her. When a young man endorses his love by honest labor, he gives it value and makes it acceptable as a purchased commodity in the market of affection; otherwise it is worthless.

PSYCHE. [*Seat, L.*] Why don't you say something, Fitts?

FITTS. [*Drops into seat, R.*] I'm dumb. By what authority do you dare-- Oh, no—I can't do the subject justice. I'll send Napier to you. Will you oblige me by letting me kill you at as early an hour as possible tomorrow?

OLIPH. Nonsense. Let us talk about living, not dying. Since I volunteered to interest myself in your behalf, I have become prospectively the natural guardian of this girl.

BOTH. What!

OLIPH. To be plain, I'm about to marry her estimable mother.

PSYCHE. Mama, marry! [*Drops into seat. Both same business*]

FITTS. [*Jumping up*] And because you are going to marry, because you propose to steep your soul in connubial bliss, no one else must have any? You refuse to share it. You're afraid there will not be enough to go around.

OLIPH. I propose to guard this girl's happiness.

PSYCHE. [*Desperately*] But there can be no happiness unless I have Fitts.

OLIPH. Hear my proposal first, then judge. Let me state the case.

FITTS. [*Threateningly*] Don't be any more personal than you can help.

OLIPH. My friend Fitts is too true, too noble, to become the pensioner of any man's bounty. He is anxious to place his wife above a position of dependence. He naturally wants to be the architect of his own fortune. To do this, I propose that he shall return to Heidelberg for one year—finish his medical course, and having mastered his profession, he shall not only have a wife, but drugs enough to kill a parish—and perhaps if he is a very good boy, a thousand pounds to make him independent of professional murder for a year or two. [*Psyche who has been exhibiting joy throughout Oliphant's speech, throws her arms around his neck at close*]

PSYCHE. You've made me so happy.

FITTS. That year of exile is a sticker. But I suppose I ought to be grateful and I am. [*Gives hand to Oliphant*]

OLIPH. [*Going to L.2.E.*] Now, having got through with an excellent evening's work, I feel myself entitled to a whiff of fresh air. This idling in Italy is very prolific of matrimony, at my age, too. [*Exit, L.2.E.*]

PSYCHE. [*Taking Fitts's arm*] Poor Fitts—a whole year.

FITTS. [*Ruefully*] If a fellow could only get one of those Philadelphia diplomas that they sell so cheap.

PSYCHE. [*Depressed*] He wants one from Heidelberg.

FITTS. I suppose nothing will satisfy him but a genuine Dutch doctor. O Psyche! [*Blubbering*]

PSYCHE. [*Sobbing*] O Fitts! [*Exeunt, L.2.E. Enter Cicely and Norcott, R.C.E.*]

CICELY. [*Admiring necklace*] It is very beautiful.

NOR. I am glad you think so.

CICELY. The workmanship is so unique.

Nor. [*Takes necklace and places it on her neck*]   It will serve to keep me in memory as well.

Cicely. [*Lightly*]   And lest I should be forgotten, take this, my miniature, set in diamonds.

Nor. [*Half protesting*]   But those stones are precious.

Cicely.   Their lustre pales before the light of love, and precious as they are, they are worthless when compared to the depths of my devotion. [*Pause*] And if aught should come between us—

Nor.   Don't let us deal in impossibilities. Nothing can ever come between us.

Cicely.   And yet I cannot repress a feeling of sadness.

Nor.   There is nothing in the situation to warrant that.

Cicely.   Unless, as I sometimes feel, excessive joy is akin to sorrow. The surfeit of conquest made Alexander weep. [*Goes L., to sofa*]

Nor.   But had he a fresh world to conquer, he would doubtless have rejoiced.

Cicely.   Do men need new worlds very often?

Nor. [*Smiling*]   I fear you are a trifle vague.

Cicely.   Come over and sit here. [*Pointing to a seat at her side. Norcott seats himself, putting his arm around her*] Not so close, there. [*Taking his arm from around her*] Do you know why I was sad this evening?

Nor. [*Smiling*]   Haven't the most remote idea.

Cicely.   Because as I watched the clouds floating across the sky, bathed a few moments only in the moonlight, to be lost in the drifting shapes of shade, I thought how swiftly across the sky of the present, our days of courtship were passing, and how soon they would be gone forever.

Nor.   To be succeeded by other and better days.

Cicely.   But I've heard so many married women regret that their courting days never could return.

Nor.   And perhaps they themselves were most to blame. Young wives kill more sentiment by their ill-advised caprice than they are willing to acknowledge. Courtship is but the vestibule to the temple of happiness where Hymen dispenses favors. Those who would taste its sweetest joys must divest themselves of every selfish thought ere they enter. To the noble mind there is more pleasure in giving than receiving. The rose would not be happier if it refused its fragrance to the world.

Cicely.   But the rose would have no fragrance to bestow if it were denied the smiles of the sun and the embrace of the warm breezes.

Nor. [*Lightly*]   My rose will never have cause to bemoan their absence.

CICELY. [*Earnestly*] I hope not, for, O Sidney, if you should change, if you would ever grow to be less kind, if you would ever take from me the love that has grown to be a part of me, what would I do?

NOR. [*Smiling*] As I will never be guilty of such a crime, there is no need to answer that question. [*Rising*]

CICELY. [*Rising*] No, but then the world is so quick to forgive men who break their vow. I have heard society make a jest of a woman's desertion. But to me it is infamous, alike in man and woman. Were I so treated, I'd revenge myself some way. No one should trample on my heart. At the very thought, my blood takes fire! [*Crosses to R.*]

NOR. [*In surprise*] Why, Cicely!

CICELY. Forgive me. [*Returning, C.*] You see what a creature of impulse you'll have to manage. [*Smiling*]

NOR. We have unfortunately drifted to an unpleasant theme. Let us dismiss it forever. Tomorrow evening remember, we go to Florence. Have you any purchase to make before starting?

CICELY. None. Yes, let me see— The little picture we both admired in the Leoni gallery yesterday.

NOR. "The Wedding Breakfast?"

CICELY. Yes, with the funny little bride.

NOR. It shall be yours. If I'm to see the artist, I must be off.

CICELY. But really, couldn't you see him tomorrow just as well?

NOR. I will not have a moment to spare tomorrow, not even to see you.

CICELY. [*In surprise*] Going to be away all day?

NOR. Yes, I have to go across the marshes nine miles and see Count Cavenna on a matter of business. I won't be back until late. The train for Florence leaves at seven.

CICELY. [*Sadly*] Across the marshes, all that way. I knew there was a disappointment awaiting me.

NOR. Your disappointment will be easier to bear when you know I share the pain, and that the cause is without a remedy. Good night. [*Offers to kiss her*]

CICELY. No, I will not say good night here. I will go to the end of the corridor with you.

NOR. [*Going up, C.*] Won't you be afraid to return?

CICELY. No, I'll be too sad to think of fear.

NOR. [*Reassuring her*] Nonsense. A day is nothing and just think of it— in three days I won't have to say good night at all.

CICELY. [*Smiling*] Three days.

NOR. Three, pretty, diminutive little days. [*Crosses to L.C. Enter Le Bois, R.3.E.*]

LE BOIS. I must lose no time in presenting myself to La Belle Blaine. These Americans carry their freedom with them and keep late hours. [*Enter Oliphant, L.3.E.*] The Scotch gentleman, Monsieur Oliver.

OLIPH. I wonder if I can sleep. [*Going, L.2.E.*]

LE BOIS. Beautiful night, monsieur.

OLIPH. Lovely.

LE BOIS. Monsieur I fear does not remember me.

OLIPH. Very well, indeed. You were with us in Venice.

LE BOIS. Exactly. I hope Ma'mselle Blaine is well and happy.

OLIPH. Ought to be—Going to be married on Thursday.

LE BOIS. Indeed!

OLIPH. If you will excuse me, sir, I will retire. I have had a very busy day. [*Aside*] I suppose Mrs. Gay is sleeping soundly. Women can stand this thing better than men. [*Exit, L.2.R.*]

LE BOIS. This marriage seems to give general joy. [*Enter Cicely, L.C.*] Ma'mselle. [*Offers his hand*]

CICELY. Baron—at last at Rome.

LE BOIS. My exile becomes painful, and I could not remain away any longer. May I flatter myself ma'mselle is glad to see me?

CICELY. I am always happy to see my friends. Have you been to Paris? [*Francesca appears with child, C.*]

LE BOIS. No. Our parting put me in no mood for the pleasure of Paris. I return to plead again. [*Francesca shrinks out of sight, L.C.*]

CICELY. It is too late, monsieur.

LE BOIS. But if you knew the depths of my devotion, how much, how ardently I love you.

CICELY. Monsieur le Baron, you must not. I am about to become the wife of another. If we cannot meet as friends, we must not meet at all. [*Enter Psyche quickly, L.2.E.*]

PSYCHE. O Cicely. [*Crosses to C.*] I want to tell you something.

CICELY. [*Reproachfully*] Don't you see the baron?

PSYCHE. Why, so it is. [*Bowing*] I'm glad to see you.

LE BOIS. And I'm delighted to see you, ma'mselle.

PSYCHE. [*To Cicely*] Come to mama's room. I've something awful to tell you. [*To Baron*] Bon soir, monsieur. [*To Cicely in whisper*] Make your hair stand on end. [*Exit, R.2.E.*]

CICELY. [*At door, R.2.E.*] You will breakfast with us tomorrow?

LE BOIS. With pleasure. [*Francesca reappears, L.C., with Child*]

CICELY. And we shall always be friends?

LE BOIS. [*With a shrug*] I am but ma'mselle's slave. Let her command— [*Kisses her hand. Exit Cicely, R.2.E.*] Too late. A clear three million francs. [*Shrugs*] Farewell, Monte Carlo and Russian war forever. [*Turning, L., faces Francesca who has come down, L.C., with Child*]

FRAN. [*L.C.*] Antoine!

LE BOIS. [*Glancing about*] Hush—sh.

FRAN. [*L.C.*] O Antoine, Antoine, is it really you?

LE BOIS. Silence! [*Looks off, R.2.*] Why have you come here?

FRAN. Why have I come here? Do you ask such a question? Where should a wife go but to her husband? For two whole years I have searched everywhere for you; now when I see you again, I forget that I am footsore, I forget that my child and yours has cried for bread. I forget everything, but that I have found the father of the child.

LE BOIS. [*Fiercely*] What do you demand?

FRAN. [*Pleadingly*] To be taken to your home and heart again—to be happy as we once were. I will never ask you to explain your cruel absence. I will—

LE BOIS. [*Comes down, R.*] Impossible.

FRAN. No, no, don't say that—Not in the presence of your child, who has prayed every night for the good Virgin to send her father back. [*Embraces Child*]

LE BOIS. Francesca, you were always a girl of sense. Don't be a fool now. Listen to me.

FRAN. [*Comes down, L.C.*] Yes, yes, anything you ask.

LE BOIS. We were always poor together. Were I to return to you, it would only be a fresh lease of poverty. I would be wretched, and you unhappy.

FRAN. [*Low and stern*] And you propose?

LE BOIS. To provide liberally for Dolores and yourself, on condition that you will return to Florence and never mention this marriage to anyone.

FRAN. [*Bitterly*] And you will marry this woman? [*Gestures, R.2.E.*] This woman whose hand I saw you kiss! You ask me to sell you to another? Never! [*Fiercely*] Your name is my honor. It shall be my shield.

LE BOIS. Since you will not listen to reason, I will do nothing. [*Going, L.*]

FRAN. I will do something. [*Starting to go, R.2.E.*]

LE BOIS. [*Catching her hand*] What do you mean to do?

FRAN. Expose you to her. [*Pointing, R.2.E.*]

LE BOIS. Do, and I shall denounce you as a lunatic and separate you from your child forever. You are poor, friendless, and a stranger; I am rich, powerful, and well known. You see, even your liberty is my gift. [*Goes up, C.*]

FRAN. You are a wretch.

LE BOIS. [*Coming down*] To prove that I am not, meet me at the old ruins across the marshes tomorrow morning at ten, and if you are wise you shall have gold enough to garment you in fashion, all your life. Come, come Fran, be sensible. I have never ceased to love you. [*He puts his arms around her. She shrinks away from him. He shrugs his shoulders, goes up, C.*] Remember the hour—across the marshes. [*Exit, L.C.*]

FRAN. [*In despair. Goes up and looks after him*] And this is the man I have loved so well. [*Turns, C.*] Hope is gone. He would separate us, Dolores. [*Clasping Child*] But no, no, children of misfortune, we will starve and die together. [*On her knees she embraces Child. Enter Cicely, R.2.E. Cicely coming down, R.*]

CICELY. It seems like a fairy tale. [*Francesca leaves Child, up L., comes down, L.C. with fierce fire in her eyes*] It will be such news in America— [*Smiles*] Such happy news. [*Sees Francesca*] Well? [*In surprise*]

FRAN. Well, it is not well, it is ill. You shrink, señorita, from the wreck you have made—fear nothing. I am not a wild beast yet. I will not destroy the beauty that has made me an outcast.

CICELY. [*In alarm*] You are mad. [*Attempts to go. Francesca steps between*]

FRAN. No, I am not mad. If I were I would not remember you so well.

CICELY. I never saw you before.

FRAN. I spoke to you at Venice, you must remember.

CICELY. Francesca!

FRAN. Ah, Francesca. Ragged and wretched.

CICELY. What has brought you here?

FRAN. Can't you guess?

CICELY. No.

FRAN. [*Uneasily. Goes up and looks around*] If I were to tell you, he would say I was mad, and then would separate me from my child, the only thing that loves me in the world. [*Drawing Child to her*]

CICELY. [*Earnestly*] Woman, I command you to speak.

FRAN. [*Coming down, L.*] You will not betray me to him?

CICELY. No.

FRAN. By all the saints you swear it?

CICELY. By all the saints; for pity's sake go on.

FRAN. I came here to seek the father of this child—my husband.

CICELY. [*Eagerly*] And you have failed?

FRAN. No, señorita. I have not failed. He is your lover.

CICELY. [*Staggers back*] My lover! [*Fiercely*] 'Tis false, a foolish wicked lie.

FRAN. [*C., raising hand*] On my soul.

CICELY. [*Grasping Francesca's hand with solemnity*] Burden not your soul with perjury, for were you an angel fresh from the golden fields of God, I would not believe you. [*Crosses to L.*]

FRAN. Because you do not wish to.

CICELY. Because it is impossible. [*Dropping in seat, L.*]

FRAN. I see you love him, too. I see you suffer, too. O señorita, pluck him from your heart. He is not worthy of a place in any woman's heart. Adieu.

CICELY. [*Rising*] Stop—give me proof. Where did you first meet?

FRAN. [*Coming down, R.*] In Florence. He was a poor painter—I his model.

CICELY. [*In a low voice*] And he married you?

FRAN. Yes—see the ring I wear, it is his. [*Holding out hand*] If the señorita will look she will see the date.

CICELY. [*Controlling herself*] No, no, go on.

FRAN. When my child was born, he sent me to Mantua where my sister lived. For weeks I got no word, and when I returned to Florence, he had gone, none knew where.

CICELY. But you met again?

FRAN. Yes, at Venice I saw him next.

CICELY. And he fled from you again?

FRAN. He came to Rome, I followed him afoot, begging my way from town to town, often helpless, always hungry.

CICELY. And here you found—

FRAN. That he had deserted me, because he loved you. [*Takes stage, R.*]

CICELY. [*Animation*] There must be some mistake. [*Going to her, R.*]

FRAN. He offerd to purchase my silence that he might wed you. He said that he could not consent to be poor any longer.

CICELY. [*Huskily*] And you—you—

FRAN. I refused and then he told me to meet him tomorrow morning where no one might see me, across the marshes at ten o'clock.

CICELY. [*Starts*] Across the marshes—are you certain he said across the marshes?

FRAN. As I am that I live. [*Goes R. and comes slowly to C.*]

CICELY. [*Aside, L.*] He said he would cross the marshes. I saw her picture with my own eyes. I saw him take his child up tenderly in his arms. How could I be so blind? [*Crosses, R. to Francesca*] I hope you do not blame me for this thing. You have suffered, I can read it in your face.

FRAN. I will forgive you, but you will not marry him?

CICELY. Marry, no, I will never see him again. [*Francesca up C.*] His name shall never cross my lips. This unholy love will not find a place of sepulchre in my desolate heart. [*With emotion. Up to Francesca*] You are hungry you say; let me relieve you. [*Offers purse*]

FRAN. Not from you, I could not take it from the hand that he has kissed.

CICELY. His child. [*Puts purse in Child's hand*]

FRAN. [*Turning*] Come, Dolores, our home is in the streets. [*Turns, L., and looks at Cicely*] I do forgive you, señorita. Come, Dolores, come. [*Exit, L.3.E.*]

CICELY. And I thought I was going to be happy. [*Enter Psyche, R.2.E.*] Psyche, go and tell Mr. Oliphant we do not go to Florence. That I have changed my mind. We must start at daybreak for Paris. [*Down, L.*]

PSYCHE. [*In amazement*] Why, has anything happened?

CICELY. Nothing; a mere trifle.

PSYCHE. [*R.C.*] But Norcott—

CICELY. [*C.*] His name must never cross your lips again. To me, he is as one dead, dead long enough to be forgotten. Why do you stare, I am not mad. I wish to God I were. O Psyche, my heart is breaking. [*Casts herself in Psyche's arms. Slips down on her knees, her arm about Psyche's waist. Music forte*]

ACT III.

SCENE: *On the Rhone. An apartment in Château Le Bois. Magnificently furnished. Through windows of F. a distant view of Marseilles. Door, L.2., leading to boudoir of Cicely. Doors, R.2. and R.3., window, L.3.E. Small table against flat, L.C. Small desk, R.1. Time, evening one year later. Music, polka. Oliphant discovered looking out of window, C. Baron le Bois reading letters at table.*

LE BOIS. Curse Belaman. Another threat. Does he expect a man to use his wife's fortune before he gets it? [*Opens another letter*] Pretty bridal favors. Well, she refused hearts, so I had to play diamonds, and if she has to pay for them, it is only fair.

OLIPH. [*Down L.C.*] Ah, baron, I almost envy you the possession of this noble pile. We have nothing in Scotland finer.

Le Bois. You now see why I wished the wedding to take place here. Nothing could be more retired and Cicely has grown so careless of display.

Oliph. [*Sighs*] A year has wrought a wondrous change in Cicely.

Le Bois. But here the excitement and worry of travel will be quite forgotten and the breezes from the Rhone will bring fresh roses for her cheeks and her domestic duties new ambition.

Oliph. I sincerely hope so. [*Enter Nichette, R.3.E.*]

Niche. The curé is below and wants to see Monsieur le Baron. [*Goes to window, C.*]

Le Bois. [*Smiling*] The curé and the notary are of some importance on a wedding day, eh, monsieur? [*Exit, R.3.E.*]

Oliph. [*Crosses to R.*] Ah, Nichette, this is a great day, it is not often you see a double wedding in this part of the country—eh?

Niche. [*Going to R.*] No, monsieur.

Oliph. Where are you going, Nichette?

Niche. To help Philemon with Ma'mselle Cicely, if she needs me.

Oliph. I don't like this marriage of Cicely's. It seems to me to lack heart on both sides. I fear she made a mistake in quarreling with Norcott, who certainly worshipped her. [*Enter Phoebe, R.2.E.*]

Phoebe. My dear, I've been looking for you everywhere. Psyche insists on exhibiting herself to Mr. Fitts a half hour before the time.

Oliph. There can be no harm in Fitts admiring her fine feathers and if it pleases her—

Phoebe. But it's against all rules. When I married Major Gay—

Oliph. Never mind Major Gay, he is a long way off. It's much better to remember our own little affair six months ago.

Phoebe. [*Shocked*] Our own little affair. That's always the way. Oliver, with you Psyche can do no wrong—and the mention of Major Gay's name drives you into a temper.

Oliph. Temper? Rubbish! I never was happier in my life except the night you asked me to marry you.

Phoebe. I? Asked you to marry me?

Oliph. No, no, I don't mean that. There's no use letting the cat out of the bag at this late day.

Phoebe. My poor nerves. I would certainly like to have a few moments' talk with Mr. Fitts before the ceremony.

Oliph. The young man is in such a transport of delight he wouldn't understand a word you said; besides, you will have plenty of time to dose him with mother-in-law.

PHOEBE. [*Reproachfully*] Dose him—is it possible you can apply such an epithet to me? Have I been a dose to you? [*Tearfully*]

OLIPH. A very agreeable dose, my dear. A sugar-coated pill. There, there. [*Kisses her*] Dry your tears.

PHOEBE. It is not easy drying a mother's tears on the day she loses her only child.

OLIPH. Now don't be hypocritical because it's the fashion. You know we are and ought to be glad Psyche is going to be settled in life so comfortably.

PHOEBE. [*Ruefully*] But young men are so wild nowadays.

OLIPH. On that score we cannot complain. Fitts has worked like a hero at Heidelberg and has fairly earned his reward. [*Enter Fitts, R.3.E.*]

FITTS. [*C.*] Ah, here we are. Ring ready; curé and notary ready. Chapel across the way crammed. How do I look? [*Turns around*]

OLIPH. At your best.

FITTS. [*To Phoebe*] Eh, mother, don't look so badly, eh?

PHOEBE. [*R.C.*] I hope you realize what a sacrifice I am making today. [*Wipes eyes*]

OLIPH. Nonsense.

FITTS. [*C.*] Come now. I hardly think it fair to look at it in that light.

PHOEBE. [*Sadly*] Am I not losing a daughter.

FITTS. And are you not gaining a son full-grown, without either a sleepless night or the aid of a nursing bottle?

OLIPH. There, do you hear that? You'll have a son.

PHOEBE. Ah, but a son is a son and a daughter is a daughter. Is not that equally true?

FITTS. Professionally they have been so regarded. [*Psyche at door, R.2.E.*]

PSYCHE. Mama, I am tired sitting up there by myself. Can't I come in?

FITTS. [*Starts toward Psyche*] Certainly—walk in—

PHOEBE. [*Coming between*] Mr. Fitts, I am sorry to have to remind you that I am still her mother.

PSYCHE. [*Still at door*] Mama, may I?

PHOEBE. Certainly not—don't you see Mr. Fitts here? How can you be so inconsiderate?

PSYCHE. [*Steps inside*] Now, mama, I don't want to be a disobedient girl and indeed I wouldn't do it if there were strangers present. [*Comes C., slowly*] And I do want to see how Cousin Cicely looks. That's a dear good mama. May I come in just a little while?

PHOEBE. [*R.C.*] May you come in—you are in.

PSYCHE. Oh, you are so good. [*Kisses her*]

PHOEBE. [*Both sobbing; embraces Psyche*] Dear, dear, child, how will I ever part with you?

FITTS. [*Making a face*] Don't cry all over the orange blossoms.

PHOEBE. He has already taken command—your mother must not even weep.

PSYCHE. [*R.*] Franklin Fitts, how can you be so cruel?

FITTS. I'm not cruel. I don't want to see you all mussed up, but if she finds any pleasure in tears, let her go it then. Shed a hogshead if she likes. If I had thought it was going to be such a wet affair, I would have worn a rubber suit.

PSYCHE. [*Aghast*] Franklin Fitts, are you sane?

FITTS. I don't know, but I'm getting pretty mad. [*Crosses to L.*]

OLIPH. [*C.*] And no wonder—this young man has been in exile a whole year and has looked forward to this day as the happiest of his life. It is neither complimentary nor pleasant to see everyone in tears.

FITTS. There's a man of sense.

PHOEBE. What have I done?

OLIPH. [*Soothingly*] Nothing, my love, that a few smiles cannot remedy.

PHOEBE. I'm sure no one could love Mr. Fitts more than I do.

PSYCHE. O mama.

FITTS. Thank you. If you promise not to cry any more today, I'll promise not to give you cause to cry again.

OLIPH. Spoken like a man. [*To Phoebe*] Come, dear. [*Crosses with her to R.2.*] Let us leave the young couple alone a little while.

PHOEBE. But etiquette.

OLIPH. They are too happy to think of etiquette, my dear. [*Exeunt, R.2.E.*]

PSYCHE. [*Crosses to L. and up, C.*] Do you think I look nice?

FITTS. [*Crosses to R.*] Nice! There are not enough adjectives to describe the general effect.

PSYCHE. There is only one thing I regret.

FITTS. [*R.*] And that?

PSYCHE. That our wedding could not have been at home in dear old America.

FITTS. We can have "Hail, Columbia" after.

PSYCHE. [*C.*] Oh, it isn't that. It would have created such a sensation in Amoskeag. The little old frame church would be crowded. The Higgins girls would be green with envy. That train creeping up the aisle. I can see just how everything would be, to the red-faced boy pumping the organ and the gray-haired sexton guarding the front door—Pshaw, it takes all the fun out of marriage to hide away like this.

FITTS. [*Coming close to her*] I hope not all the fun, my dear. The little chapel here is already filled with a curious throng, anxious to see the American marriage; and then remember we will startle the American colony in Paris, burst upon them—dazzle them.

PSYCHE. That's the only consolation.

FITTS. But, Cicely, I don't think she is very enthusiastic about our friend the baron.

PSYCHE. She isn't enthusiastic about anything any more. [*Sighs*]

FITTS. [*Solemnly*] Old love is hard to kill. You can go down into the garden of your heart and destroy all its blossoms but a few drops of remorse from the watering can of memory will bring them into bloom again.

PSYCHE. True, true.

FITTS. I hope you haven't any old roots in the garden of your heart.

PSYCHE. [*Reflectively, C.*] A few, but they withered years ago. [*Smiles*]

FITTS. [*R.C.*] Then for heaven's sake don't turn the water on them. [*Enter Nichette, L.2.E.*]

NICHE. Miss Cicely is dressed. [*Exit Nichette*]

CICELY. [*Outside*] I am quite ready.

FITTS. [*Looks off, L.*] I suppose I must evacuate. Don't be long. I'll be back in a few minutes for you. No tears now. Don't want any red noses you know. [*Exit, R.2.E.*]

PSYCHE. I don't know why she marries the baron. She don't need his money; but then Cicely is proud and the title will be something to flaunt at Newport next season. Besides, there was no way of getting rid of him. [*Enter Cicely, L.2.E.*] How lovely, you never looked prettier.

CICELY. [*L.C., very subdued*] Thanks. I'm glad my feelings are not reflected in my face.

PSYCHE. You are not ill?

CICELY. No, nor yet quite well. It will soon pass away. [*Crosses to sofa, L.*]

PSYCHE. I'm so sorry. How do you think I look? [*Turning to be admired*]

CICELY. Beautiful. Here, my dear, is my bridal present. I think it best no one should know that I gave it to you and you may need it. [*Gives check*]

PSYCHE. Fifteen thousand pounds! Fitts will just go wild.

CICELY. [*Smiling*] Your first thought is of him. Do you love him so very much?

PSYCHE. I'm going to *marry* him.

CICELY. That you think is certain proof?

PSYCHE. It ought to be.

CICELY. [*Earnestly*]   And yet, every day, facts come to light that the marriage altar is one of sacrifice as well as sacrament.

PSYCHE. [*Distressed; on her knees to Cicely*]   But, O Cicely, you do love the baron? You would not be so cruel as to marry a man you do not love?

CICELY.   Some women can only love once in their lifetime. Be sure I do the baron no injustice. He is fully aware; I have told my feelings all to him.

PSYCHE.   But you do not love anyone else?

CICELY.   No, I hope not—I hope not. [*Psyche rises and crosses to C.*]

PSYCHE.   But do you not tremble for your happiness?

CICELY.   Happiness is a rare gift. I am about to become the wife of a man of honor who has been for the last year my slave. He loves me and I respect him, and will do my duty fearlessly and faithfully. [*With emotion*] But, Psyche, I fear I am not strong enough to strangle the regrets that will rise before me—today, worse than ever. [*Crosses to table, R.*]

PSYCHE.   Regret for—

CICELY. [*Turning quickly*]   No, not for him. He is unworthy—wicked— I trust I am not so base as that. [*Sits, R. of table. Bells ring. Sadly*] Psyche, here is a little flower he gave me. It is the last link that binds me to a pleasant past. I had not the heart to tear its tender leaves apart, for it seemed to whisper to me of hope. Take it. [*Kisses it*] Poor faded flower, as scentless and dead as many a human heart. [*Gives flower*]

PSYCHE. [*C., hesitating*]   Will I send it to him?

CICELY. [*Eagerly*]   Do you know where he is?

PSYCHE.   Fitts heard from him in America.

CICELY. [*Amazed*]   In America?

PSYCHE.   He went there believing you had gone and hoping to meet you.

CICELY.   Why did you not speak of this?

PSYCHE.   His name was forbidden.

CICELY.   True, I had forgotten that. [*L., at sofa. Enter Le Bois followed by Fitts, R.3.E.*]

LE BOIS. [*Crosses to Cicely*]   Everything is ready. You are more beautiful than ever. [*Kisses her hand*]

FITTS. [*R.C.*]   Now for the final plunge.

PSYCHE. [*L.C.*]   Fitts, I feel faintish. [*Takes arm. Enter Oliphant, R.2.E.*]

OLIPH.   Mrs. Oliphant, overcome with the excitement, has lain down for a few moments but don't let this delay you. We will keep house and welcome you on your return. I wish you all happiness. [*Bells ring*]

FITTS.   Let us lead the way. [*Fitts and Psyche go to R.3.E.*]

PSYCHE.   O Fitts, it's not half so easy as I thought. [*Exeunt, R.3.E.*]

Le Bois. [*Crossing to R.3., with Cicely*] Come, Cicely, see, the moon lights us on the way. It's a good omen.

Cicely. I hope so. [*Exeunt, R.3.E.*]

Oliph. [*Goes up, C., looks after them*] Dear me. I trust Cicely is happier than she seems. As for Fitts and Psyche, they are intoxicated with bliss. Marriage after all is a capital institution; I only regret I wasted so many precious years. [*Enter Nichette, R.3.E.*]

Niche. It will soon be over. Poor madame, she looks as white as a ghost; I'm sure, if it were my wedding night, I should not tremble so.

Oliph. Ah, Nichette, you see how easily the marriage knot is tied.

Niche. Oh, yes, monsieur, it is easily enough tied. [*Sighs*] But that isn't all.

Oliph. Why do you sigh? A wedding should be wreathed in smiles.

Niche. But when one wants to get married oneself—

Oliph. Why, Nichette, it is impossible that a pretty girl like you, as plump as a partridge and as demure as a duchess cannot find a lover.

Niche. I have a lover.

Oliph. Ah, I see, not the right one—eh?

Niche. Oh, yes, monsieur. We are both willing, but what's the use in both being willing?

Oliph. I cannot see why you should not be wedded at once.

Niche. But Phillip is poor.

Oliph. With you to strengthen his arm and love to lift his heart, he can easily make his way. Besides, some friend might be found to grease the wheels of Cupid's car.

Niche. Do you think so?

Oliph. I do. How much is wanted?

Niche. Five hundred francs.

Oliph. A very modest sum. You shall have it tomorrow.

Niche. O monsieur, you are so good, so kind. [*Leans head on hand on his breast*]

Oliph. This is very pleasant but if Mrs. Oliphant should—[*Looks R.1.E.*] Egad, she is coming. There Nichette, I know you are grateful but—

Niche. Five hundred francs, let me kiss you. [*Attempts to embrace him*]

Oliph. Nichette, I am a married man and I make it a rule never to kiss a young girl, in the presence of my wife.

Niche. You are so good. [*Exit, L.U.E.*]

Oliph. Goodness and discretion are my strong points. That girl might have ruined me. [*Enter Phoebe, R.2.E.*]

Phoebe. Have they gone?

OLIPH. Yes, they are at the chapel by this time.

PHOEBE. And without my parting blessing, too? Why did you let me sleep?

OLIPH. Because your nervous system needed repose, my love, and now that you are composed, you will grace the festive board much better. Let us join the guests.

PHOEBE. Oh, it will be such a disappointment to the poor child, and etiquette demands—

OLIPH. Take my word for it, the poor child is not wasting many thoughts on anything so prosaic as her parents just now. [*Phoebe crosses to Oliphant. She takes his arm and is led, L.1.E.*]

PHOEBE. [*Regretfully*] If her father could only rise from his grave tonight.

OLIPH. I sincerely trust my warlike predecessor had too much practical good sense to do anything so ridiculous.

PHOEBE. [*Sighs*] Oliver, you are a good dear soul, but horribly matter-of-fact.

OLIPH. Just enough to balance you, my dear. [*Exeunt, L.2.E. Enter Psyche and Cicely, R.3.E.*]

PSYCHE. How you tremble!

CICELY. [*Excitedly; on sofa*] Yes, yes, I do feel cold, Psyche. Did you see anyone in the path as we turned?

PSYCHE. Of course, the path was lined with peasants. And—

CICELY. But no one in particular, no one that looked like—

PSYCHE. No, no, nor did you. This is a horrible fancy.

CICELY. Perhaps. There, there, go—return, they will miss you. [*Crosses to R.*]

PSYCHE. [*Crosses to L.3.*] But won't you come down? The supper is gorgeous.

CICELY. Say to the baron he may call for me in half an hour.

PSYCHE. [*At door, L.3.E.*] Don't be long, please. [*Exit, L.3.E.*]

CICELY. And yet I would have sworn it was he. Those eyes, blazing with a baleful fire, and that ashen face. [*Enter Norcott at window*] Who is that? [*In alarm; crosses, L., to sofa*]

NOR. [*Calmly*] It is I.

CICELY. [*Aghast*] Sidney Norcott!

NOR. [*Bitterly*] Yes, Sidney Norcott. You must pardon my mode of entry but the fine gentlemen filled the staircase and I feared perhaps my card might have been denied.

CICELY. [*Excitedly*] What could have brought you here?

Nor. [*Sarcastic*] To congratulate you. You forget this is your wedding night.

Cicely. And you forget by entering a gentleman's house, as you have done, you put your liberty in peril.

Nor. My liberty is worth little. My life I do not value as a farthing. To such as you, baroness, the world is full of precious penalties. But I am not a baron. I am but a poor painter, a dabbler in art—a bright beggar fit to amuse a grand lady for a few idle months, and then to be cast aside among the bric-a-brac of her memories.

Cicely. And you dare say this to me?

Nor. I am not a brave man, but I do not fear to speak the truth.

Cicely. Nor I to reveal it. [*Starts to C.*]

Nor. What would you do?

Cicely. Summon my husband.

Nor. Do so. They say he is a capable shot. And after the farce in Italy it is altogether fitting we should have a tragedy in France.

Cicely. Who calls our love a farce? To you it may have been, you who can speak of it with a sneer. To me it was a tragedy in which my heart was slain.

Nor. [*Earnestly*] In the name of pity, let us be honest. There is no reason why you should deceive me longer. On the night we parted, you gave me your picture set with precious stones. I have been taught by a bitter experience to value neither one nor the other. Take it. [*Gives miniature*]

Cicely. And I am equally glad to be able to return you this. [*Goes to table. Offers necklace, taking it from casket*] Had I known where it would have reached you—

Nor. I prefer you would destroy it.

Cicely. And I prefer you would do that. [*Norcott takes necklace*]

Nor. I will not torture you with my presence after tonight. We will never meet again.

Cicely. Would to heaven we had never met at all!

Nor. Amen to that, with all my heart. I then should not have lost all faith in woman and the world as well.

Cicely. [*Bitterly*] I was not prepared for such an excellent counterfeit of indignation. Were you not so base, I might even admire you.

Nor. You are an excellent judge of what is noble, madame. And as for your admiration, if it is not more sincere than your affections, it is not worth much. I merely came to show you that your perfidy has not killed me. Are you sorry? I am, farewell. I hope your title will be found worth the price you paid for it—my love. [*Goes up, C.*]

CICELY. You should have been ashamed to offer an unprotected girl a love that she could not accept without infamy.

NOR. Infamy?

CICELY. I know all—everything. I have seen your wife and helped your child. [*Sobbing*]

NOR. [*Coming down, C.*] Seen my wife? Helped my child? Are you honest? Speak. Who calls herself my wife?

CICELY. Francesca, whom I saw with you in Venice.

NOR. Can it be? Did she say so?

CICELY. Swore it—on her soul.

NOR. [*Eagerly*] And believing this you fled?

CICELY. What else could I do?

NOR. [*With emotion*] My God, Cicely, my love, my dearest life, have I lost you forever? [*Falls in chair at table, R.*]

CICELY. [*Crosses to Norcott*] It is false then?

NOR. False! How could you believe it true? See, here is her letter. [*Showing letter*] Signed Francesca, calling me her friend. [*Gives letter to Cicely*]

CICELY. [*Reading*] It is from the prison at Marseilles.

NOR. Where she is detained for the theft of a few crumbs of bread to save her child from starving. I found it awaiting me at the consul at Paris, and I hastened there to save her. At Marseilles I heard of your marriage. You see, she says after her husband's desertion I have been her only friend.

CICELY. Yes, but she swore, she took an oath.

NOR. Did she mention my name?

CICELY. She said my lover.

NOR. [*Rising*] I see it all. But she shall prove it with her own lips. You shall learn how much I have been wronged.

CICELY. [*In anguish, crosses to L.*] And now it is too late. What have I done?

NOR. [*C.*] Cicely—speak—Do you love me still?

CICELY. [*L.*] Better than my life.

NOR. You are his only in name?

CICELY. [*Quickly*] What do you mean?

NOR. I having your heart, it would be impossible to give him your hand. Will you go with me?

CICELY. [*Going*] Yes, yes, I will go. No—no—it would disgrace him. He has never injured me. I will not strike him down.

NOR. Think of our love.

CICELY. Too late—I can only remember that I am the guardian of his honor—his name.

Nor. What am I to do?

Cicely. Go at once. Think, were he to find you here, it would be death to you, to me dishonor!

Nor. But think, Cicely, we may never meet again. Farewell!

Cicely. Farewell, farewell, forever. There are footsteps on the stairs. [*In terror*] You will be discovered.

Nor. [*Out of window*] What am I to do? There are peasants beneath the window.

Cicely. 'Tis too late. What can you do?

Nor. Protect your honor at any cost.

Cicely. They are here—Sidney, my love—your life—your life—[*Enter Le Bois, R.3.E., Oliphant followed by Fitts, L.2.E. As they enter, Cicely screams and falls at the feet of Norcott; the two Servants jump in, C. window, and seize Norcott*]

Le Bois. Cicely! [*Rushes to her*] Secure the thief.

Nor. Thief!

Oliph. [*Aside to Fitts*] Not a word.

Le Bois. You cannot deny it. See! The property of my wife in your hands. [*Kneels over Cicely*]

Nor. Pardon, monsieur—it was my first offense. Pray, let me go.

Le Bois. Ay, you shall go, to the galleys. [*Fitts starts, Oliphant stops him*]

Oliph. Not a word, it is to save her honor.

ACT IV.

Scene: *Marseilles. The prison yard, large arched gateway, C. Flats in 4, prison for males, L., for females 2 to 4. Doors, R.2. and L. Stone steps under prison window, R. Large bench on female side under trees, R., also L. Sentinel seated in sentry box, R.3.; Guard pacing beyond archway, 4. Time, three days later. Francesca with three other Women discovered on benches with little Dolores, R. Dolores sleeping with head in the lap of Francesca.*

Fran. Sleep, Dolores, my pretty one, they say they will separate us but I won't believe it. They could not be so cruel. We who have hungered, thirsted, starved together. They call me a thief. They say I have forgotten the sweet precepts of religion. Perhaps I have; but to the miserable and starving, Heaven seems so far away that it is easy to forget it; but I never forget that I am a mother with your poor, pinched, pleading face before me. [*Enter Carot, a jailor, L.3.E.*]

CAROT. [*To Women*] Well, I'm going to lose most of my pretty birds. You all go on the evening boat to Toulon. [*Women go off, R.*]

FRAN. Where the galleys are?

CAROT. Ay, where the galleys are.

FRAN. [*Eagerly*] And the new prisoner, he who calls himself Remi—?

CAROT. He who attempted to rob the Baron le Bois three days ago?

FRAN. Yes, yes.

CAROT. Refuses to make any defense. Goes to the galleys for seven years.

FRAN. Will I see him there?

CAROT. You may catch a glimpse of him here. He has been granted the privilege of the yard to see some visitors. You know him?

FRAN. Yes, when he was happier. [*Sobs*]

CAROT. You weep—come—come—a lover—eh?

FRAN. No, my dearest, best of friends. [*Enter Norcott with chains, L.3.*]

NOR. [*Reflectively*] Seven years. 'Tis a long time. [*Goes to bench, L.*]

FRAN. May I speak to him?

CAROT. No. The females must keep their own side of the yard. It's a rule—penalty, bread and water for a week. [*Goes up*]

FRAN. It's worth much more to say I pity him. [*Calls*] Signor Sidney.

NOR. [*Rising*] Who calls? [*Francesca comes L.C.*]

FRAN. I, Francesca. [*Norcott crosses to C.*]

CAROT. [*C.*] Stand back, prisoner.

NOR. [*Firmly*] Your pardon, monsieur jailor, but I must speak to this unfortunate.

CAROT. [*Amazed*] Must! Come, come, your days of "must" are over. You must now *obey*.

NOR. But you have a heart, man, and what I have to say cannot injure the state or militate against justice. [*Slips coin in Carot's hand*] 'Tis my last coin. [*Jailor goes up*]

FRAN. Heaven pity you, signor.

NOR. Francesca, did you see Miss Blaine—she whom I love—in Rome?

FRAN. The American señorita?

NOR. Yes, she whom you had seen before in Venice.

FRAN. I did.

NOR. [*Eagerly*] Did you tell her aught of me?

FRAN. No.

NOR. But you spoke to her?

FRAN. I told her of Antoine's treachery, why? [*Enter a Sister of Mercy, L.3.E., and whispers to Carot. Hands him paper*]

Nor. Francesca, when you return here after a year at Toulon, you must seek out the Baroness le Bois and tell her that we are the victims of a terrible mistake.

Fran. Through me? Oh, say that you do not suffer through me.

Carot. [*Comes C. Norcott goes L.*] Prisoner, retire. You are the prisoner Francesca Brabant, [*Looking at paper*] an Italian by birth, convicted of the theft of twelve ounces of black bread from the shop of Louis Gramont and sentenced to the galleys for one year.

Fran. We knew all this before.

Carot. Personally I did, officially I am compelled to repeat it. You are the mother of the child.

Fran. What of that? [*In alarm goes to Child*]

Carot. The law and religion have mercifully conspired to save your innocent offspring from sharing its guilty mother's fate.

Fran. You would not dare to separate me from my child. [*Clutching Dolores*]

Carot. This good lady has an order for the child of Francesca Brabant. The court has ordered that it be taken to the Home for Unfortunates and saved from a vicious life.

Fran. [*Pleading*] No, no, no! If I am guilty, revenge yourself upon me in some other way. Torture me, starve me, and I will smile, but do not take her from me. It would kill me to part from her. [*Kneels*]

Carot. If you loved her, you would not wish her to go to the galleys even with you.

Fran. [*Takes Child in her arms*] Love her! She is my world. Never has she slept out of these arms. If we lodged on the roadside, she was warm on my breast, if in the street, my heart was her pillow.

Carot. Come, come, we must have the child. [*Seizing the Child*]

Fran. No, no! [*Clinging to her*] My child! Pity, pity!

Carot. There—[*Passing Child to Sister*] take her.

Fran. You shall not! [*Making a rush for Child. Sentinel comes, C., and places bayonet between*]

Carot. Back, woman! [*Sister takes Child and exit hurriedly, L.3.*]

Fran. [*Falls, C.*] Dolores, Dolores! So you have separated us at last. Fiend, I'll take your life as you have taken mine! [*Clutches Carot by the throat. Sentinel runs down and helps bind her hands*]

Carot. Now, tigress, you shall be reported for this and for this you shall serve another year.

Fran. Dolores, Dolores, Dolores.

Carot. This report will teach you better.

Nor. You will not make it, monsieur.

Carot. No? Why not?

Nor. Because you are a man and have a mother, too, who would have died for you. It was to keep her child she broke the law, it was her first and last transgression.

Carot. But her attack on me? I only carried out the law.

Nor. True, but in her agony she only knew you separated her from all she loves.

Carot. But I represent justice.

Nor. There is no justice in striking one so utterly helpless; see, she is in the dust.

Carot. But duty?

Nor. A man's first duty is to succor a stricken woman.

Carot. Do you command me?

Nor. Command, no. I but entreat. I see you soften, already you have forgiven her.

Carot. It is against all rules, but she may go this time. Rise up, it's time to prepare for Toulon. [*Upstage*]

Fran. [*Rising*] I shall never see her again. O signor, if you only knew what I suffer.

Nor. [*Assisting her*] Courage, Francesca. She will be happier with the good sisters. Remember that. Courage, courage.

Carot. Come, come.

Fran. [*Following him*] Dolores, Dolores. [*Exit, R.2.E. Shaking her head sadly*]

Nor. [*Sighs*] Poor wretch. How often are we wounded deepest through those we love best.

Oliph. [*Outside*] You see my pass is all correct. The request of the British consul signed by the governor of the prison, for self and friends.

Nor. Oliphant—I shall hear from her!

Oliph. [*Enters, L.C.*] Ah, my poor friend. [*Gives hand to Norcott*]

Nor. [*Eagerly*] How is she—Cicely?

Oliph. We have watched by her bedside for three whole days, while she tossed in delirium. Today she had a gleam of returning consciousness and her first question was of you.

Nor. But she is out of danger?

Oliph. Dr. Fitts says the worst is over unless a fresh shock should upset her nervous system.

Nor. Thank heaven.

OLIPH. If she hears of your conviction, however, she may betray the secret we have all guarded so carefully.

NOR. She must not hear of it. Tell her that I was acquitted and left France at once.

OLIPH. But her husband, who of course, we cannot take into confidence, will doubtless give her the facts.

NOR. Her physicians must warn him against so unpleasant a subject, lest a relapse—you can see what I mean.

OLIPH. But my dear friend, this family secret has been thoroughly canvassed among ourselves and all feel that you should not be permitted to suffer.

NOR. To suffer for her sake is all the happiness left for me and her honor is worth more than my freedom.

OLIPH. But the hardship—the disgrace of the galleys.

NOR. The alias I have adopted will screen my name and spare my family. As for the rest, the world without the woman I love would be as dreary a prison as they have at Toulon, the weight of my disappointment as heavy as my oar and chain.

FITTS. [*Outside*] The gentleman has a pass for self and friends. I tell you I am one of the friends.

OLIPH. [*Going up and looking off, L.C.*] It's as he says, sentinel.

FITTS. What shocking bad memories these officials have—all troubled with cerebral affections of some sort. I'd like to saw the top of that fellow's head off and see if it isn't filled with sawdust. [*To Norcott*] Ah, this is too bad. I suppose Mr. Oliphant has informed you of the family's determination to save you at any cost.

NOR. [*Earnestly*] Yes, you are my friends. But I refuse to receive it, at the price of her good name. You don't seem to understand that in any event I cannot be happy and that the story of an old lover being found in her apartments on the night of her marriage would be a rare scandal that would be heard all over Europe and America, that would last her for her lifetime. Gentlemen, I must insist nothing must be done in my behalf.

FITTS. [*To Oliphant*] An abnormal condition of the heart with slight cerebellum sympathy. [*Touches his head*]

OLIPH. Whatever he wishes.

NOR. You have been in constant attendance on her—Cicely—I mean the Baroness le Bois.

FITTS. Yes, scarcely left her bedside; when I did, my—my wife—I like the sound of *my wife*—took my place.

NOR. There is no question of her recovery?

FITTS. Very little. Fright sometimes kills, but not often. It may produce cerebro congestion and—

OLIPH. How was she when you left her?

FITTS. Much better. I left her propped among pillows talking to Mrs. Oliphant and *my wife,* seeing which I slipped out to see you. Now if cerebro—

NOR. She knew nothing of my sentence?

FITTS. Nothing, and I told Psyche—*my wife*—not to mention it under any circumstances. As I was saying, if cerebro—[*Enter Carot, R.2.E.*]

CAROT. Only ten minutes for visitors. The boat for Toulon leaves in one hour. [*Goes up to C. Exit; Fitts goes R.*]

NOR. [*Aside*] I would have liked to see her before I go to this living death.

OLIPH. Perhaps we may as well say adieu now and rest assured we will not forget you.

NOR. [*L.C.*] Tell her when she is strong enough to bear it, I shall pray for her happiness, that my last words were a blessing; that I shall not be lonely in prison for the memory of her will be my companion. I would ask you to teach her to forget me, but I am not brave enough for that. Farewell. [*Drops on bench, L. Enter Carot, C.*]

CAROT. A lady visitor for the prisoner Remi claims admission on the consul's pass as one of your friends, monsieur.

NOR. Can it be Cicely?

OLIPH. I hope not.

FITTS. Impossible! [*Enter Cicely, L.C.*]

CICELY. [*Agitated*] Where is he?

NOR. [*Opens his arms*] Cicely!

CICELY. [*Screams*] Sidney, thank heaven! And they would have sent you away without a word from me [*Reproachfully to Fitts and Oliphant. Norcott and Cicely embrace*]

NOR. It was to spare you pain.

CICELY. Spare me pain! Must I not have known it at last? Did you think I would submit to this? But for Aunt Oliphant, perhaps I would never have seen you again—

NOR. But you have been ill, and it were better that I should have gone quietly. Cicely, you are no longer a free woman, you are the wife of another. [*Releasing her*]

CICELY. Do you bid me remember that? Do you think I can forget it? Great God, it has burned itself into my brain, it has set it on fire. It has robbed me of reason, it will rob me of my life.

OLIPH. [*R.C.*] For heaven's sake, be calm. He did everything for the best.

NOR. Let us not waste the few moments we have in beating our bruised hands against the iron doors of fate. Remember we must part—so soon and—

CICELY. And do you think I will permit you to suffer, to be the companion of the low and vile, to wear this hideous garb, to drag this chain; my words must give you freedom, even at the price of my good name.

NOR. [*Excitedly*] What would you do?

CICELY. I will speak the truth.

NOR. I forbid you. Do you know what it is to have your whole life clouded with shame? Remember the world is always ready to believe the worst of women.

CICELY. But you—think of your fate.

NOR. Better the galleys for me, than your name should be the jest of Paris and London drawing-rooms, blazoned forth in every American newspaper, a warning to women, that crime cannot be hidden even behind a title.

CICELY. O Sidney, what can I do?

NOR. Your duty, come what may. [*Enter Le Bois, C.E.L.*]

LE BOIS. [*Sternly*] Baroness le Bois, what does this mean?

FITTS. [*R.*] She is suffering from delirium.

CICELY. No. We have done with lies. 'Tis time you shall know the truth.

LE BOIS. [*C.*] Why do you drop your eyes? Are you then so guilty you cannot look me in the face?

CICELY. [*Raising her eyes*] I am looking you in the face, monsieur.

LE BOIS. How comes it, madame, that I find you here, here in the arms of a self-confessed thief? [*Norcott makes gesture of protestation*] If not a thief, what then?

CICELY. I have wronged you, Monsieur le Bois, by giving you my hand when another had my heart, but I did not do it intentionally and I ask your pardon humbly on my knees. [*Kneeling*]

LE BOIS. Then this man is—?

CICELY. My lover. [*Norcott makes a movement to stop her*]

LE BOIS. [*Bitterly*] So, madame, you confess your guilt to save your paramour; you brand your husband with shame to save your lover from prison. What shall I say of you?

NOR. [*Sternly*] Nothing, monsieur. No man will assail a woman craving pardon, even by a word.

CAROT. Come, prisoners—to Toulon. [*Guard enters with Prisoners all chained to one another. Francesca, R.2.E.*]

CICELY. [*Arms around Norcott*] No, no, he is not guilty. Will not someone save him!

LE BOIS. [*C.*] Have you no shame, madame?

FRAN. [*Starts*] That voice, I cannot be mistaken—[*Rushes C.*] Yes, it is he—it is Antoine Brabant! [*Coming down, R.*]

LE BOIS. [*R.C. Aghast*] Francesca!

FRAN. [*L.C.*] Ah, Francesca, who to save your child from starving goes to the galleys.

OMNES. His child!

CICELY. [*Breathlessly*] Speak, Francesca! Do you know this man?

FRAN. Know him? Know him? He is my husband. [*Cicely rushes to Norcott, R., Francesca, R., defiantly eyeing Le Bois; Fitts and Oliphant, R. Convicts in single file up back, C. and L. Boat whistles in distance. Music forte*]

ACT V.

SCENE: *Paris. An apartment in Oliver Oliphant's house in the American colony, sumptuously furnished. Doors, L.2.E. and R.1. Distant view of the city of Paris in distance. Time, one month later. Fitts discovered at table, R., reading a newspaper. Psyche opposite, with book in lap, on sofa, L.*

PSYCHE. Franklin, dear, isn't it strange we don't hear from Papa Oliphant?

FITTS. [*Without looking up*] Yes.

PSYCHE. Just think, it is four weeks yesterday since we left that horrid old Marseilles and here we are in Paris a whole month, sealed up like sardines, afraid to show ourselves for fear that awful scandal should leak out. Dear me, if we haven't suffered enough. What with Cicely an invalid with anxiety and Papa Oliphant off in Italy, and lawyers' letters from the baron claiming Cicely as his wife, and threatening to take charge of her estates— It's simply horrible, isn't it, Franklin love?

FITTS. [*Buried in paper*] Umph! Umph!

PSYCHE. Besides, there's my whole three trunks filled with dresses, a bridal trousseau fit for a queen all lying in the fold. No chance to wear one of them, when we ought to be on the top of the Alps by this time or sailing down the Rhine. When we get off, if we ever do, it won't be a bit like a wedding tour, will it, Franklin dear?

FITTS. [*Without knowing what he said*] Yes, my love.

PSYCHE. [*In surprise*] Yes—?

FITTS. [*Sees mistake*] Certainly not—[*Reading*]

PSYCHE. It wouldn't be so bad to miss one's bridal trip if one got married every day. But the chances are, marriage only happens once in a lifetime. If it was otherwise, we wouldn't feel such a sense of loss, would we? The only thing I dread is that my satin will crease so, do you think so, Franklin love? For heaven knows, I may die before I get another, ay—

FITTS. [*Unconsciously*]   Yes, I hope so.

PSYCHE. [*Aghast*]   Franklin Fitts, you are a wretch! [*Throws book at Fitts*]

FITTS. [*In surprise*]   What did I say?

PSYCHE.   Say? You hoped I'd die before I got another new dress.

FITTS.   Nothing of the kind. I was reading the paper, my dear.

PSYCHE.   I suppose you will now set up a defense you haven't heard a word I said to you.

FITTS.   Not a syllable.

PSYCHE.   You ought to be ashamed to confess it—Scarcely a month married. [*Very injured*]

FITTS.   But, my dear, I can't take much interest in dresses and such feminine gewgaws.

PSYCHE.   Before we were married, you could take interest in *anything* that interested me.

FITTS.   But you can't expect a fellow to keep up that sort of thing *all* the time. It would be ridiculous in married men.

PSYCHE. [*Rising and crossing to Fitts*]   It was that sort of thing won me, Mr. Fitts, and I don't see anything at all ridiculous in a man being attentive to his wife. Before marriage you insisted upon reading Tennyson until I hated the very sight of blue and gold: now you mask yourself behind a stupid newspaper and I might as well talk to the sphinx. [*Snatches paper out of Fitts's hand, leaving him with small pieces which he continues to read*] But I might have expected as much from a prosaic old pill peddler. [*Crosses to L.*]

FITTS. [*Indignantly jumping up and coming C.*]   Pill peddler! Mrs. Fitts, be careful. Professional pride is very dear to me, madame, and this is a surprise.

PSYCHE. [*Crosses to Fitts*]   Your barbarity is not a surprise to me. Mama warned me of your temper; she could see through the thin veneer of your politeness.

FITTS.   She could, eh? She warned you, did she? That settles it. Into our first quarrel, your mother has obtruded. [*Enter Phoebe, R.1.E.*] So, madame, you are the nigger in the wood pile.

PHOEBE. [*Aghast*]   Nigger!

PSYCHE. [*L.*]   Mr. Fitts.

FITTS.   Oh, don't try to look me down with your indignation. You can't do it. I take my stand on my marital dignity.

PHOEBE. Mr. Fitts, are you mad?

FITTS. Yes, madame, mad as a hornet. Your daughter, this woman—

PHOEBE. [*Screams*] My child, a woman!

PSYCHE. [*L.*] He don't know what he is saying.

FITTS. I called her a woman. There is no disgrace in the title when it's worn worthily. If you deny the fact, however—

PHOEBE. My child, this is no place for you. Let us retire until his reason returns. [*Psyche starts to cross, R.*]

FITTS. [*Coming between them*] She will do nothing of the kind.

PHOEBE. She is my daughter.

FITTS. That was a good card a month ago, but as it's my play now, and I trump that with "my wife," the trick's mine. [*Goes up, C.*]

PSYCHE. [*Seated*] I couldn't have believed it. It's too awful for anything. [*Cries*]

PHOEBE. [*Seated, L., sadly*] And I have learned to love him as a son.

FITTS. [*Melting; coming down, C.*] Ladies, you have forced me to be dictatorial in order to preserve my dignity. When within one little month from the wedding day, as one may say, ere the orange blossoms have faded, ere the honeymoon is set, one is called by the wife of his bosom a pill peddler, it strikes deep. [*Takes handkerchief, wipes his eyes*] It hurts. Farewell. [*Goes, C., upstage and off, R.*]

PHOEBE. [*Sadly*] It was very wrong for you to say so. A wife should never be disrespectful to her husband.

PSYCHE. But, mama, he knew I didn't mean it.

PHOEBE. That does not exonerate you, my child. By honoring your husband you compliment yourself.

FITTS. [*Entering, up C.*] What do I hear?

PSYCHE. But he began it. I'm sure I love him too well to want to quarrel with him and a pill peddler isn't so bad after all. [*Fitts exit quickly, C.D., and returns again, up C.*]

PHOEBE. You must never repeat it. A quarrel between husband and wife is a very serious matter.

PSYCHE. [*Rising and coming C.*] But I thought everyone fought a little bit.

PHOEBE. I never did. A triumph over those we love is a very sorry victory, indeed, and not worth winning. Besides love once lost—

PSYCHE. [*L.C.*] O mama, don't say lost! [*Psyche and Phoebe have each approached, C. Fitts comes down between them with an arm around each. All sob aloud*]

PHOEBE. [*R.C.*] To think I should be the cause of this misery.

FITTS. [*C.*] To think I should have been such a brute.

PSYCHE. To think I should call my own a pill peddler. [*Sobs*]

FITTS. [*Gradually working to L.1 E.*] If you will only forgive me, my dear mother.

PHOEBE. My dear son, I have nothing to forgive.

PSYCHE. O Fitts dear, can you forgive your wicked little wife?

FITTS. Forgive you, my own precious love.

PSYCHE. I'll never do so any more. [*Sobs*]

FITTS. I don't deserve such a mother-in-law. [*Exeunt, R.1 E. Enter Napier, R.C.*]

NAPIER. [*C.*] There's been an astonishing funny time of it, since I left the party at Rome. A delightfully horrible muddle. [*Enter Fitts, R.1 E., backwards*] Why, Fitts, old boy, so you've gone and done it at last. Let me congratulate you! [*Shakes hand, Fitts still with back to Napier*] Perfectly happy, I suppose, seventh heaven and all that beastly nonsense I suppose, eh?

FITTS. Oh, yes, very happy, of course.

NAPIER. Why what's the matter with you? You look unhappy.

FITTS. No, no—nothing of that sort.

NAPIER. Why you look as though you might just have had your first quarrel!

FITTS. [*Aside*] I wonder if he suspects anything?

NAPIER. Nothing of that kind, though. Too soon for a row yet, eh?

FITTS. [*Uneasily*] Of course, entirely too soon.

NAPIER. [*Gets a look at Fitts*] But I really must apologize for my levity. I see by your face that you have been suffering.

FITTS. [*Smiling*] No, no, not at all.

NAPIER. [*C.*] This is a beastly bad business about our friend Norcott and Cicely, isn't it?

FITTS. How came you to hear of it? It hasn't got wind in Paris?

NAPIER. Bless you, no. I heard it in Marseilles from Le Bois, who seems really broken down.

FITTS. [*Eagerly*] How came you to know the baron?

NAPIER. Bless you, I knew him when he was a poor painter, before he became a baron, copying pictures in the Pitti Palace for a mere pittance.

FITTS. You knew him to be a painter?

NAPIER. Oh, yes, that's positive. But I say, you can't use my information, because I promised secrecy, you know.

FITTS. [*Coming up to Napier*] A promise of secrecy, eh? Things are getting warm. But if a woman's happiness depended upon your testimony, eh?

NAPIER. That's quite a different thing. We are not a sensitive nor a sentimental nation like you Americans, my dear boy, but there is chivalry enough left in the average Englishman to respond to a call of a woman in distress.

FITTS. I know that—Step right into my den, and we'll talk it over. [*Exit, R.2.E. Enter Cicely leaning on the arm of Nichette, L.2.E.*]

CICELY. [*Sits, L.*] That will do, Nichette—thanks. If you will be good enough to send Mrs. Fitts here. [*Nichette exit, R.U.C.*] How long and lonely are the days, silent and sad the nights. But if they are so to me, what must they be to him, toiling with the scum of Europe all day, locked in his narrow coffin-like cell at night, wearing the livery of shame. [*Rising. Enter Psyche, R.2.E.*] Is there no word from Mr. Oliphant yet?

PSYCHE. Nothing.

CICELY. He has not even written.

PSYCHE. Not a word.

CICELY. It's cruel to keep me on the rock of suspense in this way.

PSYCHE. You received a letter from the Baron le Bois last night?

CICELY. In which he denied the story of Francesca, denounced her as a lunatic and insists on seeing me.

PSYCHE. To which you sent no reply? [*Enter Nichette, R.U.E.*]

NICHE. The Baron le Bois.

CICELY. [*Goes up, C., and comes down*] Let us call Fitts. [*To Nichette in low voice*] Tell him I will see him at once.

PSYCHE. What are you going to do?

CICELY. Prevent him from calling the aid of the law to reclaim the wife who has deserted him. We must not forget we are powerless before him.

PSYCHE. You are his wife only in name.

CICELY. And in law, too. My estate is at his mercy. [*Enter Le Bois, L.C.*]

LE BOIS. At last, madame, I have the pleasure of meeting you. [*Cicely drops in seat, L.*] Is it your desire that a third party should be present?

CICELY. [*In a low voice*] Yes, monsieur. [*Psyche crosses to table, R.*]

LE BOIS. As you will. I will not ask you to explain everything, madame; your flight I prefer to cover with the mantle of charity with which your confession in the prison yard must be concealed, for, whatever restitution may be necessary, I prefer the family name shall not be covered with disgrace.

CICELY. Monsieur seems to forget he is a gentleman addressing a lady.

PSYCHE. You don't dare to question her innocence?

LE BOIS. [*Coolly*] I am speaking to the Baroness le Bois, madame. [*To Cicely*]

CICELY. [*Rising*] Baron le Bois, when I married you, I thought my heart was dead, my lover a villain. Ere the wedding bells had ceased I knew that I was mistaken in both. I determined never to become your wife in fact. You say the law gives you authority over my estate. I will not even question your word. All I ask is that you give me my freedom; release me from my heartless vow, and you shall possess everything I own.

PSYCHE. [*Rises*] But Cicely.

LE BOIS. Madame's proposal has the merit of being clear and commercial; possibly it is the only merit to which it can lay claim. That I should expect delicacy from a woman who publicly brands her husband with shame, who openly avows her love for another, is perhaps a little illogical—but—

PSYCHE. Do you dare to say—

LE BOIS. [*To Psyche*] If the madame would pardon me, I would remind her that this lady is my wife, that I am addressing myself to her.

CICELY. Then you refuse to release me?

LE BOIS. Yes, madame, your very novel proposition I have the honor of declining with thanks. [*Bows*]

CICELY. And you propose to claim an unwilling wife? You refuse me freedom, you would force me to acknowledge you as my husband while you know my heart is filled with love for another? This is monstrous.

LE BOIS. [*Quickly*] No more monstrous than your heartless desertion of me.

CICELY. Until you disprove Francesca's story—

LE BOIS. The babbling of a maniac, the story of a tramp, an idle tale told upon the threshold of a prison. Oh, I beg of you, madame, keep within the range of common sense at least.

CICELY. I am not very strong, monsieur, and I think this interview has lasted quite long enough. [*Rises*]

LE BOIS. Don't be mistaken, I don't intend to leave this house without you.

CICELY. Without me? Then you propose—

LE BOIS. To claim a wife's obedience, that's all. [*Enter Oliphant, L.C.*]

CICELY. What do you mean?

LE BOIS. You are to return to Marseilles with me at once.

CICELY. I will not go. [*Crosses to R.*]

LE BOIS. You must.

OLIPH. [*C.*] You are mistaken.

CICELY. What news? What news? [*Psyche goes, R., to Cicely*]

OLIPH. Good news.

CICELY. Thank heaven!

OLIPH. Patience, and you shall hear all.

LE BOIS. [*Going, L.*] May I inquire on what grounds monsieur dares to interfere?

OLIPH. [*C.*] If monsieur will be patient, I will answer him fully and in detail.

LE BOIS. [*Extreme L.*] You seem confident.

OLIPH. [*To Cicely*] I have been very busy during the last month and am very much fatigued, so if you will bear with me, and permit me to tell the story in my own way—

CICELY. [*Eagerly*] For pity's sake, go on. [*Sits*]

OLIPH. Thinking perhaps that what Monsieur le Bois said of the woman Francesca was true, and that she was out of her wits, I went to Florence to make some inquiry, got on the track of one Antoine Brabant, a poor artist, who on the ninth day of June 1871 married, in the Chapel of the Holy Infant, overlooking the Arno, an Italian girl from Mantua named Francesca Remini. Perhaps Monsieur le Baron may remember the little chapel?

LE BOIS. No. [*Enter Fitts and Napier, R.3.E., go R.C. at back*]

OLIPH. Nor the girl Francesca?

LE BOIS. No.

OLIPH. But monsieur cannot fail to recall the poor artist, Antoine Brabant whom Monsieur le Baron must remember quite well.

LE BOIS. [*Coolly*] I never heard of him.

OLIPH. This is very singular, for poor Antoine afterwards became the Baron le Bois. [*Sensational; all rise*]

LE BOIS. [*Smiling*] I'm sorry to spoil such a pretty picture, but I assure you, Mr. Oliver is quite mistaken—without a witness—

FITTS. [*Comes down, R.*] Excuse me, but there is a witness.

LE BOIS. Who dares say I was ever called Antoine Brabant?

NAPIER. [*Coming down, C., with monocle in eye*] I dare. I know I promised secrecy, Monsieur le Baron, but when a young woman's happiness is concerned I feel a sense of gallantry that quite absolves me. [*Goes upstage*]

LE BOIS. But I never was the husband of that woman. There was no marriage.

OLIPH. [*To Cicely*] I see you are faint. As there is a little question to be settled here before you enter into the inheritance of your happiness, I suggest that you retire for a few minutes.

CICELY. Just as you say. [*Exit with Psyche, R.E.2.*]

OLIPH. Having got rid of the ladies, let us proceed to business. I expect to prove your marriage here before these witnesses.

LE BOIS. By whom? [*Enter Norcott, R.C.*]

Nor. By me.

Le Bois. A confessed galley slave.

Nor. Yes, it is true I went to the galleys in defense of a woman's good name. You may go there for exactly an opposite reason.

Le Bois. [*Starts upstage*] I prefer to quit the apartment.

Nor. [*Stops*] You must not, sir.

Le Bois. You dare to—

Nor. I insist upon your not leaving until you have our permission to depart.

Le Bois. There is law in France.

Nor. Be careful that you escape its clutches. You deny your marriage with the girl Francesca Remini. 'Tis useless, for here is a copy of the marriage record. [*Holds up paper*]. Ah, I see you recognize it. Now, Antoine, you know the penalty for bigamy is very severe in this fair realm of France, and we have no desire to consign your elegant person to a loathsome prison, so we have a proposition to submit to you, my very good Antoine. [*Fitts and Napier behind table, Oliphant, R. of table*]

Le Bois. 'Tis cowardly to take advantage of a man alone and unarmed.

Nor. [*With dignity*] But is it not cowardly to marry a poor confiding girl whose heart you have won, and leave her to starve and beg and steal to support her child? Baron le Bois, we had all determined to send you to prison. Do you know to whom you are indebted for your freedom? [*Goes, C.D., and leads Francesca*] To this poor girl whom you have wronged more than any of us.

Fitts. There's a picture. [*Sits and writes at table, L.*]

Nor. [*L.C.*] Now, on condition that you give her one half of the entire estate of the Baron le Bois, you shall escape all prosecution.

Le Bois. [*Fitts writes*] But if I consent to acknowledge her as my wife? [*L.C.*]

Fran. [*C.*] Your wife. No, the time for that has passed. I have seen my child hungry while you rolled in riches. [*Crosses to L.*]

Nor. [*Sarcasm*] You see, even a title does not weigh for as much as an ounce of manhood in some women's eyes.

Fitts. The paper is ready for signature.

Nor. [*Takes paper*] "One half of all I possess"—very good. If you do not sign this paper in five hours, you will have to meet the penalty—seven years at least in prison and disgrace in the eyes of your emperor. [*Le Bois hesitates, looks at Francesca; crosses to table; signs, puts pen down; looks at Francesca, up C. and turns*]

Le Bois. I shall remember this. [*Exit, L.C.*]

OLIPH. It is sincerely hoped you will. [*Following him, up C.*]

FRAN. But my child, what are riches without her?

OLIPH. When I went in search of proofs, I sent a good woman to find your lost treasure, and she is here. [*Goes, C., and brings Dolores to Francesca*] Now that we have finished this business, you had better retire while I break the news to Cicely. [*Exit, R. Enter Cicely, L.*]

CICELY. Francesca here? You have heard from Toulon? He will obtain his liberty?

OLIPH. Your testimony proved very potent. I have been instrumental in taking one husband from you, let me supply the void.

CICELY. Then he has come? Where is he?

NOR. [*C.*] Here.

CICELY. Sidney!

NOR. Back to love, back to life. [*Embraces Cicely*]

CURTAIN

FAIRFAX

The text of *Fairfax* is based on a manuscript in the possession of Mr. Robert Campbell.

CAST OF CHARACTERS

EDWIN FAIRFAX, *a widower, aged 38*

DR. GUYON GAYLORD, *a bachelor, aged 40*

JAMES MARRIGOLD, *a wreck*

WEBSTER WINNE, *a tramp*

WILLIE WAGSTAFF, *a youth*

UNCLE BEN, *a house servant*

MOSES, *a young slave*

MRS. MARRIGOLD, *afterwards Miss Gladys Deane*

DIANA DORSIE, *"a real nice girl"*

MRS. SUSANNA DORSIE, *her mother*

TIBBETTS, *a dusky daughter of the South*

VIRGIE, *aged 9, daughter of Fairfax*

ACT I.

SCENE: *A hut on the bank of the Mississippi. Wood stove on which are saucepans, R.2.E. Cradle and table, L.2.E. Doors, R.2. and L.2.E., and in F.R. Large square windows in F.L.C. During progress of the act, steamboat can be seen to land; torch at gangway plank, set. Moon rises at close of act.* TIME: *1856.*

TIBBETTS. [*Discovered, leaning over baby*] Bress yer purty eyes! Dat's de only chile in dis yah worl'! Pooh sick chile! And it mustn't git up and go an lebe us, jest when we's gotten to lub ye. Heben is full enough of little angels; an' we needs one heah mighty bad. [*Sings*]

> Don't you go and lebe us for de shinin' shoh,
> We've jest done got one baby,
> And we can't git no moah.
> And, if you go an' climb up
> Dem shinin' golden sta'r,
> We may nebber see you,
> When we go away up dar.
> So don't you go and lebe us,
> For de shinin' shoh,
> For we've done got one baby,
> And we can't git no moah.

No, indeed. We couldn't done got no udder baby like dat. Humph—umph— Honey! [*Stirs up stove, and looks in saucepan*] I wondah what keeps misseh? [*Goes to window and looks out*] Dat's a dark night on de ribber! De moon don't gwine up yet. Role on, ole Mississippi! Ye a'ways seemed in a mighty hurry to git by this place. Golly. I don't wondah—[*Coming down, L.C.*] It's de meanest-lookin' place in Louisiana—suah! [*Enter Moses, D. in F.*] Hello, Moses, what ye do'n down yeh?

MOSES. [*R.C.*] All alone, Tibb? [*Winks*]

TIBB. In course, I'se all alone. Don't ye wink at me, ye Moses. [*Threateningly*]

MOSES. It done don't do ye any harm to wink.

TIBB. Well, I doesn't like it. When you niggahs wink, ye always mean something; and ye can't fin' yer meanin' in de pray'r book eider.

MOSES. Now, you Tibb gal, don't ye git up an' go to talk dat way to me. I's a Christian, I is! [*With an assumption of injured innocence*]

TIBB. You's a nice Christian! Who tole ye to come a-foolin' 'roun' me, eh?

MOSES. Why, de Good Book tole me.

TIBB. [*Surprisedly*] De Good Book! You Moses boy, you'd better not stan' up dah an' tell lies on de 'postles!

MOSES. I nevah don't tell no lies on the 'postles. De Good Book do say: lub yer neighboh—an' you's my neighboh! Isn't ye? [*Smiles*]

TIBB. You too smart to lib in dis country, Moses. You don't look out, you go right up in a fire-furnace, suah!

MOSES. You don't know what ye talkin' about. Firey char'at, you mean?

TIBB. [*Threateningly*] Don't ye shout dat way at me! I don't care if it was a skiff!

MOSES. You needn't put on so much style. I did not come down heah to see you.

TIBB. What's ye come for, den, say?

MOSES. De young Misseh Marrigold met me at sugah shed, an' she axed me to gib you dis for deh sick chile. [*Produces bottle*] It's brandy, and she done tole me, you was to gib de baby a spoonful right off, as soon as ye got it, or sooner if ye could.

TIBB. [*Amazed*] An' you cum all de way for her—for de pooh little baby down frough all dem swamps?

MOSES. I'se here, isn't I?

TIBB. [*With emotion*] Moses, I done don't hab any right to scol' you. You's a good niggah to come h'yah, to bring food for de famishin' baby. [*Wipes her eyes*]

MOSES. [*Going to her*] Dah; don't ye cry, Tibb gal. I'se only done my duty.

TIBB. [*Quite overcome*] You is a Christian, Moses! You—you—you's a true Christian. I'se got de proof now.

MOSES. [*Surprised*] How's dat, eh?

TIBB. If you hadn't been a Christian, dat bottle wouldn't have bin chuck up de cork.

MOSES. I'se mighty fon' of liquah, Tibby, dat's suah, but I—I nebber could rob a dyin' chile, dat's sartin! [*With firmness*]

TIBB. [*Going to table*] Where did you lebe de misseh?

MOSES. She said she was a-goin' to Capa-gra for de doctah.

TIBB. Dat's two mile! Dat poor woman sufferin' a good deal now. No man eber knows what trouble is, till he's a muddah hisself!

MOSES. [*Going, R.C.*] Well; I'se a goin', Tibb.

TIBB. No, you isn't; I'se afraid, all by myself.

Moses. Whar's Massah Jim?

TIBB. Down dah on dat Joe boat in de bend, drinkin' and gamblin'! while his pooh wife an' chile starve. Dat's whar Massah Jim am! [*Enter Marrigold, D. in F., somewhat under the influence of liquor*]

Moses. [*Meekly*] Hello! Massah Jim! [*Stepping back, C.*]

MARR. [*C., gruffly*] Hello yourself! What are you doing here? Say!

Moses. [*L.*] I'se come here for to bring—

TIBB. [*R., shakes her head at Moses*] Don't you tel'.

MARR. What's that? [*Turning fiercely on Tibbetts, who has put bottle behind her*] You black devil; I'll kill you, if you interfere with me. Do you understand?

TIBB. Yes, please, sir, I understan'.

Moses. Good night, Tibb gal.

MARR. [*To Moses*] Clear out! [*Exit Moses, D. in F.*] The next time I find that coffee-colored coon here, I'll put a hole in him.

Moses. [*At window*] Massah Marrigold, you's too hard.

MARR. Again, eh? [*Flings knife from table at Moses as he disappears, L.*] Thief!

TIBB. Look out; dar's only one moah knife left, to cut yer corn-dodger, Massah Marrigold.

MARR. [*At table*] Shut up! You learn this disrespect of me from your mistress. I'll teach you and her better. Where is she?

TIBB. [*Meekly*] Gone for a doctah, sir, please, for de baby.

MARR. Nothing the matter with the baby. Must have something to whine, and cry about, I suppose. Anything to eat?

TIBB. No; only de cold ham, sir.

MARR. Why didn't you get supper?

TIBB. You tooked all de money, sah, to play cyards wid.

MARR. Humph, another lie! What are you standing over there for? Come here!

TIBB. I'se a comin'. [*Moving very slowly with bottle behind her*]

MARR. What's that behind you?

TIBB. [*Innocently*] De stove, sah.

MARR. [*Angrily*] In your hand.

TIBB. [*Shows one hand*] I done got no nuffin'.

MARR. The other!

TIBB. Dar am it. [*Shows the other*]

MARR. Look here now. I've had enough of this nonsense. I'll throw you into the Mississippi if you don't mind me. What have you got, I say?

TIBB. Med'cine for de sick chile. [*Holding up bottle*]

MARR. Throw it in the river!

'TIBB. Yes, massah! [*Going to window*]

MARR. Stop! Let me see it.

TIBB. [*Aside*] Now it's done gone, suah. [*Gives it to him*]

MARR. She's killed it with her infernal quack nostrums. [*Takes out cork*] Ah, what's this? Brandy, by all that's beautiful! [*Tastes it*] Excellent!

TIBB. [*Pleadingly*] O massah! Please don't! Don't take it all from de baby—it will die if it don't get somefin' for to stren'un it. It will indeed, massah!

MARR. [*Rising*] I've a great notion to hide you—you black imp.

TIBB. [*Entreatingly*] Kill me, if you like, but give some of it to yer little chile!

MARR. Never mind the chile! You take good care of it, that's all you've got to do. I'll look after the rest. [*Exit Marrigold, L.2.E.*]

TIBB. [*Looking after him; goes to cradle*] It's sleepin' now. It was too weak to open dose purty blue eyes. I wondah why Heben sends little angels to such homes as dis? Anyway; dis one am goin' back mighty soon! [*Bell rings on the river. Tibb listens*] Dar's a boat comin' to de wood pile. [*Choruses without, distant*]

CHORUS.

Down de ribber, swift we float,
  Down de ribber, down!
On de fastest packet-boat,
  Down de ribber, down!
Good-bye, slow boat, whar ye gwine?
  Down de ribber, down!
If you want to get dar, thro's a line,
  Down de ribber, down!

[*Bell. Repeat*] Down de ribber, down de ribber, down de ribber, down.

TIBB. If misseh was heah now, we might git some liquah off dat boat, for our pooh little baby. P'r'aps de good Lord sent dat boat h'yer. He's a always doin' somefin' for de pooh! [*Bell*]

CHORUS.

[*More forte*] De possum sat on de ole coon's back,
  Down de ribber, down!
We done got dar, we can't come back,
  Down de ribber, down! [*Enter Gladys, D. in F., dressed in black with waterproof over head*]

TIBB. [*Surprised*] Back so soon?

GLAD. I ran all the way, by the cypress wood, where the trailing moss hung like black crepe from the branches, through the swamp, where the shiny reptiles hiss in the darkness. [*Throwing aside wrap*]

TIBB. Wasn't you skeered?

GLAD. I had no time for fear. How is baby?

TIBB. Just as you left her—sleepin'!

GLAD. [*Going to cradle*] How pale she is—and how cold. [*With emotion*] O baby dear, you must not die and leave your poor mama all alone! My life is desolate enough, without you it would be a desert waste. And, mama loves you so much—more than she can tell.

TIBB. [*Aside*] Poor misseh!

GLAD. Did you give her the brandy?

TIBB. [*Hesitating*] No, misseh!

GLAD. Why not? Did not Moses come?

TIBB. Oh, yes, he comed, but Massah Marrigold—

GLAD. [*Rising from her knees*] What of him?

TIBB. He tooked it.

GLAD. No, no, he could not descend so low. He could not rob his sick child—his dying child!

TIBB. [*Timidly*] Ef you don't believe me, you find him in dar—[*Pointing, L.*] wid de bottle.

GLAD. Did you tell him it was for baby?

TIBB. Yes'm.

GLAD. And still he took it?

TIBB. Yes'm!

GLAD. [*In despair*] What shall I do? Without a penny in the world; without a home, save this wretched den; without friends, save those who are as helpless as myself. O Father of the fatherless! [*Reaching up her hands in supplication*] Look down with pity upon me! Do not take my little one; it is all I have to live for—all I have to love! [*Sobs*]

TIBB. [*With sympathy*] Don't give up, misseh; don't give up!

GLAD. There is nothing to cling to! As long as there was one thread of life, one gleam of light, did I despair? No; I fought despair as I would a grim, gaunt monster that threatened to devour me. But now I find how fruitless has been the fight; how unequal has been the contest.

TIBB. [*Lifting glass off table*] Will I give some water to baby?

GLAD. Not without some stimulant; the doctor said it would be death!

TIBB. Dar am a boat at de woodpile; s'pose we try dar?

GLAD. Yes! Go, Tibbetts. They will not refuse you a few drops for a dying child. Tell them I have not a penny in the world.

TIBB. I bet I git some! [*Exit, D. in F.*]

GLAD. [*Rocking the cradle gently*] Sleep; sleep my own; it is the gift of God to those who suffer. Is she dying? [*Starting*] My child! No, no! It is only the flush of the fever fading from her face! [*Rising*] Perhaps I may find the liquor he has left. [*Going, L.*] I'll see at least. [*Exit, L.2.E. Music pp. Enter Webster Winne, D. in F., handcuffed and ragged*]

WINNE. Hello! No one in? Good! I've given them the slip at last! If they don't miss me until the boat leaves the landing, I'll cheat the state out of ten years of service. How I do hate working for the state, in a little six by eight cell. I loves the open air, an' the blue sky! There's a heap of poetry in Webster Winne! [*Sees cradle*] Hello! There is someone here! [*Going to cradle*] A baby! A sweet little dumplin'-faced darlin'; but too young to say she even saw me. Little cootsey, wootsey! How I love babies! Ah! [*With a sigh*] What a happy world this would be if it were only made up of thieves and babies! [*Starts*] Someone coming! Oh, a woman, too. Webster, my boy, don't forget yer breedin'! Always make room for the ladies. [*Going, R.2.E.*] It's the polite thing to do. [*Exit, R.2.E. Enter Gladys, L.2.E.*]

GLAD. Not a drop! Not a single drop! If Tibbetts should fail, what is to be done? [*Murmur, R.4.E.*] What does this mean?

OFFICER. [*Putting head in at window*] Did you see a man pass here, handcuffed?

GLAD. No! [*Retreating*]

OFF. Sure?

GLAD. Quite sure!

OFF. [*Turning, L.*] Come, boys; he's taken to the woods. [*Two other Men pass window, following Officer, L.4.E.*]

GLAD. Some poor wretch, on his way to Baton Rouge, has escaped! [*Goes to cradle. Enter Tibbetts with small bottle, D. in F., followed by Dr. Gaylord*]

GAY. Well, my jolly Erebus, you have landed me at last. You are not a very good guide. It is a toss-up, which is the blackest; you or the night, to be sure! [*Looking about him curiously*] I never in all my life—[*Sees Gladys, who has risen*] I beg your pardon, madam! [*Bowing politely, and removing hat*] I did not mean to be rude.

GLAD. People who live as we do, have no claim upon the consideration of the world.

GAY. [*C.*] You are mistaken, madam. The world is a coward, and always takes advantage of the poor. [*Taking off gloves*]

GLAD. [*L.*] Tibbetts, did you get the liquor?

TIBB. [*R.*] Here it am! [*Reaches it to her*]

GAY. [*To Gladys*] Your pardon. [*Takes bottle*] I know more about this than you do. I mean as a medicine.

GLAD. But sir—

GAY. Let me add, that I am a passenger on the boat, and a physician, and hearing the girl say you had a dying child here, I volunteered my services. I hope I have not—[*Taking off gloves*]

GLAD. [*Joyfully*] O sir! you don't know how glad I am, and, even though I have nothing but gratitude to offer—

GAY. [*Smiling*] Gratitude is my regular fee; and I never receive pay until I kill or cure. I presume the child is not very ill. [*Taking seat at cradle*] You women have a fashion of making a great fuss about trifles. [*To Tibbetts*] Here! You dusky daughter of the South, hold the candle.

TIBB. [*Takes candle off table; holding it very close to Gaylord*] Yes, sah!

GAY. [*To Tibbetts*] You set fire to my head, and I'll pull your wool.

GLAD. Give it to me, Tibbetts. [*Takes light*]

GAY. [*Fixing eye on Tibbetts*] That's better.

TIBB. [*Aside, going R.*] Golly! I wouldn't like to be sick whar he is!

GAY. [*Seriously*] How long has this child been ill?

GLAD. Almost three weeks.

GAY. Are you alone in the world? I mean, is your husband living?

GLAD. [*In a low voice*] He is.

GAY. How long have you lived here?

GLAD. Eight months.

GAY. I suppose you could leave this place without much regret? [*Rising*]

GLAD. Readily!

GAY. Then you will have to do so if you wish to save her life.

GLAD. Is it absolutely necessary that she should be taken away?

GAY. Absolutely. These swamps are feeding the fever. Unless she has a change of air, of fresh sea air—she will not trouble you long. [*Going up*]

GLAD. [*Who has dropped into chair, L.*] Then my child must die!

GAY. Die? I don't see that that follows. You can take it down the river over to Biloxi or Bay St. Louis, or anywhere.

GLAD. Not without money! [*In despair*] And we are penniless!

GAY. [*Aside*] The devil. [*Takes out pocketbook and selects a bill which he rolls up*] Here! [*To Tibbetts*] This is a prescription, don't you open it until I'm gone, or you will blot it. Remember! [*With sincerity*]

TIBB. Yes, sah! [*Retreating, R., again*]

GAY. [*Putting on gloves*]   Madam, the prescription in your servant's hand is the best thing I can think of now. I trust it will effect a cure. [*Bell rings*]

TIBB. [*At window*]   The boat's leben', massah doctah!

GAY. [*To Tibbetts*]   I understand. [*To Gladys*] If we ever meet again, madam, I trust it will be under more favorable circumstances. For the present, permit me to say good-bye. [*Offers his hand*]

GLAD. [*In a broken voice, rising from chair*]   I thank you, sincerely, for your kindness.

GAY.   I am only sorry I can do no better. [*Exit, D. in F. Enter Marrigold; staggers a little, D.2.E.*]

MARR.   Who was that, and what did he want?

TIBB.   It was the doctah.

MARR. [*Gruffly*]   What did he want?

GLAD.   Nothing from us; we have naught but wretchedness and rags, and no one wants either. [*Business. Gladys sinks into seat, L.C., Marrigold into chair, R.C., with back to audience, facing the door in F. Tibbetts goes to cradle and rocks it. Steamboat pushes out from landing; its green and red lights are seen through window. The chorus is repeated outside, growing more and more pp., until it finally dies away in the distance. During all this time, no action whatever on the stage. Gladys with forced calm*]   Where is the prescription, Tibbetts?

TIBB.   Here it am, misseh. [*Hands it to her*]

GLAD. [*Quietly*]   Have you got any money, James?

MARR.   Where would I get it?

GLAD. [*Unfolding note*]   I thought perhaps you would have enough to pay for the prescription.

MARR.   You're always thinking.

GLAD.   What is this? A bank note! And for fifty dollars! [*Gasps for breath. Marrigold staggers to his feet*]

TIBB. [*Amazed*]   Fifty dollahs! So much as dat?

GLAD.   More than that, it is fifty times fifty! It is the price of my child's life—of my life—of our happiness! It will bring back the light into her eyes, the glow into her cheek! O Heaven! On my knees I thank you! [*Drops on her knees, C., and bursts into tears*]

MARR.   What are you going to do?

GLAD.   Do? [*Rising*] Go away from here, with my child, this very night! [*Goes to cradle*]

MARR.   That's the way you propose to treat me, eh? After all my kindness, get up and desert me?

GLAD. [*Turning on him*] Your kindness! Let us not deal in retrospects. We have no time to talk of the past.

MARR. But I choose to talk of the past.

GLAD. Then we will talk of the happy-hearted girl you wed four years ago!

MARR. We will talk of a poor orphan governess working for my mother, whom I stooped to marry!

GLAD. [*With a smile of scorn*] And, who owes you for all she possesses tonight. You have dowered her well: you have given her a drunkard for a husband, and a hut for a home, a dull aching thing for a heart! Oh, she ought to be grateful for all this! [*Turning to cradle again*]

MARR. But for you, I would never have left my friends.

GLAD. Your friends left you—when you fell so low, it was shame to know you. It was to hide our shame, I sought this lonely shore, which I will leave tonight, forever!

MARR. No you won't! [*Forcing her*] Give me that money!

GLAD. Never! It is to purchase a passage to the pure air for our dying child, and you shall not touch a penny!

MARR. Give me that money, I say; or will I have to force it from you? [*Seizes her*]

GLAD. [*Struggling with him*] No, no, James. For our child's sake; for our poor child's sake!

TIBB. [*In terror*] O Massah Marrigold! Don't, don't, please!

MARR. There! [*Wrenching money from Gladys and pushing her from him, L.*]

GLAD. [*Fiercely*] James Marrigold; you shall not do this! I am but a weak woman, but a mother's love is stronger than ten thousand devils such as you.

MARR. [*Drawing revolver and breathless*] Must I kill you? [*Tibbetts takes Child up*]

GLAD. If you will. [*Seizing him and renewing struggle*] My life is worth nothing! [*Business. In the struggle, the weapon is discharged, and Marrigold with a shriek falls, C. at 2. Enter Winne, R.2.E.*] What have I done?

WINNE. Killed him, that's all. [*Business. Gladys snatches Child from Tibbetts, rushes to the open door. Picture*]

ACT II.

SCENE: *Exterior of Fairfax Villa on St. Johns River, Florida. House with veranda running from R.1. to R.3.E. Garden seats and table, L.2.E. Croquet*

*mallets and balls at steps, leading to veranda. Hammock under trees, L.3.E.
A thickset hedge crosses back of stage with an opening, R.4.E. and L.4.E.
River and country in the distance. Vegetation, semi-tropical. Diana dis-
covered in hammock, with a novel; Mrs. Dorsie at table embroidering.*
Time: *1859. Sunset.*

Diana. Do you like Florida, mama?

Mrs. D. Yes, my child, very much.

Diana. I don't like it as well as our old home in Virginia.

Mrs. D. Why not? [*Without looking up*]

Diana. Because it's so stupid! Nothing ever happens in Florida. No one ever dies, or gets married, or anything.

Mrs. D. Your cousin Fairfax's wife died here; and he was married here, for that matter.

Diana. Yes; but the match wasn't made here. It seems nobody ever goes courting in Florida. [*Sighs*] I wonder if Cousin Fairfax will marry again?

Mrs. D. Of course, he will. He's a young man yet, and, besides, he should have a mother for his child.

Diana. [*Getting out of hammock*] For goodness sake! Mama, don't be so matter-of-fact. A mother for his child! As if hundreds of men didn't get married without ever thinking of their children!

Mrs. D. Not men who are fit to be fathers! And those are the only kind of men girls should encourage.

Diana. But how are the poor girls going to know when a man is fit to be a father?

Mrs. D. Don't be ridiculous, Di! I don't ask you to have as much sense as other people but please don't be an idiot.

Diana. That's always the way with you, mama. I can't ask you a simple question without exciting your anger.

Mrs. D. Then don't ask simple questions.

Diana. [*Injured*] You never snap off Miss Deane that way.

Mrs. D. Because Miss Deane never gives me the opportunity. Look at her position, a mere governess, and yet she has made herself a general favorite with everybody, in less than a year. I should not be at all surprised to see her some fine day the mistress of Fairfax.

Diana. [*With animation*] Wouldn't that be splendid! A grand wedding, a royal feat, with a hundred guests, and O mama, can't you get Cousin Fairfax to do it right away? [*Pleadingly, putting her arms about Mrs. Dorsie*]

Mrs. D. [*Freeing herself*] That's just like you; not a bit of ambition. And you a Dorsie, too. I am out of all patience with you, Di! [*Exit into house, R.*]

DIANA. [*Perplexed*] I can't really understand mama. I'm sure it was she who engaged Miss Deane, and she is always praising her, and holding her up as a model. [*As if a sudden thought*] Bless me! I hope she don't want me to marry Cousin Fairfax! Oh, dear me! I could never marry a man with a baby! That would be terrible! [*Enter Willie at gate, L.4.E.*]

WILL. May I come in?

DIANA. Certainly! Why, Willie, I didn't think of seeing you today.

WILL. Miss Dorsie; if you wouldn't mind it, I'd rather not be called Willie.

DIANA. [*Amazed*] Isn't that your name?

WILL. Well, yes—that is—of course I was called that when I was a little fellow.

DIANA. I understand, when you were a baby.

WILL. Please don't, Miss Dorsie! I don't like to be reminded of my adolescent state. It always makes me feel sort of soft.

DIANA. I don't see why you should feel that way. We all had to be babies once.

WILL. [*Thoughtfully*] Yes; I suppose so. There don't seem to be any way of getting round that, does there? But, if you wouldn't mind saying Mr. Wagstaff, it would make me feel better.

DIANA. But mister is so formal, and you're only a boy yet, and—

WILL. I'm twenty; and your mama says that's three years older than you are, and everyone calls you Miss Dorsie.

DIANA. I know; but girls are like cherries, they ripen early in the season.

WILL. And are sometimes a little tart.

DIANA. Now, if you came over here to quarrel, you can go right home.

WILL. I came over to see Mr. Fairfax about the convention.

DIANA. [*With indifference*] I don't know anything about the convention; and Cousin Fairfax has been in New Orleans for a fortnight. [*Goes to table*]

WILL. I don't like to leave you like this, Miss Dorsie.

DIANA. Oh, don't mind me.

WILL. It is sort of lonesome here, isn't it?

DIANA. No, not at all.

WILL. [*Plays with his hat*] It looks lonely.

DIANA. You must never trust to appearances.

WILL. [*Hesitates*] Well, then—I'll say good day.

DIANA. Good day. [*Rising*]

WILL. It's awful lonesome over at our place.

DIANA. Then why don't you stay here?

WILL. I thought you wanted me to go.

DIANA. I never said so.

WILL. [*Eagerly*] Can I stay then?

DIANA. [*Laughingly*] If you promise to be a very good boy.

WILL. Boy! There you go again! [*In disgust. Enter Ben, R.4.E.*]

BEN. H'yar comes Massah Fairfax!

DIANA. Where? [*Running, L.4.E.*]

BEN. Right dar! Wid a strange gen'l'man!

DIANA. Why, so it is! [*Clapping her hands*] Just as natural as life!

BEN. An' twice as han'some!

WILL. Wish he had not come so soon.

DIANA. [*To Ben*] Go and tell mama that Cousin Fairfax and a strange gentleman are coming up the river path.

BEN. You bet I will! [*Exit into house, R.*]

DIANA. Quick, Uncle Ben, quick!

WILL. Can't I do something?

DIANA. [*Excited*] Yes! Stand out of the way, please! [*Enter Fairfax quickly, through hedge, R.4.E.*]

FAIR. Back again, Diana, you see!

DIANA. And I'm so glad! [*They embrace. Enter Gaylord, R.4.E.*]

FAIR. Ah, Gay, my dear old chum. I feel at home already!

GAY. [*Coolly*] If I had a pretty girl in my arms, I'd feel much at home, too!

DIANA. [*Abashed, slipping out of Fairfax's arms*] I beg your pardon! I forgot—

GAY. [*Opening his arms*] If it's only a matter of memory, it is time enough yet.

FAIR. Diana, don't you remember this gentleman?

DIANA. [*Dropping her eyes shyly*] No, sir!

FAIR. Come now, that's cruel. He used to be a great favorite of yours, in the valley of Virginia.

DIANA. [*Surprised*] Of mine?

GAY. [*With irony*] Yes; we were very friendly. You used to pull my hair, and put your fist in my mouth and kick me. [*Puts hand on stomach*]

DIANA. [*Aghast*] Kick you!

GAY. Exactly! Until your stocking came off.

DIANA. [*Amazed*] Never!

GAY. On my honor.

FAIR. [*Smiling*] I thought to be unconventional for the sake of "lang syne"; but I suppose I'll have to present you regularly. Dr. Guyon Gaylord, permit me to present my cousin, Miss Diana Dorsie.

DIANA. [*Giving her hand*] Oh, I've heard mama speak of you so much!

GAY. Yes; mama and I were chums, when you were a child. That's how I came to know you when first you wore trains, [*Makes a motion as if dancing a baby in his arms*] and we did this sort of thing for you.

FAIR. Why, Mr. Wagstaff. I didn't observe you!

WILL. I wanted to see you about the convention.

FAIR. We will talk it over after tea. This is our neighbor, Mr. Wagstaff, Doctor Gaylord.

GAY. [*Gives his hand*] I'm glad to meet you. [*Enter Mrs. Dorsie from house*]

MRS. D. Why, Edwin! Did you get back? [*Embraces him*] And Guy Gaylord, on my word!

GAY. Yes; and on your threshold, too! [*They shake hands*]

MRS. D. [*To Fairfax*] Where on earth did you find him?

FAIR. In New Orleans, quite accidentally, in a bachelor den, as might be expected.

MRS. D. Still a bachelor, eh?

GAY. Confirmed. Got the third degree of the order!

MRS. D. [*Smiling*] Just the same old Guy!

GAY. [*Assuming an air of injury*] Now come! I don't think I was ever an old "guy"! The crows may have planted their infernal feet in my face, but my heart is still free from the frost, thank heaven!

FAIR. Where is Miss Deane, and Virgie?

DIANA. Gone for a stroll along the river.

FAIR. I'll go and meet them. You'll excuse me, Guy? [*Going, L.4.E.*]

GAY. Certainly, Miss Diana, we will go in, and renew our friendship. [*Gives his arm*] I'm not too old?

DIANA. Oh, dear no! You're just right! [*Going to house*]

WILL. [*Making a wry face*] And I'm just left!

MRS. D. Mr. Wagstaff, won't you stop for tea?

WILL. Thank you; I don't feel like tea now. [*Exit, L.4.E.*]

GAY. We were very familiar once.

DIANA. [*Laughing*] When I kicked you.

GAY. Well, yes; that might be said to be a familiar footing. [*Exeunt, R.2.E.*]

MRS. D. Dear old Guy! It seems his coming has lit up the past; and I can see the sweet faces of the dear old days again! [*Sits R. Enter Winne, L.4.E.*]

Winne. Nice, cheerful place, this! I can smell supper, too, and it has a savory odor! I'll bet my life it's quail, and I never was so hungry in my life! [*Goes to steps*]

Mrs. D. [*Seeing him*] Where are you going?

Winne. [*Turning on her*] To the devil, I suppose! Am I near the end of my journey?

Mrs. D. You will find him in the first looking-glass you meet. [*Turning to house*]

Winne. Thanks! I'll go in and take a peep. [*Enter Ben from house, R.*]

Ben. No, you won't! What's you doin' 'bout h'yar?

Winne. I'm not in the habit of answering niggers!

Ben. Well, dis niggah's in de habit of makin' white trash like you move on!

Winne. [*Scornfully*] You are?

Ben. [*Facing him*] I is!

Mrs. D. My good man, you had better go.

Winne. [*To Mrs. Dorsie*] I will go for you, if you give me something to eat, and treat me like a gentleman.

Mrs. D. Ben, take him to the storehouse, and give him some food. [*Goes into house*]

Ben. Follow me. [*Going, R.4.E.*] If I had my way, I'd give you food— I'd give ye a club!

Winne. [*With a lofty air*] I prefer not to waste words on a human chattel. [*Exit, R.4.E.*]

Ben. You's de cattle youse'f! I 'spise a mean man, I don't car' what his color is! [*Exit, R.4.E. Enter Gladys and Virgie, L., attired in pretty summer goods, each with bouquets*]

Virg. Flowers are so pretty, Miss Deane!

Glad. Very!

Virg. They must be very happy!

Glad. Why do you think so?

Virg. Because they are so pretty; and the dew gives them fresh diamonds every day.

Glad. [*Going to table*] Beauty is not always happiness, my child! Only the innocent are happy! [*With a sigh*]

Virg. But you are both, and yet you sigh. [*They sit on steps, R.*]

Glad. I was thinking of the past, before I ever came to Fairfax.

Virg. Were you miserable then?

Glad. Very often!

VIRG. But here you are not so. Here, we all love you so very much; and love, papa says, makes life sweet!

GLAD. [*R.*] Yes, darling, your papa is quite right. Love alone can sweeten life; and I am very happy at Fairfax! Happier than I have ever been in my life before. So very happy, that when I come to say farewell to it forever, I fear I shall be very miserable.

VIRG. [*R.*] But you need never go away at all. [*Enter Fairfax, R.4.E.*] Oh, there's papa now! [*Running to him, C.*]

FAIR. [*Kissing her*] How is papa's little girl? [*To Gladys*] Miss Deane, I have been in quest of you. I don't see how I missed you. [*Giving her his hand*]

GLAD. We came by the lower path.

FAIR. And I went to our old retreat, under the red oaks, expecting to surprise you!

VIRG. Oh, Miss Deane never goes there when you're away.

FAIR. Indeed! [*With a glance of inquiry at Gladys*]

GLAD. [*Embarrassed*] It's so far from the house, and—and the weather has been so warm. [*Sending Virgie into house*]

FAIR. Have you been very happy in my absence?

GLAD. Virgie is always happy.

FAIR. [*Seriously*] I spoke of your happiness, and you reply as if it could be of no possible moment to me, or not even worthy of an answer.

GLAD. [*With gaiety*] What would you have me say? That your absence gave me joy? Or, that we have been very wretched, without you? If I say the last, I compliment you; if the first, I wound your pride. Prompt me, and, like the Delphic oracle of old, my answer will be but an echo of your wish.

FAIR. The Delphic oracle was a graven lie, a cheat, a pretense. And you know how I hate deceit! [*Gladys drops her eyes*] Your woman's heart— [*Taking her hand affectionately*] full of tenderness and truth, is a safer source to draw the inspiration of an answer from. Let your eyes look into mine, and say you are really glad I came back so soon!

GLAD. [*Looking up*] I am very glad you came back so soon! [*Enter Diana, from house, R. Stops on steps as she sees them*]

FAIR. [*Looking down into Gladys's face, which he holds between his hands*] You are honest with me?

GLAD. [*Earnestly*] In this at least I am. [*Fairfax kisses her*]

DIANA. Cousin Fairfax! [*Fairfax and Gladys both composed*]

FAIR. Confound that girl! I fear Miss Deane has something in her eye! [*Exit into house*]

DIANA. [*Naïvely*] Very likely a man!

GLAD. [*R.*] Diana!

DIANA. [*Laughingly*] Don't be shocked. I envy you! And so, mama was right after all! Do you know, although you two have been carrying on under my nose all this time, I never guessed it.

GLAD. There was nothing to guess. Mr. Fairfax is my employer. You must not forget that. [*Going to table and flowers*]

DIANA. As if love ever stops to think about such trifles. Besides, cousin has sense enough to see that Fairfax could not have a more accomplished mistress.

GLAD. [*Laughing*] You'll make me vain!

DIANA. But, you haven't seen the other yet; and, I don't want you to go and fall in love with him when you do.

GLAD. [*In surprise*] The other? Who?

DIANA. Dr. Gaylord; an old friend of mama's, who knew and nursed me when I was a little baby. Oh, he's just too grand for anything.

GLAD. [*Smiling*] Not too grand for matrimony, I hope.

DIANA. Oh, he's just right for that.

GLAD. But isn't he rather old for you?

DIANA. Certainly not. Men are like apples; when they are babies, they are blossoms, and look pretty on our bosoms. When they are growing, they are sour, and ought to be left alone. When full sized, and not ripe, they never agree with us; but when autumn frosts make them mellow, they are simply delicious.

GLAD. I fear the star of the Wagstaff is on the wane! [*Smiling*]

DIANA. Oh, he's a boy! A planet of the milky way.

GLAD. And yet, he was very bright a week ago. Ah, Di! Happiness is comparative, and often when we are doing our best to dazzle and delight, another star obscures our light, and gives us over to darkness and despair!

DIANA. If it is an astronomical fact, who can help it? And I don't purpose setting myself up against the whole celestial system, do you?

GLAD. [*Laughingly*] I'd rather not. [*Enter from house, R.2.E., Fairfax and Dr. Gaylord smoking*]

GAY. [*On steps*] What a delightful prospect!

FAIR. Do you like it?

GAY. It's beautiful! [*They both look toward river*]

DIANA. [*To Gladys*] That's he!

GLAD. [*Starting violently*] It cannot be! Yes, yes, it is!

DIANA. Why, what's the matter?

GLAD. [*Recovering self-possession*] Nothing!

DIANA. Let me introduce you.

GLAD. [*Nervously*] No, no, at least not now! Let us go for a walk. [*Puts her arm around Diana, and they go upstage*]

DIANA. [*Turning her head*] Good-bye!

FAIR. Where are you going?

DIANA. To the river.

FAIR. Stop a moment. [*Coming down*] I want to introduce the doctor to Miss Deane.

GAY. [*Coming down steps*] Very happy, I'm sure. [*Business. Gladys retraces her steps, coming to C. of stage, with her face averted*]

FAIR. Dr. Gaylord, this is Virgie's best friend, and governess, Miss Gladys Deane.

GAY. [*Taking her hand*] I'm delighted—[*Business. Their eyes meet, both start; Gladys drops her eyes, and trembles with excitement*] This is an unexpected pleasure. [*Serious and meaningly; she looks up into his face, appealingly. Diana comes down, L., and puts her arm about Gladys's waist at once*]

DIANA. Come. The gentlemen can join us, when they smoke out their burnt offerings.

GLAD. [*Going upstage, aside and with pathos*] He will tell him all!

GAY. [*Aside*] The very woman, or I'm in dotage! [*Exeunt Diana and Gladys, R.4.E.*]

FAIR. [*Carelessly*] Yes; Miss Gladys Deane.

GAY. [*Aside*] Under false colors, eh?

FAIR. Well, what do you think of her?

GAY. Very pretty. [*Blowing smoke*]

FAIR. And, just as pure as she is pretty!

GAY. How do you know?

FAIR. How do I know? She has been an inmate of my family almost a year.

GAY. And, before that?

FAIR. She had been teaching school in Saint Augustine.

GAY. For how long?

FAIR. [*Goes R. of table*] More than a year.

GAY. [*Quietly, falling L.*] And before that?

FAIR. [*Dropping into seat*] Lord, man! You don't expect to have a chronological record, a sort of pedigree of everyone about the place? [*Smiling*]

GAY. But, a woman whose purity you vouch for, ought to have a clear record—a record that would go back further than two years.

FAIR. Why, Guy! I thought you a better judge of human nature. Your calling makes you look always beneath the skin, and therefore, you doctors are the worst judges of human nature in the world.

GAY. And pray where do you look?

FAIR. Into the face. I would rather read a woman's eyes than feel her pulse.

GAY. But, if the case was critical, give me her pulse all the time. I see you are very fond of—the governess. [*Dryly*] Eh?

FAIR. [*Assuming indifference*] Well, yes; that is—of course she's an—

GAY. [*Leaning over table*] Angel in petticoats. I concede that. Go on! Now, for her virtues—seriatim, as the lawyers say.

FAIR. She paints splendidly!

GAY. [*Looking at him*] Her face?

FAIR. [*Snappishly*] No; landscapes!

GAY. Oh!

FAIR. Talks splendidly!

GAY. That's not a virtue in woman, it's a natural gift! Talk is her stronghold.

FAIR. She plays beautifully.

GAY. On who?

FAIR. [*Suspiciously*] What do you mean?

GAY. I mean, that I have been making a diagnosis of your case. My dear friend, you are pretty far gone—you are very ill!

FAIR. [*Amazed*] Ill—!

GAY. Oh, don't be alarmed! You'll get well. It's only heart disease. Your type is contracted by a long residence on the edge of flounces, and furbelows, and is often aggravated by drooping eyes, and bouquets on your writing-desk; with an occasional pressure of the hand, and a sigh! In fact, a sigh is a very dangerous symptom, and a kiss—is sure death! [*Solemnly*]

FAIR. Rubbish!

GAY. Young men are easily cured; all they need is a change of eyes, and perfume, perhaps. But, when it attacks an old fellow of forty, it is almost invariably—fatal! [*Sighs*]

FAIR. When you get done with this technical dissertation, I trust you will be good enough to tell me what it's all about.

GAY. I mean, that you don't want to marry a woman you don't know.

FAIR. [*Smiling*] I don't see how that could well be possible. Men are not given to marrying women they don't know, and, for that matter, doctor, you never know a woman until you do marry her.

GAY. Perhaps you're right. I had always a suspicion that it was a skin game, a sort of a pig-in-a-poke affair.

FAIR. [*Laughingly*] There is one consolation, however, the women draw blanks as often as we do.

GAY. [*Gives hand*] Let us congratulate ourselves. Speaking of that—let me have a light—thanks! I knew a woman who drew a blank once. It was three years ago, last October. I was coming down the Mississippi from Vicksburg in the Belle of Memphis, [*Enter Gladys, R.4.E., listening intently*] and we stopped at a wood pile, at Lander's Landing.

GLAD. [*Aside*] He is telling him now! What shall I do? [*In despair*]

FAIR. Yes?

GAY. I was standing at the bow of the boat, watching a party of friends play poker, when a little darkey came aboard after some liquor for a dying child, volunteering the information that the male parent had drunk the precious supply.

FAIR. The brute!

GAY. My remark exactly! Of course, I went up the bank, and into the hut, where I found matters worse than described. The little one was very ill, the mother a genteel sort of person, thinly clad and penniless; the husband drunk and ruffianly.

FAIR. A nice party. Take a light. [*Gives cigar to Gaylord*]

GLAD. [*Aside, coming down*] He must not tell him tonight! I will have a few hours more of happiness, at any cost. [*Desperately*]

GAY. [*After lighting cigar*] I prescribed for the child, was insulted by the husband, and came away.

FAIR. And the sequel? [*Gladys comes noiselessly down*]

GAY. There is nothing much to tell, only, that I am quite satisfied the heroine of the hut is—

GLAD. Excuse me, gentlemen! [*The Men rise*]

FAIR. [*In surprise*] Gladys!

GLAD. [*Smiling and lifting book from table*] I came after the book. I trust I did not disturb you?

GAY. [*Going R. Aside*] A devilish clever woman!

GLAD. Won't you join us, doctor? Diana said I should send you to her, she wants you.

GAY. I'm very glad to be in demand.

FAIR. Miss Di is sure to find some use for you, she has a wonderful gift of utilizing people.

DIANA. [*Calling from R.4.E.*] Doctor!

GAY. Coming! [*Aside, looking back at Gladys*] A remarkably clever woman! [*Exit, R.4.E.*]

GLAD. [*Going R. Aside*] I will beg his silence.

FAIR. Don't run away, Gladys. [*Gladys returning, C.*]

GLAD. Did you wish to see me?

FAIR. [*Gallantly*] I always wish to see you.

GLAD. [*Goes to garden seat, R.*] I am ready to hear anything you have to say.

FAIR. Anything I have to say! Come, that sounds frightfully commercial, and not a bit friendly. [*Lightly*]

GLAD. [*Embarrassed*] I thought you wished to speak of Virgie.

FAIR. Why should I? I know she is improving under your care.

GLAD. I think she is getting on very nicely.

FAIR. Circumstanced so favorably, she deserves but small credit for improvement. Under the soft skies and warm rays of June, we expect flowers to bloom and blossom. If she did not progress under your tuition, I should despair of her altogether.

GLAD. [*In a low voice*] It is very kind of you to say so.

FAIR. Kind words cost nothing.

GLAD. [*Warmly*] They are the coinage of good hearts.

FAIR. And good hearts are the coinage of God's merciful mint; and the only coin that will purchase a crown of eternal happiness, in this world or the next!

GLAD. Then yours is assured.

FAIR. [*Assuming perplexity*] My heart or my happiness?

GLAD. Both!

FAIR. I would be glad to think so. [*After a pause, aside*] I wonder what she is thinking of now? I don't know what to say next. If I could find the courage to—

GLAD. [*Looking up*] Did you speak?

FAIR. No, did you?

GLAD. No. [*Shakes her head negatively*]

FAIR. Lovely sunset!

GLAD. Beautiful.

FAIR. [*After a pause*] If you only knew how much I love—

GLAD. [*In surprise*] Eh?

FAIR. [*Quickly*] The sunset!

GLAD. [*Aside*] If I could only get away!

FAIR. [*After a short pause*] I am very fond of personification, and to me, night always comes as a kind mother, sandalled with silence, and robed in mists, to lull a tired world to sleep upon her dusky breast. [*Aside*] Thank heaven! I got through without mixing the metaphor.

GLAD. I fear she does not bring rest to all.

FAIR. To all except the guilty. A burdened conscience never sleeps!

GLAD. [*Shudders*] You are quite right. [*Rises*] If you will excuse me now —[*With hesitancy*] I will—

FAIR. But I haven't spoken to you yet.

GLAD. [*Respectfully*] I beg your pardon, I thought you had! [*Resuming seat, R.*]

FAIR. You can't imagine I would keep you here to talk of anything so uninteresting as night and sunsets. No, I wanted to ask you—[*Pauses*]— ask—you—if you like Fairfax as well as ever? [*Aside*] That's better than saying nothing.

GLAD. Better! It seems to me, it is the only home I have ever known. All that I knew before seems but an ugly dream, by comparison—a vague, shapeless mass of misery!

FAIR. [*Earnestly*] You wouldn't like to leave it for another home?

GLAD. [*In a low voice*] Not now; but when Miss Virgie needs me no longer, I will have schooled myself to meet the change.

FAIR. But, suppose when Virgie needs you no longer, I should need you more?

GLAD. [*Crosses, L., to table*] We will speak of that when the times comes.

FAIR. [*Impassioned, catching her hands*] The time has come, Gladys. For the past six months, I have tried to fight what some would please to call my folly. Tried to conquer my feelings, tried to convince myself that my passion was but admiration; that all I needed was a change of scene to drive you from my thoughts. But hearts are not tombs in which we can lay our loves at will. Try as I may, I find that you are ever in my thoughts, my dreams— my heart!

GLAD. [*Aside, with distress*] And, must I lose such love?

FAIR. You cannot have failed to see all this, for you have more than a woman's keen perceptions, and you are too truthful to attempt concealment.

GLAD. [*In a husky voice*] Yes, I have seen it.

FAIR. [*Eagerly*] And your answer is—?

GLAD. [*In a low voice*] I cannot give it to you now.

FAIR. [*Amazed*] Not now! Then I have been mistaken! What I thought was encouragement, was simply a clever bit of coquetry, and—

GLAD. Edwin!

FAIR. I beg your pardon! I may have prized the heart I offered you too highly—[*With a grim smile*] We are all more or less vain; [*Earnestly*] but a love as pure as mine, even if worthless else, shall not be treated as a trifle— as a thing of no value! [*Sits, R.*]

GLAD. [*With tears in her eyes*]   I will not hear you say so! Your love is a priceless boon! It came to me as a bright light in the darkness; casting out the shadows that had settled about my heart, like a crystal current, in a Sahara of sorrow, and pain and heartache. I was not worthy, but I could not dash the chalice from my parched and burning lips! I had not strength enough for that. You see, I am only a weak woman after all! [*Sinks at table, L.*]

FAIR.   Gladys, you alarm me! What does this violent exhibition of grief mean?

GLAD. [*Remembering herself*]   Mean? [*After an instant's pause*] Nothing! Why should it mean anything? [*Crosses to L.*]

FAIR.   But your words seem wild, and out of place. There is surely no one else you love better?

GLAD.   No, no; not one! Not one in all the wide world! But, the thought that I should have to leave Fairfax, go out into the hard, cold, bitter world again!

FAIR.   There is no need that you should, while I have a home, and a heart to offer you. This is no time for tears, Gladys! As the daylight fades out of the sky, let the light of your love illuminate my heart!

GLAD. [*Rocking dismally*]   If you only knew; if you only knew—[*Enter Gaylord and Diana, R.4.E.*]

FAIR.   I only want to know that you love me. [*Business. Diana comes down, R., Gaylord between Gladys and Fairfax*]

DIANA. [*In surprise*]   Why, Edwin! What have you said to Miss Deane?

FAIR.   The most important thing a man can say to a woman! That I love her, and want her for my wife! [*Turning to Diana who exhibits joy*]

GAY. [*In a low voice to Gladys*]   And you said—?

GLAD. [*Looking up into his face, appealingly, and in a voice full of pathos*] Nothing!

GAY. [*Giving her his hand*]   That was right! [*Picture*]

CURTAIN

[*Second picture: Gladys upon upper step leading to house. Diana with foot on lower one, looking at Gaylord, who is bowing to her: while Fairfax is upstage, C., tenderly regarding Gladys*]

SECOND CURTAIN

ACT III.

SCENE: *Interior of Fairfax house. Doors, R. and L.2. Large French windows reaching to the floor in F., hung in lace, and looking out on veranda, R., window partially screened by vines. Piano, R.C., table with glass aquarium, books, etc. Room elegantly furnished.*

DIANA. [*At window, L.*] It's been an awfully stupid day. I don't think I ever felt quite so miserable in all my life. Cousin Fairfax and Dr. Gaylord out fishing since breakfast and Gladys in her room with a headache—[*Enter Gladys, R.2.E.*] Oh, there you are! Are you better?

GLAD. Yes, thank you. [*Going to sofa, L.*]

DIANA. I'm so glad! Gladys dear, we women are hard to understand.

GLAD. Why?

DIANA. I do believe we are worse than the Sphinx.

GLAD. [*Smiling faintly*] In what regard?

DIANA. Why, in this. If we are not in love we are wretched, if we are in love we are miserable. If the men we love don't propose, our hearts ache; if they do—our heads ache. [*Significantly*]

GLAD. I suppose so. Have the gentlemen returned?

DIANA. No; and I think it's very selfish of them to stay away, all day, and leave us to mope.

GLAD. You must allow them some relaxation, Diana. Remember, too, they have not seen each other for so long and they naturally have a good deal to say that interests only themselves.

DIANA. If I had known we were to be left to ourselves I would not have dressed.

GLAD. [*Aside*] If I only knew the worst—this suspense is terrible.

DIANA. [*Touches key*] Ten to one, they've been talking all day about women—other women, too. Old love affairs! How I hate old love affairs. Don't you think men abominably heartless?

GLAD. [*Taking up book*] I can't say that I do.

DIANA. Of course not; because you have found your way to one. But I do hope and pray, Gladys, you are not going to put on those airs most engaged girls do.

GLAD. I fear I don't understand.

DIANA. A sort of superior, toplofty look—as if there was only one man left in the world, and you owned him.

GLAD. [*Amused*] I thought that a characteristic of matrimony.

DIANA. Oh, no! There isn't such a proprietary pride after the honeymoon. They both act then as if they had been a trifle—[*Hesitates*]

GLAD. Well?

DIANA. Swindled. [*Turns over music*]

GLAD. I fear you are cynical today. [*Enter Ben with candelabra which he places on table*]

BEN. It's hardly dark 'nough yet for de lights; but I'se a-goin' ober to Graceland dis ebenin', an' I wanted to git started early.

GLAD. [*In a whisper to Ben*] Did you give Dr. Guy my letter last night?

BEN. [*To Gladys*] I suah did! [*She passes him money*]

DIANA. What are you going to Graceland for, Uncle Ben? [*Without looking around*]

BEN. I'se got a little business ober dar.

DIANA. [*Turning around*] That is not answering my question.

BEN. [*Embarrassed*] Do you want a plain an' plump ansah?

DIANA. Certainly.

BEN. [*Smiling*] Well de fac' is, Mis Di—she's ober dar—Marfah! [*Laughs outright*]

DIANA. We know Martha's over there.

BEN. Well, she no good all by herself.

DIANA. Why not?

BEN. [*Still smiling, bashfully*] Well you see, it takes two before dar's any fun in it. [*Laughs*]

DIANA. You mean to say that you are in love with Martha?

BEN. S'pose dat's de short of it; doh I calls it "gone on her"—it seems to reach de spot bettah.

DIANA. I trust it makes up in directness what it certainly lacks in elegance. Has the affair between you and Martha been of long duration?

BEN. [*Puzzled*] I hardly t'ink I'se got your meanin'.

DIANA. Don't you understand?

BEN. [*Scratches his head*] Oh, yes, miss, I—I understan'; but I'se inclined to t'ink I don't know what you mean.

DIANA. [*A little impatient*] How long have you loved her?

BEN. Oh, eber since hog-killin' time.

DIANA. [*With a shrug*] A delicate way of fixing the date. You can go, Ben.

BEN. Yes, misseh. [*Going, L.2.E.*] I'd a notion to ask her to buy Marfah fo' me. [*Exit, L.2.E.*]

DIANA. [*Rising*] Dear me! I suppose love is such a universal malady, that even poor Martha cannot escape. [*Enter Dr. Gaylord, L.2.E.*]

GAY. Good evening, Miss Diana.

DIANA. Good evening.

GAY. Miss Deane! [*They exchange recognitions; turning to Diana*] Did you miss me much?

DIANA. [*Assuming surprise*] Why, no; were you away?

GAY. Come now; that's cruel! I thought you would be counting the minutes, and to be greeted with a look of pretty surprise and a "No; were you away?" is rather demoralizing to a fellow's vanity.

DIANA. The vanity of most men is a very robust commodity, and will survive a great many assaults.

GAY. I wish their hearts were as tough!

DIANA. You have none.

GAY. I admit it.

DIANA. [*In emphasis*] You do?

GAY. You've got it.

DIANA. Were it true, you would not say so here, would he, Gladys?

GLAD. [*Looking up from book*] What did you say? I was reading.

DIANA. I said when men declare love in public, they never mean it.

GAY. Miss Deane will hardly subscribe to that.

GLAD. I really have not got the thread of your argument; but I think when people truly love they never speak lightly of it—it is with them a thing too sacred.

GAY. [*Aside*] That's one for me.

DIANA. I really can't see why love should be enshrouded in secrecy. It's always the fault of the men.

GAY. [*Significantly*] While women frequently have the most to hide—eh? [*Gladys drops her eyes. Aside*] That's one for her.

DIANA. [*Piqued*] That's very ungallant, doctor. With such an opinion of women I don't wonder you're a bachelor.

GAY. That I am so is my misfortune. My position merits pity rather than censure.

DIANA. A truce to passion, let us talk of pain. My head aches.

GAY. I suggest ammonia.

DIANA. [*Going, L.2.E.*] I'd rather have fresh air. Nature's my physician—

GAY. He has one virtue.

DIANA. And that?

GAY. He never sends in his little bill.

DIANA. [*Gladys rises*] He's not as mercenary as the man.

GAY. But then the rascal goes naked, and has no board to pay. Now if we could—[*Diana silences him with a look, putting on her wrap at L.2.E.*]

DIANA. You're incorrigible! Come on! [*Exit, L.2.E.*]

GAY. [*Calling after her*] I'm getting my hat—go on! [*To Gladys*] I got your note.

GLAD. [*Eagerly*] I will see you tonight, before you sleep?

GAY. There is no hurry. I shall not speak until you explain.

GLAD. But you hold my happiness in your hands. I cannot live in this intense suspense. Better know the worst at once.

GAY. I will not go further than my duty to my friend.

GLAD. You deem me unworthy of him?

GAY. You can't expect a verdict—until I have heard the evidence. [*Exit, L.2.E.*]

GLAD. [*Despairingly*] His heart is closed against me, and suspicion stands on guard. But if he be not marble, my pitiful tale will move him to compassion. Oh, it seems so cruel, to be thrust from the very gates of Paradise. Have I not suffered enough? Must my path lie forever in the gloom? Is there no way to reach the glad sunlight again? [*Bursting into tears*] Oh, what have I done to deserve such disaster? [*Sinks on seat with head resting on table, L. Enter Virgie, R.2.E.*]

VIRG. Are you crying, Miss Deane?

GLAD. [*Drying her eyes*] Virgie, my darling, is that you? [*Caressing Virgie*]

VIRG. What makes you so unhappy?

GLAD. Nothing! I am very foolish—almost childish, my dear.

VIRG. Perhaps you were lonesome.

GLAD. Perhaps.

VIRG. Papa said I should come and kiss you good night before I go to bed.

GLAD. It was very kind of papa to remember me at all. [*Kisses her*] There.

VIRG. Good night, Miss Deane. [*Exit, R.2.E.*]

GLAD. Good night, my child. My child! [*After a pause*] How lightly it falls from my lips! Alas, she is not my child. Her future I hope is a fairer one than my poor dead darling knew. Ah, the little graves, the little graves that hold the jewels of so many desolate homes. They need no monuments, for the names of their hushed inhabitants have been written by the fingers of love upon our hearts. [*Wiping away a tear*]

FAIR. [*Without, L.2.E.*] By and by.

GLAD. Edwin coming! [*Rising quickly*] He must not see me now—not until my fate is decided. [*At R.2.E. Enter Fairfax, L.2.E.*]

FAIR. Ah, Gladys! Just in time, I see; for you were going away; were you not?

GLAD. [*Embarrassed*] Yes—that is—I was going to my room.

FAIR. It is too early to retire.

GLAD. But I have got something to do.

FAIR. And I have got something to say.

GLAD. But really I—

FAIR. [*A trifle hurt*] Why, is it possible you wish to avoid me?

GLAD. [*Coming C.*] Oh, no, no! Indeed I don't! Why should I?

FAIR. Why indeed?

GLAD. Nothing could be further from my thoughts. [*Giving him both hands*]

FAIR. [*Looking down into her face*] Gladys, I have remained away all day for the purpose of giving you an opportunity to think over what I said to you last night. [*She goes from him to seat, L.*] Why do you turn away? [*In surprise*] Have you no other reply?

GLAD. [*Evidently pained*] None that I can give you now.

FAIR. [*Bitterly*] And when do you propose breaking this sacred silence. [*With a forced calm*]

GLAD. In a few days—say a week.

FAIR. [*Proudly*] Why not say a century as well? Be not so mindful of my feelings, Miss Deane. It may give me pain to know the truth; but I won't give up entirely; I fancy I have pride enough to shroud my pain, and self-respect enough to bury my disappointment. [*Going L.*]

GLAD. These words are cruel, unkind—unjust! You see how you make me suffer.

FAIR. And do you think I am happy? You have led me to believe that I had a place in your affections; you encouraged me to give you my heart; and now when I am no longer master of myself, when my heart is beneath your heel, when every word you utter is as precious music to my ear, you cast me aside as a glove, no longer worthy of your hand. Is this kind or just?

GLAD. No, no Edwin! I only ask you to wait, one little week. How can you be so ungenerous?

FAIR. There is a slight even in the request. If you do not care enough for me now after all these months, a week will not be likely to work a change.

GLAD. [*Sadly*] A week often wrecks our lives.

FAIR. There can be nothing so serious impending over ours. I fail to see anything tragic in the situation at all. A plain, unpretending planter wants to wed the woman of his choice, and go sailing down the stream of time, with that calm serenity that has marked his life. She says she loves him, yet refuses to give her promise. There can be but one reason for hesitancy; it is a plain interpretation; you prefer another hand at the helm. Be it so.

GLAD. [*With a glance of reproach*]   You know how utterly untrue that is; that this wide world holds no one dearer to my heart than you. [*He advances, she puts up her hand*] It is because I love you I would have you wait; it is because I love you I would have you think. [*Going, L., to sofa*]

FAIR.   There seems something behind all this—something of which I am yet in ignorance. Gladys, can't you trust me yet; am I not worthy of your confidence?

GLAD.   I wish I were as worthy of your love.

FAIR.   Were my love a crown, I would bestow it blindly upon you, and trust you for the rest. [*Drops on his knee by her side*] Gladys, I know how impatient I appear to you; but remember my love has grown to be the fiercer part of my nature, and chafes at this rebuke.

GLAD.   Rebuke is too harsh a term; it may be only a delay.

FAIR.   There's a dangerous element in all delays.

GLAD.   It will give you time to know me better.

FAIR.   It seems to me I have known you always.

GLAD.   And still nothing of my past.

FAIR.   I'll stake my life upon its purity.

GLAD. [*Looking searchingly into his face*]   But if the tooth of scandal should assail; the best are subject to the assaults of calumny; would you still believe?

FAIR.   I'd take your word against the world.

GLAD.   My own! [*Impulsively kissing his forehead, then rising quickly and going, R., as if afraid to trust herself further*]

FAIR.   Having said as much, may I now consider I have your answer?

GLAD.   No, no! Please don't urge me further. I crave a week. It is only a little favor—and—there—[*Going to him*] don't frown again, say a week of respite, and a kind good night!

FAIR.   You love me?

GLAD.   Better than my life.

FAIR. [*Kisses her*]   A week then be it. Good night! [*At door, R.2.E.*]

GLAD.   Good night! [*Goes and gives him both her hands at R.2.E. He exits, R.2.E.*] How little does he guess the fearful struggle I have made; how little does he guess the weight of the burden he would share. [*Enter Mrs. Dorsie, L.2.E.*]

MRS. D.   I thought I should find Edwin here.

GLAD.   He has just gone. Was it for anything particular?

MRS. D.   Yes; very. Does it seem possible to you we could have used ten pounds of butter in a week? It don't seem so to me. There is something wrong.

GLAD. [*Goes to piano*] What does Hannah say?

MRS. D. Say! What can she say? Look innocent, and "wonder" as all cooks do when they can't account for things. I wanted Edwin to look over my accounts.

GLAD. Looking over them will not make them less.

MRS. D. There is some consolation in being certain, that's all. How is your head, my dear?

GLAD. [*Who has gone to piano*] Better, thank you. [*Returning, C.*]

MRS. D. If a mere proposal makes your head ache, how do you think you will withstand the thousand natural shocks of matrimony!

GLAD. Matrimony?

MRS. D. There is no need to disguise the fact from me. Diana told me all. And I'm glad of it, Gladys; you deserve just such luck.

GLAD. You are always kind. You have been a second mother to me ever since I came here.

MRS. D. Don't believe too much in second mothers my dear—try and make yourself a fitting first. But I must go—Edwin will never understand my figures in the world. [*Exit, L.2.E.*]

GLAD. [*Crosses to L.*] And it has been this way from the first. Everyone so good and kind to me, that their very kindness seems a contrast to the old life I once led—the old bitter life that I had fondly hoped had been left behind forever. [*Enter Dr. Gaylord, L.2.E.*]

GAY. You are quite alone? [*Putting hat on table*]

GLAD. [*In a low voice, sinking on sofa*] Entirely.

GAY. [*Calmly*] You see, I have come as you requested. [*Taking chair, L. of table*]

GLAD. I am very grateful for so much consideration.

GAY. Not at all. A lady in distress, whatever the circumstances may be, has always a claim upon a gentleman's time.

GLAD. And on his mercy, too.

GAY. Mercy to one is sometimes injustice to another.

GLAD. [*Aside*] How will I begin?

GAY. [*Glancing at watch*] We are losing precious time.

GLAD. You can imagine why I sent for you?

GAY. [*Calmly*] You told me in your note.

GLAD. Ah, yes! I had quite forgotten. I believe—[*Hesitates*] I mentioned that we had met before. [*Taking rose out of her head and looking at it*]

GAY. Which was quite unnecessary as I recognized you the instant I set eyes upon you.

GLAD. [*After a pause*] You were doubtless surprised to see me here?

GAY. Not at all. There is no law to prevent a woman going where she pleases.

GLAD. But my circumstances were so changed.

GAY. If you mean that you were more pleasantly situated, as far as creature comforts go, I can cordially agree with you. Your residence on the Mississippi was not particularly desirable.

GLAD. It was more wretched than you can imagine.

GAY. [*In a matter-of-fact way*] The palpable misery was bad enough without calling imagination to one's aid.

GLAD. Can you wonder that I have no desire to go back to such a life?

GAY. [*Coolly*] I certainly cannot think of anything less inviting.

GLAD. I fear you do not sympathize with my position. Your voice has something mocking in it, as if you were prepared to destroy me, and would do it remorselessly.

GAY. [*Looking steadily at her*] If necessary to save my friend—I—would.

GLAD. [*With emotion*] But I am only a woman, without a friend on earth —an orphan cast upon the world; have you no pity for me? Is it manly to assail one who never injured you! One so utterly defenseless?

GAY. [*Rising calmly*] My dear madam, let us understand each other fully. As I see it, your position is not entitled to the sympathy of any honorable man. [*She sobs aloud*] I find you here under an assumed name.

GLAD. [*Without looking up*] It is my father's name.

GAY. Be that as it may; I know you to be a married woman; I know that my friend has no knowledge whatever of your past life. He has been deceived. He has given you his love, and you have withheld the confidence he had a right to claim. As you have questioned my manhood, I ask you now, would it be manly to permit my dearest friend to marry a woman whom he does not know—and pardon my lack of delicacy if I add, whom I have reason to—

GLAD. Why pause? I have suffered so much I am callous to blame.

GAY. I do not blame you, madam; but it is not my fault if I suspect—your conduct has certainly laid you open to suspicion.

GLAD. [*Rising and looking him in the eye*] And what do you think I am?

GAY. I would prefer not to say.

GLAD. You might as well; I read it in your eyes. You deem me an adventuress—a woman without principle, eager to make a rich alliance at any cost. You believe I have craftily come here to win his heart and gain a home. You are mistaken; it is not so!

GAY. Give me some proof.

GLAD. [*Crosses to R., turning on him*] I will give you the best. I will leave this house tonight forever. I will go out into the world penniless, homeless, friendless. You cannot surely ask for more.

GAY. Without even speaking to him?

GLAD. Without even speaking to him! You don't think I would crave a repetition of this scene? O sir! I am not so fond of humiliation. Give me credit for some little gleam of grace. [*Sinking, sobbing on seat, R. of table*]

GAY. [*He looks down on her in silence a moment, then picks up the rose she has dropped. Aside*] This looks like honesty. [*Aloud*] I presume you are divorced?

GLAD. He is dead. [*Dr. Gaylord starts*]

GAY. And your child—?

GLAD. Dead, too [*Sobs*]

GAY. Utterly alone?

GLAD. Utterly!

GAY. [*After a pause*] And you came here without any design?

GLAD. I was engaged by Mrs. Dorsie; he was in Europe at the time. How could you think otherwise?

GAY. And you say you love him?

GLAD. Better than my life—to part from him will break my heart.

GAY. But you will go?

GLAD. [*Rising*] I have given you my word. [*Looking him in the eyes*]

GAY. You doubtless think me very cruel?

GLAD. I have no time to think of you, my thoughts are occupied with my own misery. [*Tries to pass him*]

GAY. [*Deferential*] Remain a moment, I beg of you! When I came into this room I expected you to weep, and beg for mercy, and I had steeled my heart against these womanly weapons; but I am only a man, if indeed a bachelor deserves the name—and I pity you from my heart! I have no desire to drive you into the streets. [*Wipes his eyes*]

GLAD. But I have determined.

GAY. And so have I. You shall remain!

GLAD. At what price?

GAY. That you shall tell Fairfax all—just as you have told me—he will forgive you—a man in love will forgive anything.

GLAD. I could not tell him now—perhaps at some future time I may find courage. In the past there is no disgrace for him! In the present there shall be no humiliation. I prefer to sacrifice myself.

GAY. A sentiment worthy of the best of women. [*Aside*] I'll soon be in love with her myself. [*Aloud*] And what do you expect of me?

GLAD. Fidelity to your friend—nothing more.

GAY. Right! But I have concluded that I can best serve my friend by giving him a noble woman's love. [*Taking her hands*]

GLAD. [*Eagerly*] You really mean it?

GAY. I do.

GLAD. [*Joyfully*] Oh, you have made me happy—so happy that I can scarce realize my joy.

GAY. I will retire until you do. [*Exit, L.2.E. Gladys bursts into a glad torrent of tears and sobs aloud till curtain*]

ACT IV.

SCENE: *Same as Act III. Dr. Gaylord and Fairfax discovered, the former with book, seated, R.C. Fairfax lying upon sofa, L.*
TIME: *Three days later.*

FAIR. What are you reading, Guy?

GAY. Paley's Philosophy.

FAIR. [*After a pause*] Why don't you get married, Guy?

GAY. That's a nice question to ask a man with a book of philosophy in his hands.

FAIR. No; but seriously! Why don't you?

GAY. Because you have determined on it? Like the fox in the fable you want everyone to lose their tail because yours has been caught in the trap. No, sir; I appreciate liberty too well! I don't intend to let any woman put me behind the bars.

FAIR. If the prison be only a pretty woman's arms, confinement could not be irksome.

GAY. If you like it so well, why postpone your wedding a whole year?

FAIR. It is Gladys's desire, not mine. If I had my way I'd be married tomorrow.

GAY. Tonight would be even better—eh? But why has she postponed your happiness?

FAIR. A woman's whim. They always want so much time to deliberate, and contemplate their happiness from a distance.

GAY. Perhaps they prefer pursuit to possession; and, by Jove, I don't wonder. Better to pursue some men a lifetime than to possess them for five minutes. [*Enter Gladys, R.2.E.*]

FAIR. Do you believe the same of women?

GAY. I do not! I confess that my opinion of women has undergone a change recently. Seeing that they have to live with your average man, I'm only astonished they retain their natural good so well.

GLAD. [*Coming down, C.*] With such sentiments, doctor, you cannot long remain a bachelor. [*Smiling*]

GAY. But suppose I am the average man.

GLAD. You are far above the average.

FAIR. [*Rising*] A compliment for you, Dr. Guy.

GLAD. It was only payment for his own. [*Pins a flower on Fairfax's coat*]

GAY. [*Aside*] The doomed are always decorated with flowers—like lambs adorned for the sacrifice.

FAIR. [*To Gladys*] Let us take a turn in the moonlight. What do you say?

GLAD. [*L.3.*] But the dew?

FAIR. [*L.3.*] Here's your wrap. [*Takes it up and puts it about her*]

GAY. [*Looking around*] Where are you going?

GLAD. To enjoy the moonlight.

GAY. Why the moon hasn't risen.

FAIR. The river is very beautiful notwithstanding.

GAY. But you can't see it for the mist.

FAIR. I did not think of that. [*To Gladys*] Did you?

GAY. Oh, go on—go on! You won't miss the moon; for you have reached that fearful crisis when love is blind, and a little silly, too.

GLAD. I'm sorry you are not coming, too; I'm sure you might.

FAIR. Why don't you come, Guy; we would be glad to have you.

GAY. Have done with hypocrisy; you know you don't want me.

GLAD. I hope Paley will comfort you.

FAIR. There's always comfort in philosophy. [*Exeunt Gladys and Fairfax, L.2.E.*]

GAY. [*Reflectively*] Yes—a great deal of comfort. One needs philosophy to guard one's loneliness. How happy they are! I wonder if bachelorhood isn't an abnormal condition? If man was intended to live alone—why did the All-wise ring in Eve on him? But then again, as soon as woman came into Paradise she raised the devil there. I don't know, perhaps it was better for Adam to have the woman and the devil than to be left to his own shift. It made things lively at least. [*After a pause*] It was very good of Gladys to give him a year of grace. It shows she is not fearful of the future; not alarmed lest she should be found out! Were she guilty she would close the bargain quickly. I wonder where Diana is? I'm afraid I am getting ridiculously fond of that girl. [*Going to window, L.F.*] There she is, talking to that young boodle Wagstaff. That boy ought to be in bed. What! Actually kissing him good night. Why it would require all my courage to do that. [*Enter Diana, L.2.E.*] Do you know, miss, you have just accomplished a very foolish piece of business?

DIANA. [*Raising brows in surprise*] I?

GAY. Yes, you.

DIANA. In what way, pray?

GAY. [*Half angrily*] By going out and standing on those steps a half hour in the dew without a wrap.

DIANA. I wasn't out there a moment. Besides you're not my guardian.

GAY. No, but I'm a physician, and I flatter myself I understand the laws of hygiene.

DIANA. Suppose I should die tomorrow; it couldn't interest you very largely. Besides, I don't want any advice.

GAY. That's a very grateful return for my solicitude, I must say. There was nothing to gain by standing out there.

DIANA. That is for me to say.

GAY. Don't be idiotic. You wouldn't throw yourself away on a boy like that?

DIANA. To marry any man is, in some sense, throwing yourself away.

GAY. Don't let us quarrel, Miss Dorsie.

DIANA. [*Petulantly*] You are always ready for a growl; it seems to be characteristic of bachelors.

GAY. [*After a pause, somewhat sadly*] I am sorry if in my brief visit to Fairfax, I have evinced such an unenviable trait; and if in any acidity of disposition, I have caused you pain, I regret it.

DIANA. [*Aside*] I do hope he isn't going to take a new tack. As long as he stormed I could keep before the wind; now I feel I am sinking.

GAY. My regret is all the more poignant when I reflect that I will not have time to create a more favorable impression, as I leave Fairfax tomorrow evening.

DIANA. [*Quickly*] Leave Fairfax! You couldn't be so cruel!

GAY. The question of cruelty is not involved. My practice will not permit of a longer stay.

DIANA. [*In distress*] But I understood you were to remain quite a long time—until the game was ready to kill.

GAY. [*Significantly*] I'm afraid the game flies too high in Florida for my aim.

DIANA. [*Roguishly*] It might fly lower if you would only linger a trifle later.

GAY. I'm afraid I've waited too long already.

DIANA. [*Impatiently*] You don't expect it to fly into your arms, do you?

GAY. If I opened them sufficiently wide—I don't see why it shouldn't.

DIANA. [*Goes over close to him*] What would you say if it did?

GAY. That I would kill it—

DIANA. [*In alarm*] Eh?

GAY. With kindness! [*Closing his arms about her and kissing her*]

DIANA. [*Escaping him*] Why what have you done?

GAY. Applied for admission to the brotherhood of benedicts—Will you initiate me now? Or will I make a fresh application? [*Offers to kiss her again*]

DIANA. Your application is filed. [*Going to him*] And you have actually done it at last—isn't it funny?

GAY. Not exactly; but it's a little easier than I supposed.

DIANA. Oh, here comes mama! Ask her now and have it over. I'll step in here and await the issue. [*Going, R.2.E.*]

GAY. I say! Don't leave me alone with her. [*Exit Diana, R.2.E.*] Egad, this is the worst part of it. I never felt so inexpressibly sheepish in my life. [*Enter Mrs. Dorsie, L.2.E.*]

MRS. D. All alone, Guy?

GAY. Yes.

MRS. D. It's too bad. Don't you feel wretched?

GAY. I have been alone so much, that it has lost its sting to a great extent. [*Aside*] How will I get at it?

MRS. D. [*As if in search of something on table*] Ah, Guy, I am afraid you have made a great mistake; a man as companionable as you always were ought to have had a mate.

GAY. If all women thought like you, perhaps I would have been married long ago.

MRS. D. No need of all women thinking so—one is enough.

GAY. [*Falteringly*] Yes, I have heard one was a dose.

MRS. D. That is a slander. Men and women, as a general rule, are both made more happy by matrimony, and remember, I speak from experience.

GAY. Do you know—take a chair—[*Places one and sits beside her*] that I am charmed to hear you speak so glowingly of the wedded state.

MRS. D. You are?

GAY. Particularly this evening.

MRS. D. [*Aside*] Dear me. I wonder what he means?

GAY. I have determined to get married myself.

MRS. D. [*Amazed*] You have! Well I never!

GAY. Yes, you have; but that don't matter now. You know I am an average good fellow, and I think if I tried very hard I could make any reasonable woman happy.

MRS. D. But you know I am quite settled and my daughter is full grown and—

GAY. I have anticipated all that. Diana has no objection if you have not.

MRS. D. I am inexpressibly grieved, Guy, to refuse you, [*Rising*] but I feel it is my duty.

GAY. [*Rising*] Upon my word, Mrs. Dorsie, I regard this as decidedly shabby treatment, and we have been friends so long.

MRS. D. But what am I to do? I don't want to get married.

GAY. Who wants you to get married?

MRS. D. [*Aghast*] What! You wouldn't dare to suggest anything else!

GAY. I would most decidedly! Say yes to me, and you can marry tomorrow if you like.

MRS. D. This is outrageous! Guy Gaylord, I always respected you; but I don't love you, never did, never will!

GAY. [*Spitefully*] I don't want you to. Who ever heard of a man being loved by his mother-in-law?

MRS. D. [*Amazed*] You don't mean me then?

GAY. You! I should hope not. [*Diana comes shyly out of room, R.2.E.*]

DIANA. [*Very meekly*] No, mama. He means me!

MRS. D. [*Sinks exhausted*] I haven't had such a fright in twenty years.

GAY. Nor I such a shock! The idea of an old woman like you—!

DIANA. You just shut up about age. She's only forty, and you're that. [*Going to her mother*] Mama, dear, may I?

MRS. D. [*Quite exhausted*] Certainly you may, my child. Doctor, you ought to have done this twenty years ago.

GAY. [*Giving Diana his arm*] Then I should not have been so happy tonight. Let us try the moonlight—[*To Diana*]

DIANA. But the dew?

GAY. It won't hurt you. [*Going, L.2.*]

DIANA. But the laws of hygiene?

GAY. You will pardon me if I say very quietly, but firmly, damn the laws of hygiene. [*Exeunt, L.2.E. Diana makes a demonstration of disapproval as they exeunt*]

MRS. D. I must go and tell Fairfax. I never was so delighted—except when I was married myself. [*Exit, L.2.E. Moon rises. Enter Fairfax and Gladys through window, L.C. in F.*]

FAIR. Did you enjoy your walk? [*Taking wrap from her shoulders*]

GLAD. [*Gaily*] Immensely!

FAIR. It was a pity we had to come home just as the moon rose. [*Sitting, L.C.*]

GLAD. [*At his feet*] But we couldn't stay out forever you know. There is a limit to all things.

FAIR. All things! I hope not; there are some things I would have last forever. [*Looking tenderly into her eyes*]

GLAD. I can't imagine what you mean.

FAIR. I mean our happiness.

GLAD. Do you fear its destruction?

FAIR. I don't know what I fear; but sometimes I feel as if such perfect content, as I have known since we have been promised to each other, is not for mortals to attain on earth—that we have filched from the future the calm of Paradise—that love has made a fairyland and given it to me.

GLAD. Don't liken our love to fairyland; for if you remember the story-books aright—there is always a spirit of evil hovering in the air.

FAIR. I believe you're right! But then the evil spirit rarely triumphs; in the end the good comes grandly home to glory.

GLAD. [*Sitting at his feet*] After many tears and tribulations.

FAIR. Which makes the fairies enjoy their new-found happiness the more.

GLAD. There is some consolation in that; isn't there? [*Smiling*]

FAIR. [*After a pause*] Do you know, Gladys, it sometimes strikes me as very strange that I have only known you one brief year.

GLAD. [*Smiling faintly*] Does it?

FAIR. It seems to me our love has had a history that goes back until it twines itself about the traditions of our childhood; a deep perspective, with a tender luminous brilliancy in the middle distance.

GLAD. [*Sadly, as if speaking to herself*] I see only shadows in the past—shadows that make me shudder.

FAIR. Then you should draw the curtain of forgetfulness between.

GLAD. It is not so easy to forget.

FAIR. Gladys, you speak as if you had suffered much.

GLAD. When women are left to fight their way through the world alone they always suffer.

FAIR. Now that the period of pain is past, let us not disturb it. [*Taking up book off table*] We can talk of something far more pleasant.

GLAD. [*Aside*] If I could only find words to frame my story, I would tell him all now, tonight.

FAIR. [*Reading*] If the heart is overweighted,
        Love will bear the burden, too,
        Love with Pity still was mated;
        Fear not foes while love is true.
        Love is stronger still than duty—
        Precious ore without alloy—
        Do not fear or tremble, beauty,
        Nothing can sweet love destroy.

GLAD. [*Earnestly. Aside*] I will tell him! He has a right to know. [*Aloud*] Edwin!

FAIR. [*Closing book and going to her*] Yes.

GLAD. Sit here, that I may look into your face while I tell you a story—my story.

FAIR. [*Sitting at her feet*] Your story! Come, you promise a treat indeed. I am ready, now proceed!

GLAD. Are you so anxious to hear the history of my past?

FAIR. Anything that relates to you is interesting. Although remember I do not ask for the information. When a man finds a nugget of precious gold, he does not enhance its value by familiarizing himself with the auriferous deposit from which it came.

GLAD. It is a story full of pain and suffering.

FAIR. Then I am willing to spare you its recital. [*About to rise*]

GLAD. [*Detaining him*] I have carried the burden alone so long, I feel the time has come when it is my duty to share it with another.

FAIR. If I can lessen your load, I am ready to relieve you.

GLAD. [*After a pause*] Before I begin, I want to free you from your promise.

FAIR. [*Amazed*] My promise!

GLAD. [*In a low, faltering tone*] If, after you have heard all, know all, you are still willing that I should be your wife, why then I shall be happier than ever. But if you feel that we should part; that we can never be anything to each other, I shall not murmur nor complain.

FAIR. There is nothing, however terrible, that would make me give you up. As for the past, I refuse to enter it. Why should we seek the cypress when we can remain among the flowers? [*Rising*]

GLAD. But I insist! It is my duty! I have been trying for the last three days to find words to tell you; I even wrote it out; but had not the courage to send it to you. Here it is. [*Taking paper from her breast and giving it to him*] Read it, and if it be my condemnation you can leave the room without a word—I ask it as a favor—perhaps the last. [*Sinks on sofa, L.*]

FAIR. [*After a long pause, during which he is undecided, glancing from paper to Gladys*] Is there aught in this paper—I mean, is it a confession of crime?

GLAD. [*Without looking up*] No.

FAIR. Thank heaven! [*After another pause*] It is a story of suffering then, and not of sin?

GLAD. Yes.

FAIR. [*Sets fire to paper from candelabra on table and watches it burn until it is reduced to ashes*] There, your story belongs to the past; in its ashes we will bury it forever.

GLAD. [*Rising*] But, Edwin!

FAIR. We will never speak of it again. [*Gladys rushes into his arms. Enter Diana, L.2.E.*]

DIANA. Oh, dear! I didn't know anything was going on, or I wouldn't have—

FAIR. [*To Diana*] Do you wish to see me?

DIANA. No; I have something awfully particular to tell Gladys 'though, and—

FAIR. It won't keep—eh? [*Going, L.2.E.*]

DIANA. I am awfully sorry to—

FAIR. Your regrets are altogether superfluous, my dear Diana. Good night, ladies. [*They bow. Exit Fairfax*]

DIANA. I know it's mean to break in on Paradise, but I couldn't wait. It's all over.

GLAD. [*In surprise*] What is all over?

DIANA. I'm engaged.

GLAD. Who to?

DIANA. Who to! As if there is another man in Florida fit to marry. I beg your pardon; I didn't think of Edwin.

GLAD. [*Smiling*] I suppose you mean Mr. Wagstaff.

DIANA. You know I don't mean anything of the kind. [*Offended*]

GLAD. Then it's Dr. Guy.

DIANA. [*Impetuously embracing Gladys*] Of course it is. I feel just like hugging everybody!

GLAD. You should have expended your superfluous energy upon him.

DIANA. I was afraid. He is not used to women yet. And he'll have to be treated carefully at first. May I take the light? I want to write it all down in my diary before I forget the particulars. [*Takes lighted candelabra*] You're not afraid?

GLAD. Not a bit. Besides the moon is up now.

DIANA. A diary is very interesting at all times; but the details of an engagement—It will be such interesting reading for the children. Won't it? [*Exit, R.2.E.*]

GLAD. [*Moonlight falls on carpet*] It seems all the happiness of the world is settling upon this house. [*Sits at table, L.*] Can fortune mean to make these favors last? [*Enter Winne through window, R. in F.*]

WINNE. All right, my hearty.

GLAD. What is that? [*Leaping to her feet*]

WINNE. It's only me! [*Grasping her by the arm*]

GLAD. And who are you? [*Making an effort to free herself*]

WINNE. No shines now! The easiest way is the best for you, my lady.

GLAD. [*Again struggling*] I'll call for help.

WINNE. Do! [*Releasing her*] Bring them all in, and let me tell them who you are.

GLAD. You know me?

WINNE. Excellently! I was at Lander's Landing one night when a woman killed a man. [*She moans*] You needn't wring your hands so piteously. I'm not going to tell on you.

GLAD. Then what brought you here?

WINNE. A trifling matter of business.

GLAD. This is no hour for business.

WINNE. Oh, I'm not overparticular in small matters. Night seems best suited to me. If I hadn't been about tonight I wouldn't have known you were here. And think how unfortunate that would have been.

GLAD. Now that you are here, what do you intend to do?

WINNE. In the first place I intend to light a candle. [*Producing candle from pocket*]

GLAD. [*Advancing on him*] You must not!

WINNE. [*Coolly*] And why not, pray?

GLAD. If anyone should come?

WINNE. [*In a matter-of-fact way*] That's just it; if anyone should come and find us in the dark it would look bad for both of us. And I have some character. [*Lights candle and places it on table*] A very comfortable home indeed. [*Looking about him*] I'd like to live here myself. But I suppose that's out of the question—eh?

GLAD. Have done with this nonsense! What do you demand of me?

WINNE. [*Coolly*] That's right! Come to business at once. You can imagine pretty nearly the nature of my demand; can't you?

GLAD. You ask me to purchase your silence.

WINNE. Guessed it the first time.

GLAD. [*Calmly*]   And what is the price?

WINNE.   Well; seeing that you are on terms of intimacy with the proprietor of all this luxury, let us say two thousand as a starter.

GLAD.   I have no money! Not a penny!

WINNE.   But you can get it from him.

GLAD.   No, I cannot!

WINNE.   Then let me get it. Let me help myself.

GLAD.   Let you rob my benefactor, let you plunder my friend? Never!

WINNE.   Come, come! Don't you be a fool. Better aid me in getting a little of his gear, than to go back to Louisiana in custody.

GLAD. [*Fiercely*]   I would sooner die, the keenest death the malefactor knows, aye, rot piecemeal in the deepest, foulest dungeon the state has reared, than to be the accomplice of a common thief.

WINNE.   And do you think I'm going to let you go scot-free? Let you roll in luxury while I tramp the highways in want of bread?

GLAD.   I am not responsible for your need.

WINNE.   I am, if I quit this house without a stiff reward. All I ask from you is to sit quietly there, while I go through the premises alone. [*Moving, R.2.*]

GLAD.   You shall not rob him! [*Seizing Winne. Candle falls on floor*]

WINNE.   Hards off, or it will be the worse for you. [*Attempts to free himself*]

GLAD.   No, no! You must not!

WINNE.   Let go, I say! [*Struggling still*]

GLAD. [*Finding herself growing weaker, breaks from him, R.2., and rushes L.2.*] Help! Help! Murder! Thieves!

WINNE.   Now you've done it! I'll see you hanged for this! [*Enter Fairfax, followed by Dr. Gaylord, Aunt Dorsie and Ben, L.2.E. Diana with candelabra, R.2.E.*]

FAIR.   In the name of Heaven, Gladys, what does this mean? [*Winne is caught at window, R.C., by Dr. Gaylord, attempting to escape*]

GAY.   This is what it means.

WINNE.   No, it isn't. It means that that young lady looking so white and innocent is a—

GLAD. [*To Winne*]   Stop! You shall not have the satisfaction. I shall confess my own sin.

OMNES.   Sin!

FAIR.   This is terrible!

GLAD.   A moment please. [*Waving them off*]

FAIR. [*Excitedly*]   Why don't you speak?

GLAD. [*In a faint voice*] I have cruelly deceived you all. My hands are stained with a husband's blood.

FAIR. Say no more! You are mad!

GLAD. Worse than mad—guilty! [*Reels and falls headlong at the feet of Fairfax*]

FAIR. [*Turning fiercely upon Winne*] You see what you have done? You have wrecked a wretched woman's life, you have hunted her to her death!

WINNE. [*Doggedly*] I have this to say—

FAIR. Say no more!

WINNE. I insist.

FAIR. Another word at your peril! [*Seizes Winne, forcing him to his knees. Picture*]

ACT V.

SCENE: *An apartment in Fairfax's house. It may be the same as Act III and IV, if desired, or a new scene at the option of the management. Doors, L.2., and windows, in F. If a new scene, there may be doors, in F., looking out onto a colonnade with awning of white and blue; landscape backing of the second act. Diana and Mrs. Dorsie discovered seated, R. Both have been weeping.* TIME: *The following morning.*

MRS. D. I cannot for the life of me realize it! What does she say?

DIANA. Nothing! She only rocks dismally to and fro, and says it is all true—every word of it.

MRS. D. [*Rising and going L.*] Well, I'll never refuse to believe anything after this!

DIANA. Did you see the doctor this morning?

MRS. D. He has been standing guard over that wretched thief, until a few moments ago I begged him to go to breakfast, and Ben has taken his place since.

DIANA. What are they going to do with him?

MRS. D. The thief?

DIANA. [*Vindictively*] Yes.

MRS. D. Take him to Saint Augustine, and hand him over to the authorities for housebreaking.

DIANA. I hope he will go to prison for life. [*Rising and going up, R.*]

MRS. D. Perhaps he has done us a great service. It would have been terrible for Edwin to have married a mystery.

DIANA. [*Coming down, R.*] Please don't talk that way, mama. Whatever is the secret of Gladys's life I feel certain she is a victim of circumstances; and that her guilt could never have been intentional.

MRS. D. I have as little disposition to condemn, my child; but facts are stubborn things and we mustn't let our feelings make us fools. [*Enter Dr. Gaylord, L.2.E.*]

DIANA. Have you seen Edwin?

GAY. No; he is locked in his own room.

DIANA. Perhaps he is sleeping?

GAY. Pain is not a sleeping potion, my dear! As I passed, I heard him pacing the floor. Poor fellow! I know he is in misery.

DIANA. Why didn't you knock?

GAY. No, no! Let the fever burn itself out, before you attempt to restore the system.

MRS. D. But a few kindly words—

GAY. The wound is too fresh for any local application, I tell you; and I don't believe in counterirritants.

DIANA. Dr. Guy, you are the most terrible man for having things your own way.

GAY. I can't help it, my dear. It's the privilege of a physician.

DIANA. Pain and physicians seem always associated.

GAY. Correct! But pain is always a little in advance. We are a rough set, I confess to you; often cross, sometimes unreasonable; but fighting fevers is not calculated to soothe the nerves, and whatever the spiteful say to the contrary, we are the ununiformed sentinels guarding the citadel of life from the cradle to the grave.

DIANA. [*Aside*] He will have the last word. [*Enter Fairfax slowly with evident traces of sorrow, L.2.E. To Mrs. Dorsie*] Mama, I'm going up to see Gladys. Will you come? [*Going, R.2.E.*]

MRS. D. Not now. [*Fairfax sinks into chair, L.*]

DIANA. Poor fellow! I feel as if I could cry my eyes out. [*Exit, R.2.E.*]

FAIR. [*In a low voice*] Where is—she?

MRS. D. Gladys?

FAIR. [*Nods his head*] Yes.

MRS. D. In her own room. Do you wish to see her?

FAIR. [*Bitterly*] No; there is no use in seeing her; it would do no good. Nothing can do any good now, everything is hopelessly lost.

GAY. [*To Mrs. Dorsie*] Leave me alone with him for a moment, please. [*She sighs heavily and exit, R.2.E. After her exit Dr. Gaylord goes over and places his hand sympathetically upon Fairfax's shoulder*]

FAIR. [*Looking up*] Well?

GAY. Matters are not as bad as that.

FAIR. Bad! [*With a sad smile*] They could not be worse; there is a limit even to misery--[*Starting up with the energy of desperation*] O Guy, my boy, you don't know how completely that woman had my heart. I had no thought that did not center in her; no hope of which she was not the inspiration; no wish that she was not at once its source and its fulfillment! And now, to think that this is the end of all! It seems like dropping from the heights of Heaven into the depths of Hell!

GAY. She is not dead yet.

FAIR. [*Hotly*] She is worse than dead. To see her in her coffin would be less pitiful—a self-confessed—I cannot say the word; it is too terrible—even for utterance. [*Excitedly*]

GAY. Calm yourself, my dear old Ned. There, now take a chair, and let us reason together. [*Fairfax drops into seat, R.*] What do you intend to do with the gentleman upstairs?

FAIR. [*Angrily, rising*] Do you mean that fiend—that wretch?

GAY. That is the party.

FAIR. I have not thought of that yet; of course he must be given over to the authorities.

GAY. [*Coolly*] That's what I thought at first.

FAIR. At first? [*Looking closely at Dr. Gaylord*]

GAY. But I have changed my mind. That fellow must go free.

FAIR. [*Amazed*] Free! He's a common thief. A fellow to whom death should be a boon.

GAY. Not a bit of doubt of that at all. He has confessed as much to me.

FAIR. [*With a shudder*] And she has been his associate! His confederate! It is terrible. [*Going R.*]

GAY. [*Going L.*] No, their meeting was quite accidental. He was fleeing from justice and ran into the poor hut which served her for a home, and thus became possessed of her secret. Their next meeting we all attended.

FAIR. And do you think I will permit the scoundrel to go free?

GAY. As you now appear to feel, you owe him no resentment; he came just in time to save you.

FAIR. True! True! [*With a low moan*] I lost sight of that.

GAY. Besides you have no desire to have her harmed?

FAIR. Harmed! If I could suffer in her place, every pang she now endures would surely be mine. Heaven knows, she has known pain enough.

GAY. More than you can even imagine. I met her in those days when she lived with him.

FAIR. [*Amazed*] You never told me that.

GAY. There was no occasion. I believe she is a more sinned against than sinning woman, and if the truth is to be told, I don't blame her for knocking the villain on the head.

FAIR. [*With dignity*] But she should not have deceived me so. I was surely worthy of some consideration.

GAY. That was a mistake, of course.

FAIR. [*Bitterly*] Mistake! It was worse—it was a crime!

GAY. [*Aside*] As a peacemaker I'm not a brilliant success. [*Aloud*] Well, am I to free the fellow? [*Going, R.2.E.*]

FAIR. For what reason?

GAY. Simply to save Gladys.

FAIR. Save her? I don't comprehend.

GAY. If we send him to prison, you know the old adage that misery loves company, and he will revenge himself on us all, by telling all, probably more than he knows. And you don't want her to go to—? [*Hesitates*]

FAIR. [*Impulsively*] Prison! No, no! You are right—quite right. Do what you think best for all concerned! [*Wrings his hands*] I don't know what we should all do, but for you.

GAY. I'm sorry I am able to do so little, when you need so much. [*Enter Gladys robed for travelling, very pale and worn, R.2.E. Fairfax, on seeing her, goes to chair, L. Dr. Gaylord presses her hand and exit, R.2.E.*]

GLAD. [*Aside, regarding Fairfax tenderly*] He turns his back upon me! Perhaps he is afraid to lift his eyes lest he should see the brand of Cain. [*Aloud and advancing, catching the table for support*] I am going away from Fairfax now, and I have come to say good-bye.

FAIR. [*Without looking up and in a low voice*] Good-bye!

GLAD. [*With emotion, after a pause*] Will you not take my hand for the last time? It will make me stronger, and I so need strength. [*Fairfax extends his hand in silence*] Thanks! You are always kind. When I am gone don't think too harshly of me. I have not done right always, but I am not wholly bad. I don't say this now in any vain hope of forgiveness—that I know is hopeless—but that you may have some little touch of tenderness for the woman you loved so wildly once—I would not go out of your heart and home utterly debased.

FAIR. Then, why did you deceive me?

GLAD. Because I was a fool. When I came here first, my history belonged to myself; it was no one's affair but my own, and when I learned to love you, how could I tell you such a sickening story? I feared you would turn from me in disgust, and to lose you—I could not think of that!

FAIR. You should have told me all.

GLAD. Did I not offer to do so? Did you not last night destroy the paper the contained it all?

FAIR. Yes, yes! But I could not imagine it as bad as this. Besides, I asked you if you were innocent of crime, if there was any shadow of guilt upon your soul, and you—what did you say?

GLAD. That I was innocent.

FAIR. Ay! You gave me your word, your solemn declaration, and I accepted it, without question. Now it is a different story.

GLAD. [*Calmly*] No; it is the same.

FAIR. The same! You forget your statement of last night—made before the whole family. [*Shudders*]

GLAD. I forget nothing.

FAIR. [*Sinking into seat*] Unhappy woman! You should pray then for some nepenthe, some deep and dark oblivion where you might lose yourself forever.

GLAD. Go on! I deserve all this. It is a part of my punishment.

FAIR. I have no desire to punish; my heart is too full of pity to think of penalties.

GLAD. [*After a pause*] You know part of my past; I feel in justice to myself you should know all. At fifteen my father died and left me alone in the world. I had all the standard accomplishments—a little French, less Latin and some music. I could paint, too, and I found little trouble in securing a position as governess in a planter's family in Tennessee. The youngest son admired me, and well—before I was nineteen I was his wife. As a boy he was dissolute, as a man he was brutal. Drink and gaming brought us to live in a miserable hut on the Mississippi, where our only child fell ill of a fever. Although his cruel treatment had destroyed all feeling for him, still I felt it to be my duty to try to save him, even at the sacrifice of myself and child. I begged, entreated, implored him to reform. I was answered by curses and blows.

FAIR. [*Fiercely, aside*] The wretch!

GLAD. Day by day I stood by the side of my dying child and watched it slowly fading from the world. It was ordered liquor as a stimulant; he robbed his dying child and appeased his own gross appetite!

FAIR. [*Aside*] Can this be true?

GLAD. One night—your friend, Dr. Gaylord, accidentally found his way to our home, and in the goodness of his heart left me money, ordering me to take my child to the sea.

FAIR. [*Aside*] God bless him!

GLAD. This money—the price of my child's life—he attempted to take from me and in the struggle which followed he was—well—he was—

FAIR. [*Looking her in the face*] Killed! Go on!

GLAD. But as I hope for Heaven, I did not do it! In endeavoring to murder me the bullet penetrated his own neck and—

FAIR. [*Fiercely earnest*] You speak the truth?

GLAD. I swear it.

FAIR. [*Aside*] Thank Heaven! [*Aloud*] And you?

GLAD. Fled—to New Orleans. There my child died, and I fell ill. When I recovered, I determined to bury the past forever, and, changing my name, began life anew. You know the rest. The world which I had given up was illuminated by your love, and I fell in love with life again!

FAIR. [*In a low voice*] A sad story indeed.

GLAD. And now, let us say farewell and part forever!

FAIR. [*With vehemence*] No, Gladys! We shall not part! In another land where we are unknown, where no whisper of this hideous past will ever dare intrude, we will love and live together!

GLAD. [*Retreating*] No—it is impossible!

FAIR. You do not love me or you would not say so!

GLAD. Love you! If all the world were offered in exchange I would refuse it. But let us not forget the barrier we cannot bridge. I should feel guilty at every glance you gave me. No, no! Our paths lie far apart. After today they will never cross again. [*Going, R.2.E. Enter Dr. Gaylord, followed by Diana and Mrs. Dorsie*]

GAY. This thief is grateful for our clemency and desires to make slight amends. [*Enter Winne in charge of Ben, R.2.E. They all face him*]

WINNE. I wanted to say before I go, that this young woman did not kill her husband at all—that she is not guilty of murder, whatever else she may have done!

GLAD. [*Eagerly*] How do you know? I saw him fall.

WINNE. Yes, and cut your stick at once. But I remained behind and nursed him back to life.

GLAD. To life—say you? Oh, this is glad good news!

FAIR. Good news! His life is a greater barrier to our happiness than even his death had been.

GLAD. I never thought of that.

WINNE. No, sir—see there is no life out of him yet! I tell you a tough customer was that same James Marrigold.

GAY. [*Starting*] James Marrigold, do you say? Is this his picture? [*Exhibiting photo to Winne*]

WINNE. That's him—sure.

GAY. Then I can testify to his death.

DIANA and MRS. D. *You* can?

GAY. Most assuredly! He died at the Hotel Dieu in New Orleans of yellow fever. I attended him and he gave me this on his deathbed, with an admonition to give it to his wife should I ever meet her. I never expected to be able to do so—but now—[*Giving it to Gladys*]

GLAD. [*Breathlessly*] And he did not die at my hands after all. I am not a—

FAIR. You are the best woman in the world.

GLAD. My life! [*Rushes, L., to his arms*]

DIANA. This is just splendid! [*Embraces Dr. Gaylord*]

MRS. D. [*Joyously*] It's really like a play!

WINNE. I suppose I can go.

GAY. Let me show you out. [*Opens the door and bows Winne out*] I say, I'm sorry I cannot invite you to call again.

WINNE. [*With mock politeness*] The regret is mutual. Farewell! [*Exit, R.C.E.*]

DIANA. And we are happy after all.

GAY. All! Except Ben, and he shall join in the general joy, if he has a wish ungratified.

BEN. Well, fac' is mas'r, if—if—

MRS. D. For goodness sake, speak out!

BEN. If you would buy Marfah—

FAIR. She shall be yours tomorrow. [*Ben dances*]

GLAD. It seems like a tale of enchanted ground.

GAY. And you and Diana are the fairies.

DIANA. And Cousin Fairfax and Gladys are?

FAIR. The happiest couple out of storybooks!

CURTAIN

THE WHITE SLAVE

The version of *The White Slave* printed here is based on a holograph "copied by Geo. J. Secor, N.Y. 1882," and owned by Mr. Robert Campbell. In addition to the main text, the manuscript also contains two scenes, a short addition for Act II, and a long scene at the beginning of Act III, which Bartley Campbell added to *The White Slave* shortly after its opening performance. It also contains the scene at the beginning of Act VI which was usually omitted after the first performances. From later copies of *The White Slave* it is evident that the play underwent many minor additions and subtractions at the hands of actors and managers. Of the plays of Campbell printed here this version of *The White Slave* is probably the only one free from such changes.

CAST OF CHARACTERS

LISA, *the White Slave*

DAPHNE, *an octoroon*

MRS. LEE, *a Virginia widow*

MISS LETTY LEE, *engaged to Jack*

NANCE, *a quadroon*

AUNT MARTHA, *a better half*

CLAY BRITTON, *a young Southerner*

JUDGE HARDIN, *who guards his family name*

BILL LACY, *deals only in horses and niggers*

JOB, *negro preacher and butler at Big Bend*

JACK HAZELTON, *a poor young doctor*

CAPTAIN STRYKER, *of the Belle Creole*

NATCHEZ JIM, *a gambler*

COUNT STRAIN, *a beat*

BANCROFT, *overseer at Osceola*

CLEM, *the other half*

P. HENRY STITCH, *a lawyer*

LITTLE JIM, *Daphne's child*

CLERK JAMIESON, *of the Belle Creole*

BARKEEPER

PASSENGER

PASSENGERS, SLAVES, ETC.

ACT I.

Scene 1st: *Drop representing Big Bend Plantation, Kentucky. Mississippi River with the Missouri shore beyond in 4. Sunset. Large windows looking out on veranda at F. at 3. Folding doors, R.3.E. & L.2.E. Large fireplace with fire burning briskly at R.2.E. Bookcase with bust of Henry Clay on top between windows in F. Sub-wall running above from L.2.E. to nearly C. of stage, 7 feet high. On top, railing two feet high, with heavy curtains depending. Large chair before fire. Long seat in front of sub-wall. Apartment elegantly furnished with antiques. Landscape. Snow storm. Enter Job, R.3.E. Time: March 1857.*

Job. [*Raking fire*] Ah! poor ol massa, your time in dis wo'ld is gettin' mighty short. [*Going to fire. Enter Aunt Martha*] Dat you Mar'fa?

Martha. Yes, indeedy. Rheumatiz couldn't pin me down no longer; I had to come up and la'n how de massa is.

Job. Berry bad! [*Shakes head dolefully*] De lamp of life is just flickerin' like a tallow dip in de west win'. A little bref from de angel ob def and he's gone.

Martha. [*Mournfully*] Deah knows we'll all miss him. De young massa is too fon' o' horses to care much for niggers.

Job. Now don't say noffin about de young massa. All young men are wile; an' no man cars much for Hebbin till he's had a tussle wid de debbil. Clay's got a good heart and I'se preached de gospel too long not to know how important dat is.

Martha. I'se got noffin to say against him. He's kind nuff to all us niggahs. So you think de ole massa will die?

Job. All flesh is grass, as de gospel says, and de harvest time for him am mighty close.

Martha. Can't none of us do noffin for him?

Job. Yes. Ye can all pray for him. Brac prayers turn as white as silver before dey get to Hebbin; and maybe dey buy as much marcy as de best. [*Goes to table*]

Martha. Glory to de Lawd! You'se a good man, Uncle Job, and I'se goin' to have a prayer meeting right off. [*Going L.3.E.*] Will you come down? Oh, dat rheumatiz!

Job. I can't leab hyar now; de 'casion am too solemn; but tell de chilern if dey don't put dere whole hearts in dem prayers, dey might as well try to ketch bass widout bait. De Lawd ain't gwine to pay no 'tention to lip salve.

Martha. No, indeedy! I'll come back an' tell you how de meetin' goes. Oh, dat rheumatiz! [*Exit, L.3.E.*]

Job. My bones is in sympathy wid you. I spec when massa dies dar am gwine to be a change hyar at Big Bend. Missa Lee habn't come all de way from Ole Virginney for noffin. [*Crosses to W.E. Enter Stitch, L.3.E., followed by Jack Hazleton*]

Stitch. [*To Jack*] Don't venture further until I feel the way. [*To Job*] Is—is Mrs. Harriet Lee of Virginia still stopping here?

Jack. [*Eagerly*] Is Miss Letty Lee with her?

Stitch. [*Stops him*] Now, Jack, my boy, you must be patient. If Mrs. Lee should dream for a minute that I had betrayed the lovely Letty's whereabouts to you, I would lose my best client.

Jack. But think of it, Stitch—

Stitch. Mr. Stitch.

Jack. To have a woman you worship—who has promised you her heart—spirited away.

Stitch. There was a proviso in the promise—her mother's consent. As to the spiriting away, she merely accompanied her mother on a business mission.

Jack. Without leaving her address?

Stitch. She didn't know where she was going.

Jack. [*Desperately*] But I must see her. [*Goes to chair*]

Stitch. Of course you must, but young men possessed of only a doctor's sign and a bit of parchment must bide their time. [*Turning to Job*] Did you say I could see Mrs. Lee?

Job. If your eye-sight is fust-class ye can.

Jack. [*Impatiently*] And Letty?

Stitch. Now my dear Jack, if you will be good enough to listen to reason.

Jack. Hang reason! It has always been the enemy of love. I can't think of anything but Letty. [*Drops into chair, R.2.*]

Stitch. [*To Job*] Take this card to Mrs. Harriet Lee [*Job takes card*] and say [*Looking about him*] I'm in the library. Am I right when I say library?

Job. Dis am de library, if dat's what ye am gettin' at. [*Going L.2.E.*]

Stitch. You have grasped my meaning with an intelligence that does you credit. [*Bows and points off L.2.E.*]

Job. [*Aside*] Bofe crazy as loons. [*Exit*]

STITCH. Now, I must insist on your retiring to the hotel at the landing until I can arrange a meeting for you with Miss Letty.

JACK. I won't move till I see her.

STITCH. Won't move? Are you mad? Do you want to ruin your uncle?

JACK. A client more or less don't matter.

STITCH. But she is more than a client, [*Excitedly*] I love her! [*Stops embarrassed*]

JACK. [*Jumping up*] Eh? At your age? [*Shakes head*]

STITCH. Age! I'm only fifty.

JACK. But you've had one wife already. Is this wise?

STITCH. Old Solomon who could double discount my wisdom had five hundred. You betray your training. You think because a man can only have some diseases once, he cannot have a plurality of anything else. Wives are not measles. Hello, who is this? [*Looking L.2.E.*] The lisping whisper of a woman's dress. What music! Now, Jack, you must go. [*Catching by collar and pushing him C.*] Now! Now! [*Enter Letty, L.2.E.*]

JACK. Don't, I say!

LETTY. [*Alarmed*] Oh, don't! Please, you will choke him! [*In distress*]

JACK. [*Breaking away*] Letty, my love, my life! [*Opens arms*] Don't you know your Jack?

LETTY. [*Amazed*] Why, Mr. Hazleton, I'm so glad! [*Embrace*]

STITCH. [*Comes down L.*] Now, she's choking him! If the old lady should come! [*Looking off L.2. nervously*]

LETTY. How did you know I was here?

JACK. Uncle Stitch there—

LETTY. [*Excitedly*] Told you! Of course he did! The dear good old soul! [*Throws her arms around Stitch*]

STITCH. [*Returning embrace warmly*] Sweetest, darling, petite—

JACK. [*Indignantly*] Here, quit that! [*Taking Letty, R.*] What do you mean, sir?

STITCH. The young lady didn't object, and I found it rather pleasant. Hello! [*Going L.2.*] The rustle of a woman's dress again. Fly!

LETTY. It's mama's step; where shall we go?

JACK. Behind here; we can sit in the window and the curtains will conceal us.

LETTY. Oh, Jack! This is perfect Paradise. [*Behind curtain*]

STITCH. If I had a family history—if my name was Randolph or Curtis or anything but puny plebeian Stitch, I might make a conquest of this excellent woman's heart. [*Letty laughs*] Stop that giggling! What a fool I was to bring that Jack!

MRS. LEE. [*Enters L.2.E. and bows to Stitch*] You are very prompt.

STITCH. [*Bowing*] In a matter of business always.

MRS. LEE. Take a seat. It was a long journey, but I couldn't trust a stranger. [*Sits L. of table*]

STITCH. [*Sits R. of table*] I am at your service.

MRS. LEE. I want your advice in a matter where my daughter's interests are concerned.

STITCH. Exactly. [*Puts hand on her caressingly*]

MRS. LEE. [*Reprimanding*] Mr. Stitch! [*Withdraws hand*]

STITCH. I beg pardon! [*Bows low and sits*]

MRS. LEE. The husband of my eldest sister, the owner of this place—

STITCH. You refer to Judge Hardin?

MRS. LEE. Yes. He is dying. For years he has been an invalid; indeed, ever since the death of his daughter, an only child, which sad event occurred in Italy seventeen years since, he has been the victim of the deepest melancholia. He has not been able to leave this house for six years.

STITCH. Indeed! [*Abstractedly stabs himself with a pen*] Oh!

MRS. LEE. The estate has been managed by an adopted son, Clay Britton.

STITCH. The name is familiar.

MRS. LEE. He is the son of Judge Hardin's old law partner, and while good hearted and all that, is, I fear, too fond of the race course and bad company. Indeed, [*Sighs heavily*] I fear he has involved the estate to such an extent that I dread a settlement.

STITCH. Is there a will?

MRS. LEE. There is—but I have not seen it.

STITCH. Are you—

MRS. LEE. No, I'm not mentioned, but the judge told me he had settled something on Letty. I fear it is but a trifle for I think he is disposed to give the bulk of his property to Lisa, the housekeeper's child.

STITCH. [*Surprised*] White or colored?

MRS. LEE. An octoroon girl to whom for some reason he has given the training of a lady, and thereby created a great deal of scandal.

STITCH. Is this Lisa handsome?

MRS. LEE. Very! No one would believe she had a drop of African blood in her veins.

STITCH. [*Pause*] Mother of—of Lisa, pretty?

MRS. LEE. A quadroon almost white; but why do you ask?

STITCH. [*Affecting air of wisdom*] I thought perhaps if her mother was beautiful, Lisa might have a closer claim upon the judge—

MRS. LEE. You think Lisa might be his own child?

STITCH. Under the peculiar institution—that is—

MRS. LEE. I know such things have occurred, but not so in this case. The only time I spoke to him of Lisa he refused to answer, but murmuring his dead child's name, turned his face to the wall and wept.

STITCH. There seems to be some mystery here.

MRS. LEE. There is, and I want you to solve it if you can, and as for your pay—

STITCH. Don't speak of it.

MRS. LEE. But I prefer—

STITCH. No, no! I know lawyers are a sordid set, but oh, how I adore— [*Tenderly, half rising*]

MRS. LEE. Eh? [*In surprise*]

STITCH. [*Relapsing*] The idea of doing something unselfish for one whom I—[*Half rising*]

MRS. LEE. [*Reprovingly*] Mr. Stitch!

STITCH. So thoroughly esteem. [*Sits down. Mrs. Lee rises, Letty laughs without, L.3.E.*]

MRS. LEE. [*Looking at Stitch who is embarrassed*] What was that?

STITCH. [*Rising and going C.*] That? The birds singing in the naked boughs. The poor little birds that have sought shelter from the snows in vain.

MRS. LEE. Sentiment is not becoming in a lawyer, Mr. Stitch. You are stopping at the hotel at the landing, I suppose?

STITCH. I am.

MRS. LEE. We will make room for you here tomorrow. [*Gives hand*] Goodbye.

STITCH. [*Aside*] A hint to go. [*Aloud*] Goodbye. I'll call tomorrow morning. [*In a whisper at curtains*] Hist, Jack, follow me. [*Looks tenderly at Mrs. Lee who has gone to fire-place*] Oh, to be exiled from the things we love! [*Exit, L.3.E.*]

JACK. [*Comes from behind curtains with Letty on tiptoe*] Farewell, my own. [*In a whisper*]

LETTY. [*In a whisper*] Oh, Jack, must you go! [*He kisses her and exits L.3.*]

MRS. LEE. What was that, Letty?

LETTY. [*Innocently*] The wind, I think.

MRS. LEE. No; it was not the wind.

LETTY. Was it a familiar sound, mama?

MRS. LEE. Very familiar and as reprehensible as familiar. [*Looks at Letty suspiciously. Enter Lisa, R.3.E. Music*]

LETTY. What's the matter, Lisa? Is uncle worse?

LISA. Much worse. I fear he has but a few hours more to live.

MRS. LEE. For pity's sake you needn't cry so much. You're well taken care of—freedom papers and a fortune. I like people to be sincere.

LISA. Oh, madam, I hope you don't think—

MRS. LEE. [*Significantly*] I think those who have managed to improve every opportunity to the exclusion of others who have natural claims, are capable of a little hypocrisy, [*Goes R.3.E.*] when it serves for a mask.

LISA. What have I done?

MRS. LEE. Done! Robbed my child! Brought reproach on this house.

LETTY. [*Shocked*] Don't, mama.

LISA. [*In a low tone*] In what way have I done this?

MRS. LEE. By seizing on an old man's weakness and winning his heart. I can't say you alone are guilty, but it lies between yourself and scheming mother.

LISA. [*With feeling*] 'Tis false.

MRS. LEE. Don't dare! You forget who you are. Your white skin and dainty rearing cannot obliterate the fact that you belong to a race of slaves.

LETTY. [*Appealingly*] Mama!

MRS. LEE. [*Haughtily*] Come, Letty. [*Exit, R.3.E. Lisa stands with hands locked and head bowed, silently gazing on the floor*]

LETTY. [*With sympathy*] Don't mind her, Lisa, she will be sorry some day. Please forget it. [*Exit, R.3.E.*]

LISA. [*Pause*] Forget it! Forget what I am! Do what I will, hope what I may, the curse of Cain still clings to me! [*In despair. Enter Nance, L.2.E.*] Oh, how wretched I am!

NANCE. What is the matter, my child?

LISA. [*Bitterly*] Nothing. I have only been reminded of my heritage; of the doom attendant on the birth of a slave. Mother, I owe this to you!

NANCE. [*Amazed*] To me, Lisa?

LISA. Ay! To you! My white face made you vain of your offspring, and you took advantage of a good master to rear me like a lady. Didn't you know that the farce couldn't last? That beneath the mask of beauty that was my bane flowed the tell-tale current, that sooner or later must seek the light?

NANCE. It was my master's wish.

LISA. Yes; he thought it was kind to fill an octoroon's mind with false hopes! To bid her heart go out to those so far above her that it makes her dizzy when she comprehends the distance. Why didn't you insist on my being kept in my place; among my own race, so ignorant that I would never realize the depths of my degradation. [*Falls into chair, R. Music*]

NANCE. Lisa, I have never seen you this way before. Who has spoken to you? Was it Clay?

LISA. Clay! Oh, no! Thank God! Not Clay! It would kill me if he were to speak so! [*Weeps*]

NANCE. [*Sits at table*]   I fear I have discovered your secret, my child. You love Clay Britton.

LISA. Yes, I do love him! Love him as one may love the stars that we know we cannot reach. It was my slavish nature, I suppose, to love, dog-like, whoever gave me a kind word; but I was young and full of a vague hope that I see now was worse than madness. [*Goes to sofa, L., and sits*]

NANCE. You don't know how hard it is to hear this from your lips! It makes me feel guilty! I can't look you in the face! Lisa, child, forgive me! [*Kneels before sofa*]

LISA. No! No! Not on your knees to me! Forgive me for speaking so cruelly to you, you who have always been so good, so kind, so tender; I did not mean it; but oh, I had to speak, my heart was so full! [*Goes to fire-place*]

CLAY. [*Outside*]   Hold my horse. [*Enters, L.3.E.*] Ah, Lisa, is that you? How is the judge? [*Lays aside hat*]

LISA. [*In a low voice with forced calmness*]   Worse.

CLAY. I'm sorry. [*Stops to think at table C.*]

JOB. [*Enters, R.3.E.*]   Missa Nance, de massa want you all by yourself.

NANCE. Yes, Job, I'm going. [*Exit, R.3.E. Job exits, R.3.E.*]

CLAY. [*L. of table*]   I'd like to go to him, but perhaps he wants to say something to Nance in private.

LISA. [*At fire-place*]   He will be glad to see you; he was complaining only today that he had not seen you for a long time.

CLAY. It's too bad, but I went off with Lacy to the races at Memphis and—

LISA. Lost your money.

CLAY. How do you know?

LISA. You never win where you are with him.

CLAY. [*Incredulously*]   Do you think that my friend—

LISA. Is not your friend at all.

CLAY. Nonsense. A woman's prejudice. Why, Lisa, next to you, I haven't a better friend on earth than Bill Lacy. By George, I'm sorry to hear the judge is worse, and I away! It looks like ingratitude to one who has been better to me than a father!

LISA. Go to him now and say just what you have said to me; it will do him more good than all the drugs in the world.

CLAY. I'll try it. I don't know what we would do at Big Bend but for you. [*Goes R.3.E.*] Lacy will be here directly, but never mind. [*Exit, R.3.E.*]

Lisa. [*Scornfully*] Lacy! A wretch who boasts that he never deals in anything but "horses and niggers." A villain who under the guise of friendship robs his friend at cards and leads him to destruction. Before Clay knew him, he was a strict business man; now Big Bend takes care of itself, and even Clay's very nature seems changed. I've tried to warn him, but what am I? A leaf in a storm. [*Music. Enter Nance and Clay bearing between them the tottering form of Judge Hardin, whose long white hair and beard falls upon his breast and shoulders, R.3.E.*]

Judge. [*In a feeble voice*] Before the fire. I feel cold, and the heat and light will do me good. There! [*Lisa arranges arm chair and falls on her knees before the Judge as soon as he is seated. Red medium from fireplace. Nance, R. of chair, and Clay, L.*] It is nearly over. [*Closes eyes wearily*] The long, long fight for a life that has no sunshine left. [*Sees Lisa looking up into his face*] Who is that? [*Nervously*]

Nance. That is Lisa.

Clay. Don't you know Lisa? Nance's child?

Judge. [*As if wondering*] I thought it was Grace, my poor dead child; she whom we buried years and years ago. You remember, Nance, the lonely funeral—the little grave under the tall poplars at Florence? And her child— her child. [*Closes his eyes with a moan*]

Clay. [*Surprised, looks searchingly at Nance*] Her child? She had no child.

Nance. It is a fancy of his—his mind has given away.

Lisa. [*To Judge*] Don't you know me? Lisa.

Judge. [*Pause, scans her face*] Yes, my dear, dear child, I know you very, very well. [*Places hand on her head*] Will you be sorry when I am no longer here to trouble you?

Lisa. [*In a broken voice*] I'm losing my only friend.

Judge. No! No! Nance is still here, and [*Turning, sees Clay bending over him*] Clay. He will always be your friend. See to it, my boy, son of my best friend, see to it. Guard Lisa from harm as if she were my own child.

Clay. You have been all in all to me; I will be only too glad to do anything you ask.

Judge. That is all I wish. I have given Lisa and Nance their freedom papers and an annuity. You will pay it regularly, won't you?

Clay. [*In low voice*] Yes.

Judge. I know you will. You are an honest lad. See to the poor slaves, they have been faithful to me and mine. [*To Lisa*] Go with Clay for a few minutes; I want to speak to Nance alone—quite alone. [*Lisa rises, her face buried in her hands, and exits, L.2.E., with Clay, sobbing*]

NANCE. [*In a whisper*] They are gone.

JUDGE. See that no one is listening, Nance, my girl; see that no one is listening.

NANCE. [*She looks about and then returns to Judge*] We are quite alone.

JUDGE. Nance, I had a dream last night—a strange dream. [*Music*] We were on a ship going to Europe. Grace, my beautiful only child fresh from school, and yourself just as we were years ago. Everything was the same. She was singing softly to me; my hand rested on her chestnut braids, and her little head close to my heart. Then we came to land and I stood in Florence on that dreadful night when the marquis fled, and my daughter became a mother without the name of wife; then I fell to cursing him and his, and as I spoke the Heavens above opened and from the crystal gates of God came a voice saying "Forgive! Forgive! And save, oh, save my child!" It was Grace's dear sweet voice, and with its music still in my ears I awoke. [*This is said with great effort*]

NANCE. [*Stroking his head*] It was a good dream; and before you go to join Miss Grace you *will* save Lisa, her child, won't you? [*Pleadingly*]

JUDGE. What do you mean?

NANCE. Tell her the truth, that she is not my child, that she is your own flesh and blood—free born white woman.

JUDGE. Hush-sh! No, no! Do you want me to write shame upon the grave of my dear dead. Would Lisa be happier were she to know the truth?

NANCE. But justice—

JUDGE. Justice to the living—justice to the dead forbid it. I have made Lisa free, as she has always been, and you as well. In a foreign land you can live happily, your secret safe, my name unsullied. You will do this, Nance, for my sake, for *her* sake! [*Pleadingly*]

NANCE. If you ask it.

JUDGE. [*Excitedly wringing his hands*] I do ask it. And now swear it. [*Raising right hand solemnly*] As you hope for Heaven, as you fear Hell. You solemnly swear to me, to me who now stands on the brink of the grave, within the dark shadows of death, that you will never betray my dead child's secret, never reveal her shame.

NANCE. [*Sinking at his feet*] I swear!

JUDGE. If you ever break this awful oath I will burst the bonds of death to meet you face to face; remember that, remember that! [*Sinks back exhausted*]

NANCE. O! you are not dead, master, you are not dead!

¶JUDGE. Hush-sh. You will find in that box in the book-case, which this key will open [*Gives her key*], your freedom papers and Lisa's. There is also a package containing a curl of Grace's hair and a letter from Lisa's father.

NANCE. From the marquis?

JUDGE. Yes, a whining letter asking my forgiveness, for the wrong he had done my child.

NANCE. And you?

JUDGE. Treated it with contempt; but I kept it, I kept it to revel in the anguish of his written remorse! Call Lisa and Clay now, [*Gasping*] and Mrs. Lee. [*Nance, weeping, goes L.2.E. and passes out an instant. Enter Lisa followed by Clay quickly. She goes at once to his side. Nance re-enters, L.2. and exits softly, R.3.E.*]

LISA. See how pale he is! Is he dying?

CLAY. [*Sadly*] I fear the time has come. [*Turning away his head*]

JUDGE. [*In a very weak voice*] Lisa, come, come closer to me.

LISA. My heart is breaking. [*Burying her face on his breast*]

JUDGE. Clay will take care of you—he has promised—and Nance—cling close to Nance. I can't see you. [*Enter Mrs. Lee, followed by Letty, followed by Nance, R.3.E., while Job enters, R.3.E., with candelabra*]

MRS. LEE. Is he dead?

CLAY. Not yet.

JOB. All the people have comed up from der cabins and dey would like to sing a hymn for pooh ole massa.

MRS. LEE. [*To Judge*] Your people want to sing a hymn for you. Shall they? [*Judge nods his head affirmatively*]

NANCE. [*Starts L.3.*] Shall I bring them in?

MRS. LEE. Let them remain in the hall. [*Job goes out L.3.E. and the plantation hands sing soft and low a hymn. Job returns during song at conclusion, and while it is pp. the dying man falls back rigid*]

CLAY. It is all over. [*Hymn. Lisa sobs. Job falls upon his knees at table. Mrs. Lee bends over Judge, R. of chair. Clay turns his face away leaning against back of chair. Nance drops on sofa, L. Slow curtain*]

ACT II.

SCENE 1ST: *Same as Act I.*
TIME: *April 1857.*

JOB. [*Discovered*] Dar am no use talkin', I'se afraid Big Bend's in mighty bad luck. It's free weeks since pore old massa died, and noffin seems as it us't to was. Ev'ry niggah on de place war's his heart in his boots, an goes trampin' round on it all day. [*Sings*]

> Down in de co'n feel I hears dat mournful soun;
> All de darkies am a-weepin',
> Massa's in de cole, cole groun'.

[*Goes to R. window and wipes his eyes*] Yes, indeedy, down in de cole, cole groun'. [*Aunt Martha and Clem outside quarreling, L.3.E.*]

MARTHA & CLEM. You is to blame! No, I isn't! No, I isn't! Yes, you is! You is. [*They enter L.3.E., Martha holding dead hen by the legs*]

CLEM. Don't you lift that poultry to me.

MARTHA. Den you take car. I bust ye up, ole man. [*Threateningly raises hen to strike*]

JOB. [*Angrily to Martha*] Stop dat! Do you suppose de good Lo'd made dat ole hin for you to strike yer husband? W'r ye gwine to get your forgiveness?

CLEM. [*Excitedly*] She don't car for forgiveness! De debbil has been stirrin' dat ole woman up for—for a week.

MARTHA. Don't ye done tell me dat. I'se been an angel long 'nuff.

JOB. [*Desperately to Martha*] Shut yer business!

CLEM. I said—

JOB. Shut yer business! [*After a pause*] Ye ought to be ashamed. Two ole people like you is—married forty years, fightin' like two coons up a sycamore. What's de Bible say? Brudderin should live in peace and harmonies together.

CLEM. It's easy for brudders to live in peace, but a man dat could lib forty years wid dat woman widout fightin', he's a wingless angel; he is—

MARTHA. Ye didn't talk dat way when ye was suckin' roun' to get me to marry you. Den ye was full ob mean sweetness.

CLEM. I nebber sucked roun'.

MARTHA. Ye did suck roun'.

CLEM. [*To Job*] Did I suck roun'?

MARTHA. Yes, ye did, jis' as suck as suck could be.

CLEM. I lebe it to preacher Job. Did I?

JOB. [*Trying to remember*] I disrecolleck. Forty years ago when ye bofe come to me an' asked me to trust ye for a marriage, I think it was suck and suck all roun'.

CLEM. Well, dat's all over, ah! We come up hy'ar to get a divorce, right off.

MARTHA. Can't be too soon for me.

Job. My chilr'n, divorce is a bad business. It's like sawing off a man's head to cure de toof ache, besides I don't know what de Bible says on dat question. 'Pears to me it's berry silent, terrible silent!

Clem. You tied us togeder, didn't ye?

Job. 'Cordin' to de Scripters, I did.

Martha. Den ye can let us loose just de same.

Job. I'se afraid de lettin' loose'ness is left to ole Judge Peters on de hill.

Clem. Dat ole debbil?

Job. Dat's jis' as it should be. De Lo'd jines togeder an' de debbil lets loose again.

Martha. I tell ye what it is; I isn't gwine to live wid dat ole rooster [*Indicating Clem*] any longah. I'se been 'posed on long nuff. [*Wipes eyes. Enter Lisa, L.2.E.*]

Job. [*To Martha*] Shut your shut up, before Miss Lisa. [*Pushes Martha up stage*]

Lisa. [*In surprise*] Why Martha, what is the matter?

Job. Dey's quarrelled, Miss Lisa; dey want divorce.

Lisa. What for?

Martha. His dog's all de time killin' my hen. Dar's a bird I'se raised from de shell. [*Holding up hen*] When it done doan' hab no moah fedders dan a tadpole, I made a roost for it on the head of my bed. Dat made him mad. He was jealous ob dat bird, and growled and made all sorts of false complaints. He was allus pickin' at it.

Clem. Who picked me in the eye in de night time?

Martha. You' 'magination.

Clem. My 'magination didn't pick a hole in my eye-lid, did it?

Lisa. Is this all?

Martha. He robs my hen-roost, too.

Clem. An' you stone my dog, too.

Lisa. [*Reproachfully*] And for this you want to get a divorce? To be separated after living together for forty years? Why, Aunt Martha, have you forgotten when you were sick with fever how Clem sat up and nursed you?

Clem. An' fed her on eels—long eels, too.

Martha. [*Subdued*] No, I'se not forgotten.

Lisa. And are you going to let a miserable chicken separate you?

Martha. [*Humbled*] I don't lay no store by de chicken. It's a poah breed anyhow. [*Looks tenderly at Clem*] If Clem's agreed to make it up— [*Hesitatingly*]

Job. Ob co'se he is. [*To Clem*] Go and gib her yer forgiveness.

Clem. I'se been wronged by dat woman who I'se nursed like a baby.

LISA. Hasn't she done the same for you? I've known her to share your labor in the fields all day, and wash all night for some white folks at the landing that you might fare better than the rest. [*Goes up C.*]

MARTHA. [*Through her tears*] I've had hunks of gingerbread on dat ole man's table free times a week. [*Martha and Clem look at each other an instant*]

CLEM. [*In tears*] I'm sorry dat my dog kill yer hen.

MARTHA. Oh, Clemie!

CLEM. Let's go back to de cabin and lib in peacefulness. [*He opens his arms and Martha rushes into them and they exit, L.3.E., weeping together*]

JOB. [*Looking after them*] If people would disremember de ole kindness, dar wouldn't be many divorces. [*Looks at Lisa, who has dropped into chair*] She did it all; she's allus doin' some good. Youse sad, Miss Lisa? [*Going to her*]

LISA. [*From a fit of abstraction*] Oh! no, not sad. But Mama Nance and I are going away—away across the sea, among strangers, and the thought that I shall never see dear old Big Bend again—[*Crosses to L.*]

JOB. [*Half sadly*] We've had mighty good times hyar. I mind when massa comed back from ober de ocean, whar he lef poor Missy Grace—you was a little bright-eyed baby then. I'se the fus' party larned ye to took youah fust step. Jest ober dar, I stood ye up against de chair. Ye were mighty car'ful about lettin' go, but I just whistled "Jim Crow" and before I got done, ye broke loose an fell into dese arms laughin' like a little sinnah. [*Laughs*]

LISA. [*Happily*] And when we went fishing in the Willow Creek with Clay.

JOB. 'Xactly. He ust get discorged, an' roll up his pantaloons an wade in an scar de fesh 'way.

LISA. And how we used to drive the sleepy old cows through the wood and meadow land, wading knee deep in the clover that seemed to be holding up its red lips to be kissed, while the wild flowers like gossamer chalices filled with dew, made the rosy morning fragrant. I can hear the birds calling yet, "To weet, to woo" in the branches of the cottonwood.

JOB. Stop, Missa Lisa. You'se a witch.

LISA. And see the river flashing in the sun. Do you remember, too?

JOB. Yes, indeedy!

LISA. [*With enthusiasm*] And down in the bottom, near the river, where we used to catch the horses, and, with only their silken manes for a bridle, gallop off like mad.

JOB. [*Laughing*] Jes' so! Jes' so! I see ye disremember eberyting.

LISA. I remember, too, when the canoe turned adrift with me in it, and went floating into the red sunset, how Clay swam out and rescued me at his own peril.

JOB. Yes, indeedy, when he was a leetle fellow, he was monstrous fond of ye.

LISA. [*Sighs and crosses R.*] Things have changed since then.

JOB. [*More seriously*] Yes, ye can't be boys and gals foreber. [*Enter Clay, L.3.E.*] Hy'r's Massa Clay, now. [*Going out. Lisa is about to exit, R.3., when Clay stops her*]

CLAY. Don't run away, Lisa, I have something to say to you. [*Earnestly*]

LISA. [*Returns slowly C.*] I am listening. [*In a low voice. Exit Job, L.2.E.*]*

CLAY. [*After a pause*] What do you think of me?

LISA. That's such a strange question, and I hardly know how to answer it.

CLAY. [*Nervously*] You don't believe me capable of a crime, do you?

LISA. No, I would not believe it if it were sworn to.

CLAY. Not if I were to confess it?*

LISA. I don't understand.

CLAY. I have been a weak, wicked fool. I have betrayed the trust reposed in me. I have, while acting as agent for the dead master of this house, buried the estate in debt, and robbed you all.

LISA. [*Breathlessly*] How?

CLAY. By neglect of my duties; by the gaming table; and by the race course. I did not know how bad it was until today, when I tried to raise some money on the land, and found three mortgages were about to be foreclosed. I only wish I were dead.

LISA. [*In a steady voice*] Is it as bad as that?

CLAY. It is worse. Of your annuity I fear I can never pay a cent.

LISA. Let not that trouble you for a moment. I had no claim on this estate. I have my liberty and that is all I ask.

---

* The dialogue which appears between the asterisks was in the first version of the play. Later Campbell substituted the following lines:

CLAY. [*Moodily*] I beg your pardon, but I'm nervous and excited—and humiliated. [*Drops into chair, L. of table*]

LISA. [*Surprised*] Humiliated? [*With sympathy*] I hope there is no cause for that.

CLAY. [*Bitterly*] Yes, but there is cause. I have a confession to make to you.

LISA. Not to me, Clay, I beg of you. Let me think of you only as I have known you, a kind, generous—

CLAY. [*Rising*] Stop. I am neither. You have seen me through the vision of your own noble nature, and in the radiance of its white light, mine has been illuminated. Oh, Lisa, girl, I would give the world to be the man you think I am.

CLAY. Lisa, the late judge refused to have you treated as a slave. I have no wish to penetrate the mystery that he guarded so zealously; but my duty was to obey him, and above all to be an honest man. I have not done so and the blush I feel now burning on my cheek does not even faintly express the shame I feel at this moment. [*Covers his face with his hands, sinks into chair*]

LISA. What do you intend doing?

CLAY. If the worst comes, I will go North where I am unknown and work at my profession, out of the proceeds of which I can repay those whom I have robbed. I never had the training of a planter—and—

LISA. Oh, Clay! You don't know how I pity you.

CLAY. [*Rising*] I have no claim on your pity. Why don't you say something bitter? It would make me feel less mean.

LISA. Don't speak in that despairing way. Out of all this evil good may grow. It may teach you who your true friends are—and—

CLAY. Whoever else may be, I know you are one! [*Taking her hand*] Your friendship is of a kind that has created halos around the heads of less saintly women. I am not worthy of a thought from you. Lisa—I—[*Pause*]

LISA. Well? [*Looks up into his face*]

CLAY. Suppose that I should say that I—[*Pause*] Pshaw! [*Drops her hands*] I'm still a fool! [*Goes R.3.*] Always will be one. If Lacy comes, tell him I am waiting for him in my own room. [*Aside*] God bless her! [*Exits, R.3.E.*]

LISA. If I could do anything!—But I can't. And still he clings to Lacy. Were I to tell him how his friend had insulted me. But then I have no rights! What am I? [*Bitterly*]

LACY. [*Enters, L.3.E., coolly comes down to Lisa*] A very pretty girl.

LISA. I did not ask your opinion, sir!

LACY. I know that, but I volunteered it; I am always liberal. Come, come, now Lisa, you needn't turn up your delicate nose at me. I have been your friend. When people said you were airy, and condemned the judge for spoiling you, I said: "That gal is a Hardin sure, and if Nance is her mother, why—"

LISA. Stop. You have no right to discuss such a subject at all. To mention it so coarsely before my face is an insult.

LACY. Don't you be a little fool. I have always admired you, and perhaps you might do worse than become the mistress of a farm in Kentucky and a plantation in Mississippi.

LISA. Mr. Britton is waiting to see you in the next room. [*Points, R.3.E. Enter Stitch, L.3.E.*]

LACY. Time enough for him. I'll tell you what I'll do; give me a kiss right here, and I'll give you that little diamond there. [*Holds out right hand for inspection*]

STITCH. [*Takes Lacy's hand*] Very pretty one it is. How many carats? [*Looks up at Lacy. Lisa exits, L.2.E.*]

LACY. [*Takes hand away and goes R.3.E.*] You're an ass; a confirmed old ass.

STITCH. [*Amazed*] I? Do you know what I do to a man who insults me?

LACY. [*Returning threateningly*] No!

STITCH. [*Fearful*] I—I—ask him to—

LACY. Fight? [*Putting hand in hip pocket*]

STITCH. No, certainly not. I ask him firmly but politely to—apologize.

LACY. And does he?

STITCH. If he is a nice respectable gentleman, he always does.

LACY. Do you know what I do when I run across a nobby old nuisance like you?

STITCH. Oh, I say!

LACY. I always pull his nose. [*Seizes Stitch's nose and pulls him to chair, R. of table. Enter Mrs. Lee*]

STITCH. [*With difficulty*] There! There! [*Sits in chair*]

LACY. [*Throws card at him*] There's my card if you're not satisfied. [*Exits, R.3.E.*]

STITCH. I don't want your damned old card. If there was law enough in Kentucky to imprison a mosquito, I'd have that fellow arrested. Seems to me he's the man of the mortgage, curse him.

MRS. LEE. Mr. Stitch. [*Stitch jumps up*] Who is that gentleman who just left the room?

STITCH. A friend of mine.

MRS. LEE. He seems familiar.

STITCH. Oh! he knows me.

MRS. LEE. So you've got back, Mr. Stitch.

STITCH. I have, my dear.

MRS. LEE. Dear?

STITCH. Beg pardon, really, it came involuntarily to my lips.

MRS. LEE. [*Bows and sits, L. of table, Stitch, R.*] You went to the Courthouse?

STITCH. On horse-back—ten miles—correct.

MRS. LEE. And there found that there were mortgages on the place.

STITCH. I did.

MRS. LEE. [*Impatiently*] Well?

STITCH. Well? [*Elevating his eyes*]

MRS. LEE. For goodness sake, why don't you tell me the facts?

STITCH. My dear—[*Rising*] I beg your pardon. [*Sits*] Permit me to say I thought you were getting them out of me on a direct examination very cleverly.

MRS. LEE. Who signed those mortgages?

STITCH. Young Britton.

MRS. LEE. I thought the judge's own signature would have been necessary in that case.

STITCH. [*Smiles at her*] Very well put, but the young rascal had power of attorney to sign for him; you see?

MRS. LEE. Are they heavy?

STITCH. [*Assuming professional air*] As well as I could judge, my love. [*Rises*] I beg your pardon. [*Sits*] They will pretty thoroughly eat up this magnificent estate of Big Bend. Of course, I mean at a forced sale—under the hammer.

MRS. LEE. And Letty's share?

STITCH. Gone—not a dollar.

MRS. LEE. And we have wasted four weeks here besides your bill, which—

STITCH. Don't let that disturb you. [*Pause*] Let me be frank with you; to labor for those we love is solace to the soul, reward far beyond—

MRS. LEE. For pity's sake, talk sense; don't address me in that ridiculous fashion as if I were a jury. [*Impatient gesture*]

STITCH. [*Subdued. Aside*] I won't.

MRS. LEE. Have you nothing more to say? [*Crosses R.*]

STITCH. Nothing; unless you permit me to dwell upon a tender theme that has filled my heart for the last year. Here let me declare, [*Drops on knees. Mrs. Lee shows annoyance*] that one thought, one vision alone has ever filled—[*Enter Letty followed by Jack*]

LETTY. Oh, come in, Jack; you needn't fear—[*Sees Mrs. Lee and Stitch and stops suddenly*] Mama! [*Embarrassed, Jack looks at ceiling, Stitch rises and looks troubled, from one to the other*]

MRS. LEE. Mr. Hazleton here!

JACK. [*Tries to be at ease*] Yes. [*Smiles faintly*] How do you do? [*Offers hand which is not taken*]

LETTY. [*Nervously*] Yes, mama, this—is—is Jack.

MRS. LEE. [*To Stitch*] I suppose, sir, that this is some of your work. A mean little piece of treachery to wed my daughter to your worthless nephew.

JACK. Worthless!

STITCH. My dear Mrs.—

MRS. LEE. Hold your tongue!

LETTY. My Jack, a doctor in good standing, worthless?

MRS. LEE. Yes, very good standing. Standing in Grimm's drug shop, when he isn't ogling the girls in Peter's grocery.

JACK. Mrs. Lee, if you weren't Letty's mother, I wouldn't stand it. Even doctors must have a beginning and I've already got—

MRS. LEE. A tin sign on a frame shanty.

STITCH. [Laughs loudly] His name on a tin sign and his patients on marble slabs! You had him there.

MRS. LEE. [To Stitch] Don't you be a fool!

JACK. Mrs. Lee, you object to my suit because I am poor; but poverty is not perpetual, and with her love to fight for, I am certain to make my way. In any event you have no right to insult me.

LETTY. And I don't care what any one says, I will never, never, never, marry any man but Jack.

MRS. LEE. How dare you talk to me in this manner! Come with me! [Goes L.2.E.] Come, miss! [Points to L.2.E.]

LETTY. [Going slowly, L.2.E., to Jack] I wish I was married, then I could do as I like. Jack, don't you go back to Virginia until I see you again! [Disposed to cry] Will you?

JACK. No, my dearest. [Letty crosses to door, L.2.E. Letty throws kiss to Jack and exits. Mrs. Lee looks at Jack who is scratching his head. Stitch turns his back to audience. Picture]

MRS. LEE. As for you Mr. Stitch—

STITCH. Yes, my dear.

MRS. LEE. You can return to Virginia as soon as you like. [At door with sarcasm] You are no doubt a true friend, Mr. Stitch, and I am very sorry that I cannot appreciate your friendship. [Exits, L.2.E.]

STITCH. So am I! Well, sir. Well, sir, you have pretty effectually cooked my goose. I could have married that woman, if you had kept your absurd puppy love in the background. [Takes hat]

JACK. Would you marry a woman with such a temper?

STITCH. I like temper in a woman, especially when it has 500 acres of good Virginia land attached to it. It relieves the monotony of life [Goes L.3.E.]

JACK. What will I do now?

STITCH. Do? Do what you please now. Hang yourself and go to the devil! [Exit, L.3.E.]

JACK. Stitch is a ridiculous old fraud, but I won't allow him to cast me off like that. [Exit, L.3.E. Enter Clay followed by Lacy, R.3.E.]

LACY. I can see only one way out of this and that is to do as I suggest.

CLAY. But I hate to part with the slaves. Most of them were born on this place; some of them have been companions in all my boyish sports; besides they are all so attached to Big Bend and—

LACY. Therefore you are willing to become a beggar for them. Don't you see that you can't keep them? If you let the land go and the old homestead, what use will you have for these niggers?

CLAY. [*In despair*] You are right, I suppose. Oh, why didn't I see this sooner.

LACY. Don't weaken now. You have had your fun and luck ran against you; that's all, but it may turn any moment and you'll be on top of the heap again.

CLAY. You propose then—

LACY. To buy the niggers at the highest figure, $18,000, cancel my mortgages on them which is three thousand more, and with this money you can save Big Bend from a forced sale, and get on your feet again.

CLAY. I—ah—I had rather part with half the estate. Take that now and I—

LACY. [*Lighting cigar*] Excuse me. I never deal in anything except niggers and horses, and you know I'm giving you an outside figure, for niggers are down. Why, only last month I sold a woman off my place in Mississippi, and she kicked up such a devil of a row in the market about being separated from her husband that she went for six hundred dollars—ought to have brought a thousand easily. You can't depend on a nigger.

CLAY. [*After a pause*] Lacy, I have determined never to sit down to a gaming table again; I am a good lawyer, I know, and in all our transactions I have acted honestly and paid every penny, haven't I?

LACY. Like a little man. [*Blowing a cloud of smoke*]

CLAY. You have been winning largely of late of me as well as of others, and if you will only loan me $15,000, I will pledge my soul to its payment.

LACY. That's all right, old man, but my plan is the easiest for you, and more business-like. I prefer it.

CLAY. Then you refuse?

LACY. I prefer to put it in another shape.

CLAY. [*Bitterly*] Then you insist on the purchase of my people?

LACY. [*Carelessly*] I'd like to have my money.

CLAY. So you shall. Every cent.

LACY. When?

CLAY. Now! Make out a memorandum of sale and I will sign it; I am too nervous to write myself. [*Rising and crossing R.*]

LACY. That's business! [*Takes up pen from table and writes*]

CLAY. [*Pacing stage, R.*] What a miserable fool I have been! The glamour of the race track, the excitement of faro, the friendship of heartless hypocrites who called themselves friend. Had I taken Lisa's advice—

LACY. [*Holds out paper*] Read it. I didn't name the slaves. I just said all those now attached to Big Bend plantation. That will do?

CLAY. [*Glances at paper without taking it*] I suppose it will.

LACY. [*Passing over roll of bills and filling out check*] Here are $1,500 and this check covers the balance. [*Rises*] I am glad you are taking the right view of this, Clay. [*Clay comes from window and sits L. of table*] You have no objection to my giving the niggers notice at once?

CLAY. [*At table, signing receipt*] I should rather you would wait a day or two.

LACY. But I want to ship them off tomorrow. I don't feel quite safe with so much property within a few hours of free soil.

CLAY. You have the right to do what you please, but you will excuse me if I refuse to share a scene that cannot but be full of pain to me. [*Going R.3.E.*]

LACY. Nonsense! Why, old man, a blubbering nigger is no more to me than a yelping dog.

CLAY. [*Sarcastically*] I'm sorry I cannot boast of such delicacy of feeling. [*Crosses to door, R.3.E.*]

LACY. Now I hope this little transaction won't interfere with our friendship.

CLAY. Such sincere friendship as ours has been ought to be cherished above every other consideration. [*Exit, R.3.E.*]

LACY. [*After a pause*] He's mad now! Never mind, he'll soon get over it.

BAN. [*Enters, L.3.E.*] Well, how did you come out?

LACY. I own every nigger on Big Bend.

BAN. Good. I knew you'd fetch him. [*Enter Job, L.2.E.*]

LACY. I say Uncle Job, go down to the quarters with Bancroft here, and tell the people that I've bought 'em all and that we're going to start for Mississippi tomorrow on the Sunny South. [*Music*]

JOB. [*Amazed*] Bought all de people!

BAN. Every nigger on the place.

JOB. [*With feeling*] But not me, Massa Lacy, not pooah ole Job. I'd die if I war taken away from Big Bend. 'Deed and 'deedy I would.

LACY. I said all, didn't I?

JOB. My ole missy's grabe in hyar, and by dar mudder, my two chilen; I hope to lie thar, too, some day. Don't take me away, don't. Please, massa Lacy. [*Weeps*]

Lisa. [*Enters, L.2.E.*] Weeping Job? What for?

Job. [*Rising*] Massa Lacy has done gone an bought eberybody on de place, and gwine to take dem down to Mississippi right off.

Lisa. [*To Lacy*] Is this true?

Lacy. You can bet your life it is.

Lisa. I didn't think Clay was capable of such a thing. I thought he would have let every vestige of Big Bend go before he would part with his people.

Lacy. Now he couldn't help it; he had to do it; but you needn't worry, I'll take good care of you; only I won't have any airs.

Lisa. [*Proudly*] Care of me! What have you to do with me?

Lacy. I own you, that's all.

Lisa. By what right?

Lacy. This bill of sale [*Shakes paper*] which reads, "I hereby sell, etc., all the slaves of Big Bend to William Lacy." All! Don't that look like business?

Lisa. That does not include me. Job, tell Nance to come here, quick! [*Job exits, L.2.E.*]

Lacy. Why don't it include you? [*Change music*]

Lisa. Because I am a free woman—made so by Judge Hardin—and I defy you. [*Cross to R. Enter Nance followed by Mrs. Lee, L.2.E. Enter Stitch, L.3.E., who comes down L. of Nance*]

Lacy. [*Sneeringly*] Free, are you? Where are your freedom papers?

Nance. Here on my breast where they have been since I got them. [*Draws out package of papers, one of which falls and is covered by the foot of Mr. Stitch unnoticed*]

Lacy. [*Carelessly*] The date?

Nance. February the 9th.

Lacy. They are worthless!

Nance. You lie!

Lacy. [*Clenching fist*] I'll strike your back for that! Ask that lawyer there. He can tell you that when those papers were made out, I held a mortgage on the property which renders freedom papers null and void.

Lisa. [*To Stitch*] Is this true?

Stitch. I fear it is. [*Nance goes up*]

Lisa. [*Crosses to Stitch*] And I am this man's slave? The creature of his will, subject to his whim; to be beaten like a dog. Oh, why don't someone in pity kill me! [*Wrings hands*]

Nance. [*Moans*] Lisa, I must speak!

Mrs. Lee & Stitch. Well?

Nance. My God, I cannot! I cannot!

Mrs. Lee. Poor girl!

CLAY. [*Enters, R.3.E.*] Lisa, in tears! What has happened?

LACY. I have just told her of my purchase.

CLAY. It docs not include her.

LACY. My bill of sale says "All."

CLAY. But she has her freedom papers.

LACY. I had a mortgage on her when they were made out. [*Lisa moans*]

CLAY. But you know there was no thought of her when that mortgage was made, and you would not take advantage of—

LACY. She is my slave under the law. Bancroft—[*Bancroft is about to go C. Lisa shrinks toward Nance*]

CLAY. The first man who places a hand on that poor girl, I'll kill with as little mercy as I would a reptile. Lisa, come here! [*She rushes to him and falls on her knees, clinging to Clay*]

LACY. The law!

CLAY. Law! There is a higher law—a law of right, mercy and justice, a law written on the throne of God and in the hearts of men—all others I despise. [*Picture*]

ACT III.

SCENE 1ST: *Exterior of Lacy's house at Osceola Landing. House with vine-embowered low veranda running from L.1. to L.3.E. Roadway leading to landing at 3. Profile shows negro quarters and river beyond with cotton field stretching between at 4. Dark sunset drop in 5. Large bell with rope attached at R.3.E. During the action the sun sets. Profile boats go up and down river in the distance at nearly close of act the stars come out and moon rises. The red glare of steamboat torch is seen off L.4.E., and the Mississippi boatmen's song is heard faintly in the distance.*
TIME: *August 1857.*

CLEM. [*Enters with banjo, L.U.E., over platform, down C. run wiping brow*] Dis yar field business is gwine to tell on de ole man, and dis Mississippi climate is not 'greeable to a Kaintuck raised niggah; 'sides since Martha's come'd up yar at de big house, it's berry lonesome at de ole cabin foh me. I tell you what it is, widout a woman, no house is furnished, and widout a little ob dar chin music a cabin is mighty empty! I'll jest let her know I'se heah. [*Sits on stump, C., and sings song, accompanying himself on the banjo. Martha enters from house, L., and begins dancing, and finally says*]

MARTHA. Oh, dat rheumatiz. [*Clem rises and puts banjo on garden seat, R. Martha sits on stump, C.*] Dat ole man ob mine. Dare he is playin' like an angel in de front row ob de heavenly choir.

CLEM. I know'd ye'd come when ye'd har de ole man's voice.

MARTHA. I'se been lookin' foh ye eber since de sun set. How is ye?

CLEM. Lonesome, awful lonesome. Fac is, Martha, I'se been married man too long to stand dis livin' lone buziness. Like weaning a baby without a bottle.

MARTHA. I miss you, too, Clem. Eben yer cold feet that used to make me so mad winter nights would be some comfort now.

CLEM. [*Moved*] I go home from de field now, an dar is no face in de cabin doah; no fire on de hearthstone; no kind voice hollerin' "Look out whar yere putting dem big hoofs on my scrubbin'." [*Wipes his eyes*]

MARTHA. [*Moved*] Don't cry, Clem. When Massa Lacy comes back from New 'Leans, I'll ask him to let me go back to my deah old man again.

CLEM. No. You'se bettah off heah, an Lacy's quarters is not de place foah women, not like old Big Bend. You'se right. How de little rascal does brighten up tings. Kiss me, Martha. [*Kisses her*] Now don't let us feel gloomy any moah. Let's amuse ourselves.

MARTHA. Dis seems like de sweet foolishness ob courtin' days again, when you used to come an' seranade me.

CLEM. [*Putting his arms around her*] Yes, an hole ye in de middle like this. [*Squeezes her*]

MARTHA. Yah. Keep still, ye tickle me. Ah, Clem, you'se up to yer old tricks again, I see. I tell ye it takes some men a long time to get old.

CLEM. Yes, an' some wimen, too. However, I'll serenade ye agin. [*Goes up to get banjo*] Hallo, here's ole Job an' all de folks comin'. [*Music. Enter Job, L.U.E., followed by field hands*]*

JOB. I know it do her h'art good to heah de old familiar voices from Big Bend; she tole me it would for her heart is hebby, sad and lonely. She says to me: "Job, never min' yer rags an' de cruel way Massa Lacy treat ye; it's only a little way till we all reach home agin. Don't expec' happiness till ye do."

CLEM. Did she mean Kaintuck?

JOB. No, she didn't! She meant de home on de gol'en shores ob de good Lo'd whar dar's plenty room for weary niggahs on de back benches.

OMNES. Bress de Lo'd.

MARTHA. Did she tell ye if she h'ard from young Massa Clay yet?

JOB. No, indeedy! I h'ard at de landin' de udder day [*Looks around and drops into whisper*] dat Massa Clay was put in jail fo' in'fering wid a mastah an' his slaves.

---

* This opening scene of Act III was added by Campbell after the play had been copied. The act originally began with Job's, "I know," etc.

MARTHA. Jes' for takin' Missa Lisa's part? Dat waz sad.

JOB. [*Nods*] Ump-um. Now chillen, rise your voices before Massa Bancrof' comes and drives ye off.

CLEM. We'se done our work and what has Massa Bancrof' got to do wid us now?

OMNES. Dat's me! Dat's me!

JOB. What's he go to do wid ye? Ye ign'nt niggahs. He owns ye; he's your oberseer. I'se tellin' for yer comfort to sabe yer hide from de whippin' post. Is I right, Marfa?

MARTHA. You is always right, Uncle Job, always.

JOB. Now den. "De old Kaintucky Home" whar we war all so happy. [*Quintette sings "My Old Kaintucky Home." All join in the chorus*]

> Weep no more, my lady,
> Weep no more today,
> And I'll sing one song
> For my old Kaintucky home,
> For my old Kaintucky home
> Far away.

[*They go singing off R.3.E. Job drops into a bench during song and remains there with head upon his breast. Enter Lisa from house, L.2.E. Lisa looking after slaves. Job, who has arisen*] Missa Lisa, how's ye gittin' on?

LISA. Badly, Job!

JOB. I'se mighty sorry for dat.

LISA. These three weeks I have spent here have been full of torture. First I thought Mother Nance would be with me; but instead, he sent her to the slave market in New Orleans to be sold among strangers. [*Drops into seat*]

JOB. I heard him say to Massa Bancrof' dat she made ye more stubborn, and he's have to get rid ob her. [*Pause*] 'Scruse me, missa, but dey say down in de fiel's dat you's gwine to be lady hyar, an' dat Missa Daphne gwine to be sent away as soon as Massa Lacy come back f'om New 'Leens. Is it so?

LISA. [*Scornfully*] Mistress of this house! Not as long as that broad river rolls so swiftly to the sea. [*Points to river*]

JOB. To go down dat ribber don' mean 'scape. Ye haf to go up it, far, far up Norf.

LISA. [*Desperately*] There's a shorter path to freedom in its depths.

JOB. Oh! I hope dat ye nebber be driven to take ye own life, Missa Lisa. De gospil's dead down on dat sure. De hour o' deliberance is bound to come. [*After a pause and twisting his hat in his hands*] It's gettin' on to supper time down in de quarters, an' I 'spose I'll have to bid ye good bye.

LISA. Good bye, Job, and God bless you for your good, kind heart.

JOB. [*Going R.3.*] Thankee, missa! Doze Mississippi niggahs is goin' to hab a dance tonight an' when dey's at it I'se gwine to get de boys to come hyar wid dere banjos an' serenade ye. Good bye! [*Boat whistles*] Yes, I is shuah. [*Exit, R.3.E. Boat comes up, R. to L., whistles and rings bell as she disappears R.U.E.*]

LISA. [*Lisa looks L. Goes up and looks after boat*] A boat from below coming to the landing; I hope it has not brought my tyrant back.

DAPHNE. [*Enters from house, L. Fiercely*] So, you're looking for him, too? You want to be the first to greet him. [*Turns R.*] Oh, you needn't put on your queenly airs and try to look me down. I'm only Daphne, half French, half fool! But I know the scheme.

LISA. [*Indignantly*] Scheme!

DAPHNE. [*C.*] I saw through it from the first. I'm to be driven into the fields, and my child either sent with me, or sold. It's the old programme! I took the place of one he had grown tired of. She died broken-hearted, but I'll not submit so tamely! [*Grinding her teeth*]

LISA. I don't quite understand you.

DAPHNE. Five years ago when I came here first, I was as young and pretty as you are. Yes, I was! Yes, I was!

LISA. What have I to do with all this?

DAPHNE. [*Turns on her*] Do with it! So much have you to do with it, that for the last three weeks I have had all I could do to fight down a desire to kill you. [*Clenching her fist, and facing Lisa*] I have stood at your bedside when the white moonlight fell upon your face, and you were fast asleep, and tried to summon up strength enough to strangle you. Do you know what saved your life? A tear upon your cheek and the word "home" upon your lips. It recalled brighter days to me. Days in dear old *La Fourche* in the green country of eternal summer, and I fled like a weak fool weeping from your side. [*Weeps, Crosses R.*]

LISA. Poor creature!

DAPHNE. [*Turning quickly*] I don't want your pity! when you are mistress here, when you have taken my place—

LISA. Your place, Daphne! That time will never come. I am a miserable wretched octoroon, like yourself, but sooner than become the mistress of this man, I'd die.

DAPHNE. Mon Dieu! Then you don't love him?

LISA. Love him? I despise him.

DAPHNE. But when he returns and speaks kindly to you, and tells you how he worships you, as he will, you will be like me, the creature of his caprice.

LISA. Never!

DAPHNE. I said so, too, at first.

LISA. You shall see!

LITTLE JIM. [*Music. Enters L.3.R. and running to Daphne*] Mama, save me! Save me! [*Enter Bancroft with whip, R.3.E.*]

DAPHNE. Jim! My child!

BANCROFT. [*Attempting to drag Jim from Daphne*] Give me that young rascal.

DAPHNE. [*Fiercely*] No! I'll not!

BANCROFT. Why do you interfere?

DAPHNE. Because I am his mother.

BANCROFT. Why don't you learn him better than to throw sand into the sugar pans? Mother or no mother, I'll teach him better! [*Lifts whip*]

LISA. [*Coming between them quickly*] Please don't!

BANCROFT. Stand aside, or I'll let you have it.

LISA. Strike! If life means living among such scenes as this, death is welcome.

LACY. [*Enters, L.3.E., with linen duster on arm*] Hello, what does all this mean?

BANCROFT. Jim has been in the habit of going to the sugar house and throwing sand in the pans.

LACY. Did you give the young rascal a whipping?

BANCROFT. I was going to, but Lisa interfered.

LACY. [*To Lisa*] You shouldn't have done so.

LISA. [*Going up*] Perhaps not.

BANCROFT. She's always interfering with the discipline of the place. [*Go up*]

LACY. She must not do so any more. Daphne, take Jim into the house. [*Daphne going L. As Daphne passes him going into house, in undertone to her*] The devil's got into you of late. Take care or I'll beat him out of you.

DAPHNE. [*Tenderly*] But Bill, remember how much I love you.

LACY. That will do—Go. Go, I say. [*Exeunt Daphne and Little Jim to the house*] We can get along without you, Bancroft.

BANCROFT. [*Aside at R.2.E.*] Things have got to be straightened out hyar. [*Exit, R.3.E.*]

LACY. [*After a pause*] Now, Lisa, I want to come to an understanding with you. I have given you your own way in everything here, and have tried to treat you like a lady, but you must not interfere with the rules governing this plantation.

LISA. [*Quietly*] In what way have I offended?

LACY. Well, you had no business mixing yourself up in that matter of Little Jim.

LISA. [*With irony*] Then you deem it an offense to step in between your own flesh and blood, poor innocent child, and the scourge of an ignorant ruffian.

LACY. The child's mother was there.

LISA. [*Fiercely*] Yes. There a shackled slave, more helpless than even the child; but were he mine—

LACY. [*Soothingly*] Now, now! There's no need of working yourself up to white heat. Sit down. [*She drops into seat*] Lisa, you are taking the wrong way with me. I may be a little rough and quick-tempered; but you can make a different man of me.

LISA. I?

LACY. Yes, you. Ever since I saw you first, I admired you, and if the law of the state would permit it, I would marry you gladly. But—it don't—and— [*Hesitates*]

LISA. [*Calmly*] Well?

LACY. But of this house and all this land, a full mile along the river and three back to the bayou, with the cane and cotton fields, you shall be mistress.

LISA. And Daphne?

LACY. Oh, I'll send her away. She never was fit for anything but the fields; but you're different. You can grace a mansion. I'll fix up Osceola like a bit of fairy-land. There shall be new carpets, soft laces and silks for yourself, and you can gallop over all these acres on the best horse-flesh the Blue Grass region ever bred.

LISA. [*Rising*] And pay for it all in the degradation of my womanhood. It is too much! I can't afford so high a price.

LACY. [*Excitedly*] Remember you are my slave.

LISA. Were I ten thousand times your slave, my answer would be the same.

LACY. I can send you to the fields to work all day among the common niggers—a hoe in your hand, rags upon your back.

LISA. Rags are royal raiment when worn for virtue's sake, and rather a hoe in my hands than self contempt in my heart.

LACY. [*Angrily*] Don't insult me [*Clenching fist*] or you will rue it. I'll put you so low—

LISA. A woman cannot fall lower than to live with a man she does not love—cannot even respect.

LACY. Dare you tell me this to my face!

LISA. I dare tell you more! That you ruined Clay Britton! That I despise and loathe you as I would any other common thief!

LACY. [*In a rage, raises his fist*] I'll murder you! [*Between his teeth*]

LISA. It would be the greatest boon you could bestow upon me.

LACY. [*Pause. Conquering himself*] You have been spoiled, but I'll tame you, you'll crawl to me for mercy yet! You prefer a hoe in your hand! You shall have one! Under the blazing summer sun you shall toil from dawn till dark! You shall be fed on corn! Sleep on straw! Lodge in the humblest hut! I'll teach you who you are! [*Going R.2.*] I'm going now to make room for you there. Bancroft will be your escort and I will greet you on your arrival. You have made your choice. Let us see how bravely you will bear the burden. [*At R.2.E.*] She Devil! [*Exit, R.2.E. Bell rings and the glare of a torch is seen off L.4.E. A voice outside L.3.E. sings the following, accompanied by banjo*]

Lovely Sally.

My love she was a yaller gal
An dearly she lub me.
Dey used to call her beautiful,
Sweet Sal of Tennessee.
Her eyes were bright as stars at night,
Her mouf jist like a rose.
She did agree to marry me
As soon as I propose. [*Song dies out pp.*]

LISA. [*Ringing. Looking L.3.*] A boat at the landing for New Orleans! If I can only reach it! I'll make the attempt! [*Starts up L. and suddenly stops*]

CLAY. [*Enters L.U.E.*] Lisa! [*Chord*]

LISA. Is that you, Clay? [*Retreats, R.*]

CLAY. Yes! [*Pause*] Have you no word of welcome for me?

LISA. [*Coldly*] Why should I welcome you, one to whom I owe so little? But for you I would have been a free woman, a happy hearted girl. [*Pause*] Well, why don't you speak?

CLAY. I prefer to be silent.

LISA. Have you no defense to offer?

CLAY. [*In a low voice*] None!

LISA. You have no other plea then, than guilty to the charge that you betrayed an old man's faith; brought misery on us all?

CLAY. None!

LISA. [*After a pause, pleadingly*] Oh, Clay, speak. Say something! Give me some little chance to say I forgive you.

CLAY. I don't deserve forgiveness. I have been a weak wicked fool. Yes, worse—a thief.

LISA. Thief! Oh, no!

CLAY. [*Drop in seat*] Why not? Have I not robbed you of your dower [*Rises*] to enrich a race of wretches? Stripped you of your freedom for one day of feverish excitement!

LISA. [*Tenderly*] But you are sorry—

CLAY. Sorry! In my prison cell where Lacy had me sent for interfering with his rights as a master, I had time to think—think of my past life—of you—of the happy childhood we had known together; time to make the discovery that I had made a slave of the dearest being on earth to me.

LISA. [*Excitedly*] You—you love me?

CLAY. So well that I have come here to take you out of bondage or share it with you.

LISA. But you forget what I am.

CLAY. I forget everything—but that I love you.

LISA. Clay, I am no longer a slave. The knowledge that you love me has made me free. [*They embrace*]

CLAY. [*Nervously*] You shall be free indeed. The boat I came down on is still at the landing bound for New Orleans. As the last plank is drawn aboard, we will board her.

LISA. But in New Orleans?

CLAY. We will get off before reaching there, and, hailing the first boat going up the river, escape.

LISA. I will be ready in a moment. [*Goes into house, L.2.*]

CLAY. Haste! We have not much time to lose. [*Goes up C. Exit Lisa, L.2.E. Enter Bancroft, R.2.E.*]

BANCROFT. It will do me good to drag the lady Lisa down to the quarters. She'll find that Osceola [*Music*] isn't Big Bend.

CLAY. [*Bancroft kneeling to tie shoe. Clay coming down run*] She will—eh? [*Seizing Bancroft from behind*]

BANCROFT. Here, what are you going to do?

CLAY. Make you a prisoner! [*They struggle fiercely. Bancroft succeeds in drawing revolver, but Clay seizes his wrist, and strikes it out of his grasp*]

BANCROFT. Help! Help!

CLAY. [*Forcing Bancroft into out building, R.2. Bolts door. Lisa and Daphne enter at same moment from house, L.2.E.*] Now, Lisa, for freedom.

LISA.   Farewell, Daphne! God pity you, poor girl. [*Going with Clay, L. up stage to 3. Enter Lacy, R.2.E. Rushes to C. Daphne picks up revolver dropped by Bancroft, and points it at Lacy*]

LACY.   What do you mean?

DAPHNE.   To kill you, if you attempt to bring her back. [*Picture*]

CURTAIN

[*Second Picture: Boat going down stream from L. to R. at 4. Boatman's song pianissimo. Daphne lying on stage. Lacy standing over her with revolver*]

SECOND CURTAIN

ACT IV.

SCENE 1ST: *Interior of the cabin of the Belle Creole. Clerk's office, L.1. Bar, R.2. Small table near bar. Monte table near clerk's office. Heavy drapery at 3, dividing ladies' cabin from saloon. Noise of escape pipe and distant roll of thunder during act, becoming more violent at close. As curtain rises, ladies and gentlemen dancing in ladies' cabin while the negro cabin boys in white jackets play for them. Captain Stryker, Count Strain and Natchez Jim with others at table, L. Bar-keeper with others at poker table, R.*

TIME: *Night. Two days later.*

CAPT.   [*Sitting*]   There, we will see what luck that will have. [*To Strain who is shabbily genteel and who is leaning on him*] What do you take me for? A hitching post?

COUNT.   [*With a little falsetto laugh*]   I beg your pardon—really. [*Laughs*]

CAPT.   That's all right, count, but don't do it again. Go on, Natchez, deal 'em.

NAT.   [*Dealing*]   I never saw such luck. The dealer, gentlemen, is out over three hundred dollars. Lost again.

COUNT.   [*Laughs, reaching on table*]   My way at last—really.

CAPT.   I'll trouble you not to catch a crab on that ere bet.

COUNT.   [*Laughs*]   Captain, that was my money, really.

CAPT.   Well, I'll swear I put it on the queen.

NAT.   Of course ye did. What are ye giving us, count?

COUNT.   I don't want to dispute your words, gentlemen, but I thought really—

NAT.   Don't someone want to deal a while? I'm getting tired.

COUNT. I will take your place with pleasure; but you will have to play light against me, really. [*Change places*]

CAPT. What do you call light? We don't play for buttons.

COUNT. [*Dealing*] Now, gentlemen, make your bets.

CAPT. Fifty on the ace.

NAT. One hundred on the deuce and ten on the queen.

COUNT. [*Laughs*] Rather heavy, gents, rather heavy—really.

NAT. Deuce wins.

COUNT. [*To Natchez*] There's sixty-five dollars. I'll pay you the other thirty-five as soon as I get my money from the safe in the office. Put it there for safe keeping; I always do, [*Laughs*] really.

NAT. [*Threateningly*] Say, what do ye mean? Do you think yer playing with a lot of bald-headed old women? Pay up!

COUNT. Didn't I say you'd have to play light? Really—

CAPT. Very light indeed to suit your empty pockets.

NAT. Has he any money in the office, cap?

CAPT. Not a picayune.

NAT. See here! [*Taking Count's arm and leading him down L.*] What do you think of a man that sits for a banker without a cent?

COUNT. Well—really—

CAPT. He thought he'd win the first time, I suppose.

NAT. I ought to put a hole in you!

COUNT. You'd never forgive yourself—really.

NAT. 'Twould only be wasting lead to shoot you like a gentleman so I'm going to kick ye out like a loafer.

COUNT. [*Laughs*] Thank you—but really it was only a—just a joke.

NAT. So is this. [*Crushes hat over Count's eyes and kicks him off, L.2.E. As he kicks the second time, Stitch is just coming in, L.1.E., followed by Mrs. Lee, and receives the kick in the stomach*]

STITCH. [*With grimace*] What do you mean, sir?

NAT. Excuse me, I didn't mean it.

STITCH. [*Indignantly*] Didn't mean to! That's a great satisfaction to me! What are you kicking for, anyway?

NAT. [*Coolly, menacing him*] Now I've apologized to you, but if you want more satisfaction, step out on the guards.

STITCH. There's a lady present.

NAT. I beg your pardon. [*Lifts hat to Mrs. Lee*]

STITCH. Very fortunate thing for you that the presence of this lady—

MRS. LEE. Mr. Stitch, I beg you will not renew the quarrel.

Stitch. [*Scowling at Natchez*] For your sake, I'll be patient. [*Natchez gives him a look of withering contempt and retires to bar. Capt. Stryker has joined the group at table, R.*]

Mrs. Lee. What time do we arrive at Osceola? [*Stitch and Mrs. Lee on bench in front of office*]

Stitch. I think about twelve. Captain, what hour will the boat reach Osceola landing?

Capt. [*Pauses to think*] Well, let me see. We are about ten miles below Orange Grove and it's now ten o'clock. We'll get there in the neighborhood of midnight.

Mrs. Lee. Isn't that rather slow work?

Capt. Yes'm, it's not up to the best mark of the "Belle Creole"; but the river is three miles wide here and the current is very stiff. [*Turning to table*]

Mrs. Lee. [*To Stitch*] I'm just dying to confront that rascal, Lacy.

Stitch. So am I. He did a shabby thing on me once, and I imagine I see him wriggle when I put the machinery of the law upon him.

Mrs. Lee. I hope there will be no loop-hole left for him to crawl through.

Stitch. Nary a loop.

Mrs. Lee. But the law is weak in many respects and one never can tell.

Stitch. There is nothing stronger than the law, my dear Mrs. Lee, except love. That universal law—

Mrs. Lee. Now didn't you promise not to speak of any such thing on this journey?

Stitch. But if you will—

Mrs. Lee. But I won't do anything of the kind. O, dear—I believe this trip is just a conspiracy to give you the opportunity of worrying me to death.

Stitch. [*Music*] I'm silent.

Capt. [*To Mrs. Lee*] This is the last dance. Can I have the honor? [*Offers his arm*]

Mrs. Lee. It will be a pleasure. [*She takes his arm and goes to ladies' cabin where they dance*]

Stitch. See how she smiled on him! Oh, if she would only smile that way upon me! I hope Jack is making good use of his time with Letty. I have given him the opportunity of his life. [*Enter Nance, L.1.E., with child, about to pass Stitch going C.*] What, Nance! [*Aside*] Very lucky! [*Aloud*] Where did you come aboard?

Nance. At Red Church with Mrs. Col. Breen, my new mistress.

Stitch. And this, I suppose, is the child of your new mistress? [*Chucking child under chin*]

Nance. Yes, sir! Have you heard anything of Lisa lately?

STITCH. Yes, indeed, something of importance, too, but I can't tell you yet. By the way, I may want you, and if I do, what is your address?

NANCE. Col. Breen's plantation near Vicksburg in the bend. [*Music ceases. Card party breaks up*]

STITCH. Very good!

NANCE. 'Tis bed time! Good night, Mr. Stitch. [*Exit Nance, C., through curtains. Enter Count, L.C.*]

STITCH. Everything seems to conspire in my favor. [*Yawns*] I'll lie down myself. [*Goes to bar, is about to take a whiskey straight*]

COUNT. Ah, my dear old chum, just taking a night cap, eh?

STITCH. Do I know you?

COUNT. Well, we're sort of drinking acquaintances—really.

STITCH. I never encourage vice in others, therefore, I always drink alone. [*Drains glass*] I'm glad to have met you. Good night! [*Offers hand*]

COUNT. [*With contempt*] I never shake hands with a man that drinks alone. [*Drops into chair, L.U., and falls asleep*]

STITCH. [*Retires, L.1.E.*] Bad night! [*Lightning*] Very bad night! [*Steam whistle. Stitch goes to stateroom, yawning as he goes. Bar closes. Curtains are drawn together. Lights one-third down. Lightning. Boat whistles. Enter Captain from behind curtains, C.L., comes down C. and speaks to clerk Jamieson, who enters from stairway*]

CLERK. What are we stopping here for, captain?

CAPT. [*Goes into office*] It's a hail from the shore at Orange Grove. [*Clerk begins to figure on slate, and look over bills of lading. Bell rings on hurricane deck and small bell in engine room tinkles. Captain exits, L.1.E., buttoning his coat tight about himself as he goes out. Lightning and thunder and more wind*]

CLAY. [*Enters with Lisa from stairway. Bell rings again*] Sit here, Lisa, until I get you a room.

LISA. [*Seated, L.C.*] Oh, Clay, I'm so nervous.

CLAY. [*In a low voice*] You have nothing to fear. The darkness of the night kept people away from the landing. Once you get a stateroom, you can feign illness 'till we reach Cairo.

CLERK. [*In office*] Where are you going, sir?

CLAY. Cairo.

CLERK. Lady your wife, I suppose?

CLAY. No, my sister.

CLERK. Then you want two rooms. [*Looks over book*] I'm sorry, but we haven't got a room in the ladies' cabin. If you sit up until we reach Osceola we can fix you nicely.

LISA. [*Starting*] Osceola!

CLAY. Hush—sh. [*To Clerk*] You have passengers then for Osceola?

CLERK. [*Carelessly*] Two! Man and old woman! Separate rooms. Just suit you.

CLAY. Yes, that will do.

LISA. [*Hoarse whisper*] Who can these be? Daphne and—

CLAY. No. No. [*To Clerk*] Very bad night. [*Thunder*]

CLERK. [*At his books*] Terrible—a regular deluge.

CAPT. [*Enters, L.1.E., takes off hat and shakes it at L.1.E.*] That rain is coming down the short way. There's nothing to take on at Osceola, is there?

CLERK. Twenty bales of cotton.

CAPT. That's rather a mixed cargo, isn't it? The boiler deck full of turpentine and sperm oil, and the lower deck full of cotton. Rather dangerous, eh?

CLERK. [*Coming out of office*] I know it; but Dale & Bullock, our agents in New Orleans, made out the bill of lading; that lets us out.

CAPT. Certainly! If she burns up, the owners are responsible, and if they lose—[*Shrugs shoulders*]

CLERK. As long as this rain lasts there's not much danger of flying sparks anyway.

CAPT. [*To Clerk*] I see the bar at Red Devil's Island is covered up to the trees, there must be over sixty feet of water here, and over three miles wide. [*Whistles twice and bell rings*] Osceola, eh?

CLERK. [*Coming out of office. To Clay*] Now, sir, you can have your rooms as soon as we leave the landing.

CLAY. Thank you. [*Bell rings*]

CAPT. [*Going L.2.E. with lantern*] Come on, Jamieson.

CLERK. Aye! aye! sir! [*Captain and Clerk exit down stairs*]

LISA. [*Excitedly*] Oh, Clay! If anyone should come aboard, what would we do? [*Small bell rings*]

CLAY. Be calm! We need not remain here.

LISA. Where will we go?

CLAY. Out on the guards where we can remain till the boat is in mid stream again. [*Terrific crash of thunder and vivid flash of lightning. Lisa in affright clings to Clay*]

LISA. What a storm! I never have seen anything half so terrible.

CLAY. Have no fear. I have seen many such in this region.

STITCH. [*Enters from L.1.E. with satchel, enveloped in overcoat, yawning*] Seems to me I haven't slept five minutes.

LISA. [*In alarm*] Mr. Stitch!

CLAY. Turn your back quickly. He might betray us! Come! [*Exit, R.1.E.*]

MRS. LEE. [*Enter in wrap with very small satchel*] This is a fearful night and an awful hour to go ashore in a strange place.

STITCH. [*Takes Mrs. Lee's satchel*] Let me have your satchel. It isn't Paradise, I assure you.

MRS. LEE. Can we go to the house at once?

STITCH. No, we wouldn't be made very welcome by Mr. Lacy. There's a store at the landing they tell me, where I think, considering our mission, we will be more comfortable.

MRS. LEE. Oh, dear! Oh, dear!

STITCH. Do you mean me?

MRS. LEE. Mr. Stitch, have some sense! Calling you "dear" indeed. [*Exit, L.1.E. During this scene there is a singsong air sung by the deck hands off R.3.E. Bell rings at Mrs. Lee's exit*]

CAPT. [*Enter with Lacy, upstairs R.C.*] We expect to be in Cairo Sunday morning. You will reach Hickman Sunday afternoon! [*Small bell*]

LACY. I hope so.

CAPT. But do you think the runaway has gone there?

LACY. Can't tell. They got off the boat in which they escaped at Orange Grove, but disappeared there, and of course they've caught an up-river boat before this.

CAPT. More'n likely. Will you have a drink? [*Thunder*]

LACY. Bar's closed, isn't it?

COUNT. [*Awakens, aside*] Somebody said drink? [*Sees Captain and Lacy*]

CAPT. [*Enters office*] We always keep a private bottle in the office. [*Hands out bottle through ticket window*]

COUNT. [*About to use Lacy's glass*] Thanks!

LACY. [*Regards Count severely*] Who is this fellow?

COUNT. A perfect gentleman, sir. Secretary of legation once and had a seat—

CAPT. [*To Count*] Well, just take another, will ye?

LACY. Go to the devil! [*Hurls Count, C.*] Here's yer health, cap.

CAPT. [*Drinks*] I'm looking at ye.

COUNT. [*Aside ruefully*] So am I. [*Enter Clerk with lantern from stairway shaking rain off his hat*]

CAPT. [*To Clerk. Coming from office*] Under full headway again, eh?

CLERK. Yes, sir! [*Enter Natchez, C. Enter Lisa and Clay, R.1.E., followed by passengers. Lacy stands, back to R., and therefore is not recognized by Clay. Clay, R.C., Lisa, R. of Clay*]

CLAY. [*To Clerk*] Can you let me have the state-rooms now, sir?

LACY. [*Turns quickly*] That voice! Lisa!

LISA. Lost! [*Turns face away and draws veil over head*]

CLAY. [*Grasps her by her wrist, in a whisper. Music*] For God's sake, silence.

LACY. Captain, land this boat! The runaway slave I told you of stands there! [*Points to Lisa*] And this man aided her escape.

CAPT. [*To Clay*] Is this true?

CLAY. [*Looking him coolly in the face*] Not one word.

LACY. See how she trembles and hides her face. She will not deny she is my property.

CLAY. She is a lady, and your rudeness has frightened her. That's all.

CAPT. Let us see her face.

CLAY. [*To Lisa*] Look at them. No one here shall harm you. [*Lisa uncovers her face and looks fixedly at Lacy*]

LACY. [*To Lisa*] Are you not my slave?

LISA. [*Calmly and in low voice*] No!

LACY. Did you never see me before?

LISA. Never!

CLAY. This is an outrage, captain!

CAPT. Certainly! I see it is! This lady is a genuine white woman!

NAT. [*To Lacy*] I say, old man, you've been drinking.

LACY. [*To Natchez angrily*] What right have you to interfere?

NAT. [*To Lacy*] The right to see fair play, and this little gal's going to have it.

LACY. [*To Captain*] If you don't put those people off at Osceola, I'll sue you and this boat. That's my remedy. Now do as you please!

CLERK. [*To Captain*] We can't afford to take any risk?

CAPT. [*Reluctantly*] I suppose not.

CLAY. [*Nervously*] You don't mean to say that you're going to put us off at Osceola at mid-night in a tempest.

CAPT. I'll have to, but it will only be a delay of a day or two, for there's just as good law for white people in Mississippi as anywhere on earth.

CLAY. But my business is most urgent.

CAPT. Sorry, but I can't help it. [*To Clerk*] Jamieson, tell Bill to land her. [*Exit Clerk. L.1.E.*]

LISA. [*In despair*] Oh, Clay, what will we do? What can we do?

CLAY. Die together, if need be!

NAT. That's pluck and I'm with ye to the end! Don't leave the boat!

CLAY. Captain, I refuse to go ashore here!

CAPT. Then you'll go by force!

CLAY. Force then it will have to be!

CAPT. [*Men come from below*] Here Jim, Bill, Sambo, put that man and woman ashore. [*Negroes rush at Clay*]

CLAY. [*Appealing to men*] Boys, we are in the midst of the Mississippi; there is no law can reach us but the law in the hearts of all true men, there is an unwritten law that says all women have a claim upon our pity and protection. In the name of that claim I call upon you all to defend this poor orphan girl!

OMNES. Right! Right!

LACY. I know nothing of an unwritten law, but the law of this land, which I respect, gentlemen, declares this woman to be my property and thus I claim her! [*About to seize her*]

CAPT. [*To Mate and Men*] Take that man and woman [*Indicating Clay*] downstairs! [*They seize Clay, struggle begins*]

LISA. [*Cries out*] Clay!

CAPT. Someone take the girl. [*Man with lantern attempts to seize Lisa. Natchez seizes his lantern and hurls it downstairs*]

CLERK. [*Rushing upstairs*] Fire! Fire! [*Explosion. Picture*]

CURTAIN

SECOND TABLEAU: *From the moment the curtains are drawn together in the previous tableau the carpenters set second tableau by placing set waters up to 2, hanging drop curtain in 4 representing a Mississippi river scene at night with a terrific thunder and lightning storm raging. As soon as curtain descends, the scene is carried down to 1st entrance, where a cut drop representing a group of live oaks hung with festoons of moss completes the scene. A working boat containing Count Strain, Captain Stryker, two Ladies and Lacy moves from R.2. to L.2. as curtain rises. Scene very dark, only the flash of lightning illuminating it. Red glare from burning boat. Count and Stryker at oars. Lacy standing up in boat.*

LACY. I'm sure they remained on the boat. Let us go back and take them off.

COUNT. I saw them after everyone had escaped clinging to a burning spar.

CAPT. They've been burned to a crisp by this time. Thank Heaven, no one shared their fate.

COUNT. Except that yellow woman, the nurse. Let us pull for the shore, cap.

LACY. I think I see something floating there.

CAPT. [*Looking*] Yes! Cotton bales! Come on, count, for the shore.

LACY. I'd like to save Lisa, she's worth two thousand dollars.

COUNT. I'd like to save the Count Strain. He's all I've got in the world. Not so hard on that oar, cap, now pull. [*Boat pulled off, L.2.E. Red glare of burning boat fades out and deepens in the darkness. Music. Cotton bale, burning, floats from L. to R. at 3. When it is fairly off stage, a spar with Lisa lashed to it, her face upturned, and Clay with one arm thrown around the spar, while with the other he holds up Nance, floats from L. to R. Only the blue flashes of lightning lighting up their faces when 2/3 across stage*]

ACT V.

SCENE IST: *Red Devil Island in the Mississippi. Back to 3, where the river begins, live oak, sycamores, and willows. The spar from the wreck at 3. Fire, C. at 2. Lisa sitting on log. Nance stretched on the ground beside fire. Day begins to break and sun rises. The sun is not seen, only the glow in the sky which is produced by gauze drop. A boat, illuminated, passes down the river from R. to L. at 4.*

TIME: *Night, two days later.*

LISA. [*Music*] How long and lonesome the night has been—the second we have spent on this desolate island with only a dreary waste of rushing waters in our ears—and death by starvation staring us in the face. [*Sees boat*] A boat bound down the river. [*Waves burning brand three times*] They pay no attention to the hail, or else they do not see it. [*Drops on log, L. Boat passes, L.*]

NANCE. [*Arising*] Are you awake, child?

LISA. Yes, I didn't sleep all night.

NANCE. You ought to try to sleep. It will give you strength to stand the hunger.

LISA. Why should I wish to live longer?

NANCE. There may be happiness for you yet.

LISA. Happiness! A miserable slave; hunted like a wild beast, driven like a dog. If it were not for Clay, I would gladly give up the struggle now and lie down here and die.

NANCE. [*Rising*] Don't despair like that, Lisa. You don't know how it stabs me to the heart. [*Weeps*]

LISA. [*Going to her*] No, no! Don't let me cause you a tear. You are not to blame for my misery. It was only in despair that I cried out against the chance that made me the child of a poor wretch who could not even call her flesh and blood her own. Forgive me! [*Embraces her*]

NANCE. Lisa, look me in the face, child. You have never doubted that I was your mother, have you?

LISA. Never! [*Change music*]

NANCE. Suppose I should say that I was not your mother, would you believe me?

LISA. No! No! No! [*Goes away*]

NANCE. [*Following her*] But suppose I should say that your mother was white, and free, and beautiful. Your father—a—

LISA. [*Shrinking*] I would think it was the delirium of starvation.

NANCE. [*Looking around and in a whisper*] Lisa, do you believe that the dead can come back?

LISA. No!

NANCE. They do! I have felt them near me when alone at night; so close that their garments brushed mine, and in the silence I have heard their voices; low voices like the faint wail of the winds in the trees, and sometimes I thought I heard them whispering to each other. [*Looks around and moves closer to Lisa*]

LISA. This is but your imagination.

NANCE. No, it is not, for sometimes they are with me days and days, and always when I want to speak and tell you something, I have—what was that?

LISA. Only the falling of a leaf. How you tremble.

NANCE. [*Kneels*] Oh, if I could only speak!—Only tell you all! There, don't you see the shadow of the dead! Oh, master, let me speak! Let me speak! I cannot see her suffer so. No! No! I will keep my oath. Forgive me! Forgive me! [*Falls to the earth moaning. Enter Clay, R.2.E.*]

CLAY. What has happened, Nance?

LISA. Starvation has turned her brain—she is raving mad.

CLAY. [*Bending over Nance*] Poor creature! Nance, look up! Don't you know me! Clay?

NANCE. Very well! 'Tis past and gone now. Let me go.

LISA. [*Coaxingly*] Stay here by the fire.

CLAY. [*To Nance*] There is hope for you yet, Nance. If the worst comes and we are discovered, you can return to your good master. [*Sun rises*]

NANCE. Return and leave Lisa? Never! Chance has reunited us; fate alone can separate us. [*Exit, L.2.E.*]

CLAY. Our only hope is to be taken off the island on the channel side; and no boat seems disposed to land here. Besides, but for those willows there [*Points L.3.*], we could be seen from the landing very distinctly.

LISA. [*To Clay*] What kept you so long away?

CLAY. I had hoped to find game of some kind to keep us from starving until all idea of pursuit is given up.

LISA. And you found?

CLAY. Nothing.

LISA. [*Wearily*] It seemed as if you would never return.

CLAY. It was only half an hour.

LISA. Hours are sometimes centuries when counted by the beating of anxious, weary hearts. [*Boat passes, going from L. to R. at 4*] See, Clay! There is a boat bound up the river. Here, take this; [*Looses white handkerchief from her neck*] it will serve for a signal.

CLAY. [*Waving 'kerchief over his head*] I fear it is useless! [*Boat stops, faint tap of bell*]

LISA. She stops! [*Eagerly*]

CLAY. Yes!

LISA. [*Boat backs a little*] She is backing! [*Breathlessly*]

CLAY. At last, Lisa! At last! [*Embrace fervently*] Why doesn't she come? They seem to be consulting with the pilot. She moves ahead again! Ah, I see. There must be a bar between the channel and the island which renders a landing impossible. [*In despair*]

LISA. Then there is no hope left! [*Drops on knees at his feet holding his left hand. Boat disappears*]

CLAY. Courage! Courage! We will go over to the point and build a raft and reach the main shore tonight.

LISA. But on the property of Lacy we could not escape detection.

CLAY. He believes we have perished on the "Belle Creole" and that may give us a chance. [*Looks up R.*] My God!

LISA. [*Leaping to her feet*] What have you seen?

CLAY. The boat is landing at Osceola.

LISA. [*In a low voice*] Well?

CLAY. Well, don't you understand? They will report seeing us and suggest our rescue.

LISA. Yes, and then?

CLAY. Lacy will divine at once the truth. In any event, we will be in his hands again. [*Looks off*] Yes, a skiff starts out from the shore. They pull straight for the head of this island. [*Goes R., leaves Lisa, C. Rowing sounds, faint at first, then louder*]

LISA. What are you going to do?

CLAY. What can we do, if overpowered by superior numbers? [*Sits on log. Music*]

LISA. Clay, you have told me again and again that you loved me. That even the dark drop that stains the red current of my veins is not a barrier strong enough to keep your heart from going out to me. Did you speak the truth when you told me this?

CLAY. [*Earnestly*] Yes! No truth ever spoken was half so true.

LISA. What was my reply?

CLAY. I cannot now remember.

LISA. I said the knowledge that you loved me had made me free. I could have said much more. I could have told you that even when a lisping child I ran to your embrace, the germ of love was in my heart although I knew it not. I might have said that as I grew to girlhood's noon, that flower expanded in the sunlight of your smiles and tenderness of your speech until it burst into beauty and filled my soul with a fragrance that made life a dream. I was only an octoroon, but I rose above my place and in the ecstasy of bliss forgot I had imprisoned in my nature the inheritance of Cain.

CLAY. Lisa, I—

LISA. Let me speak, for we have but a moment left, and I have now so much to say to you.

CLAY. Go on!

LISA. I wanted to make myself worthy of you!

CLAY. Haste! The boat is almost here!

LISA. [*Speaking quickly*] Before it comes, I beg a favor in payment of this toil.

CLAY. Anything you ask! Speak! [*Music*]

LISA. Here, take this! [*Offers knife*]

CLAY. A knife! For what purpose?

LISA. [*Clinging to him pleadingly*] I want my love to give me liberty.

CLAY. Impossible. Horrible!

LISA. Oh, don't say that!

CLAY. I cannot kill the only woman I have ever loved!

LISA. [*On her knees*] But would you doom her to a living death? To years and years of hopeless misery, to die at last alone?

CLAY. No! No! What shall I do?

LISA. [*Baring her breast*] Bury that gleaming blade in this breast and set me free.

CLAY. I cannot! I cannot!

LISA. I hear their feet upon the leaves. In mercy, strike!

CLAY. [*Wrought up to fearful excitement*] Yes, I will strike! But before your spirit has reached the skies, mine will be with you! [*Raises dagger over her head*]

LISA. Clay, a moment more, until I pray!

CLAY. Heaven have mercy on us both! [*Lifts dagger*] I cannot strike while you are looking in my eyes!

LISA. [*In low voice*] Now!

CLAY. [*Flings knife down and goes R.*] My God, I cannot! I cannot!

LISA. [*Grasping knife*] Then I must!

CLAY. [*Rushing to her side*] Self-destruction is a coward's act! Be brave enough to live! [*Takes knife from her and flings it away. Picture*]*

ACT VI.

SCENE 1ST: *Drawing room in Lacy's house at Osceola, beautifully furnished with cane furniture trimmed with Tiffins to match silken drapery on the windows. French windows in F. looking out on veranda, through which backing of 3rd Act can be seen. Folding doors, L.2.E. Large window, R.2.E. Picture on easel. Piano, etc. Orange tree and tropical flowers in window, R.3.E. Daphne discovered asleep on sofa, R. Martha bending over her.*

MARTHA. Pooah Daphne! Shot down in her tracks by de man she lubed 'case he wanted to lub annuddah woman. I tell ye I wouldn't stan' it neidah. No, I wouldn't. If dat Clem war caught foolin' 'roun' anybody else, I'd skin him like a coon! I'd make his har very light on de scalp. I tell ye a woman haf to protect herself in dese times.

JOB. [*Enters R.3.E.*] How is de pooah chile now?

MARTHA. Gettin' weakah an' weakah.

JOB. [*Over Daphne*] She's makin' a strong struggle to hol' on to dis worl'; but it's no use. It's slippin', slippin', right out of her grasp. [*Goes R.*]

MARTHA. You see de lawyer down at de stoah?

JOB. Yes, indeedy! He was gwine home today wid Mrs. Lee, 'case he's giben up all hope ob Lisa 'scapin' from the Belle Creole. But I suppose he won't. I begged him not to go, "For," say I to him, "Daphne she goin' to die shuah, and if you don' stay here and have Massa Lacy 'rested, he nebber get punished nohow."

MARTHA. An' what did he say?

* Act is sometimes ended with the following. Continue from last speech.

LACY. [*Enter with four others, R.2.E.*] Found at last! [*Enter Nance, L.3*]

CLAY. [*To Lacy*] Back, on your life.

LACY. This woman [*Indicating Lisa*] is my slave and I demand my rights.

NANCE. [*Coming C.*] You have no rights, for this woman is not a slave.

OMNES. Not a slave!

NANCE. No, nor never was. She is a free born white woman! [*Picture*]

JOB. "If de gal dies I hab him punished," says he, an mor'n dat, he was talkin' to de sheriff 'bout it den.

MARTHA. Sheriff heah?

JOB. Sittin' on his horse 'fore de stoah now, Missah Lee, too, takin' great interest in Daphne. I tell ye it's gwine hard wid him if she dies.

MARTHA. Where is Massa Lacy now?

JOB. At de shoah, waitin' for a boat I seed comin' to take him up de ribber. I think he's a skeered about Daphne dyin'.

DAPHNE. [*Awakening and in a weak voice*] Jim! Jim! Where is my child?

MARTHA. He's done gone out to play in de garden, missy. Does you want to see him?

DAPHNE. Oh, yes, I want to see him so much. He is the only one in all the wide, wide world that ever loved me.

JOB. [*Aside to Martha*] Bring in de chile. [*Exit Martha*]

DAPHNE. My life has been such a wasted one. I wonder why such creatures were ever born at all?

JOB. It's God's will an' foah a wise purpose; 'sides, Daphne, you hab not been raised ign'ant like most ob de people at Osceola an' you've sabed many a pooah debbil, an dese people am all prayin' for ye now. [*Distant hymn*] Hear dem singin' now at de quarters?

DAPHNE. Poor creatures! I did the best I could with my surroundings, I hope Mon Dieu will remember that.

JOB. You bet He will. De Lo'd nebber forgits our temptations, an how we war fixed on dis arth. His angah isn't half so big as His marcy. He's said so as offen as I hab finger and toes.

DAPHNE. [*Low*] Where is your master?

JOB. Gone up de ribber by this time, I suppose.

DAPHNE. Did he know I was dying?

JOB. [*Sadly*] He knowed you was bery low, missy.

DAPHNE. Did he speak of me or leave any word?

JOB. Not as I knows on.

DAPHNE. Do you think he is sorry for what he has done?

JOB. Well, he's an odd sort of fish. I don't think he cares much.

DAPHNE. [*Covers face with hands*] If it were not for Jim, I would be glad to go. Poor little Jim!

JOB. Doan feah foah Jim. He'll get along shuah. He's lively 'nuff.

DAPHNE. [*Moans in pain*] Oh, Job, let me hold your hand!

JOB. [*Gives hand*] Dar it am, missy.

DAPHNE. When I am gone, Jim will have no home but the quarters, and he will be lonely and ragged, I know; but, Uncle Job, you'll remember me when you see him so, and speak a kind word to him! Won't you?

JOB. [*With emotion*] 'Deed I will!

DAPHNE. And being a preacher, Job, tell him of Heaven, and how to get there, and if he ever asks for me, as perhaps he will, tell him how much I loved him, and that I am waiting for him there. Do you promise, Job?

JOB. It is my duty, Daphne, an' I always tries to do dat.

MARTHA. [*Enters with little Jim, R.3.E.*] Heahs Jim now.

JIM. [*Runs to Daphne's open arms*] Don't sleep any longer; come and play with me.

DAPHNE. [*Brokenly*] Our playing days are over, Jim!

JIM. Ain't you goin' to play never no more with me?

DAPHNE. Oh, yes, I'll be near you when you play and when you sleep. Our Heaven would not be Paradise, if poor mothers were denied the privilege of watching over the lonely little ones left behind. Job, I'm getting faint. I can't see any of you now. Take me—take me to my room. I'll be better there.

JOB. [*Raising her from sofa*] Lean on me. [*Exit with her, L.3.E.*]

MARTHA. [*Takes her other arm*] Let me take Jim.

DAPHNE. No, no! Let him stay with me to the last! It will only be a little while now! [*All exit, L.3.E. Enter Mrs. Lee and Mr. Stitch, R.3.E.*]*

MRS. LEE. Do you really think she'll die?

STITCH. Every one says so.

MRS. LEE. Well, it's a fitting climax to a succession of horrors. First the death of Judge Hardin and Clay's sale of the slaves; then the fearful discovery of Lisa's history; then the burning of the Belle Creole; and now Daphne must die for aiding the poor child to escape from that wretch Lacy. It is simply terrible! I don't know how I have stood up under it all!

STITCH. [*Shaking head*] It has been a regular hurricane of striking events, that's very true.

MRS. LEE. Dear knows, it has changed my views of life a great deal. I do wonder why some one don't come to receive us? I feel like a fool!

STITCH. I'll ring for them. [*Hunting bell*]

MARTHA. [*Enters, R.3.E., with letter*] I'se bringed up a letter for ye, Missy Lee.

MRS. LEE. [*In surprise*] For me? [*Takes letter*]

MARTHA. It just comed ashore on de Lady Franklin, de fines boat on de—

---

* This foregoing scene between Martha, Job, Daphne and Jim was usually omitted in performances of *The White Slave*. The act usually began with the entrance of Mrs. Lee and Mr. Stitch.

STITCH. Close your fly trap! Who cares anything about boats now?

MARTHA. [*Aside*] I wonder how poor Daphne's comin' on, poor chile! [*Exit, R.3.E.*]

MRS. LEE. [*Finishing letter*] Well! There's more of it!

STITCH. More of it? More of what?

MRS. LEE. [*In despair*] Read it! My only child, too!

STITCH. [*Reads*] "Dear Mama: We got married the evening you left. Jack and I couldn't stand it any longer. We know you will forgive us, dear mama." [*Speaks*] Very touching!

MRS. LEE. Touching! Forgive indeed! Don't be a fool, Mr. Stitch. Elbow-glazed, shiny-kneed, country doctor, too! [*Weeps*] And you are glad of this I suppose?

STITCH. Not at all! [*Wiping his eyes*]

MRS. LEE. In Heaven's name what are you crying for?

STITCH. I'll have to begin de nova. The arrangement was that I should marry you first; then Jack was to have a chance. Now, I suppose you'll blame me for this, and—and—Oh, what I suffer for your sake. [*Cries*]

MRS. LEE. [*Wiping her eyes*] You suffer! Wasn't she my only child?

STITCH. And mine—

MRS. LEE. Sir! Am I not left alone in the world?

STITCH. You are! You are!

MRS. LEE. What am I to do? [*Pushes him away*]

STITCH. Don't remain alone. Have I not offered you my heart and home? Don't wrap yourself up in second mourning wretchedness and pine away like a tender flower on a withered stem. Rather come to the hot house of my love where you can bloom perennial. [*Drops on knee*]

MRS. LEE. Mr. Stitch, if you only knew—how ridiculous you look.

STITCH. I know it, but I am too desperate to care.

MRS. LEE. But please get up!

STITCH. Never, until I have your answer!

BAN. [*Enters, R.3.E.*] Here! What do you people want here in this house? We've had trouble enough with you, and old Nuggs will have to leave that store at the landing for giving ye lodgings.

STITCH. We are here in the cause of humanity, sir. Don't think you can shoot poor women with impunity, even if you do own them. No, sir! Not while law and justice reigns.

MRS. LEE. Bravely spoken! [*Stitch bows to her*]

BAN. [*Contemptuously*] Well, you're a sight.

STITCH. [*Indignantly*] A sight?

BAN. [*Tumult, R.2.E.*] Hello! What's this? [*Look off R.2.*]

STITCH. [*Look off*] It's Clay and—yes it is, by Jove, Lisa.

MRS. LEE. Lisa? Where? [*Enter Lacy, Lisa, Clem, Nance, Clay and Natchez, R.3.E.*]

BAN. You found 'em, eh?

LACY. Yes, on Red Devil Island. I have sent for the sheriff to give Mr. Britton into custody for nigger stealing; as for the slave, Lisa—

NANCE. It is false. She is no slave. She is a free born white woman.

LACY. Yes, you have repeated that crazy story without rhyme or reason in it, until I'm sick of it.

MRS. LEE. It might be true, sir, after all.

STITCH. [*Aside to her*] Not a word.

LACY. If true, where is her proof?

CLAY. Speak out. If Lisa is not your child, whose child is she?

LISA. Oh, please answer!

NANCE. [*In agony*] All I can say is that she is not my child; that no blood of my race stains her veins. Is not that enough?

CLAY. That is worse than nonsense! Nance, look at that poor girl! [*Indicating Lisa*] How can you remain silent when her liberty, her life is at stake?

LISA. Oh, if you ever loved me, and I know you do—

NANCE. Better than myself!

LISA. In the name of the days, when we were all in all to each other.

NANCE. You torture me. My lips are sealed by a solemn oath given to the dead.

LACY. [*Jeeringly*] And this is the proof. Her word.

NANCE. There were other proofs which I lost the night the slaves were sold at Big Bend.

LACY. Of course you did! They haven't been found yet, have they?

STITCH. Oh, yes, they have!

LISA & CLAY. Found! Speak!

STITCH. The paper fell into my hands. Being a lawyer, I felt certain I was a better custodian than Nance, so I kept it and went to work.

NANCE. Give them to me!

STITCH. Excuse me. I am not oath bound, therefore, can explain matters here a great deal more satisfactorily than you can.

LISA. [*Eagerly*] Yes, yes, and you—

MRS. LEE. Hush, my dear. Let Mr. Stitch proceed.

STITCH. [*Smiles and bows to Mrs. Lee*] Here is the package. It contains a baptismal record of the child of Marquis De Bernaugre and Grace Hardin, also a tender letter from the father of the infant dated ten years after, saying that he had repented of the wrong done that child's mother, and expressing a desire to have the infant restored to him. That letter, Judge Hardin never answered.

CLAY. And that child is—

LISA. And I—

STITCH. [*To Lisa*] You are that daughter—a free born white woman. [*Mrs. Lee and Lisa embrace. Nance falls on her knees and hides her face in Lisa's garments. Enter Job followed by Martha, L.2.E. Job whispers in Stitch's ear. Enter Sheriff, R.3.E.*] Dead? Sheriff, you have just come in time!

LACY. Yes, to arrest the man who steals niggers!

STITCH. There is a graver matter than stealing niggers to be attended to first! Sheriff, I charge that man, William Lacy, with having killed an octoroon girl named Daphne at Osceola on the Mississippi on the evening of June 9, 1857.

BAN. 'Tis a lie, the woman is living.

LACY. [*To Stitch*] Idiot!

JOB. Go in dat room dar and see if she is. She died in dese arms five minutes ago.

LACY. [*Starts, R.*] Come, Bancroft, I want to see you.

CLAY. You can't leave this room!

LACY. [*Angrily*] Who will stop me?

CLAY. I will! [*Sheriff & Natchez seize Lacy*]

STITCH. Remove him to the veranda, sheriff, if you please. We want to have a little family reunion here, and he's not invited. [*Sheriff, Lacy, Count Strain, Natchez, Jim, and plantation Hands all exit, R.3.E.*]

JOB. De debbil gets his own at last.

STITCH. [*To Bancroft*] We would like to use that chair, and a little fresh air would do you good.

BAN. [*Going to Stitch*] We owe all this to you, you little shrimp! [*Exit, R.3.E.*]

STITCH. Shrimps are very good in season.

LISA. It is all so strange and sudden that I can scarcely believe that I am free—that you are all my dear good friends! [*Sees Clay*] And you, Clay?

CLAY. Your lover still! [*They embrace*]

STITCH. [*To Mrs. Lee*] I am waiting for your answer.

MRS. LEE. Mr. Stitch, you're a fool, but I'm proud of you! [*Gives her hand. Two shots heard in quick succession. Enter Job, R.3.E.*]

CLAY. Well, what has happened?

JOB. Massa Lacy tried to shoot the sheriff, an' de sheriff killed him.

CLAY. They should have permitted the law—

STITCH. My dear Clay, the law is all right, but let justice have a little show once in a while. Eh, my love? [*To Mrs. Lee*]

MRS. LEE. Mr. Stitch!

CLAY. Now that Osceola has lost its master, the place will be sold, and when it is, Lisa, we will become the purchasers of all our slaves, and together, we will return to our home in old Ken-tuck. [*Enter Martha with Little Jim*]

LISA. [*Taking Jim's hand*] And take poor Daphne's child with us.

CLAY. Yes!

MRS. LEE. But won't Lisa go to Paris to her father?

CLAY. On a visit, but I know that she will prefer to live at—

LISA. Big Bend with you. [*Picture*]

CURTAIN

MAN AND WIFE
AND OTHER PLAYS

A series in twenty volumes of hitherto unpublished plays collected with the aid of the Rockefeller Foundation, under the auspices of the Dramatists' Guild of the Authors' League of America, edited with historical and bibliographical notes.

BARRETT H. CLARK
GENERAL EDITOR

Advisory Board

ROBERT HAMILTON BALL, QUEENS COLLEGE
HOYT H. HUDSON, PRINCETON UNIVERSITY
GLENN HUGHES, UNIVERSITY OF WASHINGTON
GARRETT H. LEVERTON, FORMERLY OF NORTHWEST-
ERN UNIVERSITY
E. C. MABIE, UNIVERSITY OF IOWA
ALLARDYCE NICOLL, YALE UNIVERSITY
ARTHUR HOBSON QUINN, UNIVERSITY OF
PENNSYLVANIA
NAPIER WILT, UNIVERSITY OF CHICAGO

A complete list of volumes, with the names of plays contained in each, will be found at the end of this volume.

MAN AND WIFE

& Other Plays

BY AUGUSTIN DALY

EDITED WITH INTRODUCTORY NOTES AND PLAY LIST
BY CATHERINE STURTEVANT

INDIANA UNIVERSITY PRESS
BLOOMINGTON

ACKNOWLEDGMENTS

To all who have given of their time and wisdom to aid in the preparation of this volume, the editor is happy to express her gratitude. The assistance rendered by librarians in many cities has been invaluable. Especial thanks are due to Professor Napier Wilt, whose knowledge of the American theater in general and of the Chicago theater in particular has been most helpful; to Miss Lucile Gafford, who generously permitted free use of her notes on the Boston theater; and to Mr. Barrett H. Clark, whose knowledge of the drama and whose patience with the laggard are alike unbounded.

CONTENTS

INTRODUCTION

Forty years have elapsed since Augustin Daly died in Paris, June 7, 1899, in his sixty-first year. They have been eventful years in the history of the world and of the theater, but they have brought little change to Daly's reputation as one of America's foremost producers and directors. As a man Daly seems to have become a vaguely legendary figure, compounded of more than the usual amounts of temperament and tyranny. Distinctly less nebulous are the managerial talents and achievements which have upheld Daly's fame. His love of beauty, his extravagance and courage, and his phenomenal ability in picking and training actors resulted in productions noted for the luxurious splendor of their sets, in lavish revivals of the classics, in breathtaking enterprises such as the European tours, and, above all, in casts that were uniformly praised for their perfection.

Unfortunately, with the exception of the classics, the plays were generally not worthy of the superb productions given them. Many of the pieces produced at Daly's theaters were emanations from the manager's own pen. If Daly was the author, however, he was usually not the sole, or what is more important, the first and original author of the plays to which his name was attached. The originals of most of Daly's plays—adaptations or dramatizations would perhaps be a better term—have been identified. In fact, the number of plays for which no source whatever is known is so few that one suspects lack of information on one's own part rather than originality on Daly's.

Before condemning Daly, however, let us remember Ambrose Bierce's definition of a dramatist—"One who adapts plays from the French." In his dramatizations and adaptations Daly carried the good old dramatic tradition of plagiary and patchwork to its logical extreme. The fact that he dared to call one of his plays an "original adaptation" from a play by Sardou and another "an original play . . . based upon the latest work of S. H. Mosenthal" shows that he saw little difference between his practice of borrowing all he wanted from a single play and the habit of other American dramatists of helping themselves from the general stock of tried and true characters and situations. To Daly's credit it must be said that he generally confessed the source of his inspiration even though the confession was frequently made in terms somewhat too general to suit the historian.

In the long list of plays which follows, the editor has perforce fallen in with Daly's generous views on authorship. To have limited the list to strictly original work would have been practically to abolish it. Certainly it would have been robbed of all interest and value. To have drawn the line between plays of greater and lesser originality was impossible as many of Daly's plays and their sources were not available. The only alternative has been to include everything produced, original plays (if any), adaptations, dramatizations, and even those revisions of the classics that Daly considered of sufficient importance to have privately printed. Though the editor has erred deliberately on the side of inclusiveness, she has made no attempt to include all the plays to which Daly contributed a scene or two, but to which he laid no claim. A few of the early plays mentioned by Judge Daly have had to be omitted because no definite record of their production could be found. Imperfect as it is, the editor hopes that this list of Augustin Daly's plays may be suggestive of an interesting epoch in the American theater.

LIST OF DALY'S PLAYS

THE plays are arranged chronologically according to the date of first production. After the title a brief description of each play is given, including, whenever known, the type (usually taken from a playbill or a review); the number of acts; the names of the collaborators, if any; the source or sources; the date of the first production (if outside New York City, the date of the first production in that city is also given); and the name of the series in which the play was published or the year in which it was privately printed.

Valuable collections of Daly material are available in the New York Public Library and in the Brander Matthews Dramatic Museum at Columbia University. The manuscripts of many of Daly's plays are owned by Samuel French. These, unfortunately, were not accessible to me, but a partial list of them, including only those plays not published in trade or private editions, may be found in the Play List of Arthur Hobson Quinn's invaluable *History of American Drama from the Civil War to the Present Day*.

Other sources of information which were useful in the preparation of this list and the notes on the plays were the following: Joseph Francis Daly's *Life of Augustin Daly*, Edward A. Dithmar's *Memories of One Theatre*, *The Diary of a Débutante* attributed to Dora Knowlton Ranous, George C. D. Odell's *Annals of the New York Stage*, T. Allston Brown's *History of the New York Stage*, H. J. Eldredge's *"The Stage" Cyclopaedia*, and, of course, the newspaper files of the period.

Leah, the Forsaken. Melodrama. 5 acts. From *Deborah*, a play by S. H. von Mosenthal. Boston, Dec. 8, 1862; New York, Jan. 19, 1863. Pub. by French and by Dicks. Priv. pr. 1886.

Taming a Butterfly. Farce. 3 acts. In collab. with Frank Wood. From *La Papillonne*, a play by V. Sardou. New York, Feb. 25, 1864. Priv. pr. 1867.

Lorlie's Wedding. Pastoral drama with music. 5 acts. From *Dorf und Stadt*, a play by C. Birchpfeiffer, based on *Die Frau Professorin*, a tale by B. Auerbach. Boston, Mar. 2, 1864; New York, Mar. 28, 1864.

Judith, the Daughter of Merari. Tragic play. 5 acts. In collab. with Paul Nicholson. Prob. based on *Giuditta*, a play by P. Giacometti, and *Judith*, a play by F. Hebbel. New York, Apr. 4, 1864.

Daly and Nicholson may have had a third collaborator. The playbill lists Daly as sole author. Judge Daly credits his brother and Nicholson. The drama editors of the period say that Daly asked (and they imply that he received) aid from Nicholson and also from one De Lisle (or De Lille), a *New York Herald* writer.

The Sorceress. Melodrama. 5 acts. Prob. from *La Sorcière; ou, Les États de Blois,* a play by A. Bourgeois and J. Barbier. New York, Apr. 26, 1864.

Griffith Gaunt; or, Jealousy. Drama. 6 acts. From the novel by C. Reade. New York, Nov. 7, 1866. Pub. by Wemyss in a 5-act version.

Hazardous Ground. Comedy. 4 acts. From *Nos Bons Villageois,* a play by V. Sardou. Newark, Feb. 22, 1867; Brooklyn, Mar. 11, 1867. Pub. by Wemyss and French.

Under the Gaslight. Sensational drama. 5 acts. New York, Aug. 12, 1867. Pub. by Wemyss, Lacy, and French. Priv. pr. 1867.

The emotional pattern is said to have been inspired by Lester Wallack's *Rosedale;* the railroad scene by an English play, *The Engineer.* On Feb. 28, 1881, the play appeared in Boston in a 4-act version which, according to the playbill, had been "Re-Written, Re-Arranged and Re-Constructed, by the Author, Mr. Augustin Daly, expressly for Oofty Gooft (Mr. Gus Phillips)."

A Legend of "Norwood"; or, Village Life in New England. Dramatic comedy. 4 acts. In collab. with Joseph W. Howard. From *Norwood,* a novel by H. W. Beecher. New York, Nov. 11, 1867. Priv. pr. 1867.

Pickwick Papers. Comedy. 4 acts. From the novel by C. Dickens. New York, Jan. 22, 1868.

A Flash of Lightning. Sensation drama. 5 acts and 10 tableaux. Plot device from *La Perle Noire,* a play by V. Sardou. New York, June 10, 1868. Priv. pr. 1885.

The Red Scarf; or, Scenes in Aroostock. Sensation drama. 3 acts. Brooklyn, Oct. 12, 1868; New York, Nov. 30, 1868.

Frou Frou. Comedy. 5 acts. From the play by H. Meilhac and L. Halévy. New York, Feb. 15, 1870. Pub. by French.

Fernande. Comedy. 4 acts and 4 tableaux. In collab. with Hart Jackson. From the play by V. Sardou. New York, June 7, 1870.

No two sources agree upon the authorship of this adaptation. At the time of the first performance the playbill credited it to N. Hart Jackson and Myron A. Cooney. When the play was given at the Union Square Theatre "by special permission of Augustin Daly," June 4, 1873, the bills named only Jackson. When it was revived at Daly's Theatre in 1879, they listed only Daly. The likelihood seems to be that the play was translated by Cooney (cf. the *New York Times,* Mar. 21, 1872) and adapted by Jackson and Daly.

Man and Wife. Emotional drama. 5 acts. From the novel by W. Collins. New York, Sept. 13, 1870. Priv. pr. 1885.

The Red Ribbon. Sensation drama. 4 acts. Chicago, Oct. 10, 1870.

This seems to be the play written for Mr. and Mrs. E. E. Tiffany which Judge Daly gives under the title *Sanya; or, The Red Ribbon,* a "Polish revolutionary drama," and which Professor Quinn believes to be identical with a manuscript play *Rhoda.* During its Chicago performances (the only ones I have been able to find), the play was known simply as *The Red Ribbon* and the scenes, according to the *Chicago Times,* were laid in Spain during the rebellion of 1868.

Come Here; or, The Débutante's Test. Dramatic sketch. 1 act. From *Komm Her!* a play by F. von Elsholtz. New York, Oct. 15, 1870.

Horizon. Frontier play. 5 acts and 7 tableaux. New York, Mar. 21, 1871. Pub. in A. G. Halline's *American Plays, 1935.* Priv. pr. 1885.

No Name. Dramatic comedy. 4 acts and 5 tableaux. From the novel by W. Collins. New York, June 7, 1871.

Daly's part in this dramatization is not entirely clear. Contemporary reviewers offer contradictory evidence, some of them crediting it to Daly, some to Collins, and some to both men. Judge Daly and the advertisements support the latter view.

Delmonico's; or, Larks up the Hudson. Comedy. 3 acts. Revised from *Taming a Butterfly, q.v.* New York, June 20, 1871.

Also known as *Delmonico's at Six.*

Divorce. Modern society drama. 5 acts. From *He Knew He Was Right,* a novel by A. Trollope. New York, Sept. 5, 1871. Priv. pr. 1884.

Article 47. Emotional drama. 5 acts. From *L'Article 47,* a play by A. Belot. New York, Apr. 2, 1872.

Roi Carotte. Fairy spectacle. 4 acts and 20 tableaux. From the fairy operetta by V. Sardou with music by J. Offenbach. New York, Aug. 26, 1872.

Round the Clock. Local sensational folly. 4 acts and 12 tableaux. In part from *La Tour du Cadran,* a vaudeville by H. Crémieux and H. Bocage. New York, Nov. 25, 1872.

The title sometimes included a subtitle, *New York by Dark.*

Alixe. Emotional comedy. 4 acts. From *La Comtesse de Somerive,* a play by T. Barrière and A. Régnauld de Prébois. New York, Jan. 21, 1873.

Roughing It. Kaleidescopic drama. 4 acts, 11 tableaux, and a transformation. Said to have been founded on a popular Parisian revue. New York, Feb. 18, 1873.

Uncle Sam; or, The Flirtation. Comedy. 4 acts. From *L'Oncle Sam,* a play by V. Sardou. New York, Mar. 17, 1873.

Madelein Morel. Emotional drama. 4 acts. From *Madeleine Morel,* a play by S. H. von Mosenthal. New York, May 20, 1873. Priv. pr. 1884 (as *Madelaine Morel*).

The Parricide. Melodrama. 6 tableaux. From *Le Parricide,* a play by A. Belot based on *Le Parricide* and *Dacolard et Lubin,* novels by Belot and J. Dautin. New York, Dec. 17, 1873.

Folline. Comedy. 4 acts. From *La Maison Neuve,* a play by V. Sardou. New York, Jan. 27, 1874.

Monsieur Alphonse. Society drama. 3 acts. From the play by A. Dumas, *fils.* New York, Apr. 14, 1874. Priv. pr. 1886.

What Should She Do? or, Jealousy. Society drama. 5 acts and 6 tableaux. From *Germaine,* a novel by E. About. New York, Aug. 25, 1874.

The School for Scandal. Comedy. 5 acts. From the play by R. B. Sheridan. New York, Sept. 12, 1874; revived with slight alterations Jan. 20, 1891. Pub. by French. Priv. pr. 1891.

Daly's arrangement seems to have been similar to one used at the Prince of Wales Theatre, London, earlier in the year. In both versions the scenes were so ordered as to form five acts of a single scene each. Daly had, of course, produced *The School for Scandal* before 1874, but not in a version adapted by himself.

The Two Widows. Comedy. 1 act. From *Les Deux Veuves,* a play by F. Mallefille. New York, Oct. 10, 1874.

The Critic. Conceit. 1 act. A condensed version of Sheridan's play. New York, Oct. 10, 1874. Revived Dec. 26, 1888 under the titles *Rehearsing a Tragedy, A Tragedy Rehearsed,* or *A Tragedy Rehearsal.* Priv. pr. 1889.

Yorick. Romantic tragedy. 3 acts. From *Un Drama Nuevo,* a play by M. Tamayo y Baus. New York, Dec. 5, 1874. Typewritten copies at Harvard and University of Pennsylvania libraries.

The Merchant of Venice. See below under date of Nov. 19, 1898.

The Big Bonanza; or, Riches and Matches. Farce-comedy. 4 acts. From *Ultimo,* a play by G. von Moser. New York, Feb. 17, 1875. Priv. pr. 1884.

The New Leah. Melodrama. 4 acts. Revised slightly from *Leah, the Forsaken, q.v.* New York, Nov. 22, 1875.

Pique. Society drama. 5 acts. From *Her Lord and Master,* a novel by F. Marryat Lean. New York, Dec. 14, 1875. Priv. pr. 1884.

Life. Comedy. 4 acts. From *Le Procès Veauradieux,* a play by A.-C. Lartigue and A. Hennequin, and *Loulou,* a play by H. Meilhac and L. Halévy. New York, Sept. 27, 1876.

The American. Society drama. 5 acts. From *L'Étrangère,* a play by A. Dumas, *fils.* New York, Dec. 20, 1876.

Lemons; or, Wedlock for Seven. Comedy. 3 acts. From *Citronen,* a play by J. Rosen. New York, Jan. 15, 1877. Priv. pr. 1877.

Blue Glass. Farce. 3 acts. From *Epidemisch,* a play by J. B. von Schweitzer. New York, Mar. 12, 1877.

The Princess Royal. Romantic play. 4 acts and 10 tableaux. From *L'Officier de Fortune,* a play by J. Adenis and J. Rostaing. New York, Mar. 31, 1877.

Vesta. Romantic tragedy. 5 acts. From *Rome Vaincue,* a play by D.-A. Parodi. New York, May 28, 1877.

The manuscript of a 3-act version made by Daly for Fanny Davenport is owned by the Princeton University Library.

The Dark City. Sensational play. 5 acts. From *Les Compagnons de la Truelle,* a play by T. Cogniard and L.-F. Nicolaïe. New York, Sept. 4, 1877. The complete title as given in the playbills was *The Dark City! and Its Bright Side.*

L'Assommoir. Melodrama. 5 acts and 9 tableaux. From the novel by É. Zola and its dramatization by W. Busnach and O. Gastineau. New York, Apr. 30, 1879.

Judge Daly says that this was "the French dramatization of Zola's novel done over into English by Mrs. Olive Logan Sykes," but the advertisements and playbills say it was adapted by Daly from the novel and the French dramatization. The title appears both as *L'Assommoir* and *The Assommoir.*

Love's Young Dream. Comedietta. 1 act. From the French. New York, Sept. 17, 1879. Priv. pr. in *Three Preludes to the Play*.

Although this was published as by Augustin Daly, it may have been the work of someone else—possibly of Daly's brother, Joseph Francis Daly.

An Arabian Night; or, Haroun al Raschid and His Mother-in-Law. Farce-comedy. 4 acts. From *Harun al Raschid,* a play by G. von Moser. New York, Nov. 29, 1879. Priv. pr. 1884 as *An Arabian Night in the Nineteenth Century*.

The Royal Middy. Operetta. 3 acts. In collab. with Frederick Williams, with additional music by Edward R. Mollenhauer. From *Der Seekadett,* a comic opera with music by R. Genée and libretto by F. Zell (C. Walzel). New York, Jan. 28, 1880.

Der Seekadett seems to have been derived from a French vaudeville, *Le Capitaine Charlotte,* by J. F. A. Bayard and Dumanoir (P.-F. Pinel), or from a common source.

The Way We Live. Social comedy. 4 acts. From *Wohlthätige Frauen,* a play by A. L'Arronge. New York, Apr. 10, 1880.

Tiote; or, A Young Girl's Heart. Melodrama. 5 tableaux. Trans. by Frederick Williams. From *La Petiote,* a play by A. Poitevin. New York, Aug. 18, 1880.

Needles and Pins. Farce-comedy. 4 acts. From *Starke Mitteln,* a play by J. Rosen. New York, Nov. 9, 1880. Priv. pr. 1884.

Zanina; or, The Rover of Cambaye. Oriental comedy. 3 acts. With several new musical numbers by E. R. Mollenhauer, a Hindu interlude by H. W. French, and lyrics by F. Williams. From *Nisida,* a comic opera by A. West and F. Zell (C. Walzel), music by R. Genée. New York, Jan. 18, 1881.

Quits; or, A Game of Tit for Tat. Farce-comedy. 4 acts. Said to be from a play by J. Rosen. New York, Sept. 7, 1881.

Royal Youth. Comedy. 5 acts. From *La Jeunesse de Louis XIV,* a play by A. Dumas, *père,* slightly revised by A. Dumas, *fils*. New York, Oct. 22, 1881.

The Passing Regiment. Farce-comedy. 5 acts. From *Krieg im Frieden,* a play by G. von Moser and F. von Schönthan. New York, Nov. 10, 1881. Priv. pr. 1884.

Odette. Emotional drama. 4 acts. From the play by V. Sardou. New York, Feb. 6, 1882.

Mankind. Melodrama. 5 acts. From *Mankind; or, Beggar Your Neighbour,* a play by P. Meritt and G. Conquest. New York, Sept. 5, 1882.

Daly apparently condensed and rearranged the play considerably and may have added a farcical element.

Our English Friend. Farce-comedy. 4 acts. From *Reif-Reiflingen,* a play by G. von Moser. New York, Nov. 25, 1882. Priv. pr. 1884.

She Would and She Would Not. Comedy. 4 acts. From the play by C. Cibber. New York, Jan. 13, 1883. Priv. pr. 1886.

Serge Panine. Comedy of manners. 5 acts. From the play by G. Ohnet. New York, Feb. 1, 1883.

Seven-Twenty-Eight; or, Casting the Boomerang. Farce-comedy. 4 acts. From *Der Schwabenstreich,* a play by F. von Schönthan. New York, Feb. 24, 1883. Pub. by Roorbach and by Dick and Fitzgerald. Priv. pr. 1886.

Dollars and Sense; or, The Heedless Ones. Farce-comedy. 3 acts. From *Die Sorglosen,* a play by A. L'Arronge. New York, Oct. 2, 1883. Priv. pr. 1885.

The Country Girl. Comedy. 3 acts. From the adaptation by D. Garrick of *The Country Wife* by W. Wycherley, with additions from *Love for Love* by W. Congreve. New York, Feb. 16, 1884. Priv. pr. 1898.

Red Letter Nights; or, Catching a Crœsus. Farce-comedy with songs. 4 acts. From *Ein Gemachter Mann,* a play by E. Jacobson, with music by G. Michaelis. New York, Mar. 12, 1884.

A Woman's Won't. Farce. 1 act. From *Gott sei Dank, der Tisch ist Gedeckt,* a play by M. Röttinger based on *Dieu Merci, le Couvert est Mis,* a play by L. Gozlan, based on *Eigensinn,* a play by J. R. Benedix. Philadelphia, May 2, 1884; New York, Feb. 28, 1885.

A Wooden Spoon; or, Perdita's Penates. Farce-comedy. 4 acts. From *Roderick Heller,* a play by F. von Schönthan. New York, Oct. 7, 1884.

Love on Crutches. Comedy. 3 acts. From *Ihre Ideale,* a play by H. Stobitzer, said to have been based on an idea by L. Schücking. New York, Nov. 25, 1884. Priv. pr. 1884.

The Recruiting Officer. Comedy. 3 acts. From the play by G. Farquhar. New York, Feb. 7, 1885. Priv. pr. 1885.

A Night Off; or, A Page from Balzac. Farce-comedy. 4 acts. From *Der Raub der Sabinerinnen,* a play by F. (and P.?) von Schönthan. New York, Mar. 4, 1885. Pub. by Dick and Fitzgerald and by Roorbach. Priv. pr. 1885.

Denise. Problem play. 4 acts. From the play by A. Dumas, *fils.* New York, Apr. 21, 1885.

Living for Show. Comedy-drama. 4 acts. From the German. Boston, Dec. 7, 1885.

The Merry Wives of Windsor. Comedy. 4 acts and 11 scenes. From the play by W. Shakespeare. New York, Jan. 14, 1886. Priv. pr. 1886.

The version used at this time seems to have been shorter than the one produced by Daly on Nov. 19, 1872, which, according to the playbills, consisted of 5 acts and 12 scenes. Textual changes were also made for the purpose of "expunging from the text whatever might perchance be offensive to fastidious refinement."

A Wet Blanket. Comedy. 1 act. From *La Douche,* a play by P. Bilhaud and J. Lévy. New York, Feb. 13, 1886. Priv. pr. in *Three Preludes to the Play*.

A Sudden Shower. Comedy. 1 act. From the French of F. Beissier. New York, Feb. 18, 1886. Priv. pr. in *Three Preludes to the Play*.

Nancy and Company. Farce-comedy. 4 acts. From *Halbe Dichter,* a play by J. Rosen, from an idea by B. Busch. New York, Feb. 24, 1886. Priv. pr. 1884 and 1886.

After Business Hours. Farce-comedy. 4 acts. From *Sammt und Seide,* a play by O. Blumenthal. New York, Oct. 5, 1886. Priv. pr. 1886.

Love in Harness; or, Hints to Hymen. Farce-comedy. 3 acts. From *Le Bonheur Conjugal,* a play by A. Valabrègue. New York, Nov. 16, 1886. Priv. pr. 1887.

The Taming of the Shrew. Comedy. 5 acts and induction. From the play by W. Shakespeare with a few of Garrick's alterations. New York, Jan. 18, 1887. Priv. pr. 1887.

The Railroad of Love. Comedy. 4 acts. From *Goldfische,* a play by F. von Schönthan and G. Kadelburg. New York, Nov. 1, 1887. Priv. pr. 1887.

A Midsummer Night's Dream. Comedy. 5 acts. From the play by W. Shakespeare. New York, Jan. 31, 1888. Priv. pr. 1888.

The Lottery of Love. Farce-comedy. 3 acts. From *Les Surprises du Divorce,* a play by A. Bisson and A. Mars. New York, Oct. 9, 1888. Priv. pr. 1889.

The Under Current. Melodrama. 4 acts. New York, Nov. 13, 1888.

In an interview which appeared in the *New York Times* of Oct. 25, 1888, Daly is quoted as having said that *The Under Current* was begun ten years before in an attempt to combine the sensational incidents of *A Flash of Lightning* and of *Under the Gaslight*. The full title, which was seldom used, was *The Under Current of Human Life and Human Passion*.

Rehearsing a Tragedy. See *The Critic,* Oct. 10, 1874.

The Inconstant; or, The Way to Win Him. Comedy. 4 or 5 acts. From the play by G. Farquhar. New York, Jan. 8, 1889. Priv. pr. 1889.

The evidence as to the number of acts is contradictory. It was printed in 4 acts, but it seems to have been produced, at least in the beginning, in 5 acts.

An International Match. Farce-comedy. 4 acts. From *Cornelius Voss,* a play by F. von Schönthan. New York, Feb. 5, 1889. Priv. pr. 1890.

Samson and Delilah. Farce-comedy. 3 acts. From *Un Conceil Judiciaire,* a play by A. Bisson and J. Moineaux. New York, Mar. 28, 1889.

The Golden Widow. Comedy. 3 acts. From *Marquise,* a play by V. Sardou. New York, Oct. 2, 1889.

Roger la Honte; or, A Man's Shadow. Melodrama. 4 acts. From an English version, *Roger La Honte; or, Jean, the Disgraced* (later known as *A Man's Shadow*) by R. Buchanan, of *Roger-la-Honte,* a play by J. Mary and G. Grisier based on a story by Mary. New York, Oct. 8, 1889.

The Great Unknown. Farce-comedy. 3 acts. From *Die Berühmte Frau,* a play by F. von Schönthan and G. Kadelburg. New York, Oct. 22, 1889. Priv. pr. 1890.

As You Like It. Comedy. 5 acts. From the play by W. Shakespeare. New York, Dec. 17, 1889. Priv. pr. 1890.

Miss Hoyden's Husband. Comedietta. 1 act. From *A Trip to Scarborough,* a play by R. B. Sheridan based on *The Relapse* by J. Vanbrugh. New York, Mar. 26, 1890.

The Last Word. Comedy. 4 acts. From *Das Letzte Wort,* a play by F. von Schönthan. New York, Oct. 28, 1890. Priv. pr. 1891.

The Prodigal Son. Pantomime. 3 acts. From *L'Enfant Prodigue,* a pantomime by M. Carré, *fils,* music by A. Wormser. New York, Mar. 3, 1891.

Love's Labour's Lost. Comedy. 4 acts. From the play of the same name by W. Shakespeare. Mar. 28, 1891. Priv. pr. 1891.

Daly's first production of a 5-act version of this play on Feb. 21, 1874, was widely advertised as its first performance in the United States.

Love in Tandem. Farce-comedy. 3 acts. From *La Vie à Deux,* a play by H. Bocage and C. de Courcy. New York, Feb. 9, 1892. Priv. pr. 1892.

Little Miss Million. Farce-comedy. 4 acts. From *Das Zweite Gesicht,* a play by O. Blumenthal. New York, Oct. 6, 1892. Priv. pr. 1893.

A Test Case; or, Grass versus Granite. Farce-comedy. 4 acts. From *Die Grossstadtluft,* a play by O. Blumenthal and G. Kadelburg. New York, Nov. 10, 1892. Priv. pr. 1893.

The Hunchback. Comedy. 5 acts. From the play by S. Knowles. New York, Nov. 29, 1892. Priv. pr. 1893.

The Belle's Stratagem. Comedy. 3 acts. From the play by H. Cowley. New York, Jan. 3, 1893. Priv. pr. 1892 and 1893.

Twelfth Night. Comedy. 4 acts. From the play by W. Shakespeare. New York, Feb. 21, 1893. Priv. pr. 1893.

The Orient Express. Farce-comedy. 3 acts. In collab. (?) with F. C. Burnand. From *Die Orientreise,* a play by O. Blumenthal and G. Kadelburg. New York, Jan. 31, 1895.

The evidence as to Daly's share in this adaptation is not entirely clear. When the play was first produced at Daly's London Theatre, Oct. 25, 1893, Daly was not mentioned as coadapter, nor did his name appear on the playbills when, despite its English failure, it was given in New York fifteen months later. On the other hand, a press notice which appeared shortly before the New York production declared it to be Daly's adaptation; it was copyrighted in 1913 as by Burnand and Daly; and a manuscript version owned by Mr. Barrett H. Clark seems to be in Daly's handwriting.

Two Gentlemen of Verona. Comedy. 4 acts. From the play by W. Shakespeare. New York, Feb. 25, 1895. Priv. pr. 1895.

A Bundle of Lies. Farce-comedy. 3 acts. From *Der Höchste Trumpf,* a play by K. Laufs and W. Jacoby. New York, Mar. 28, 1895.

The Transit of Leo. Comedy. 3 acts. From *Das Schosskind* (or *Aus Berlin, W.*), a play by B. Köhler. New York, Dec. 10, 1895.

The Countess Gucki. Comedy. 3 acts. From *Komtesse Guckerl,* a play by F. von Schönthan and F. Koppel-Ellfeld. New York, Jan. 28, 1896. Priv. pr. 1895.

Much Ado About Nothing. Comedy. 4 acts. From the play by W. Shakespeare. New York, Dec. 23, 1896. Priv. pr. 1897.

The Wonder! A Woman Keeps a Secret. Comedy. 4 acts. From the play by S. Centlivre. New York, Mar. 23, 1897. Priv. pr. in *Two Old Comedies,* 1893.

The Tempest. Comedy. 4 acts. With music by Arne and Purcell, arranged by F. Ecke; also with music by K. Taubert. From the play by W. Shakespeare. New York, Apr. 6, 1897. Priv. pr. 1897.

Number Nine; or, The Lady of Ostend. Farce. 3 acts. In collab. (?) with F. C. Burnand. From *Hans Huckebein,* a play by O. Blumenthal and G. Kadelburg. New York, Dec. 7, 1897.

It is by no means certain that Daly had a hand in this adaptation. Neither the advertisements, the playbills, nor the reviewers credited him with a share in it. Daly, however, copyrighted it in 1897 as a comedy from the German by Burnand and himself, and this statement of joint authorship is repeated by the administrators of Daly's will.

Cyrano de Bergerac. Romantic drama. 5 acts. From the English translation by G. Thomas and M. F. Guillemard of the play by E. Rostand. Philadelphia, Oct. 3, 1898.

The Merchant of Venice. Comedy. 5 acts. From the play by W. Shakespeare. New York, Nov. 19, 1898. Priv. pr. 1898.

The version produced by Daly, Jan. 11, 1875, with E. L. Davenport as Shylock, was not advertised as his. It had 4 acts and 4 scenes.

MAN AND WIFE

A Play in Five Acts

Based on a Novel by Wilkie Collins

MAN AND WIFE

MAN AND WIFE was the sixth of the great successes which began in Boston in 1862 with *Leah, the Forsaken*. It was the second to be produced in the Fifth Avenue Theatre, which Daly had leased from Jim Fisk in 1869. *Frou-Frou*, the hit of Daly's first season, had come only after strenuous and not too encouraging months of struggle in building up a company and a clientele. *Man and Wife*, "an original dramatic arrangement in five acts of Wilkie Collins' romantic novel," opened the second season, September 13, 1870, most auspiciously. The dramatization may not have been entirely the work of Daly as the advertisements said that the American manager merely adapted the Englishman's own version. On the other hand Collins's dramatization, according to a review of the London production on February 22, 1873, differed materially from Daly's.

Whether Daly contributed largely or scantily to the play, his Fifth Avenue Theatre company was an important factor in the play's success. Clara Morris, a newcomer to the New York stage, was greatly praised for her work as the wronged "Anne Sylvester." Miss Morris's appearance in this rôle was due to its refusal by Agnes Ethel—a refusal which is said to have been based on its alleged immorality. Others who were markedly successful in their parts were James Lewis and Mrs. G. H. Gilbert. Kate Claxton made her stage début at this time as a croquet player without lines. The complete cast will be found on page 6.

Although the fine performance of Clara Morris was the principal topic of the reviews, generous praise was bestowed on the play itself. William Winter, after dilating upon the theater with "its glancing lights, its flashing mirrors, its burnished hydrants, . . . and its new drop-curtain," declared:

The drama proved to be exceeding interesting and effective. . . . In this instance the task [of dramatization], if not entirely and perfectly accomplished, has been carried a very long way toward brilliant fulfillment. . . . "Man and Wife" . . . owed its success, on Tuesday, to this among other causes—the refining influence of its spirit. Something of the debt, though, was due to its romantic interest, as the crystallization of a fine story, and something to the worthy efforts of the players.—*New York Tribune*, Sept. 15, 1870.

Man and Wife ran for slightly more than two months, closing on November 19. It was, however, repeated several times later in the season. January 3, 1874, Ada Dyas made her first appearance with Daly's company

in the rôle of "Ann Sylvester." The next revival occurred in December of
the same year. Business was not good in 1874 and *Man and Wife* was being
used to fill gaps. In February 1877 some of Daly's actors presented the play
in brief engagements at the Grand Opera House and the Bowery Theatre.
The next and apparently final revival of the play by Daly was for a few
matinées in November and December of 1879.

Outside of New York, Daly's *Man and Wife* had to compete with a
number of other dramatizations. Versions by Frank Mayo and Fred Williams
preempted the Boston theaters, both being seen there in November 1870.
The only Boston production of Daly's play, of which I have record,
occurred in 1877 when it was given by amateurs as a benefit for sufferers
in the Cuban war. Chicago on the other hand saw Daly's version first. A
Chicago company played it at Aiken's Museum from December 5 to 17,
1870. The *Times* in its review the next day noted that Daly had adhered very
closely to the text of the novel, "some of the lines of entire scenes being
exact reproductions of the original." As a play *Man and Wife* was "odd,
attractive, and without being sensational, thoroughly dramatic." On June
10, 1872, Frank Mayo brought his version of the story to Chicago and the
newspapers were again cordial. The following year a third rendition of the
novel was seen in Chicago on September 29. This time *Man and Wife*
elicited a savage attack from one of the critics who was apparently motivated
by dislike of Wilkie Collins rather than by any defect in the work of the
adapter, H. A. Webber. Many years later, April 28, 1894, Marie Wainwright
was advertised to appear in Daly's version in one of Chicago's minor houses.

In the British Isles, where, according to *"The Stage" Cyclopædia*, C. H.
Stephenson had preceded Daly by a little less than two weeks with a dramatization produced in Belfast September 2, 1870, there were a number of other
versions. Collins's own was produced by the Bancrofts February 22, 1873,
and ran for more than five months. It is interesting to note that Collins
omitted the attempted murder at Salt Patch which formed the sensational
last act of most, if not all, of the American dramatizations. In addition to
Collins's version there were several others which were produced in Britain
in the 'Eighties and one in the 'Nineties. None of these were as late,
however, as the Chicago performance of 1894.

Burlesque skits of *Man and Wife* seem to have been more popular in
New York than elsewhere. At least I have found no record of parodies being
given in Boston or Chicago, whereas four different minstrel troupes in
New York and Brooklyn played with the piece before the end of the
1870-71 season.

Webber's version was copyrighted in 1874 and published by A. D. Ames.
None of the others seem to have been published. The libraries of the Uni-

versities of Pennsylvania and of Chicago both have mimeographed copies of some version of the play. Chicago's copy, and I presume it is similar to Pennsylvania's, differs radically from both Webber's and Daly's versions. Daly printed his play privately in 1885.

The present edition of *Man and Wife* is based on the printing of 1885. In this play as in the others in the volume, spelling, capitalization, and punctuation have been modernized in conformity with the policy adopted for the whole series. The stage directions and the abbreviations of speakers' names have also been changed somewhat in the interest of uniformity and modern typographical style. With the exception of a few corrections of obvious misprints or misreadings, especially in Bishoprigg's lines, which Daly took almost verbatim from the novel, the dialogue of the play has not been touched. In the few cases where words seemed to be lacking or where emendations seemed necessary, the editor's additions have been enclosed in brackets.

The cast of characters which follows is a synthesis of the cast as given in the printed edition and as listed in a playbill of the early weeks of the run.

DRAMATIS PERSONAE AND ORIGINAL CAST

GEOFFREY DELAMAYN, *the "man"*   MR. D. H. HARKINS

ARNOLD BRINKWORTH, *his friend*   MR. JOS. POLK

SIR PATRICK LUNDIE   MR. JAMES LEWIS

BISHOPRIGGS, *"with one eye moist and merry"*   MR. W. DAVIDGE

JULIUS DELAMAYN   MR. ARTHUR MATTHISON

MR. MOY, *Geoffrey's London solicitor*   MR. GEO. F. DE VERE

NUMBER 1   MR. GEO. PARKES

NUMBER 2   *The "Choral Gentlemen"*   MR. H L. BASCOMB

NUMBER 3   MR. F. CHAPMAN

CAPTAIN NEWENDEN   MR. J. H. BURNETT

PERRY, *the trainer*   MR. G. F. BROWNE

JONATHAN, *who knew where he "would go to if he told a lie"*   MR. W. H. BEEKMAN

JOHN THOMAS, *the "traditional" footman*   MR. PIERCE

ANNE SYLVESTER, *the "wife"*   MISS CLARA MORRIS

BLANCHE LUNDIE, *her friend*   MISS FANNY DAVENPORT

LADY LUNDIE   MISS KATE NEWTON

HESTER DETTHRIDGE, *the dumb cook at Windygates*   MRS. G. H. GILBERT

MRS. GLENHARM   MISS LINDA DIETZ

JO, *a young lady for croquet*   MISS KATE CLAXTON

MISS ELLERSLY   MISS GERTRUDE KELLOGG

HOPKINS, *Lady Lundie's French maid*   MISS ROBERTA NORWOOD

MRS. INCHBARE   MAD. LESDERNIER

MISS LITTLE   MISS LOUISE VOLMER

ACT I: "THE PROMISE OF MARRIAGE!" THE SUMMERHOUSE AT WINDYGATES.

ACT II: "THE EXTINGUISHED CANDLE!" SCENE 1: THE HALL AT WINDYGATES. SCENE 2: THE SCOTCH INN.

ACT III: "DONE!" SCENE 1: THE LIBRARY AT WINDYGATES. SCENE 2: THE HALL AT WINDYGATES. SCENE 3: THE LAWN AT SWANHAVEN.

ACT IV: "MAN AND WIFE." THE LACE PARLOR IN PORTLAND SQUARE.

ACT V: "DIVORCE." THE PAPERED ROOM AT SALT PATCH.

ACT I.

SCENE: *Interior of the summerhouse at Windygates. The grounds seen through the arch, C., entrances at L.D. and R.1.E. Light waltz heard at rise of curtain. Rustic sofa, R.H. Rustic chair up. Sofa and rustic table, L.H., downstage, with croquet mallets and balls. Enter Geoffrey and Julius, L.1.E.*

GEOF. [*R.*] We're private enough here, I guess. What's the row?

JUL. I've just left father. As you know, he's very sick—as I know, he's nearer death than his own iron will admits. Well, father is willing to give you a last chance. If you don't take it, my doors are closed against you as well as his.

GEOF. Out with it then, and don't be long about it.

JUL. [*L.*] I won't be five minutes. Here it is in plain words: Father consents to see you again, if you choose to settle in life and marry the woman he has chosen for you. Refuse, and you go to ruin your own way. [*Geoffrey pausing in contemplation*] Isn't the prospect pleasing to you?

GEOF. [*Seated, R.*] To me? Oh, yes, but I was just thinking what a certain young lady not far from here would say, if she could hear your silvery temptation.

JUL. I have nothing to do with any degrading connections which you may have formed. I have only to put the matter before you exactly as it stands, and to leave you to decide for yourself. The *lady* father proposes for your consideration, is Mrs. Glenharm. Birth and fortune—she has both. Her union is a ten thousand a year; father will make it fifteen thousand if you are lucky enough to persuade her to marry you.

GEOF. [*Arousing himself from thought*] If she don't, to a man who's going to run in the great race at Fulban, there are plenty as good as she is, who will. That's not the difficulty. Bother that! [*Taking a letter from his pocketbook and showing it to Julius*] The trouble's here.

JUL. What's that?

GEOF. [*Withdrawing the letter and throwing himself into a chair with a laugh, holding his head downwards*] Only a love letter, that's all.

JUL. [*Crosses to R.*] I tell you again I have nothing to do with your difficulties. Take the rest of the day to consider what I have said to you. If you decide to accept the proposition, I shall expect you to prove you are in earnest by meeting me at the station tonight. We will travel back to London together. There is nothing more to be said. If you join me at the station tonight, I will do all I can to help you. If I travel back to London alone, don't trouble yourself to follow—I have done with you. [*Exit, R.1.E. Music · till all on. Geoffrey twirls the letter in his hand a brief second after Julius goes off, following him with his eyes, then he opens and reads aloud*]

GEOF. [*Reading*] "Your conduct to me is cruelty itself. Consider, in your own interests, consider before you drive the miserable woman who has trusted you to despair. You have promised me marriage by all that is sacred. I insist on nothing else, than to be what you vowed I should be—what I have waited all this weary time to be—your wedded wife. My mind is made up to endure this suspense no longer. Geoffrey, remember the past—be faithful, be just to your loving wife. Anne Sylvester." [*Restoring it to his bosom*] That's scarcely what the newspapers would call light reading for summer, I should think. [*Rising*] Thunder and lightning, but here's a mess for a fellow—a threat from the governor, an appeal from Anne. Will it be best to heed the threat or the appeal? [*Music. Laughter and music without*] Whichever, this isn't the time to decide; a croquet party is coming. [*Music, forte. Attempts to exit, R.1.E. Enter Nos. 1, 2 and 3 with Mrs. Glenharm, Sir Patrick, Lady Lundie, etc., all chatting and laughing, with parasols up*]

No. 1. [*R.C., turning to R.*] I say, by Jove, there's Delamayn now. I say, Del. [*Geoffrey expresses disappointment*] Old boy, we just want you.

No. 2. Aw—ya'as, Delamayn, we just want you.

No. 3. Ya'as.

ALL. Come, Delamayn, you can't be spared. [*Enter Blanche, C.L.*]

BLAN. Now, then, good people, silence if you please; we are going to choose sides at croquet. Business, business, business.

LADY L. [*In door, L.*] My dear, words have a meaning even on a young lady's lips; please don't call croquet "business." [*Comes down*]

SIR P. [*In door, L.*] I hope you don't call it pleasure. [*Comes down, L.*]

BLAN. [*Motioning both to be quiet*] I head one side, ladies and gentlemen, and Lady Lundie heads the other; we choose our players turn and turn about. Mamma has the advantage of me in years, so mamma choose first.

LADY L. [*L.C., aside*] Ah! I'd send you back to the nursery, miss, if I was your real mother, instead of being merely your stepmother. [*Turning and running her eye with eyeglasses over the guests and singling out Anne, who enters at this moment*] I choose Miss Sylvester. [*All guests turn and look at Anne, who advances slowly*]

ANNE. [*Upstage*] Thank you, Lady Lundie. I would rather not play. [*Lady Lundie assumes an air of surprise. Both look at each other with looks of distrust*]

LADY L. [*Sharply*] Oh! Indeed, considering that we are here for the purpose of playing, that seems rather remarkable. Is anything wrong, Miss Sylvester?

ANNE. [*L.*] Nothing is the matter. I am not very well this morning. But I will play if you wish it.

LADY L. I do wish it. [*Anne bows, moves to one of the entrances to summerhouse and looks off*]

BLAN. Now it's my turn. I choose Mr. Delamayn. [*Geoffrey advances, Anne turns and on seeing him tries to repress emotion, clutches back of rustic chair. Lady Lundie watches her without being noticed by the others*]

GEOF. [*Down on her R.*] Thanks very much. But couldn't you additionally honor me by choosing somebody else? Croquet is not in my line. [*All laugh*]

LADIES. [*All*] Why, Mr. Delamayn!

No. 1. [*R.C.*] Aw—a—boat race is more in your line, old fellow.

Nos. 2 and 3. [*R.*] Ya-as.

BLAN. [*Petulantly, L.C.*] Can't we interest you in anything but severe muscular exercise, Mr. Delamayn? Must you always be pulling in a boat race, or flying over a high jump?

GEOF. [*Good humoredly*] Just as you please. Don't be offended, only let me smoke. I miss my smoke. I thought I'd step away a bit and have it. All right, I'll play. [*Enter Arnold; stands behind Blanche's chair*]

BLAN. Oh, smoke by all means. I shall choose somebody else. I won't have you. [*Looking around R., not seeing Arnold*] Whom shall I choose? [*Nos. 1, 2 and 3 regulate themselves, and advance a step*]

ARN. [*In a whisper, C.*] Choose me. [*Down to R. of Blanche*]

BLAN. [*Breaking into a smile, turning towards him*] You? [*Then rising, poutingly*] Why, you are going to leave us in an hour's time!

ARN. [*Same, pleadingly*] I am coming back the day after tomorrow.

BLAN. You play very badly.

ARN. I might improve if you would teach me.

BLAN. Might you? Then I will. [*Turning to rest*] I choose Mr. Arnold Brinkworth.

No. 1. By Jove! [*Nos. 1, 2 and 3 drop their glasses and turn away disgusted*]

BLAN. Now it's your turn again, mamma.

LADY L. [*Up and down, L.*] Well, I choose for my second partner, Sir Patrick.

BLAN. Why, mamma! what can you be thinking of? Sir Patrick won't play; croquet wasn't discovered in his time.

SIR P. [*Down R.C. to table*] In my time, my dear, people were expected to bring some agreeable quality with them to social meetings of this sort. Here [*Taking up a croquet mallet from the table*] is one of the qualifications for success in modern society, and here [*Taking up a ball*] is another; very good. Live and learn. I'll play, I'll play.

LADY L. [*L.C.*] I knew Sir Patrick would play to please me.

SIR P. [*Bowing with satirical politeness*] Lady Lundie, you read me like a book—I may say with Dryden—

"Old as I am, for ladies' love unfit,
　　The honor of beauty I remember yet." [*Lady Lundie bows,
pleased, and joins Blanche and the ladies*]

No. 1. [*Crosses to C.*] Aw—I say—hold on! Dryden never said that, by Jove.

Nos. 2 and 3. Wobinson's right—Dryden couldn't, by Jove!

SIR P. [*To No. 1*] Do you know Dryden better than I do, sir?

No. 1. Know him? Ha—ha!— Know him?—he—he! I should say I did—rowed three races with him, and trained with him, too. [*Crosses to R.*]

Nos. 2 and 3. That's so.

SIR P. [*L.C.*] Then let me tell you, sir, that you trained with a man who died nearly two hundred years ago.

No. 1. [*R.C.*] Say, Barow, what does he mean? I am speaking of Tom Dryden, of Corpus. Everybody in the University knows *him*.

SIR P. I was speaking of John Dryden, the poet; apparently everybody *out* of the University doesn't know *him*!

No. 1. Bless me, you don't say so. Give you my word of honor I never heard of him before in my life! I say, don't be angry with me—I'm not offended with you! [*Taking out cigarettes*] Got a light?

SIR P. [*In disgust*] Don't smoke.

No. 1. Don't smoke! How the deuce do you get through your spare time? [*Sir Patrick turns up in disgust*] I say, do you know?

No. 2. Weally, no!

No. 3. Fact, no.

BLAN. Come, Mr. Delamayn. Come, ladies, let's begin the game. Take any mallets from the table. [*Running to Sir Patrick*] Mr. Brinkworth—uncle—give me an arm apiece.

SIR. P. Leave Mr. Brinkworth with me, I want to speak with him.

BLAN. Oh, uncle! [*Pouting in byplay. Arnold joins them and they get to R. Ladies and Gentlemen exeunt. As Geoffrey is following, Anne suddenly crosses his steps, in a low voice speaks. Lady Lundie and Mrs. Glenharm joining with Nos. 1, 2 and 3. Playing party appear at back and play*]

ANNE. [*L. of Geoffrey, upstage*] You got my letter?

GEOF. Yes.

ANNE. In ten minutes the summerhouse will be empty—meet me here.

GEOF. Do you think it safe?

ANNE. I insist upon it. [*Exit after party. Geoffrey, R.U.E.*]

BLAN. Well, I agree, uncle. But mind, Mr. Brinkworth is to be released the minute I call him.

ARN. [*Aside and slyly*] Call me soon, [*She pouts*] please. [*Blanche smiles, and is going*]

SIR P. Agreed! Agreed! [*Exit Blanche after party*] Mr. Brinkworth, your father was one of my dearest friends. Let me make a friend of your father's son.

ARN. O Sir Patrick! [*Holding out his hands*]

SIR P. I have taken a liking to you; you're not like the young fellows of the present time. I shall call you Arnold—you mustn't return the compliment, and call me Patrick! I'm too old to be treated in *that* way. [*Sir Patrick touches a spring in the knot of his ivory cane, a little gold lid flies up and discloses the snuffbox hidden inside. He takes a pinch and chuckles satirically*] Well, how do you get on here? Who are your friends?

ARN. I have only one friend at Windygates, he came here this morning, like you—Geoffrey Delamayn. [*Sir Patrick looks disappointed*]

SIR P. Your choice of a friend rather surprises me.

ARN. We were schoolfellows together, at Eton. Geoffrey saved my life, Sir Patrick. [*His voice rising and his eyes brightening with honest admiration of his friend*] But for him, I should have been drowned in a boat accident. Isn't that a good reason for his being a friend of mine?

SIR P. It depends entirely on the value you set on your life.

ARN. It's an obligation I can never repay.

SIR P. Well, he'll make you repay one of these days with interest, if I know anything of human nature. [*At this point Geoffrey appears at the entrance to the summerhouse. A smile of pleasure passes over his face as he sees the place is occupied. He has a flower in his mouth. He is about retreating again, when Mrs. Glenharm enters. Sir Patrick motions silence to Arnold. Sir Patrick gets R.C.*]

MRS. G. Is that the use you make of a flower when I give it to you—mumbling it in your teeth as if you were a horse?

GEOF. If you come to that, I am more of a horse than a man. I'm going to run in a race, and the public are betting on me. How! How! Five to four.

MRS. G. [*Taking him by the arm, and turning him to go out*] Five to four! I believe, Sir Patrick, he thinks of nothing but betting. You great heavy creature, I can't move you. You're not going to let go of my arm; you're to take me. [*Exeunt together. Sir Patrick follows them up and smiles disdainfully*]

SIR P.   There's pretty stuff for a slayer of hearts.

ARN.   [*R.*] You speak rather bitterly, sir; what has Geoffrey done to offend you?

SIR P.   [*L.*] He presumes to exist—that's what he has done! Don't stare; your friend is the model young Briton of the present time. I don't like the model young Briton. I don't see the sense of crowing over him as a superb national production—because he is big and strong, and drinks beer with impunity, and takes a cold shower bath all the year round. Let's change the subject. I know nothing to the prejudice of your friend, Mr. Delamayn. Is he the only attraction for you, here, eh? [*Blanche calls from outside "Mr. Brinkworth." Arnold starts as if to go*] Ah! that's the attraction, is it? [*Arnold looks confused. Blanche appears at door, L.U.E.*]

BLAN.   Mr. Brinkworth, I shall want you directly. Uncle, it's your turn to play.

SIR P.   Bless my soul, I forgot the play. [*Looks about; sees his mallet and ball left waiting on the table*] Where are the modern substitutes for conversation? Oh, here they are. [*He bowls the ball out before him, and tucks the mallet under his arm, as if it were an umbrella*] Who says that human life is a serious thing? Here am I with one foot in the grave, and the most serious question before me now, is, shall I get through the hoops? [*Exit, L.U.E.*]

BLAN.   [*Entering. Arnold shy*] What has Sir Patrick been saying to you?

ARN.   [*R. Still shy and after a moment's irresolution*] Sir Patrick is a terrible old man; just before you came in, he discovered one of my secrets by only looking in my face. [*He pauses, rallies his courage, then comes headlong to the point*] I wonder if you take after your uncle?

BLAN.   [*Aside, gaily*] He is going to make me an offer, and he has about a minute to do it in. He shall do it. [*Aloud*] What! Do you think the gift of discovery runs in the family?

ARN.   I wish it did.

BLAN.   Why?

ARN.   If you could see in my face, what Sir [*Pauses as he is about to make another attempt. Cries of "Oh, Sir Patrick!" outside*]

BLAN.   [*Impatiently*] Well, if I did look in your face, what should I see?

ARN.   You would see that I wanted a little encouragement.

BLAN.   From me?

ARN.   Yes, if you please.

BLAN. [*After gazing off, then around, and satisfying herself that they will not be interrupted, then whispers to him*] Well, consider yourself encouraged [*He takes her hand in rhapsody*] within limit!

ARN. [*With ardor*] Consider *yourself* loved without any limit at all! [*Blanche struggles to release her hand, he holds it more tightly*] Do try to like me a little. [*Pleadingly*] I am awfully fond of you.

BLAN. Did you learn this method of making love in the merchant service?

ARN. [*Seriously*] I'll go back to the merchant service, if I have made you angry with me.

BLAN. [*Demurely*] Anger, Mr. Brinkworth, is one of the bad passions. A young lady who has been properly brought up, *has* no bad passions. [*Loud cries from the players outside: "Mr. Brinkworth," "Arnold," "Game." Blanche tries to push him out*] There, go; they are calling. [*Crosses to R.*]

ARN. [*L.H.*] Say something to encourage me before I go; one word will do; say yes.

BLAN. [*Shaking her head*] Quite impossible; if you want any more encouragement, you must speak to my uncle.

ARN. I'll speak to him before the game is out, if I have to pick him up in my arms and bring him here. [*Cries outside: "Mr. Brinkworth"*]

BLAN. Go, and mind you get through the hoops. [*Blanche has both hands on his shoulders, her face close to his; Arnold catches her around the waist and kisses her. Before she recovers herself, Arnold gives her a last squeeze and runs out, L.U.E.*] Oh, the darling fellow! I wouldn't have anyone know it for the world, but I'm ready to jump out of my skin for joy! [*Blanche sinks into chair, runs towards entrance, meets Anne, who enters, looking off scene*] Oh, Anne! [*Anne looks in her face, smiles sadly, then looks off*] What is the matter, Anne?

ANNE. [*L.*] Nothing.

BLAN. There is something the matter; is it money—bills to pay? I've got plenty of money. I'll lend you what you like.

ANNE. No, no, my dear.

BLAN. I tell you all *my* secrets. Why are you keeping a secret from me? Do you know that you have been looking anxious and out of spirits for some time past? Perhaps you don't like Mr. Brinkworth? No? You do like him? Is it my marrying, then? You fancy we shall be parted, then; as if I could do without you; of course, when I am married to Arnold, you will come and live with us. [*Anne draws suddenly away from Blanche*]

ANNE. [*Crosses to R.*] There is somebody coming—look! [*Arnold appears in doorway*]

BLAN. You are not yourself, and I must know the reason of it. I will wait till tonight, and then you shall tell me all. And there's a kiss for you in the meantime. [*Crosses to C., joining Arnold*] Well, have you got through the hoops?

ARN.   Never mind the hoops, I have broken the ice with Sir Patrick.

BLAN.   What! Before the whole company?

ARN.   Of course not. I have made an appointment to speak to him here. [*They go off laughing, L.U.E.*]

ANNE.   Is the time coming when even Blanche will see what I am in my face? [*With a sudden cry of despair, she throws up her hands and lays them heavily against the wall, and rests her head on them, with her back to the light; at the same moment Geoffrey enters and stands in the doorway, smoking*]

GEOF.   [*L., suddenly and advancing*]   I have come, as you made a point of it, but mind you, it is not safe. [*At the sound of his voice, Anne turns towards him. A change of expression appears in her face, and she slowly advances with terrible composure and terrible contempt*]

GEOF.   Well, what have you got to say to me?

ANNE.   [*Turning to him*]   Mr. Delamayn, you are one of the fortunate people of this world; you are a nobleman's son—you are popular at your college—you are free of the best houses in England. Are you something besides all this? Are you a villain and a coward?

GEOF.   [*Struggling to subdue his temper*]   Come, keep your temper.

ANN.   Keep my temper? Do *you* of all men expect me to control myself? What a memory yours must be? Have you forgotten the time when I was fool enough to think you loved me, and mad enough to believe you could keep a promise?

GEOF.   Mad is a strong word to use, Miss Sylvester. [*Murmurs of rippling laughter without, and the croquet party seen at the back, rolling the balls. Anne tries to shut out sounds of gaiety and dries her tears. Geoffrey gently arranging tobacco in his pipe*] Go on. [*She strikes the pipe out of his hands*] Look here—there is no need to quarrel; you know I don't want to break my promise, but it's to your interest as well as mine to wait till my father has provided for me. Here it is in a nutshell. If I marry you now, I am a ruined man.

ANNE.   Geoffrey, my whole future is in your hands. Will you do me justice? [*She goes nearer and lays her hand persuasively on his arm*] Haven't you a word to say to me? No answer, not even a look? [*She waits a moment more, a marked change comes over her, she turns slowly to leave the summerhouse*] I am sorry to have troubled you, Mr. Delamayn. I won't detain you any longer. [*Crosses to R. He looks suddenly after her, stretches out his hands as she passes him and he clutches her, turning her to him and looking into her face as he grasps both her hands*]

GEOF. Where are you going?

ANNE. [*Looking him full in the face*] Where many a miserable woman has gone before me—out of the world.

GEOF. Do you mean that you will destroy yourself?

ANNE. Yes. I mean that I will destroy myself!

GEOF. [*Pushes one of the chairs in summerhouse to her with his foot and signs to her to take it*] Sit down. [*Roughly*] Sit down! [*She obeys him*] What do you want?

ANNE. You know well enough.

GEOF. [*After taking a turn and back*] Look here, Anne, I have got something to propose. [*She looks up*] What do you say to a private marriage?

ANNE. I consent to a private marriage.

GEOF. Very well, will you wait a little?

ANNE. Not a day.

GEOF. Where's the hurry?

ANNE. [*Rising, vehemently*] Have you ears, do you hear how Lady Lundie speaks to me? My dismissal from this house may be a question of a few hours. [*Laughter heard outside*]

GEOF. [*Glancing towards lawn where players are still seen*] Hush, they will hear you.

ANNE. [*Going*] Let them hear me; when I am past hearing them, what does it matter? [*Throws his hands off*]

GEOF. [*Detaining her*] Say what you want and I'll do it. Only be reasonable. I can't do it today.

ANNE. You can.

GEOF. What nonsense you talk!

ANNE. I have been thinking about it ever since we came to this house. I have got something to propose to you. Will you hear it or not?

GEOF. Speak lower.

ANNE. Will you hear it or not? [*Crosses. A loud clapping of hands now heard outside amid laughter, and Blanche is heard calling for Anne*]

GEOF. There, they are coming. I told you we'd be followed.

ANNE. Wait till I stop her on the steps. [*Exit hurriedly, L.U.E. Geoffrey looks for a means of escape, seeing door, R., tries it. It is bolted, he forces it with his knee and is about to exit when Anne returns and touches him on the shoulder*] You may want it before long; you don't want it now. I have secured a respite of five minutes; in that time or less Lady Lundie's suspicions will bring her here. For the present shut the door.

GEOF. [*Closes door*] Come to the point. What is it?

ANNE. One question first. Lady Lundie has invited you to stay at Windygates. Do you accept the invitation, or do you go back to your brother's?

GEOF. Why do you ask?

ANNE. Because we must both leave this place today.

GEOF. If we go away together, good-bye to my prospects and yours, too.

ANNE. We will leave separately, and I will go first. Wait here an hour after I have gone to save appearances, and then follow me.

GEOF. Follow you? Where?

ANNE. Four miles from this is a lonely mountain inn.

GEOF. [*In surprise*] An inn!

ANNE. The place I mean is the loneliest place in the neighborhood; it's kept by a respectable Scotch woman.

GEOF. Respectable Scotch women, who keep inns, don't cotton to young ladies who travel alone.

ANNE. I have provided for everything. I shall tell the landlady I am on my wedding tour, I shall say my husband is sightseeing on foot, among the mountains in the neighborhood.

GEOF. [*With a sneer*] She is sure to believe that.

ANNE. [*L.*] She is sure to disbelieve it, if you like. Let her. You have only to appear and to ask for your wife and then is my story proved to be true. Leave me to do my part. Will you do yours?

GEOF. Give me a minute to think.

ANNE. Not an instant. Once for all is it yes or no?

GEOF. [*Savagely*] Where is the inn?

ANNE. [*L., putting her arm in his and whispering rapidly*] Pass the road on the right that leads to the railway. Follow the path over the moor and the first house you come to after that, is the inn.

GEOF. What's the name of the place?

ANNE. Craig Fernie.

GEOF. Who am I to ask for at the door?

ANNE. For your wife. I shall do my best to avoid giving any name, and you will avoid making a mistake, by asking only for me as your wife. Is there anything else you want to know?

GEOF. Yes. How am I to know you have got away from here?

ANNE. If you don't hear from me in half an hour from the time I have left you, you may be sure I have gone. Hush!

LADY L. [*Without*] She is here, I am sure.

SIR. P. [*Without*] Well, well. [*Anne points to door, R. Geoffrey exit quickly as Lady Lundie and Sir Patrick enter L.U.E., and Anne is closing the door after Geoffrey*]

LADY L. [*Outside to Sir Patrick*] Observe, Miss Sylvester has got rid of somebody! I was sure she was not alone! [*Sir Patrick looks directly opposite to Geoffrey's exit and at the ceiling*]

Sir P. [*L.*]   Why, I don't see anyone else here but you and me.

Lady L. [*Pointedly, L.C.*]   May I inquire, Miss Sylvester, if your sufferings are relieved? Blanche said you were not feeling well.

Anne.   I am no better, Lady Lundie.

Lady L. [*As if not understanding*]   I beg your pardon.

Anne. [*Near door, R.*]   I said I was no better.

Lady L.   You appear to be able to stand up. When *I* am ill, I am not so fortunate. I am obliged to lie down.

Anne.   I will follow your example, Lady Lundie. [*Crosses to L.*] If you will excuse me, I will leave you and lie down in my own room. [*Anne exit, L., bowing to Lady Lundie and Sir Patrick*]

Lady L. [*R.C.*]   After what I have already told you, Sir Patrick, of Miss Sylvester's conduct, may I ask whether you consider that proceeding at all extraordinary?

Sir P. [*L.C., touching the spring in the knot of his cane, takes a pinch and chuckles*]   I consider no proceeding extraordinary, Lady Lundie, which emanates from your enchanting sex.

Lady L.   Sir Patrick, I beg you to observe that I am speaking seriously and expect a serious answer.

Sir P. [*L.*]   My dear Lady Lundie, ask me for anything else and it is at your service. I have not made a serious reply since I gave up practice at the Scottish bar. At my age nothing is serious except indigestion. I say, with the philosophers: "Life is a comedy to those who think, and a tragedy to those who feel." [*Taking Lady Lundie's hand and kissing it*] Dear Lady Lundie, why feel?

Lady L. [*Snatching her hand away, crosses to L.*]   When you are next called on, Sir Patrick, to judge of Miss Sylvester's conduct, unless I am mistaken, you will find yourself compelled to consider it something beyond a joke. [*Exit into garden, L.2.E.*]

Sir P. [*Looking after her*]   Were there ever two women yet with a quarrel between them, who didn't want to drag a man into it? [*Arnold enters, L.3.E. Sir Patrick crosses to R.*] Let them drag me in, if they can! [*Sits R. taking snuff. Arnold hesitating. Sir Patrick dusting his shoes with his handkerchief; his back towards him*]

Arn. [*R.*]   I hope I'm not in the way, Sir Patrick?

Sir P.   In the way? Of course not! Bless my soul, how serious the boy looks! [*Sits, C.*]

Arn. [*L.*]   I asked leave to consult you in private, sir, and you kindly said you would give me the opportunity, before I left Windygates.

Sir P.   Aye—aye—to be sure, I remember, well here is the opportunity, and here I am with all my worldly experience at your service. [*Arnold hesi-*

tates to speak] Don't hurry yourself; collect your ideas. I can wait—I can wait.

ARN. [*Stammering*] You have been very kind, sir, in offering me the benefit of your experience. I want a word of advice.

SIR P. Suppose you take it sitting; get a chair. [*Arnold goes for one. Sir Patrick watches him, then aside*] Wants my *advice*! The young humbug wants nothing of the sort—he wants my niece.

ARN. [*Sitting and moving uneasily in chair*] I am only a young man, and I am beginning a new life.

SIR P. Anything wrong with the chair? Begin your new life comfortable and get another.

ARN. There is nothing wrong with the chair, sir; would you—

SIR P. Would I keep the chair in that case? certainly.

ARN. I mean would you advise me?

SIR P. My good fellow I'm waiting to advise you. I'm sure there's something wrong with that chair! Why be obstinate about it? Why not get another?

ARN. Please don't mention the chair, Sir Patrick, you put me out. I want, in short—curious question—I want to be married.

SIR P. That's not a question; it's an assertion. You say "I want to be married," and I say "Just so," and there's all of it.

ARN. Would you advise me to get married, sir? That's what I meant.

SIR P. Oh, that's the subject of the present interview, is it? Would I advise you to marry? eh! Two courses are open to us, Mr. Arnold, in treating that question. May I begin by making an inquiry relating to your past life?

ARN. Certainly, sir.

SIR P. Very good again. When you were in the merchant service, did you ever have any experience in buying provisions, sir?

ARN. [*Surprised*] Plenty of experience, sir.

SIR P. Don't be astonished. I'm coming to the point. What did you think of your moist sugar when you bought it at the grocer's?

ARN. Think? Why I thought it was moist sugar to be sure.

SIR P. [*Slapping him on the knee. Arnold lets his hat drop, continues trying to reach it without taking his eyes off Sir Patrick*] Marry by all means. You are one of the few men who can buy [?try] that experiment with a fair chance of success. Don't you understand me?

ARN. I don't see what moist sugar has to do with my marrying?

SIR P. You don't? Well, I'll show you. You go to the tea shop and get your moist sugar. You take it on the understanding that it *is* moist sugar. But it isn't anything of the sort. It's a compound of adulterations, made up to look like sugar. You shut your eyes to that awkward fact and swallow your adulterated mess in various articles of food, and you and your sugar get on together in that way, as well as you can. Do you follow me so far? [*Arnold nods "yes"*] Very good. You go to the marriage shop and get a wife. You take her on the understanding—let us say—that she has lovely yellow hair, that she has an exquisite complexion, that her figure is the perfection of plumpness, and that she is just tall enough to carry the plumpness off. You bring her home, and you discover that it's the old story of the sugar again. Your wife is an adulterated article; her lovely yellow hair is dye, her exquisite skin is pearl powder, her plumpness is padding, and that three inches of her height are in the bootmaker's heels. You shut your eyes and swallow your adulterated wife as you swallowed your adulterated sugar, and I tell you again, you are one of the few fortunate men who can try the marriage experiment with a fair chance of success.

ARN.   That may be all very true, sir, of some young ladies; there is one I know of, who is nearly related to you, and who doesn't deserve what you have said of the rest of them.

SIR P.   Is this female phenomenon my niece?

ARN.   Yes, Sir Patrick.

SIR P. [C.]   May I ask you how you know that my niece is not an adulterated article, like the rest of them?

ARN. [*R.C.*]   I love her.

SIR P.   That's the most convincing answer I ever heard in my life.

ARN.   I'm in earnest. Put me to the test, sir—put me to the test! [*Rises, crosses to L.*]

SIR P.   Oh, very well, the test is easily put. My niece has a beautiful complexion. Do you believe in her complexion?

ARN.   There's a beautiful sky above our heads. I believe in the sky.

SIR P.   Do you? You were evidently never caught in a shower. In the meantime, what do you think of my niece's figure?

ARN.   Oh, come! There can't be any doubt about that. Any man with eyes in his head can see it's the loveliest figure in the world.

SIR P.   Of course it is, my good fellow! The loveliest figure in the world is the commonest thing in the world. It varies in price, and when it is particularly seductive, you may swear it comes from Paris. Now, Blanche's figure, for instance, how much of it comes from Nature and how much from the shop? I don't mind. Do you?

ARN.   I'll take my oath every inch of it!

SIR P.   Shop?

ARN.   Nature.

SIR P. [*Rising*]   If I ever marry and—hem—have a son, that son shall go to sea. [*Taking Arnold's hands*] My dear fellow, if you have Blanche's consent, you have mine.

ARN. [*In ecstasy*] Have I? [*About to run off. Geoffrey is now seen at back upon the lawn, as a Groom enters, R., with a letter in his hand. Arnold pauses*]

SIR P. What do you want?

GROOM. I beg your pardon, sir, I have a message for Mr. Geoffrey Delamayn from his brother; they told me I should find him hereabouts. My master said it was very important; I should deliver this immediately.

ARN. [*To Sir Patrick*] I haven't seen him, have you?

SIR P. [*Crossing to L.*] I have smelt him ever since I have been in the summerhouse. There is a taint of tobacco in the air—suggestion, disagreeable suggestion to my mind, of your friend, Mr. Delamayn. I'll leave you to find him, if you please. [*Exit, L.2.E.*]

ARN. If you are right, we will find him at once. [*Geoffrey and Mrs. Glenharm cross behind, R. to L. Arnold going to L.U.E.*] Geoffrey!

GEOF. [*Outside*] Hellow!

ARN. [*Pointing to Groom*] You're wanted, come here. [*Geoffrey enters, C.L., and on seeing Groom*]

GEOF. [*Crossing to C.*] Oh, it's you! Well, what is it?

GROOM. This from your brother, sir, and word that the train leaves in thirty minutes, and he is waiting. [*Meantime Geoffrey hastily opens the letter*]

GEOF. [*Calmly*] By Jove, I had forgotten my promise to Julius. [*To Groom*] That will do—go! [*Exit Groom, R.1.E. Suddenly*] The deuce! Anne expects me, too. Curse my luck. [*Throws pipe down, sits R.C.*]

ARN. Is there anything amiss, Geoffrey?

GEOF. I'm in the devil's own mess.

ARN. [*L.*] Can I do anything to help you? [*Geoffrey starts as with a sudden thought, glances sideways at Arnold, then reflects a moment, then turns hastily and slaps Arnold on the shoulder*]

GEOF. I say, old fellow, do you remember when the boat turned keel upwards in Lisbon Harbor?

ARN. [*L.C.*] Do you think I can ever forget that you swam ashore with me and saved my life?

GEOF. [*R.C. Aside*] If I should only get him to go with a message to her. [*Aloud*] One good turn deserves another, don't it?

ARN. Only tell me what I can do.

GEOF. [*Looks around to see if they are alone*] You know the governess here, don't you?

ARN. Miss Sylvester?

GEOF. Yes. I've got into a little difficulty with her, and there isn't a soul I can ask to help me but you.

ARN. You know I will help you! What is it?

GEOF. It isn't so easy to say. Never mind, you're no saint either, are you? You'll keep it a secret of course! Look here, I've acted like an infernal fool and all that; she has gone to a place four miles from this, and we settled I was to follow and marry her privately this afternoon. That's out of the question now. While she is expecting me at the inn, I must be on the road to London with my brother. Somebody must tell her what has happened, or she'll play the devil, and the whole business will burst up. I'm done for, old chap, unless you help me.

ARN. It's dreadful, old boy.

GEOF. [*Crossing to L.*] Enough to knock a man over, isn't it? [*Picking up his pipe*] Got a match?

ARN. I hope you won't think I'm making light of your other business; but it seems to me that the poor girl has the first claim on you.

GEOF. The first claim on me? Do you think I am going to risk being cut out of my father's will? Not for the best woman that ever put on a petticoat.

ARN. You know best. [*A little coldly*] What am I to say to her? I am bound to do all I can to help you, and I will.

GEOF. [*R.*] Say, say? I'm half distracted and—wait a bit, tell her to stop where she is until I write to her.

ARN. Can't you write to her now?

GEOF. What's the good of that?

ARN. Consider for a minute and you will see. To present myself to this lady as your messenger, seems exposing her to a dreadful humiliation.

GEOF. Perhaps I'd better write. Have we time to go into the house?

ARN. No, the house is full of people, and if you are going to London, the train's nearly due now. Write at once and write here; I have got a pencil.

GEOF. What am I to write on?

ARN. Anything; your brother's letter.

GEOF. That's full. [*Looking in his pockets and taking out Anne's letter. Sits*] This will do, it's one of Anne's own letters to me. There's room on the fourth page. If I write, you promise to take it to her? Your hand on the bargain? [*Arnold gives his hand, sits*] All right, old fellow, I can tell you how to find the place as we go along in the gig. [*Looks up*] By-the-by, there's one thing that is important.

ARN. What is it?

GEOF. You mustn't present yourself at the inn in your own name, and you mustn't ask for her in her name.

ARN. Whom am I to ask for?

GEOF. She has planned to tell them that she expects her husband to join her. If I had been able to go, I should have asked at the door for "My wife." You are going in my place.

ARN. [*Simple wonder*] And I must ask at the door for "My wife," or I shall expose Miss Sylvester to unpleasant consequences?

GEOF. [*Eagerly*] You don't object?

ARN. Not I. I don't care what I say to the people of the inn. It's the meeting with Miss Sylvester that I'm afraid of.

GEOF. I'll put that right for you, never fear. [*Going to table and scribbling rapidly*] Will that do? No, I'd better say something spooney to quiet her. [*Then writing the following*] "Dear Anne! Just called to London by my father; stop where you are, and I will write to you. Trust the bearer. Upon my soul, I'll keep my promise. Your loving husband that is to be. Geoffrey Delamayn. Windygates, Aug. 14th, 4 P.M." [*Rising*] That will do the business. [*Hands it to Arnold*]

ARN. This is rather short.

GEOF. Have I time to make it longer?

ARN. Perhaps not.

GEOF. Come, we haven't a moment to lose. [*Rushing towards R.1.E.*]

ARN. I can't leave Blanche without saying good-bye. Where is she? [*Sir Patrick entering, L.U.E., with Blanche*]

SIR. P. [*L.C.*] Here she is; here I am. In fact, here we both are. [*Arnold crosses to Blanche*]

BLAN. [*C.*] Going?

ARN. I shall be back right away. It's all right; Sir Patrick consents. Good-bye. [*Blanche detains him by the arm*]

GEOF. [*Going, R.1.E.*] We shall be late. Come! Good morning, governor. Good morning, Miss Blanche. [*Exit, R.1.E., Arnold following, Blanche kissing her hand to him as he goes off, R.H.*]

BLAN. [*Pointing, returning to Sir Patrick, who is in C.*] Why is Arnold going away with that brute?

SIR P. Brute? Oh, you mean the Hon. Mr. Delamayn! You don't like him?

BLAN. I hate him. [*Striking chair pettishly*]

SIR P. [*Aside*] She is a young girl of eighteen and I am an old man of seventy! Curious that we should agree about *anything*; more than curious that we should agree in disliking Mr. Delamayn! [*Aloud*] Why, Blanche, Blanche! One would think Arnold had gone out for a voyage around the world—you silly child, he will be back again tomorrow.

BLAN. I wish he hadn't gone with that man. I wish he hadn't got that man for a friend.

SIR P. [*C.*] There, there! Come back to the house; croquet is over and dancing commencing. Dance it off, my dear. Dance it off.

BLAN. No, I'm in no humor for dancing. I shall go upstairs and talk about it to Anne. [*Music. Lady Lundie enters, followed by Nos. 1, 2 and 3, Mrs. Glenharm, and party*]

LADY L. [*L.C.*] You will do nothing of the sort!

BLAN. [*C.*] What?

LADY L. I forbid you to mention that woman's name again in my hearing. My worst anticipations are realized—Miss Sylvester has left the house. [*Blanche confronts Lady Lundie, and then turns towards Sir Patrick, and falls despairingly in chair, C. Mrs. Glenharm and Jo hasten to R. and L. of chair, Swells cross to L.E., Captain Newenden to two Ladies, L. Quick curtain*]

ACT II.

SCENE 1: *Anteroom at Windygates, gold table, with flowers in vase, L.C., chairs, R. and L. of it. Sir Patrick enters at L.*

SIR P. Much is to be said for, and much is to be said against a single life, but this I take it is certain, a man's married friends can't prevent his leading a life of a bachelor, if he pleases. But they do take devilish good care that he shan't enjoy it. Now I've got to stir about in this matter of Miss Sylvester's disappearance; assume all responsibilities, and do all that's necessary to be done, as if all these women were my wives, and all the girls my daughters. I'm afraid I can't control my sister-in-law, for I've noticed, that when one woman takes a dislike to another woman, she will bend heaven and earth to discover her frailties. [*Lady Lundie enters, L.1.E., followed by Hopkins*]

LADY L. Well, Sir Patrick, I have lost no time.

SIR P. Hum—how do you get on with your examination of the servants?

LADY L. None of the men know anything. The sly, deceitful creature—she must have laid her plans well, to elude every eye. Jonathan! [*Suddenly calling*] Where is Jonathan? [*Jonathan entering sullenly, R.1.E.*]

JON. Here I be, my lady. [*Hopkins passes behind*]

LADY L. [*L.C.*] Take your place, there, Jonathan; I am about to question you, Jonathan.

SIR P. Pardon me, Lady Lundie; before you go further, I think it is proper to tell you that this is a free country, and you have no right to investigate Miss Sylvester's actions.

LADY L. [*Warmly*] Before I lay my head on my pillow this night, Sir Patrick, I mean to know where that unhappy person is; she was Blanche's companion—she was under this roof—I'm morally responsible for her, and I must be satisfied. It is my duty. Jonathan! [*Jonathan, who has been chatting with Hopkins, draws up*]

Jon. [*R.*] Ees, my lady.

Lady L. I am about to examine you.

Jon. Please, my leddy, I ain't got nuthin on me; I ain't took nuthin.

Sir P. Her ladyship means that she wishes to question you; speak the truth.

Jon. Ees, sur. [*Stupidly*]

Lady L. You know that it is wrong to lie, Jonathan?

Jon. Ees, mum. [*Stupid surprise*]

Lady L. You know where you will go to, if you tell a lie?

Jon. Ees, mum—I will go to hell.

Lady L. How dare you?

Sir P. Silence! you rascal.

Jon. Well, you mustn't ax me, if I mustn't speak.

Sir P. [*Rises. Crosses to L. Laughs*] Well, I leave you to your agreeable task. I wish you luck. [*Aside*] Ah, my poor brother Tom! To think that you married that woman. I never knew till now, how much you must have sighed for the peace of the grave! [*Exit, L.1.E.*]

Lady L. Jonathan, do you know anything about Miss Sylvester's leaving the house? [*Crosses to Sir Patrick's chair*]

Jon. Ees, mum.

Lady L. Ah! we are getting to it at last; where did she go?

Jon. I don't know.

Lady L. How do you know she went?

Jon. Hopkins told me.

Lady L. Hopkins, what did you tell him?

Hop. Me lady, I have never told him nothing but what everybodee knew already.

Lady L. But I want to know what he knows.

Hop. La, my lady, he is fol; he don't know nossing whatshowever.

Jon. Ees! [*Grinning*]

Lady L. Attend to me; what do you know of yourself, apart from what Hopkins told you?

Jon. Eh! [*Eyes rolled in astonishment*]

Hop. He no comprend.

Jon. Ees, I understand. You means what does I know as how nobody else but I knows. Ees, I understand—well, I don't know nothing.

Lady L. Then go out of this, this instant, you booby. Hopkins, where is Hester Detthridge?

Hop. In the kitchen. She knows nossings, my lady.

Lady L. How do you know that?

Hop. Why she nevare speak—she hear nossing—she is dumb and she is stupid.

Jon. Ees, that she be, and bewitched, too.

Lady L. Silence! Go tell her I wish to speak with her.

Jon. I be afraid.

Lady L. What?

Jon. I be scared o' her. She be a witch. She ha got an evil eye.

Hop. I think he is right.

Lady L. Go instantly and tell her to come here. [*Exit Jonathan, going foolishly, R.1.E.*] What fools you all are about this woman Detthridge—a poor, dumb creature.

Hop. My lady, you no feel scared of her, eh? Not a little bit, when she comes in so pale, so cold, so still—ugh; when she never speak, but write all down on ze little slate dat hang by her side, eh?

Lady L. Of course the woman is queer, and a puzzle, and all that, but then she's dumb, and that's always queer.

Hop. You think she is dumb?

Lady L. Certainly—don't you?

Hop. Vell, I tink I sometimes hear a noise in her room dat sounds like a cry.

Lady L. Why, dumb people cry—don't they?

Hop. Yes, dumb cry; but dis was a sound—ah!—it freeze my blood—I tell you, my lady, she is bad—mysterious—fatal—what is dat scar on her forehead?

Lady L. That's where her drunken husband struck her one day.

Hop. Her husband is dead?

Lady L. Yes—so she says.

Hop. Exact—I should expect to die myself if I should strike her—she look fatal.

Lady L. Ah, the poor wretch is here. [*Music. Hester enters, R.1.E., followed by Jonathan, who gets back from her glance*] I wish to speak with you. [*Hester bows slowly, takes up slate and pencil, and waits, her eyes cast down*] Do you know that Miss Sylvester has left the house? [*Hester bows*] Do you know at what time she left it? [*Hester bows. Lady Lundie leaning forward*] Have you seen her since she left the house? [*Hester bows. Lady Lundie quickly*] Where? [*Hester writes on slate and holds it out. Lady Lundie motions to Hopkins to read it, without touching it*]

Hop. [*Leans over and reads*] On the road to the railway, near Chew's Farm.

Lady L. Did Miss Sylvester see you? [*Hester shakes her head*] Did she go to the railway? [*Hester shakes her head*] She went towards the moor? [*Hester nods*] Where did she go to then? [*Hester writes*]

Hop. [*Reading from slate*] She took the footpath to Craig Fernie.

Lady L. [*Jumps up*] There is but one place a stranger could go to there— the inn. She has gone to the inn. Have you reported this to anyone else? [*Hester bows*] What! Do you mean you have told someone else? [*Hester bows*] Someone, then, has questioned you? [*Hester bows*] Who was it? [*Quickly. Hester writes. Hopkins is about to read, when Lady Lundie snatches it. Hopkins crosses to L. Lady Lundie reads*] Miss Blanche. [*Drops the slate*] Here, Hopkins!

Hop. [*Down L.*] Ees, madam.

Lady L. Go to Miss Blanche's room; tell her I wish to see her—to wait for me there—and on no account to stir out—quick!

Hop. Ees, madam, I run. [*Runs out L.*]

Lady L. Here, you Jonathan. Go at once to Sir Patrick, and tell him I wish to see him in my room—quick! [*Exit Jonathan, R. Lady Lundie stops and sees Hester*] You have done wrong to tell anyone but me what you saw. *I* am your mistress, [*Hester bows*] and Miss Blanche is not. You are very much to blame. I have threatened to discharge you on account of your eccentric ways, your comings and your goings, your mysteries and fol-de-rols—and if I find you committing another such fault—[*Hester, who has looked sternly at Lady Lundie until she says "fol-de-rols," commences to write*] You have no right to answer anybody's questions. [*Hester hands her the slate*] What is this? [*Reads*] You had no orders not to answer! You keep nobody's secret but your own! [*Hester bows*] Hoity-toity! It seems that it don't need a tongue to be insolent. This settles the question. I've threatened before, but now you pack, and when your month is up you go. [*Music till Hopkins is on. Hester looks at her, bows, turns and walks out, totters at doorway, and supports herself out by the wall. Exit, R.1.E. Hopkins enters, L.1.E.*]

Hop. Oh, madam, Sare Patrick and ze gentlemens are come dis way.

Lady L. [*Relaxing*] Oh, Hopkins, my nerves are all unstrung. [*Goes off, R.1.E., in affected weakness, supported and comforted by Hopkins*] I really can't see Sir Patrick now.

Hop. Madam. [*Exit with Lady Lundie, R.1.E. Swells 1, 2 and 3 enter, L., followed by Sir Patrick*]

Swells. [*All together, as they enter*] Don't incommode yourself. Don't let us put you out. Anything will do for us, you know, my dear boy.

No. 1. For my part I'm just the fellow to have in a house when there's a row—nevah see anything—nevah hear anything—nevah say anything—nevah think anything!

No. 2. Neithah do I.

No. 3. Nor I, by Jove!

No. 1. Nevah think anything of anything.

No. 2. Always take an explanation.

No. 3. Stow myself where I'm not in the way.

Nos. 1 and 2. Just my way exactly—yaas!

Sir P. Gentlemen, you are too good, you lift a great weight off my shoulders. Ha, ha! Things are a little mixed just now here, ladies all nerves, you know.

No. 1. Yaas—had 'em myself, bad—yaas!

No. 2. Know what they are.

No. 3. Oh, yaas.

Sir P. [R.] So, you see, it's left to me to entertain you. I'm to keep you lively. I'm to occupy your minds.

No. 1. Oh, that's easy.

No. 2. Yaas—easy.

No. 3. Easy—yaas.

Sir P. That's what I thought, so now as we're all together—why—[Hopkins enters, and whispers to him] Eh, all right. I'll come at once. Gentlemen, I'm sorry, but another phase of this domestic crisis calls me away for a few minutes. I'll just see Lady Lundie and be with you. Meet me on the lawn. [Exit, R.1.E.]

Nos. 1, 2 and 3. Certainly—yaas. [All face and follow him to the door, and then turn and saunter back to C.]

No. 1. Wonder whether domestic crisis won't kill old boy.

No. 2. I'll bet on the old boy.

No. 3. [Betting book out] Done for a hundred.

No. 1. [Ditto] I back crisis against old boy.

No. 2. Two to one on old boy. [All enter bets with eyeglasses up, books and pencils all same size]

No. 1. Hundred to fifty that domestic crisis in conjunction with Lady Lundie lays old boy out.

No. 2. Make it thirty and I'll do it.

No. 3. I'll take fifty.

No. 2. Then I will. [Nos. 1, 2 and 3 all writing] Hundred to fifty—domestic crisis and old girl—too much, old boy. [Exit, L.1.E., writing in book. Clear and change]

SCENE 2: *The lonely inn at Craig Fernie. Large, old-fashioned window at back. Anne discovered seated at table, C., her head buried in one hand, while from the other hangs a purse. Mistress Inchbare standing primly, L.C. Bishopriggs at back, listening, while pretending to dust.*

MRS. I. [*L.H.*] Weel, weel, sae let it be. Bide awhile and rest ye, we'll see if your husband comes. I'll just let the rooms to him, instead of lettin' them to you. [*Exit Mrs. Inchbare, L.2.E. As she goes out, Anne raises her eyes red with weeping. Bishopriggs pretends to be very busy dusting, Anne hearing him, turns*]

ANNE. [*R.C., concealing tears and sharply*] What are you doing there?

BISH. [*L.*] Eh? Am just doostin' the things and settin' the room in decent order for ye.

ANNE. For me? Did you hear what the landlady said?

BISH. [*L.*] Never fash yourself about the landlady; your purse speaks for ye, my lassie; in' wi' it into your pocket; sae long as the world's the world, while there's silver in the purse, there's good in the woman.

ANNE. [*Rising*] What do you mean by speaking to me in that way? [*Goes to armchair*]

BISH. Hech—hech—sit ye doon, sit ye doon. Am I no' to be familiar wi' ye when I'm auld enough to be a father to ye, till further notice? Sit ye doon, and don't take the armchair; your husband will be comin', ye ken, an' he's sure to want it. [*Exit, L.2.E., with a profound wink. Anne watches him out, then looks at her watch, then goes to the window and looks out*]

ANNE. No, not a sign of him. [*Throws herself on sofa near window*] Will he keep his promise?

MRS. I. [*Outside*] Show the gentleman the room.

BISH. [*Outside*] Aye, aye—this way, sir.

ANNE. Someone is coming up. Is it he? [*Runs to door, listening*]

ARN. [*Outside*] Lead on. I'm after you.

ANNE. No, it is a stranger's voice. They are bringing him here. [*Runs to room, R.2.E., exit, and shuts herself in. Door, L., opens, Bishopriggs enters, showing in Arnold, L.2.E.*]

ARN. [*L.*] Nobody here. Where is she?

BISH. Eh, yer gal. De leddy's just in the bedchamber nae dout.

ARN. In there, eh? [*Aside*] Now, how the deuce am I going to get her out of there?

BISH. How are you to get her out? I'll show ye how. [*Advances to door, R.2.E., and knocks*] Eh, my leddy, here he is in flesh and bluid. Mercy preserve us, do ye lock the door of the nuptial chamber in yere husband's face? [*The door is heard unlocking. With a finger to his nose, and confidentially to Arnold*] I'm awa' afore she fa's inter yere arms. Rely on't, I'll no come in again without knocking first. [*Exit door, L.2.E. Anne opens the door timidly as Bishopriggs exits*]

ANNE. [*Stepping on the threshold*] Mr. Brinkworth. [*Arnold remains silent and becomes nervous. Anne advances a step and shuts the door*] What do you want here?

ARN. I—I—have got a letter for you. [*Takes a letter from pocket and offering it*]

ANNE. [*Refusing the letter*] I expect no letter. Who told you I was here? Is there a watch set on my actions, and are you the spy?

ARN. [*Quietly*] You haven't known me very long, Miss Sylvester, but you ought to know me better than to say that. I am the bearer of a letter from Geoffrey.

ANNE. [*R., impulsively*] Did Geof—[*Coldly*] Do you mean Mr. Delamayn?

ARN. [*L.*] Yes.

ANNE. What occasion have I for a letter from Mr. Delamayn?

ARN. Miss Sylvester—it's no use beating about the bush. If you won't take the letter you force me to speak out. I am here on a very unpleasant errand. I begin to wish from the bottom of my heart I had never undertaken it.

ANNE. Go on.

ARN. Try not to be angry with me. Geoffrey and I are old friends; Geoffrey knows that he can trust me.

ANNE. Trust you? [*Springing forward with a look of horror*] Has he told you?

ARN. [*Earnestly*] Please read this letter. [*Anne pushes back the letter*]

ANNE. [*R.*] You don't look at me. He has told you.

ARN. Read this letter in justice to him, if you won't in justice to me. [*She takes it*]

ANNE. I beg your pardon, sir. I understand my position at last. I am a woman doubly betrayed. Please to excuse what I said just now, when I supposed myself to have some claim on your respect. Perhaps you will grant me your pity; I can ask for nothing more. [*Opening the letter*] My own letter! In the hands of another man!

ARN. Look at the last page.

ANNE. [*After reading*] Villain! Villain! Villain! [*Crushing the letter and casting it towards the fire, and sinking in a chair with her back to Arnold*] He has deserted me!

ARN. Don't take it in that way, pray don't. It's dreadful to hear you. I am sure he has not deserted you. Come, cheer up a little.

ANNE. [*In chair, R.C.*] Didn't you say he had told you everything? [*Turning to Arnold*]

ARN. [*L.H.*] Yes.

ANNE. Don't you despise a woman like me?

ARN. Does a man live who can think of his mother and despise women? [*She turns away weeping*] All I want, Miss Sylvester, is to be of some service to you, if I can. You will hear from Geoffrey tomorrow, or next day. I know he means to write.

ANNE. For heaven's sake, don't speak of him any more. How do you think I can look you in the face? [*Checking herself impatiently*] What am I saying? What interest can you have in this miserable state of things? I have something else to say to you. Did you see the landlady when you came in?

ARN. No. I only saw the waiter.

ANNE. The landlady has made some absurd difficulty about letting me have these rooms, because I came here alone.

ARN. She won't make any difficulty now. I have settled that.

ANNE. You?

ARN. Certainly. Geoffrey told me, when I came here I was to ask for you as my wife.

ANNE. [*In alarm*] You asked for me as your wife?

ARN. Yes. I haven't done wrong, have I? As I understand it, there was no alternative. Geoffrey told me you had settled with him to present yourself as a married lady, whose husband was coming to join you. Don't suppose I object to this little stratagem. I am serving an old friend, and I am helping the lady who is soon to be his wife.

ANNE. [*Rising suddenly*] Pray, don't think of me any longer.

ARN. In your situation who else am I to think of?

ANNE. [*Laying hand on his shoulder*] Blanche!

ARN. Blanche?

ANNE. Yes, Blanche. I know of your offer to her. I know that you are engaged to be married to her.

ARN. [*Cheerily*] You don't expect me to go after that? Come and sit down again, and let's talk about Blanche. [*Anne declines with a gesture of impatience. Arnold continues without noticing it*] You know all about her habits and her tastes, and what she likes and dislikes. It's most important that I should talk to you about her. When we are husband and wife, Blanche is to have all her own way in everything. That's my idea of the whole duty of man—when man is married. You are still standing. Let me give you a chair?

ANNE. [*Declining the chair*] Whatever we have to say about Blanche, Mr. Brinkworth, must be said at some future time. I beg you will leave me.

ARN. Leave you?

ANNE. Yes, leave me to the solitude that is best for me, and to the sorrow that I have deserved. Thank you, and good-bye!

ARN. If I must go, why I must! But why are you in such a hurry?

ANNE. I don't want you to call me your wife again before the people of the inn.

ARN. Is that all? What on earth are you afraid of?

ANNE. I have two reasons to be afraid—one that I can't give, and one that I can. Suppose Blanche heard of what you have done? The longer you stay here—the more people you see—the more chance there is that she might hear of it.

ARN. And what if she did? Do you think she would be angry with me for making myself useful to you?

ANNE. Yes, if she was jealous of me.

ARN. That's impossible!

ANNE. Sir Patrick would tell you that nothing is impossible where women are concerned. You can't put yourself in Blanche's place—I can. [*Seriously*] Once more I beg you to go; come, let us say good-bye. [*She holds out her hand to him, at the same time a loud knock is heard at the door, L. Anne, in alarm, throws herself in chair*]

ARN. [*After looking at her an instant*] Come in! [*Knock repeated*] Are you deaf? Come in! [*Bishopriggs partly opens the door, showing his body and knocks again*] What the deuce are you waiting for? I told you to come in! [*Bishopriggs entering with tablecloth on his arm and tray in his hand*]

BISH. Eh! now d'ye think I've lived in this hottle in blinded ignorance of hoo young married couples pass the time when they're left alone? Twa knocks at the door, and trouble in opening it after that, is just the least ye can do for them. Whar dije think, noo, I'll set the places for you? [*Anne rises in disgust and goes to the window*]

ARN. One at the top and one at the bottom, I suppose.

BISH. One at the top and one at the bottom? [*Setting table*] Deil a bit of it! Baith yer chairs as close together as chairs can be. Hech! Hech! Haven't I caught 'em after goodness knows how many knocks at the doors? Dinin' on the husband's knees and stimulating a man's appetite by feeding him at the fork's-end like a child, eh! [*With a heavy sigh*] It's a short life wi' that nuptial business, and a merry one. A month for yere billing and cooin' and a' the rest of yer days fur wondering ye were such a fule and wishing it was a' to be dune over again. Ye'll be for a bottle of sherry wine, nae doot, and a drop of toddy afterwards, to do yer digestion on? [*Anne beckons to Arnold, and he joins her at window*] Ay! Ay! Gang tae yer dearie! Gang tae yer dearie! And leave all the solid business o' life tae me! I've scripture warrant for't. [*As he is about to cut a loaf of bread, sees the crumpled letter on the floor*] What's that I see yoner—mair litter in the room after I've dusted and tidied it wi' my own hands? [*He picks up the paper slyly*] Eh! What's here? Written on it in ink, and written on it in pencil? Who may this belong tae? [*Looks around cautiously*] Here it is clean forgotten and dune wid. Noo what would a fule do if he found this? A fule would licht his pipe wi' it, and then wonder whether he wad have done better to read it first. And what wad a wise man do in a similar position? [*He puts it in his vest-pocket with a sly wink, then aloud*] Am gaun tae bring the dinner in and mind ye there is nae knockin' at the door possible when I've got the tray in baith my han's, and mair's the pitty the gout in both my feet. [*Exit, L.2.E. Anne and Arnold come down*]

ARN. You see, we can't help it. The waiter has gone to bring the dinner things in. What will they think in the house if I go away already and leave "My wife" to dine alone?

ANNE. [*Crossing down R., bitterly*] A curse seems to follow me. This will end ill—and I shall be answerable for it. [*To Arnold*] You may leave your excuse to me. Do you go by the up train or down?

ARN. By the up train. [*Bishopriggs enters suddenly with tray containing dinner. Anne separates suddenly and goes up. Arnold following her*]

BISH. I warned you baith! It was a clear impossibility to knock at the door this time. Don't blame me! [*Setting table*] The sherry wine hoo, sir! I kin but what it may be corkit? I main tae taste and try. [*He drinks a large tumblerful from the decanter, then fills it up with water and puts water on sideboard*] Eh! It's addin' ten years to the age of the wine. The turtle doves will be none the wiser, and I am, myself a glass of wine the better. Praise Providence for a' its marcie! [*Aloud*] Dinner's servit, my leddy! [*Gets R.*]

ARN. [*Coming down*] Where will you sit?

ANNE. Anywhere. [*Impatiently snatching up a chair and placing it at the bottom of the table*]

BISH. [*Politely but firmly puts chair back in place*] Lord's sake! What are you doin'? It's clean contrary to a' the laws and customs o' the honeymoon, to sit as far away frae your husband as that! [*They sit, Bishopriggs takes off cover of one dish, and Arnold is about to help from it when Bishopriggs slaps the cover down again suddenly. Wind begins*] Is there naebody gaun tae say grace?

ARN. Come, come, the fish is getting cold!

BISH. For what ye're gaun tae receive may ye baith be truly thankful! My conscience is clear noo. Fa' to! Fa' to!

ANNE. Send him away! His familiarity is beyond endurance!

ARN. You needn't wait. [*Lightning*]

BISH. [*Crossing to L., and whispering to Arnold*] Take her on the knee as sune's ye like. I'll think o' something else and look at the prospect. [*Winks, goes to window, and as he does, wind and lightning*] Ma certie, it's well ye caim when ye did. It's ill gettin' to this hottle in a storm.

ANNE. [*Turning in alarm*] A storm coming?

BISH. Eh! ye're weel hoosed here, ye needn't maend it. [*A knock at the door, wind heard again. Mrs. Inchbare enters*]

MRS. I. I have just look in, sir, tae see ye've got what ye wanted.

ARN. Oh! You are the landlady? Very nice, ma'am, very nice.

MRS. I. Ye'll excuse me, sir. I wasna in the way when ye came here, or I should ha'e made bould to ask the question which I maun een ask ye noo. Am I to understand that ye hire these rooms for yourself and this leddy, yer wife? [*Anne is about to speak. Arnold, by a sign, silences her*]

ARN. Certainly, I take the rooms for myself and this lady here, my wife.

ANNE. This gentleman—[*Arnold stops her*]

MRS. I. This gentleman! I'm only a puir woman, my leddy—d'ye mean yer husband here? [*Lightning and wind. Arnold a third time motions Anne. Mrs. Inchbare stares fixedly. Anne after a struggle speaks*]

ANNE. My husband! [*Casts her head upon table*]

ARN. [*Aside to Anne*] Never mind, I know what it is, and I'll see about it. [*Rising, to Mrs. Inchbare*] She's always like this, ma'am, when a storm is coming. We'll send for you if we want your assistance.

MRS. I. At your ain pleasure, sir. Nae offense, my leddy! You remember that ye came here alone and that the hottle has its ain gude name to keep up. [*Exit stiffly, L.2.E.*]

ANNE. I'm faint! Give me some water!

ARN. [*Seeing none on the table, to Bishopriggs*] Get some! [*Exit Bishopriggs, L.1.E.*]

ANNE. [*Rising*] Mr. Brinkworth, you are acting with inexcusable rashness! That woman's question was an impertinence! Why did you answer it? Why did you force *me*?

ARN. Why didn't I have the inn door shut in your face, with a storm coming up, and without a place in which you can take refuge? Scruples are out of place with such a woman as that landlady! Let's change the subject. The water is a long time coming—try a glass of wine. [*Anne goes up, C.*] No? Well, here is Blanche's health [*He takes some of the wine himself*] in the weakest sherry I ever drank in my life. [*Bishopriggs enters with water, L.2.E.*] Well, have you got the water or did you use it all for the sherry?

BISH. Is that the way ye talk of the oldest bottle of sherry in Scotland?

ARN. Have you brought the water?

BISH. I have brought the water. There it is! [*Puts it on table and exit, L.D.; Arnold gets R. As Arnold advances with water, Anne comes down*]

ANNE. This suspense is unendurable! Mr. Brinkworth, you must leave me at once; ring the bell and ask the waiter about the trains. [*Anne crosses, R. Vivid flash, crash of thunder*]

ARN. Pleasant weather to travel in—Bishopriggs tells me the last train has passed for the night. What's to be done now?

ANNE. You must take a coach and drive! [*Thunder and lightning and rain*]

ARN. Do you hear that? If I ordered horses, do you think they would let me have them in such weather as this? And if they did, do you suppose the horses could face it on the moor? No, Miss Sylvester! I am sorry to be in the way, but the train has gone, and the night and the storm have come. I have no choice but to stay here. [*Anne clasps her hands and goes towards window*] Shall we have the candles, and shut out the weather? [*Closes shutters*] I'll promise to go away—the first thing in the morning. Do try and take it easy, [*Lights candle*] and don't be angry with me. Come! Come! You wouldn't turn away a dog, Miss Sylvester, on such a night as this! [*She turns on him with a smile and holds out her hand, which he takes*]

ANNE. Nothing can make matters worse than what they are, and nothing can justify my inflicting my own wretchedness on you, Mr. Brinkworth.

ARN. We'll have a pleasant evening of it yet. [*He rings the bell*] I've got it. We'll kill time as our cabin passengers use to kill it at sea. [*Bishopriggs enters*] Waiter—a pack of cards!

BISH. [*Aghast*] What?

ARN. A pack of cards!

BISH. Cairds? A pack of cairds? The deevil's allegories in the deevil's own colors, red and black. I wunna execute yer order. For ye ain soul's sake, I wunna do it! Ha ye lived to your time of life, and are ye no awakened yet to the awful sinfulness o' gambling wi' the cairds?

ARN. Just as you please. If I don't get the cards though, you will find me awakened—when I go away—to the awful folly of feeing a waiter.

BISH. [*Suddenly altering*] Does that mean that you are bent on the cairds?

ARN. Yes, that means that I am bent on the cards.

BISH. I take up my testimony against 'em, but I'm no telling ye that I canna lay my hand on 'em if I like. What do they say in your country, "needs must," when the devil drives? [*Exit, L.1.E.*]

ANNE. [*Rising as Bishopriggs goes off*]   Oh, Mr. Brinkworth, I am unequal to this struggle! Let us proceed no further with this farce! Think! For Blanche's sake! Think, is there no way out of this?

ARN. [*Sitting calmly*]   Blanche again? I wonder how she feels in this storm!

ANNE.   I won't let this deception go on. I'll do what I ought to have done before, come what may of it. I'll tell the landlady the truth. [*Music. Goes to door, is about to open it, when noise of whip is heard outside*]

ARN.   Hallo! More travellers [*Goes to window*] in this weather! [*Lightning and rain*]

ANNE. [*Starting from door*]   Can it be Geoffrey?

ARN.   Not Geoffrey! Whoever else it may be, not Geoffrey! [*Mrs. Inchbare enters, L.2.E.*]

MRS. I.   Eh, mistress! Who do you think has driven here to see ye from Windygates Hoose, and been overtaken in the storm?

ARN.   Who is it?

MRS. I.   Who is't? It's just the bonny young leddy—Miss Blanche herself! [*Lightning and wind*]

ANNE.   Ah! [*Starts as if to warn Arnold*]

MRS. I.   Eh, mistress! You'll find Miss Blanche a bit baulder than to be skirt at a flash of lightning! That girl! Ah! The bonnie birdie! [*Exit Mrs. Inchbare, L.*]

ANNE. [*Catching Arnold by the arm, looking terrified at door, L., and pointing to door, R.*]   Go! Go! Blanche must not see you! [*She blows out the candle. Arnold exit, R.U.E. A vivid flash of lightning. Blanche enters, R.U.E.; she runs with a cry of joy and embraces Anne. Mrs. Inchbare follows her to door. Quick curtain*]

ACT III.

SCENE 1: *The library of Windygates. Door, C., open, looking upon lawn. Curtain recesses, R. and L. Table, C., with lamp, magazines, and seats; bookcases at back, R. and L. Geoffrey and Arnold discovered. Arnold, head buried thoughtfully on table, C., Geoffrey, filling his pipe.*

GEOF. [*R.*]   I've promised already not to breathe a word to any living soul of your having been to the inn, what more do you want?

ARN. [*L.*]   I am anxious, Geoffrey. I was at Craig Fernie, remember, when Blanche came there. She has been telling all that happened, poor child, in the firm persuasion that I was miles off at the time. I swear I couldn't look her in the face; what would she think of me if she knew that I was there, hiding all the while she was with Anne. My mind misgives me, I don't know why.

GEOF. Mind? It's flesh, that's what's the matter with you. You're a stone over your right weight. Mind be hanged! A man in healthy training don't know that he has a mind. Take a turn with the dumb-bells, and a run up hill, with a greatcoat on. Sweat it off, Arnold, that will set you right, sweat it off! [*Geoffrey goes to window, L.H., opens curtains in recess, and smokes. Blanche enters, C., looks disgusted on seeing Geoffrey*]

BLAN. [*Sitting in armchair, R.H.*] Oh, dear! What shall we do until lunch time? I want a mild excitement. Arnold, come here; suppose you read me some poetry!

ARN. [*Crossing to her*] While he is here? [*Pointing to Geoffrey*]

BLAN. Pooh; he's only an animal; we needn't mind him!

ARN. You're as bitter this morning as Sir Patrick himself; what will you say to me when we are married, if you talk like that of my friend?

BLAN. [*R., stealing her arm in his*] I shall always be nice to you.

ARN. Whose poetry shall I read?

BLAN. Anybody's! I am dying for poetry; I don't care whose, and I don't know why!

ARN. [*Picking a book from table*] How'll this do? *Paradise Lost,* by John Milton. Have you ever read Milton?

BLAN. No. Is he nice?

ARN. I don't know! Let's try him! No educated person ought to be ignorant of Milton. Let's be educated persons. [*Sits by table, L.*] Where shall I begin?

BLAN. At the top, of course! Stop! You mustn't sit all that way off! [*Arnold brings a stool and sits at her feet*] You must sit where I can look at you. That's it! Now begin!

ARN. [*Reading in monotone*] "Of man's first disobedience and the fruit of that forbidden tree whose mortal taste brought death into our world, and all our woe, and loss of Eden, sing heavenly muse."

BLAN. Beautiful! What a shame to have Milton all this time in the library and never to have read it! We will have mornings with Milton, Arnold. He seems long, but we are both young, and we may live to get to the end of him. Do you know, dear, now that I look at you again, you don't seem to have come back to Windygates in good spirits.

ARN. Don't I?

BLAN. I know: it's sympathy with me, I'm out of spirits, too!

ARN. You?

BLAN. Yes; after what I saw at Craig Fernie, I grow more and more uneasy about Anne. [*Arnold, growing nervous, looks toward Geoffrey, and then dips hurriedly into Milton*]

ARN. Let's go on with Milton. [*Quickly*] "In the beginning how the heavens and earth rose out of chaos, or of Zion hill."

BLAN. Do wait a little; I can't have Milton crammed down my throat in that way. Besides, I have something to say. Didn't I tell you that I consulted my uncle about Anne? He told me I might be quite right in suspecting Anne's husband to be an abominable person. His keeping himself out of my way was a suspicious circumstance; and then there was the sudden extinguishing of the candles when I first went in; I thought it was done by the wind. Sir Patrick suspects it was done by the horrid man himself, to prevent me from seeing him. What do you think?

ARN. I think we had better go on. We'll never get through Milton at this rate.

BLAN. Oh, don't worry about Milton; that last bit wasn't as interesting as the other. Is there any love in *Paradise Lost*?

ARN. I don't know. I see something about Adam.

BLAN. What's the use of Adam? You can't have any love till Eve comes in. But go on, and be quick!

ARN. [*Reading*] "In the beginning how the heavens and earth rose out of chaos, or of Zion hill."

BLAN. You read that before.

ARN. I'll try the next page. [*Reading*] "Say first what cause moved our grandparents in that happy state."

BLAN. [*Starting up pettishly*] I can't bear any more. [*Crosses to L.*]

ARN. [*R.*] What's the matter now?

BLAN. [*C.*] That happy state! What does that happy state mean? Marriage, of course, and marriage reminds me of Anne. [*Crosses to L., turns on him, catches the book between his hands, and closes it*] I won't have any more *Paradise Lost;* it's painful; shut it up! See here! [*Drawing him confidentially to her*] This is a secret: Anne may come to me privately today while you are all at luncheon; if she doesn't come and if I don't hear from her, then the mystery of her silence must be cleared up, and you must do it.

ARN. I?

BLAN. Don't make difficulties. There is nobody but you, and to Anne you go tomorrow, if I don't see or hear from her today. [*Lady Lundie calls Blanche, C.R.*]

ARN. [*Crossing to L., faintly, and almost dropping Milton, as he turns towards table to put book away*] If Geoffrey doesn't get me out of this—I shall begin to be profane. [*Enter Lady Lundie, L.C.*]

LADY L. [*L.*] What are you doing here?

BLAN. [*R.*] Improving my mind. Mr. Brinkworth and I have been reading Milton.

LADY L. [*C.*] Can you condescend, after reading Milton all the morning, to help me with the invitations?

BLAN. If you can condescend, Lady Lundie, after feeding the poultry all the morning, I must be humility itself after only reading Milton. [*Exit Blanche and Lady Lundie, R.1.E., latter bowing low to Arnold. When they have departed, Arnold, after a moment of irresolution crosses to Geoffrey*]

ARN. [*L.C.*] I say, Geoffrey, have you heard what Blanche has been saying to me about Miss Sylvester?

GEOF. [*L.*] Some of it.

ARN. Did you hear Blanche say that she meant to send me to that devilish inn tomorrow, if she failed to get news from Miss Sylvester today?

GEOF. No.

ARN. Then you know it now. That is what Blanche has just said to me.

GEOF. Well?

ARN. Well; there's a limit to what a man can expect even from his best friend. I hope you won't ask me to be Blanche's messenger tomorrow. I can't and won't go back to the inn, as things are now.

GEOF. [*Sulkily, after a pause*] Well?

ARN. Well—all that is done and ended. It rests with you now to get me out of this difficulty I'm placed in with Blanche. Things must be settled with Miss Sylvester today!

GEOF. Things shall be settled! [*Rises and crosses to R.*]

ARN. *Shall* be? What are you waiting for?

GEOF. I am waiting to do what you told me.

ARN. What *I* told you?

GEOF. Don't you remember you advised me to consult Sir Patrick before I married her. I am waiting for a chance with Sir Patrick.

ARN. And then?

GEOF. [*Significantly*] And then you may consider it settled. [*Voices outside. Arnold offers his hand, Geoffrey pretends not to see it. Voices of Swells and Sir Patrick heard outside*]

ARN. Why there's Sir Patrick now. I'll tell him you want to speak with him. [*Exit Arnold, L.C. As he goes out the voices greet him: "Hallo—come here, Brinkworth!" and "I say, old fel." As he goes off, Geoffrey hastily seats himself at the table and hurriedly writes, then reads aloud*]

GEOF. Let me see if I remember all that Arnold has told me. He asked for her by the name of his wife, at the door of the inn. He said at dinner before the landlady and waiter: "I take these rooms for my wife," and at the same time he made her say he was her husband. After that he stopped all night. What do lawyers call this in Scotland? A marriage! [*Folds the paper and puts it in his pocket, as Nos. 1, 2 and 3 enter, followed by Sir Patrick and Arnold*]

No. 1. I say, Delamayn, we want you. Here is Sir Patrick running a regular muck at us. Calls us aboriginal Britons. Tells us we ain't educated. Doubts if we could read, write or cipher if he tried us. Says because a chap likes a healthy out-of-door life, and trains for rowing, running and wrestling, and the rest of it, and don't see his way to stewing over his books— he's safe to commit all the crimes in the calendar—murder included. Saw your name down for the foot race, and said when we asked him which way he'd bet, he'd take any odds we liked against you at the other race at the University, meaning, old boy, your degree.

No. 2. Aw—such bad taste, you know!

No. 3. Weally nasty, by Jove!

GEOF. Oh, I guess Sir Patrick didn't mean what he said.

SIR P. [*R.*] Oh, yes, I did.

GEOF. [*Angrily*] You point me out before all these people—

SIR P. One moment, Mr. Delamayn. I admit that I may have been wrong in directing the general attention to you; I apologize for having done that, but I don't retract a single word of what I have said on the subject of your health.

GEOF. [*L.*] I wish you were twenty years younger, sir!

SIR P. Why?

GEOF. I'd ask you to step out on the lawn there, and I'd show you whether I'm a broken down man or not.

SIR P. God bless me! [*Getting out of the way*]

ARN. [*Down between, interposing*] Geoffrey, remember you are invited here in the character of a gentleman, and you are a guest in a lady's house.

SIR P. [*Good humoredly*] No, no; Mr. Delamayn is using a strong argument, that is all. If I were twenty years younger and did step out upon the lawn with you—you would probably punch my head well, but the result would not affect the question between us, in the least. However, accept my excuses once more for having been so free and public in my remarks, and don't forget my warning. [*Geoffrey turns and crosses to R. of No. 1 with a sneer*]

No. 1. [*To Sir Patrick*] I say, no gammon there—all sound—there's blood for you. Let's go and have a game of croquet. Come! I say, Wobinson, come let's have a wun! [*Nos. 1, 2 and 3 go off, Sir Patrick wanders to window, Arnold following*]

GEOF. [*R., aside to Arnold*] I say, do you think I have set the old fogy's back up?

ARN. [*L.*] Do you mean Sir Patrick?

GEOF. [*Nodding*] I haven't put that little matter to him yet about marrying in Scotland, you know. Suppose he cuts up with me if I try him?

ARN. Make him an apology. Sir Patrick may be a little irritable and bitter, but you'll find him just.

GEOF. All right! [*Sees Arnold off, and then goes to Sir Patrick, and touches him on the shoulder*] I say!

SIR P. What do you want?

GEOF. I want to make an apology. Let bygones be bygones, and that sort of thing. I wasn't guilty of any intentional disrespect towards you, sir. Forgive and forget; not a bad motto, eh?

SIR P. [*Rising*] Not a word more, Mr. Delamayn. Accept my excuses for anything which I may have said too sharply on my side, and let us by all means forget the rest. [*Sits*]

GEOF. [*Brings a chair near Sir Patrick; after moving off, returns*] I beg your pardon. Could you give me a word in private?

SIR P. [*Bowing, and then aside*] Humph! What can he want with me?

GEOF. It's about a friend of mine. He's in a scrape—my friend is—and I want to ask your advice.

SIR P. Hem! You are quite sure you are applying to the right person in applying to me?

GEOF. You are a Scotch lawyer, ain't you?

SIR P. Certainly!

GEOF. And you understand about Scotch marriages, eh?

SIR P. [*Suddenly turning*] Is that the subject you wish to consult me on?

GEOF. It's not me, it's my friend.

SIR P. Your friend, then?

GEOF. Yes. It's a scrape with a woman here in Scotland. My friend don't know whether he's married or not.

SIR P. [*Aside*] Humph! Is there any connection, I wonder, between the position of Blanche's friend, and the position of Mr. Delamayn's friend? Something may come of this. [*Aloud*] Your friend doesn't know whether he is married to the girl or not, eh? Did he mean to marry her?

GEOF. No.

SIR P. Humph! Are you at liberty to mention names?

GEOF. No.

SIR P. Places?

GEOF. No.

SIR P. Were your friend and the lady at some time in the present year travelling in Scotland together.

GEOF. No.

SIR P. Living together in Scotland?

GEOF. No.

SIR P. What were they doing together in Scotland?

GEOF. They were meeting each other at an inn.

SIR P. Oh! Which was first at the rendezvous?

GEOF. The woman was first. Stop a bit. [*Taking his own memorandum from his pocket*] I've got a bit of a note here. Perhaps you'd like to have a look at it?

SIR P. [*Reading*] "He asked for her by the name of his wife at the inn door; he said at dinner, before the landlady and waiter, I take these rooms for my wife; he made her say he was her husband at the same time." Was that done jocosely, Delamayn, either by the lady or the gentleman?

GEOF. No. It was done in downright earnest.

SIR P. You mean it was done to look like earnest, and so to deceive the landlady and waiter?

GEOF. Yes.

SIR P. Humph! Am I to understand that the lady claims, on the strength of the circumstances which you have mentioned to me, to be your friend's wife?

GEOF. Yes. [*He pauses; Sir Patrick remains in reflection*] Well, what's your opinion?

SIR P. You wish me to decide on the facts with which you have supplied me, whether your friend is married or not?

GEOF. [*Eagerly*] That's it.

SIR P. Well, my experience is, that every single man in Scotland may marry any single woman at any time and under any circumstances. In short, after thirty years' practice as a lawyer, I don't know what is not a marriage in Scotland.

GEOF. [*Triumphantly*] In plain English then—she's his wife?

SIR P. Don't rush to conclusions, Mr. Delamayn. I have only told you what my general experience is thus far.

GEOF. [*Clouds up despairingly, then suddenly*] Look here! Suppose my friend had another lady in his eye?

SIR P. Yes.

GEOF. As things are now, would you advise him to marry her?

SIR P. As things are now, certainly not.

GEOF. That will do for him and for me. [*Goes to window recess, L.*]

SIR P. [*Looking after him*] I don't know who your friend is, but if your interest in this marriage is an honest and a harmless interest, I know no more of human nature than the babe unborn. [*Exit, C. Arnold enters, C.L., bows to Sir Patrick*]

ARN. All right, Geoffrey?

Geof. [*Without looking up*] Yes, all right. [*Malignantly*] Sir Patrick has said just what I want him to.

Arn. No difficulty about the marriage?

Geof. None.

Arn. No fear of Blanche?

Geof. [*Tapping him on the shoulder significantly*] She won't ask you to go to Craig Fernie again. [*Going*]

Arn. Are you going there?

Geof. [*Stopping, smilingly*] Where?

Arn. [*R.*] Why, to see Miss Sylvester!

Geof. [*C.*] Humph! [*Turns to go*]

Arn. Why don't you answer me?

Geof. Enough of being worried about Miss Sylvester! Miss Sylvester's my business, not yours. [*Going*]

Arn. [*Dropping his hand on his shoulders*] Gently, Geoffrey. Don't forget that I've been mixed up in that business without seeking it myself.

Geof. There's no fear of my forgetting; you have cast it in my teeth often enough.

Arn. [*L., dignified*] Mr. Delamayn, when you come to your senses, I'll remember old times, and receive your apology. [*Goes up*] Till you *do* come to your senses, go your way by yourself, I have no more to say to you. [*Bows stiffly, and exit, C.*]

Geof. Ha! I'd like to wager a hundred to one, my smart lad, that you'll want to see me again, before I want to see you. Humph! I see my way clear of that girl now—thanks to sweet Scottish laws—and the lovely widow is as good as mine. [*Exit, C.R., lighting his pipe. Sir Patrick and Blanche enter at R.1 E. door*]

Blan. Now, uncle, I've been watching you for the last minute or two, and do you know what I've seen?

Sir P. [*L.*] You have seen an old gentleman in want of his lunch.

Blan. I have seen an old gentleman with something on his mind. What is it?

Sir P. Suppressed gout, my dear.

Blan. That won't do. I'm not to be put off in that way, uncle. I want to know!

Sir P. Stop there, Blanche! A young lady who says she "wants to know" expresses very dangerous sentiments. Eve wanted to know, and see what a mess she got herself into, and all the rest of us. I'll be back directly, my dear, as soon as I get my lunch. Suppress your curiosity until then. Suppressed curiosity is as good as a dose of medicine. Try it! [*Exit, L.1 E. Music. Blanche throws herself on seat by window, L., pettishly*]

BLAN. That's always the way with uncle; just when I want to know—
[*Anne appears in doorway, C., looking around, bonnet on, pale and faint*]
And a simple answer would satisfy me. [*She turns, sees Anne, C., rises with a joyful exclamation, runs and embraces her*] This makes amends, love, for everything! You answer my letter in the best of all ways, you bring your own dear self. [*Anne staggers; Blanche, alarmed, runs for a chair, Anne sinks into it, near R.H.*] Oh! Anne! Anne! What can have happened to you? My darling, you look so faint and strange. [*Anne kisses her on the forehead*] You're tired! [*Kneels, R. of Anne*] I'm sure you're tired! Have you walked here? You shan't go back on foot! I'll take care of that!

ANNE. I don't go back, Blanche. I have left the inn.

BLAN. Left the inn? With your husband?

ANNE. A curse seems to follow me wherever I go. I am the cause of quarrelling and wretchedness everywhere, without meaning it. The old man who is head waiter at the inn has been kind to me, my dear, in his way, and he and the landlady had a quarrel; he has lost his place in consequence. I have missed a letter at the inn—a very important letter—I must have thrown it aside and forgotten it. I told the landlady, and she fastened a quarrel on me, so I thought it best to leave Craig Fernie. I hope and pray I shall never see that place again!

BLAN. Come upstairs, and rest in my room. You're not fit to travel.

ANNE. [*Rising*] I can't stay. I have come here to find out something, if I can. Will you tell me?

BLAN. What is it?

ANNE. Who are the gentlemen staying in the house? [*Blanche looks at her in surprise*] Run their names over, Blanche, I have a reason for wishing to know.

BLAN. Well, to begin: there's Mr. Arnold Brinkworth and that hateful friend of his, Mr. Delamayn. [*Anne on hearing Geoffrey's name, sinks to seat, her head falling on her breast and half fainting. Blanche kneels anxiously*] Let me run and get you some wine; you will faint, Anne, if you don't take something. I shall be back in a moment, and I can manage it without anyone being the wiser. [*Exit, R.1.E. As Blanche goes out, Geoffrey saunters in, C., in reflection. Anne hears his step and starts up. They confront each other*]

ANNE. [*L.*] Geoffrey! [*He expresses great annoyance, but says nothing*] Pray forgive me for coming here. [*He looks hard at her, then turns away*] I have done nothing to compromise you, Geoffrey. I got your letter, but you promised I should hear from you again, and I never heard, and it was so lonely at the inn. [*She stops; staggers against table*]

GEOF. [*C.*] What do you want?

ANNE. I am broken by what I have gone through. Don't insult me by making me remind you of your promise!

GEOF. You claim my promise after what you have done at the inn?

ANNE. [*Bewildered*] The inn? What have I done at the inn?

GEOF. I have had a lawyer's advice. Mind you, I know what I am talking about.

ANNE. [*Vacantly*] What did I do at the inn? [*Then resolutely, and advancing a step*] Do you refuse to marry me?

GEOF. I marry you? Why you're married already to Arnold Brinkworth! [*Anne gazes at him blindly a moment, then with a cry drops at his feet near C. door. Looking at her*] Done! [*Enter Blanche, R., Hester, L.; Geoffrey hurries out, C., as Hester passes L., and Blanche from R., with a glass of wine. Latter sees Anne, and with a cry runs to her*]

BLAN. Oh! Anne! Anne! [*Hester crosses from L. to C.; looks after Geoffrey. Close in*]

SCENE 2: *Table and chairs carried on. Anteroom at Windygates. Music. Enter Sir Patrick and Arnold, L.1.E., arm in arm.*

SIR P. [L.] I have a word to say to you, Arnold, before you become a married man. Do you remember what Lady Lundie said while the topic was on the table?

ARN. [R.] She told me what I can't believe, that Geoffrey Delamayn was paying attention and was likely to be married to Mrs. Glenharm.

SIR P. Exactly. I observed that you appeared to be startled by what my sister-in-law had said; and you declared that appearances must certainly have misled her. Now, are you at liberty to tell me why the mere report that your friend was likely to marry Mrs. Glenharm roused your indignation?

ARN. No; it is a secret.

SIR P. Committed to your honor?

ARN. Doubly committed to my honor.

SIR P. What do you mean?

ARN. I mean that Geoffrey and I have quarrelled since he took me into his confidence. I am doubly bound to respect his confidence after that.

SIR P. You have had very little experience of the world. Are you sure you are acting wisely in keeping his secret from me? Are you sure you will not repent the course you are taking tonight? Think, Arnold, think before you answer.

ARN. I feel bound in honor to keep a secret; nothing can alter that.

SIR P. Well, there's nothing more to be said on that point, then. Now as to your marriage—but, perhaps you object to be married?

ARN. Object? If Blanche will only consent I will take her to church as soon as she comes downstairs.

SIR P. Ha, ha! That's the right spirit, and it's just possible, if Lady Lundie consents and the lawyers hurry, you may be married this day week.

ARN. The lawyers! What have they got to do with it? Oh! I know, the settlements. Come into the library, Sir Patrick, and I'll soon settle the settlements. A bit of paper and a dip of ink—I hereby give every blessed farthing I have got in the world to my dear Blanche—sign that, stick a wafer on at the side, clasp your finger on the wafers—I deliver this my act and deed—and there it is done.

SIR P. Really! Among your other superfluities do you happen to have such a thing about you as a lawyer? [*Arnold feels in his pocket*]

ARN. Well, I have two not far off.

SIR P. One will do. Go into the library there, summon one of your legal friends to your aid, and we'll settle the whole of the legal business before breakfast tomorrow. [*Pushes Arnold off*] There, there, go; no time to lose. Now, if Lady Lundie has no objections to throw in the way, my little Blanche may be made happy in a week, and I shall have leisure to devote to clearing up this mystery about Anne Sylvester and very likely get a clue to her missing letter, which I have no doubt that rascal Bishopriggs has got hold of. [*Lady Lundie enters, R., attended by her maid, who wheels in a chair*] I am afraid my request for an interview disturbed you?

LADY L. A little pressure here. [*Hand to head*] Sir Patrick, pray sit down. Duty finds me accessible; from a poor weak woman duty must expect no more. Now, what is it? [*Sir Patrick hesitates*] If it is anything painful, pray don't hesitate. I am quite prepared.

SIR P. We won't call it a painful matter. Let us say it is a matter of domestic anxiety—Blanche!

LADY L. [*R.*] Blanche's heartless secrecy, Blanche's undutiful silence. I repeat the words: heartless secrecy, undutiful silence. I took her in my arms and folded her to my bosom; I sent everybody out of the room. I said, "Dear child, confide in me." And how were my advances, my motherly advances met? I have already told you, by heartless secrecy, by undutiful silence.

SIR P. She was probably afraid to speak.

LADY L. Afraid? You can't have said that. I have evidently misapprehended. You didn't really say "afraid."

SIR P. I said she was probably afraid, since the cause of her anxiety was about Miss Sylvester.

LADY L. I can run out of the house; I can fly to the uttermost corners of the earth, but I cannot hear that person's name mentioned. No, Sir Patrick, not in my presence—not while I am Mistress at Windygates.

Sir P. Well, she—

Lady L. Sir Patrick, stop! Stop there! I won't have the name mentioned. Say, "the person," if you please—"the person."

Sir P. Well, "the person" has mysteriously disappeared, left the house, in fact, after having a painful interview with Blanche in the library.

Lady L. [*Using salts*] The library? I undertook to control myself, Sir Patrick. Anything missing from the library?

Sir P. Nothing missing, Lady Lundie; but "the person" herself, she—

Lady L. Sir Patrick!

Sir P. I beg your pardon. "The person" has written a farewell letter to Blanche, and has mysteriously disappeared, leaving Blanche extremely distracted. All we can do to divert Blanche's mind is to turn Blanche's attentions to some other subject of reflection, less painful than the subject which occupies her now. Do you agree with me so far?

Lady L. I don't understand you, Sir Patrick. Be so good as to explain yourself.

Sir P. No, it would be asking too much. Even with your high standard of duty it would be asking too much.

Lady L. Nothing which you can ask me in the name of duty can be too much.

Sir P. No, no. Let me remind you. Human mind has its limits.

Lady L. A Christian gentlewoman's sense of duty knows no limit.

Sir P. Very good. Assuming that Blanche is like most other human beings, and has some prospect of happiness to contemplate, if she would only be made to see it, are we not bound to make her see it?

Lady L. If my stepdaughter had any prospect as you describe, I should, of course, say yes; but Blanche's is an ill-regulated mind. An irregulated mind has no prospect of happiness.

Sir P. Pardon me! Blanche *has* a prospect of happiness. In other words, Blanche has a prospect of being married; and what is more, Arnold Brinkworth is ready to marry her as soon as the settlements can be prepared. [*Lady Lundie expresses unconcealed chagrin; Sir Patrick watches her; she rises after a pause and an effort, and after a little silvery laugh continues*]

Lady L. My dear Sir Patrick! You have wasted much precious time, and many eloquent words in trying to entrap me into giving my consent when you might have had it for the asking. I think the idea of hastening Blanche's marriage an excellent one. I am charmed to transfer the charge of such a person as my stepdaughter to the unfortunate young man who is willing to take her off my hands. The less he sees of Blanche's character, the more satisfied I shall feel of his performing his engagement to marry her. Pray, hurry the lawyers, Sir Patrick, and let it be a week sooner, rather than a week later, if you wish to please me. [*Rises*]

SIR P. [*After a profound and courteous bow*] I believe every word of that charming answer. Admirable woman, adieu! [*Exit Lady Lundie, R.1 E., with Hopkins. As he is going off*] Gad, if I don't hurry, she may change her mind. The mother-in-law is a queer invention, as full of flaws and dangers as a second-hand steam boiler. [*Exit, L.*]

SCENE 3: *Music. Swanhaven portico, L.U E. Balustrades at back. Avenue of trees, R. Rustic table, R., and chairs. Enter Bishopriggs from house with a basket of wine, following John Thomas who carries a picnic basket.*

JOHN. Here, you—follow me down to the Swan Lake, where they are to have the picnic! [*Going*]

BISH. [*Putting down basket and resting*] Hech! Hech! Bide a wee till my legs be rested.

JOHN. Let me have the wine basket there. There's not so much danger of your resting so long with the sandwiches. [*Changes baskets and goes off, R.U.E. Bishopriggs makes a grimace after him, then sits*]

BISH. [*Sits*] The mean doalin' villain! Hont wi' ye. [*Taking letter from his pocket*] Aye, aye, it's safe eno'! I did well to keep the dockiment, the puir leddy at the inn threw on the floor. Two letters in one wi' "Anne Sylvester, yer loving wife," at the bottom o' one, and "Your loving husband that is to be, Geoffrey Delamayn" at the end o' t'other. I said tae mysel' at the time, "who kens but there'll be a reward offered for it ane o' these days," and sure enough when I engaged my services at this bonny hoose o' Mr. Julius Delamayn, the first news I hear is the match that's making between the braw widder Mistress Glenharm and Mr. Geoffrey Delamayn's ainsel'. Hech! Hech! Who knows but the leddy or the gentleman wad like tae buy this bit of paper like? [*Rising*] Eh! Eh! There may be the worth of a fi' pun note in this tae a puir lad like me. [*As he is going off, he meets Blanche coming from R.U.E., in summer hat, parasol, etc.*] Eh, my bonny miss! Are ye starving in this land of plenty? Can I serve you wi' a goose, pray, and some truffles? [*Turning up napkin*]

BLAN. [*R.*] No—nothing. [*Aside*] I'm sure this is that old man of the inn. I wonder if he's got that letter about him, that Sir Patrick says is so important for us to find for Anne's sake. [*Sitting, R., and aloud*] Do you remember me at the inn on the night of the storm?

BISH. [*Fighting shy*] I'm no' sayin' I canna' remember ye, miss. Whar's the mon wad mak' su an answer as that tae a bonny young leddy like you?

BLAN. [*Taking out her purse*] There is something I wanted to say to you. A friend of mine, whom you were very kind to, had a loss while she was staying at the inn.

BISH. Aye, aye! Like enough. Fra the mistress doon, they're kiddle caddle at the inn sin' I left 'em. What may it ha' been that she lost?

BLAN. She lost a letter.

BISH. When you say lost, d'ye mean stolen?

BLAN. Oh, no! Not stolen, only lost. Did you hear about it?

BISH. Wherefore could I hae heard about it? Tell me this, me young leddy. What sets ye tae coming tae me for your friend's lost letter?

BLAN. Sir Patrick. Sir Patrick thought you might have *found* the letter and not remembered about it again until after you left the inn.

BISH. [*Aside*] The dour auld deevil kens no better now that he'd clap me in jail if I own it tae havin' the wee dockiment.

BLAN. [*R.*] Well, is Sir Patrick right?

BISH. [*R.C. Taking up his basket and going*] Richt? He's as far awa' frae the truth as John O'Groat's hoose is frae Jericho.

BLAN. You know nothing of the letter?

BISH. Deil a bit I know o' the letter. The first I ha' heard o' it is what I hear noo. Excuse me, young leddy, the folks are starving below for their goose, frog and truffles. [*Exit, R.U.E.*]

BLAN. [*Rising*] Dear—dear me! I'm afraid I've done wrong as usual. Sir Patrick wanted to question the old man himself, and there I'm afraid I've gone and frightened him off. Blanche Lundie, you are a little fool, and I'd cut your society entirely, if you were not about to marry Arnold Brinkworth; and to tell the truth, I do love that dear fellow so, that I tolerate any amount of nonsense in his wife, if he can. [*As she is going off, L.U.E., First Lady enters from the house. Enter Geoffrey, lighting his pipe after looking around*]

GEOF. No one about here? Perry not come yet. A man can have a good chance to think. Think! There's the rub. I don't pride myself much on being able to think, and it's very well I don't; and whenever I do get into a heavy brain trot, I'm sure to break up by having Mrs. Glenharm run in my head. Hang the whole business—I can't get out of it. Arnold has certainly got himself mixed up with Anne. Those Scotch laws settle the fact that everything in Scotland is unsettled when you come to talk of "man and wife." Oh, if I could think the end of it! Stop! There's the clubs! My mind's in a muddle! I'll try the clubs. Here! John Thomas! [*John enters, L.*] Where are my clubs, you rascal? Where did you put them?

JOHN. Right here, sir, in the hall.

GEOF. Bring them out. My mind's muddled, that'll clear it. [*John enters with clubs and dumb bells, staggering under their weight. Geoffrey relieves him*] Why, you poor miserable rascal, can't you even carry them? [*John exit, L. Geoffrey takes off coat and picks up clubs, and exercises furiously round stage, singing out "Phew! Phew!" then throws them down suddenly*] I have it! I have it! [*Puts on coat*] I'll elope! I'll take Mrs. Glenharm and go to France! That's the way! Why didn't I think of it before? [*John enters, L.U.E.*]

JOHN. Please, sir, Mr. Perry has just come.

GEOF. My trainer? Tell him to come out here. He'll clear my head with a punch or two. Send him out. [*John exit, L.*] It's a capital plan! Marry Mrs. Glenharm in France, and then—then what? [*Pauses*] How am I to keep Mrs. Glenharm all her life away from England—and then Anne can follow me all over the Continent and bother me. That won't do. My head's going round again. I must cool off. [*Takes off his coat*] Thunder and lightning, Perry, where are you? [*Enter Perry, L.U.E., from house*]

PER. Aye, aye, sir! Here I am, and no mistake.

GEOF. [*Knocks his hat off*] You rascal! Have you brought the gloves?

PER. [*Astonished*] Well, I never see anybody say good morning like that before.

GEOF. Perry, my head's going round. I want a bout. None of your child's play. Fight as if you were in the ring with orders to win.

PER. You want a round with the gloves? You vants it all work and no play? Werry well, sir! As the grocer said to the fly when he spread the molasses on the fly trap, you shall have vat you vants.

GEOF. Quick, you rascal! [*Seizes gloves from carpetbag which Perry opens, and while Perry is slowly taking off his coat and laying it over a chair, and putting his hat down, Geoffrey dances around him, Perry dodging*]

PER. All right, sir. Vaer yourself hout, sir—spar away, sir—just keep it up till I come in, sir. Now, sir. [*Suddenly gets gloves on, faces him and gives him a blow which knocks him against table, then dances round him*]

GEOF. [*Recovering*] Hit hard! Harder, you beggar, or I'll withdraw my patronage and you'll go to the dogs.

PER. Well, sir. I've got a family to support, but if you will have it, why— [*They spar. Geoffrey gets Perry's head in chancery and is about to hit when he pauses*]

GEOF. I've got it.

PER. You've got *me*, you mean.

GEOF. [*Releasing him, putting on his coat and sitting to rest*] If she and Arnold are married by Scotch law, as Sir Patrick gave me the hint, I'm free, and why bother my head about it. [*Mrs. Glenharm enters, R.U.E. Perry gathers up gloves, etc.*]

Mrs. G. [*Tapping him on the shoulder*] Ah! You bad boy! Have I found you at last?

Geof. Well, now you have found me, what's the good? I've got to go with Perry, the race is near, and I can't idle any more. Perry says so. [*Crosses to C.*]

Mrs. G. Don't talk to me about Perry. A little vulgar wretch. Put him off. [*Geoffrey shakes his head*] You won't? Do you mean to say you are such a brute that you would rather be with Perry than with me?

Geof. The betting's 5 to 4, my dear, and the race comes off in a week's time from this.

Mrs. G. Oh! go away with your Perry. I hate you. I hope you'll lose the race! [*Crosses R. in pique, then turns towards him*] And mind this, don't presume to say "My dear" to me again.

Geof. [*Putting his arms around her waist*] It ain't presuming half enough, is it? Wait a bit. Give me till the race is over and then I'll presume to marry you.

Mrs. G. You? You will be as old as Methusaleh if you wait till I am your wife. I daresay Perry has got a sister. Suppose you ask him. She would be just the right person for you.

Geof. All right. Anything to be agreeable to you. I'll ask Perry. I say, Perry. [*Perry looks up, winks, then carries clubs into house*]

Mrs. G. What a funny man you are. I never met anybody like you before. Won't you take me to the lake?

Geof. Can't. Perry is waiting for me.

Mrs. G. Perry again? [*Turning away vexed*]

Geof. Yes.

Mrs. G. [*Slapping him on shoulder with fan and breaking it*] There! My poor fan broken. You monster. All through you.

Geof. [*Picks up fan and puts it in his pocket*] I'll write to London and get you another. Come along. Kiss and make it up. [*Looks around to see if they are alone, then gives her a kiss on both cheeks*] With kind compliments from yours truly.

Mrs. G. How dare you do that? I shall claim Mr. Delamayn's protection if I am to be insulted in this way. [*Coquettishly starting away and then leaning on his arm with a smile*] How rough you are, Geoffrey. Come, put him off. Never mind Perry for this once. Take me to the lake.

Geof. No.

Mrs. G. You brute.

Geof. Do you want me to lose the race?

Mrs. G. Yes. [*Goes to seat and throws herself into it. Geoffrey after a pause goes to her, she turns from him*]

GEOF. See here. Don't be a fool. [*Mrs. Glenharm puts handkerchief to her eyes*] Come, now, I've got something to say to you. [*Puts his arm around her waist, she looks up, smiles and rises*] You're just the sort of a woman I like, and there isn't a man living loves you half as much as I do.

MRS. G. Oh! Geoffrey, if you could only be always like this. Do you really love me?

GEOF. Don't I? [*Taking her towards L.U.E.*] Come along, I'll see you to the house.

MRS. G. But—but—Geoffrey—shan't—I see you again?

GEOF. Yes, after my run when I've got my toggery on. Now go. [*He looks after her; she runs off just as Perry appears behind, scowling at her*] Come along, Perry, and help me win your money. [*As they are going out, L.U.E., Bishopriggs enters, R.U.E.*]

BISH. Praise Providence for a' his maircies, there's Mr. Delamayn's ain sel. I wonder what he'll give me for the letter? [*Takes letter from his pocket. Perry turns and sees him, stops Geoffrey*]

PER. Hello! What do you want here? [*Bishopriggs bows and scrapes*]

GEOF. Who the devil are you?

PER. A spy, sir, sent to time you at your work. [*Geoffrey starts forward, lifting his fist. Bishopriggs scampers off*] You can't do that, sir. The man's too old. No fear of his turning up again. You've scared him out of his wits. [*They exeunt, L.U.E., laughing. Bishopriggs hobbles on again*]

BISH. Praise Providence for a' his maircies. I've got twa strings, as they say, to ma' bow. I trow the woman's the canny string of the twa and will een try twanging o' her. [*Going, L.U.E. John enters from house*]

JOHN. [*In doorway*] Mr. Bishopriggs, there's a fine leddy in the hall asking for you by your own name.

BISH. A leddy, ye ne'er-do-well! Do ye come to a decent 'sponsible mon like me wi' sic a Cyprian overture as that? What di ye take me for? Mark Antony that lost [the] warld for love (the more fool he), Don Jovanny, or the blessed Solomon himself? Awa' wi' ye tae yer pots and pans and bid the wandering Venus that sent ye go spin. [*Music. Anne puts John aside and enters, L.U.E., down steps*]

ANNE. You had better tell the servant I'm no stranger to you.

BISH. Ma ain sister's child! Go yer ways, Tummon. The bonny lassie's my ain kith and kin. [*Exit John*] Lord save us and guide us, what brings ye here? [*Anne comes down*]

ANNE. [*L.*] I have come to ask you for something.

BISH. Aye, aye, what may it be ye are wanting o' me?

ANNE. I want the letter lost at Craig Fernie.

BISH. [*R., after a pause*] I dinna ken what ye're drivin' at.

ANNE. [*R.C.*] You have got my letter [*With sternness*] and you are trying to turn it to a disgraceful use. I won't allow you to make a market of my private affairs. You have offered a letter of mine for sale. I insist on your restoring it to me before I leave this place.

BISH. I'll no waste precious time in brushing awa the fawse breath o' scandal when it passes my way. It blows to no purpose, my young leddy, when it blows on an honest man like me.

ANNE. I have learned enough by this time to know that the one argument that prevails with you is the argument of money. If money will spare me the hateful necessity of disputing with you, poor as I am, money you shall have. [*Bishopriggs attempts to speak*] Be silent! If you choose to own the truth and produce the letter, [*Takes money from her pocket*] I will give you this as your reward for finding and restoring to me something that I had lost. If you persist in your present prevarication, I can and will make that sheet of note paper you have stolen from me nothing but waste paper in your hands. You intend to seek a purchaser in Mrs. Glenharm. I intend to seek Mrs. Glenharm myself and reveal to her all that letter contains. What has Mrs. Glenharm to purchase of you then?

BISH. Mercy presairve us! Is it even you yersel' that wrote the letter to the mon ca'd Geoffrey Delamayn and got the wee bit answer in pencil on the same sheet? Hoo in heaven's name was I tae know that were the letter ye were after when ye came in here? Gi ye back yer letter? Ma certie, noo I know it is your letter. I'll gi it back wi a' the pleasure in life. [*Opens his pocketbook, takes letter out. Anne offers him money*] Hoot toot, I'm no that clear in my mind that I ought to take yer money. Eh? Weel, weel, I'll e'en receive it as a bit memento o' the time when I was o' some sma service to you at the hottle. Ye'll no mind writing me a line in the way of receipt, ye ken, to clear me o' any further suspicion in the matter of the letter. [*Anne snatches the letter from him and throws money on table*]

ANNE. You need no receipt. There shall be no letter to bear witness against you. [*About to tear letter*]

BISH. Tear it if you will. It matters nothing to me, but, young leddy, tak' ma word, that dockiment is worth more than scrap paper.

ANNE. [*Rising*] I will keep the letter. [*Folds it, puts it in her bosom, going, stops in C.*] One thing more. Do you know where Mrs. Glenharm is now?

BISH. You're no really going to Mrs. Glenharm?

ANNE. That is no concern of yours. You can answer my question or not. Just as you please.

BISH. Eh? My leddy, yere temper's no what it used to be in the auld time at the hottle; aweel, aweel, ye ha' gi'en me yer money, and I'll e'en gi ye back gude measure for't on my side. Mrs. Glenharm is no above twa rod frae here. Bide a bit and I'll send her to ye in a jiffy. [*Aside as he goes off. Anne sinks in a seat, R.*] Hech, hech, I trow I hae gone out for wool and come back shorn. My certie! There was nothing left for't when madam's fingers had gripped me, but to slip through them as soon as I could. [*Exit, L.U.E.*]

ANNE.   So near. Am I so near her? Heaven give me strength to pursue my sacrifice to the end. His wife that is to be. Yes! [*Rising*] Well, be it so. She may marry him without a breath against it to dread from me, [*Mrs. Glenharm enters, L.U.E., Bishopriggs with her; he points to Anne, then goes off*] so long as he unsays the words and undoes the deeds that throw an obstacle between the marriage of Arnold and Blanche.

MRS. G.   I think I understood that you are so good as to have come to see me. You look tired; won't you take a chair? [*Anne sits as if about to faint*] It's so awkward. There's no one here to introduce us. Might I ask your name? [*Sits, L.C.*]

ANNE.   I am speaking, I believe, to Mrs. Glenharm? [*Mrs. Glenharm smiles and bows*] I have come here by permission of Mr. Julius Delamayn to ask leave to speak to you on a matter in which you are interested.

MRS. G.   Indeed. I am interested in so many matters. May I ask what this matter is?

ANNE.   I wish to speak to you about an obstacle that might prevent the consummation of what I am given to understand is your dearest hope.

MRS. G. [*Using eyeglass*]   Pardon me, my memory of faces is a bad one. Have we ever met before?

ANNE.   Never.

MRS. G.   And yet you want to speak to me about something which is only interesting to myself and to my most intimate friends?

ANNE.   You understand me correctly. I wish to speak to you about Mr. Geoffrey Delamayn. [*Mrs. Glenharm rises quickly*] Of a letter which was offered you for sale. The person who wrote to you offering to sell you that letter is no longer in possession of it.

MRS. G. [*Rising excitedly*]   The man who wrote to me spoke of something else besides a correspondence. He spoke of a woman. [*One step*] I understand you—you are the woman. [*One step. Music till end*]

ANNE. [*Rising*]   Mrs. Glenharm, I warn—[*More gently*] no, I entreat you not to take that tone to me. Pray bear with me a little longer. I admit that you have guessed right. I own that I am the miserable woman who has been ruined and deserted by Geoffrey Delamayn.

MRS. G. [*Advancing on her*]   It is false! He has never wronged you! It is all a plot to injure him in my eyes. I'll summon the servants. [*Crosses to R.*] I'll have you driven from the grounds. [*Turns to go into house. Anne hurries and places herself between steps and Mrs. Glenharm. A moment's pause. Mrs. Glenharm draws back a step*]

ANNE. Listen to me.

MRS. G. Listen to you? You have no right to be in this house. You have no right to force yourself in here!

ANNE. [*L.*] Take care, Mrs. Glenharm. I am not naturally a patient woman. Trouble has done much to tame my temper; but endurance has its limits.

MRS. G. You shameless woman! You are married already to Arnold Brinkworth!

ANNE. Did Geoffrey Delamayn tell you that? [*Mrs. Glenharm turns away contemptuously, Anne advances and repeats*] Did Geoffrey Delamayn tell you that?

MRS. G. [*R.*] He did tell me.

ANNE. He lied!

MRS. G. I believe *him*. I don't believe *you*.

ANNE. You believe I am Arnold Brinkworth's wife?

MRS. G. I am certain of it.

ANNE. You tell me that to my face?

MRS. G. I tell you to your face, Geoffrey Delamayn disowns you. You are Arnold Brinkworth's wife. [*R.*]

ANNE. Say no more. I came to you with mercy in my heart—you fill it with revenge. While I live you will never see Geoffrey Delamayn again! I swear it! I swear it!

MRS. G. I shall be his wife the day after the race. I am going to him in London to warn him against you.

ANNE. You'll find me in London before you, with this in my hand. [*Mrs. Glenharm attempts to pass again, Anne warns her back imperiously*] I forbid your marriage to Geoffrey Delamayn. I insist on his performing the promise he gave me. I have it here in his own words, in his own writing. His plaything, did you say? His WIFE before this week is out! [*Music. Off. Tableau*]

ACT IV.

SCENE 1: *Portland Place. Elegant interior. Divan, C. Large table, L. Sofa, R. Chairs, R. and L. Bronzes, etc. Lady Lundie on divan, C. Blanche on chair, L., her head buried in her hands.*

BLAN. [*Rising*] I can't believe it—I won't believe it—you're trying to part me from Arnold—you're trying to set me against my dearest friend. It is infamous! It is horrible!

Lady L. I was prepared for this outbreak. [*Blanche walks to and fro*] These wild words relieve your overburdened heart, my dear Blanche. I can wait. I can wait.

Blan. [*Facing Lady Lundie*] You and I never liked each other. I have always taken Anne's part against you. I have shown you plainly—rudely— I dare say, that I was glad to get away from you. This is not your revenge, is it?

Lady L. [*Rises, passing her arm around Blanche*] Oh, Blanche! Blanche! What thoughts, what words!

Blan. [*Sinking in chair*] I am mad, Lady Lundie; you bear with mad people—bear with me. I love *him*, I love *her* with all my heart.

Lady L. [*Trying to compose her*] My dear Blanche, can't you see that your interest and my interest in this matter are one?

Blan. [*R.*] Don't repeat it.

Lady L. I must repeat it. I have told you that Arnold Brinkworth was privately at Craig Fernie with Miss Sylvester in the acknowledged character of her husband—you refuse to believe it, and I am about to put it to the proof. Mr. Geoffrey Delamayn is also anxious for an investigation. This woman (Mr. Brinkworth's wife) has brought accusations against Mr. Delamayn which must be cleared before he marries Mrs. Glenharm. The investigation is to take place in this room, today—in fact, presently. Have you the courage to be present—to have the truth confirmed, or do you fear the test?

Blan. [*Rises*] If I believed him guilty, Lady Lundie, I should *not* have the courage. I believe him to be innocent. I *will* be present, even though the truth should break my heart. [*Bell*]

Lady L. As you please, my dear, but I fear the ordeal will test you more than you think. However, you can't meet strangers in this state. Come to your room and compose yourself. Your eyes are positively inflamed. Tears! and all for a man! Blanche, as a woman, you are unworthy of the nineteenth century, and unless you stop all that nonsense, as a wife you will be a disgrace to any free and enlightened country. Come, dry your tears. [*Exit, with Blanche, R. arch. Hopkins is seen to cross at back and then reenter, C.R., showing in Sir Patrick and Mr. Moy, who enter shaking hands*]

Hop. Wait—Sir Patrick—will you please valk in here and wait—nobody else have yet arrived. [*Curtsies and goes off, C.*]

Sir P. [*L.*] Quite an accidental meeting, both of us first on the grounds, eh? We lawyers are not often accused of such punctuality—eh, Moy? Ha, ha! and not often found guilty—ha, ha!

Mr. Moy. Ha, ha! Not often, Sir Patrick.

Sir P. How is your client since his breakdown at the race?

Mr. M. Mr. Delamayn is recovering but slowly, Sir Patrick.

Sᴵʀ P.   It was a bad break in his health.

Mʀ. M.   It is useless to conceal it now, he has had a narrow escape from a paralytic stroke.

Sᴵʀ P.   That was what I dreaded when I spoke to him at Windygates.

Mʀ. M.   When he dropped on the race course I firmly believed we should find him a dead man. His physicians positively assert he will never recover. Paralysis is hanging over him. How long he may live is impossible to say, much depends upon himself. In his condition any violent emotion may kill him at a moment's notice. [*Bell*]

Sᴵʀ P.   Will he be sufficiently himself again to leave his bed and come out? Is it likely that he will be able to keep his appointment here, today?

Mʀ. M.   Quite likely. [*Hopkins crosses at back, reenters with Captain Newenden*]

Sᴵʀ P.   Thank you; you know he was quite as eager as any of us for the investigation at which we are to assemble this morning, and—living or dying —he has as much at stake in it as any of us. [*Seeing Captain, bows to Mr. Moy, who goes to table and busies himself with papers. Sir Patrick shakes Captain's hand and brings him forward, L.*] Charmed to have the pleasure of meeting you, Captain Newenden.

Cᴀᴘᴛ.   Delighted to have the honor of making your acquaintance, Sir Patrick.

Sᴵʀ P.   I think we could settle this in two minutes.

Cᴀᴘᴛ.   My own idea perfectly expressed.

Sᴵʀ P.   State your position, captain.

Cᴀᴘᴛ.   With the greatest pleasure. Here is my niece, Mrs. Glenharm, engaged to marry Mr. Geoffrey Delamayn. All very well; but there happens to be an obstacle in the shape of a lady. Do I put it plainly?

Sᴵʀ P.   You put it admirably, captain. But for the loss to the British Navy, you ought to have been a lawyer. Pray go on.

Cᴀᴘᴛ.   You are too good, Sir Patrick. Mr. Delamayn asserts that this person in the background has no claim on him, and backs his assertion by declaring that she is married already to Mr. Arnold Brinkworth. Lady Lundie and my niece assure me, on evidence which satisfies *them,* that the assertion is true. The evidence does not satisfy *me.* I hope, Sir Patrick, I do not strike you as being an excessively obstinate man. [*Bell*]

Sᴵʀ P.   My dear sir, you impress me with the highest opinion of your capacity for sifting human nature.

Cᴀᴘᴛ.   This is my course: I refuse to sanction my niece's engagement until Mr. Delamayn has effectually proved his statement, by appeal to witnesses, of the lady's marriage. This was to be done on Saturday. Today is Saturday—

here I am to hear it done. Will it be done? [*Hopkins, as before, showing in Anne, closely veiled*]

SIR P. Captain, in ten minutes you shall have your answer. Pray be seated. [*Seeing Anne, goes to her. Captain goes to Mr. Moy, shakes hands, then crosses to seat, L. Sir Patrick brings Anne down C.*] Forgive me, my dear Miss Sylvester, for thinking first of Blanche's happiness and having insisted upon your presence here. Since I made the request, I have seen the dreadful sacrifice as *you* see it. I ask myself, have I any right, has Blanche any right—

ANNE. [*R., as if to assure him*] Yes, if Blanche's happiness depends upon it, say no more.

SIR P. Remember what may be the consequences. Do you feel strong enough to go on?

ANNE. Thank you, Sir Patrick, I am more than ready, I am eager to go on. [*Lady Lundie and Blanche enter, R.1.E. Anne and Blanche both start forward to greet each other. Blanche is withheld by Lady Lundie and submits. Anne turns away sadly to Sir Patrick, who leads her to R., while Lady Lundie and Blanche take seats, L. Ring as before. Hopkins crosses behind*]

LADY L. My stepdaughter is here in direct defiance of my entreaties and my advice. Persons may present themselves whom it is in my opinion improper that she should see. Revelations will take place which no young woman in her position should hear. She insists on it, Captain Newenden, and I am obliged to submit. [*Both sit, L. Hopkins enters, showing in Geoffrey, who is frightfully pale. He bows to Lady Lundie and Blanche, then sits apart, at L., above table*]

SIR P. Where the deuce can that boy Arnold be? [*Hopkins crosses as before*] He never was so late before, particularly when Blanche was to be on the grounds. [*Hopkins ushers in Arnold. He stands C. a moment. Sir Patrick advances to meet him. Arnold's eyes seek for Blanche, who had been the first to catch the first glance of him, but when he enters, casts down her eyes and pretends not to see him. Arnold gently advances, releasing himself from Sir Patrick, who follows him, however. As Arnold comes towards Blanche, Lady Lundie rises and interposes*]

LADY L. Not yet, Mr. Brinkworth.

ARN. [*After a pause, glancing from Lady Lundie to Blanche, who lifts her eyes to him and then turns away weeping*] I won't distress you. [*Sir Patrick takes his hand and draws him towards R.*]

SIR P. Come, my boy, don't be put down by that; see, there's Miss Sylvester.

ARN. [*Fretfully, turning away from Anne*] I wish to heaven I had never set eyes on her.

SIR P. Lay-the saddle on the right horse—wish you had never set eyes on Geoffrey Delamayn. [*Sir Patrick directs him to a seat, then turns to Lady Lundie*] Lady Lundie, are all the persons present whom you expected to see here today?

LADY L. [*With a bitter tone and look at Anne*] All whom I expected, here? More than I expected.

SIR P. I am here to act on behalf of my friend, Mr. Arnold Brinkworth, whom I beg leave to present you to, Mr. Moy, as repellant in the charge which has been made against him, and which I declare to be false, and unjust and malignant.

MR. M. [*Rising*] And I, rising on behalf of my client, Mr. Geoffrey Delamayn, charge that Arnold Brinkworth was married on the fourteenth day of August, of this year, at a place called Craig Fernie, in Scotland, to a lady named Anne Sylvester, now living and present among us, as I understand, at this moment.

SIR P. Since you assert this Scotch marriage, it rests with you to begin. [*Sits*]

MR. M. The object of our meeting here is, if I am not mistaken, of a two-fold nature. In the first place it is thought desirable by a person who has a special interest in the issue of this inquiry, [*He looks at the Captain, who suddenly becomes attentive*] to put my client's assertion, relating to Mr. Brinkworth's marriage, to the proof. In the second place, we are all equally desirous—whatever differences of opinion may exist—to make this informal inquiry a means, if possible, of avoiding the painful publicity which would result from an appeal to a court of law.

LADY L. [*Rising*] I beg to inform you on behalf of my stepdaughter, that we have nothing to dread from the widest publicity—we consent to be present at what you call "this informal inquiry," reserving our rights to carry the matter beyond the four walls of this room.

ARN. [*Rising excitedly*] After what Lady Lundie has said, I think I ought to be allowed to say a word on my side. [*Sir Patrick rises*] I only want to explain how I came to go to Craig Fernie at all, and I challenge Mr. Geoffrey Delamayn to deny it if he can—that it was he himself who asked me to go there on his own business. Do you dare deny this, sir?

MR. M. [*Calmly to Geoffrey*] You are not bound to answer unless you wish to.

GEOF. [*Stolidly*] I deny every word of it. [*Arnold sinks back aghast*]

MR. M. I trust, Sir Patrick, we have had enough of assertion. Suppose we proceed in the legal way, now?

SIR P. [*Rises*] As you say, Mr. Moy, let us proceed in the legal way. Arnold Brinkworth, answer for yourself, in the presence of the persons here assembled; in all that you said, and all that you did, while you were at the inn of Craig Fernie, on the 14th of August last, were you solely influenced by the wish to make Miss Sylvester's position as little painful to her as. possible, and by anxiety to carry out the instructions given to you by Mr. Geoffrey Delamayn? Is this the whole truth?

ARN. It is the whole truth, Sir Patrick.

SIR P. On the way, when you went to Craig Fernie, had you not, a few hours previously, applied for my permission to marry my niece?

ARN. I applied for your permission, Sir Patrick, and you gave me it.

SIR P. From the moment you entered the inn to the moment you left it, were you absolutely innocent of the slightest intention to marry Miss Sylvester?

ARN. No such thing as the thought of marrying Miss Sylvester ever entered my head.

SIR P. This you say on your word of honor as a gentleman?

ARN. [Rises] On my word of honor as a gentleman.

SIR P. [To Anne] Was it a matter of necessity, Miss Sylvester, that you should appear in the assumed character of a married woman, on the fourteenth day of August last, at Craig Fernie Inn?

ANNE. I went to the inn alone, Sir Patrick. The landlady refused, in the plainest terms, to let me stay there, unless she was first satisfied that I was a married woman.

SIR P. Which of the gentlemen did you expect to join you at the inn— Mr. Arnold Brinkworth or Mr. Geoffrey Delamayn?

ANNE. Mr. Geoffrey Delamayn.

SIR P. When Mr. Arnold Brinkworth came in his place, and said what was necessary to satisfy the scruples of the landlady, you understood that he was acting in your interest from motives of kindness only, and under the instructions of Mr. Geoffrey Delamayn?

ANNE. I understood that, and objected as strongly as I could to Mr. Brinkworth placing himself in a false position on my account.

SIR P. Did your objection proceed from any knowledge of the Scottish law of marriage, and of the position in which the peculiarities of the law might place Mr. Brinkworth?

ANNE. I had no knowledge of the Scottish law. I had a vague dislike and dread of the deception which Mr. Brinkworth was practising on the people of the inn, and I feared it might lead to some possible misinterpretation of me on the part of a person whom I dearly love.

SIR P. That person being my niece?

ANNE. Yes.

SIR P. And from first to last you were absolutely innocent of the slightest intention of marrying Mr. Brinkworth?

ANNE. [*Rises*] I answer, Sir Patrick, as Mr. Brinkworth has answered; no such thing as the thought of marrying him ever entered my head.

SIR P. And this you say on your oath as a Christian woman?

ANNE. On my oath as a Christian woman. [*Sits. Sir Patrick sits. Mr. Moy rises*]

MR. M. I waive my claim, Sir Patrick, to put any questions on my side. The marriage which they deny I am now waiting to prove—not by assertion on my side, but by an appeal to competent witnesses.

SIR P. Do you wish to produce your witnesses at once? I have not the least objection to meet[ing] your views—if it is understood that I am permitted to return to the proceedings as interrupted at this point. [*Mr. Moy consults with Captain, and then Lady Lundie, then rises*]

MR. M. Reserving my right of objection, Sir Patrick, I beg you to go on.

SIR P. [*Rises*] Blanche, my dear, I have a question to ask you, which you can answer or not, entirely as you please. [*Lady Lundie and Mr. Moy talk together; Lady Lundie seems to object, Mr. Moy consoles her*] You have heard what Arnold Brinkworth has said, and what Miss Sylvester has said— that Arnold who loves you, and that sisterly friend who loves you, have each made a solemn declaration—recall your past experience of both of them, and tell me do you believe they have spoken falsely?

BLAN. I believe, uncle, they have spoken the truth.

MR. M. [*Rises*] Ha, ha! Sir Patrick, I must really object, you know. This is quite out of the usual course.

SIR P. Well, object as much as you please, and register your objections, but I have some questions to ask Miss Lundie, and if she has no objections I will proceed with her.

BLAN. Ask me anything you please, uncle. [*Mr. Moy and Lady Lundie turn aside, disgusted*]

SIR P. You believe what Arnold Brinkworth has said—you believe what Miss Sylvester has said—you know that not even the thought of marriage was in the mind of either of them, at the inn—you know whatever else may happen in the future, that there is not the most remote possibility of either of them consenting to acknowledge that they ever have been, or ever can be, "Man and Wife." Is that enough for you? Are you willing, before this inquiry proceeds any further, to take Arnold's hand and to leave the rest to me? [*Mr. Moy and Lady Lundie rise, she advances as Geoffrey lifts his head with a sudden start*]

BLAN. [*Advances*] I hope you will not think me ungrateful, uncle. I am sure that Arnold has not knowingly done me any wrong. But I can't go back to him until I am first *certain* that he is free to make me his wife.

LADY L. [*Embracing her with an outbreak*] My dear Blanche, well done, my dear Blanche!

SIR P. [*Aside*] Ha, ha! You bad, foolish girl—if you only knew what you are forcing me to.

LADY L. We have had enough of irregularity. I for one object to more.

MR. M. We don't presume to restrain you, Sir Patrick, by any other limits than those which, as a gentleman, you impose on yourself.

SIR. P. Do you object to my speaking to your client?

MR. M. To Mr. Geoffrey Delamayn?

SIR P. Yes. [*Anne makes a move, Mr. Moy invites Sir Patrick to proceed by a gesture of assent*] You are seriously interested in this inquiry, and you have taken no part in it yet. Take a part in it now. Look at this lady.

GEOF. [*Banteringly and without moving*] I've seen enough of her already.

SIR P. You don't look at her! Well, I rather thought you would be ashamed to. I would, myself, under the circumstances. I wish to ask you to carry your memory back to the fourteenth of August. Do you deny that you promised to marry Miss Sylvester privately at Craig Fernie Inn?

MR. M. [*Rising*] I object to the question. My client is under no sort of obligation to answer it.

GEOF. [*To Mr. Moy*] I shall answer it if I like. [*To Sir Patrick*] I do deny it.

SIR P. You deny that you promised to marry Miss Sylvester?

GEOF. Yes.

SIR P. I asked you just now to look at her.

GEOF. And I told you I had seen enough of her, already.

SIR P. In my presence and in the presence of the other persons here, do you deny that you owe this lady, by your own solemn engagement, the reparation of marriage?

GEOF. [*Rises. Raises his eyes to Anne, and savagely*] I know what I owe her!

MR. M. [*Advancing to him. Aside to Geoffrey*] Control yourself, or I will throw up your case.

GEOF. [*Savagely at Anne*] But for you I should be married to Mrs. Glenharm; but for you I should be friends with my father; but for you I should have won the race. I know what I owe you!

SIR P. [*Rising and leading Anne down*] I must speak to you, instantly.

LADY L. What does this mean?

MR. M. It means that I have not been properly instructed. Sir Patrick Lundie has some evidence in his possession that seriously compromises Mr. Delamayn's case. He has shrunk from producing it hitherto—he finds himself forced to produce it now. [*To Geoffrey*] How is it you have left me in the dark?

GEOF. I know nothing about it.

SIR P. [*Taking a letter from his pocketbook*] I have done all that can be done. I have left nothing untried to prevent the necessity of producing this letter which, I have assured you, proclaims you both by Scotch law and English law to be Geoffrey Delamayn's wife.

ANNE. [*R.*] I feel your kindness greatly, Sir Patrick. You must produce it now.

SIR P. Take it back; I can't produce it. I dare not ask you to declare yourself that man's wife.

ANNE. Blanche?

SIR P. Not even in Blanche's interest! Not even for Blanche's sake! Destroy it and rely on my silence.

ANNE. I have something to ask you, Sir Patrick, before I destroy it. Blanche refuses to go back to Arnold, unless she returns with the certain assurance of becoming his wife. If I produce this letter, she may go back today. If I declare myself Geoffrey Delamayn's wife, I clear Arnold Brinkworth at once and forever.

SIR P. [*After a pause*] Well, since you are resolved, let us not prolong this. [*They return to seats*]

ANNE. [*R.C.*] Must I speak for myself, Sir Patrick, or will you—I wish it as a last favor—speak for me?

SIR P. You insist on appealing to the letter in your hand?

ANNE. I am resolved to appeal to it.

SIR P. Give me the letter. [*Anne gets back to seat*]

MR. M. Do you know what this is?

GEOF. No!

SIR P. [*To Blanche*] A short time since I proposed to you to return to Arnold's protection, and to leave the termination of this matter in my hands; you have refused. Thanks to a sacrifice to your interests and your happiness on Miss Sylvester's part—which I tell you frankly I have done my utmost to prevent—I am in a position to prove positively that Arnold Brinkworth is a single man, as far as this lady is concerned.

MR. M. Do you claim on a promise of marriage?

SIR P. I do. Loose and irregular as the Scotch law is, a written promise of marriage between a man and woman in Scotland, marries that man and woman eternally and irrevocably. What stronger contract do you want than this gentleman's signature to these words: [*Music. Reading*] "Stop where you are, and I will write to you. Trust the bearer. Upon my soul I'll keep my promise. Your loving husband that is to be, Geoffrey Delamayn." And with this evidence in my hand I declare this lady to be now and to have been on the 14th of August last, Mr. Geoffrey Delamayn's wedded wife. [*All start up. Blanche rises horrified, Arnold goes to Sir Patrick, Lady Lundie goes to Captain. Anne stands down R.C.; Geoffrey slowly rises; Mr. Moy takes letter from Sir Patrick, looks over it and then crosses to Anne*]

Mr. M. On the faith of this written promise of marriage exchanged between you in Scotland, you claim Mr. Geoffrey Delamayn as your husband.

Anne. I claim Mr. Geoffrey Delamayn as my husband.

Mr. M. Enough, Sir Patrick, I understand you. Madam, I sincerely respect you.

Geof. Is it settled? [*Sir Patrick goes to Anne*]

Mr. M. To all practical purposes it is settled.

Geof. Has the law of Scotland made her my wife?

Mr. M. The law of Scotland has made her your wife.

Geof. Does the law tell her to go where her husband goes?

Mr. M. Yes! [*Geoffrey utters a low laugh and beckons Anne to him. She obeys*]

Blan. Oh, Anne! Anne! [*Runs and throws herself in Anne's arms*]

Anne. Happy days are coming, my love. Don't think of me. [*Kisses her and passes her to Arnold, to whom Blanche in pantomime appeals. To Arnold*] You did not befriend an ungrateful woman. Today I have proven it. [*She bends her head gently, then turns to Geoffrey*] I am here, what do you wish me to do?

Geof. Mrs. Geoffrey Delamayn, come home!

Arn. I can't see this sacrifice go on. [*Starting forward. Sir Patrick follows*]

Geof. Ha, ha! [*Putting Anne behind him and interposing between them*] The law tells her to go with her husband! The law forbids you to separate "*Man* and *Wife.*" [*Quick curtain*]

ACT V.

Scene: *The papered room at Salt Patch. Bureau, R. Sofa, R. Mantel, L. Two gas jets. Bed, C. Enter Perry, shown in by Hester, R.D.3.E.*

Per. Is this Mr. Geoffrey Delamayn's house? Well, it's not very nobby. Same place I trained him in the last week before his race, ah! He hired it from you, I believe. [*Hester bows*] And you're dumb and can't speak? Lord, how it must worry a woman to be dumb! [*Hester places chair for him, C.*]

Thank you. Is Mr. Geoffrey's wife here? Did he bring her here? [*Hester bows*] It's a nice place for a honeymoon, I *don't* think. You live with her as a companion, I suppose. [*Hester bows*] Well, if you will just tell Mr. Geoffrey I'm here according to promise, I'll be much obliged. [*Hester goes to table and touches bell*] She don't seem to like my being here alone. Afraid I'll run off with the valleyable furniture—no doubt. Ah, that's his tread! [*Music stops. Geoffrey enters, R.U.E., dressed carelessly, face pale, hand unsteady; his look is wild and preoccupied*] Well, sir, you see, I've come.

GEOF. [*C. To Hester, but not looking at her*] Give me some water. [*Crosses to C., Hester pours some in glass; he takes it with shaking hand*]

PER. Little nervous, sir—off training.

GEOF. Eh? Yes! That is—no, well, your business? You have seen the lawyer I sent you to?

PER. Yes, sir; and he was what you may call a lawyer. None of your respectable men, but up to all sorts of sharp dodges. He's the regular sporting man's lawyer.

GEOF. Yes. You said he sticks at nothing? Well—his answer?

PER. H—m. [*Looks at Hester*]

GEOF. You may speak before her. I wish her to hear.

PER. Oh, very well, sir! I thought as it concerned your wife—

GEOF. Go on!

PER. Well, sir, I asked him what you told me about—about the divorce.

GEOF. Well?

PER. Well, sir, he said at first it was easy, that Mr. Arnold Brinkworth, calling of her his wife, and staying at the inn with her all night, did the business, and you could get a divorce from the courts to pack her off.

GEOF. Oh, he said that?

PER. Yes, sir. Then he sent for the landlady of the inn and for that rum old cove, the servant, and questioned them. But they broke down. They said as how Arnold and the lady took supper together, but there wasn't no familiarities whatsoever. That wasn't no ground of divorce. Then he nosed around and moused about, and turned over the matter in his mind, and said it was no go—it was a fluke.

GEOF. Then he gives it up as hopeless?

PER. He says, sir, as how you couldn't divorce a mosquito on such evidence.

GEOF. Then the law be hanged! I'm done with it. You may go.

PER. All right, sir. Anything more, sir?

GEOF. No—clear out.

PER. You'd better take my advice, sir: get in condition—try a little exercise —train a bit—get the muscles up.

GEOF. [*Violent*] Curse the muscles, and you and your training. It's broken me down body and soul. Look at me—the sinews of a tiger and the strength of a child. The fool was right who told me I was gone inside. I feel it. [*Crosses to R.*]

PER. Not so bad as that, sir.

GEOF. Perry, I feel sometimes as if the ground, my footing, the earth, and all that's in it, were slipping from me. My eyes grow dim and my head reels. Twice I have felt it—then a numbness seizes me. Just before you came in I raised this arm to the chimney piece to reach for a lamp—my hand fell back as if it had been loosed from my shoulder. They call it paralysis. Do you know what it is?

PER. No, sir—and I don't want to.

GEOF. Then to give up all that's worth having and live like a milksop, for these doctors tell us that, if we live like men, as we are, we are bound to drop down dead, and all that sort of thing. There, clear out. [*Crosses to L.*]

PER. All right, sir. I'm sorry, sir.

GEOF. Get out!

PER. [*With agility*] Oh, yes, sir! [*Exit, R.3.E.*]

GEOF. [*Locks the door and turns to Hester*] You heard him? [*Hester leans on table and bows*] I am tied to her for life, and the law is powerless to cut the knot. Now see here! [*Takes a little billet-doux from his pocket*] Here is a woman, young, handsome, rich, who would be mine if this creature were out of the way. This came yesterday as soon as I brought that precious creature here. This is the woman I have lost; what do you think of it? You don't answer? [*Hester looks up after drying her eyes, and points to her mouth*] Dumb, eh? [*Hester takes up slate as if to write, Geoffrey takes her arm; she looks up; he gazes at her*] I want no writing, I want words. [*Hester looks at him amazed. Geoffrey sits*] There must be no fooling here; I know you. [*Hester smiles*] You don't believe it? You are a widow! Your husband's name was Joel Detthridge! [*Hester looks at him*] He was a worthless drunken wretch. He followed you from place to place, from year to year—one morning he was found dead in his bed. [*She catches his arm*] He died a natural death—he slept alone, the doors, the windows, the chimneys were closed—so no one could kill him. The room he slept in might have been such a one as this. [*Looks around; she looks around shuddering*] You see, I know you. [*Hester reassured, smiles*] Stop! You were a free woman when he died; but something still followed you from place to place, from year to year. [*Hester horrified, starts back*] From your husband's death you spoke no more. The doctor said the shock had made you dumb. It was so, was it? Or was it this phantom which followed you? [*She retreats and crosses to R., he follows and catches her hand; she shakes her head and tries to get away*] The words that could not come from your lips, flowed from your hands in the watches of the night with no one to see you. You traced the awful story of your crime in this confession. [*Takes paper from his pocket. Hester utters a stifled cry, tears herself away and tries to get the paper. Geoffrey seizes her and she struggles*] It is useless. The paper is mine. Last night, by accident, I saw you—followed you—found you senseless by your desk, and this beside you.

HES. [*On her knees; clutching*]   It is mine! Give it me! Give it me!

GEOF.   Aha! The dumb speak! The miracle is wrought.

HES.   You have robbed me! I will have your life! Help! Help!

GEOF.   Another cry—and to the first one who comes I give this paper. You know it; 'tis the confession of the murder of your husband!

HES.   He was a fiend! He cursed me, beat me, broke my heart, and dragged me down to rags and misery.

GEOF.   I will do you no harm, but you must tell me how you killed him.

HES.   Oh, speak no more of that!

GEOF.   On one condition.

HES.   Condition? [*Half demented*]

GEOF.   Yes. Look at me! As you were, I am tied to a being whom I hate, who stands between me and freedom.

HES.   Oh, no! No, no! You would not kill her?

GEOF.   *I* will not, but YOU must.

HES.   I?

GEOF.   One more crime is the price of your safety. Look! Did I not say it was in such a room as this your husband lay that night—the doors, the windows fastened—his bed was there [*Points to bed*] and through that wall—

HES.   No! No! No!

GEOF.   Then nothing is to be done except to give this paper into the hands of the magistrates. I bring them here. Here, gentlemen, is the house of blood, and here the murder was done. Seven years ago she planned the deed, and strangled him as he slept. Here is the wall, which day by day she worked at until its hollow was covered only by this paper, [*Goes to wall*] feel it, gentlemen—nothing but a slip of paper covering the place by which she entered by his bed—the napkin steeped in water was in her hand—he slept—she trod softly to his side—in one moment—[*He suits the action to the words*]

HES. [*Cries out in terror*]   No more! No more! Do with me as you will. [*Falls at his feet and clasps his arm*]

GEOF.   You consent? 'Tis well. [*Gate bell heard, both pause*] Someone comes—go see who it is—stay—your looks are too wild—I will go with you.

But remember it is agreed between us! [*Both exeunt, R.H. Anne enters door opposite with a letter in her hand, L.2.E.*]

ANNE. [*Pale and weary, supports herself to chair*] I thought I heard voices here. No one? Nothing but solitude, which seems peopled with dangers for me. Two days alone with him, and with that fearful woman, whose glance seems to come from the— Only this [*Takes letter from her bosom*] to comfort me. From Blanche. [*Kisses it*] Dear, dear Blanche. [*Reads*] "As we understand it, you are kept a close prisoner by your husband. My uncle, Sir Patrick, is almost beside himself with alarm and vexation. He has asked Geoffrey to consent to a separation, which he refuses. What can his motive be? We know he does not love you, why, then, does he insist on keeping you so closely with him? Arnold says we must find a way to get you away. We have all been concocting a plan to help you. We will have a carriage and horses ready at the back of the garden, every night. It was Arnold's suggestion. I love him so much." [*Pauses*] Dear little angel, how happy she is. [*Reads*] "We mean to make a final attempt to see you, to-morrow. Sir Patrick, Arnold and I will come. If Geoffrey refuses to let us in, we will apply to a magistrate; so keep up your courage and all may yet be well." All may yet be well? Perhaps! But I feel myself standing on the brink of an unknown danger. This house—so deserted! What room is this? I never was here before. Ah! this window! It looks out upon the garden! What noise was that? [*Looks out*] A carriage stands beyond the wall. It may be Blanche. [*Geoffrey enters, R.D., closes it, stands by it. Anne comes down fearfully, C.*]

GEOF. [*Hesitatingly, and as playing a part*] Anne.

ANNE. Well.

GEOF. There are some friends of yours below. Do you wish to see them?

ANNE. If you will let me.

GEOF. Why do you say "If you will let me"? You may do as you please. You don't consider yourself a prisoner, do you?

ANNE. I do not know what to think. Since I have been here—two days now—I have seen no one but that silent woman, who speaks not and answers not.

GEOF. If you want to go, say the word [*Anne makes a step forward*]— and I'll go anywhere with you. If you want to send any message, I'll take it for you. I know I have acted strangely, but then I have been sick, you know. But I have been thinking over everything last night, and today I am a new man. I—[*Hesitates and watches effect of his words*] I beg your pardon for what I have done to you.

ANNE. Can this be true? Are you in earnest? [*Looks at him sternly*]

GEOF. [*Drops his eyes and fumbles with his hands*] Yes. You can rely on me. I want to make a good husband. Give me a chance, you know. Stay here with me, I want to make it up. Think over it, will you?

ANNE. [*Aside*] I know not what to think.

GEOF. I will show up your friends. You see I don't keep you very close. [*Pushes open door and calls*] Come up, this way!

BLAN. [*Without*] Come along, uncle! Come, Arnold! Where is she? [*She enters, R. She and Anne rush to each other's arms and embrace*] Oh, my dear darling; oh, my precious; oh, my dear Anne. [*Kisses her. Geoffrey and Arnold exchange a slight and cold bow. Enter Sir Patrick and Arnold, R.D.*]

SIR P. Very glad to see you, Anne. Really thought I shouldn't have the chance. [*Snuffs and looks at Geoffrey, who stands by door, his eyes cast down*] You see, Arnold? [*Anne puts out her hand to Arnold, who takes it*]

ARN. [*To Anne*] How-de-do, Miss Sylvester—I mean Mrs. Delamayn. I am very glad to see you, you don't look well.

BLAN. For shame, Arnold.

ARN. Well, she don't.

SIR P. Don't cast her down.

ANNE. Dear friends, he is right, I must show what I feel. But I ought to look happy, since I see you again.

BLAN. Come, Anne, let us go into the garden. [*Aside to her*] I have something to tell you. [*They move towards door, R.H., Geoffrey interposes*]

GEOF. [*C.*] I beg your pardon. My wife is not well. The doctors advise her not to go out except in a carriage.

BLAN. [*L.C., aside to Anne*] Oh, the brute! He don't want me to talk with you.

SIR P. [*R.C., aside to them*] I'll get him away. You stay with Anne. Leave it to me.

GEOF. [*Aside*] There's some plot here.

ARN. [*To Blanche, aside*] Why not come right out and ask her to bolt with us? That's the square way.

BLAN. Oh, you don't understand what it is to be man and wife; she can't leave him that way.

ARN. When I'm married I hope *mine* won't leave me anyway.

GEOF. [*L., who has edged around to listen*] You see, Miss Lundie, my wife is perfectly free here. I am glad there are witnesses to hear me. [*Looks around furtively to Arnold and Sir Patrick*] She can do what she likes. [*Draws her arm through his*] She don't hate me, she don't fear me, and we agree perfectly.

SIR P. [*R., aside to Arnold*] What a precious rascal!

ARN. [*R.C., aside to Sir Patrick*] Pure humbug.

GEOF. [*Crosses to C.*] We've lived here two days, and only it's been lone-some, she has got nothing to complain of. We are going to be quite happy together. I want you all to bear witness for me, I love her.

SIR P. H—m. [*Aloud*] I'm delighted to hear it, Mr. Delamayn, and now, if you will just give me your arm, we can take a turn about in the garden, and I'll tell you—[*Crosses to C. and stops. Puts his arm through Geoffrey's; Anne slips hers out, and turns to Blanche*]

GEOF. Thank you, I'm not well, and the doctor don't like me walking in the garden.

SIR P. [*C., vexed*] Egad, it must be devilish unhealthy in this neighbor-hood—everybody sick.

GEOF. Yes, it *is* somewhat unhealthy.

BLAN. Come over here, Anne, by this sofa. [*Anne brings sofa down, R.H.*]

ANNE. [*Aside*] He will prevent us exchanging words. [*Geoffrey watches them with uneasiness*]

SIR P. [*Trying to engage his attention*] I wanted to say, Mr. Delamayn. [*Geoffrey not heeding*] I say I wanted to say—that when I came here my purpose was to observe—

GEOF. [*Abruptly breaks from him, crosses to sofa, where he eyes both suspiciously*] I have no secrets from my wife, why should she have any from me?

BLAN. [*Aside*] Oh! the provoking creature. [*Aloud*] I'm sure we have no secrets to tell. [*Touches Anne with her foot*] I only asked Anne where her bedroom was.

GEOF. [*Suddenly*] What do you want to know for?

ANNE. [*Quickly*] And I was just going to tell her it was at the other side of the house, the east side.

ARN. [*Whom Blanche taps with her parasol to make him take notice*] The east side? All right!

SIR P. [*L., aside, making memo in his book*] The east side? All right!

BLAN. And I was only asking her, if she ever got alarmed at night by burglars or anything, how she would give a signal.

GEOF. Give a signal?

BLAN. [*Excited*] I mean how she would let her friends know.

ARN. Yes; you know she could put a light in her window.

GEOF. Ha, ha! While I am there, while I'm in the house! What are you talking about? Do you see any alarms or enemies, or other here?

SIR P. Quite right. [*Crosses to Blanche*] My dear! Mr. Delamayn is quite right; Anne, don't mind Blanche. There being no burglars or enemies, and you not being frightened, you will not have to put lights in your window.

GEOF. Thank you, Sir Patrick. I don't understand this, but I think you are trifling with me. If so—

ANNE. [*Crosses, past Blanche, interrupting him*] My dear friends! J understand your solicitude for my happiness, but [*Glances at Blanche*] I fear nothing.

GEOF. You hear her? She fears nothing.

ANNE. [*Aside to Sir Patrick, as she gives her hand*] Do not desert me!

SIR P. We will watch for the light.

BLAN. Good-bye, love! Come, Arnold—until tomorrow, darling!

ANNE. And the day after?

BLAN. You will come to us. It's our own wedding day. [*Hides her face in Anne's shoulder*]

ANNE. My own darling! [*Kisses her*]

SIR P. Good night! Pleasant dreams! Don't forget the old riddle. What is that which goes round and round the house all night and never touches the house, eh? Ha, ha!

ARN. Ha, ha! I know the answer; it's a carriage. [*Geoffrey glances suspiciously at all*]

SIR P. Oh! Hang the boy. Good night! [*Exit, scolding Arnold, who hangs his head. Blanche once more kisses Anne, and exit. Anne and Geoffrey alone*]

GEOF. [*L.*] Well, you see I gave you liberty to [see] your friends.

ANNE. I thank you. [*Goes toward the door she entered, L.*]

GEOF. This is to be your room tonight. [*Music*]

ANNE. How? This?

GEOF. This! The other in the east side is exposed. Besides I have taken the bed down, you cannot sleep there.

ANNE. What is the meaning of this change?

GEOF. My pleasure; what is there so wonderful in changing a room? [*Rings bell on table. Hester appears with tray, with lighted candle, pitcher and glass, her face averted from both*] Do what you can to make my wife comfortable; she sleeps here tonight. [*Hester starts and clinches her hand*] What is the matter? Is this room unfit?

HES. No. [*Crosses to L.*]

ANNE. She speaks!

GEOF. [*L.*] Yes, she has found her voice. If it displeases you, don't fret about it. After tonight you will hear it no more. [*Exit, U.E., R.H. door*]

ANNE. [*Comes to Hester, who turns away her head*] What does he say? Are you going to leave here tomorrow? [*Hester, wrung by internal agitation, merely bows*] I am sorry for that. You are at least a woman, and in this prison [*Looks around*] it is at least a protection to see a woman's face. Although you seem so cold and distant, I think you will not harm me. Oh, I am very, very miserable! [*Bursts into tears and sinks into chair*]

HES. You know me not, trust me not! I am accursed!

ANNE. Whatever you be—at least do not help to crush me. I am defenseless. [*Rising and looking about cautiously*] Tell me, do you know why this room is given to me tonight?

HES. [*With an effort*] No.

ANNE. Have I any danger to fear?

HES. [*The same and coldly*] No.

ANNE. How am I to be assured of that?

HES. The key is on the inside of your door; lock it; draw the bolts. The window is fastened—what more safety do you want?

ANNE. True, what is there to fear? [*Calmer*] You may retire. First see if the bed is aired. [*Hester goes toward the bed, pauses as if she saw an apparition, recoils slowly and dropping the light staggers against table*] Where is the light? [*Turns astonished*] Hester, where are you? [*Hester evades her and starts out by door, which she closes after her*] Gone! Stay, I have matches. I saw them. [*Gets matches from mantel, lights gas jet near window*] Gone! What is the meaning of this? [*Runs to both doors and bolts them*] At least I am secure. All is silent. The light in the window! Ah, I can give the signal! [*Pauses and starts*] This is not the room! I am then cut off from all help but Thine. Oh, save me! [*Sinks on her knees*] All is quiet! No one stirs! [*After a moment rises*] Oh, for the daylight! [*Goes to door, listens; goes to window, feels its fastenings*] I must be prepared for everything, prepared for flight, if need be, or to struggle for my life. [*Pours out and drinks water; goes to gas and turns it down*] What a bitter taste that water has. [*Goes to bed and lies upon it. Music. She turns over once or twice, and then her arm drops as if she slept. The wall paper by head of bed rolls up slowly, disclosing aperture, through which another room is seen with Geoffrey in the opening. He enters cautiously, and then beckons Hester, who enters fearfully, her eyes fixed on bed*]

GEOF. Can the wall paper be fastened again, when we go out? [*Hester bows*] Have you the napkin? [*Hester goes to washstand and wets napkin*] What did you put in the pitcher of water? [*Hester shows phial. She stands C., her gaze riveted on bed*] What are you looking at? [*She points to head of bed*] Come to your work. [*She does not stir*] Confound you, what is the matter? It is too late to go back now! [*Takes napkin from Hester*] Give me the napkin! [*Anne stirs; they pause. Hester, in pantomime, entreats him to come away; he shakes her off and advances to the bed by R.*] It is too late, quick! [*Music. As he advances to bed, Hester moves to L. As he is about to place the napkin over Anne's face, she springs forward, arouses the sleeper and clasps her in her arms. Anne terrified, clings to her*]

HES.   Awake! Awake! There is death in the room!

ANNE.   Great heavens!! [*Geoffrey springs back*]

HES. [*Helping Anne from bed*]   Call them in, quick, quick, from the window!

ANNE. [*At window*]   Help! Help! [*Geoffrey springs towards her. Hester interposes*]

GEOF.   Curses seize you both! [*Loud crash. Making toward R.U.E.*] They have broken down the door.

ANNE.   Oh, Blanche! [*Going up*]

GEOF.   Silence! [*Darting towards C.*] Ah! [*Falls across chair and rolls over. Blanche runs from C., followed by Arnold and Sir Patrick. Hester falls on her knees by window*]

GEOFFREY   HESTER
    ARNOLD
        SIR PATRICK   BLANCHE AND ANNE

CURTAIN

DIVORCE

A Play of the Period, in Five Acts

DIVORCE

T HE third season of the Fifth Avenue Theatre opened September 5, 1871. The play was *Divorce,* a society play based on Anthony Trollope's wearisome novel, *He Knew He Was Right.* Although Daly treated his materials more freely than was his custom, introducing a new subplot and many new characters as well as transposing the locale to the United States, the main plot and the two principal characters were essentially the same as they were in the novel except for a reconciliation just before the final curtain. The divorce phase of the play was Daly's, and although it provided some very popular comic scenes and characters, it weakened the force of the main plot by making the wife more independent of her husband's delusions than was Trollope's heroine.

The critics at once proclaimed the success of the play.

The subject . . . is a real live one, and certainly its treatment evinces rare delicacy and skill and a thorough knowledge of society of the present day. . . . The play is a very long one . . . [but] there is not a weak or uninteresting scene in it. . . . It is superfluous to say that such an array of dramatic talent has rarely been seen in a theatrical company before in one performance. . . . The scenery of the play . . . was most vociferously applauded.—*New York Herald,* Sept. 6, 1871.

William Winter praised—with reservations. The topic, "matrimonial troubles," was one of "invariable and unfailing attractiveness to the average mind." But Winter's mind was not average and the lesson of "forbearance" did not redeem *Divorce.*

The lesson is not astonishingly novel, and it has been taught with less prolixity, in other and better plays than "Divorce." . . . The work of the playwright . . . has been skillfully done. There may be a question whether art ought to invite public attention to minute vivisection of matrimonial infelicities; but that question is rather a tender one, and we do not incline to ponder upon it now. . . . Mr. Daly's company proved very strong, and did everything needful for the success of the piece.—*New York Tribune,* Sept. 6, 1871.

The cast was indeed a strong one as the critics acknowledged. According to Judge Daly, *Divorce* had been written "expressly to display the talent of all the members of the company." Those who made particularly good impressions included D. H. Harkins as "Adrianse," William Davidge as "De Witt," James Lewis as "Jitt," Fanny Morant as "Mrs. Ten Eyck," Clara

Morris as "Fanny Ten Eyck," Fanny Davenport as "Lu Ten Eyck," and Mrs. Gilbert as "Mrs. Kemp." Five members of the cast, according to the playbill, were making their first appearances with the Fifth Avenue Theatre Company. These were Louis James, Henry Crisp, W. J. LeMoyne, Owen Fawcett, Mary Cary, and Ida Yerance. The complete cast will be found on page 79.

The sets received an amount of praise unusual even for a Daly production. Winter mentioned specifically the beauty of "views of Long Island Sound, the Hudson, and the ruins of St. Augustine," and a number of the critics alluded to the applause bestowed upon the sets by the audience. When the play was revived April 15, 1873, one of the critics was so impressed with the Florida scenes that he declared that hereafter he would "prefer Florida scenery on the stage to seeing it in Florida."

The strength of the company, the current interest of the theme, the beauty of the sets, all combined to make *Divorce* the outstanding hit of the day. Not only was it Daly's greatest success up to that time, but, according to Professor George C. D. Odell, it surpassed in number of continuous performances—two hundred from September 5, 1871, to March 18, 1872—any comedy previously seen on the New York stage. Its life was by no means ended by the termination of its initial run. It was revived briefly at one or other of the Daly theaters almost every year until Daly retired from management in the autumn of 1877. After the failure of *Newport* at the opening of Daly's Theatre in 1879, *Divorce* was hastily rehearsed and put into performance with Ada Rehan in the rôle of the volatile "Lu Ten Eyck." By this time the critics were no longer inclined to treat the play seriously. Though one or two still thought *Divorce* "a strong play and a good play," most of them agreed with the critic who wrote:

There is nothing very great about "Divorce." The amount of intellectuality thrown over it has always been discounted by the satin covered furniture of the scenes and the handsome dresses of the actresses.—*New York Telegram*, Oct. 1, 1879.

The levity with which this revival of his "lavishly upholstered melodrama" was received seems to have discouraged Daly. At any rate, he never put it on again in his own theater. I have no record of any later New York productions, but I suspect that the play lingered in the minor theaters for some time. Indeed, it must have done so if there was any truth in the statement printed in 1892 in connection with a Philadelphia revival of the play that it had reached a total of six hundred performances in New York City.

The popularity of *Divorce* was not, of course, confined to New York. In fact Professor Odell says that during the initial run there was one week when *Divorce* was being performed simultaneously in New York, Boston, Philadelphia, Buffalo, and St. Louis. Some time later a performance of the play was reported to have been given aboard ship by officers of the U.S.S. *Macedonian* at Yokohama.

In Chicago *Divorce* was first announced for performance the week of October 9, 1871, but Mrs. O'Leary's cow caused a postponement to November 6 when it opened at the Globe Theatre with a company headed by Blanche DeBar. The rhapsody elicited by this performance follows:

A few days ago there was not a theatre in existence in Chicago. On Monday night the city could boast of a new play, one of the best modern dramas ever produced, splendidly put upon the stage, and acted by a company rarely, if ever, surpassed before the fire. . . . The new play, "Divorce," which has created an extraordinary interest in New York and Boston, is evidently destined to include Chicago in its triumphs. The author of it is a genius. . . . Not a dull or valueless episode occurs in the progress of the plot.—*Chicago Tribune,* Nov. 8, 1871.

Civic pride was undoubtedly responsible for much of the uncritical spirit of this review, but *Divorce* always seemed to get good notices in Chicago. Throughout the 'Seventies and into the 'Eighties there were productions by various companies, including Daly's own on June 8, 1874. As this was the first appearance of the Fifth Avenue Theatre Company in Chicago, the members of the cast got most of the attention and praise. The play was merely a strong example of the "millinery drama."

Divorce was equally, if not more, popular in Boston. The first production at the Globe, October 17, 1871, ran for four weeks with a supplementary week at the holiday time; the last, at the Castle Square Theatre, November 21, 1898, not only filled the house but drew standees.

Ten years after its first production in the United States Daly's play was produced in Edinburgh, December 12, 1881, with Linda Dietz. Of this production an English critic wrote:

If Mr. Daly's manner of developing his plot is somewhat crude, and the incidents are throughout cumbered with a considerable quantity of superfluous dialogue, still, looking to the work as a whole, we have a production possessing a fair amount of interest for the general playgoers. . . . Of the literary merit of the drama we cannot speak highly.—*London Era,* Dec. 17, 1881.

Divorce had fewer imitators than did *Man and Wife,* probably because more of the play was original work and so could not be copied with impunity. There was at least one imitation, nevertheless—a four-act piece entitled *Divorced,* which featured a divorce lawyer. According to the copyright entry *Divorced* was the work of Sam Ryan and G. W. Murray. It was produced in

Chicago, February 23, 1874. Several burlesques of Daly's play also appeared, one by J. F. Poole having the novelty of being in verse.

Daly never published his play but it was printed "as manuscript only" in 1884. That privately printed edition is the basis of the present text and of the cast of characters which follows:

DRAMATIS PERSONAE AND ORIGINAL CAST

ALFRED ADRIANSE, *who regarded marriage as an episode and found it fate* — MR. D. H. HARKINS

CAPTAIN LYNDE, *a friend in need, indeed, and a friend in the way* — MR. LOUIS JAMES

REV. HARRY DUNCAN, *successor to the martyrs* — MR. HENRY CRISP

DE WOLF DE WITT, *an excellent authority on the management of wives* — MR. WM. DAVIDGE

TEMPLETON JITT, ESQ., *of the New York bar* — MR. JAMES LEWIS

MR. BURRITT, *ex-policeman and private detective* — MR. W. J. LEMOYNE

PAM, *his partner* — MR. JOHN BURNETT

JUDGE KEMP, *a relic of the last generation* — MR. D. WHITING

DR. LANG, *late of Bloomingdale Asylum* — MR. GEO. DEVERE

JIM, *with a new system for naturalizing aliens* — MR. OWEN FAWCETT

RICHARD, *Adrianse's man* — MR. G. GODFREY

CHRISTMAS, *one of the emancipated* — MR. F. CHAPMAN

GUINEA, *another of the same sort* — MR. W. BEEKMAN

MRS. TEN EYCK, *a mother of society, who has provided well for her two daughters* — MISS FANNY MORANT

MISS LU TEN EYCK, *who made the Newport match* — FANNY DAVENPORT

MISS FANNY TEN EYCK, *who got the best catch of the season after all* — CLARA MORRIS

GRACE, *"Our Niece," for whom we must find something after the dear girls are provided for* — LINDA DIETZ

FLORA PENFIELD, *a bud of the Florida groves* — MARY CARY

MRS. KEMP, *the partner of the relic* — MRS. G. H. GILBERT

KITTY CROSBIE, *who was satisfied with her own "way"*   IDA YERANCE

MOLLY, *the nurse*   NELLIE MORTIMER

NELLIE, *the help*   KATE CLAXTON

JENNY   LOUISE VOLMER

ALFRED, *a child*   GERTRUDE

WEDDING GUESTS, VISITORS, ETC.

ACT I: MRS. TEN EYCK'S CITY RESIDENCE IN WAVERLY PLACE. "GIVEN IN MARRIAGE!"

ACT II: ALFRED ADRIANSE'S SUMMER LODGE ON LONG ISLAND; WITH VIEW OF THE SOUND BY SUNSET AND MOONLIGHT. "THE STRIFE BEGUN!"

ACT III, SCENE 1: MRS. TEN EYCK'S MANOR OF THE HUDSON. "THE HUSBAND TAKES THE LAW IN HIS OWN HANDS!"
SCENE 2: AN APARTMENT IN THE VILLAGE INN.
SCENE 3: SAME AS SCENE 1.

ACT IV, SCENE 1: ST. AUGUSTINE, FLORIDA. THE OLD SPANISH TOWN. "TWO PURPOSES."
SCENE 2: THE OLD CONVENT RUINS. "THE LAW RETALIATES!"

ACT V: ELEGANT PARLORS AT DE WITT'S IN NEW YORK. "THE DIVORCED!"

ACT I.

SCENE: *Parlors at Mrs. Ten Eyck's, on Waverly Place, near the park. The rooms old-fashioned and hung with pictures. Furniture old-fashioned, but well preserved. Arch C., through which, from the L., all entrances from the exterior are made. Doors, R. and L. Time, afternoon; date, just after the summer season at the summer resorts. C. from L., at the rise of curtain, Nellie enters, followed by the Rev. Harry Duncan. She takes his hat and gloves, while he speaks.*

DUN. [*L.*] No one visible; but all is bustle upstairs, eh?

NEL. Yis, sir—yer riverince, I mane.

DUN. [*L.*] You may announce me as soon as you like, Nellie.

NEL. [*R.*] Who to, sur? Shure, missus is gone out.

DUN. What, gone out, and her daughter to be married in a couple of hours?

NEL. Something forgot, sir, and the darling, Miss Louise, is upstairs, sir, a-fitting on the dresses. Oh! She do look beautiful, to be shure, and Miss Fanny is getting on her bridesmaid's dress, sir, and she do look beautiful as well. Miss Crosbie and the other bridesmaids, they—

DUN. Do look beautiful, too?

NEL. Yis, sir, that they do.

DUN. [*Looking at his watch*] Well, they'll be in plenty of time, and— [*Looks slyly at Nellie*] Miss Grace, how about her dress?

NEL. [*Despairingly*] Oh, sir! she's not to be bridesmaid.

MRS. TEN EYCK. [*Outside*] Back in excellent time. We'll have them in here, Edward.

NEL. Missus is back. [*Retreats to R. Duncan rises. Mrs. Ten Eyck enters, C., followed by Captain Lynde*]

MRS. T. Place them here, Edward. [*Captain places a very few parcels on table, R.*] Ah, my dear Harry! I knew you'd come; you couldn't wait for us. [*She puts a couple of parcels on table as she speaks*]

CAPT. [*Languidly*] Hello, reverend father.

DUN. [*Meets Mrs. Ten Eyck, C., shakes hands*] I wanted to make one more call in the old way before I received dear Miss Lu at the church.

MRS. T. So good of you; isn't it, Edward? [*She crosses to Nellie, R., gives her bonnet and shawl. Nellie takes them off, R.1.E.*]

CAPT. Very thoughtful; but the clergy are always doing the right thing.

MRS. T. Confess now, Harry, you feel a little nervous at the idea of performing your first marriage service! [*Recrosses to Duncan*]

DUN. I do. I'm afraid I shall shake so, that the whole thing will be invalid.

MRS. T. Oh, you boys—you boys! But the dear girls were all determined you should officiate, and it is so fortunate you were ordained just before darling Louise was engaged.

CAPT. [*Down, C.*] Ye—es! He was at the seminary getting ready for Lu, while she was at Newport getting ready for him.

MRS. T. [*Tapping him with her fan*] Irreverent fellow. Don't mind him, Harry.

DUN. Oh, I don't! I never do.

CAPT. [*C.*] Only a little pleasantry. Ministers are so grave, they want brightening up.

DUN. Has the happy bridegroom, Mr. De Witt, arrived yet?

MRS. T. Oh, he'll not be here till the last moment, of course. He never hurries.

CAPT. Lucky fellow. He waited, and you see what a good thing he got by it. Widower for twenty years, and now he has the finest woman, except her mother, in New York.

MRS. T. Did you ever—what a blunt fellow. For shame!

CAPT. Oh, I'm privileged, you know. I'm out of the way of all the proprieties. Too poor to get married! It's understood, I'm to have my privileges on that account.

MRS. T. [*Crosses to C.*] So you can, you great baby. Now, excuse me, while I devote the rest of the day to my darling. I'll send Grace down to entertain you. Poor Grace!

DUN. She's not to be a bridesmaid.

MRS. T. You know? Oh, well, she'll be a bride herself yet. We must do something for Grace, Harry.

CAPT. [*Going up*] When our two daughters are provided for.

MRS. T. [*Laughs*] Oh, you monster! How disagreeably you tell the truth. But you must help me, Harry; you know, Grace is my poor sister's only child. I will be a mother to her; and we must get her a real good husband.

DUN. [*Eagerly*] Yes!

MRS. T. [*C.*] Somebody with money.

DUN. Oh!

MRS. T. Think over all the rich bachelors and widowers in your church. You can manage it; it shall be a secret between us. Where are those parcels? Oh! [*Gathers them up*]

Dun. [*Recovering*] Oh, by the way, I forgot—I met an old friend of ours today.

Mrs. T. [*Carelessly*] Ah!

Dun. I think he will call on you.

Mrs. T. [*Same*] Tomorrow, I hope. Not today.

Dun. It's Alfred Adrianse. [*Sits R. of L. table*]

Mrs. T. [*Suddenly turning at C., and drops one of the parcels, which Captain picks up*] Ah!

Dun. He has just returned in his yacht from the Mediterranean.

Mrs. T. [*Seriously*] Alfred Adrianse returned! [*Coming down, R.*]

Dun. Met him this very morning. Impulsive, quick, petulant as ever, and a bachelor still. [*Sits, L.*]

Mrs. T. He said he would call today?

Dun. Yes, and he inquired particularly after Fanny. [*Nellie enters, C., and goes towards R.1 E.*]

Mrs. T. [*As if preoccupied*] We shall all be most happy to see him. Ah, Nellie! [*Nellie bows, crosses to her*]

Nel. Yes'm!

Mrs. T. Tell Miss Fanny to go to my room and wait for me.

Nel. I will, m'm. [*Exit, R.D.*]

Mrs. T. [*To herself*] Alfred Adrianse returned!

Capt. [*Presenting parcel*] You dropped this.

Mrs. T. [*Takes it*] Thank you, Alfred. [*Exit, R.1 E.*]

Capt. [*Winks to Duncan*] You heard her call me Alfred. That's your friend's name. Who is he? The duchess seemed to be struck by your news.

Dun. Oh! Alfred Adrianse is an old story.

Capt. Old story? Why, I know all the old stories of this family. Yet, stop; it was while I was at the West, eh?

Dun. Yes. He was supposed to be in love with Fanny.

Capt. And what were Fanny's sentiments?

Dun. She wasn't allowed to have any sentiments on the subject, as she was merely a schoolgirl then, and his attentions were very properly discouraged, so he swore he'd never marry, bought a yacht and disappeared in it.

Capt. Is he rich? [*Gets L., back of table*]

Dun. Sixty thousand a year.

Capt. Young man?

Dun. Yes—but as eccentric as the—as a badly made skyrocket.

Capt. Happy Alfred! On sixty thousand a year, a man can be all fireworks. But I tell you what—his time has come.

Dun. What do you mean?

CAPT. Didn't you notice the duchess's face at your news? She'll make a match for him.

DUN. Not with Grace—Miss Grace.

CAPT. Grace? Pooh! No, his original flame, Fanny. [*Goes up. Grace enters, C., from R.*]

GRACE. Didn't I hear someone say "Miss Grace"?

CAPT. [*Points to Duncan*] For further particulars inquire next door. [*Goes up and sits in rear parlor*]

GRACE. [*Down R.*] Aunt Clara said you were here, and that I must entertain you in her place.

DUN. [*L.*] I should have thought you were all too busy.

GRACE. [*C.*] Oh, I've done my share. Cousin Lu looks so lovely and so bright, such a contrast to cousin Fanny, who looks so lovely but so grave. But, then, wedding dresses make everyone look lovely.

DUN. Particularly to the happy man whose love is crowned by the marriage.

GRACE. [*Sighing*] Aunt Clara tells me that love need have very little to do with it.

DUN. You don't believe that?

GRACE. I don't want to. She says it's enough to respect a husband. But I think respect is like a cold luncheon in a dark dining-room, while love is like a delicious picnic in the woods.

DUN. [*Flattered*] Could a young wife and husband live on picnics, do you think?

GRACE. Of course, in the summer, but there's the winter. [*Sits at table, L.*]

DUN. Yes, there's the winter. [*Aside, R.*] It's no use, she's thoroughly imbued with the selfish principles of her aunt; she'll marry a wealthy sexagenarian, and be satisfied. Women of the world are all oysters, they look out for some old wreck to fasten on and vegetate.

GRACE. But for my part, unless I loved I'd never marry.

DUN. [*Eagerly*] Nor I! [*Coming L.*]

GRACE. I would be content to wait.

DUN. [*Taking a chair a little distant*] So would I, but not too long.

GRACE. [*Sighs*] Most young men are so poor.

DUN. [*Sits R. of L. table*] Yes, it's a disease incident to youth.

GRACE. My idea is this: A young lady needn't close her heart to a young gentleman who loves her, because neither of them is rich.

DUN. [*Drawing a little nearer*] My sentiments exactly.

GRACE. They can love on, and hope on.

DUN. I will. I—I mean they can.

GRACE. And when, in the course of years, he has made his way up—

DUN. [*Drawing nearer*] Your aunt will come down.

GRACE. [*Starts up*] Gracious! I'm not speaking of myself. [*Crosses to R.*]

DUN. No?

GRACE. No!

DUN. Oh!

GRACE. I'm speaking of some abstract person.

DUN. [*Sighs*] I wish I could find an abstract person.

GRACE. Oh, Mr. Duncan, you oughtn't to think of such things.

DUN. Why not?

GRACE. Aunt Clara and I have been talking about you, and we have made up a little plot to find you a real nice girl somewhere in your congregation.

DUN. [*Coldly*] Indeed! Thank you, and was this your own idea?

GRACE. No, it was Aunt Clara's.

DUN. [*Turns away*] Aunt Clara takes a great deal of trouble.

GRACE. She is all heart. [*Slowly and meaningly, crosses to him*] She has told me your secret, too.

DUN. My secret?

GRACE. Yes, that you are going to find for me some old bachelor or widower, who—

DUN. That will do, Miss Grace. Your aunt's secrets are not kept long. [*Goes to R., and sits. Bell heard*]

GRACE. [*Going to L., hurt tone*] So it is true then! I wouldn't believe her at first! The hypocrite! I actually thought he took an interest in me on his own account. Aunt is right. I've no business to love.

CAPT. [*Rising at back*] Hullo, I say, here's the bridegroom. Whew! How he has improved. Been at his glass all day, no doubt? [*Comes down to C.*] Why, Grace, what's up? As an old friend of the family, I can't see that dull face on such a happy day. [*Duncan goes up to R. Captain looks from one to the other, then*] They've been at it, too, just as I suspected. What a fool the man is—not a dollar, nothing but his pedigree to boast of. Must break this up. [*Puts his arm about Grace, and in baby tone*] Come, my little Gracie, it mustn't pout any more. [*Takes her up to L.*]

DUN. [*Comes down*] If I wasn't a clergyman, I'd hate that officious rascal with his "friend of the family ways." [*Gets to R. Nellie enters, C., ushering in De Witt*]

NEL. I'll tell 'em you've come, sir.

DE W. Thank you—stop—[*Gives her box from pocket*] Take this, my child.

NEL. For me, sir? Oh, thanks!

DE W. For you? No, for Miss Louise. Quick, run up with it. [*Nellie exit, C. and R. De Witt sees others*] Ah! Good day, good day.

Capt. [*Grace goes up*] My dear boy, how splendid you look. [*Shakes him by the hand*] Glad to see you. Lu is dressing—soon be down. [*Goes up to Grace, L.*]

De W. Thank you. [*Aside*] How infernally familiar he is. "Lu is dressing," as if he had just come down from helping her to do up her back hair. [*To Duncan, who is down R.*] Well, reverend sir, my fate is soon to be in your hands. Is this the first time you ever married a couple? [*C., crosses to table L.*]

Dun. I regret to say it is.

De W. Don't regret it. Don't be nervous. If you forget anything, I'll help you out. I've been married before, you know. [*Takes Duncan's arm, and goes up*] Ah, Miss Grace. [*Up to L.*]

Lu Ten Eyck. [*R.C., outside*] Oh, where is he, where is Harry?

De W. That's Miss Louise's voice.

Grace. [*Coming down between the two gentlemen*] Oh, dear, she's coming down here.

Capt. Yes, and she's calling for the reverend Harry. [*Crosses to him*]

Grace. [*Coming forward, to De Witt*] She thinks there's no one here, but him and me. Run away, Mr. De Witt, you mustn't see her. [*Runs to him*]

Capt. Yes, conceal yourself. Pantry—no—under the piano. [*They put him up, R.*]

De W. [*Flurried*] The deuce! [*All upstage, R., but Duncan. Lu enters, C., from R.*]

Lu. Is he here? Oh! There he is. [*Down to Duncan, who is crossing to L.C.*] Oh, Harry, I know I'll never go through with it, and I want you to tell me all I'm to do, and when I'm to do it, and—[*As she goes for chair sees De Witt*] Oh, you are here?

De W. [*L.C., coming to C.*] My dear Miss Louise. [*Captain comes down to R.*]

Lu. [*C.*] Oh, don't look at me, it's not proper—go away.

Capt. Go away, sir! Calm yourself, my dear!

De W. Where shall I go?

Lu. Oh, you needn't go away, sit down and turn your back. [*Turning herself round in circle and self-admiringly*] Well, how do I look, now you've seen me? [*Crossing to Captain*]

De W. [*Upstage to R.C.*] Charming! Charming!

Lu. Not you. I mean the captain, he's got such good taste. [*To De Witt*] Why don't you do as I told you? [*De Witt up to R. table, and sits*]

Grace. [*L.C.*] Oh, Lu, don't be foolish.

Lu. [*C.*] What do you know about it—were you ever married?

Grace. [*Sighing*] No!

Lu. [*Crossing to L. corner*] Then don't interfere—take up the train a little; so. [*Grace assists*] Now, how does it do? [*Walks over towards De Witt and passes him, C., without looking at him*] Not too long, eh?

Capt. [*Glass to eye*] Not a bit.

Lu. [*Down to Captain*] Now mind, sir, you've seen me two hours before it's time.

Capt. [*Bows and kisses her hand*] I'm deeply sensible of the privilege.

De W. [*Aside at R. table*] If that fellow dares to show himself at my door, after I'm married, I'll have it slammed in his face. [*Crosses C. Lu and Captain go to Duncan, who is up R. Grace joins them. Mrs. Ten Eyck enters, R.C.*]

Mrs. T. Why, Louise, I'm shocked. How could you—O Mr. De Witt, [*Shakes hands*] what spirits she has. How lovely the dear child looks. [*Emotionally*] To part with her takes more than common fortitude, Mr. De Witt.

De W. [*R.C.*] True, and you bear it in an uncommon manner, Mrs. Ten Eyck.

Mrs. T. [*L.C.*] It is our duty to yield to the affections of our children, and when Louise's ideas were once fixed, I had nothing to do but give way.

De W. My dear madame, I am under eternal obligations to you.

Mrs. T. Come, daughter, we must repair this little inadvertence, by retiring at once.

Lu. [*R.C., between Captain and Duncan*] Yes, ma!—Well, good-bye all, till we meet at the wedding march. [*To Duncan*] I won't forget, now. [*To Captain*] Oh, you tease. [*Demurely, when led off by Mrs. Ten Eyck*] It isn't long to the hour, Mr. De Witt.

De W. My dear Miss Louise, so soon to be mine!

Lu. Ah! [*Sighs quizzically, looks back at him, exit, R.C.*]

De W. I believe she does love me, and if she does, she may do what she likes.

Mrs. T. [*L.C.*] Just a little temper, dear girl. [*All come down*]

De W. [*R.C.*] Temper is an excellent quality, ma'am. It gives a thousand opportunities for the most delicious thing in life, making up after a quarrel. It serves to keep impertinences at a distance, when they become distasteful to a husband [*Looks at Captain*], and it adds new beauty to a pretty face.

Mrs. T. [*L.C.*] My ideas most admirably expressed. It is what I have tried to tell dear Fanny.

Grace. [*Down R.*] And why Fanny, aunt?

Dun. [*Near her*] Hush, that's another of her secrets.

Capt. [*Seated L. of table*] I understand that, Mr.—Mr.—[*Pretends to forget*] Mr. Adrianse had quite a temper of his own. [*Mrs. Ten Eyck looks suddenly at him penetratingly*]

DE W. Mr. Adrianse! Ah, a friend of the family?

Mrs. T. I hope so; he was once. I felt for him the affection of a mother, but he couldn't have his own way, and so—well you see Fanny was but a child, then, and I had to tell him she was too young; then he told me I had wrecked his life, and away he went to China or somewhere.

Capt. Now he brings the wreck home again. [*Bell heard*]

DE W. [*Slowly crosses to Captain*] Perhaps we had better repair him thoroughly, and find him a mate for his next voyage.

Dun. [*Aside to Grace*] Vulgar old fellow.

Mrs. T. Poor Alfred, I hope his health has not suffered by his distress of mind.

Dun. He was in tiptop spirits when I saw him this morning.

Mrs. T. I fear it was only feigning. [*Nellie enters, L.C., with card*]

Nel. [*Handing it*] Gentleman in the reception room, ma'am.

Mrs. T. Alfred Adrianse. I thought so—show him up here, Nellie. [*Exit Nellie, L.C.*]

Capt. Now let us see if he is reduced to a skeleton.

Grace. For shame, captain, how can you be so unfeeling! [*Mrs. Ten Eyck whispers to Grace, and she exits, R.2.E.*]

Capt. Oh, we fellows who dare not fall in love, may laugh at those who can. It's a toss-up who has the best of it. [*Alfred Adrianse enters, C., preceded by Nellie, who exits, C.R.*]

Mrs. T. [*Meeting him*] My dear Alfred, how glad I am to see you.

Al. Thank you, Mrs. Ten Eyck, I have looked forward to this pleasure for a long time.

Mrs. T. Be as you have always been, like one of my children. You see Harry. [*He crosses to R., shakes Duncan's hand heartily*]

Dun. [*R.*] How do you do, again, Alfred?

Al. [*To Mrs. Ten Eyck*] To think Harry would ever be a churchman; why we used to box together, at college, and he was never without a black eye.

DE W. [*L.*] That fitted him for wrestling with the evil one.

Mrs. T. Allow me, Mr. De Witt, Mr. Adrianse. You know Captain Lynde?

Al. I have not the honor.

Mrs. T. [*R.C.*] True—he was fighting the Indians on the prairies, when—

Capt. When Fanny was at school.

Mrs. T. I want you to become acquainted, I know you will like each other. I don't know what we should ever do without Edward. [*Crosses to him*]

Al. Delighted, I'm sure.

Capt. Most happy, I'm sure.

AL. [*Low to Duncan*] Who is he?

DUN. [*Same*] Nobody! Butterfly!

AL. Butterfly! More of a wasp, I should think.

CAPT. [*Starts to go C.*] I'm for the smoking room—who comes?

DUN. I'll keep you company.

DE W. And I, for I want to talk with the reverend father. [*All three go up and stop C., looking back at Alfred, who is joined by Mrs. Ten Eyck*]

DUN. Looks splendid after his travels. [*Goes up*]

CAPT. [*Takes out his cigar case and offers to Duncan, who declines*] Bet you ten to one his next journey will be his wedding tour. [*Offers to De Witt, who declines*]

DE W. Rather young to be married, eh? Man wants to be more settled.

CAPT. [*Takes out cigar, puts up case*] Wish he'd do it! Man with sixty thousand a year must give good dinner parties. [*All exeunt, C. and L.*]

MRS. T. [*L. of R. table*] Now that we are alone, my dear Alfred, let me assure you again that the news of your arrival is the best I have heard for at least two years. Your call is a token of forgiveness, is it not?

AL. [*R.*] I forgive? Why, it was you I offended, and I have come back to act more like a man, to ask your pardon, and to say that whatever becomes of me, I shall feel that you have always acted right.

MRS. T. Surely, you have no thought of leaving us again.

AL. In ten days I go to Corea. You know I have nothing to do now but to look for sensations.

MRS. T. Oh, how disappointing. I hoped I should find in your company some solace for the loss of my daughter.

AL. [*Hesitatingly*] She is to be married today?

MRS. T. Yes.

AL. [*Confused*] Of course, it was foolish for me to call, but I did not know. You see, I only arrived last night.

MRS. T. Exactly.

AL. I heard about it first at the club.

MRS. T. The dear girl was the belle of Newport, and only her first season, too.

AL. Then she left school?

MRS. T. Last winter.

AL. [*Aside*] It is Fanny, then.

MRS. T. Mr. De Witt fell in love the instant he saw her.

AL. De Witt—that was his father who was here a moment ago.

MRS. T. [*Biting her lips*] No, that was the bridegroom himself.

AL. What, that old gentleman?

MRS. T. [*Trying to smile, but embarrassed*] Oh, love is blind, you know. Besides, the dear girl aspires to be a leader in society, which is impossible without wealth; and that, marriage must give her. You are so candid, Mr. Adrianse, you see you force me to be so, too.

AL. I beg pardon. I did not intend to wound you. But it seems so like a sacrifice. Poor Fanny, she must have greatly changed.

MRS. T. No, Fanny has not changed. She is the same foolish, romantic thing as ever. Romantic as lovely, my dear Alfred. "No, mamma," she often says to me, "since I left school I have seen no one I could love." So ridiculous, you know.

AL. Then, in spite of these sentiments, she sacrifices herself to Mr. De Witt for position.

MRS. T. [*Rises*] Sacrifices herself to Mr. De Witt! [*Aside*] He thinks it is Fanny. [*Aloud*] Sacrifices! Alfred!

AL. [*Rises*] You are surprised, but I have the right to speak, now that she can never be mine.

MRS. T. Well, then, what interest can you now have?

AL. This—that I never ceased to love her, that I came back determined again to ask—

MRS. T. Stay, Alfred. In honor I can hear no more.

AL. Why not?

MRS. T. [*L.*] Because you are laboring under some strange mistake. Because it is Louise who is to be married to Mr. De Witt. Fanny's heart is still free.

AL. [*R.*] Fanny not to be married! I thought, of course, hearing that Miss Ten Eyck was to be married, that—

MRS. T. You thought, of course, everyone must love Fanny, because you—but there—[*Puts her hand to her mouth*]

AL. [*Eagerly*] Finish the words—because I love her. I do, deeply, sincerely.

MRS. T. Hush, you impetuous boy. You are almost as bad as she is herself. [*Sits R. of L. table*]

AL. You think me impetuous? Well, I am, even reckless. I came to New York to stay, but when I heard that Fanny was about to be married, I resolved to remain but two days, then to sail for Corea. Half doubting my reception, I called, as I thought, for the last time.

MRS. T. Why, you strange boy.

AL. I love Fanny still, and as you can forgive anything in me, I ask for her again.

MRS. T. [*Affecting surprise*] My dear Alfred!

AL. I know you don't want me to have her; you refused me once. But now or never. I won't marry anyone else.

MRS. T. This is so unexpected.

AL. You must give me my answer.

Mrs. T. But I must ask Fanny.

Al. Let me see her?

Mrs. T. [*Rises*] No, I must speak to her. It is two years since you met; you are almost a stranger. Two years ago she was but seventeen, and childish impressions fade so soon. [*Crosses to R.*]

Al. Tell her then I love her; that she shall go with me to Corea, or all over the world.

Mrs. T. And if she wishes to stay home?

Al. I'll sell my yacht, I'll do whatever she pleases. I'll join Harry in the smoking room and await your reply. [*Going up L.*]

Mrs. T. What now?

Al. [*Returning*] I've given orders to have the "Hope" ready to sail day after tomorrow. You say you like me, but you don't seem to trust me. If you do, let me marry Fanny.

Mrs. T. I don't know how to manage boys, I never had any. I suppose the way is to let them do as they please; go, you self-willed fellow, I'll send for you. [*Captain appears, C.*]

Al. My happiness is with you. [*About to go*] Do let me ask her? No? then plead my cause as though it were your own. [*Sees Captain*] Don't tell that party, will you?

Mrs. T. Who? Eh! Edward, why he's as harmless as a kitten.

Al. Never mind. This is between you and me.

Mrs. T. Enough, it's our secret. [*Sits at R. table*]

Al. [*Going out and shaking hands with Captain without stopping*] Smoked your cigar already? [*Exit, C. and L.*]

Capt. Ya-as—what's the matter? [*To Mrs. Ten Eyck, comes down*] Popped for Fanny?

Mrs. T. [*R.*] Don't be so disagreeable—what if he has?

Capt. [*L.*] Knew he had soon as he shook hands. He don't like me, and he wouldn't shake hands unless he was so nervous he didn't know what he was doing.

Mrs. T. You spoilt fellow! Still I suppose I ought to put up with everything from you *now*. Fanny was your favorite, and here she is asked for.

Capt. And so you noticed it, did you?

Mrs. T. [*R., advancing*] Oh, I have eyes; but you have behaved admirably; you knew it was impossible, and so you were content to be *only a friend*.

Capt. It's all owing to your admirable manner of teaching me how hopeless it was for a man with nothing to marry a girl with nothing.

Mrs. T. Thanks, my dear Edward, you are indeed a man of honor.

Capt. And now let's call her. [*Goes to R.D.*] Fanny!

Mrs. T. What are you doing? He'll hear you.

CAPT. Oh, he won't get jealous if I call his wife, will he?

MRS. T. [*Stage, L.*] But he's not married yet, remember that. [*Fanny enters, D.R.2.E.*]

FAN. Well, here I am. [*Crosses to C.*]

CAPT. [*Takes her hand*] Come to the altar of duty and be sacrificed.

MRS. T. [*Stage, L.*] Edward, you are carrying this too far.

FAN. Why are you so impatient, mamma? [*Captain pantomimes in a comical way that a proposal has been made for her*] What is all this mystery? You are too funny.

CAPT. [*Mock, dramatic*] She will explain all. [*Goes up and off, L.*]

FAN. All what? [*Comes over to Mrs. Ten Eyck*]

MRS. T. My love, the greatest surprise is in store for you.

FAN. Nellie told me about it.

MRS. T. Nellie told you!

FAN. Yes, that Alfred had called. [*Looking up C., goes up a little*] Is he gone?

MRS. T. No, he will remain here today, if you choose.

FAN. If I choose?

MRS. T. My darling child, he has proposed for you.

FAN. For me?—Now?—Here?

MRS. T. This very moment. You know his impulsive nature. He has come home after two years' absence more devotedly in love with you than ever. [*Sits with Fanny, L.*]

FAN. But he hasn't seen me since I was a schoolgirl—since you—

MRS. T. My dearest he *is now* his own master. His father's death left him everything—he is most eligible; if I had toiled season after season to secure your lifelong happiness, my child, I could never have found so splendid a fortune as this.

FAN. But, mamma—

MRS. T. I told him, of course, that I must consult you—that everything depended on your heart. I had to say that, of course. [*Smiling*]

FAN. Of course.

MRS. T. He is waiting for your reply now.

FAN. What? Without seeing me? He ought to have come to me first. He used to have courage enough once.

MRS. T. Hush, my dear, be reasonable; what answer will you give him if I send him here?

FAN. I don't know till I hear his question, of course.

MRS. T. You silly girl, you must accept him.

FAN. [*Turns away*] I don't know whether I love him.

Mrs. T. I'm sure you were perfectly ridiculous two years ago.

Fan. [*Turns towards her*] I don't know whether he truly loves me.

Mrs. T. I never saw such devotion—such passion, I may say.

Fan. I wish to see for myself.

Mrs. T. Fanny, do not throw away your happiness by these girlish coquetries.

Fan. I coquettish, mamma?

Mrs. T. Then it's some romantic stuff. For heaven's sake, Fanny, don't be romantic—don't!

Fan. [*Bitterly*] Romance! I don't know what it means, except to marry the wrong man because you love him.

Mrs. T. I expected to hear something like that next.

Fan. [*Angrily*] Have I ever said I loved anybody?

Mrs. T. [*Rises*] Yes. This very Alfred! Tut, tut, tut, what creatures you all are—whenever you should not love, you do, and when you ought to, you won't. Come, come, I'm certain you'll like him again after you are married. I must interfere for your own happiness and insist. [*Fanny crosses to Mrs. Ten Eyck*] What a contrast to your sister; she marries a man old enough to be her father for position, and like a sensible girl is happy. I don't insist upon your being happy, but I expect you to be sensible.

Fan. [*Laughing*] That is very reasonable, mamma.

Mrs. T. There, I like to see you laugh. If Alfred were to see you now, he would fall at your feet. Let me call him in. Nellie!

Fan. But, mamma—[*Nellie enters, R.C.*]

Mrs. T. Ask Mr. Adrianse to come to the parlor. [*Nellie exit, R.1.E.*]

Fan. But, mamma—

Mrs. T. There, compose yourself. He'll be here in a moment.

Fan. Not now, not now. I haven't seen him for two years. Perhaps I may not like him.

Mrs. T. You would be sorry for that? [*Fanny crosses, R., nods*] After all, then, you do love him. [*Kisses her*] There, let me go.

Fan. But, mamma—

Mrs. T. [*Going*] No, darling, I leave you to your own happiness. [*To Alfred, who enters, C.*] She is there.

Al. She *will* receive me, then?

Mrs. T. Have courage. I have no influence over her heart, perhaps someone else can find the way. [*Taps his cheek and exit, R.C.*]

Fan. [*Sits, R.C.*] He's there, and I'm afraid to look.

Al. Dear Fanny. [*Chair, C.*]

Fan. [*At table, R.*] The same voice.

AL. [*Aside*] How lovely she is in that dress, her bridesmaid dress. [*Stands beside her chair; aloud*] It is two years since we met, but it has not been my fault. [*Sits*]

FAN. Has it been mine?

AL. No, it was not yours, it was my misfortune. I commenced to love you too soon.

FAN. Oh, you must have forgotten that.

AL. Today proves I have not.

FAN. Two years make a great difference.

AL. [*Takes chair next her*] True, it has increased my affection. I can't hide my feelings from you. Fanny, I loved you when a girl; as a woman, I love you still, deeply, devotedly. May I speak on?

FAN. Mamma has given you permission.

AL. Will you permit me?

FAN. Of course, I shall listen.

AL. Why are you so reserved? When you were a girl—

FAN. I don't remember half I did when I was a girl. Many foolish things, no doubt.

AL. You loved to hear me speak of my love, of our prospects.

FAN. That was all silly, was it not, for a little thing like me to do?

AL. It was Heaven for me! And then you remember you let me give you a ring, our engagement ring, we called it.

FAN. [*Laughing*] Which I took off whenever I went home, and put on whenever I went out.

AL. [*Takes her hand*] It's not here now.

FAN. I took it off when you went away, for good.

AL. Because you were resolved to forget me. [*Drops hand*]

FAN. Well, it would have become too small. My fingers all had to grow, you know. It's a pity, isn't it, we get too big for all those things of girlhood, even for its love.

AL. No, the love can grow with us, as mine did. Don't tell me that yours is a thing of the past.

FAN. What can I tell you, when I've had no time to think?

AL. Do as I do—never think. Trust your happiness to me. I will leave mine in your hands.

FAN. And yet you hardly know me. [*Giving both hands*]

AL. I am sure you are the one destined to make me happy. I never loved anyone else. I went away hating everybody. I don't know why I came back, except to see you once more, and then leave New York forever. I thought once I had forgotten you, but now I feel that I can't be happy without you. I promise you'll never regret it. Do say yes.

FAN. And you choose to take all the consequences?

AL. Yes, because the consequences will be that I shall love you more and more. Don't delay longer, for until you say yes, I shall be miserable.

FAN. If you won't give me time to think.

AL. You'll have plenty of time to do that afterwards. Do say yes.

FAN. Well, then—

AL. Yes.

FAN. Yes! [*Alfred kisses her hand impulsively. Mrs. Ten Eyck enters*] There's mamma.

MRS. T. My darling!

AL. [*Presses Mrs. Ten Eyck's hand*] At last I have her.

MRS. T. [*To Fanny*] You have made me so happy, and him, too.

FAN. And myself.

MRS. T. [*Crosses to Fanny*] Don't be selfish, darling. That is enough happiness for one day. [*Exit, R.1.E. Fanny turns as she goes. Alfred runs, kisses her hand*]

AL. This morning I was going to Corea, now I find myself in Heaven. [*Duncan enters, C.*] Harry, just the fellow I want to see. I'm to be married.

DUN. Everybody gets married, and I can't. When is it going to be?

AL. Just as soon as my ardent appeal can make it. A week, if I can't do it sooner. And you shall marry us, my boy.

DUN. Just wait and see how I get through with this one today. It's all going out of my head. I know I'll drop the book.

DE W. [*Outside*] All right, I'll find them.

DUN. [*Gets L. corner*] Here comes the unfortunate man whose fate is in my hands. [*De Witt entering, C.*]

DE W. The happy hour approaches. [*Grace entering, R.*]

GRACE. [*To Duncan*] Not gone yet?

DUN. [*Watch in hand*] I have fifteen minutes, and that will be just in time. [*Captain enters C. from L.*]

CAPT. Everybody ready? Ah! [*To De Witt*] Nervous, old fellow? [*Drawing on gloves*]

DE W. No, sir, I'm not. [*Captain crosses to L. and up. Mrs. Ten Eyck enters, C.R.*]

MRS. T. Here we are at last. [*Lu, C.R., followed by two Bridesmaids and elderly Groom*]

LU. What are we waiting for, ma?

MRS. T. For Fanny.

LU. Why, she was ready an hour ago.

MRS. T. Something has happened during the last hour.

Lu. Oh, Lord, she isn't sick! Not sick at the last moment, to spoil the whole thing.

Mrs. T. No, but within the hour Fanny's condition has changed. She has accepted Alfred Adrianse.

Lu. Oh, the darling. Where is she? [*Fanny enters, R.D. Lu runs and embraces her*] Oh, you dear, delightful little thing. I'm so glad. I won't be so lonely, if you are married, too.

De W. [*L. corner*] Ahem!

Mrs. T. [*L. of De Witt*] She never thinks of what she says.

Al. [*R. of Fanny*] If this were only our wedding day. Have pity on me, and don't delay it.

Capt. [*Up C., at back*] Now, Fanny, go to your groomsman. [*Comes down, C.*] Here I am, Miss Lu. [*They go upstage*]

Fan. [*To Alfred, who is annoyed*] Don't be jealous. I don't go to the altar with him for life, as I shall with you. [*Fanny goes to Groomsman*]

Mrs. T. Come, we shall be behind time.

De W. [*Offers arm to Mrs. Ten Eyck*] I shall have the honor. [*All pair off. Grace takes Alfred's arm*]

Grace. Won't you take me?

De W. [*Last downstage*] I'm the happiest man in the world.

Mrs. T. And I'm the happiest mother. [*Music of wedding march. All off towards C. Nellie enters, R.1.E.*]

Nel. Oh, good luck to ye! [*Throws shoe as they exeunt. Quick curtain*]

ACT II.

Scene: *Country residence of Alfred Adrianse on Long Island. Grounds in front of the house, the portico and entrance to which is upon the R. of the scene; view of the Sound in the distance. The time is sunset deepening into evening. Three years have elapsed since the preceding act. Fanny and Grace enter from the L.1.E., as if from walk. Fanny carries her hat in her hand. Grace wears hers.*

Fan. [*R.*] So now you have the whole thing.

Grace. [*L.*] I don't think it is so very serious. Your husband has merely expressed a wish that you should not encourage Captain Lynde's visits to your house; every husband might do the same thing. One would think that Lynde still looked upon you as an unmarried woman.

Fan. [*Crosses to seat, R.*] I suppose no one can control Captain Lynde's thoughts. It is time to interfere when I forget that I am a wife.

Grace. Oh, Fanny! Alfred didn't mean to hint at that.

Fan. [*Seated, R.*] He couldn't act worse if he did. What will people say if I begin to grow distant with such an old friend, and particularly such a good friend of mamma's.

Grace. Never mind what people say; you should think only of your husband. [*Sits*]

Fan. You know nothing about it; you have not been a wife so many years, or you would rebel against the slavery to which women are subjected by a husband's caprice. Time alters opinions.

Grace. Well, you told me you had been perfectly happy while you were away traveling all over the world in your husband's yacht.

Fan. So I was—so we both were, and so I have been since our return home; but while I was innocently enjoying the society of all the old friends who come to visit us, this sudden fancy of Alfred's comes to destroy all.

Grace. [*Looking off*] Hush! he's coming.

Fan. Alfred?

Grace. [*Seriously*] No! [*Rising. Captain appears on veranda, smoking cigarette*] Why does he leave everybody in the house to come out here.

Fan. [*Laughing*] Why—because he prefers to take the air, I suppose.

Grace. Come with me to the library till Alfred returns.

Fan. [*Rising*] Nonsense—I won't run away. I am not afraid.

Capt. [*From portico*] I've been looking all over for you—for both of you. Grace, somebody's been calling you this half hour.

Grace. I'm going. [*To Fanny*] Don't stay here alone.

Fan. Grace, you are as bad as Alfred. [*Sits*]

Grace. I am only prudent. [*Going*]

Capt. [*Coming down*] Sorry you have to go.

Grace. [*Pettishly*] So am I. [*He gives a look at her, as she exits*]

Capt. [*Throws away cigar*] Thought she'd never go. [*Aloud*] Been hunting you both all over the lawn.

Fan. Why?

Capt. Got a secret for you.

Fan. A secret—what is it?

Capt. Just come from your mother. She's in a flutter about your sister Lu. Something horrible just up, and she wanted your advice. Gave her mine, but, as usual, she didn't seem to think it first-rate.

Fan. If everybody knows it, it's not a very great secret.

Capt. Nobody knows it but she and I. We let you in as Number Three. I say, can't you make room for one more?

Fan. What, in the secret?

Capt. No, on that seat.

FAN. Oh, I'm tired, and want it all for myself. I learned all sorts of lazy habits abroad. There's a chair over there.

CAPT. No, I'd rather lean over this and talk.

FAN. As you please.

CAPT. [*Leaning over back of her seat*] Lu's in a heap of trouble. Old De Witt is as bad as ever. [*She turns away with a shrug of unconcern*] Don't that interest you?

FAN. [*Wearily*] Oh, I've heard it so often.

CAPT. Yes, they quarrel every day, perhaps every hour, when they're at home; but this is worse than anything yet. Rumpus must follow.

FAN. Lu is very foolish.

CAPT. Can't say I think so; your mother don't. Look at this. [*Takes letter from his pocket*]

FAN. A letter—from whom?

CAPT. From your mother to a lawyer.

FAN. What folly is this? [*Takes it*]

CAPT. [*Gets away, L.*] Old story. When a husband and wife can't agree, they call in a lawyer to make it worse than ever.

FAN. But mother's lawyer is Mr. Remsen; this is addressed to Mr. Templeton Jitt.

CAPT. Yes, new man. Different kind of business; Remsen, like a family physician, does very well for ordinary cases. When you want a legal surgeon, you call in Jitt; he's an amputator.

FAN. A what?

CAPT. Cuts off members, figuratively speaking. Takes out a rib, that is, procures divorces.

FAN. [*Rising*] Mother cannot be so imprudent. It is shocking. [*Crossing to L.*]

CAPT. Ah! Don't talk so loud. Give me the letter.

FAN. What are you going to do with it?

CAPT. Send it, of course.

FAN. Promise me not to do so until I have seen mamma.

CAPT. I will wait for your orders. But mind, not a word of this to Adrianse.

FAN. And why not to Alfred?

CAPT. Because, in the first place, I don't want anybody to think I'm mixed up in any quarrel between husband and wife, and, in the next place, because your mother desires it to be kept quiet.

FAN. But I have no secrets from my husband.

CAPT. This is *not* YOUR secret; will you promise?

FAN. And suppose I do not?

CAPT. Then I must obey orders, and mail it.

FAN. [*After hesitating a moment, gives back letter*] I promise.

CAPT. [*Takes her hand*] Thanks, my dear Fanny.

MRS. T. [*Outside*] Never mind, I'll find her.

CAPT. Your mother. I'll step one side until you speak with her. [*Goes up and off, R.U.E., bows. Mrs. Ten Eyck entering from house*]

MRS. T. Ah! there you are.

FAN. Mamma, what is all this about Lu?

MRS. T. Ask me, my love! Louise has actually gone and taken a step which I consider dreadful.

FAN. But it is you that wrote to the lawyer.

MRS. T. [*Sits on seat, R.*] My dear, Louise had already written to him, asking him to call.

FAN. Are matters so bad, then, between Mr. De Witt and her?

MRS. T. They have always been bad. She has had her own way in everything, and yet she is not satisfied; she says he is not attentive, that he neglects her! She is jealous.

FAN. [*Smiles*] What, of old Mr. De Witt?

MRS. T. Well, my dear, these old men are only men after all. He was said to be a very gay widower.

FAN. And yet you allowed Lu to marry him.

MRS. T. She had nothing to do with his life as a widower. We can't demand Sunday-school certificates from grown men, my dear, when they ask for our children. [*Crosses to L.*]

FAN. But surely since his marriage he has behaved properly.

MRS. T. I believe Louise's suspicions are all fancy.

FAN. Who is this Mr. Jitt she has sent for?

MRS. T. That is the most dreadful part of it, my love. He is some wretch who advertises in the papers to procure divorces without publicity. I thought I should have dropped when she told me. [*Sits, L.*]

FAN. Lu is disgracing herself. What is this letter which you have given to Edward?

MRS. T. I wrote it as soon as I could get the man's address from your sister. "My child," said I, "you'll break my heart," but she didn't seem to care. I've written to tell the wretch not to come, that everything is settled.

FAN. That was right.

MRS. T. As for Lu, I've told her I wouldn't permit any more talk of divorce between her and Mr. De Witt. She has no children, and in the event of a separation the court wouldn't allow her enough to live decently on. Then she became worse than ever.

FAN. [*Aside, smiling*] I don't wonder.

Mrs. T. [*Rises*] What did you say?

Fan. [*Smiling*] You think of the practical results so much.

Mrs. T. [*Business tone*] And who else is to think of them! I won't have her thrown back upon me with a pitiful two or three thousand a year, while that old wretch, her husband, dashes about like a bachelor with his half million of money. [*Crosses to R.*] It would all be different if she had a child, as you have; no, no, when it is proper to have a separation I will manage it. For the present they must be reconciled, although I admit old Mr. De Witt is not a very delightful creature to—[*De Witt enters, R.2.E.*] Ah, my dear, dear child, where on earth have you been? [*Takes his arm. Fanny goes up into house*]

De W. Been! I've been sulking.

Mrs. T. Sulking! Why, I wanted you to cheer me up. You have such a youthful flow of boyish spirits, that I quite look on you as my son.

De W. I'm afraid I'll have to be a very undutiful son, then, and run away.

Mrs. T. Where to?

De W. Home—New York. The fact is I don't seem to please Lu much when we're among strangers.

Mrs. T. Please her? And she doats on you.

De W. She won't notice me one moment, and then blows me up the next.

Mrs. T. It's her girlish nonsense. You wouldn't have her moping and poky like an old woman.

De W. No, I know she's a girl. But I've been married before, I know how wives ought to act. [*Crosses to L.*]

Mrs. T. I believe your first wife belonged to our generation, twenty years ago or so. Girls are different nowadays, my dear De Witt. They have more of their own way.

De W. [*Gallantly, R.H.*] I wish they had more of their mother's way.

Mrs. T. [*Curtsies. Quickly*] Thanks, but we must put up with them. You are so kind and indulgent.

De W. I thought I was, but she says I'm a brute. I'm too phlegmatic, too quiet, too—the fact is, I'm not young enough for her.

Mrs. T. Oh, De Witt! How can you! You'll tell me I'm an old woman next.

De W. I can't help it. Lu wants some young chap who will fall out, quarrel, cry, kiss, make it up, quarrel and forgive again ten times a day. I could when I was young. I can't now. I want rest. That makes her angry. Then she loves to be jealous.

Mrs. T. But she is not jealous.

DE W. I know it, but she likes to think she is. It's her nature. If I gave her cause she'd be delighted—be miserably happy. As I don't, she frets. Now what am I to do?

MRS. T. [*Sobbing*] Do? Can you ask? Bear with her, poor child. In a few years she will lose all that. We get old soon enough. Let us have a little youth. [*Handkerchief to eyes*]

DE W. There, there, don't mind me.

MRS. T. [*Same*] Poor Lu, so young, so inexperienced.

DE W. I'll make it up, Mrs. Ten Eyck. I won't go.

MRS. T. Humor her little faults, De Witt.

DE W. I will. I will.

MRS. T. Let us find her, poor child. Come. [*About to take his arm. Fanny enters from house*] Ah, excuse me a moment. [*Aside to Fanny*] Fanny, my love, do you know if Edward has posted my letter to that lawyer.

FAN. No, I stopped it, until I saw you.

MRS. T. Quick, then, find him, he must catch the mail tonight.

FAN. [*Looking off, R.U.E.*] There's the captain now. [*Calls him*] Captain!

MRS. T. What nonsense. Call him Edward, nobody calls him captain, and you always—

FAN. But, mamma, since I'm married—

MRS. T. Stuff, my dear, an old friend like him!

FAN. Oh, well. [*Calling*] Edward! Edward!

MRS. T. Run and meet him. Tell him to hasten to the post. [*Fanny runs off, R.U.E.*] Come, De Witt, let us find Lu, and begin your excellent system of forbearance. [*Exeunt in house*]

FAN. [*Heard in distance*] Edward! Edward! [*Adrianse and Duncan enter, L.I.E.*]

AL. You see?

DUN. Yes, I see.

AL. He is here still. When I went to the city yesterday, I expressly said to her, I don't like that man, I don't like his familiarity with you. If you wish to oblige me, discourage his visits.

DUN. Well, that can't be done at once; you can't take a gentleman by the back of the neck and turn him out. She may be complying with your request, and doing it gradually.

AL. Does this look like it? Calling him to her, calling him over and over again?

DUN. That was because he didn't hear her.

AL. [*Throws himself in seat*] But by his name—Edward, as if—

DUN. Well, it *is* his name—suppose it had been Patrick?

AL. How is he to be discouraged if she calls him back whenever he leaves her side.

DUN. [*Sits L. of Alfred*] You forgot, her mother and old De Witt were here.

AL. Yes, and she left them to seek him alone. I tell you my wishes are not respected. She is my wife, and my will ought to be law, particularly when it concerns a man whose conduct might give rise to talk.

DUN. But I confess I don't see—you know he is an old friend of the family.

AL. What rights that gives him he may have. I ask him to the house when I ask her mother.

DUN. Oh, well, tell him to go.

AL. [*Rises, and walking to L.*] You talk like a child. How can I make myself a laughingstock, ordering a man to leave the house; he'd talk about me all over New York. It's my wife's business. Women know how.

DUN. [*R. on seat*] But she don't encourage him.

AL. How absurd you are. Of course she don't. Do you think I'd live with her a day if she encouraged him? Thank heaven, I don't suspect my wife.

DUN. [*Rising*] Then all is well.

AL. All is not well, while I am annoyed by that man coming between her and me. [*Fanny entering from house*]

FAN. My dear Alfred. [*Runs to him*]

AL. [*Coldly*] Well, Fanny. [*She looks at him a moment, then draws back her hand, which was on his shoulder. Alfred walks up and down, L.*]

FAN. Grace and I were looking for you both long ago. The train has been in this half hour. Where have you been, Harry?

DUN. We walked up, instead of driving. I called at Messerroles for the things. You will have quite a party tonight for baby's birthday. Where's Grace? [*She motions towards house*] I must run off to find her. [*Aside, crosses to Alfred*] Do be good now—you noticed she called me by my Christian name, too. [*Fanny goes up to L.*]

AL. [*Crossing to seat, R.*] You are an old friend of mine.

DUN. And Lynde is an old friend of hers. Do be decent now, make it up for the sake of your guests tonight. [*Exit into house, R.*]

AL. [*By seat*] Why do you stand over there?

FAN. [*Advancing to L.*] You hardly noticed me when I spoke to you. I suppose you feel towards me as you did when you left me yesterday morning.

AL. [*Rises, advances to her*] As I live, Fanny, I came back today resolved to show you that I loved you more than ever, but expecting to find my wishes complied with.

FAN. I have done all that lay in my power.

AL. How can that be, when I heard you calling that man; and you have just left him.

FAN. I have not just left him, I could not find him.

AL. Why did you go to seek him?

FAN. Because he—I cannot tell you.

AL. You cannot tell me. Take care, Fanny, you are touching dangerous grounds.

FAN. Not at all. I promised to keep his secret, that is all.

AL. His secret? So, then, there are secrets between you; up to this time I considered you blameless.

FAN. [*Indignantly*] Have a care in your turn. You have not gone as far as that yet.

AL. I will have nothing more between you and that man. You shall not see him again, do you hear?

FAN. Yes, I hear you, Alfred. [*Sits, L.*]

AL. You are periling your own reputation by such conduct.

FAN. [*In seat, L.H.*] Go on. [*Tremulously*] Let me hear the worst you think of me.

AL. You are destroying my happiness and you will ruin your own.

FAN. [*Rises*] You have destroyed my happiness by your passionate caprices. Do you know what your words mean? If I am fit to be told that I must not see any man living, I am not fit to be any man's wife.

AL. [*Up and downstage*] I have the right to regulate your conduct to other men.

FAN. I do not care what you do. I am willing you should send everyone out of the house.

AL. [*Stage, R.*] It rests with you to discourage the man.

FAN. I will do nothing more. I care no more for him than for any other old friend of my childhood. I am conscious of no guilt, and I suspect nobody's motives. If he comes here I will treat him decently. If you drive him away and we chance to meet, I shall treat him as I always do. [*Enter Captain, R.U.E., hurriedly*]

CAPT. [*Comes down C.*] Ah! Fanny, heard you'd been looking for me. [*Sees Alfred*] How are you old fel—[*Holds out his hand, Alfred takes it reluctantly*]

FAN. [*Crosses L. to Alfred*] Make some excuse to take me away. Give me your arm. [*Captain eyes them with glass*]

AL. I'm not going to run away as if I were afraid of him.

CAPT. I wanted to see you myself, about—you know; getting late you know, the letter—[*She takes no notice*]

AL. Do you wish to disgrace us? Look at the way he stares at us, as if he was about to laugh in my face.

FAN. I thought you wished me to offend him.

CAPT. [*Advancing*] When will you talk over that little matter, Fanny?

AL. [*Crosses to him*] If you like to wait in the house, we'll soon be in.

CAPT. [*Crosses C. and up*] Thanks, there's some hurry, you know. I can drive down to the post though, if time presses. [*Lights cigarette and exit into house. Fanny takes stage C.*]

AL. [*Advancing to her*] You have told him pretty much all he wants to know by your conduct.

FAN. What am I to do to please you? I can bear this no more. [*Going up R.*] He shall leave here tonight. I will make him go.

AL. I will have no vulgar scenes. If you are anxious to go to him about your secret, go, but make up no farce with him about his expulsion on account of my jealousy!

FAN. When you are calm again you will recall that. For the present my course is fixed. [*Exit, R.2.D.*]

AL. [*As she is going*] What course is that? [*As she exits without replying, throws himself in seat, R., buries his head in his hands*] There is a curse hangs over marriage after all. For all these years we seemed to agree in everything. I was as happy as my fondest dream, but this miserable little question of my right to advise and guide her separates us in a moment. [*Rises, savagely*] Curse the scoundrel, I wish he'd never been born. [*Sits R. Jitt enters, L.U.E.*]

JITT. Hem! Excuse me, sir, is this Mr. Adrianse's place?

AL. Yes.

JITT. Mrs. De Witt on a visit here at present?

AL. She is.

JITT. Hem, I should like to see her.

AL. [*Turns away*] Give your card to the servant.

JITT. Well, I've hardly got the sort of card to go up into a parlor with. Nothing but my business pasteboard. [*Produces one*] "Templeton Jitt, Attorney and Counselor-at-law, Proctor in Admiralty, Commissioner for all the States. Divorces procured without publicity." Hardly the sort of bombshell to throw into a host's parlor that, eh?

AL. [*Quickly, R.*] You are a lawyer?

JITT. Yes, and wanted particularly quick, too, I should reckon, by the summons. Do you happen to know the lady?

AL. Mrs. De Witt, yes. Did she send for you?

JITT. Oh, things must be in a precious state. Is she regularly hurt bad?

AL. Hurt bad?

JITT. Black and blue—all over bruises—cruel treatment, you know! Also more serious crimes against the matrimonial laws.

AL. [*Turns away*] I don't comprehend. I'll call my wife.

JITT. Bless me. I hope you are not the husband. What a puddle I have got into.

AL. [*Returning*] What husband?

JITT. De Witt.

AL. Mr. and Mrs. De Witt are guests of mine. They are in the house at this moment.

JITT. You don't mean to say they've made up again? That is too shabby. After bringing me all the way here.

AL. [*Calls*] Richard!

JITT. Eh! He's calling the servants. I wonder if he means anything summary. [*Richard enters, R.2.E., from house*]

RICH. Yes, sir!

AL. Show this gentleman into the library, and take his card to Mrs. De Witt.

RICH. Yes, sir. This way, sir!

JITT. [*Crosses to C.*] A thousand times obliged. Have a card, sir? Happy to return politeness by anything in my way. [*Offers card. Alfred takes it and throws it on seat, R.*] He may be good for a fee some time or other. Lead on, Richard.

RICH. This way, sir!

JITT. All right. I always follow precedents. [*Exeunt, R.2.E. Music of waltz is heard in house. Alfred comes slowly to seat, R., picks up card*]

AL. So, then, domestic trouble begins to eat its way into all our houses. [*Mr. and Mrs. Kemp appear, L.U.E.*]

MRS. K. [*R.*] Not a soul to receive us, I do declare.

AL. [*Rises, and puts card thoughtlessly into his pocket*] Why, yes. I'm here, Aunt Kemp. How do you do, and you, Uncle Syl. [*Crosses to C.*] I was half afraid you wouldn't come.

MRS. K. We never miss anything in this way, you know.

KEMP. We have lived so long in the country that we should be dead and buried if we didn't keep up our visiting, you know. There's the music. Waltzing, eh? I must see to that. I'll go right in. [*Going gaily*]

MRS. K. Wait a bit, father.

KEMP. [*Coming back gaily*] All right, Susie, just as you say.

MRS. K. Who's here? [*Old man continues dancing to the music quietly*]

AL. Not many yet, it's early. You are the first from Hempstead way.

MRS. K. I mean stopping with you?

AL. Fanny's mother, De Witt, and his wife.

MRS. K. And Neddie Lynde, as I live. I see him through the glass there. It is he, isn't it?

AL. Yes!

KEMP. [*Near window*] I see you. [*Shakes his finger. Chorus of girls inside*]

OMNES. Oh, if it isn't Mr. Kemp, I declare. Did you ever?

KEMP. Aha, I'm with you. See here, Susie, you can spare me, just a minute. There's a kiss till you come. [*Going*] Aha, you rogues, look at this. [*Chorus of girlish laughter at his exit. Music stops*]

MRS. K. Father's as wild as ever, ha, ha! How on earth did you come to know Neddie Lynde? Did he visit Clara's when you were there?

AL. Yes, constantly.

MRS. K. Not married yet, I suppose.

AL. [*R., gloomily*] I suppose not.

MRS. K. You don't like him—neither do I; but I have my reasons, and you have not. He's a fool.

AL. A very dangerous one, I believe.

MRS. K. It's not the danger in the man, it's the effect he produces. He never got a woman to fall in love with him yet, but he can ruin her good name in a week by making everybody believe she has—and all through his familiar ways.

AL. Dear aunt, I only wish Fanny could hear you; she refuses to believe anything against Lynde.

MRS. K. I hope you haven't said anything to her against him; that's not the way, you foolish boy, to make a woman dislike a man. [*Music*]

AL. No?

MRS. K. No. Has he been worrying you?

AL. I don't want to say anything to make you think Fanny—

MRS. K. And I wouldn't think Fanny—if you did; she's a blessed good girl. The best I ever saw. I'll talk to her. [*Turns to R.*]

AL. You've taken a load off my mind.

MRS. K. [*Laughs*] I hope I haven't put the load all on my own shoulders. However, I guess I know how matters are, and I'll drop a word in Fanny's ear if I can. [*Kemp runs in from window*]

KEMP. I say, Susie.

MRS. K. Did you ever hear a name sound so funny for an old woman? Well, father, what is it?

KEMP. I want you to dance.

MRS. K. With whom?

KEMP. With me, of course. I wouldn't let anyone else. When I get old, you can dance with all the young fellows you like. Come along, quick, they are going to begin. [*Runs in, R.2.E.*]

AL. Take my arm.

MRS. K. Nonsense. I can run faster than you can; let me try—oh! Well. [*Laughs, takes his arm; they go in together. Stop Music. Jitt and Lu enter from R.U.E.*]

LU. We can talk here better than in the library; no one will overhear us. [*Goes to garden bench*]

JITT. [*L.*] As you please; but it is hardly the place for a consultation. Nature is all very well, but it has a depressing effect on law.

LU. Oh, rubbish! Sit down.

JITT. Ah, excuse me. [*Goes L., blows a little whistle, and is answered*]

LU. Mercy on me! What's that?

JITT. That's—that's only Burritt; the regular thing, ma'am. Burritt is a private detective, invaluable in these matters. [*Burritt enters, L.U.E.*]

BUR. All right, sir. Here I am—handy.

JITT. [*To Lu*] I think you said that old gent with the white hair was your husband. [*Points through window, R.*]

LU. [*In maze*] Yes, but—

JITT. Excuse me. Burritt, look at that gentleman standing by the window. [*Taking him upstage, and points to window*]

BUR. I see him easy enough.

JITT. Mark him, then. [*Burritt watches window*]

LU. What is all this? What do I want with a detective?

JITT. We shall see, ma'am, we shall see.

LU. [*Sits on bench, R.*] But I insist upon your sending that dirty man away.

BUR. [*Advancing, L.*] All regular, ma'am, I assure you. Everybody has us.

LU. But I don't want to have anything to do with detectives.

JITT. Never engaged in this sort of thing before, then? Never been divorced, eh?

LU. Why, I've only been married three years.

JITT. Very fortunate lady, ma'am. The way things go nowadays, a very long period of connubial felicity. But to judge by your letter, your time's come at last. [*Sits, L.C.*]

LU. I'm a perfectly wretched woman. [*Sits, R.*]

JITT. Let's come to the point, then. [*Draws chair near C., Burritt stands beside him*] You talk, I'll listen. Don't be afraid to speak. To begin, you want to get a divorce from your husband. What's your ground? [*Burritt gets out his notebook and pencil*]

Lu. What's my ground?

Jitt. Yes—your legal grounds.

Lu. Why, I leave all the legal grounds to you. You are a lawyer.

Jitt. Ah, I see; I'm to work up the case. [*Slyly*]

Lu. You are to do whatever lawyers do, I suppose.

Jitt. The old style of thing; eh, Burritt?

Bur. Old game, sir. She's a deep one. It's my opinion, she's been there before.

Jitt. You must give us some clue, ma'am. Your husband is pretty gay, eh?

Lu. Not a bit of it.

Jitt. But he goes out—you don't know where?

Lu. No, he doesn't.

Jitt. Whom do you suspect. Got your notebook, Burritt?

Bur. I'm there!

Lu. Suspect of what?

Jitt. Why—hem—what—particular lady?

Lu. Why, you vulgar creature, what do I know about such things?

Jitt. Then it is a case of cruelty.

Lu. Yes.

Jitt. Inhuman conduct. Unsafe and dangerous to live with him; mere separation. Revised Statutes—Part Second, Chapter 8, Article 4. And nothing else?

Lu. What! Isn't that enough? No.

Jitt. [*Disappointed*] Oh!

Bur. [*Shuts up book*] Ah! [*Disgusted*]

Jitt. Poor stuff—eh, Burritt?

Bur. Very common, sir.

Jitt. You can't get a divorce in full for that, you know. You only get a separation.

Lu. Well, that'll do—anything.

Jitt. But, then, you can't marry again.

Lu. Who said I wanted to be married again? I wouldn't be married again for anything; once is a dose.

Jitt. Ah!

Bur. [*Long whistle*] Oh! [*Puts up notebook*]

Jitt. Odd case, this, Burritt.

Bur. Most remarkable, sir.

Lu. What astonishes you so much?

Jitt. Well, hem, I've procured about a thousand divorces in my time, and you are the first lady who didn't want one in order to marry somebody else.

Lu. The horrid things. All I want is to be independent, to live as I please, and to have a liberal allowance; he must give me a liberal allowance, mustn't he?

Jitt. What's he worth?

Lu. [*Carelessly, as she rises*] Half a million. [*Burritt opens book again*]

Jitt. [*Rises*] Half a million? Whew! This is out of the common run. [*Aside*] Five thousand dollars fee at least. [*Aloud*] You are a lucky woman. He shall pay you—let me see. Burritt, what do you say?

Bur. Ten thousand a year would sound tidy.

Lu. That would do very well, indeed. [*Rises*]

Jitt. With your appearance, ma'am, I think I could guarantee more; if you'll only come into court, I think I could make it fifteen. What a—a splendid figure, Burritt, to fling at a jury, eh?

Bur. Lovely, sir, perfectly irresistible.

Lu. No, I won't have anything to do with it.

Jitt. All legal, ma'am—quite legal.

Lu. And remember, Mr. De Witt is not to know anything of this till it's all done.

Jitt. Eh? [*Looks at Burritt, who scratches his head*] We have to give him notice, serve him with a summons, as we call it.

Lu. But I don't want him to know anything until I get the divorce; he'd tell ma, and she'd stop it.

Jitt. Can't be done, ma'am.

Bur. [*L.*] It used to be did, but that's all over now. Courts too strict—States Prison—**no go.**

Lu. [*R.*] But you said in your advertisement that you would procure divorces **without publicity.**

Jitt. [*C.*] I meant without getting it in the papers, without having it come before a court and jury. We get it done by a referee.

Lu. What's that? Some kind of a machine?

Jitt. Yes'm. A machine referee.

Bur. A referee machine.

Lu. And it's as good that way, as the other way.

Bur. Oh! Copper-bottomed—A 1.

Jitt. [*Sits, L.*] And now, if you'll give me the points of the cruelties. Tell me what he does. Get your notes ready, Burritt.

Bur. Here we are, sir.

Lu. [*Sits, R.*] He's perfectly outrageous, he finds fault with my extravagance—says my dressmaker's bills are too high, and that my appetite for jewelry will ruin him. A month ago we had a quarrel, and he didn't come home to dinner—in fact, he didn't come home till one o'clock—I locked myself in my room, and when I refused to let him in, he abused me through the keyhole.

JITT. It's heartrending. What did he call you? [*Clutches Burritt's hand, he leans forward*]

Lu. He said I was a goose. [*Both disappointed*] Then all the next week I refused to speak to him, and he sat back and laughed at me; then when I wouldn't relent, he went out of town, and stayed two days. But I revenged myself; I went to every store I knew of, and bought everything I could think of, and when he came back I showed him the bills, and he laughed at me, and said he'd keep the amount out of my allowance, and he has exasperated me every day since, to the last degree of frenzy, by keeping as cool as ice, while I was boiling over. At last, my patience gave way, and I told him I would leave him, and wrote to you.

JITT. Is that all?

Lu. All! Isn't that enough?

JITT. Come, now—try and remember—didn't he fly into a passion?

Lu. Never. That's what makes me so mad.

JITT. But he did call you several opprobrious epithets?

Lu. Yes, he called me a goose repeatedly.

JITT. But he prefixed some qualifying adjective, eh? He was profane, eh? Come, now. What kind of a goose did he call you?

Lu. Nothing. Just plain goose.

JITT. [*Eyeing her, then reflectively*] Plain goose—well, put it down, Burritt.

BUR. Down she goes, sir. Plain goose.

JITT. And he never used any violence?

Lu. [*Starts up with tone of implied threat*] I'd like to see him!

JITT. Never locked you up?

Lu. No, indeed—he couldn't.

JITT. Never prevented your family visiting you?

Lu. He wouldn't dare to. [*Goes up*]

JITT. Burritt, this is a very weak case.

BUR. It's a fraud, sir, that's my view of it.

JITT. The court would throw the papers at our heads.

BUR. Oh, it wouldn't do, no ways.

JITT. I regret to say, Mrs. De Witt, that you have no case; you couldn't get a decree of divorce for that, any more than you could get a paper of tacks.

Lu. [*Stage, R. and back*] You mean to say that I have no redress for my husband's cruel conduct?

JITT. [*Still seated*] I mean to say that the law don't see it.

Lu. But I will. [*Hits his hat with her fan. Burritt takes note of damages*] Have a separation—I will—I will. I won't be abused in this way all my life. Is there no other way?

Jitt. [*Rises*] I'll think it over. Eh, Burritt?

Bur. Yes, sir, we'll give it our consideration.

Jitt. [*Hat behind him*] Where can I see you in two or three days?

Lu. We return home to New York, tomorrow. Come into the library, and I'll give you the address.

Jitt. You are very good. I'll put my mind on it.

Lu. Come this way, so as not to be seen. It wouldn't do to take your friend through the parlors, he isn't just the figure for a quadrille. [*Exit, R.1 E.*]

Jitt. Coming, Burritt?

Bur. Thankee, no. I'll wait about here—too hot in the house. [*Jitt exit, R.2 E.*] There's no knowing what odd plants I might come across here. [*Lights his pipe and goes off, R.U.E., observing Fanny and Captain, who enter, R.2.E., followed by Mrs. Ten Eyck*]

Capt. There's no use talking further, my dear Fanny. I might as well go now as any time; he won't treat me any better if I stay.

Mrs. T. I never heard of such conduct. Edward has always been so kind, so brotherly.

Capt. Well, you know, I can't help it if he's jealous. So it's best for me to go. I'll do whatever you say, though.

Fan. And I insist upon your remaining.

Mrs. T. Fanny, would you have Edward exposed to daily annoyance, such as he has just submitted to? [*Crosses to her*]

Fan. [*Seated, L.*] I would have no publicity about our domestic concerns. If Edward goes away suddenly, talk will be made, questions will be asked, and you know, however innocent she may be, blame will fall upon the wife.

Mrs. T. Well, then, perhaps Edward had better stay—at least for a while.

Capt. No, I'm only in the way, I'm only an object of suspicion to your husband; I'd better go. Good-bye, Fanny, don't begin to think, as your husband does, that I'm to blame for all the—

Fan. You are to blame for nothing. Won't you remain for my sake?

Capt. I am going for your sake. All will blow over when I'm out of the way. I should like to hear that you are happy; you might just drop me a word, just a line, to say: "All's well!" I should be so glad of that.

Fan. [*Crosses to Mrs. Ten Eyck*] I will tell mother all—she is my confidant; you can ask her.

Capt. [*Going up, L.*] Thanks for so much, then. Good-bye. [*Going up*]

Mrs. T. See Edward to the gate, Fanny.

FAN. I'm going to, mamma.

MRS. T. You can come in by the back way; I'll watch for you.

FAN. I will return this way; I'm not afraid that anything I do should be known to all the world. [*Exit, L.U.E., taking Captain's arm*]

MRS. T. I will be home tomorrow, Edward; come and see me as soon as I get there. [*Towards house*] I'd better go as soon as I can in my turn, for after he's sent all his wife's old friends out of the house, he'll show her mother the door. [*Alfred enters from house*]

AL. Where is Fanny?

MRS. T. Fanny—why, didn't you leave her in the house?

AL. She left me to come out here.

MRS. T. Well, you must watch her for yourself. When my daughters marry, I can't do that duty for their husbands. [*Crosses, R., upstage*]

AL. There is no occasion for bitterness. I'm not a very brutal husband yet.

MRS. T. Don't tell me that, Mr. Adrianse, after you have driven one of your wife's and one of *my* best and truest friends from your house tonight by your cruel jealousy.

AL. [*Pleased*] What—is he gone?

MRS. T. Yes, he *is* gone, and let me tell you that, if you particularly value your character as a gentleman, you will have it pretty severely tested by society in a very short time. [*Exit into house*]

AL. Gone—that is some comfort at least. But I shall have the whole exposure that I dreaded unless I prevent it. [*Burritt comes from behind house, going L.*] It's foolish to hesitate now, and beat about the bush. I'll see him myself, and make him understand. [*Sees Burritt*] Here, my man, whose servant are you? Do you know Captain Lynde?

BUR. [*Keenly*] Captain Lynde? Is that the one they call Edward? [*Alfred turns away, as if biting his lips*] I heard the ladies call him Edward. He's gone down to the gate with the one they call Fanny. Precious sweet on him, she is, too, I should judge.

AL. [*Seizes him violently*] You scoundrel!

BUR. Now, don't, sir; you'll only shake yourself to pieces that way. If I've offended you, I beg your pardon. I may have seen too much; but that's our business. I'm a detective.

AL. A detective? What brought you here?

BUR. Mr. Jitt, he brought me.

AL. Hark you, then, my man, the less you see, and the less you say about what you see, the more it will be worth to you. [*Gives money*] Go!

BUR. [*Touches hat*] All right, sir. [*Aside, as he goes off*] I guess he's the one they call Alfred. [*Exit, L.1.E.*]

AL. [*Looking off, L.*] It was that way they went. If I dared to follow— perhaps I should know the worst—know whether my wife—[*Turns towards house. Mrs. Kemp enters, R.2.E.*]

MRS. K. Talking to Fanny? Where is she? I saw her slip out after Neddie, and I thought it a good chance to catch them together and give them a little good advice.

AL. I'm afraid that's useless now; the man has concluded to go at last, and my wife is taking what, I suppose, may be called an affectionate farewell. [*Bitterly*]

MRS. K. Nonsense! What has happened to you? There, go along, I hear her coming; go in, I tell you. [*Pushes him into house. Fanny and Kitty Crosbie enter, L.U.E.*]

KITTY. [*L.*] How odd to meet you down there. Do you know, George never got home at all, and I was afraid I couldn't come, but I drove over myself. Won't I pay him off for that, though.

MRS. K. Very bad language, young woman.

KITTY. Lord, if it isn't Cousin Kemp. Why, Cousin Kemp, how are you? [*Crosses and kisses her*]

MRS. K. About as well as you flighty things will let me be with your new ideas about the management of husbands.

KITTY. Well, I don't trouble myself about managing mine, I let him manage himself. Only married a year and a half and quite independent of every restriction. Have my own company, my own flirtations, in short, quite my own way.

FAN. And George?

KITTY. Oh, he has what he wants—his own way. I make it a point of advising all the girls I know to do as I do when they get married: have your own way; if you stop to think what will please your husband, you'll live in hot water all your life.

FAN. You are not very wrong. It's best to give up the task at once; a wife never does the right thing.

KITTY. And if she does, it's either too late or too soon, or the wrong way, or not done well. It's impossible to meet a husband's whims; my rule cures him; I never mind his wishes, and he soon gives up wishing.

MRS. K. [*Seated, R.*] Well, I've lived forty years with my husband.

KITTY. Lord, how did you manage it?

MRS. K. [*Rises*] We tried to bear with each other's failings. If he was jealous, I was circumspect. If I was jealous, he was devoted; instead of abusing each other, we tried to remedy the trouble, and so we've lived to this time without a quarrel.

KITTY. Oh, mercy! A sermon. [*Crossing to window*] I never listen to one.

Mrs. K. You don't—why not?

Kitty. [*Laughs*] It might change my views, and I'm too well satisfied to risk that. Come, Fanny. [*Exit, R.2.E.*]

Mrs. K. [*Stopping her*] One moment, my love, Eddie Lynde has gone away, and you are not friends with your husband.

Fan. Who told you that?

Mrs. K. He did!

Fan. Does he begin to publish our quarrel? I can spread the news as well as he. [*Crossing to R.*]

Mrs. K. [*Takes her hand as she crosses*] He only wanted me to advise you.

Fan. Advise me to do what? I have already done everything he wishes.

Mrs. K. But things are worse than ever!

Fan. That is his fault.

Mrs. K. You have not implicitly obeyed his wishes.

Fan. Don't use that word to me, I can't bear it.

Mrs. K. Why, my dear, it's the duty of a true wife.

Fan. Right or wrong?

Mrs. K. Right or wrong.

Fan. This is your doctrine?

Mrs. K. I have lived by it forty years.

Fan. Then listen to mine. Just so far as it is right I will obey his wishes. If I am in doubt, I will give him the benefit of that doubt and still comply, [*Alfred appears, Mrs. Kemp motions him back*] but if he outrages my feelings, insults my friends and suspects my honor, I will resent it with all my power to the day of my death. [*Crosses to L. Music tremolo till end*]

Al. [*Advancing*] That is your determination?

Mrs. K. [*Crossing C. between them*] Hush, both of you. [*To Alfred*] This was not for your ears. [*Enter Mrs. Ten Eyck, R.2.E.*]

Fan. It might as well be spoken out. I take nothing back. [*Goes to Mrs. Ten Eyck*]

Mrs. T. [*L.C.*] My poor child. [*Embracing her.*]

Al. You forget that I have some rights. Among them—[*Crosses to C.R.*] I am master of my own house. This quarrel is between my own wife and me; we will settle it without interference. You must take my views of her duties, or you must leave the house. [*To Mrs. Ten Eyck*]

Mrs. T. I told you. It's my turn now to go. I can overtake Edward. [*Going, L.U.E.*]

Fan. Mother, stay where you are. [*Crosses to Alfred*] Will you apologize for this insult to my mother?

Al. [*Crossing to R.*] No!

FAN. [*Taking her mother's hand*] Then we will go together. [*Alfred takes stage to R.H., with a wave of the hand signifying "Do as you please." Mrs. Kemp makes a step to interfere, she is waved off, she turns to console Alfred*]

ACT III.

SCENE 1: *The interior at Hyde Parke. At R.C. a large arch, through which is seen a chamber, bed partly visible; window near it in flat, L.C., doors through which the woody country is seen. Doors, R. and L. Music. Molly is discovered dressing Alfred, a child about 2½ years old. Jim, dressed as a tiger, is looking on.*

MOL. Now do let me put the things on ye, Master Alfred, it's the provoking time I have with you anytime, but when ye're going out, shure you've no match for contrariness.

JIM. It's all the want of paternal correction, Molly. If he had a father to welt him, he'd precious soon stop his pranks.

MOL. Shure, it's a thousand pities the father and mother couldn't agree. It's a warnin' to us young girls.

JIM. Not if you haven't got the vicious propensities of the *aristocracy*. Poor people can't afford to separate.

MOL. Thrue for ye, it's only the rich folks ken indulge in such luxuries; we have to live together for economy.

JIM. Look at Bonyparte and Josephine, how they separated; it's a foreign and disgraceful practice.

MOL. Shure, but it's slander we're talking, though; sure the master hasn't separated from the missus.

JIM. Well, what's the difference; she's been down here three months, and he's never come near her. Do you suppose a square man would act like that? Do you suppose, if I was married, I would?

MOL. I suppose it all depinds on the woman you were married to.

JIM. That's so, Molly, and it depends on a young woman what I has in my eye now.

MOL. Ah! Don't be looking at me that way, you decaiver. Let me dress the child for ye to take out. Put your hands away, will ye?

JIM. All right, hurry him up. He's becoming an object of curiosity to the neighborhood already; the baby without a father, as they call him.

MOL. Who called him that?

JIM. Why, I got the word from a strange-looking fellow that's been talking with us down at the stable.

MOL. A stranger, is it? An' what's he got to say about Master Alfred?

JIM. Why, no later than day before yesterday, there was a sort of chunky chap, with short hair, a cross between a farmer and a horse-jockey, who came over to the stable, and says he to me—[*Burritt, who has appeared at C.D., from L., and overheard the last words*]

BUR. Good morning!

JIM. [*Startled*] Eh!

MOL. [*Frightened*] Merciful gracious presarve us—who's that?

BUR. I said good afternoon!

JIM. [*Aside to Molly*] That's him.

MOL. Who—who do you want to see, if you please?

BUR. Oh, nobody, I was only passing—

MOL. Thin pass on, if ye plaze.

BUR. Time enough. Folks in?

MOL. Yis, sir, the folks is in. If ye've no business here you'd better go on; if you don't, shure I'll call the master.

JIM. Yes, and if he can't settle you, I'll lend a hand.

BUR. Don't come too near me, bobby, or I'll blow you away. Pretty child, that. Looks like his father. Come here, bubby!

CHILD. [*Clings to Molly*] No!

BUR. Don't be afraid of me, sonny, I'm a friend.

MOL. None of your decait now.

BUR. I'm a friend of his mother's, I tell you; look at this. [*Shows letters*] A little note for the lady herself—Mrs. Adrianse.

MOL. Shure, so it is.

BUR. Didn't I tell you I was a friend.

JIM. [*R.C., to Molly*] Don't believe him. [*To Burritt*] Where'd you get it?

BUR. I won't tell you, I'll tell the pretty girl there; you've no business with the lady's secrets, but I guess the girl knows 'em. Let the girl alone for that.

MOL. Jimmy, just stand forninst the dure. Don't go far.

JIM. I won't. There's no telling when I may be wanted. I'll be handy. [*Goes up to door, L.C.*]

BUR. [*Gets close to her, affecting mystery*] This here's from Captain Lynde.

MOL. Shure he's the foine gintleman.

BUR. Tiptop fellow; the ladies all love him, don't they?

MOL. He has such a way wid him. Shure, they couldn't help it.

BUR. Now you see, he gives me this letter, and he says, "See the pretty girl, and give it to her to give her mistress."

MOL. So I will. Jimmy, take the child.

BUR. Where's he going?

MOL. Out for a drive.

Bur. With his mother?

Mol. No, with Jimmy and the coachman. Take him along, Jim.

Jim. [*C.*] All right, Master Alfred. Come along, my hearty. [*Aside to Molly*] I say, keep your eyes open, and your mouth shut, with that fellow. I don't like him. [*Carries the child out on his shoulders, L.C.*]

Bur. [*Calling after him*] Take precious care of him, Jimmy—how I loves the pet—I'm fond of children myself. [*To Molly*] I say, if I was you, I wouldn't let Mrs. Ten Eyck or Mrs. De Witt see you give this letter to your missus. I guess it's pretty private and all that. I say, how is the duchess, as they call her? You see I know the whole family. All pretty mad at Adrianse, ain't they—he was a bad fellow, wasn't he—they call him pretty hard names, now, I dare say, eh?

Mol. I don't listen at doors, and I can't say. If you know so much, you can't want any stories from me; give me the letter. [*Going, R.*] Shure, is there an answer?

Bur. Yes—I'll wait for it. [*Molly runs off, R. door, he looks after her, then takes out notebook*] Now for my wady megum. Plan successful—saw the captain—pretended to be general errand porter—bait took—hired me for confidential messenger—promised me fifty dollars—paid fifty cents down— first service, gave me letter to carry to Mrs. Adrianse; I did so—looked through it with my double microscope investigator, found it to be a request for leave to call and tender his consolation—commenced "Dear Fanny," and ended: "Your affectionate friend, Edward." There. [*Closes book and rises*] Now for my personal observations. Front door opening on garden—bolt lock—small bed—large bed—little shoes—little hat—nurse and child's room. [*Comes forward*] Good enough.

Jitt. [*From room, L.2.E.*] That's it. That's it, exactly.

Bur. What's that? Blessed if it ain't Jitt's voice. I hope he ain't on the other side. It would go agin me to circumvent him. [*Sneaks up back. Lu enters, L.D.2.E.*]

Lu. Here's the room, sir, you can look at it. [*Jitt enters, L.D.2.E.*]

Jitt. Just about the size, not too much furniture, therefore not too dangerous for the experiment.

Lu. [*Sees Burritt*] Why there's your dirty man, again.

Jitt. Eh? Why, Burritt!

Lu. What did he come for? I told you in my letter I only wanted *you*.

Jitt. [*Aside*] Hem! What does he want? [*Burritt signs to him*] Excuse me. [*To Lu*]

Lu. [*Crosses behind, and off, L.2.E.*] Well, you call me when you get rid of him. [*Goes off, gathers her skirts from Burritt*]

Jitt. [*L.*] What is it? What are you doing here?

Bur. [*R.*] One word, governor, whose side are you on?

Jitt. That lady's.

Bur. Oh, then you ain't into the Adrianse quarrel?

Jitt. No, I'm not retained in that.

Bur. All right, then, that's my job.

Jitt. Can't you get me in?

Bur. You can do it yourself, now you're here. Go for the wife and her mother; things have got to come to law, yet. I'm for the husband. I always like to know there's a gentleman on the other side to work agin.

Lu. [*Looking out*] Ain't he gone yet?

Jitt. [*C.*] Get out, now.

Bur. [*R.*] I'm waiting for an answer to a letter I brought, but I don't mind the grass outside. Your servant, ma'am. [*Goes out and throws himself on grass, smoking*]

Lu. [*L.*] I thought he'd never go. I don't want to meet any horrid creatures in the business, but yourself. [*Both sit*]

Jitt. Shan't occur again. Now to the point. Your husband made up for his former brutality by paying all your bills, asking your pardon, and taking you on an overland excursion to California and Utah?

Lu. Yes, it was splendid while it lasted, but when we came back he got to be just as bad as ever—in fact, worse.

Jitt. Any violence?

Lu. Only to my feelings.

Jitt. Suspicious? Jealous?

Lu. Just the reverse. He says I may do what I like. I may buy all New York up, and beggar him—says all he can do is to submit to my whims. Did you ever hear such outrageous language?

Jitt. Yes, he's as bad as he was before, no doubt about it. In fact, my dear madam, you can never be happy with him, and you must get a divorce somehow.

Lu. I must have it. I have suffered in silence, but I can bear it no longer.

Jitt. Have you tried whether your husband would consent to a separation?

Lu. No, I want him to propose it, so I can go into hysterics, and touch his heart.

Jitt. And he won't?

Lu. No, he won't, and yet he goes on torturing me with his pretended resignation.

Jitt. Well, I see nothing left for you but to put in operation the little stratagem I suggested; you must lead him into some ebullition of anger, in which he will forget himself.

Lu. But suppose he forgets me, too?

JITT. If he does, his case is settled. If he'll only give you a pinch on the arm, or a shove with the hand, or a box on the ear—but that is too great a legal luxury to expect.

LU. What if he should?

JITT. I undertake to get you a cast-iron divorce for the faintest tap on the cheek.

LU. It's no use—he'd never do it.

JITT. Try him.

LU. He never flies into a passion, he never has any ebullitions of anything.

JITT. Oh, bother, you don't make an effort.

LU. I don't?

JITT. Of course not. You're an angel. I'll bet now you've never alluded to his age—to his ugliness—of course not. Have you ever told him of the splendid young fellow you'll marry, when he's gone under? I thought not.

LU. He'd only laugh at me, and tell me I didn't mean it. That's how he always crushes me, by telling me I never mean any harm.

JITT. Well, you just try it as an experiment. If you don't, then make up your mind to endure him as your lifelong tormentor.

LU. But he's always in such good humor.

JITT. If you can't get him out of it you are not up to the average of wives. [*Rises*]

LU. He'd provoke a saint.

JITT. You mustn't let him provoke you. Make an effort; I'll be by, we have the girl here for a witness, too—you must have witnesses to his brutality, you know. We'll be concealed, and at the moment he's worked up to an ungovernable rage we'll break forth and confront him.

LU. You are sure it will succeed?

JITT. Of course it will, and as for the result—I pledge you my honor. [*Bows low*]

LU. Your honor? Well I might as well take it, for you don't seem to need it much in your business.

JITT. Ha, ha! very good. [*Aside*] Just like the rest of 'em, when we show 'em the way out of their troubles, they always joke us on our roguery. [*Fanny enters, R.D.*]

FAN. Where is the person who brought this letter? [*Molly entering after her*]

MOL. I left him just here, ma'am. [*Exit, R.*]

JITT. I beg pardon, I think the person you inquire for is outside. Here, Burritt.

BUR. [*Gets up and comes forward*] Good enough. [*Jitt goes up to Lu. Mrs. Ten Eyck enters, R.D.*]

MRS. T. Fanny, what are you about to do?

FAN. To send my answer, mamma. Edward says he wishes to see me; I tell him he may come. [*Burritt leaning against door enters the conversation in his book*]

MRS. T. [*R., low*] Take care, my dear. This may give rise to scandal. He has not been here yet, I have kept him away. We must avoid everything that excites gossip.

FAN. I won't submit any longer to be shut up like a nun. I left Alfred because of his tyranny. Under my mother's roof, at least, I can be free.

MRS. T. But you must be politic, dear, your position is not settled.

FAN. [*Impatient movement*] Take this letter to Captain Lynde.

BUR. [*Taking letter*] This blessed minute, missus. [*Puts letter in his note-book*] Good enough. [*Exit, C.*]

FAN. I'm not playing a game of skill against my husband. I wage no war with him and have no plans. I am his wife still, and when he acts justly towards me, I am ready to go to him. I do him no harm in receiving a letter from an old friend, nor in answering it, nor in receiving Edward. Come, Lu, let's go on the lawn, we may meet baby. [*Goes to window*]

LU. [*To Jitt*] Don't go. De Witt will be here soon and I want to have this all over with. [*Comes to Mrs. Ten Eyck*] Now, ma, do be polite to Mr. Jitt, please. Don't act as if you'd never seen him before.

MRS. T. [*Crossing to L.C., to Jitt*] Pray be seated, sir. [*To Lu, L.C.*] Will you never be done with this nonsense about lawyers and divorces! You see the difficulty your sister's in?

LU. [*C.*] She's left her husband. I suppose I can do what I like with mine now. You didn't tell her it was nonsense.

MRS. T. Well, a more ungrateful girl! You deserve to be left to yourself.

LU. That's what I want.

FAN. [*Comes down to her*] Come, Lu, don't talk any more about it.

LU. [*R., weeping*] Well, but ma thinks because you have a matrimonial difficulty, nobody else has a right to one.

FAN. You foolish girl, come. [*Leads her up*]

LU. You know that I am wretched. [*Sinks on Fanny's shoulder*]

FAN. Yes, love, I do.

LU. And that I must have a separation and, and—[*Sobs. Grace enters, L.C.*]

GRACE. Why, Lu, what's the matter?

LU. Nothing. [*Snappishly*] Go up to your room. You are young and un-married and mustn't know everything, oh, oh, oh! Come, Fanny, let's go.

FAN. At last. [*Exit, L.C., with Lu, laughing*]

GRACE. [*Comes down R.C.*] Why, Aunt Clara, what's the matter?

MRS. T. Nothing. More of Louise's nonsense. Grace, my love, I want you to watch from your window and when you see Edward Lynde coming, go out and meet him before Fanny does.

GRACE. What, is Edward coming here after all the trouble?

MRS. T. He has asked permission and Fanny has foolishly given it. But until something is definitely settled between her and Adrianse they must not meet; it will only give a color to Alfred's suspicions. Tell him so.

GRACE. I had better get Harry Duncan to see him, too. We've both been making up how to reconcile Fanny and Alfred.

MRS. T. Nonsense, I don't like this getting into corners with Mr. Duncan, and this secrecy. You must discontinue it, and I don't approve of your inter- fering between Fanny and her husband at all.

GRACE. But, aunt, he said it was a work of Christian charity.

MRS. T. Christian charity is his business as a clergyman, but it's not yours. A young lady has nothing to do with these matters. [*Crosses to C.*]

GRACE. [*R.*] But, aunt, you have just told me to speak to Eddy Lynde about the same thing.

MRS. T. It's altogether different; when I tell you to do anything you may rely on its being proper.

GRACE. [*Pettishly*] And when I act on my own impulse, I suppose it's very improper.

MRS. T. [*Dignified*] That will do; go to your own room till Edward comes. [*Goes up to door*]

GRACE. [*Going, R., aside*] I'll ask Harry if he thinks it's improper. I'll believe what he says. Clergymen must know better than anyone else what's right, and he says he's always glad to advise me. [*Exit, R.1.E.*]

JITT. [*Who has been making several attempts to talk to Mrs. Ten Eyck, at last, rising*] I must get into that quarrel somehow. [*Aloud*] Beg pardon, but I don't think you like me. [*She turns away*] I thought not. But suppose, my dear madam, I have information concerning your very sad domestic afflictions which may be of service.

MRS. T. [*Sits, R.*] Information about whom?

JITT. You must be aware, of course, that we divorce lawyers have peculiar experience in these matters, and know the proper treatment for all the dis- orders of the matrimonial constitution.

MRS. T. [*Laughs*] I hardly think the present little matter demands much scientific legal treatment.

JITT. That shows how little you suspect what proceedings Mr. Adrianse is taking.

MRS. T. [*Rises, with curiosity*] Proceedings—how?

JITT. Hem! My information was acquired in my capacity as lawyer.

MRS. T. Well?

JITT. According to the—hem!—rules of the profession, it can only be imparted in my capacity as lawyer.

MRS. T. I suppose it only requires the capacity of a human being with a tongue in his head to tell what you know.

JITT. Ah, I see, you are ignorant of law. Of course, then, you don't know that I must be your legal adviser before I can speak?

MRS. T. I imagine you wish to be *hired* by me.

JITT. We don't call it hired when we speak of lawyers; we call it retained. I have no objection to be retained in the defense of a lady so deeply injured as your daughter is by a wicked and malevolent husband. Put her cause in my hands, and I will insure success.

MRS. T. But she has no cause as yet; there is only a slight misunderstanding.

JITT. [*Oratorically*] It is the cloud presaging the storm! By and by there will be lightning, and the tempest will burst.

MRS. T. How poetical! [*Laughs*]

JITT. You laugh? You think that I am trifling. What if I, unprofessionally, come to the point at once and tell you I know of a plot against your daughter, by which Mr. Adrianse—

MRS. T. [*Serious and anxious*] A plot—what is it?

JITT. Am I to be retained, to be consulted, to have charge of this matter?

MRS. T. If it is so serious, I must have legal advice.

JITT. I am retained then?

MRS. T. Yes, yes. [*Crosses to L.*] But the plot? [*Sits R. of L. table*]

JITT. A month ago, sitting in my office in New York, Mr. Adrianse entered, pale as a ghost, and threw my card on the table. "I come to you," says he, "to find the address of that detective."

MRS. T. He wanted a detective?

JITT. I gave him the address, he found Burritt—

MRS. T. And retained him?

JITT. We call it employing when we speak of detectives. He employed Burritt exclusively, paying him $25 a day—a large figure.

MRS. T. Well?

JITT. Well, what was he employed for? Don't start, compose yourself; I've seen that detective today here. He was the messenger who brought the letter from the captain to your daughter, and carried back the answer.

MRS. T. Good heavens! Then Alfred will know all.

JITT. He has got copies of both letters by this time, no doubt.

MRS. T. But the man came from Captain Lynde.

JITT. Of course; he first worms himself into the captain's confidence, and notes down every word he utters; next, he acts as messenger, brings the letter to your daughter, and hears all she's got to say; I suppose by this time he's accumulated evidence enough to go to a jury.

MRS. T. This is infamous!

JITT. So it is; but we have learned it in time to circumvent the plotters.

MRS. T. What do you advise?

JITT. See Captain Lynde and warn him; see your daughter and warn her; see Burritt and bribe him; I know the ropes, I've been at it all before.

MRS. T. Your confidence quite reassures me; what step shall we take first?

JITT. Go find your daughter; I will seek the captain and Burritt.

MRS. T. She's in the garden—I will go at once. [*Exit, L.C.*]

JITT. [*Takes out memorandum-book*] "Adrianse *vs.* Adrianse." Retained this day for wife—advised, um, um. [*Writing*] Two daughters—two divorces. Why can't every family do as well? It would make our profession as lucrative as a politician's. [*Enter Lu, C.*]

LU. He's coming! He's coming!

JITT. The captain?

LU. No, De Witt; he's coming over the lawn. I'm ready to drop.

JITT. Don't drop. [*Aside*] I'd quite forgotten about our friend De Witt. [*Lu sinks in chair*]

LU. Don't desert me now, Mr. Jitt, I feel so weak.

JITT. Don't, don't feel weak; I don't know what to do with weak women— there's nothing about 'em in the statutes. Wake up, this is just the time to give my plan a trial.

LU. Oh, yes! [*Starts up*] I'm to put him in the closet for a witness, while I slap your face.

JITT. No, no—you've got things mixed. Lord! She's out of her head. I hear him coming. [*Lu screams and sinks in Jitt's arms*] This is the biggest case I ever had on my hands. [*Molly runs in from R.*]

MOL. Oh, Lord! was it you, ma'am, that screamed? Shure, she's fainted!

LU. [*Recovering, gets L.*] No—I'm better now.

JITT. Then think of business—your husband's coming; let me arrange for you. This girl will make a first-rate witness, won't you?

MOL. Shure, I can make first-rate cake; but I never made a witness.

JITT. Well, some witnesses are cakes, sure enough. Come here; I want you to go into that room and close the door; if you hear any loud talking, you must remember what is said; if you hear sounds of violence, you must run out on the instant—do you understand?

MOL. Faith, I do, aisy enough. But are you and the master going to have a fight? Sure, I think he'll warm you.

JITT. Go in and be quiet.

MOL. That I will. [*Going*] Well, it's quare, anyhow. [*Exit, D.R.1.E.*]

JITT. Now, summon up your courage; remember your wrongs. Talk to him as only a wife can talk—get him to burst into a paradoxysm of rage, and he bursts the chain that binds you to him, forever. [*Exit, L.1.E.*]

LU. I know I'll make a mess of it. [*Sinks in chair, L.*] I'm as cold as ice— I wish I'd never been such a fool. [*De Witt enters, C.L.*] After all, De Witt is not so bad.

DE W. Why, Lu, my love?

LU. [*Seated, L.*] Oh—is that you?

DE W. I thought I'd run over and see you, although you told me on Tuesday you didn't care if I never came again. I know, of course, it was more of your silliness, and here I am again. [*Leans over chair and kisses her*] You dear little goosey.

LU. He's treating me like a child again. You think I am silly, do you?

DE W. [*Going to table and putting down hat and duster*] That's what you've called yourself a dozen times. Come, let's be friends. [*Returns and offers hand*]

LU. [*Rises*] It's contemptible to rake up the confessions I made in our little reconciliations. De Witt, you are a mean man.

DE W. Are you going to be as bad as ever, birdie, or, is this only a little storm that will clear away?

LU. Bad! I'm bad, am I? What'll you call me next, I wonder? What do you mean by bad, sir?

DE W. Oh, I only meant in comparison with your other moods.

LU. I'm only comparatively bad, am I? There *are worse*, are there? Oh, thank you, very much!

DE W. I wouldn't get in a rage for nothing. Just say, am I welcome or not?

LU. No, you're not!

DE W. [*Movement*] Then I'll go back.

LU. [*Seizing him*] No, you won't.

DE W. [*Laughing*] Then I won't. Anything to please you.

LU. Anything to torment me, you mean; you love to do that. [*Trying to weep, violent sobs*]

DE W. [*Approaching*] Lu, let me just say one word.

LU. [*Retreats to L.H.*] Keep your hands off me—I'm afraid.

DE W. [*Astonished*] Afraid of what?

LU. I'm afraid of your violence.

DE W. The violence of my love?

Lu. No, sir, of your anger. You are full of suppressed rage; I see it in your face. I'm afraid of you, I tell you.

De W. Ha, ha, ha! This is too good! Afraid of my violence; why, with my rheumatism you'd double me up in no time.

Lu. Likely, indeed, you *old* men are just as vicious as you can be.

De W. Old men, eh? You married me, old as I am.

Lu. With all your rheumatism, and the gout, and goodness knows what all, you'd like to box my ears often.

De W. [*Severely*] Lu—stop—you wish to make me angry.

Lu. Oh, we'll have a storm presently; Mr. Amiability can't keep his temper forever, I see.

De W. Oh, you want to try my patience, eh? Very good. [*Laughs*] But you see I knew what to expect before I married a young wife, and prepared myself.

Lu. You provoking wretch, do you mean you prepared for outbursts of temper on my part?

De W. I did. I had an organ-grinder to play all day under my window— I hired a saw-filer to file his saws a couple of hours, each day, in my back yard—I invested in some wildcat stock, and otherwise exercised my fortitude, until the wedding day.

Lu. [*Savagely, close to him*] Then you mean to say that I have a bad temper—that I'm a scold—that my voice is like a saw-grinder, and an organ-filer, and that I'm a wildcat—do you, do you?

De W. [*Laughing*] Not exactly. You misinterpret.

Lu. [*Fanning herself violently*] You dare to use language like that to me—and you won't get angry.

De W. [*Laughs*] I should be a fool to get angry with a little simpleton.

Lu. I'm a fool, am I?

De W. Oh, I don't go so far as to say that.

Lu. You'd provoke your wife if she were a saint.

De W. [*Laughing*] I should like a saint to try on.

Lu. Oh, this is too much, you deceitful, abominable—take that—[*Slaps his face. Jitt and Molly burst out, De Witt holding his face, looks from one to the other, Lu walks up and down in rage*]

Jitt. [*Oratorically*] Miserable man, what have you done? [*Crosses to C.*]

De W. [*R.*] Eh?

Jitt. With one blow you have shattered your domestic happiness to fragments, you have called upon your head the scorn of men, you have aimed a stroke at civilization, you have struck at the holiest of creation, and you have broken half a dozen statutes at a single blow!

De W. What is the idiot talking about?

JITT. Behold your victim! She flew to your bosom for protection. [*Lu sinks on chair, L.*] You have felled her to the earth. Coward!

DE W. I felled her to the earth? Are you mad?

LU. [*Aside to Jitt*] Don't say any more. It's all wrong.

JITT. What's wrong?

LU. There's a mistake.

JITT. A mistake?

LU. Instead of it being my ears that were boxed—

JITT. [*Aghast*] Well?

LU. It was his.

JITT. How could you—you make me look like a fool. [*Stage, up and down, C.*]

LU. We both do.

MOL. [*Near Lu*] Shure, I think I begin to understand now, ma'am, ah! worra, worra, more power to your arm.

LU. Molly, leave the room instantly.

MOL. I will, ma'am. [*Aside, going R.*] Aha! They all do it; wait till I get a husband! [*Exit, R.2.E.*]

DE W. [*Coming down, C.R.*] I think I understand. This was a plot of some kind against me, and this crazy person, here—

JITT. [*Comes down, C.*] Hem! Jitt, sir. Templeton Jitt, attorney and counselor, your wife's legal adviser, divorces procured without publicity, my card, sir? [*Crosses R.*]

DE W. [*C., tossing card aside, seriously*] I see. It is as bad as that, is it? I thought you a wayward child—[*Lu turns*] Don't speak, I can't bear to hear the voice of a deceitful woman. You wish to have a separation? You may have it; your lawyer here will tell you the way; get it as quickly as you can. I will fix an allowance with which you will be satisfied, and as you need money now, I leave it here [*Places wallet on table, L.*], and so I go back to the city. [*Exit, C., off L.*]

LU. [*Up after him. Jitt crosses to take money*] Oh, De Witt, don't go.

JITT. [*Hands her the wallet*] Cheer up, it's all right, at last.

LU. [*Flying at him, and throws wallet at him*] You miserable, little, plotting creature, you have ruined me! [*Angrily towards him*]

JITT. [*Behind table*] Be calm! It's all right, you are free, I'll get you the divorce in six weeks.

LU. I don't want it.

JITT. What? You must have it! I'm not going to let you lose so good an opportunity; it may never occur again.

LU. [*R.*] I shall never see him any more?

JITT. Oh, yes, you may, after you are separated.

LU. I have lost everything by my folly!

JITT. I'll get you ten thousand a year.

LU. My conscience reproaches me; he is all kindness and goodness.

JITT. So he is. We don't meet such men every day, we must make the most of them when we do. [*Puts wallet in pocket*]

LU. [*Weeping*] I'll write to him tonight, I'll explain all.

JITT. Send the letter to me, I'll take it [*Aside*], and take care of it.

LU. Will you try and see him?

JITT. I will. [*Aside*] I'll serve the papers on him myself.

LU. [*Sobbing*] Do all you can for me.

JITT. Rely on me.

LU. [*Going, R.*] Bring him back to me. Oh! Oh! Tell him, I'll do everything to please him; I never knew how generous he was, and how foolish I am; I'll put up with one new dress a week! Oh! Oh! Oh! I'll never say a cross word to him again. Oh! Oh! You mean little spider! I hate you! [*Exit, R.1E.*]

JITT. Splendid! That case goes on smoothly. I'll have 'em divorced before they know it. [*Goes up. Fanny and Captain enter, L.C.*] My fair client and the gay deceiver, I must see Burritt and give him a hint. [*Exit, L.C.*]

CAPT. [*L.*] It was so good, so kind of you to permit me to come once more.

FAN. I resolved to see you against everybody's advice, because I wish to show them I am superior to any scandal that may be uttered. [*Drawing her hand away*] Do not come often; you may wish to come, because you say you always like to see me; yet that is all wrong; I am a wife and you are not my husband.

CAPT. That's a bitter truth to my ears. But I will do anything to make you happy.

FAN. It will not make me happier for you to be away; but it will please the world, and it will perhaps satisfy my husband.

CAPT. You will grieve a little, then, when I am gone?

FAN. [*R.*] I shall be sad to think a causeless jealousy has driven you from your home, for mamma's house has always been your home.

CAPT. And I had hoped to be so happy here, and to make you so happy. Only think, I had arranged for a little water party for this evening on the lake—men all hired, and the boats—and came to ask you all.

FAN. There is no harm in that. If mamma and Lu and Grace consent, we'll go.

CAPT. I shall always look back on this night as the happiest in my life. [*Gently takes her hands*]

FAN. Foolish fellow! You ought to have a wife to love; you would be good to her.

CAPT. I shall never marry, because I can love no one, as I—but there.

FAN. I'll go find mamma. [*Turns away, going up*]

CAPT. [*Crosses to R.*] And if she refuses? But she won't refuse me.

FAN. Not if you promise her to never call again. Make it your own proposal.

CAPT. It shall be done as you wish.

FAN. [*Leads him to L.*] Go into the library till I call you.

CAPT. [*Crossing to L.D.*] Good-bye for a little while. [*Taking her hands*] What a villain the man must be who causes you a moment's pain.

FAN. [*Smiling*] You would not, I suppose?

CAPT. I would lay down my life for you. [*He stops to kiss her hand, she withdraws it*]

FAN. I believe you. Go—mamma is coming. [*He exits, L. Duncan enters, C.*] What—is it you, Harry?

DUN. [*L.*] Yes, it's I.

FAN. Where have you been for the last week? [*She sits at table, R., picks up book and turns over leaves during scene*]

DUN. [*Aside*] Now that I am face to face with her, I can't find courage to mention my unpleasant errand. [*Aloud*] I've been doing duty as a sort of missionary [*Aside*] to the uncivilized and barbarous husband. [*Grace runs in door, R.2.E.*]

GRACE. I thought it was you. I saw you when you were way down the road. [*Aside*] I'm so glad you've come; I've got something to tell you.

DUN. [*L., whispering*] What is it?

GRACE. [*C., whispering*] Auntie is awful mad about our interesting ourselves about Alfred.

DUN. [*Same*] She is?

GRACE. [*Same*] Yes—she calls it interfering, and scolded me awfully. Be prudent.

DUN. [*Same*] But I ought to tell Fanny what her husband says; I owe it as a duty to them.

GRACE. [*Same*] You owe it as a duty to me, not to get me blown up about it. Alfred's big enough to deliver his own messages.

DUN. [*Same*] Well, I've put my foot in it.

GRACE. [*Same*] Then try and keep the rest of your body out of it, eh? Here's Aunt Clara; not a word about Alfred, or I don't know what'll happen.

DUN. I'll try. [*They separate and look embarrassed. Mrs. Ten Eyck enters, C.L.*]

MRS. T. [*Goes to Fanny*] Fanny, you did wrong to elude me; you know I wished to see you before Edward came.

FAN. [*Coldly, still turning over pictures*] I am always doing wrong, mamma; I suppose I shall never do the proper thing any more.

MRS. T. Well, it's done and can't be helped; we must make the best of it—why, Harry.

DUN. [*His manner is embarrassed all through the following scene, exchanges glances with Grace*] Delighted to see you, very, that is, I hope you are well.

MRS. T. Why, what's the matter?

DUN. Oh, nothing, nothing.

MRS. T. [*Looks at Grace, aside*] There is something behind all this; he must have come with a purpose, and the little minx has warned him. [*Aloud and sweetly*] Be seated, Harry. Grace, get Harry a chair. [*Crosses and sits R. of L. table*]

GRACE. [*Places a chair for Mrs. Ten Eyck first*] Oh, yes, auntie.

DUN. [*When she brings it, L., aside*] She seems all right.

GRACE. [*Same*] Don't be too sure.

MRS. T. [*Sits, L.C.*] Have you seen any of our old friends in the city? [*Grace crosses beside Mrs. Ten Eyck's chair*]

DUN. [*L.*] Hem, not particularly.

MRS. T. [*Carelessly*] Anything interesting stirring?

DUN. Um, no, nothing. [*Grace delighted*]

MRS. T. [*Aside*] He has seen Alfred and he's full of the subject.

GRACE. [*Down C.*] Harry's tired, auntie; I know he'd like to row me about the creek, wouldn't you, Harry? Let's go.

DUN. [*Up*] Certainly, most happy. [*Starts C.*]

MRS. T. Oh, don't run away. [*They stop*] Well, I see you are bent upon it, go along you foolish things.

GRACE. [*Going*] Come, Harry. [*Both C.*]

MRS. T. By the way, Harry, you've seen Alfred?

DUN. Ah, Alfred! [*Looks at Grace, Fanny looks up*]

GRACE. Oh, dear, it's all up now.

DUN. [*Aside*] I needn't say what he said. [*Aloud*] Yes, I saw him a little bit.

FAN. When did you see Alfred, Harry?

DUN. Today!

MRS. T. Ah, in the city?

DUN. Oh, no, just down in the village here.

FAN. [*Closes book and eagerly*] So near?

DUN. Yes, he said he wanted to be near.

MRS. T. His wife?

DUN. No, his child.

Mrs. T. [*Severely*] Indeed!

Grace. [*Despairingly*] You've done it.

Dun. Have I? I wish I were dumb. Tell me what to say.

Mrs. T. Do you know that Edward Lynde is here?

Dun. Yes, I saw him as I came in.

Fan. [*R.*] I suppose it would be considered very improper for him to call.

Dun. [*Looks at Grace, she nods eagerly*] Oh, very, yes, very—very improper.

Fan. [*Severely*] And the fact of the impropriety will be duly reported to my husband.

Dun. [*Grace shakes her head*] Oh, no, not at all! I won't say a word about it.

Grace. [*L.C.*] You know, Harry, we none of us wanted Edward to come.

Mrs. T. Grace, this does not concern you. [*Grace looks up cross and sullen*] Of course, we did not wish him to come, but it was natural, being an old friend, that he should call. You can tell Alfred this on your return. At least treat us fairly, although you are his agent, you know.

Dun. [*With dignity*] But I'm not his agent, I don't like the word. Any gentleman may bring a message from another.

Fan. [*Seated, R.*] A message—you have a message from Alfred?

Dun. [*To Grace*] You see, [*Doubtfully*] I can't tell a lie and say no!

Grace. [*Up L.C.*] That's the inconvenience of being a clergyman.

Fan. If Harry does not wish to speak, I will not press him. If his message is not fit to be uttered by him, it is not fit to be heard by me.

Mrs. T. [*L. at table*] I insist upon the whole truth.

Grace. [*L.C., whispers*] Try and soften it.

Dun. [*Whispers*] A good idea, I'll soften it. [*Aloud*] Of course, it's foolish for him to get angry about Lynde, but the fact is, the thought of his being near his wife maddens him, and he swears he will never—

Grace. [*Low*] Soften it, soften it—for goodness sake.

Dun. [*Low*] I will. [*Aloud*] That he can never receive Fanny again if she receives Lynde. [*Low*] Was that soft?

Grace. [*Despairing*] Too soft! [*Going up*]

Dun. Don't leave me.

Fan. [*R., at table*] That is his fixed resolve?

Mrs. T. [*Crossing to her*] My child, you cannot be thrown off like that. It is criminal to marry a girl and then cast her off for such a trifle.

Dun. [*Advancing, L.C.*] There's another thing—he spoke about you.

Grace. Why couldn't you leave that out?

Dun. But I think it very appropriate, I just remembered it.

Mrs. T. [*Breaking from Fanny, who has tried to restrain her*] I will hear it, my love. Well, sir, about me?

Dun. [*Crosses to C.*] He says you encourage Fanny in her determination to oppose his wishes, and that you render a reconciliation impossible.

Mrs. T. I have a right to stand by my child, since she has stood by me at the sacrifice of her home. I have not been an enemy of your friend so far, Mr. Duncan. I have done the best I could for him, but if he affronts me further, let him look to it.

Dun. *Mr. Duncan!* I'm scratched out. [*To Grace*]

Grace. [*L.*] We are both lost.

Mrs. T. Grace, it is very unbecoming in you to remain here listening to all this.

Grace. [*To Duncan*] I told you so. She's going to send me away.

Mrs. T. Grace!

Fan. [*Stage, R.*] Let him finish first, mamma. I do not care how many hear the shame with which he loads me in sending such messages.

Dun. I have kept the rest back, but I suppose I ought to say it all since I have said any part of it.

Fan. [*R., turns, clings to her mother*] The worst is to come.

Dun. [*L.C.*] It is for you alone.

Fan. Speak it aloud.

Dun. He says that if after this warning you continue to receive the visits of Captain Lynde—[*Pause*]

Fan. [*Scornfully*] Well, the penalty?

Dun. He will consider you unfit to have charge of his child.

Fan. Of his child?

Dun. [*L.C.*] And he will take forcible means to remove the boy to his own home.

Fan. Take my child! Mother, do you hear? He would not dare! Let him touch my child if he can.

Dun. *My* duty is done.

Fan. [*Crosses to R.C.*] Tell him from me that all is over between us. He has branded me with the last mark of disgrace, I am unworthy to rear my own child. If there is justice in the land I will have it upon him if he dares to take Alfred from me. [*Throws herself on Mrs. Ten Eyck's neck*]

Dun. It shall be my last message, and then I have done with the quarrel.

Mrs. T. [*Crosses to Duncan*] It would have been better if you had never undertaken it; I may forgive you, Mr. Duncan, but until I do, I prefer that we should not meet again.

Grace. [*At L. table*] Oh, aunt, you are going to forbid him the house?

Mrs. T. Yes, and to show him the ungrateful part he is playing towards us all, I forbid you to speak to him again.

Grace. Oh, aunt. [*Sinks in chair*]

Dun. [*Takes hat from chair*] What I did I thought it right to do. If I am right, I am willing to wait for the future to justify me. [*Advancing*] Good-bye, Grace, perhaps all will yet be well, if not, forgive me any pain I have caused you and try to forget me.

Scene 2: *An apartment in the village inn. Alfred enters, following Burritt from R.*

Bur. Well, sir, I've returned from the little expedition as you see, sir; the worst is come.

Al. The worst?

Bur. Your fears was correct, sir.

Al. That scoundrel then visits there?

Bur. Worse than that.

Al. Speak out, then, what is the worst?

Bur. She writes to him, they correspond; their infamy, sir, is got itself down to black and white.

Al. What! I'll not believe it.

Bur. I took the letters, sir; got myself hired by the captain, as I loafed about the place he's stopping at; got copies of both letters, sir. Do you want to see 'em?

Al. Do you think I wish to drive myself mad? No—destroy them. I only want to be convinced that I have not misjudged her, that she is hiding a guilty heart beneath this effrontery, and then—You say you were hired by the man—did you speak of me in any way?

Bur. Just enough to draw him out. He said he pitied you, kind of him, wasn't it, sir? Called you "poor fellow," and said you was a little touched up here. [*Points to forehead*]

Al. [*Crosses to L.*] Enough! Enough!

Bur. I pretended I'd been groom at Mrs. Ten Eyck's and knew a little of the story.

Al. I tell you I wish to hear no more. Curse my fate that makes me use such instruments as these to do such work. [*Duncan enters, L.*] What! Harry back already?

Dun. [*Moodily, gets C.*] Yes.

Al. [*C.*] What answer does she send—you need not say anything about—about that man, curse him—I know all about that; Burritt has told me.

Dun. [*C.*] Burritt?

AL. The detective; there he is.

BUR. [*R.C.*] Servant, sir.

DUN. [*Crosses to C.*] What? You have employed a detective, you have put a hound on your wife's footsteps? Alfred, this is cowardly.

AL. I must know all.

DUN. For shame! You do her an infamous wrong.

AL. Oh, you believe in her still, do you? Get married, and you'll understand women better.

DUN. I tell you, your wife is above suspicion; why, she showed me the letter Lynde wrote her.

BUR. [*R.*] Corroborates me, sir, you see.

AL. [*C.*] Oh, she did; which letter?

DUN. How do I know which letter?

BUR. The one there was least harm in, no doubt, sir.

DUN. Confound you, you rascal, what do you mean? If you utter another word, I'll throw you out at the window.

BUR. Nice language for a parson—I don't think.

AL. Come, come, the man serves me; I won't have him abused.

DUN. I tell you what it is, Adrianse, it's my solemn belief Fanny would do everything you wished, if you didn't threaten her, and insist upon obedience and all that nonsense.

AL. Has she not left my house? Has she not encouraged that man to visit her? I tell you there shall be an end of all this. What is her answer to my message?

DUN. [*C.*] Just what I expected. Since it was a threat, she will make no promise, and she will keep her child.

AL. [*Crossing to R.*] Will she? Burritt!

BUR. Ready, sir!

AL. Come to my room.

DUN. Then you don't wish me to serve you any longer?

AL. No, you pretend to be my friend and you take their part against me. I was a fool to send you there!

DUN. And I was a fool to go.

AL. [*Crosses back to C.*] You have made me feel that I have no friend but myself, and such as I pay to serve me! Come, Burritt.

DUN. Don't take the trouble to leave the room in order to get rid of me. [*Aside*] I've made a bad day of it, and I think I'd better retire from the world. [*Aloud*] Good-bye, old fellow. If it's any consolation, you may know that I'm about as wretched as you now. [*Aside, going*] This is the result of my first missionary work. The South Sea cannibals couldn't have treated me worse. [*Exit, L.1.E.*]

AL. Now he is gone—to business. The child must be taken from her.

BUR. Good enough, sir. We can get a *habeas corpus* first thing in the morning, and bring it into court.

AL. You fool! Do you suppose I mean to crawl through the dirty byways of the law to get my own flesh and blood?

BUR. But the law is the only way.

AL. Do I look like a man who would sit biting his nails and gnawing his lips behind a fool of a lawyer, in a court, when I can reach out my hand and take what I want? [*Going, R.*]

BUR. But it ain't legal.

AL. [*Turns back with vehemence*] I'm no lawyer, but I understand this: Wherever I can lay my hand on my child, I can take him—the others must go to law to get him from me.

BUR. Yes, sir, that's so.

AL. They watch him well, but I will have him. Come! [*Crosses to R.H.*]

BUR. What, tonight?

AL. They have got the alarm; tomorrow he may be out of my reach.

BUR. It's a risky business, sir, for me. I'm not a father, and if I break into houses it's felony.

AL. How much money do you want?

BUR. Perhaps I can figure it up as we go along.

AL. Name your price, then, for it must be done tonight. [*Exeunt, R.*]

SCENE 3: *Same as Scene 1. Darkness grows quite dense as scene progresses. Captain, Mrs. Ten Eyck and Fanny enter from R., with shawls, hats, etc., attired for the water party.*

CAPT. [*C., assisting Mrs. Ten Eyck with shawls*] I'm so glad you consented to come, you'll find the sail pleasant.

FAN. [*R., putting her hat on*] Mamma wishes us all to lock ourselves up, as if we were in a convent.

MRS. T. [*L.*] Well, my dear, say no more about that. If you will have your way, you must take the consequences.

CAPT. [*C., up a little*] The only consequence will be a delightful excursion and a glorious evening altogether. [*Grace enters, R.1.E.*]

GRACE. Here's your heavy wrap, aunt. [*Crosses to her*]

MRS. T. Thank you, my dear.

CAPT. [*Laughing*] Grace looks very ungracious.

MRS. T. [*Going up, L.C.*] I rely upon you to console her.

GRACE. I don't want consolation. [*Goes to Fanny*]

Capt. [*C.*] That's lucky, for I mean to devote myself to Fanny. [*Carriage heard*]

Fan. That's baby. I'm so glad he came before we went out. [*Upstage, looks off through door*]

Mrs. T. Why so, he's perfectly well.

Fan. I'm foolish, perhaps, but I did so want to see him, to know I had him still with me.

Mrs. T. What nonsense! Don't let that ridiculous talk of Harry Duncan's annoy you. Come, we must be going. [*Lu enters, R.1.E.*]

Lu. [*Dressed*] I'm ready, if you are. [*Throws herself in chair, R.*]

Capt. What, another melancholy face?

Mrs. T. I really don't know what's come over Lu.

Lu. Ruin and wretchedness has come over Lu, that's all. Don't trouble yourselves about me; otherwise I'm quite well.

Capt. Gad, it's lucky I proposed this excursion; the house would become a perfect hospital in a few days.

Fan. [*C.*] You all go. I want to see Alfred. I'll follow you. [*Crosses down, L., Mrs. Ten Eyck goes up*]

Capt. [*Crosses to her*] Oh, now—I say, don't back out at the last moment.

Fan. I'll come. Don't be afraid of that.

Mrs. T. Let us leave her, I understand her feelings. Give me your arm.

Capt. With pleasure. [*Aside, as he is going up*] This knocks my projected *tête-à-tête* in the head. [*Gives arm to Mrs. Ten Eyck and they go off, C.*]

Lu. Come, Grace, you are miserable, too, ain't you?

Grace. Yes, that I am.

Lu. Come along with me, then; we can talk over our ruin and wretchedness together. [*Both exeunt, C.L., passing Molly, who enters, followed by Jim, carrying the child in his arms, closely wrapped in shawls. Fanny runs up and meets them*]

Fan. Ah, my baby.

Mol. Whist, you'll wake him!

Fan. Is he asleep? [*Takes child tenderly*]

Jim. Fell asleep on the way home.

Fan. My darling—my darling! Who shall take you from me? [*Kisses child*]

Mol. Shure, ma'am, let me take him to his room.

Fan. No, I will take him; run and light the lamp. [*Both exeunt into room, R.C., up steps*]

Jim. Well, she loves her baby better than she loves her husband, that's clear. But they are all that way; soon as there's a baby, the old man has to

take a back seat. [*Carriage heard*] Who's that? Company at this hour?
[*Turns up lamp on table, R.*] There—can't see who it is. [*At door, L.C.*]
Old style wagon—old lady getting out. [*Mrs. Kemp entering, L.C.*]

Mrs. K. Well, Jim, that you? Don't stare so; where are the folks?

Jim. [*R.*] Gone out.

Mrs. K. What, everybody? [*Down, L.*]

Jim. Everybody but Mrs. Adrianse. She's going right away, though.
Upstairs with the baby now.

Mrs. K. Tell her I'm here; she's the one I want to see. [*Jim exit into
room, R.C.*] Rather glad the others are out of the way. If I didn't think I'd
do some good, I'd never have given my old bones such a rattling as they've
had on that road tonight. [*Fanny enters, followed by Jim*]

Fan. Why, Mrs. Kemp, what a surprise!

Mrs. K. [*L.*] Well, my precious, and how's the diamond of diamonds?

Fan. [*C.*] Baby's very well, indeed. Asleep now.

Mrs. K. [*Low*] Send that gaping goose away.

Fan. James, wait for me at the gate; I wish you to walk down to the
boat with me.

Jim. [*Upstage, R.*] Yes'm. [*Aside*] That's the way—company's always
coming when the family's going out. [*Exit, L.C. window. Fanny makes
her sit*]

Mrs. K. [*Sits, L., Fanny kneels*] My love, I've come eight miles in an
hour, which is rather hard on my venerable dobbin, to see you. I couldn't
wait till tomorrow, and you'll know the reason why, when I tell you that
Harry Duncan came for me.

Fan. [*Reserved at once*] Harry Duncan—who sent him?

Mrs. K. His own good heart, which prompts him to try every means of
saving you and your husband.

Fan. Mr. Duncan has already received discouragement enough in this
house for his interference.

Mrs. K. Yes, and he got worse from your husband. He's a martyr—poor
boy; he resembles that early Christian who was ground up between two
millstones.

Fan. Well, the meaning of all this?

Mrs. K. [*L.*] That I have come to continue his work. As I'm not in love
with any young person here, your mother can't punish me as she did him.
You must make it up with your husband.

Fan. It is useless to say that. If I were willing, he has gone too far for me
ever to recall our former love.

Mrs. K. If you can't love him, you can't, of course. But you can always
do your duty.

FAN. And that duty is?

MRS. K. To go to him at once!

FAN. And ask his pardon for having offended?

MRS. K. No, you needn't ask his, and he needn't ask yours. Go back to him, open the door, walk in with your child, "Well, Alfred, here we both are," that's all you have to say.

FAN. And make a solemn promise never again to see any man whom he dislikes?

MRS. K. Well, that's not hard, is it?

FAN. Close the door against my mother?

MRS. K. That'll come all right yet. Your mother won't die of it—I'll come over and console her.

FAN. You are trifling with me.

MRS. K. Because it is only a trifle which is making all this trouble. I know the effect upon husbands of a little submission. Give way to their wishes but the slightest bit, and they'll really let you do as you please—fight them step by step, and they become as obstinate as jackasses.

FAN. [R.] But if I go back, it will be an acknowledgment that I'm in the wrong.

MRS. K. So you are as long as you stay away.

FAN. You don't know the sting which suspicion of unfaithfulness causes a wife.

MRS. K. Don't I? There's not a wife in the world—no matter how ugly she may be—that her husband does not believe to possess some dangerous attraction for other men.

FAN. I have tried to do everything, tried to meet his changing fancies, but in vain; his torment comes from within. He was never meant for a husband, at least, not for mine.

MRS. K. That's free-love doctrine and nonsense. He was meant for what he is, and you must make the best of it. Come—there's a dear girl—listen to my advice.

FAN. I will try once more, if you think it for the best; I will write to him.

MRS. K. Go, and take the child.

FAN. No, no! I must be certain first that I will be allowed to keep him. I mean to send baby away tomorrow; I won't leave him here till I know what to expect.

MRS. K. No faith in your husband, eh? Confidence all gone? Well, you may write; but if you don't put any heart in your letter, it will be useless.

FAN. I'll write. Don't fear for the rest. If Alfred would but say the word, and lift the mantle of shame he has thrown about me. I could still respect, still love the father of my child. [In Mrs. Kemp's arms]

Mrs. K. Good! My little pearl, and he shall do it, too; I'll see to that. [*Jim appears at door*]

Jim. [*Getting R.C.*] They've sent for you, ma'am.

Mrs. K. Run along, my dear, and I'll be off, too. [*Starts up*]

Fan. You are not going to stop with us tonight?

Mrs. K. No, I'm going to see your husband and make love to him on your account.

Fan. Tonight? Now?

Mrs. K. Certainly, I never stop when I've made up my mind. Come, I'll drive you to the boat, and be off.

Fan. You have raised my courage so—I feel as if I—

Mrs. K. As if you could come with me. [*Fanny nods*] Come, my pet, that's like a true woman.

Fan. Yes, I will make the sacrifice; it will be all the greater, because I risk a last affront.

Mrs. K. No fear! Things begin to brighten.

Fan. I will follow you in all things.

Jim. [*Up R.*] Shall I wait for you, ma'am?

Fan. No—go back to the boat, tell Captain Lynde I beg to be excused—that—that—I am ill. Come, my dear friend, I will go anywhere you wish. [*Going up, C.*]

Mrs. K. Come, my darling; unless I am greatly mistaken, tomorrow will find you an entirely happy woman. [*Exeunt, L.C. window*]

Jim. [*Solus*] "Tell Captain Lynde I'm ill." I wonder who the lies are charged to in the next world which servants are compelled to tell in this. There's some game up. Nobody left in the house now except the baby and nurse. [*Goes to room, R.C.*] I say! [*Molly, top of steps, appears folding baby's things*]

Mol. Well!

Jim. All right there?

Mol. Yes.

Jim. We're all out down here. I'll turn the light down, you come and lock up after me.

Mol. Shure, I won't come down till you're gone.

Jim. Why not?

Mol. Because you'd be talking nonsense to me, and keepin' me away from the baby.

Jim. What's the harm? All the nurses leave the babies; so the comic papers say.

Mol. Go 'long wid ye, now. [*Putting things on chair*]

Jim. Ah, come down.

MOL. What'll I come for?

JIM. To hear what I've got to say to you. [*Turns lamp down on R. table*]

MOL. Don't do that! I'm afraid of you in the dark. [*Coming down, Jim clasps her, R.*]

JIM. I've got you.

MOL. [*L.*] If it wasn't for fear of waking the baby I'd scream. Ye know ye've got the advantage of me.

JIM. Walk down a little way with me.

MOL. I can't leave the child.

JIM. [*Closing the doors, L.C., and bolting them*] Come by the back door, and sit there with me.

MOL. What for?

JIM. I want to ask you an important question.

MOL. What's that?

JIM. [*Hesitating, clasping her waist and leading her, L.1.E.*] How would you like to be naturalized and become an American citizen?

MOL. An American! Shure, can I drop the Irish?

JIM. Of course—get naturalized.

MOL. How'll I get naturalized?

JIM. By marrying me.

MOL. Faith it's an expensive job, then. [*Exeunt, L.1.E. Music till end. Stage quite dark. Burritt appears at window, muffled up and using dark lantern. He tries the door, L.C. It does not yield. He returns to window, raises sash, enters quickly and softly, looks round, and then returns to window and beckons Alfred*]

BUR. [*L.*] Rather chilly these nights, sir.

AL. I do not feel it. Where is the child?

BUR. In there.

AL. Go and open the door. [*Goes off, R.*]

BUR. [*Down L.C., unlocking the door*] I don't like this, it's a thief's job.

MOL. [*Outside, L.H.*] Who's there?

BUR. He's waked the nurse. [*Puts lantern down. Molly enters, L.1.E.*]

MOL. It's so dark. I thought I saw someone moving in baby's room. I'm nearly dead with fright.

BUR. [*Seizing her*] Silence, or I'll shoot you! [*Molly screams. Fanny runs in, C.*]

FAN. What fear was it impelled me to return? Molly! [*Molly makes an effort to speak. Burritt places his hand over her mouth*] What was that? [*Noise of chairs overturning. Child calls out, "Mamma!"*] My boy! [*She runs and turns up lamp. Alfred comes down with child*]

CHILD. [*Seeing Fanny, stretches out its arms*] Mamma! Mamma!

FAN. Alfred! Husband! What would you do?

AL. Burritt, clear the way.

FAN. [*Clutching his arm*] You shall not take him from me.

AL. [*Trying to shake her off*] Let go!

FAN. Where are are you taking my child?

AL. From the miserable wretch who disgraces him and me.

FAN. Give him to me! Give him to me!

AL. Look your last on him. You will never see him more. [*Throws her off. Fanny screams, falls, C. Mollie runs to her. Alfred and Burritt exeunt with child, L.C.*]

ACT IV.

SCENE 1: *St. Augustine, Florida. An old house, on the outskirts of the old town. Music. Pam is discovered upon steps of house, R., smoking a pipe. Enter Burritt, from L.*

PAM. [R.] Well, seen him?

BUR. Yes, and got the sack at last!

PAM. Don't want you any more?

BUR. No. Paid me in full, and told me to get out; said that now he had his child, and was in a hiding-place so clean out of the world as this, he didn't fear nobody; didn't want no help.

PAM. Then it's all up with us.

BUR. Lights turned out, and the pianny shut up. We can get back to New York as lively as we like. We've made all we can ever make out of Mr. Adrianse. [*Christmas, a negro, enters, L., with a bag, or valise*]

CHRIST. Mass' Burritt, Mass' Adrianse send me with your bag, tell me to take it down to town for you.

BUR. All right, Christmas. [*Aside to Pam*] That darkey's sent by Adrianse to see that we clear out of these parts; you go on; I've got to pay my board bill here, I'll follow.

PAM. [*To Christmas*] Come along, Santa Claus! You go ahead.

CHRIST. All right, massa! Dis de way. [*Exit, R.*]

PAM. [*Cautiously coming back*] I say, Burritt.

BURR. Well!

PAM. [R.] I've got a notion we can make something of this Adrianse business yet.

BUR. [L.] No! How so?

PAM. [*Mysteriously*] Go over!

Bur. Go over what?

Pam. Sell out to the other side.

Bur. What! To his wife and mother-in-law?

Pam. Exactly. They'd pay five thousand dollars down to know where he's hiding with the child.

Bur. Do you want to insult me, young feller? Lookee here, didn't I take you on, three months ago, to learn you how to become a detective, didn't I?

Pam. [*Abashed*] Yes, sir, you did.

Bur. Then, recollect this—our reputation is everything. If we was ever found out going over to the enemy, nobody wouldn't never trust us. We travel on the confidence of the public. Go, young man, never hint no such thing no more.

Pam. All right, cap, I ask your pardon. I'll run on and catch up with the nigger. [*Exit, R.*]

Bur. I wonder if he suspects me, and was pumping. There he goes, if he stops once, or leaves the road, I'll know he's gone back to Adrianse—no, he's caught up with the—[*Mrs. Ten Eyck enters from house, L.E.*] Ah! arternoon, ma'am! [*Meeting Burritt*]

Mrs. T. [*L.*] I saw you through the blinds, in company with your assistant, but thought it prudent not to show myself.

Bur. [*R.*] Quite right, too. He's a very evil disposed young man, and he might go back to the other party and blow on us.

Mrs. T. You've just come from the ruins?

Bur. Yes'm, and a precious tumble-down old place it is for anybody, let alone a gentleman born, to hide himself in.

Mrs. T. And you assure me solemnly that my daughter's husband and child are there, and that I shall find them today.

Bur. Well, ma'am, when I wrote to Mr. Jitt, in New York, to tell you to come down here if you wanted to get on the track, I acted square.

Mrs. T. [*Giving money*] Here is the first instalment of your pay, the rest you shall have when the child is ours.

Bur. Did you act on the hint I threw out about Adrianse having gone out of his head—clean crazy?

Mrs. T. It was most timely. Your friend, Mr. Jitt, immediately applied for an order of the court to take him into custody.

Bur. [*R.*] Lord, what a spry fellow that Jitt is. Have you brought the doctors with you?

Mrs. T. One, Dr. Lang. He is accustomed to insanity in every form.

Bur. He'll have to get someone to help secure Adrianse. Luney as he is, he's a hard bit to tackle.

Mrs. T. In that case we had better take advice. Doctor, doctor, won't you come here a moment? [*Calling off at house. Dr. Lang entering from house*]

Dr. L. At your service, my dear madam.

Mrs. T. This person can tell you the state of our patient.

Dr. L. [*Eying him sharply, crosses C.*] Ah! You have seen Mr. Adrianse?

Bur. [*R.*] Yes, sir, and strangely he do act, I tell you.

Dr. L. [*Crosses C.*] He acts strangely, does he? How strangely?

Bur. Like a regular lunatic, sir.

Dr. L. That's your opinion. I want the facts.

Bur. Well, sir, in the first place, he don't say much—he's disinclined to conversation.

Dr. L. [*Smiling, glancing towards Mrs. Ten Eyck*] With you?

Bur. Yes, sir! The fact is, although I've done him a heap of work in my line, and some of it precious dirty, too, he hasn't treated me lately like one gentleman should another. He always seemed to despise me, and you know if it is despisable to do dirty work, it's just as despisable to pay for it.

Dr. L. [*C.*] Despised you, eh? Although you served his purposes so well.

Bur. Yes, he did; and yet I stuck to him until I found he was beginning to prepare to get ready for to commence to kick me out, and then I thought he was beginning to lose his reason, you see, to become a lunatic; and I considered, as I ought to do him the favor to return evil for good, and let his wife and his friends know where he and the child were concealed.

Dr. L. Oh, you always had a good heart, Burritt.

Bur. Oh, bless you, sir, I throw that in. It ain't business, but I throw it in; but, sir, believe me or not, he's gone crazy. I swore to it in the affidavits as were sent on—and I stick to it. The niggers all call him mad—Miss Penfield calls him mad—and she ought to know.

Mrs. T. [*L.*] Miss Penfield? And who is Miss Penfield?

Bur. Belongs down here—daughter of an old navy officer—lives near the ruins, and goes over there to draw 'em. She's very fond of the babby; she's the only person Mr. Adrianse allows to come near him.

Mrs. T. This seclusion, this cautiousness—are they not additional proofs of madness, doctor?

Dr. L. They point that way, of course; but what we must be convinced of is that his insanity is mental, of which the common evidences are delusions.

Mrs. T. What delusion could be greater than that his wife was false to him, when he could not even give the slightest proof of it?

Dr. L. A good many sane men, my dear madam, have suspicions of that sort without having legal evidence of the fact.

Mrs. T. But his was not suspicion, it was certainty; ask this man.

Bur. Certainty! Why, bless your medical buttons, he told me he was *sure* she had dishonored him.

Dr. L. Does the boy's health suffer?

Bur. [*R.*] Why, I says to him, says I—governor, you'll kill that boy.

Dr. L. And his answer?

Bur. [*R.*] He will live as long as his father. We will die together.

Mrs. T. [*L.*] You hear! No sane man would say a thing so heartless as that. Are you not satisfied now that you are justified in proceeding under the warrant?

Dr. L. I have proof enough to arrest him; we will see how he acts when we have done so.

Mrs. T. Burritt spoke of some assistance in securing the madman.

Dr. L. Well, let Burritt be the man to do it. [*Claps him on shoulder*]

Bur. It would rather go agin me, sir, to make a prisoner of the man that I worked for in a confidential capacity.

Dr. L. There's your soft heart again, eh?

Bur. But, then, he never made no friend of me. After all, why shouldn't I do a real good action and help him to a safe, decent lodging. This place is a killing him, and the baby, too.

Mrs. T. Come, let us lose no time.

Dr. L. [*Looking towards house*] Won't your daughter want to accompany us?

Mrs. T. It's better she should not. The sight of her husband, pale, sick, and perhaps subjected to violence, might overcome her; she knows nothing of the warrant we have for his arrest. I had to keep that from her too.

Bur. [*L.C.*] Ladies *is* rather chicken-hearted—all except you, ma'am; you are the gamest I ever see.

Dr. L. [*Crosses to him*] Lead the way, we will follow you. Take my arm, Mrs. Ten Eyck, we won't forget our manners, even when we are in the woods. [*All exeunt, L.1.E.*]

SCENE 2: *The old Convent ruins in St. Augustine. Alfred, the child, enters mounted, L.2.E., on the the back of Christmas, and driving Guinea.*

Child. Get up there, get up!

Guin. Now, horsey, begin to kick, and young massa beat him. [*They gallop around*]

Child. Whoa! Whoa!

Christ. [*R.*] G'wan' away, you young niggah, you is too frisky for the chile. You tink little massa want fast horse already? No, Massa Alfred play wid ole niggah, old family hoss—no play—dere now, see me! [*They play, Christmas takes reins in his mouth and leads round stage*]

CHILD. You ain't fast enough.

GUIN. [*Dances step or two*] Dere; didn't I tole you? G'lang yer superranerated ole wooly hoss; young massa want Dexter, me Dexter, first half mile in eleben seconds, second half in four hours, here de gait, here we go, fine span of blacks. [*Gallop around again*]

CHILD. Get up! That's it. Get up! [*Flora enters, L.2.E., carrying sketchbook*]

FLORA. What a racket you are making! Come to me, Alfred.

CHILD. [*Running to her*] I'm tired.

FLORA. [*L.*] I told you so; take him down to the water and let him sail his boat.

CHILD. No, I'll go with you.

FLORA. Where do you want me to go?

CHILD. To the river.

FLORA. [*Advancing downstage*] But perhaps papa wouldn't like it.

CHILD. Let's run away, then. [*Goes to Guinea and Christmas, who run with him towards C., when Alfred enters, R.2.E.*]

AL. [*Nervously and half savagely*] Where are you going?

GUIN. Only down to the ribber, sar!

CHRIST. Dat's all, massa.

AL. Give him to me. Have I not forbidden you to stir with him from this place? Get off to your work—go! [*Christmas and Guinea slink off, giving a couple of steps of their dance for Child, as they exeunt, off L. Alfred goes with Child, R., and sits. Flora sits by tree, L., and opens her book, then puts it down and comes to him*]

FLORA. Blame me. I told them to take him. I thought the fresh breeze would do him good; see how pale he is.

AL. You had no right. I must keep him again within the house.

FLORA. Oh, what a cross face! [*Stooping to Child*] Poor little angel. You wouldn't bury him in that gloomy place?

AL. If I can live there, he can. You took advantage when I was sick and brought him out; all that must stop now.

FLORA. Why, you ungrateful person! This is how I'm to be treated as soon as you get well, is it? After all my nice nursing; now, confess, wasn't I good to you, and did you deserve it?

AL. I didn't care what became of me. I wished to die; why didn't you let me?

FLORA. [*Lightly, kneeling to Child*] Oh, oh, oh! I'm shocked. Come, Alfred, put your fingers to your ears, papa is saying naughty things—papa is bad, he won't have any friends. [*Pulling Child affectionately to her, L.H.*]

AL. [*Sadly*] No!

FLORA. [*Changing tone*] You can make them wherever you go, even here —ever such good friends, if you would but think so.

AL. Yes, I can find more traitors to steal away my last happiness, the love of my child.

FLORA. [*Kneeling by boy and at Alfred's feet*] Tell me, little darling, would you not like to have friends?

CHILD. I want mamma.

FLORA. [*Looking up in surprise*] He speaks of her as if she were living.

AL. So all children speak of the dead.

FLORA. And she *is* dead—truly?

AL. I told you truly. I have no wife. [*Bows his head on his bosom*] She is dead.

CHILD. [*L.*] Papa, mamma is not dead.

FLORA. No, darling! [*Aside to Alfred*] Let him remain in ignorance. It is so cruel to undeceive him.

CHILD. Shall I see mamma again?

FLORA. Yes, my darling. [*To Alfred*] Let him believe so. [*To Child*] Yes, my darling, for a mother and child who love so much will surely meet again.

AL. [*Turning away*] Enough—speak no more of her.

FLORA. [*Rising*] Now, I have wounded you. I did not mean that. I would make you happy if I could. [*Child crosses to bank, L.H., and looks over pictures in portfolio*]

AL. Learn this: for the dead we have tears—for those whose sin has killed them—none.

FLORA. She was unworthy, then—even of pity?

AL. [*Tone of agony*] Peace, peace! Do not wring my secret from me. If I should speak of her, I should go mad. The thought of her has nearly made me so.

FLORA. But she was beautiful—he remembers that. [*Points to Child*] Even beauty is forgotten. You men have hard hearts. [*Sits next to him on bank*]

AL. You have learned this, have you? It is the cant of your sex, you begin early to adopt it.

FLORA. [*Light, gay tone, tempered with occasional seriousness*] But you have; don't tell me. All men think women ought to be as wise and as cold as they are. I couldn't be. If you had married me, you would have broken my heart, too.

AL. What makes you think so? You are different from her. Pshaw! What am I saying—you are but a child!

FLORA. Oh, no I'm not. I know I could fall in love—and when that comes, one is a woman. [*Rises*]

AL. [*Rises, takes C.*] Do not hasten that time. Keep it away from your life.

FLORA. [*Coquettishly*] For how long?

AL. Forever! If you have to do as I do, fly from the world.

FLORA. But I couldn't, and you cannot.

AL. [*Gloomily*] Humph!

FLORA. [*Playfully*] Do you think that these ruins, this solitude, your gloomy looks can frighten away love? If I were in love, they wouldn't frighten me.

AL. [*Smiling, rises*] You believe, then, love can do all things?

FLORA. Everything, even to bringing a smile where it has not been seen perhaps for years.

AL. [*Still smiling*] You could love like that perhaps?

FLORA. Ah, you smile still! And you, when you loved, was it not like this?

AL. [*Gloomily again, goes back to seat*] Speak no more of the past.

FLORA. Then the future. Will you always be alone? Not a single gleam of sunlight in the ruin there?

AL. Nor here! [*Sits*]

FLORA. [*Sitting beside him, taking his hand*] Let me tell you your future?

AL. It is not hard.

FLORA. No; so you shall learn it all. One day you will become weary of this place—of all about you—of me! You will say, "Good-bye, little friend," and you will go, I know not where, but some place where bright eyes and rosy cheeks will greet you. Away in the North—you will love again, you will marry, and I—[*Rises and takes C. sadly*]

AL. [*Tenderly*] Well, and you—[*She hides her face in her hands*] Why, you are not weeping? [*Drawing her hand towards him*]

FLORA. [*Pettishly*] Let me alone. [*L.*]

AL. [*R.*] Come—why these tears?

FLORA. [*Pettishly*] I'm not crying. [*Playfully*] Was I crying? Well, it was because I was foolish. [*Laughing archly*]

AL. [*Still tenderly*] There, the sun is setting; you must return home. I will go into my Timon's cave. Come, Alfred.

FLORA. I may come tomorrow?

AL. Tomorrow? Yes.

FLORA. And you are not angry with me?

AL. Angry—how could I be?

FLORA. Let me kiss little Alfred goodnight. [*Child runs to her*] There! [*Kisses him*] Good night!

CHILD. Good night. I love you.

FLORA. You love me—why?

CHILD. Because you make papa so happy. [*Crosses to Alfred. Flora looks at Alfred, smiling, yet abashed, he takes her hand*]

AL. I believe he almost speaks the truth. Good night, little friend. [*Exeunt, R.2.E. Flora looks after him; suddenly Fanny appears, L.2.E., stands upstage, L.C. Tableau for a moment*]

FLORA. [*R.*] If it were so. But he would despise me if I were to betray my secret. [*Turns to go, confronts Fanny, who stands motionless*] A stranger!

FAN. [*L.*] To you, yes, but not to your thoughts. From that grove I have unwillingly heard all.

FLORA. [*Naïvely*] Mercy on me! I thought we were alone.

FAN. Have no fear of me.

FLORA. [*Dignity*] I have no fear of anybody. I am *mistress* of all this place, of the ground you stand upon. What should I fear?

FAN. Perhaps that the love which you have so badly concealed should be known.

FLORA. And if it were, where is the harm?

FAN. You admit, then, you love this man.

FLORA. I admit nothing to you. What business has anyone to question me or him? I am free to do as I please—so is he.

FAN. [*Scornfully*] Doubtless, since he listens to you!

FLORA. [*R.*] You speak as if you knew him. What do you know of him? What have you to do with the matter at all?

FAN. Only to ask a favor, which, perhaps, you will not refuse. [*Flora thoughtfully crosses L.*] If your designs are upon him, they are certainly not upon his child. If one came who had the right to ask it, would you assist her to take away the child?

FLORA. [*Stage, L.*] To take away the child he guards so well! I know you now. You are one of those enemies whom he fears. [*Turning short on her*]

FAN. [*Wretched*] I am one of those enemies.

FLORA. [*Goes to her, tenderly*] You belong to his family, you are related to him?

FAN. I am his wife, the mother of his child.

FLORA. [*Starts back*] His wife! Oh, what have I done? How mad I have been. Oh, forgive me—forgive me!

FAN. [*Gazing sternly at her*] I do not regard you. I come only for my child. [*Going towards R.*]

FLORA. [*Impetuously*] But you shall hear me. You come in time to save me from my own folly, to spare him a crime. But it was all your fault, why did you leave him? [*Going to bank, L., sitting and burying her head in hands*]

FAN. Ask why his mad unreasoning heart made him an exile from his home.

FLORA. [*Sinks on tree, L.*] But it is dreadful, all this. If I were a wife I would not leave my husband unless a rival—but I would have no rival.

FAN. [*Approaching her*] And if he discarded you?

FLORA. I would follow him wherever he went. I would find him.

FAN. As I have done, and find another woman in my place.

FLORA. No, no! [*Starts up*] I will make my error good; I will bring him to you. You shall see how good a friend I can be.

FAN. It is useless, he will not see me. [*Crosses to L.*]

FLORA. [*Crosses to R.*] Let me but try. I know he loves you—because he does not love me.

FAN. [*R.*] I only wish to see my child.

FLORA. [*Running off, R.2.E.*] Wait here, I'll find him. [*Returning*] You mustn't hate me, I'm too little and too silly to hate; there, I'll bring him to you. [*Exit, R.2.E.*]

FAN. [*Solus*] Will he see me? There must have been a Providence directing my unwary steps that led me to this place. How still the air! Away from all the scenes that recall his anger—alone with me—perhaps the feeling of the old days will return, perhaps his love, not dead, but sorely wounded, may revive. He spoke to that woman, but without a single accent of affection. Ah, if he had but paused before he disowned me, if he had but sought to know the truth, this humiliation had been spared him and me. A footstep! I tremble! [*Retires. Flora enters, followed by Alfred, they cross to bank, L.*]

AL. My mind is ill at ease. What is this you have to tell? Speak quickly!

FLORA. How impatient you are! Sit down here. [*Leads him L.*] Just as impatient as I would be if I were married and my husband, long-lost to me, were coming back again.

AL. [*L. by bank*] You speak of feelings you know nothing of. I have trifled too long. Tomorrow you shall not come.

FLORA. [*Smiling sadly*] Tomorrow I will not come.

AL. [*L.*] I must be left in peace, or I shall seek it elsewhere.

FLORA. You shall and I will help you to it.

AL. Silly child, what jest is this?

FLORA. Proof, that even in these ruins—in this solitude, love can find you out.

AL. [*One step forward*] I will hear no more.

FLORA. Only one word, and that the truest I ever spoke and the happiest for you. Little Alfred's mother is here.

AL. [*L., down*] My wife! [*Fanny appears*] Fanny!

FLORA. Now I have made amends. [*Runs out, R.*]

AL. [*Looks around nervous and suspicious*] You are alone?

FAN. Alfred! Have you no welcome for me? [*Offers her hand*]

AL. [*L.*] You have found me at last.

FAN. Did you not know in your heart we must meet again? Have you not thought in your heart: If she comes it will be proof that she is faithful?

AL. [*His back towards her*] I have thought that you would find me out in time, because you wanted your child.

FAN. Is it not your child that I love?

AL. I have no thought of myself. If you come, it is because you have a mother's instinctive love. All women have that, even the worst.

FAN. I have no reproaches to heap on you; spare me now.

AL. What should I say to reproach you? You see me an exile from home, a man dragged down by grief and sickness. What words of mine can add to your remorse?

FAN. [*R., quite in front of him, throwing her arms about his neck*] Oh, Alfred, tell me that you do not believe me guilty of any sin.

AL. [*Calmly*] I have said that I have no charge to make.

FAN. But in your heart—in your own heart, you do not think me the vile woman you have made the world believe me?

AL. [*Calmly*] In my heart, I have tried to defend you. [*Releasing himself from her arms*]

FAN. [*Clasping her hands in agony*] And you will not say one word?

AL. [*Petulantly*] It is useless. I am not well. Even this is too much for me. [*Crosses to R.*] Though I was willing to see you. [*Music. Flora appears at R. with child, it runs to Fanny*]

CHILD. Mamma!

FAN. My darling! [*Clasps him, sinking on her knees. Alfred stands C., looking away*]

CHILD. I have loved you all the time, mamma.

FAN. Did you think mamma would never come? All the nights long she has been praying to Heaven for this happy moment.

AL. [*R.*] You might have been happy.

FAN. [*Stretches out one hand*] I thank you for this.

AL. Come, bring him into the house.

FAN. You will let me enter?

AL. [*Up R.*] I can deny you nothing with my child in your arms. [*Burritt steals in, C., rushes forward and snatches the child, which he passes to Mrs. Ten Eyck, who follows after him, accompanied by Dr. Lang*]

BUR. [*C.*] Secure the child!

AL. [*R.C.*] My God! What's this? A plot?

DR. L. [*Interposing*] Be composed, we will do you no harm.

MRS. T. Fanny, come away. [*Alfred glares at Fanny*]

FAN. [*L.*] As Heaven is above me, Alfred, I did not know of this. [*Alfred makes an angry dash towards her. Dr. Lang interposes*]

AL. Who are you?

DR. L. I am a physician.

MRS. T. Charged with your custody.

DR. L. I have a warrant for your apprehension as an insane person, and must enforce it.

AL. [*To Fanny*] This is your plot! You come to me like a thief.

FAN. I swear to you—

AL. [*R.*] Silence! would you have me strike you to my feet?

DR. L. Secure him! [*Burritt seizes him behind. Alfred struggles wildly, and is borne to the ground. The Child cries, "Papa, oh, papa!" and is held by Mrs. Ten Eyck. Fanny throws herself on her knees beside Alfred, who repulses her with gesture of scorn. Curtain, quick*]

ACT V.

SCENE: *Elegant parlors in the city house of De Witt. Time, evening. Everything rich, gay and tasteful. Duncan and Grace enter in wedding dress, L.2.C.*

DUN. [*R.*] Only a few moments more, and I shall be sure of my happiness. It seems to me it is not secure until I hear the words, "I pronounce you man and wife."

GRACE. [*R.*] Why you haven't anything to fear now, you frightened fellow; here we are, the carriages are outside, the church just around the corner, and nobody in the world objects.

DUN. Add, too, a couple of hundred invitations out, the parlors lighted, supper downstairs, the music in the hall, and above all—my determination to be married, no matter who objects.

GRACE. But it *was* so sudden after all, wasn't it? Button this for me, Harry. [*Offering glove*] To think we took advantage of auntie being away and we left alone to ourselves.

DUN. Then we had De Witt and Lu to encourage us.

GRACE. [*L.*] How nice it will be to ask Fanny to come with little Alfred, and live with us. Poor Fanny!

DUN. Do you know what I began to fear at the last moment?

GRACE. What was it?

DUN. That Fanny's unhappy experience would frighten you from every thought of wedding me.

GRACE. Ah, but you are reasonable; you are not jealous. Sit down here. [*Sit on tête-à-tête, C.*]

DUN. Yes, I am. I'm terribly jealous. If anybody else in trowsers were to fall in love with you—I don't know what I wouldn't do to him.

GRACE. I don't mind that, that's nice; but Alfred, you know, visited his jealousy upon his wife.

DUN. Poor fellow, he's helpless enough now.

GRACE. If I were Fanny, I know what I would do.

DUN. What would you do?

GRACE. Take him away from his prison, for I know it's a prison; they may call it an asylum—but it has iron bars and great gates, too. I wouldn't let the father of my child be treated so.

DUN. How can she help it? The law puts him there.

GRACE. [*R.*] No law can stand in the way of a wife's love.

DUN. Well, I blame Mrs. Ten Eyck for all this.

GRACE. No, you mustn't. Aunt Clara, I know, did what she thought was best.

DUN. There is nothing personal in what I say. I shall have no mother-in-law, nor you neither. We are independent orphans, and if we quarrel, which Heaven forbid, we shall make it up again easily by ourselves.

GRACE. And auntie mustn't come to see us after we are married? [*Pouts*]

DUN. Oh, yes, as an aunt.

GRACE. But—[*Rises*]

DUN. Ah, rebellion—[*Rises*]

GRACE. But I ought to look upon her as my mamma—not as a mere aunt.

DUN. Remember you are going to be a model wife—wife of a clergyman—pattern to the parish, an awful responsibility.

GRACE. But I mustn't commence now, must I?

DUN. Yes, practise early—say "aunt"—come, that's a good girl.

GRACE. Just let me have a little of my own way now, only once before we are married.

DUN. [*Looking at watch*] Well, that's just for ten minutes. [*Enter Mrs. Ten Eyck, R.C.*]

MRS. T. [*C.*] My darling Grace!

GRACE. Well, auntie!

MRS. T. [*With affection to Duncan*] Oh, Mr. Duncan, my last daughter has gone, too.

Dun. [*L.*] Why, what has happened to Fanny?

Mrs. T. Can you not understand? [*Embraces Grace*] Have I not always looked upon you, Grace, as my own child?

Grace. Yes, auntie.

Mrs. T. You need not have been so precipitate, my dear. All the time I was away I intended your young hearts should be made happy on my return, for I had already forgiven Harry.

Grace. And Harry had forgiven you, too, auntie.

Mrs. T. [*C.*] Forgiven me!

Dun. [*L.*] Say no more about it, my dear Mrs. Ten Eyck.

Grace. And he will always love you as—

Dun. As an aunt. I told Grace just before you came in, that as an aunt—

Mrs. T. Thanks, my dear Harry.

Grace. And when we build an addition to our house—

Mrs. T. [*Subdued vexation*] I shall be welcome, no doubt.

Grace. Oh, yes. You can come and live with us, then.

Dun. [*Aside*] I shan't enlarge it till I'm tired of life.

Mrs. T. [*C., ironically*] Ah, well, my loves, you will be happy. You are both poor, and therefore dependent on each other. You can't afford to disagree, so you will be happy. [*R.*]

Grace. And if I should ever need a friend—a *confidante*—

Mrs. T. Confide in Harry. Let no third person step between you. [*Crosses to C.*]

Dun. We won't. We shall keep so close together there won't be room.

Mrs. T. I have but one word of advice.

Grace. Yes, aunt. [*Crosses to C.*]

Mrs. T. Bear with each other's faults. It will be a hard task, I have no doubt, but it is the only way to have perfect peace. [*Goes up*]

Dun. [*Mock gravity to Grace*] I feel much chastened in spirit.

Grace. [*Same to Duncan*] Bear with my faults.

Dun. [*Same*] Yes. I'll take half of them at once and we'll be an even match. What a little stab she gave us.

Mrs. T. [*Upstage near door*] Come, my dears, the wedding party is waiting for you. Ah, a few short years ago, how happily my children were married. [*Advancing*] And then see how they suffered—what misery has been theirs. And, now, you are going to walk in the same path.

Grace. Oh, dear, don't say that.

Mrs. T. I mean you are going to be married; you don't know what is before you. [*Goes up*]

DUN. [*To Grace, crosses to C.*]   I know what I should like to leave behind us. She is cutting us up.

MRS. T. [*L.*]   But whatever betides, you have my sympathy. Come, my children. [*Aside, going up*] I think I have repaid their impertinence. [*Exit, C. and L.*]

DUN. [*Going up with Grace*]   What do you say now, Grace, to having her for a mother?

GRACE.   I think that she had better be considered as an aunt.

DUN. [*Kisses her*]   Bravo! [*Exeunt, C. and L. Kemp enters, R.1.E., goes C., looks off after party, then returns, R.*]

KEMP.   They are all gone. [*Fanny enters, R.1.E., leaning on Mrs. Kemp*] Don't be afraid! Stop here a bit, Susie, and I can catch up to them—plenty of time. [*Goes up and comes down, R.*]

FAN. [*R.*]   You cannot tell how these lights, the bustle and the gaiety of the wedding preparations trouble me.

MRS. K.   There, you are nervous again.

FAN.   No, I am past that; the feeling is cold and deadly—it is remorse. [*Crossing to seat, C.*]

KEMP.   Remorse? Nonsense! Why should you feel remorse?

FAN. [*Sinks on seat, C.*]   Everything seems clearer to me now. I see with anguish every hasty step, every false suggestion, every unwise counsel that I took. I retrace my short wedded life pace by pace; I say to myself, "Here I might have stopped, and all would have been well—this I might have left unsaid, and now be happy."

MRS. K. [*R.*]   Let me paint a different picture, my love; your husband was rash, self-willed, unthinking.

FAN.   Of whom do you speak? I only see now a man broken by misfortune, dragging out a living death. If I turn from that, I see only the generous, loving, happy heart that took me for a wife—believed, trusted, and was deceived.

MRS. K. [*L.*]   All is not yet hopeless.

FAN.   Day by day, they tell me so; but they say no more.

KEMP.   Cheer up. Dr. Lang called on me only yesterday to say that Alfred was making most rapid progress towards a cure.

FAN. [*Gazing calmly in his eye*]   Do you believe Alfred was really mad?

KEMP.   Yes, the doctors—

FAN.   The doctors thought they had conclusive proofs of his insanity, because he fell into ungovernable rage when we took his child. What think you would I do, if men came to tear that child from me now? Sit smiling—

talk reason—suffer the outrage; or fly like the tigress in defense of its young—
mindful of nothing but to save its own?

Mrs. K.   Then you believe—[L.]

Fan. [*Rising*]   That every day he lingers in that prison is an outrage on
justice.

Kemp.   Well, if I may be allowed to speak freely, I think your mother—
For a more hard-hearted, interfering—! But there, Susie don't approve of
violent language, and I'm done.

Fan.   What was I—the blindest tool that ever wrought unconsciously her
own destruction! Swayed by a puff of pride; listening to the devil of per-
versity. [*Rises*]

Mrs. K. [*R.*]   And you have no blame, then, for your mother?

Fan. [*C.*]   No blame, save for myself; my mother's course is run. [*Throws
herself in Mrs. Kemp's arms*] Your words are vain; only when he can hear
me, can forgive me, shall I find peace.

Mrs. K. [*L.*]   What do you propose to do?

Fan.   Liberate him, set him free, and ask him to choose what reparation
he exacts.

Mrs. K.   Perhaps, after all, his request would be unreasonable. He might
only ask you to refuse to see some man he did not like.

Fan.   You jest at my misery?

Mrs. K.   No, I only see Edward Lynde coming this way, and the source
of all the trouble flashed upon me.

Fan. [*Drying her eyes*]   If I asked you to let me speak with him alone,
would you think it strange?

Mrs. K.   With all my heart. [*Kissing her forehead*]

Kemp.   Certainly! We'll just be in time at the church. Come, Susie!

Mrs. K. [*Aside to Kemp, as they go out*]   There is hardly any fear of
leaving them alone now. [*Captain enters, C. and L.*]

Capt. [*To Mr. and Mrs. Kemp*]   What! Not gone to the wedding?

Mrs. K. [*Crosses to him*]   Can't you get money enough to go to Salt Lake?

Capt.   No—can't say where I could raise it. Why?

Mrs. K.   Because I think you have done mischief enough in this part of
the world. Don't look at me like a fool; you know what I mean—and you
ought to be ashamed of yourself to come here. Come, Sammy!

Kemp.   All right, Susie, dear. [*Exeunt, C. and L.*]

Capt. [*Comes down, L.*]   That's a downright old-fashioned, vulgar scolding. What can she mean? [*Sees Fanny*] I beg your pardon! [*Recognizes her*]
Why, Fanny, this is an unexpected pleasure. I feared you wouldn't be
visible tonight, but I see, Grace's wedding. You couldn't resist, weddings are

fascinating; and when a fellow is too poor, like me, to marry, he sees it done by others with peculiar zest.

FAN. Edward, is it possible for you to speak seriously?

CAPT. [*Eyeing her through glasses and aside*] Broken up—deucedly broken up, or perhaps it's the dress. [*Aloud*] Why I always talk sense.

FAN. [*C.*] If there be in your nature a single chord that vibrates to the touch of remorse, listen to me.

CAPT. [*Sits*] My dear Fanny, you may play on all the chords. I don't know if there's any tuned to remorse, but I think not. At all events I never use it. Come, don't look so doleful. Play a lively air.

FAN. This, at least, you will bear in mind. In your playday world, among the toys with which you pass your useless hours, I have no longer a place.

CAPT. [*Gets round, while speaking, to R.H.*] It's the old doll and sawdust story over again, and I don't want to hear it. I can't go down into the tomb before my time, no matter how many agreeable young ladies ask me to come down a while and talk sense there. I'd rather give 'em a hand to help 'em out. Come, now, what do you say? Jump out and let's have a little sunshine.

FAN. [*Half to herself*] Is it possible I have permitted my husband's happiness to depend upon my encouragement of such a man as this?

CAPT. Oh, your husband! You don't want that misery raked up again If he's coming back, of course I'll go off again, but if he's not, why the same old plane of friendship, you and I—[*Sits on arm of chair, puts arm about waist*]

FAN. [*Rises, stage, L.*] I tell you, between you and me there is no longer any friendship—no past—no future. The step I should have taken once, I now take, late as it is—we must never see each other again. It is now my own wish, not the command of a husband, and for that reason it is earnest and irrevocable. [*Crosses to R.*]

CAPT. [*Rises, down C.*] Well, this is a riddle.

FAN. [*R.*] They tell me that once before you kindled this flame of jealous misery, but that the victims fled from you and were saved. This time behold the end.

CAPT. Oh, I say now, I didn't steal your child nor put Adrianse in a madhouse. Don't blame me for that.

FAN. I do not blame you, I pity you, and I implore you—

CAPT. [*Comes toward her, feelingly, L.*] You implore me to see you no more?

FAN. [*Indignantly*] No, sir! but to remember this: that soon every door must be closed against you, if it is known that you bring only wretchedness to its threshold. If you would have other friends, be warned in time. As for me, think of me no more. We are strangers henceforth and forever. [*Exit, R.1.E.*]

CAPT. I oughtn't to have let her preach at all; she got an advantage over me at the last. American women are pretty fair at intrigue, but they haven't the courage to carry it out like Frenchwomen. Perhaps they'll get it in the course of time. [*Looks at watch*] Half-past, the wedding will soon be over. [*Draws on gloves*] Just in time to join 'em, and give the bride a kiss. I wonder whose carriage I shall go into. [*Looks off*] By Jove, it must be De Witt's, for here they come. Haven't seen them since their last row. What a pair of doves! [*Lu and De Witt enter, C. and L.*] Good evening, delighted I am sure. [*Lu looks at him, and passes with averted head. He stands astonished, using glass. Lu sits, L., putting on gloves*]

DE W. [*C.*] You see, the family is not disposed to smile upon you.

CAPT. [*R.C.*] By Jove, you know, I'm very badly treated. Here's two houses gone. Where am I to go when I want to go out?

DE W. I've been thinking, captain, that with the assistance of several large capitalists—married gentlemen—I'll start a joint stock company for your benefit.

CAPT. [*R.*] No!

DE W. Name of company: "The Captain Lynde Joint Stock Relief Association"; object—to raise money enough to get Captain Lynde married, and put out of the way. Every married man with a pretty wife will be sure to take a share.

CAPT. Good idea! Capital notion, old fellow. Try it! I'll drop around to your house every evening and talk it over.

DE W. No, I only talk business at my office; all my business acquaintances may call there—you understand?

CAPT. Ya'as—think I do. What hour tomorrow will it be agreeable for you to have your nose pulled?

Lu. [*Jumping up, crosses to C.*] Tell him anytime, De Witt. But don't try it by yourself, captain; it's too much for one—let it out by contract. [*Crosses to R.*]

CAPT. Haw! I will. Bye-bye. [*Going up, C.*] I say, have you seen that lawyer lately—I think they call him Jitt. [*Lu crosses to R., indignant*] Oh, you don't want to, either, I suppose. Made it all up. Well, but look out for Jitt, he's been running all over, trying to find you—better see him. [*Very mysterious*] Bye-bye! Don't forget Jitt—see Jitt. [*Exit, C. and L.*]

Lu. [*R.*] I wonder you had the patience to talk to the booby.

De W. What does he mean by telling me to see Jitt? [*Coming to her*]

Lu. [*R.*] Some of his mischief. [*Lovingly*] We have done with Jitt.

De W. So we have.

Lu. You threw the law papers he gave you into the fire, didn't you?

De W. I did. When I looked at them, I saw it was a suit for divorce he had brought in your name against me, so I kicked him out, threw them in the fire, and then I went to find you.

Lu. [*Lovingly*] The brute. I told him to see you and make it up.

De W. Instead of which he was trying to make it worse.

Lu. [*Same*] But we settled it ourselves, didn't we, love? How delightful it is for married people to trust each other! Can't they put all the divorce lawyers somewhere, and keep 'em where they won't do any damage?

De W. We will keep them outside of our doors, my love, and they'll never damage us.

Lu. Isn't it perfectly splendid to make up again on the very day Grace and Harry are married? It'll be like our own wedding. How nice it was of you to give them the wedding reception.

De W. I thought you would like it. I'm so happy, too. I must—I must have one kiss.

Lu. Somebody's coming!

De W. Let 'em come! [*Salutes her, when Jitt enters, C. from L., in great haste, followed by Burritt*]

Jitt. Stop, I forbid it! [*Aghast*]

Lu. Oh, dear! it's the horrid wretch.

Jitt. Unhappy creatures! What are you doing?

Bur. I think they was hugging, governor.

De W. Confound you! What business is this of yours? Get out of my house directly.

Lu. Both of you.

Jitt. [*Advancing, L.C.*] My afflicted friends, excuse my agitation! But this very day I learned that you had come to town together; that you were about to live together. My mind shuddered at the awful consequences.

Lu. [*R.*] What awful consequences?

Jitt. Is it possible my letter to Long Island didn't reach you?

Lu. I haven't been there for a month.

De W. Will you get out?

Bur. [*L.H.*] Don't go, governor; you're in the performance of a moral duty. Don't go!

Jitt. I won't!

DE W. [*R.C.*] You don't like to see us happily reunited, eh? It's bad for business, eh? Look here, sir! [*Takes Lu's arm*] And look here, sir! [*Kisses her*]

JITT. Wretched couple! Do you not know that you are divorced? [*Lu screams and faints on De Witt*]

DE W. Did you say divorced?

JITT. I said divorced. Here are the vouchers. You are no longer man and wife!

LU. You little wretch! [*To Jitt, C.*] Do you mean to tell me that this paper divorces us?

JITT. I do!

BUR. Flattens the old man clean out, mum.

LU. Then there—and there—and there! [*Tears it*] Now we are married again. [*Crosses to De Witt, throws arms around his neck*]

JITT. [*L.C.*] Stop! It's immoral! Tearing the papers won't do it.

BUR. [*L., picking up pieces*] Besides being a felony for to destroy the records of the court.

DE W. [*R.*] My love, we're in a very bad fix.

LU. [*R.C.*] Oh, what are we to do, what is to be done? [*Turns suddenly to Jitt*] You hear, sir! What are we to do?

JITT. Legal advice demanded. Consultation fee one hundred dollars.

LU. [*Seizes him by collar*] I'll give you a consultation fee, tell me directly what is to be done?

JITT. Ah, ugh! [*Choking*]

LU. Come, now.

JITT. What are you to do? Why get the decree set aside?

DE W. [*R.*] How long will that take?

JITT. Two or three weeks.

LU. We'll have it done. [*Suddenly to him*] Go directly and do it.

DE W. Isn't there any shorter way?

JITT. None, unless you get married over again.

LU. [*To De Witt*] We'll do it tomorrow.

DE W. We will, my love, and as for you, sir, leave the house. [*Crossing, threats to Jitt*]

JITT. [*L.C.*] You'll pay for this violence, Mr. De Witt. Burritt, you're a witness. Your wife, sir, choked me while you stood by consenting, aiding and abetting.

DE W. Will you get out, at once, or shall I do a little more on my own account?

JITT. No, sir, you need not, sir; come, Burritt, bring the fragments of the judicial decree. You'll hear from me, sir—I'll have justice yet, sir.

DE W. I hope so, and when you get it, I'll come and see you hung with pleasure.

JITT. Ugh! Come, Burritt! [*Exeunt through C. and L.*]

BUR. [*Steals back*] If you want a confidential agent, sir, one as can tell you the full extent of the villainy of that man Jitt in this matter—

DE W. Will you go out, or shall I call the servants?

BUR. Oh, no, sir! Not on my account. Well, this is as ungrateful a crowd as ever I see. [*Exit C. and off L.*]

LU. [*R.*] It's too much. To think it should come to this; to think I'm not married now after all. Lord, lord, De Witt, what's my name now?

DE W. I don't know, my love.

LU. I don't believe I've got any. [*Goes up*]

DE W. Come along, I'll give you one right off. It's not too late, we'll get married with Grace and Harry. Ha, ha! What a life of adventure.

LU. Once divorced, twice married, and the last one a great deal better and nicer and funnier than the first. Come along. [*Exeunt, C. and off L. Jenny enters, L.2.E., with child Alfred*]

JEN. There's nothing more to be seen now, Master Alfred, they've all gone off to church, and it's time for you to be going upstairs to bed.

CHILD. [*L.*] I want to wait for mamma.

JEN. Your mamma don't go to weddings, my darling; you'll see her before you go to sleep—here she comes now. [*Fanny enters, R.1.E.*]

CHILD. [*Crosses C.*] I was waiting for you, mamma.

FAN. Yes, love.

CHILD. May I stay up with you? I only want to say my prayers to you—then I'll go.

FAN. Mamma will come up to you, darling, and when you pray, remember poor papa.

CHILD. Come soon, mamma. [*Kisses her*]

JEN. I found this letter for you, ma'am. I thought I'd bring it up. [*Gives letter, then takes Child's hand*] Come, pet. [*Exeunt, R.2.E.*]

FAN. [*Sitting, C.*] From Dr. Lang. [*Opening letter*] The only comfort left me is to read his cold but honest words. [*Reads*] "I cannot say that you ought to come here to see your husband. His restoration to health is not far distant, but I beg you to wait until he is himself anxious to see you or the child. When that time comes, I am certain your meeting will be a happy one. Meanwhile trust to me as his friend and yours." [*Lets letter fall in lap*] "Wait until he is anxious to see you or the child. When that time comes, your meeting will be a happy one." How I have prayed for it, until my brain, turned with hope and fear, conjures up unreal visions of happiness, or pictures an everlasting despair. [*Her head falls upon her arm, as she bows upon chair. Alfred and Dr. Lang appear at back, from L. They pause, see Fanny and converse. Dr. Lang's manner is that of a friend. Alfred is calm and self-possessed*]

AL. Leave me for a little while, my friend, I will join you below. [*Dr. Lang retires, after warmly pressing Alfred's hand*] Fanny! [*Advances, R.*]

FAN. [*Starts up, L.*] Alfred! [*Screams, runs to his arms*] You are here. Free!

AL. [*C., gently releases himself*] Today I was strong enough for the first time to leave the doctor's house. I have sought you, for I have a few words to say.

FAN. [*Gently bowing her head*] Speak, Alfred.

AL. I know now that you were not concerned in taking my child by force. Dr. Lang has told me all that. For what I then said in my violence, I ask your pardon. [*She sinks on seat*] I also know that my imprisonment was not your work; may Heaven and you forgive me the unjust maledictions that I heaped upon you in my passion.

FAN. I forgive you everything.

AL. [*Repressed emotion*] You have my—our child.

FAN. [*Quickly*] Let me bring him to you. [*Runs R., and calls off*] Alfred!

AL. [*R.C.*] Stay! It is needless—I have not finished. In this paper provision is made for him and you. All I have I give. [*Fanny sinks in chair*] Thus, your future is provided for. This other paper is signed by me, and needs only your hand. It is called a deed of separation. In it I renounce authority over you and him. It is the perpetual guaranty of your absolute freedom. [*Going, C.*]

FAN. [*Rising*] These forms affright me! You have not spoken of yourself.

AL. Have I not made reparation enough?

FAN. I ask none, I ask what is to become of you—my husband?

AL. [*Faltering and nervous*] I have not settled it at all; my purpose is to find some retreat, where I can trouble you no more.

FAN. [*R.*] What can I do—what can I say, to prove to you that I have loved you—that I have been faithful from the beginning to the end?

AL. It is not needed; I see clearly, the fault was mine; it is best we should part.

FAN. [*R.*] We cannot part. Say that you forgive me—say that you believe in my truth!

AL. [*Points to papers*] Are not these enough? The world will see in them confession of your honor, acknowledgement of my wrong against you.

FAN. I want none of these. [*Tears papers*] I confess every other sin against you—but I have been faithful in every thought and deed.

AL. Be satisfied. I believe you to be as pure as the heaven above us.

FAN. And you will leave me after that? Tell me the promise I must make, the vow I must keep for the future, as the price of your returning love. For your child's sake you cannot leave me. Two lives—two futures hang upon a word! Alfred! Husband! I beseech you!

AL. I have thought it all over. The past is like a gulf—from either side our arms stretch forth to meet in vain. What power can bring forgetfulness, and unite us in a new life?

FAN. [*R.C., sinking on her knees, and bowing her head*] Heaven, have pity on us! [*Child runs in from R.E.*]

CHILD. Why, it's papa! Oh, papa! Have you come? [*Alfred with a cry takes the child up into his arms*] Oh, mamma, how glad you must be! [*Alfred releases the child, who runs to Fanny*] Papa will never go away again, will he, mamma?

FAN. Pray to him, darling. [*Alfred, after a struggle, turns and holds out his arms to her*]

AL. Fanny!

FAN. Alfred! [*They embrace. Music. Wedding party enter, headed by Grace and Duncan, Lu and De Witt following, Kemp and Mrs. Kemp next. Kitty Crosbie, Bridesmaids and Gentlemen after. Tableau*]

CURTAIN

THE BIG BONANZA

A Comedy of our Time, in Five Acts

From the German of Von Moser

THE BIG BONANZA

THE BIG BONANZA was not ill-named. At the time it was produced, Daly was in financial straits. The first Fifth Avenue Theatre had burned on January 1, 1873, and the new Fifth Avenue which opened on Twenty-eighth Street near Broadway after a short season at 728 Broadway, had fallen upon hard times.

The play was a bonanza to Daly in more ways than one. Not only did it relieve the momentarily desperate situation at the new Fifth Avenue Theatre, where it was acted for the first time on February 17, 1875, but it was the beginning of that long series of farce-comedies adapted from the German which were for many years the delight of New York. The original of *The Big Bonanza* was Gustav von Moser's *Ultimo,* which had appeared in Berlin in 1874. Daly followed the situations and characters of his original very closely, though transposing the scenes to New York City. The lines he rendered more freely by giving the sense rather than a literal translation of the German. The significance of *The Big Bonanza* in Daly's career is heightened by the fact that it introduced as a member of the Fifth Avenue Theatre company a young man from a well-established theatrical family of Philadelphia, John Drew. The newcomer was welcomed by most of the critics, one of whom thought he had talents that could "scarcely fail to raise him to a position of prominence as an interpreter of light comedy" (*New York Dispatch*). Another, somewhat more harsh, declared that he had "intelligence, self-possession and a certain odd sense of humor which is attractive," but he lacked "that finish and culture which are required on New York boards for the portrayal of 'walking gentlemen's' parts" (*Daily Graphic*).

Concerning the play itself, there was a marked difference of opinion, the majority of the critics disapproving pretty strongly. William Winter was caustic.

As a piece of dramatic construction or literary composition, as a picture of life and character, it has no claim to consideration. The dialogue drivels through four acts of hopeless commonplace in which there is not one spark of wit, not one bright thought, not even a gleam of smartness. The play can hardly be said to have a plot. The story involves itself without any cause, and is straightened out at the end without any reason. . . . The whole mixture is like fragments of a multitude of farces shaken up in a kaleidoscope.—*New York Tribune,* Feb. 18, 1875.

The *Herald* recognized that "the public requires this quality of dramatic composition," but thought that "it might, however, be worth while producing better work of the same class, if they are to be found." The same viewpoint was expressed somewhat more superciliously by another critic six months later when Daly revived the play in a supplemental summer season with Maurice Barrymore making his New York début in John Drew's rôle of "Bob Ruggles."

"The Big Bonanza" is one of the most remarkable instances on record of the appetite of the average American for "hash" that is warmed up. This voluminous farce was received with unbounded delight by the public. The allusions to the stock market threw all the ablebodied men into paroxysms of pleasure, and the quasi-fashionable dresses and airs of the female players were accepted as proofs supreme of histrionic genius.—*New York World,* Aug. 24, 1875.

Such critical snobbishness was assailed by the *Daily Graphic*:

["The Big Bonanza"] is the same sort of piece as "Saratoga," "Diamonds," and other plays of Bronson G. Howard's—pieces, by the way, most ingeniously and maliciously attacked by our local critics. There is a place on every modern stage for a class of pieces which is neither farce nor comedy but which has many of the characteristics of both. People go into a place of amusement to be amused, and bright dialogue, eccentric characterizations and queer and unexpected situations are sure to be pleasing. . . . The plot of "The Big Bonanza" is not worth giving, but the play abounds in humorous situations, and is constantly moving the audience to merriment. It is well mounted, the costumes are superb, and it was very admirably represented by the members of Mr. Daly's company.— Feb. 18, 1875.

The Big Bonanza was not as popular as *Divorce,* but it received 137 performances, closing the New York season on June 28, 1875. Cast changes were numerous toward the close as many of the regular members of the Fifth Avenue Theatre company left with Daly before the end of the play's run on a tour to San Francisco. The new piece was an important item in the repertoire of the touring company. In Chicago, where it was given for slightly more than two weeks beginning June 14, it was welcomed for its "downright roaring fun" in spite of being "dreadfully talky." "'The Bonanza,'" said the *Chicago Times,* "is scarcely up to what it was expected to be, and . . . is not likely to astonish the natives." San Franciscans, native or otherwise, failed to be impressed by the play when the Daly troupe arrived at the Golden Gate the latter part of July. Its failure here might be attributed to the production, only a few weeks before, of *Bulls and Bears,* Bartley Campbell's version of the same piece, were it not that all of the plays of the repertoire suffered in the same way. When the play was given in Boston, October 18, 1875, with a Boston Museum cast headed by William

Warren, a slipshod attempt seems to have been made to localize the production. Boston stores and, in some instances, Boston streets replaced New York stores and streets. It is not impossible that other revisions were made in the play from time to time, as the number of acts, as reported by the critics, varies from four to six and the printed version, though claiming five acts on the title page, actually has but four.

The play kept the stage in New York for about three years, chiefly as a starring vehicle for James Lewis. The last New York performance of which I have record occurred May 2, 1878, at the Park Theatre. Both Chicago and Boston, however, had performances in minor houses in 1885, and in the latter city a revival featuring William Courtleigh as "Bob" was favorably received on July 10, 1899.

As was usual with Daly's successes, *The Big Bonanza* was an inspiration to other playwrights. In addition to Campbell's rival, and not too successful version, there was at least one burlesque which was produced in Boston under the title of *The Two Bonanzas* several months before the Boston Museum gave its localized version. Sol Smith Russell appeared in the burlesque.

The privately printed edition of 1884 is the basis of the present text.

DRAMATIS PERSONAE AND ORIGINAL CAST

JONATHAN CAWALLADER, ESQ., *banker, broker and bondholder; in fact, the representative of "Money"* — MR. CHARLES FISHER

PROFESSOR CAWALLADER, *his cousin, an "A.M.," "M.S.," "F.G.S.," etc.; in short, the representative of "Brains"* — MR. JAMES LEWIS

UNCLE RYMPLE, *a sagacious old soul* — MR. W. DAVIDGE

BOB RUGGLES, *straight from the Big Bonanza (his first appearance in New York)* — MR. JOHN DREW

JACK LYMER, M.D., *in want of practice and a patient* — MR. B. T. RINGGOLD

MR. ALPHONSUS DE HAAS, *a scion of the ancient family of De Haases* — MR. GEORGE PARKES

MOUSER, *a party who lives by furnishing "points"* — MR. OWEN FAWCETT

CRUMPETS, *a valuable family retainer* — MR. J. W. JENNINGS

TAFFERTY, *upholsterer* — MR. W. BEEKMAN

IZARD, *cashier* — MR. J. DEVEAU

JOHN, *porter* — MR. SULLIVAN

MRS. LUCRETIA CAWALLADER, *wife of the banker, with a soul above money* — MISS ANNIE GRAHAM

EUGENIA, *her daughter, heroine of a romance beginning at the depot and lasting for eight blocks with unexpected results* — MISS FANNY DAVENPORT

MRS. CAROLINE CAWALLADER, *wife of the professor, with a soul above science* — MRS. G. H. GILBERT

VIRGIE, *her daughter, heroine of a romance tinged with dissolving views* — MISS EMILY RIGL

MLLE. DEVINCEY, *"Modes Parisienne"* — MISS NINA VARIAN

MRS. BALDER, *with a "Floor to Let"* — MISS NELLIE MORTIMER

ELIZA, *a maid at the banker's* — MISS GRIFFITHS

ACT I.

SCENE: *Parlor in the house of Jonathan Cawallader on Madison Square. Elegant furniture; bay window, L.; doors, R. Door, C., open, showing hall and street door beyond. Crumpets enters from R., carrying a wine-cooler with a pint and quart bottle of champagne on ice. He comes to table at C., as Lucretia enters from C.*

LUC. Crumpets! What are you doing with that thing in here? What is it?

CRUM. Wine on ice for Mr. Cawallader, ma'am. The usual bottle and a half. Master's standing order, ma'am. Half bottle if he comes home alone, whole bottle if he brings a friend.

LUC. Didn't I tell you never to bring them in here? Take them away instantly.

CRUM. All right, ma'am. [*Crosses to R.*] Only master'll order 'em up again the minute he comes in.

LUC. [*Sits L. of C.*] Take them away, I tell you—instantly! [*Exit Crumpets, R.*] The parlors, at least, shall not be desecrated by Mr. Cawallader's bacchanalian orgies. How did I ever marry a person with so little feeling? But he was young then. All young men are sentimental, when they're courting—but the poetry goes out of them, when they take to slippers and neglect their hair. [*Crumpets enters, C.L.*]

CRUM. Mr. Rymple, ma'am. [*Rymple enters, C.L.*]

RYM. [*Pushing past Crumpets, cheerfully*] I'll announce myself, Crumpets. [*To Mrs. Cawallader*] Ah, my dear Lu, I came to see you as fast as I could. I got your note this morning, and here I am.

LUC. I'm so glad you've come, Uncle Rymple. [*To Crumpets*] Not at home, Crumpets.

CRUM. Yes, ma'am. [*Exit, C.R.*]

RYM. Now, what is it, Lucy, eh? Another trip, eh? Do you want to go to Saratoga again, eh?

LUC. Saratoga? [*Not comprehending*]

RYM. [*R.*] Yes; don't you remember—last summer—when Cawallader wanted to go to California, and you preferred Saratoga, I dropped in occasionally every evening and called his attention to your precarious state of health and the necessity for the waters, eh?

LUC. Oh, yes, and we managed that capitally. You did it like a darling old uncle, as you are. But this time it is a more serious undertaking.

Rym. Ah! I see. A trip to Europe. You really need it. You are actually looking very ill.

Luc. [*L.C., laughs*] Am I? Well, I can be restored by a very simple and homely remedy.

Rym. Eh! So! And what's the remedy?

Luc. You! Only you!

Rym. Eh! And what's the matter to be cured?

Luc. My husband. [*Sits L. of C. table*]

Rym. I'm afraid he'll baffle my skill. [*Sits R. of table*]

Luc. You know, uncle, that for the last few years, since Eugenia went away to school, Mr. Cawallader has acquired a good many bad habits, and I have indulged him, perhaps, more than I ought.

Rym. Cawallader is a perfect model of a husband.

Luc. Oh, yes, but he has all sorts of notions about taking what he calls solid comfort.

Rym. Goodness me! What does he do?

Luc. He lives all over the house, makes a lounging place of the parlors, and has his lunch, his wine and his cigars everywhere.

Rym. Dear, dear!

Luc. We have no system. He insists on doing what he calls enjoying his own home. It was all very well, when we were alone. But our darling Eugenia is coming home fresh from school, full of the romance, of the poetry, and the dreams of a refined existence, and Mr. Cawallader's ways will either spoil the poor child if she is not wholly ethereal in soul, or will shock her, if her nature is as sensitive and delicate as mine was—once.

Rym. Why not hint it to him gently?

Luc. He is not susceptible to delicate approaches. He has no poetry in his soul.

Rym. That's bad! No poetry, eh? Sho!

Luc. [*Impressively*] The way to touch him is to excite his apprehensions about his health. You must do it, uncle. Cawallader is a practical man; convince him that champagne and cigars will cut him off suddenly, and you have him.

Rym. [*R.*] But they don't. [*Rises*] I like a glass of wine and a good cigar myself. How can I convince *him* of what I don't believe?

Luc. [*Sentimentally*] Would you hesitate to give air and sunlight to a fading rose? To nourish a drooping bird? To save your little pet, Eugenia?

Rym. But, my dear, suppose we wait and see if she droops, before we begin to humbug your husband.

Luc. [*Rises*] You never refused me a favor before, Uncle Rymple.

Rym. I didn't say I wouldn't help you, dear; but, when it comes to down-right lying—

Luc. Oh, uncle, how can you call it by that name?

Rym. [Scratching his head] The thing's no better than its name. It was christened too long ago to change now.

Caw. [Outside] That'll do, Crumpets! That'll do! See that you obey me.

Luc. There he is! [Crosses to R.] Remember what I asked! Commence at once! [Cawallader enters, R.]

Caw. You there, my dear? What, Uncle Rymple? The very man I wanted to see. [Lucretia exit, R.D., first making gesture to Rymple]

Rym. [Aside, L.] Now, he wants to see me.

Caw. You are quite a stranger in the daytime. Want anything? Anything I can do?

Rym. Well, you see, I was worried about Lucretia's health, and so I called —and—[Aside] Now, the lying begins.

Caw. She's in capital health; you ought to hear her scold.

Rym. I hope you feel quite well. Do you feel quite well? Really—do you now?

Caw. Do I? Yes, I do. What makes you look at me so?

Rym. Your color, that is, your skin, appeared to be a little—just a little bilious. [Aside] Mercy on me, how I am going it!

Caw. Bilious? [Laughing] Oh, no!

Rym. Your eyes are very queer!—Very!

Caw. Are they?

Rym. Yes. [Aside] Now I've got him.

Caw. I know what it is.

Rym. What is it?

Caw. [Touches bell] I haven't had my lunch yet.

Rym. [Aside] Mercy on me! [Crumpets enters, C.L.]

Caw. [L.] Crumpets, the large bottle, and two glasses.

Crum. Yes, sir. [Exit, R.]

Caw. [Rubbing his hands] It tastes so much better, when you have a friend to help you. [Slaps Rymple on back]

Rym. [Laughs, takes hat from sofa] Oh, I'm afraid you'll have to drink it alone.

Caw. You're not going?

Rym. I must.

Caw. Nonsense. Put down your hat and stay to lunch.

Rym. My dear nephew, when a man arrives at a certain age he must be careful. I never lunch. It might be fatal.

Caw. Stuff! When a man arrives at a certain age, he must eat and drink the more.

Rym. [*Aside*] He's right!

Caw. What's the matter?

Rym. Nothing. If you insist on your bottle, let's go to the dining-room, or your study—or let's go to the Brunswick.

Caw. Not a step out of this. Here's everything we want. [*Crumpets brings in a tray, with bottle on ice, glasses, box of cigars and a taper, which he lights*] Fill the glasses, Crumpets. [*Sits at table*] Come, uncle, your favorite. [*Pushing a glass of wine to him*] Napoleon Cabinet!

Rym. [*Mouth waters*] Napoleon Cabinet! [*After a struggle, puts on his hat and buttons his coat*] No, I'm going.

Caw. Just one glass before you go.

Rym. [*Hesitates, looks off where Lucretia went out. Takes his hat off*] Well, to please you—only a taste. [*Sighs, looks off, sits, puts his hat in his lap, and spreads his handkerchief over it*] Um! What a color! [*Sips*] Um!

Caw. How do you like it?

Rym. Delicious!

Caw. Take Mr. Rymple's hat, Crumpets. Nothing sets a man up like a glass of champagne.

Rym. My opinion, exactly. [*Remembers Lucretia and looks off*] That is—if it don't disagree with the liver.

Caw. [*Taking cigar from box*] And, after the wine, a good cigar.

Rym. [*Looking off*] Smoking? You mustn't smoke!

Caw. Why not? [*Surprised*]

Rym. Cigars affect the nervous system injuriously—the cardiac nerves—[*Crumpets lights match*]

Caw. The cardiac moonshine. If it hurts your cardiac nerves to smoke, don't do it. But as for mine—[*Puffs*]

Rym. [*Inhaling the smoke*] Those are splendid cigars. [*Snuffing*] Actual perfume.

Caw. Take one. [*Pushes box towards him*]

Rym. [*Coquetting with a cigar*] Beautiful shape. I wonder how they smoke! [*Reads label*] Ne plus ultra. [*Looks off as before*]

Caw. Yes. [*Smokes. Exit Crumpets*]

Rym. As you insist, I don't mind a puff or two. [*Lights it suddenly and puffs vigorously, hugging his knees with his hands*]

Caw. How do you like 'em?

Rym. Delicious!

Caw. [*Sipping and smoking*] Do you know, uncle, this is the most delightful hour of the day to me. And yet my wife says—

THE BIG BONANZA

RYM. [*Struck by remorse*] His wife! [*Looks off as before, and puts down his cigar and glass*]

CAW. What's the matter?

RYM. Don't you think you'd enjoy this sort of thing better at the club or somewhere?

CAW. The club? No—no clubs for me. A marble floor—marbled-top tables—spittoons—a crowd of noisy fellows at your elbow. Give me home! Quiet, peaceful and comfortable. Come, uncle, I'll give you a toast. [*Fills glasses*] Here's to home and comfort.

RYM. [*Agonized and looking off*] Home and comfort. [*Drinks hurriedly and puffs cigar*] Ha, ha! [*Recklessly*] Home and comfort. [*Lucretia enters, R.*] Mercy on me!

LUC. [*At back of table*] Here's a pretty parlor scene. Smoking, drinking and toasting. This is too much.

RYM. [*Putting his glass and cigar down, stage, R.*] L—L—Lucretia!

CAW. Well, what's the matter now?

LUC. [*To Rymple*] Is this the way you keep your promise?

RYM. My dear Lucy—I assure you—

LUC. [*Crosses to window, L., fanning smoke with her handkerchief*] Pah! What a fog!

CAW. [*Coolly*] Yes; uncle smokes very rapidly.

RYM. Oh, you tempter—I—I—good afternoon, Lucy. [*Runs to door*]

CAW. [*Crosses to R.*] Here, uncle, take your cigar with you.

RYM. Oh, you! [*Exit precipitately, C.L. Cawallader laughs*]

LUC. [*L.*] What a horrid atmosphere! [*Opens window, L.*]

CAW. Oh, my dear—my rheumatism—

LUC. It's your own fault. I don't care to be suffocated.

CAW. [*R.*] You needn't come into the room.

LUC. The vile smoke pervades the whole house. It's impossible to keep one spot sacred to purity and poetry.

CAW. Now, Lucretia, please don't begin with your poetry.

LUC. [*Sarcastically*] I forgot. I must come down to the level of your own understanding. [*Peremptorily*] Jonathan—I wish to speak seriously to you. Will you sit down, and listen like a sensible person?

CAW. Certainly—if I can find a sensible person to listen to. [*Crosses to L., shuts window, then sits*] Now, go ahead.

LUC. [*R., both sit*] You know that Eugenia returns home from school tomorrow. My Eugenia—my only child.

CAW. [*L.*] I don't see anything very shocking in that. Go on.

Luc. [*R., tenderly and enthusiastic*] She comes to us fresh as a newly budding rose. She commences a life full of hope and promise. She will be admired and courted by everyone that sees her.

Caw. Do you think so?

Luc. Picture her enslaving hundreds of hearts! At last her own is captivated—and a favored suitor plucks the trembling flower from its parent stem.

Caw. You mean, in plain English—somebody will come and ask me for her?

Luc. Someone comes to lay the treasures of his heart's devotion at her feet.

Caw. Let him come. I'm not alarmed.

Luc. He comes, I say, his heart full of love; and he finds himself in an atmosphere of cigar smoke. He stands paralyzed at the portals, and what will you say then?

Caw. Why, if he's the right sort of a fellow, I'll put him in a chair, open a fresh bottle of champagne, hand him a cigar, and make him comfortable.

Luc. [*Indignant, rises*] And you believe that he will see in you the father of his heart's idol? [*Crosses to L.*]

Caw. [*R.*] I'll wager he'll see in me the father-in-law of his heart's idol. [*Rising*] Come, come, Lucy, I've had my poetical days—and, if they're over —remember we married young.

Luc. [*Heavy sigh*] Ah! You've changed since then.

Caw. Well, and so have you. [*Puts his arm round her waist and draws her gently down front*] But let us go back to those pleasant days. Do you remember once upon a time, when the little girl whom we are expecting home tomorrow, was a little, tiny baby, hardly a year old? I was going out one evening—as I used to do—to my club, to drink and smoke with the fellows there, and I went to your room to kiss you good-bye; you were sitting near the cradle—baby was awake, and looked up at me with its big eyes, as if to say, "I know you—you are my papa! Take good care of my mamma and of little me, papa." Well, I put down my hat and my cane, and I went back to my study. There I began to work and to toil. Sometimes I sat up half the night—sometimes the whole night—with a good will, working for her and for you. You see, [*Drawing her to him and kissing her*] that was my poetry.

Luc. [*Shrugging her shoulders*] All that has changed now.

Caw. So it has. Heaven has blessed my labor. We have all we need and more—and so I take my little rest—indulge myself in my old days with a glass of wine and a good cigar.

Luc. But to sit here carousing with my stupid old uncle!

Caw. [*Down C.*] Poor old uncle, with his white hairs and his honorable years! He, too, has the right to take his comfort, although he has lost everything, not for want of toil, but for want of a hard heart. But come, come, dear. We've nothing to fear. Eugenia will be too sensible to encourage a dandy, who faints at any odor stronger than cologne.

Luc. Dandy? You call every young man of delicate susceptibilities a dandy!

Caw. My dear, if my daughter sets her heart upon any creature with the face of a man—the whims of a woman—the heart of a chicken—the dress of a fool, and the actions of a monkey—don't let me see him, or I shall begin to talk plainly. [*Crosses to L.*]

Luc. Hush. Here's Mr. De Haas! [*De Haas enters, C.L., carrying very large bouquet, meets Lucretia, kisses her hand*]

De H. [*C.*] He, he, he! I beg pardon. I hope you're quite w-w-well, Mr. Cawallader.

Caw. [*L. Gazes at him quizzically*] Quite. Thank you.

De H. It looks like an intrusion to call so early, but I wished to be among the first to offer my felicitations.

Luc. [*Surprised*] Your felicitations?

Caw. And whom are you going to felicitate, Mr. De Haas?

De H. Miss Eugenia, of course! I hope she will accept my bouquet. It's small, I know, but there's a big funeral on hand, today, and the florists have run out of w-w-white flowers.

Luc. But Eugenia will not be home till tomorrow.

De H. [*C.*] Yes—I know—it is excusable in you to arrange this little period of r-r-rest for Miss Eugenia, after her journey; but I couldn't wait. I found out your secret. I know she's here. [*Titters*]

Caw. [*Aside*] I see how it is. He's drunk—intoxicated with the smell of his bouquet. There's a young man of delicate susceptibilities for you.

Luc. But, Mr. De Haas, Eugenia has not yet arrived.

De H. Oh, but I s-s-saw her.

Caw. You saw her?

De H. Yes, in the street—with a young man.

Luc. Eugenia! My Eugenia, in the street with a young man?

De H. A rather seedy-looking young man. [*Crosses*]

Luc. [*To Cawallader*] My dear!

Caw. [*Rises*] Of course. The porter, carrying her trunk.

De H. [*R.*] Yes, he was there—the porter was there—but he was walking behind her and the young man.

Luc. But where—where was this?

De H. Just at the depot.

Caw. Ah—I see—you offered her your assistance, and dismissed the shabby young man?

De H. I couldn't, you know, Mr. Cawallader. I would have given worlds to do so, but I couldn't; I had on my twelve o'clock suit and dark gloves, so I hurried home and put on my three o'clock suit, and g-g-got this bouquet to present to her on her arrival.

Caw. [*C., aside to Lucretia*] There's poetry for you. [*Bell heard*] That's her now, I suppose. [*Eugenia, outside, C.L.*]

Eug. Papa! Mamma! Here I am! [*Runs in, in elegant travelling suit, very girlish; long braids down back*] Oh, dear mamma! [*Kisses and hugs her*] Here I am at last. [*Lucretia gets R.C.*]

Caw. My dear little girl.

De H. [*Crosses, R.C.*] My dear M-M-Miss Cawallader. [*Presents bouquet*] Permit me to offer you—

Eug. [*Crosses, R.C.*] Why, it's Mr. De Haas. They are lovely.

De H. He-he-he!

Luc. For goodness sake, Eugenia, tell me how it is you came so soon.

Eug. [*Laughs*] I know you expected me tomorrow. I did it on purpose to surprise you. The idea came to me ever so long ago, and it was so romantic, I couldn't resist it.

Luc. [*To Cawallader*] So romantic. [*Crosses to L.*] She gets that from me.

Caw. She certainly never got anything like it from me. [*To Eugenia*] My dear little daughter, I do not like surprises. Surprises by a grown-up daughter are dangerous.

Luc. [*Reproachingly*] Jonathan!

Eug. No, mamma, papa is quite right. Surprises may turn out dangerous things, and so may romantic ideas. I found that out today. Before, when I used to come home from school, there was always someone at the train to receive me, and to look after my baggage; today, I found myself all alone in the great big depot—a crowd of people pushing me about one way—another crowd pushing me another way—my valise so heavy I could hardly drag it along—a dreadful crowd of men shaking their whips at me, and shouting something—I don't know what—a policeman telling me to "go that way"— car conductors calling me to "come this way," until, finally, I was rescued by a splendid young man, who saw my helplessness. Could anything have been more fortunate, papa?

Caw. Yes. A splendid old man would have been better.

Eug. [*Archly*] I don't know about that. The young man said to me, "I beg pardon, miss, can I be of service?" I said, "Thank you, I am standing here like Scipio on the ruins of—of—[*Looking for the word*]

De H. Jerusalem.

Luc. Rome.

De H. The Hellespont. He-he-he!

EUG. No, sir! Carthage! Then he offered me his assistance *so* sweetly that I couldn't refuse. Then I told him I only lived a little way off. Then he took part of my things and gave the rest to a porter, and then we came along.

DE H. That was when I saw you!

EUG. [*R.C.*] Did you see us?

DE H. [*Titters*] Yes. I was on the other side of the street.

EUG. I didn't notice you—but I suppose that was because the young gentleman was so lively and entertaining.

LUC. [*Aside, glancing at Cawallader*] Ahem!

CAW. Very romantic! She gets it from you.

EUG. At first I was very quiet, for I was vexed, you know, to be under any obligations to a stranger, but he made me laugh so much by his fun. I never heard such funny stories.

DE H. [*Aside*] He must have been a negro minstrel. [*Titters*]

LUC. [*Weakening*] A chair, if you please, Mr. De Haas.

CAW. No more surprises, I hope, daughter!

EUG. Yes, indeed, papa! A dreadful one!

LUC. [*Starting up*] What?

EUG. Just as we were turning one of the street crossings, I hadn't noticed the crowd of carriages driving by, and all of a sudden—I didn't know how it was—I was beneath the feet of a pair of horses, which he was holding back by the curb. Oh! it would have been more than a surprise, papa, if he had not been there.

LUC. My salts, Mr. De Haas, please!

DE H. [*Crosses, L., to Lucretia*] Here are mine, my dear Mrs. Cawallader.

EUG. But it was all over in a moment, and we ran on chatting as if nothing had happened. But when we came to the house, and I turned to bid him good-bye and thank him, I saw that his coat sleeve was torn and his hand bleeding, and his face was so pale, I begged him to come in, but he refused and went away, leaning on the arm of the porter.

LUC. [*Rises*] I hope he's not seriously injured.

EUG. But he may be, papa, for he trembled all over when I shook hands with him.

CAW. I don't wonder.

EUG. And his coat was all torn.

DE H. He did look quite seedy all over.

EUG. I didn't look at his dress, Mr. De Haas. [*To Cawallader*] He had such lovely blue eyes, papa.

CAW. I'm glad to hear it. I wish you had learned his name.

EUG. Oh, I know his name, papa. His name is Robert Ruggles.

DE H. [*L.*] Ruggles, Ruggles—h-h-how common.

CAW. At all events we are greatly indebted to the young man.

EUG. I should think so, papa. Not only in thanks, but in money, for he paid the porter—I forgot all about it. Never mind, I can make him a little present. You must find out his address, papa, and thank him in person.

CAW. I shall do so, my darling.

EUG. And you must be particular in learning whether his accident is serious.

CAW. Oh, certainly—certainly!

EUG. Poor fellow! Perhaps he'll need a doctor.

CAW. Of course—of course.

EUG. And he'll want somebody to nurse him, you know, papa.

LUC. Pray, be done, child. Your father will attend to the matter. You must go up to your room now. [*Crosses to R.*]

EUG. So I must, dear papa. [*Kissing him*] You are not angry with me?

CAW. Not at all, my pet. But no more surprises.

DE H. [*Crosses to her*] My d-d-dear Miss Cawallader, permit me to offer you my sincere congratulations and—

EUG. [*Interrupting*] Oh, yes; I'll take your bouquet with me, Mr. De Haas.

DE H. And let me assure you that the j-j-joy I feel at seeing—

EUG. [*Same*] They are the loveliest flowers. Bye-bye. Come, ma. [*Exit with Lucretia, R.D.*]

DE H. [*Follows her*] Is more than I can express, and the simple tribute—[*When she is off*] the—the—[*C., comes down to Cawallader*] It must be delightful to have Miss Eugenia again under the parental roof, Mr. Cawallader.

CAW. [*Politely*] Yes.

DE H. She is looking exceedingly well.

CAW. [*Kindly*] Yes.

DE H. And s-s-seems in excellent spirits.

CAW. [*Slight yawn*] Yes.

DE H. [*Biting end of handkerchief*] It must be a joy to have such a daughter. I wish I had one.

CAW. Do you?

DE H. Fine weather today.

CAW. [*Politely*] Yes.

DE H. [*Sits R. of table; looks at watch*] But I must be going.

CAW. Yes—but what's your hurry. Sorry to lose you. [*Gets De Haas's hat and presses it on him*] Can't you stay longer?

DE H. I hardly l-l-like to intrude today.

CAW. [*Politely*] Not at all. Good-bye.

DE H. Yes—precisely. Good-bye. I'll call again. [*Exit, L.C.*]

CAW. Crumpets! [*Crumpets appears, comes down, removes wine, etc., exit R.*] Thank goodness, he's gone. The older children grow, the more trouble they bring. Here I was setting aside tomorrow for running about town looking up furnished rooms for some old friends who are coming up to stay, and now I must spend it hunting up this Mr. Ruggles. Where the deuce shall I find him? Directory first—Crumpets! Oh, here it is, had it here this morning. [*Gets book at table, L.*] Let us see, A—A, B—B, C—C, F— G—H—H, P—Q—R—. Here we are, R—Ra—Ri—Ru—Rug—Ruggles. Ruggles, Robert, undertaker; that's not the man, I'll be bound. Ruggles, Robert, colored; oh!—Ruggles, Robert, junk; that can't be he. By the way, what extraordinary occupations the Ruggles take to: Ruggles, Robert, whitewashing; Ruggles, Robert, hoop-skirts; Ruggles, Robert, police; Ruggles, R., simply R.—wet-nurse! Tut! tut—that can't be the man. Pshaw! [*Closes the book with a bang and throws it on the table*] Might as well look for a needle in a haystack. [*Lucretia enters, R.D.*]

LUC. What's the matter?

CAW. Unsuccessful search for Ruggles in the directory. Confound the fellow—why didn't he choose a better name? [*Crumpets enters, C.L., with salver and cards*]

CRUM. Professor Cawallader, Mrs. Caroline Cawallader and Miss Cawallader.

LUC. [*R., quickly*] We are not at home, Crumpets.

CAW. My dear, we must be at home to Cousin Cornelius Agassiz.

LUC. Oh, pshaw! Well, Crumpets, what are you standing there for?

CRUM. Are you at home, ma'am, or are ye not at home? I don't know.

LUC. [*Pettishly*] Show them in, stupid. [*Crumpets exit, C.L.*] I think the professor is a perfect old poke, and Caroline is as haughty as Trinity steeple, with her nonsensical airs. To be sure, Virgie is a nice girl, but how she can live with that stepmother of hers—and her father is completely henpecked in his own house. Ah! My dear Caroline! [*Goes warmly to Mrs. Cawallader, who enters, followed by Professor and Virgie. Lucretia kisses the Ladies*]

LUC. What an age since we saw you, and dear Virgie, too!

CAW. Hallo, Cornelius!

PROF. Good afternoon, Cousin Jonathan.

MRS. C. [*Shaking hands with Cawallader*] The professor is so immersed in his latest scientific explorations, that we can hardly find time to visit a friend.

VIR. [*After kissing Cawallader*] I am so anxious to see cousin Eugenia! [*The Ladies talk aside*]

CAW. [*To Professor*] Just think of it, professor, Eugenia has got home!

Prof. Got home? Where has she been?

Caw. Where has she been? Why, to school for the last four years!

Prof. Oh, ah—yes—when is she going back?

Caw. Why, she's home for good. Wake up—wake up, old boy. Come down from the planets.

Prof. Well, why didn't you say so at first? Bless my soul, how you do keep things to yourself. [*Crosses to R.C.*]

Luc. [*To Mrs. Cawallader and Virgie*] Come up to her room, she'll be delighted to see you.

Mrs. C. [*To Professor, aside*] Now remember. Try and pass an hour with your cousin without quarrelling with him as you always do.

Prof. [*Aside to her*] I? I never do.

Mrs. C. The last time you were here, you nearly upset the dining-table between you. Remember, I forbid it. [*Aloud to Lucretia*] I'm with you, my dear. Come, Virgie, my love. [*The Ladies exeunt, R.D.*]

Caw. Haven't seen you for days and days, Cousin Cornelius!

Prof. Well, to tell the truth, I was a little afraid to come—you were so excited the last time I was here.

Caw. [*Quickly*] I excited! Permit me, professor. I never get excited.

Prof. Well, somebody did. It wasn't I—I'll swear to that. I make it a rule to take things calmly, a course which my habits of study and seclusion render exceedingly easy.

Caw. You mean to say that, as I don't pore over books or lock myself up in the house—

Prof. There you go! Your invariable custom is to put a false construction on everything I say. I, who make it a rule—

Caw. Well—well—well, let's drop the subject. [*Cordially*] Take off your coat, professor. [*Assists him*] There! Now sit down and be comfortable.

Prof. Thank you! And now let me ask you how our good, dear, old Uncle Rymple is?

Caw. In the best of health. He was here today.

Prof. I'm very glad to hear it. The old gentleman must be getting on in years. Let me see—

Caw. Seventy-three.

Prof. Sev-en-ty-three. Ah! [*Shakes his head gloomily, stops suddenly*] Why do you look at me so?

Caw. I?

Prof. [*Warmly*] Yes, you! Do you think that I mean to insinuate anything about Uncle Rymple's last will and testament because I simply ask you his age?

Caw. I never dreamt of such a thing.

PROF. You have such a habit of looking at me, when I speak. I'm sure I don't care whether he's named me in his will or whether he hasn't. I make it a rule—

CAW. [*Interrupting*] Now, my dear professor, don't get provoked at my looks.

PROF. [*Excited*] Provoked! I make it a rule never to get provoked. I am not provoked! [*Angrily*]

CAW. [*Soothingly*] All right, then—all right. I was afraid from your tone—

PROF. [*Very angry tone*] My tone? You couldn't have got such an idea from my tone. I make it a rule to control the inflections of my voice. Besides, do you suppose that when I come to ask a favor of a man I would address him in a provoked tone? It's nonsense—nonsense!

CAW. Very well, then, so be it. And, by the way, as you mentioned a favor, how can I assist you? [*Patting him kindly on the shoulder*] How much?

PROF. Let me see. It's rather a large sum—quite a large sum. Three hundred dollars.

CAW. [*Hand in pocket*] Three hundred—let me see.

PROF. If it's too much—I make it a rule—

CAW. Oh, dear no! I was only thinking whether I had it in my pocket or whether—[*Examines wallet*] Here are three hundred.

PROF. Much obliged. [*Cawallader smiling*] You are smiling. What is there to laugh at about a man's poverty? [*Angrily, as he pockets the money*]

CAW. Oh, nothing. I was only thinking.

PROF. [*R.*] Thinking—what were you thinking?

CAW. [*Cheerfully*] Of the time when we were both beginning life. You were a student and I a clerk. You went to college at nine. I went to the office at seven. You got home at three. I got home at ten. You used to tease me, and say, Jonathan, you are wearing yourself out. And I smile, when I think I'm not worn out yet!

PROF. And I am, eh? Is that what you mean? Because you have amassed riches and I have only amassed knowledge! Is that what you mean? [*Cawallader leans back in chair and whistles*] What did you say?

CAW. I? Nothing.

PROF. Oh, I can read your looks. [*Rises*] You believe yourself the cleverest of the two. But let me tell you, there's a vast difference between a man who simply makes money and a man who toils with his brain.

CAW. [*Nettled*] Is there?

PROF. [*Ironically*] Now, you're getting excited.

CAW. [*Excited, rises*] No! But you seem to think that a merchant or banker who makes money does no brain work.

Prof. [*R.*] Work! Good heavens! At one o'clock you go on 'Change; you say I take that, or I take this—and an hour afterwards you walk off with your pockets full.

Caw. And I don't need brains for it, eh? What do you get for your reading and writing, day and night? What has it brought you?

Prof. [*R.*] The consciousness of progress in an elevated pursuit. If I didn't prefer glory to gain, I'd employ my faculties on your petty business, and I'd wager that I'd make more money in half the time, than all your bankers and brokers.

Caw. [*Crosses to R.*] You would?

Prof. I would. In four weeks I'd have a million.

Caw. Oh, this is too much! [*Rises, jumps up and rings the bell. Crumpets enters, C.R.*]

Crum. Mr. Izard, sir, from the office, with a telegram.

Caw. [*R.*] Izard, the cashier. The very man! Tell him to come in. [*Crumpets exit, C.L.*]

Prof. What's the matter now?

Caw. [*Crosses to Professor*] Wait a moment, you'll see. [*Izard enters, C.R.*] Ah, Izard, anything important?

Iz. [*Giving letter, R.H.*] A cable from Hamburg, sir, you'll be glad to see —thought I'd leave it as I went up town.

Caw. [*Opening envelope*] Thank you, Izard, excellent. [*Unfolds it*] Allow me, Izard, to make you acquainted with Professor Cawallader. [*They bow*] Professor Cawallader, Izard, has just deposited thirty thousand dollars with us. [*Taps his pocket, as if he had it there*] He wishes to speculate on 'Change. He will retain control of the operations, and instruct you day by day how to invest, and you will send him a statement every evening.

Iz. [*R.*] Yes, sir. [*Bows to Professor and Cawallader. Aside*] Nobody would have supposed he had so much money. [*Aloud*] Is that all? [*Cawallader bows*] Good day, sir. Good afternoon, sir. [*To Professor, who bows awkwardly. Izard exit, C.L.*]

Prof. [*Going up*] I understand you, and I accept your challenge. [*Rises and buttons his coat*] You have treated me systematically like a child. I will show you that it is child's play to make money. For the next four weeks I shall descend to your petty trade of haggling and shaving.

Caw. You believe that fortunes are made by haggling and shaving? I warn you that all your gigantic intellect will be taxed to escape with the clothes on your back and the hair on your head.

Prof. [*Getting warm*] Pah! Pah!

Caw. [*Getting excited*] Why, any of the brokers on 'Change could write as good a book as you, any day.

PROF. [*Excited, up and down stage*]   Could they?

CAW. [*Ditto*]   It's nothing but paste and ink, after all. I do more writing than you every day.

PROF. [*Ditto*]   Writing! Bills! Checks! Notes! Rags—nothing but rags. It takes no genius to cheat, I fancy.

CAW. [*Ditto*]   Cheat! This is too much. In four weeks you'll—But don't come near me when the money's gone!

PROF.   Now you're throwing your paltry three hundred dollars in my face.

CAW.   You're out of your senses.

PROF.   Now don't get mad!

CAW.   Mad! [*Raps Professor's hat on table with stick*] Who's mad?

PROF. [*Making for his hat*]   My hat!

CAW.   That's right, save it. You'll want it, in four weeks. [*Throws chair aside*] Cheat! Cheat indeed!

PROF.   By this day month—[*Rapping on table with stick*]

CAW.   You'll be in the almshouse. [*Rapping on table. Lucretia, Mrs. Cawallader, Virgie and Eugenia enter, precipitately, R.D.*]

MRS. C.   Professor!

VIR.   Papa!

LUC.   Jonathan!

EUG.   Father!

PROF. [*Shaking his stick*]   In four weeks!

MRS. C.   Cornelius!

PROF.   Let me alone! [*The wives seize their husbands; the young ladies get between beseechingly*]

CURTAIN

[*For second tableau: Professor in doorway, his wife and daughter pushing him off; Cawallader on sofa, Eugenia and Lucretia about him*]

SECOND CURTAIN

ACT II.

SCENE: *Parlor in Professor Cawallader's house. Very plain, a sort of study and parlor combined. Professor's desk, R., door, C., door, R. Plain chintz furniture. The Professor is at his desk, R., looking over accounts on large sheets. He rises and knocks his head.*

PROF.   How can any human being possibly understand this confounded stock jargon. First it takes what the papers call an "upward tendency," and I buy, whereupon it "fluctuates," and I dance in doubt. Then it takes a "plunge," and I sell, then it "rallies," and my misery begins again. [*Looks at paper*] "Lake Shore," that's another concern I've dipped into. They told me on the street it was a lively stock; money to be made in it by a man of brains. Well, I invested and found it so lively I couldn't catch anything for a week. Then it "declined" and I caught it. [*Looks at paper*] "Northwest." That gives a definite idea of what you've got, don't it? I bought five hundred "Northwest's," and now I don't know at which point of the compass to look for my money. [*Mouser enters, C.R., with a bundle of shabby books*]

Mous. [*R.*] I've got it, professor. I've got 'em.

Prof. Eh? What? What have you got?

Mous. [*Opens package*] The work you have been looking for so long. "Killbobbin's Treatise on the Geological Formations and Encrustations of the Rocky Ridge of the Great Northwest." [*Hands them all to him*] A splendid copy—only two or three dozen leaves missing—and very cheap.

Prof. [*Throws books aside*] Hang the Geological Formations of the Rocky Ridge. Have you got the Post?

Mous. [*Astonished, crosses to L.*] Yes, sir; here it is. [*Gives it, then aside*] Sent me a month ago to hunt that book up, and now pitches it aside to read newspapers. He never read a newspaper before. [*Picks up books and puts them on table*]

Prof. [*Who has feverishly opened the paper to the money article*] "The market opened lively with a demand for speculative shares by those who have been 'short' of the leading stocks"—now what the devil does that mean?

Mous. [*Amazed*] Stocks? Shares? Short? Why, sir, that's what I hear continually at my bookstand down near the Exchange. The brokers collect round my corner every day.

Prof. Do they? Then you must know all about it. I have observed that you are very intelligent for a secondhand bookseller, Mouser. And so you've heard the brokers talk, eh?

Mous. Oh, yes, sir! Oh I've got the whole of Wall Street by heart. I know their secrets.

Prof. [*R., ardently*] Indeed, tell me—[*Checking himself*] I merely ask out of curiosity, you know. Now, for instance—what does "Short" mean, eh?

Mous. "Short," sir, is when you haven't got it.

Prof. Oho! Then I suppose "Long" means you've got too much of it?

Mous. Yes, sir.

Prof. [*Aside, looks at paper on desk*] I think I must be long.

Mous. And if I had money now, sir, I know where I could double it in a month.

Prof. [*Catches his arm*] Do you? Where? [*Excitedly*]

Mous. Why, sir, no later than yesterday, I heard two gentlemen talking confidentially.

Prof. [*Catches his arm*] Yes.

Mous. [*Turns round in pain*] Oh!

Prof. I beg pardon. Go on. You heard two gentlemen—well?

Mous. They were talking, and says one to the other in a whisper, "If you want to clear a big pile—sell Bonanza!"

Prof. Sell Bananas?

Mous. [*L.*] No—Bonanza.

Prof. What's Bonanza?

Mous. The stock of the big silver mine just discovered out West, and the two gentlemen agreed that Bonanza stock would take a turn in a month— and there were millions to be cleared.

Prof. Is it possible? [*Aside*] Here's a valuable piece of information. How can I sell Bonanza? I must sell Bonanza, and right away. But how can I sell it, if I haven't got it? [*Aloud*] Thank you, Mouser, much obliged. That's all this morning, Mouser. [*Aside*] Sell Bonanza. [*Coming down, L.*]

Mous. [*Going up*] I say, sir. [*Fingering his hat*] The information I gave you; you know what they call it on the street, sir?

Prof. No; what do they call it?

Mous. "A point." I've given you a point, sir; and when a man gives another man a point, sir, why he naturally expects—hem—hem—

Prof. Does he? Is that the custom, Mouser?

Mous. Oh, yes, sir! always on the street.

Prof. [*Doubtfully*] This is in the house, you know. However, here's a dollar, Mouser, for this point.

Mous. Thank you, sir. All right, sir; I'll go down to Wall Street right off, sir, and get a few more points for you.

Prof. Do.

Mous. [*Aside*] Murder! To think the governor's going into that line. Oh, I'll give him points. [*Exit, R.1.E.*]

Prof. [*Rubbing his hands*] Sell Bonanza! This is the first practical step I've taken yet. Now I see my way clear. Sell Bonanza! I must write to Izard at once and give orders. To sell Bonanza, I must get Bonanza to sell; and, of course, the more I have the more I sell. I see it all now. I'll write to Izard and order him to purchase all the Bonanza he can get, no matter what it costs. Oh, I'm a fool, am I? We'll see. Sell Bonanza. [*Exit, R. Virgie enters, C.L.*]

Vir. Papa! [*Calling after him*] There he goes, talking to himself as usual. And I wanted to speak with him about Jack. [*Jack enters, C.L.*]

Jack. Professor not here? [*Sees Virgie*] I beg pardon. [*Embarrassed*] I expected to find your father.

Vir. [*R.*] And are you frightened at finding only me?

Jack. Oh, no indeed! It's just what I—[*Checks himself*] was afraid of—I mean I hoped to—that is, to see him. I wanted to ask him a question about some chemical combinations. I have a case, a very important case, but as he isn't here, I'll—

Vir. [*R., coquettishly*] Don't go away. You and I are very old friends, Jack, and we've known each other so long, yet you treat me almost as a stranger whenever we meet, and I have to begin our acquaintance all over again every time. [*Archly*] I begin to think, Jack, that you don't like me, or you'd get acquainted and stay so.

Jack. [*Making a plunge for her*] Not like you, Virgie! Oh! if you knew!

Vir. [*Half scared*] I think it would be more friendly if you were to sit down.

Jack. Yes. [*On edge of chair*] Sometimes I can talk. There was last Saturday, I came to ask your father about—potash, and you came in—and we were alone! And I began to explain to you. [*She turns her head away, he rises*] There! you're angry again?

Vir. No, I'm not.

Jack. You tur-turned your head away.

Vir. Then, I'll look at you.

Jack. [*Sits again*] Please don't—it drives all my wits away. What was I saying?

Vir. [*Fervently*] You came to see father, and I came in.

Jack. Yes, you came in and knocked the potash all out of my head.

Vir. [*Archly*] But something came in its place, didn't it?

Jack. Ye-es, brains. [*With energy*] I say brains, because I have been a fool for years not to see that I—I—loved you.

Vir. [*Rising, stage, R.*] Oh, Jack!

Jack. I'll go at once if you're mad. [*Darts for door*]

Vir. Oh, no, please! I'm not angry.

Jack. [*Returns*] I thought you were going to call your mother.

Vir. [*Half laugh*] Mamma knows all about it!

Jack. [*Nervous*] You told her what I said to you last Saturday?

Vir. Every word.

Jack. I shall never dare to look her in the face again.

Vir. [*Taking his arm*] Oh, mamma is all right—but papa—

Jack. [*Terrified*] You didn't tell him?

Vir. No, but mamma did.

Jack. [*Nervously looking around*] I think I'd better go before he comes in.

VIR. [*Catching his hand*] No, it's all over with him. He simply said: "My daughter shall never marry a doctor—"

JACK. [*L., dropping into chair*] I knew it! Why do all parents object to their daughters marrying doctors? How do doctors ever get married? And yet some of 'em do.

VIR. You didn't let me finish. He said, "My daughter shall never marry a doctor without a practice."

JACK. [*Annoyed, crosses to R.*] Without a practice!

VIR. [*Taking his hand*] Forgive me, Jack.

JACK. Forgive you! It's not your fault—it's mine.

VIR. I'm not afraid to wait, Jack. The practice must come. If I knew anybody that was sick, I'd make 'em send for you.

JACK. If you were only sick.

VIR. Jack!

JACK. I mean if your mother was only sick.

VIR. Jack!

JACK. [*Taking her hand*] So I could come every day to see you. [*Mrs. Cawallader enters, C.R.*]

MRS. C. [*R., gaily*] Why, doctor!

JACK. [*C.*] Ma'am—Mrs. Ca—I—

MRS. C. [*R.*] I'm glad you called, doctor.

VIR. He called to see papa, and ask him about—about—

JACK. But as he is not in—[*About to go*]

MRS. C. Oh, yes, he's in. I'm very glad you've come. The professor certainly needs distraction. For the last few days, ever since our visit to Cousin Jonathan's, he has been gloomy and excited by turns. I fear he is not well.

JACK. I'm so glad to hear it.

MRS. C. Glad to hear it?

JACK. Sorry to hear it.

MRS. C. And yet he seems active, too. Is out every day—all day.

JACK. Let us hope for the best. He may be taken down suddenly.

VIR. [*Indignantly*] Jack!

MRS. C. Taken down suddenly? [*Professor enters with a bundle of papers, R.*]

PROF. Oh! *You* are there, are you?

JACK. [*R.C., tries to feel his pulse*] Good morning, professor.

PROF. Mornin'. [*Surly; snatches his hand away, sits at desk*] .

JACK. What a reception. [*Aside*]

VIR. [*Crosses to Professor*] Jack wishes to consult you, papa, about some chemical combinations.

PROF. [*Busy writing*] I've no time to think of chemical combinations.

JACK. I really beg pardon for intruding. [*Crosses to Professor*]

PROF. [*Turning to him*] You must have a great deal of spare time on your hands. Where are your patients?

JACK. [*Ruefully*] I don't know. I think they must have some other doctor!

PROF. Rubbish. Here you are—a young man full of health and strength—bothering about chemical combinations and stuff, when you might be hard at work making money.

JACK. I am hard at work, sir, but I don't make money. I've lots to do—but the people are too poor to pay me. I was up all last night—brought two poor fellows through—but they had nothing to give me but thanks.

PROF. [*Ironically*] Ve—ry well; ve—ry well. Go on.

JACK. [*Gaily*] I actually *did* think I would get a fee yesterday morning. Sent for to attend a guest in a hotel. He was in a high fever. He rolled about and insisted on having water—wouldn't take anything else—so I gave him a pint; went back this morning and found him gone.

PROF. Killed him, eh? Dead?

JACK. No. Paid his bill and left the hotel. He was cured. It seems he was a salesman in a wholesale liquor house—the water acted like magic on his system, which was unaccustomed to the fluid.

PROF. [*Abruptly*] Do you know anything about stocks?

JACK. Stocks? No, sir.

PROF. Not acquainted down Wall Street?

JACK. Very sorry, sir. No.

PROF. So am I. [*Turns to his desk*]

JACK. [*To Ladies*] Now he's angry with me.

MRS. C. [*Aside*] Don't mind him. It's his way.

JACK. [*To Professor*] Perhaps if I call again in a few days to get your opinion on some experiments in chemicals—a joining of two bodies—

PROF. No time in a few days.

JACK. Next week?

PROF. No—next month—next month. I've matters of importance on hand now.

JACK. [*Aside, to Ladies*] That's plain enough. Not for a month, a whole month without seeing you!

MRS. C. [*Aside, to Professor*] You are very rude to the doctor, Cornelius.

PROF. Can't help it.

MRS. C. [*To Jack*] Call again as soon as you can or please.

VIR. [*L., half aside to him*] I shall be at home all day tomorrow, Jack.

JACK. Good-bye, Virgie. [*Crosses to each*] Good-bye, Mrs. Cawallader. Good-bye, professor. I'll call on you in a month.

PROF. [*Snarling*] In a month. Better put it down in your visiting book.

JACK. Yes, sir. [*Takes out book, drops hat, picks it up, drops book, stoops, drops all, picks up book and puts it on his head, backs off, trying to put his hat in his pocket. Virgie follows him off, C.R.*]

PROF. [*R.*]   Idiot!

MRS. C. [*Bringing Virgie's hat from table, L.*]   Have you a moment's leisure, Cornelius?

PROF. [*Sits, reading stock list*]   Big Bonanza firm.

MRS. C.   I want you to look at this hat, dear.

PROF.   Oh, don't bother me.

MRS. C.   That's what you said to me yesterday.

PROF.   Don't you see I'm busy?

MRS. C. [*C.*]   Now don't get excited.

PROF. [*Violently*]   Excited? Excited? I make it a rule never to get excited. What *is* the matter? [*Gets up and throws down paper*]

MRS. C.   Look at this hat.

PROF. [*Looks at her with scorn, then grabs the hat, pulls at it, tumbles it inside out*]   Well? [*Mrs. Cawallader snatches it from him*]

MRS. C.   You monster!

PROF.   What about the hat?

MRS. C.   It's Virgie's new hat. I want one just like it in lilac.

PROF.   Well, get one in all the colors of the rainbow! What do I care!

MRS. C.   Oh, very good. Give me the money.

PROF.   Money? Do you think I'm made of money? I won't be ruined by your extravagance.

MRS. C.   Extravagance? When I pinch myself in every conceivable way? When I buy the cheapest things, and turn every dress I have four times. When I—

PROF. [*Taking out wallet*]   There, stop this infernal clatter!

MRS. C. [*Observing wallet*]   A pocketful of money, as I'm a living woman! [*Professor hastily closes the pocketbook, and puts it into his right-hand pocket. Mrs. Cawallader walks around him, observing*] And you tell me continually that you haven't a cent!

PROF.   Oh, well, here, take that. [*Gives bond*] Don't talk to me any more about money for two years.

MRS. C.   What's this?

PROF.   Money, or as good as money. It's a bond.

MRS. C.   What bond?

PROF.   Wa-bash!

MRS. C. [*Returning it*]   Wa-bash—all bosh.

PROF.   Oh, you're mighty particular—here's another, perhaps you will like it better, C. C. and I. C.

MRS. C. What's C. C. and I. C.?

PROF. Coffee, cakes and ice cream.

MRS. C. I won't have it. I want money.

PROF. [*Carefully selecting three or four pieces of currency*] Well, there, hold your apron. There's a dollar and a half; now go and buy just as many bonnets as you want to.

MRS. C. Cornelius, you are becoming a miser. You are amassing wealth and concealing it from your wife.

PROF. [*R.*] Well, somebody must save. You don't. You drain me of every dollar. First it's for Virgie, then it's for yourself—then it's for your everlasting relations.

MRS. C. My relations? What do you mean?

PROF. Isn't there your precious nephew?

MRS. C. Robert?

PROF. Yes, Robert. He ought to be called "Robber!"

MRS. C. He's been to California for a whole year.

PROF. Of course he has. I ought to know it. Didn't I give him the money to go there? But I didn't grudge that.

MRS. C. Yes, you did.

PROF. No, I didn't. I'd pay him handsomely to go to China. But now he's back again—for more, I suppose.

MRS. C. You don't know. He may be a rich man, now—they say the silver mines are inexhaustible.

PROF. He'll exhaust 'em. Talk about the Big Bonanza. He'd go through it in a week. If he'd made his fortune, he'd have been to see us first thing, and now it's a week since he wrote to tell us of his arrival, and not a sight of him yet.

VIR. [*Outside, C.R.*] Bob! Oh, Bob! Is it you?

BOB. [*Outside, C.R.*] Why, Virgie!

MRS. C. Why there he is now. [*Bob and Virgie enter, C.R.*]

BOB. Here I am! Kiss me, auntie! Shake hands, uncle! Back again, you see. Why, Virgie. [*Holding her off*] What a woman you've grown to be. What big eyes, and ever so much more beautiful than when I left you all a year ago.

PROF. [*Stepping between*] Ahem—yes, very much so!

BOB. [*R.*] My dear uncle. [*Taking his hand again*]

PROF. [*R.C., surveying him*] The same suit of clothes you went away in; and rather a shabby suit, too.

BOB. Oh, don't look at the outside, uncle. Here, Virgie, here's something I brought for you. [*Dives into his pocket, crosses to her*]

VIR. Something for me?

Bob. [*Still diving, gets L.C.*]   It's not much, but it's something. [*Produces shell*] There!

Vir. [*Pleased*]   A shell!

Mrs. C. [*Disappointed*]   A shell!

Prof. [*Disgusted*]   A shell—a sell. [*Goes up to desk*]

Vir. [*Takes it, admiring it*]   Oh, how lovely!

Bob. [*Crosses to her*]   Do you see that gleam in there? It reminded me of your eyes. I thought of dashing my worthless brains out down a Colorado precipice, one day—but I looked in that shell—thought of you—and made up my mind to come home again. One of these days I'll have it set in gold as a locket for you. [*Virgie kisses the shell*]

Mrs. C.   Set in gold! Dear Robert.

Bob.   Yes, I've come back determined to. make my fortune.

Mrs. C.   And I know you'll succeed.

Prof. [*Spins round on chair*]   Come back to make your fortune! What did you go away for? What have you been doing?

Bob.   You shall hear. [*All sit*] You know I went away with a thousand dollars and my railroad ticket in my pocket. [*Mrs. Cawallader being near the Professor, he looks at her suspiciously, and changes his pocketbook from his R. to his L.H. coat pocket*]

Prof.   A thousand dollars!

Bob.   Yes. You gave me seventy-five and Aunt Carrie gave me the rest— [*Professor surprised, looks at Mrs. Cawallader*] all she had. Well, I went West. First, it was railroad—railroad—railroad—for six days. Then, it was wagon—wagon—wagon—for ten days. Then, mule—mule—mule—for a week. Then, it was walk—walk—walk—for the balance. But I struck the mines at last.

All.   Struck the mines!

Bob.   I mean I got there. That's the way the miners talk, you know. The very first fellow I saw had a mine for sale.

Vir.   Oh, how fortunate.

Bob.   Wasn't it? He inquired my object in emigrating. Heard I wanted to make a fortune. You're just the person I've been looking for, says he. I'm in want of a superintendent for the richest silver mine around the Bonanza. I like your looks. I'll take you. To place you above temptation, as you'll have to handle millions, I'll give you five thousand dollars a month.

All.   Oh!

Bob.   I only require, says he, security for your honesty and fidelity. How much ready money have you about you? A thousand dollars, says I. Hand it over, says he—willingly—and he pocketed the cash. I arranged to meet him that night to go to the mines. *He* had to leave just then to look after another concern ten miles below. I waited for him. [*Stops*]

ALL. Well?

BOB. I guess he died on the way back. That was the last I saw of him. I went to look up the mine. Not any. It was a sell—humbug. I had been carbined.

ALL. Robert—carbined?

BOB. I mean rifled—cheated. That's the way the miners talk.

VIR. Oh, what *did* you do then?

BOB. [*Shrugs shoulders*] Well, I had rather a hard time. A little starvation—a little sickness—a few nights out on the plains—

MRS. C. But you found friends?

BOB. One.

MRS. C. Bless him—who was it?

BOB. Myself. [*Rises*] I went to work. Not at five thousand dollars a month, but at three meals a day. [*Professor turns away in disgust*] Regular pay. It was a luxury.

VIR. Poor Bob! [*Bob and Virgie embrace, Professor starts from his seat, snatches Virgie from Bob, and makes her sit in the chair at desk*]

BOB. Poor Bob! Rich Bob. For I've found out how to make a fortune. To make it anywhere—here as well as out West—all the world over. Work!

PROF. [*Crosses to Bob*] And so that's the luck you've had?

BOB. Luck? My dear uncle, I've been smothered in luck! How many fellows survive such experience, and here I am back among you, healthy and hearty! [*All turn and look away*] Ha, ha! [*Looks round on all*]

PROF. [*L.*] And ready to eat three meals a day here. And so you've come back to be a burden on us?

BOB. Eh?

PROF. What can you do here?

BOB. The very first day I got back I went out prospecting. I've got a place, if not a placer. For one week I've been up at six and to bed at twelve. I share the lodgings of my old chum, Jack, and my first week's salary lies in my pocket like a nugget in a shaft. In a short time, say twenty years or so— [*Looks at watch*] Eleven already! I must be off. Had business up this way, and ran in. Back to office. Report. Then dinner with Jack at twelve. Then at it again till night.

MRS. C. [*Crosses to him*] You need not hurry. [*Taking his hand*] You must take dinner with us. [*Looks at his hand*] Where is your ring? Your mother's ring? You haven't lost it?

BOB. No. That's a good story. You see, the day I arrived at the depot I was looking about, wondering where I should go first, when I saw a young lady also looking about—evidently wondering where *she* should go. So I offered her my assistance. I got a porter to take her luggage and the rascal wanted his pay. I had no money, and so I had to pledge the ring. But I'll have it again today. [*Slaps pocket*] Fortunately, they wouldn't lend me much on it.

PROF. Another humbug awaiting you on your arrival.

VIR. But, papa, Bob was quite right, if she needed his assistance.

MRS. C. It was his duty.

VIR. [*Turning on seat each time*] The same dear Bob as ever!

PROF. [*Swinging her back*] The same old Bob! Pah!

BOB. No. Not the same. The old Bob is left out there—at the Big Bonanza —lazy Bob—idle Bob. Good-bye, Aunt Carrie. Good-bye, Virgie. [*Kisses both*] Good-bye, uncle. You'll see there's a new Bob in old New York. [*Exit*]

ACT III.

SCENE 1: *Plain apartment in humble lodging. Bachelor's room. Wardrobe, C., with cheap clock on it. Window, R.C., Door, L.C. Fireplace and mantel, R. Table up C., and chairs, R. and L. Small table, R. Mrs. Balder discovered dusting, goes to window and takes down notice, "Apartments to let," which had hung there.*

MRS. B. There, everything is ready for my new tenant. [*Jack enters, L.D.F.*]

MRS. B. Good morning, doctor. [*Jack flings himself down, R., dispiritedly and throws his hat on table, R.*]

JACK. Good morning, Balder.

MRS. B. I've rented the room, doctor.

JACK. I'm glad to hear it, for your sake. Now you'll get a good rent for it.

MRS. B. And the room upstairs will be much snugger for you, too, and less to pay.

JACK. Certainly; when must we move?

MRS. B. [*Very fussy all through*] Not till tonight. The family comes tomorrow, early. The gentleman that took the rooms for them will be here today to see if everything's arranged. He seems a very respectable old gentleman—so fatherly and good. It's quite a pleasure for a poor widow with children to see such a fatherly body.

JACK. Very well; very well. [*Rises and walks impatiently over to L.*]

MRS. B. Tut loo! I was forgetting. [*Goes up to basket*] See what's come for you since you went out.

JACK. [*Astonished*] A basket of wine for me! [*Examines it*]

MRS. B. And this letter. [*Gives letter from her pocket*]

JACK. A letter, too. [*Bob bursts in gaily, L.D.F.*]

BOB. Ah! Jack! [*Sees wine*] Hollo! what in the—I say, Jack, explain the presence of these distinguished foreigners in our humble lodging. [*Elevating and examining two bottles critically*]

JACK. [*Shows letter*] Only think! From my patient—the liquor merchant —in the hotel. He begs to be excused for his hurried departure, and asks my acceptance of half a dozen of champagne. Remove the tempters!

BOB. Noble fellow! I say, Jack, I bet his medicine will be better to take than yours. [*To Mrs. Balder. Hands her the two bottles, which she replaces in basket*] Anon, we will partake. [*Crosses to R.*]

MRS. B. Yes, sir. Lor, what spirits he do have, for a young man as works as hard as he does. [*Exit, L.D.F.*]

JACK. [*Sits L. of C. table*] I say, Bob, I feel awfully unhappy.

BOB. [*Sits on table*] Then I'll cheer you up [*Takes both his hands*] by saying I've been to uncle's, have seen Virgie, your little sweetheart, and am dying to congratulate you.

JACK. Congratulate me on what? On my prospects! Oh! [*Despondent*]

BOB. [*Coming forward*] Take heart, old fellow! Look here! [*Produces greenbacks in small roll*] My first week's salary. It comes at last, my boy. It comes. [*To money, as he admires it*] Oh, you magnificent works of art! When I look at you, and remember that the newspapers and members of Congress call you rags! But I notice nobody throws you away!

JACK. [*Rises*] I'm glad of your good luck, Bob.

BOB. So am I; and now to divide. There are just twenty—here's your half.

JACK. [*Indignant*] Robert!

BOB. John, what's the matter now? Didn't we agree to live together, and share everything in common?

JACK. [*L.*] But not money.

BOB. Not money? The deuce! There's nothing one can so easily divide. If you refuse, I give you notice I'll quit on the first of the month. [*Coaxing*] Come—come, old fellow, take half of my money, and I'll take half of your champagne. Is it a bargain?

JACK. Yes. [*They divide money and pocket it; crosses, R.*]

BOB. [*Sits, L. of C. table*] What a lucky thing your patient sold wine and not boot blacking. Think of a present of a dozen bottles of Day & Martin!

JACK. [*R. of C., table*] It would have been all the same to me.

BOB. What a fit of blues; you were lively as possible this morning.

JACK. I've been to the professor's.

BOB. [*Seated L. of table*] Well, was Virgie out?

JACK. No. But the professor was worse than ever, much worse, almost showed me the door, and actually told me not to call for a month.

BOB. Oh, you must have misunderstood him. [*Crosses to R.*]

JACK. [*Pettishly*] Misunderstood him! [*Crosses to L., and sits*]

BOB. I always do. That's the only way to get along with him. [*Mrs. Balder enters, L.D.F.*]

MRS. B. Oh, my goodness sakes! [*Gets between them*] Did anyone ever hear of such a misfortune?

BOB and JACK. What is it?

MRS. B. You know the tailor and his wife across the way? You were in there last week, doctor. Poor people!

JACK. Yes. What's the matter? Has he fallen downstairs and broken his leg?

MRS. B. No, sir. Worse than that.

BOB. His wife's fallen downstairs and broken her leg?

MRS. B. No, sir. Worse than that, too.

BOB and JACK. What is it? What can be worse?

MRS. B. Twins!

JACK. You don't call that a misfortune?

MRS. B. Twins—and he's about to be turned out in the streets for his rent, and them with seven children.

BOB. [*Sitting on table, R.*] Turned into the street, with twins?

JACK. [*Aside to Mrs. Balder, beckoning her L.*] Sh! Come here, don't say anything to Bob; here are ten dollars, give them to the tailor.

MRS. B. [*Exclaiming*] Oh! [*Jack stops her mouth*]

BOB. [*Gyrating*] Pst! [*Beckoning Mrs. Balder, she crosses to R.*] Don't mention this to Jack. He's a little close. Here are ten dollars, give 'em to the twins.

MRS. B. [*Same*] Oh! [*Bob stops her mouth*]

BOB. [*Singing*] "Beautiful isle of the sea," etc. [*Hums*]

MRS. B. Heaven be praised! They won't be turned out. I'll run and give 'em the money. Heaven bless you, gentlemen!

JACK and BOB. [*Hurrying her round and round to door*] Now be off. Run to the tailor. Remember the twins. Quick! [*They whirl her off, L.1E.*]

JACK. The woman's crazy, Bob.

BOB. [*Going R.*] Oh, mad! Mad! [*Looking at clock*] But I say, Jack—time for dinner—we must be off to dinner.

JACK. So we must. [*Aside*] I'll have to borrow from Bob!

BOB. [*After recollecting, R.*] Dinner! and I haven't a cent, and my ring at the pawnbroker's. I'll have to ask Jack. [*They approach each other*]

JACK. Talking about dividing a little while ago, Bob—

BOB. Suppose we divide again, Jack?

JACK. Five dollars apiece—

BOB. Plenty after all.

JACK. So— [*Holds out his hands*]

BOB. Hand over— [*Holds out his, their hands meet*]

JACK. Eh? I asked you!

BOB. I gave my ten to the twins.

JACK. And I gave mine to the tailor.

BOB. [*Laughs*] Jack, you're an extravagant fellow. [*Sits, L.*]

JACK. You are very improvident. [*Sits, R.*]

BOB. Well, there's one comfort, the twins will have a double allowance. [*Knock at door*]

JACK and BOB. Come in! [*De Haas enters, L.D.F., eyeglass on, coolly surveys them both*]

BOB. [*Points to Jack*] There's the doctor. [*Aside*] He looks sick.

DE HAAS. [*To Jack*] Ah! Mr. Robert Ruggles!

JACK. There's Mr. Ruggles.

DE H. Ah! Happy to make your acquaintance, Mr. Robert Ruggles. My n-n-name is Haas—De Haas.

BOB. Haas, eh? [*Aside*] When shall we three meet again. [*Aloud*] Take a seat and recover yourself.

DE H. [*Aside*] Evidently extremely poor! [*Looks around*]

BOB. [*Watching him*] The new tenant, I suppose.

DE H. You were fortunate enough, Mr. Robert Ruggles, to render an important service to a young lady, a few days ago.

BOB. [*Rises, surprised*] If you allude to the young lady I met at the depot—

DE H. At the depot—quite right. [*Bob brings chair and he sits*] The yer-yer-young lady is a relation of mine, Mr. Robert Ruggles. She related to me all about the horses and carriage; it was very amusing, we laughed excessively over it. Ha, ha, ha!

JACK. [*Reproachfully*] My friend nearly broke his arm. [*Rises. De Haas eyes Jack through his glasses coolly*]

BOB. It was nothing serious.

DE H. You mentioned your name, Mr. Robert Ruggles, and I promised my cousin to make inquiry for you. She authorizes me to give you this little token of her gratitude, as she will probably never have an opportunity of thanking you in person. Mr. Robert Ruggles [*Hands a packet*], w-w-will you be good enough to accept it?

BOB. [*Hesitating*] I didn't expect! Indeed it's very kind.

DE H. Pray take it, Mr. Robert Ruggles. [*Bob takes it*] There, the matter is settled.

JACK. [*Calmly*] Like any other business.

DE. H. [*Again surveying Jack*] Just so. [*To Bob*] I have the honor to wish you a very good morning, Mr.-Mr.-Ruggles. [*Bowing and backing out, L.D.F.*]

BOB. Oblige me by presenting my thanks to the young lady! [*Treads on his toes several times bowing him out. De Haas exit, Bob turns and grasps Jack's hand*] Jack! My dear Jack! Do you hear—a present, a keepsake! from her! [*Kisses it*]

JACK. [*Dryly*] Who is this cousin?

BOB. Never mind the cousin; she can't help the sort of cousins she has, nobody can help their cousins. Did I not tell you—she is as good as she is beautiful. Those eyes could not speak an untruth. [*Kisses packet*] Oh, Jack! [*Hugs him*]

JACK. [*C., solemnly*] Bob, you're in a high fever!

BOB. I am. [*Feels packet*] What can it be? It's soft, Jack, it's soft! Feel it! No, don't! Let's look at it. [*Opens letter*] A pocketbook, worked by her! [*Kisses it*] Eh, Jack?

JACK. Eh?

BOB. My initials! "R. R."

JACK. [*Laughing*] Radway's Relief.

BOB. Worked by her hands. Her delicate little fingers toiled upon it for me. What can I do to show my joy?

JACK. [*As Bob dances to him*] Anything but hug me. [*Keeping him off with chair*]

BOB. I'll work twice as hard now; I'll work all night. Jack, what can a fellow do all night, to make money?

JACK. Well, you might try your hand at draw poker.

BOB. Oh, you dear little letters! This shall be my talisman.

JACK. Be calm, Bob, be calm. Think of De Haas.

BOB. A fig for De Haas. What shall we do, Jack? Let's sing.

JACK. Sing away! But, stop. Why don't you examine the book? There may be something in it.

BOB. [*Struck with the idea*] I never thought of that; so there may. [*They sit at table, C., opens book cautiously*]

JACK. Easy now.

BOB. Nothing in there.

JACK. Try the next.

BOB. Ah! No!

JACK. Not so fast.

BOB. Easy! Easy!

JACK. There's something.

BOB. [*Taking out a little parcel*] Wrapped in paper.

JACK. [*Guessing*] A love letter! [*Bob opens paper carefully*]

BOB. Nonsense.

JACK. A lock of her hair.

BOB. [*In dismay*] Money!

JACK. A hundred dollar bill. [*They look at each other, and their faces fall*]

BOB. Do you know, Jack, this vexes me—hurts me. It's an insult. Here, you can have it. [*Pushes it over*]

JACK. [*Pushing it back*] No, thank you.

BOB. Money—from her!

JACK. Payment in full.

BOB. Jack, there's some mistake here.

JACK. [*Takes up note*] Hundred dollar bills never come into pocketbooks by mistake.

BOB. [*Takes book from him*] I certainly told her I was poor, and she has told her father, and her father, who has no heart—

JACK. But plenty of money.

BOB. Placed it here without her knowledge.

JACK. What will you do?

BOB. Write to him and return his money.

JACK. Yes!

BOB. Better still, I'll go to him.

JACK. And they'll have something more to laugh at.

BOB. Jack, this almost breaks my heart.

MRS. B. [*Outside*] This way, sir! [*Mrs. Balder enters, followed by Cawallader, who looks around the room. Mrs. Balder speaks, aside, to Bob and Jack*]

MRS. B. This is the gentleman that took the rooms for some friends, who are coming up to New York, on a visit. [*Bob and Jack nod and sit at table, R., conversing, not observing others, Jack trying to cheer Bob*]

CAW. You'll excuse the intrusion, gentlemen, but I wished to look at the rooms.

JACK. [*Without looking round*] Certainly, sir; no trouble, I assure you.

CAW. [*To Mrs. Balder*] The family will arrive from Peekskill tomorrow. I will be responsible for their rent. A very nice place. [*Sees basket of champagne on floor, takes out a bottle and puts on glasses to examine it*] What's this? Old acquaintance! "Goulet dry." I haven't tasted "Goulet dry" for an age.

Bob. [*To Jack*] I have an idea. That old gentleman looks like a man of the world, and a father of a family to boot; I'll ask his opinion. [*Crosses to Cawallader*] I beg your pardon.

Caw. [*Replacing bottle*] I beg *your* pardon. You indulge in capital champagne, I see.

Bob. Have a glass with us. Mrs. Balder, another glass.

Mrs. B. Yes, sir. [*Gets one from mantelpiece*]

Caw. [*At back of table*] You are very kind, but—

Bob. No excuses. You call at our lodgings, you can't refuse our hospitality.

Caw. Yes, but—

Bob. We have a favor to ask of you.

Caw. Oh! If you put it that way.

Bob. [*Handing him a glass*] Your health.

Caw. [*Sipping like a connoisseur*] Excellent! Do you know, young gentlemen, that your wine is excellent? My regards! [*Drinks*]

Jack. [*L.*] And now, Bob, state the case.

Caw. But I'm a perfect stranger.

Bob. So much the better, you'll be impartial.

Caw. Very good, but let us clear our heads for the hearing. [*Fills his glass*] Now, then. [*Sipping*]

Bob. [*R.*] There is a young man.

Caw. [*Sips*] Quite dry.

Bob. Eh? Oh! And a young lady.

Caw. [*Sipping*] Not too sweet.

Bob. [*Indignantly*] How do you know?

Caw. I refer to the wine. [*Sips*]

Bob. Oh, excuse me! [*Takes his glass away*] I want you to concentrate your intellect on the facts.

Caw. You are a couple of odd ones.

Jack. The facts are these: the young gentleman assists the young lady in a moment of peril, and her father, instead of thanking him, gives him money.

Caw. [*Reaching for his glass*] The father is an unmannerly old donkey.

Bob and Jack. [*Slap him on back*] You are right! [*Bob fills glasses*]

Jack. But now the question is: what shall he do with the money? I say, give it to the poor.

Caw. And I say—don't keep it.

Bob. [*Slaps him again*] Right again! I'll take it back to the unmannerly old donkey myself. [*Rises*]

Caw. And you'll do exactly what you should.

BOB. Then, we'll have another glass all round. [*Refills*]

CAW. [*Eyeglass on, examining label*] Where did you get this wine?

BOB. My friend here is a doctor and got it from one of his patients.

CAW. [*Taking bottle*] Let's drink the health of the patient.

BOB. Stop! That's my bottle, and was dedicated to a young lady. Let the doctor open another bottle to his patients. [*Jack gets another bottle*]

CAW. [*Laughing*] Upon my word, we get on very well together for strangers. Nevertheless, let's finish your bottle. Here's to the young lady. [*Drinks*] What is your business, my young friend, if I may be allowed?

BOB. Clerk in a commission house.

CAW. [*Attentively*] Good situation?

BOB. [*Crosses to L.*] Yes. [*Looks at watch*] By Jove! I must be back to the office. You remind me that I'm not my own master. [*About to go*]

CAW. [*Restraining him*] Wait a moment. It's very pleasant here.

BOB. [*Crossing*] Impossible. Time is money. Punctuality is the soul of business—and so on. Would like to stay, but I've only fifteen minutes.

CAW. Just five minutes more.

BOB. Not a second! [*Gets his hat. Jack puts the clock back*]

CAW. [*R.*] Oh, yes, you will! Listen to me! I am in business, and I make you an offer.

BOB. [*C., stepping back and eyeing him suspiciously*] What is it?

CAW. I like you.

BOB. [*Aside to Jack*] He begins like the old swindler at the mines about his Big Bonanza.

CAW. You please me exceedingly.

BOB. [*Same*] The same old dodge.

CAW. [*Surprised*] Eh? Come in my office, and, as the position I will offer you is one of great responsibility, your salary—

BOB. [*Laughs*] That'll do! It's very nice, my dear sir, but it won't do. I'm up to all that. I've been taken in before, sold and got a receipt in full.

CAW. [*Amazed*] Taken in! Sold!

BOB. Go West, old man! Go West! They are still verdant and confiding on the plains, but as for me, I want no more splendid offers. My motto is slow and sure. Hard to get, but safe to come. So, bye-bye, old fellow. [*Shakes Cawallader's hand, who is now smiling*] Bye-bye, Jack, I'm off. [*Going, returns to Cawallader*] I say, old boy, be virtuous—give over these tricks, and you will be happy. Bye-bye. Ha, ha, ha! [*Exit, Jack following him to the door, L.F.*]

CAW. Well, of all—[*Falls in chair*] of all the rascals I ever met. Ha, ha, ha! [*Jack takes Cawallader's arm*]

JACK. Come in and take another glass of wine to the health of my friend. [*Exeunt singing, R.1.E.*]

SCENE 2: *At Cawallader's. Same as Act I. Afternoon. Lucretia and Eugenia discovered sitting, embroidering or sewing.*

EUG. [*L.*] I wonder where Mr. De Haas can be. I wonder if he has seen Mr. Ruggles.

LUC. [*R.*] Eugenia, do pray cease this continual reference to Mr. Ruggles.

EUG. But, mamma, he keeps continually coming up in my mind.

LUC. But you are too old, now, to say everything you think. A girl of your age must be more careful than a mere child at school.

EUG. Oh, dear! I used to want to grow up and be independent. Now I wish I was so little again, that I might do what I liked. [*De Haas enters, shown in by Crumpets*]

CRUM. Mr. De Haas. [*Exit, C.L.*]

EUG. Oh, Mr. De Haas, I'm so glad you've come! [*Jumping up and running to him*]

DE H. I am t-t-truly delighted.

EUG. We were dying to hear if you succeeded in finding the young gentleman.

LUC. [*Remonstrating*] Eugenia!

DE H. The address was q-q-quite correct. I found the young man. Lives with another disagreeable person, in a flat. I have arranged everything.

LUC. Thank goodness, that painful affair is disposed of.

EUG. But what did he say?

LUC. Eugenia—my dear!

EUG. I mean, was he quite well—quite recovered?

DE H. Mr. Robert Ruggles seemed to be enjoying very good health.

EUG. Oh, pshaw! Why don't you tell us what he said?

LUC. [*Rising*] I'm surprised at you, Eugenia. I allowed you to embroider that present for the—the person, who, of course, cannot appreciate the gift. But now the matter is disposed of, and I beg you won't mention it again. Besides, you forget that Mr. De Haas invited you to visit the Academy of Design today. [*Rymple enters, C.L.*]

EUG. [*R.*] Mr. De Haas is very kind, but I promised to go with Uncle Rymple—didn't I, uncle?

RYM. [*R.C.*] Good morning, my darling.

EUG. [*Aside to him*] Say I did.

RYM. She did. She did, indeed.

EUG. [*Aside to him*] You promised to take me to the Academy.

RYM. Promised to take her to the Academy. [*Crosses, R.C.*] I love the opera! What's played today?

EUG. [*Same, pulling his coat*] No—no—the other Academy—pictures!

RYM. Well, they're both good.

EUG. [*Pulling him*] We must go at once, uncle, no time to lose. Good-bye, Mr. De Haas.

RYM. Good-bye! Good-bye! [*Eugenia and Rymple run off, C.L.*]

DE H. He, he, he! She is charming!

LUC. With a will of her own, I'm afraid.

DE H. So like her esteemed p-p-papa. By the way, is he at home now?

LUC. Mr. Cawallader is just about going downtown. But that reminds me, you don't approach my husband in the right way to gain his favor.

DE H. I would be so delighted, if you would only give me a suggestion on the subject.

LUC. You always tell him the gossip of the clubs and society—for which he cares nothing. Now if you would engage him on commercial topics—about business.

DE H. An excellent idea. I'll study up financial subjects.

LUC. And there's another hint. You are too studiously polite. I've heard Mr. Cawallader say that he loves a frank, open, careless nature, and that the man who asks for Eugenia, must be so carried away by affection, as to be almost beside himself.

DE H. Beside himself! Gracious, must I double myself?

LUC. He once said to me, I'd like the young fellow to be so enthusiastic as to hug me when I said "yes."

DE H. Wouldn't he be satisfied if I hugged Miss Eugenia?

LUC. [*Frowns, crosses to R.*] Why, Mr. De Haas!

DE H. I beg pardon!

LUC. It is not a subject of jest. I am only endeavoring to assist you in gaining his consent. [*Melting*] For you have a poetical nature, and I am sure you would make Eugenia happy. [*Going*] Don't forget my advice.

DE H. I'll d-d-do better—I'll act on it. [*Kisses her hand*]

LUC. [*Romantically*] Farewell! Remember. [*Exit, R.D., 1.E.*]

DE H. It's becoming very complicated. The mamma must be fed on poetry, and the papa must be hugged; I never hugged anybody, much less a banker, and I don't know how to begin! [*Makes a few motions with his arms, going L. as if practising. Cawallader enters, C.R., sees him, watches him*]

CAW. What are you doing there?

DE H. I—oh! I-I-I'm taking a little exercise. [*Practises*] But I'm very glad to see you, Mr. Cawallader.

CAW. Humph!

DE H. I want to open an account. I want to invest, and if you'll only advise me—

CAW. Advise you, eh? You want to invest, eh? What do you want to invest in?

DE H. Well, I'd like to talk it over with you. As we are business men, why in a few minutes—

CAW. [*R.*] Are you a business man?

DE H. I flatter myself. He, he, he!

CAW. I thought you knew nothing about money except how to spend it.

DE H. Oh! Y-y-you've entirely mistaken my character. I'm a business man, a frank, open, careless business man, with a frank, open, affectionate nature.

CAW. The deuce you are! Do you know what exchange is?

DE H. Of course! A fellow gives me something, and I give a fellow something.

CAW. Do you know what discount is?

DE H. Y-y-yes. It's what the other fellow keeps for himself.

CAW. Do you know what a balance is?

DE H. Certainly. It's what a fellow always owes his tailor. He, he, he!

CAW. Do you know what credit is?

DE H. I ought to. It's so hard to get.

CAW. And you wish to do business with me, do you? Good morning. [*Exit, R.D.*]

DE H. I have evidently not made a favorable impression. Perhaps I should have begun by hugging him. [*Practises gesture of hugging, crossing L. Crumpets enters at back, sees him and imitates him. At last De Haas turns*] Ah! I say, Crumpets!

CRUM. Yes, sir.

DE H. Look me in the eye, Crumpets. [*Makes a dart towards him, Crumpets jumps back*]

CRUM. Lor, sir!

DE H. I can't do it. I want more practice. [*Exit, C.L., practising, Crumpets follows a few steps imitating*]

CRUM. He's drunk. Drunk at eleven in the morning! [*Exit, C.L. Eugenia and Virgie enter, C.R., embracing each other*]

VIR. [*R.*] I'm so glad I found you home; what a lovely dress!

EUG. I wish I could get back to short skirts again.

VIR. Nonsense! Why?

EUG. Because I have to be a young lady when I wear these things, and mamma preaches at me night and day. I can't tell everything I should like to.

VIR. If you can't tell her, tell me.

EUG. O Virgie, that would be so nice! But you won't laugh at me?

Vir. Your confidences shall be sacred.

Eug. If I told you a secret, would you make fun of me?

Vir. Have you got a secret? I've got a secret, too. How sweet! Do you cherish a favored image? Do you love, too? Confide in me and we'll be happy.

Eug. Oh, how sensibly you do talk, so different from mamma. [*Embracing her*] Have you been in love?

Vir. [*Sighs*] Yes.

Eug. Are you in love now?

Vir. Alas, yes!

Eug. Oh, that's splendid. [*Embracing her again*] Tell me all about it, I'm dying to know. At school all the girls were continually talking about love, but none of us could explain it. How does it commence?

Vir. [*R.*] Commence?

Eug. Yes. It must have a beginning. Everything's got a beginning. Hasn't love got one?

Vir. Yes, it had a beginning; when I met Jack first.

Eug. Jack! Is his name Jack?

Vir. At night when I closed my eyes, instead of darkness, as it used to be, I saw his form. I thought and dreamed of him. I could see and think of nothing else.

Eug. [*Frightened*] Oh!

Vir. What's the matter?

Eug. Nothing. I said oh, because *I* never see anything, when I close my eyes. Is that the beginning of love?

Vir. At first his image comes to us dimly and faintly, then lustrous with a glory that brightens and brightens, until it pours forth a flood of radiance.

Eug. [*Scared*] Virgie, let's talk of something else.

Vir. But you asked me.

Eug. [*Slowly shaking her head*] We never knew anything about that at school. [*Cawallader enters, C.R.*]

Caw. [*C.*] What, Virgie! You are quite a stranger!

Vir. [*R.*] I wanted to see you, uncle, because you told me once if I ever needed your advice and assistance—

Caw. Certainly. I'm not only your uncle, but your godfather, and I mean to see that nobody makes you unhappy.

Eug. [*Embracing Cawallader*] You'll help her, won't you, papa?

Caw. If I can.

Vir. Well, uncle, you must know there is a young gentleman who used to come to our house—

Caw. Where under the sun do all the young gentlemen come from?

VIR. To be brief—

CAW. Your father and mother object to him?

VIR. Oh, no! On the contrary, father was very friendly with him, and so was mother, but—

CAW. [*Aside to her, and indicating Eugenia*] Can Eugenia hear the rest of the affair?

EUG. [*Who has overheard*] Can I? Of course I can! His name is Jack.

CAW. Oh, if his name is Jack, go on then.

VIR. But since the day father called here last, and saw you, everything is changed. He treats everybody with rudeness.

CAW. [*Smiling*] So! So! I understand.

VIR. And I don't know what to do, unless you will see father.

CAW. Impossible, my child.

EUG. But, papa—

CAW. Impossible for the present, but in the course of a month—

VIR. A month! That's just what papa said to Jack. He forbade him to come for a month. What is going to happen in a month?

CAW. [*Laughing*] You'll see. You'll see.

EUG. Papa, you are laughing! [*Reproachfully*]

CAW. [*Pats her cheek*] Don't fret, my dear. Everything will come right in a month; come with me, Virgie, and tell me about the young gentleman. [*Going*] I don't want Eugenia to hear about such things just yet. [*Exit with her, R.D.*]

EUG. [*Alone*] But Eugenia knows all about it. When Virgie spoke just now about the beginning of love, I thought I was going to faint. But no. It's impossible, and yet I shall be afraid to shut my eyes after this for fear— [*Closing them suddenly*] There he is! [*Opens them, jumps and looks around*] I must think of somebody else; I'll think of everybody else. [*Crumpets enters, C.L.*]

CRUM. A gentleman, miss.

EUG. Papa has gone to the library.

CRUM. So I told him, miss, and he said very well. Then I told him Mrs. Cawallader was not at home, and he said very good; and I told him nobody was visible but you, miss, and he said so much the better, and to tell you, that Mr. Robert Ruggles—

EUG. [*Eagerly*] Mr. Robert Ruggles! To see me? [*Checks herself*] Show him in, Crumpets.

CRUM. Show him in, miss?

EUG. Didn't you hear me? Show him in, directly.

CRUM. [*Surprised*] Yes, miss. [*Goes off, looking back*]

Eug. Mr. Robert Ruggles come to see me! Oh, I know I look a perfect fright. [*Runs off, L.U.E. Bob enters, C.L., well dressed; morning dress; limps a little*]

Bob. [*Sits R. of table*] Not here. Thank goodness! Then I can sit down a moment. Jack's clothes fit me very well, but his boots—ouch! [*Sits and nurses his foot*] Particularly the left. What a devil of a shape Jack's left foot must be. I've limped every step here, and it's getting worse and worse. [*Eugenia enters, L.U.E., bashfully, but smiling and delighted*]

Eug. I hope I have not kept you waiting.

Bob. [*Rising*] Oh! [*Limping*] Excuse the liberty I've taken.

Eug. Papa and mamma will be as glad to see you, as I am.

Bob. I'm rejoiced to hear it, Miss—Miss—

Eug. My name is Eugenia.

Bob. Beautiful name! [*Advancing*] Oh! [*Foot*]

Eug. Won't you be seated?

Bob. [*Quickly*] With the greatest pleasure. [*Sits R. and eases foot*] I came today to thank *you,* and to—

Eug. Oh, it's not worth mentioning. If my little gift pleases you—

Bob. I believe it will bring me good fortune. [*Takes pocketbook from his pocket*]

Eug. I'm sure I embroidered a good wish for you with every thread.

Bob. Thank you. But there was something in it.

Eug. [*Aside*] He means the verses I wrote and slipped into it.

Bob. I would give the world that you had not misunderstood me, Miss Eugenia, and if, in self-defense, I must speak of the contents of this book—

Eug. [*Worried*] Didn't—didn't you like them?

Bob. [*Firmly*] No, I did not!

Eug. I didn't think you would be so harsh to me for the folly, the presumption. I knew, of course, that in strict propriety, my action might be blamable, but my intention was good.

Bob. [*About to rise*] Oh! [*Nurses his foot*]

Eug. [*Aside*] He is disgusted with my forwardness. [*Aloud*] Then you have come to return me—

Bob. [*Firmly*] I have!

Eug. [*Coldly*] Give it to me, then! [*Both rise, she takes the book*]

Bob. [*Pleading*] Don't be angry!

Eug. Oh, no! Certainly not. [*Puts it in her pocket*]

Bob. But you don't understand. I don't wish to return the book—it is mine—I would not part with it for my life itself. Keep the contents, but do not take the book from me!

Eug. [*Looking at him*] You are very strange.

Bob. [*Pleading*] Perhaps I seem so; but please give me back the book. Take out the contents, and give me the keepsake—that is all I ask.

Eug. [*Opens book*] There is nothing in it.

Bob. Yes, here! [*Taking it*] The money—a hundred dollar bill—take it.

Eug. A hundred dollar bill! [*Takes it*] And the other—

Bob. Was there another? Then I suppose De Haas kept that. There was only one, when he gave it to me.

Eug. Money in my pocketbook—who put it there?

Bob. I know I did not.

Eug. And my verses?

Bob. Verses!

Eug. Can it be possible? No, it is too mean—too—

Bob. What's the matter?

Eug. And you thought me capable of sending you money! [*Throws it down*]

Bob. No, I did not think so; but you spoke of verses.

Eug. The verses which I put in here, and which have been taken out, and this dreadful money put in their place! Who has done it? Oh, sir, I understand, now, how you must have felt!

Bob. Verses! From you? Taken out? What rascal stole my property? [*Stage, R.*] Where is he?

Eug. I don't know; but I have a copy of the verses—the one I made first. I wrote them over and over before I sent them! You shall see them. Wait one minute, I'll get them. [*Runs off, L.1.E. He runs, limping, after her*]

Bob. Verses! Now I feel relieved. That money burnt into my very heart! But verses—written by her! [*L.H. De Haas enters, C.L.*]

De H. [*Aside, R.*] Crumpets told me—

Bob. Confound these boots!

De H. [*R.*] You here?

Bob. The very man! Explain, sir, [*Fiercely*] who put the money in the pocketbook, and where are my verses? [*Advances*] Oh! [*Limps*]

De H. [*Eyeing his foot*] You s-s-seem to suffer internally.

Bob. [*Aside*] Yes, and infernally! [*Aloud*] Sir! I have been defrauded!

De H. Sir!

Bob. Oh! Don't put on that air with me! What did you mean by it?

De H. I meant to save a thoughtless young lady from an indiscretion.

Bob. By what right?

De H. I was not willing that my future wife should compromise herself in that fashion.

Bob. [*Overcome*] Your future wife?

De H. Yes!

Bob. [*Stunned*]   That alters the case.

De H.   I should think so! [*Aside*] I've just told Mrs. Cawallader all about it. [*Exit, C.L.*]

Bob. [*Nursing his foot*]   His future wife, why not? I've been a fool, that's all; she has treated me as a warm-hearted girl would treat a friend. But she loves him, and she will marry him. [*Eugenia reenters with paper*]

Eug.   Here it is; but don't laugh at me. [*He rises*]

Bob. [*Seriously*]   I—I—thank you, but—

Eug.   Won't you take them, then?

Bob.   I cannot.

Eug.   So grave; what has changed you?

Bob.   Forgive me that I have been so mad as to—but now I know all.

Eug. [*Aside*]   Did anyone ever—[*Stage, L.*]

Bob.   The only one who has the right to tell me so, informs me that you have done wrong.

Eug.   Whom do you mean? Has papa been here?

Bob.   Your father—no—your future husband.

Eug.   My future husband—who—who—who?

Bob.   Mr. De Haas. He was here—and—

Eug.   He! That donkey! Oh, this is beyond everything! I could—[*Bursts into tears*]

Bob.   You are crying, Miss Eugenia. [*Limps to her*]

Eug.   Go away—I don't like you, now.

Bob.   Don't cry. I can't see you cry. You are angry with me? [*She shakes her head in her handkerchief*] With him? Shall I do anything? Say anything, only speak to me!

Eug.   That horrid wretch. I never could love him, and now I hate him.

Bob.   But you are going to marry him.

Eug. [*In a rage*]   I'd die first. Never—never—never! But mamma likes him, and that's the reason—he—he—[*Tears*]

Bob.   Your mother favors him? Have you no father?

Eug. [*Crying*]   Oh, yes; I've got one.

Bob.   But he will not condemn you?

Eug.   He's always good to me, but he treats me like a child, and if mamma says the word—oh—oh—I know how it will all end. [*Tears*] They will make —m—m—me—and I shall die. [*Exit, L.1.E., crying. Bob limps after her*]

Bob.   No, no, no. Let me speak to him. Let me see your mother. She is gone. [*Coming down*] No, let me see De Haas, just let me talk to him. Where did he go? [*Cawallader enters, C.R.*] The old gentleman. [*Limps up and grasps his hand*] What are you doing here?

Caw.   The very question I was going to ask you.

Bob. Then you are acquainted here?

Caw. Slightly.

Bob. Then you know the father, the proprietor, the head of the house?

Caw. My most intimate friend.

Bob. [*Slaps him on the back*] The very man of all others; come, sit down. Make yourself at home. [*They sit*] You know his daughter?

Caw. Daughter!

Bob. Lovely girl; in short, an angel.

Caw. Do you think so?

Bob. Somebody must speak to the old gentleman—open his eyes to the true state of affairs, and you are the man to do it.

Caw. What are his eyes to be opened to? What have you to do with his daughter?

Bob. I met her at the depot.

Caw. [*Astonished*] You?

Bob. Why, I told you the whole story yesterday.

Caw. Me—not a word!

Bob. Yes, I did! Why, you remember! You said yourself the father was an old donkey! Don't you recollect? He sent the money in the pocketbook, and you advised me to send it back to him.

Caw. You received money from—[*Checks himself*]

Bob. How dull you are!

Caw. Yes; I am a little confused.

Bob. [*Rises*] That comes of your drinking so much champagne in the middle of the day.

Caw. [*Aside*] Gad, if my wife could hear him, she'd be delighted.

Bob. Don't mumble to yourself. Advise me what I should do.

Caw. [*Picking money from the floor*] I suppose this is the money?

Bob. [*Dashes it out of his hand*] Don't bother with that. We are talking about the young lady.

Caw. Well?

Bob. They are forcing her to marry a person she despises.

Caw. Are they?

Bob. His name is De Haas, and a precious ass he is.

Caw. Indeed! [*Astonished*]

Bob. Her mother has set her heart on it, and her father—the donkey, you know—he stands by and sees her sacrificed under his very nose.

Caw. [*L.*] But I say—where did you learn all this?

Bob. Never mind where. That's none of your business; your business is to see the father, speak to him—wake him up.

Caw. But—

Bob. Do it your own way; only tell him his daughter's happiness is at stake, and if he wishes to save her life, he must take this rascally De Haas by the collar and show him the door.

Caw. But there's his wife.

Bob. Is he afraid of his wife?

Caw. [*Quickly, L.*] Oh, no!

Bob. Tell him that this rascal has insulted him under his own roof, and without asking his consent, has boldly declared himself the future husband of his child.

Caw. Declared it? To whom?

Bob. To me!

Caw. This is becoming interesting.

Bob. Isn't that ground enough to show him the door?

Caw. Oh, ample!

Bob. And if he refuses [*Firmly*], I'll step in; I'll see the mother, and then there'll be the devil to pay.

Caw. [*Delighted, aside*] What a magnificent fellow!

Bob. But if the governor is willing to make a stand—if he insists on being master in his own house, I'll back him; I can be a lion in defense of beauty in distress. [*Starts up, foot*] Oh! Murder!

Caw. [*Rising*] It seems the lion has a weak spot.

Bob. Oh! [*Sinks in chair, R., nursing his foot. Crumpets announces, C.L.*]

Crum. Mr. De Haas! [*Comes down, R.*]

Bob. [*Jumps R.*] Let me get at him.

Caw. [*Stage, L.*] Sh! Leave him to me. [*De Haas enters, C.L.*] You wish to see me, sir?

De H. [*With a burst of feeling, and rushing towards Cawallader*] Mr. Cawallader!

Caw. [*Stepping back*] Hold on!

De H. Don't restrain me, I'm an open, frank, careless fellow; I wish to show you the depth of my affection. [*Embraces him at a jump*] Pardon my emotion. I'm obeying the dictates of my heart. [*Another dive*]

Caw. [*In a rage*] Then, let me obey the dictates of my heart. There's your hat. There's the door. I'm also a frank [*Turns him*], careless [*Turns him*], open fellow [*Hurries him to door*], and if I ever see you here again— [*Exeunt, C.L., with De Haas*]

Bob. [*Grasping Crumpets' arm*] I say, my good fellow, who is that old gentleman?

Crum. Him, sir? That's Mr. Cawallader, my master.

Bob. Her father! I'm a dead man! [*Sinks in a chair, Crumpets goes off, C., practising the embrace gesture*]

Scene 3: *Hallway in Professor's house. The Professor enters with hat on, and umbrella under his arm, putting on gloves as if to go out, with a newspaper in his coat pocket, R.1.E.*

Prof. I believe, if any man of brains were to engage in this stock business for half a year, he'd be prostrated mentally and physically for life. Now I begin to understand, why a lower order of intellects succeed so well in speculation. They can't grasp the bewildering perplexities, and so they survive. Here's this morning's paper, [*Taking it out and slapping it*] a family newspaper, containing the stock quotations. In it I have just read that the great Seal Oil Company pays 12 per cent dividend, and yet its stock sells for 63 cents on the dollar. Now where is the logic, the common sense, the arithmetic of those facts? A stock that pays 12 per cent dividend, ought certainly to be above par. [*Mrs. Cawallader outside, R.1.E., calls "Professor." He folds paper*] Oh, why didn't I slip out at once? I don't know which worries me the most, her questions, or this confounded business. [*Mrs. Cawallader enters, R.1.E.*]

Mrs. C. Out so early, dear?

Prof. So early? Yes. I'm tied to the wheel and go around with it. [*Slapping the paper*] A man sits down day after day, to read this financial hodgepodge, and finds it results in nothing but ghastly nonsense; when I've finished my morning dose of it, I have to go out and take a walk.

Mrs. C. Can I assist you to make it out, whatever it is?

Prof. No, you can't.

Mrs. C. Pray, don't get excited. I only made a civil offer, I'm sure.

Prof. The old cry—don't get excited. Stick pins in me, and beg me not to get excited.

Mrs. C. If that's the way you receive my efforts to assist you—

Prof. Your efforts? If I wanted a cake baked, your efforts might be of some account. But this is business. Do you understand anything about business? No, you don't. Then you are only bothering me, and you might as well stick pins in me,, as bother me when I'm worried already.

Mrs. C. [*Aside*] And I was trying to get him in a good humor for Virgie's sake. I'd better postpone discussing her affair with Jack.

Prof. [*Looks at watch*] Where the deuce can Mouser be, half an hour behind his time?

Mrs. C. [*Sweetly*] Won't you wait for him, dear? [*Buttoning his coat, etc.*] I wish to ask you about—

Prof. About what?

Mrs. C. [*Quickly*] Now don't be so—[*Checking herself and sweetly*] Do you remember, love, saying the other day, when we spoke of money, that you could not spare any because you anticipated a call on you from Bob?

Prof. Well, what of it?

Mrs. C. Well, you see, Bob gets on very well without assistance—and so I thought, as we have often talked of getting a new set of furniture—

Prof. [*Angrily*] A new set of furniture! Are you crazy?

Mrs. C. Come into the parlor—look at the sofas and chairs, and then call me crazy.

Prof. I won't go into the parlor, nor look at anything. Some other time.

Mrs. C. That's what you always say.

Prof. I guess the sofas and chairs will last for a week or so longer!

Mrs. C. But when, dear, when will you see about them? I saw the most exquisite parlor set at Pottier & Stymus's on Tuesday, only five hundred dollars, and a lovely, a perfectly lovely set, only fifteen hundred.

Prof. Fifteen hundred fiddlesticks! Don't talk to me! Fifteen hundred dollars!

Mrs. C. Well, but the five hundred?

Prof. Don't talk to me about any such nonsense for a month.

Mrs. C. For a month! Gracious me, Cornelius—always in a month. What's going to happen in a month? [*Doorbell rings*]

Prof. That's Mouser, now. [*Holds door open*]

Mrs. C. That dirty creature again. What does he want here, every morning and evening? [*Mouser enters, L.1.E.*]

Mous. Morning, professor. Morning, ma'am.

Prof. Come in, Mouser. Come into the parlor, we'll be quiet there. [*Crossing*] Excuse me, my dear. [*Exit with Mouser*]

Mrs. C. In a month—what does it mean? There's something on the professor's mind, and I'll discover what it is, if I have to shave his head. [*Exit, R. Music*]

Scene 4: *Same as Act II. Enter Professor and Mouser, C.R.*

Prof. [*L.*] Now, Mouser, any points?

Mous. [*Rubbing his hands*] What did I tell you about Bonanza, eh?

Prof. Anything new?

Mous. It's working; you'll be a millionaire in a week.

Prof. What is it—what is it?

Mous. Haven't you heard? [*In a tone of triumph*] A hundred and eighty-seven!

Prof. A hundred and eighty-seven! You don't say so! What's a hundred and eighty-seven?

Mous. Bonanza! When I told you to sell, it was three hundred and five.

Prof. Was it?

Mous. When are your contracts due?

Prof. What contracts?

Mous. Your sales.

Prof. I haven't made any sales yet. But if you think it's a good time, I'll sell now.

Mous. Sell now! Why nobody'll buy now.

Prof. The devil they won't!

Mous. You've missed a fortune! Why didn't you take my advice?

Prof. I did take your advice.

Mous. I told you to sell.

Prof. Well, I had to buy before I could sell, didn't I? And I bought that very day.

Mous. Bought! [*Horrified*]

Prof. Yes—and I've been buying ever since, every share that was offered, deliverable today! Nobody would deliver before today. Why, what's the matter, Mouser? [*Observes Mouser's face, which has undergone horrible convulsions*]

Mous. Oh, you infernal fool!

Prof. Mouser!

Mous. You've been done—sold—swindled!

Prof. Swindled! Sold!

Mous. I told you to sell, and you bought.

Prof. But I didn't have 'em then to sell.

Mous. Neither did the sharks you bought from. Don't you know the first rules of the game?

Prof. No, I'm afraid not.

Mous. Afraid not! And you speculating in stocks!

Prof. But what's to be done—why didn't you tell me? What's the end of it all?

Mous. The end? You're squeezed.

Prof. Squeezed? Have I lost everything?

Mous. Lost everything? Yes, and more, too! I'm done with you!

Prof. Don't desert me, Mouser.

Mous. Good morning. [*Going*]

Prof. Mouser—my good Mouser, what is to be done?

Mous. Have you any money left?

Prof. I don't know; not much I guess.

Mous. Have you the nerve for a desperate attempt?

Prof. [*Faintly*] I'll try.

Mous. There is one thing left. Keep it up. Bull the market.

Prof. Bull the market! Mercy on me, what's that?

Mous. Go on! Buy Bonanza.

Prof. And be doubly ruined.

Mous. It's your only chance. Buy all that's offered. They may think on the street that you have private and valuable information about Bonanza, and the price may go up—and then—

Prof. Yes—then?

Mous. Sell—sell as fast as you can.

Prof. If I only get a chance once—how I would sell!

Mous. Come with me.

Prof. Wait. [*Buttons up*] Now. [*Doorbell rings*] Who's that? [*Rymple enters, L.1.E.*]

Rym. My dear nephew!

Prof. Another time. I'm going out.

Rym. But—

Prof. Millions of dollars hang on every moment. I can't wait. Mrs. C. will be with you in a moment. Come, Mouser! To the street!

Mous. And remember—bull Bonanza.

Prof. I will—I'll bull Bonanza! [*Both exeunt, L.1.E.*]

Rym. Bull Bonanza! Poor boy! Speculating in stocks! Bull Bonanza! Poor boy! They'll toss him. [*Enter Mrs. Cawallader and Virgie, C.R.*]

Rym. Ah! My dear Carrie! And my pretty pet! And so your husband is speculating in stocks! Dear me—dear me!

Mrs. C. [*R.*] Cornelius speculating?

Vir. [*L.*] Papa speculating?

Rym. [*C.*] Don't you know—hasn't he said anything to you?

Mrs. C. Not a word!

Rym. It's too true. Izard told me yesterday. You know Izard?

Vir. Uncle Cawallader's cashier?

Rym. Yes. I was at the office, and he said to me in a sly tone, "The professor is going to be a millionaire!"

Vir. and Mrs. C. A millionaire!

Rym. He has an immense sum in deposit with Izard. Immense!

Mrs. C. [*About to faint*] Virgie, catch me!

Vir. Oh, mamma!

Mrs. C. [*Recovers, vigorously*] Are you sure?

Rym. Izard showed me your husband's orders for buying stocks—hundreds and thousands of shares.

Mrs. C. Hundreds of thousands! Oh! [*About to go off again*] But where did he get the money?

Rym. [*C.*] I knew for some time past, that he had money; and so do you. You knew it, now don't pretend. [*Smiling, gleefully*]

Mrs. C. I?

Rym. Of course! You know that, ever since I failed in business and became too feeble to continue, your husband has always joined with Cawallader to supply my wants. Cawallader told me so. Every time I asked him for a favor, he says to me, "Remember, you are indebted to the good professor for half of this, but he don't like it to be mentioned; so don't speak to him about it, but always come to me," and I always went to him, and never even thanked your husband.

Vir. Oh, mamma! It is only a kind deception of uncle's. Papa has always been struggling to keep a roof over our heads.

Mrs. C. No, my child. My suspicions tell me there is truth in it all. [*To Rymple*] How much money has Cornelius embarked in these vile speculations?

Rym. A large sum—thousands and thousands, I guess.

Mrs. C. Oh, the deceitful monster! But there shall be an end of it. Speculations, indeed! Thousands and millions squandered in stocks, and his wife and daughter in rags!

Vir. Oh, mamma!

Mrs. C. [*Walking about*] In rags, and our furniture in holes, and the—oh, this is too much! Has he gone out?

Rym. [*Following her*] Yes. To Wall Street. To bull Bonanza.

Mrs. C. [*Shrieks*] What? More extravagance, I suppose. But I'll put a stop to it.

Rym. Don't be violent! Don't be rash! Wait a little while, and in a month or so—

Mrs. C. [*Shrieks*] What—in a month or so? That settles it! Virgie!

Vir. Mamma!

Mrs. C. [*To Rymple*] Will you do me a favor, Uncle Rymple?

Rym. With pleasure, my dear child; but nothing rash—

Mrs. C. Go down to Pottier & Stymus's at once.

Rym. Pottier & Stymus's?

Mrs. C. [*Feels in her pocket*] Here's his card! Tell him you come from me, and simply say, "The Orange Puffs!"

Rym. The Orange Puffs?

Mrs. C. He'll understand!

Rym. But—

Mrs. C. If you don't go, I'll go myself.

Rym. I'll go! I'll go! But nothing rash, promise me, nothing rash!

Mrs. C. I'll take care of that. Remember, the Orange Puffs!

Rym. Orange Puffs! Bull Bonanza and Orange Puffs! They're both mad! [*Exit quickly, L.1.E.*]

Vir. [R.] What are you going to do, mamma?

Mrs. C. We have been wronged, my poor child, but the day of retribution is at hand! I have ordered a new set of furniture.

Vir. Without papa's consent?

Mrs. C. His consent? With his millions? Go to Lord & Taylor's at once!

Vir. About the dresses?

Mrs. C. Tell them to send up their very latest styles from Worth's.

Vir. All of them?

Mrs. C. All of them! We'll select them here, my poor darling. You shall be happy! Jack shall be happy! The money shall benefit somebody besides these wretched speculators.

Vir. [Looking L.] There's papa at the door; I hear his key.

Mrs. C. Run at once to Lord & Taylor's! I'll see your father alone.

Vir. [Aside] I'll send a little note to Jack, too. [Exit, C.R.]

Mrs. C. I wonder he has dared to look me in the face! [Professor enters, L.E., very dejected]

Prof. I went out to bull Bonanza, and I'm gored myself. Mouser is to follow me with the latest from the scene of battle. [Sinks in chair, L.]

Mrs. C. Cornelius Agassiz! [Severely]

Prof. Oh! You're there!

Mrs. C. Have you ever had a truer friend than your wife, Agassiz?

Prof. Now what the devil's the matter?

Mrs. C. Do you confide in your wife? Do you share your happiness with her?

Prof. Happiness? Share it? I think she keeps it all to herself.

Mrs. C. [Effusively] Oh, Cornelius! You deprive yourself and her—[Sinking on her knees beside him and embraces him]

Prof. Oh, behave yourself! Don't make a damned fool of yourself. I don't want to be pounced upon!

Mrs. C. Pounced upon?

Prof. Yes, pounced upon! [Starts up] It really surprises me, when I think how patient I am. When I go out—when I come in—when I sit down—it's always the same!

Mrs. C. I will not disturb you any more, my dear!

Prof. Glad to hear it.

Mrs. C. Go when you please, come when you like, sit down or stand up—it shall be all the same to me. I shall have plenty to do, without consulting you.

Prof. Visions of happiness!

Mrs. C. Only—don't be astonished.

Prof. Eh?

Mrs. C. I say—don't be astonished!

Prof. Astonished at what? [*She commences to unpin tidies from chairs*] I say, look here, you ain't going to begin housecleaning now, are you?

Mrs. C. Go on with your business—I'll attend to mine! [*Jerks tidy off his chair*]

Prof. Look here! Don't flap those things about my back, will you? [*Bell rings*] Who's that?

Mrs. C. The dressmaker!

Prof. The what?

Mrs. C. The dressmaker! Are you deaf?

Prof. Oh! I'm dumbfounded! [*Mlle. de Vincey, modiste, enters, preceded by Virgie, and followed by two Girls with large boxes*]

Vir. Here we are, mamma.

Prof. Who are these people?

Mlle. D. Vel, I declare! Who is zis gentleman, mademoiselle?

Vir. This is my papa. [*Professor grunts and turns aside*] It's the dresses from Lord & Taylor's, pa.

Mrs. C. [*Sweetly*] Don't mind Mr. Cawallader. What have you brought?

Mlle. D. Ve have brought ze *manteaux*, madame, you vere looking at ze day before ze yesterday. Open ze cartons, ladees! [*The Girls open boxes, Mlle. de Vincey takes out a cloak*] I vill try you first, mademoiselle! [*Tries sack on Virgie*] It is vere becoming. Do you not zink so, madame?

Mrs. C. [*R.*] Lovely!

Vir. Oh, papa! Isn't it lovely?

Prof. Don't bother me!

Mlle. D. Now yours, madame! It fits *perfection*.

Mrs. C. How do I look, dear? [*L.C., and round*]

Prof. Like an old scarecrow.

Mlle. D. [*C.*] I beg *pardon*, monsieur, zis is ze latest style.

Prof. [*L.*] Hold your tongue; who spoke to you?

Mlle. D. *Mon dieu!* Ze savage!

Mrs. C. We'll take these.

Vir. Oh, papa, I'm ever so much obliged to you.

Prof. What the devil—

Mlle. D. Zese two vill be exact three hundred and seventy-five dollars.

Mrs. C. Very well; send the bill in on the first of the month. We'll call this afternoon, and look at some silks for dresses.

Mlle. D. *Oui* madame, I have ze honor, madame. *Bon jour,* monsieur.

Prof. Go to the—

Mrs. C. Professor! [*Mlle. de Vincey screams and runs off, followed by Virgie and two Girls*]

PROF. Now, Mrs. C., perhaps you'll explain—

MRS. C. Certainly—in a month. [*Tafferty, a smart-looking salesman, enters, C.L., followed by four Porters*]

TAF. Ah! Good morning, Mrs. Cawallader! We're prompt you see. This is the room, I suppose.

MRS. C. Yes, sir.

TAF. And this is the old set you wish us to allow for on the bill?

MRS. C. Yes; it's rather old—but—

TAF. Rather. We have the carts below, and will carry it off at once. John, load these. [*The Porters seize chairs and commence to carry them off*]

PROF. Good lord—what is all this?

MRS. C. [*Triumphantly*] My business, my dear. Don't be astonished.

PROF. The woman's mad! [*As he is about to sit down in successive chairs, the Porters carry them off. In despair, he throws himself in arm-chair, L. Tafferty jerks it from under him, and takes it off*]

TAF. The new set will be here in a few minutes, ma'am. [*Exit after Porters*]

PROF. Stop, you robbers! Where are the police? Not even a stool to sit on. Woman, what does this mean?

MRS. C. Can't you see? I've ordered the new furniture.

PROF. New furniture! And I'm beggared!

MRS. C. We understand. [*Laughs*] Bonanza.

PROF. A beggar, I tell you! I'm ruined!

MRS. C. Certainly—ha, ha, ha!

PROF. How are these things to be paid for? [*Music. Jack enters with Virgie, hand in hand*]

JACK. My dear professor, I have just heard; Virgie has told me all. Believe me, no one rejoices more than I do, to know that you are a rich and prosperous man. [*Offers both hands*]

PROF. [*Starts back*] He's mad, too!

JACK. I know how many years you have toiled in the interests of science, and now that you are reaping your reward—

PROF. Reaping my reward! I tell you all—

MRS. C. [*Placing Virgie's hand in Jack's*] She is yours, Jack. The first act of our prosperity is to make you both happy.

VIR. Dear papa!⎫
                    ⎬ [*Both kneel*]
JACK. Dear professor!⎭

PROF. [*Runs and grasps his hat*] This is a madhouse. There's something in the air. I begin to feel it. It's beginning to unsettle my reason. Let me go out—[*Tafferty appears, C., with a chair*]

TAF. Now, boys, lively!

PROF. [*Staggers back*] More of it!

MRS. C. The new furniture, love. Orange puffs—ten pieces—fifteen hundred dollars.

PROF. Oh! [*Porters enter with the set of furniture. Two appear in doorway with a sofa. Professor makes a dash for the doorway, sinks on sofa, and is brought down, C., swooning*]

ACT IV.

SCENE: *Elegant drawing room in Cawallader's house, supposed to be en suite with the scene of the first act, but more richly decorated and furnished. Girandola on piano, bookcase upstage. Time, evening, just after dinner. At a table, R., is Lucretia sitting upon a sofa, R. At piano, C., are Bob and Eugenia. He is playing very softly, a study. Cawallader is in easy chair, L., talking with Rymple. Lucretia is looking over papers.*

RYM. When did you take him into your office?

CAW. The very day after he called here first.

RYM. He looks a bright lad. [*Looks furtively at Bob*]

CAW. I never saw anyone like him. He gets at the meaning of everything in the business, at the first word of instruction.

RYM. Steady?

CAW. Spends every evening here.

RYM. He plays chess capitally.

CAW. Why don't you play with him?

RYM. Because—[*Pointing over his shoulder*] That's the only chess he plays now.

EUG. [*To Bob*] How beautiful that is? You call it "The Dream"?

BOB. Yes; you haven't heard the second part; I don't like it; it's too loud. That is the "Awakening."

EUG. [*Gently*] Don't play that yet. Let us have the dream over again. [*They play*]

CAW. He seems to be rather fond of that laborious occupation.

RYM. I know he'd rather play chess with me, for when I got your permission to invite him here to a game or two of an evening, he jumped at it.

CAW. Suppose you ask him now.

RYM. It's no use; when he leaves the piano, he has to read to your wife.

CAW. She seems to have taken quite a fancy to him.

RYM. So she does, but don't let it distress you.

CAW. I don't. I'm only sorry for you. You have no one to checkmate.

RYM. Not even the professor. I can never get him to sit down with me now. He's worried. Have you had a quarrel?

CAW. I haven't seen him for a month.

RYM. And you're sure there's nothing between you?

CAW. So far from that, they are coming here tonight.

LUC. Come, Eugenia. Isn't it time to read?

EUG. In a moment, mamma.

RYM. [*Rising*] They are going to read. I'm off. [*Crosses to C.*]

CAW. Don't you like reading?

RYM. Ivanhoe? No; when we get old, we love to hear new things. When I hear them read Ivanhoe, I seem to be as old as Isaac. I'll come back by and by, and see the professor. [*Goes up and stops a moment at piano, to chat, then exit, C.*]

CAW. [*Solus*] My wife begins to like him. If I only knew how to encourage her. I guess the old way is the best—to oppose her fancy. That will do the business. [*Rises*]

EUG. [*Comes down*] Dear papa! How happy you look tonight. [*Kisses him*] Somehow you seem so full of pleasant thoughts these days. I believe you like me more than ever.

CAW. [*Smiling*] Perhaps. [*She goes up*]

LUC. [*Coming C.*] This is the fourth evening you've been at home this week. What in the world will your board of directors do?

CAW. [*Assuming gruffness*] I say, is that young man going to spend the night here again?

LUC. Why not? Have you any objections?

CAW. He seems to be indispensable.

LUC. He reads very well, don't you think so?

CAW. Too loud, disturbs me, when I look over the papers.

LUC. Oh, Jonathan! If you only had a little poetry in your soul! [*Goes to chair, R.*]

BOB. Shall we begin? [*To Lucretia*]

LUC. [*Going R.*] Come to this table, then we'll disturb no one. Will you bring the light here, Mr. Ruggles? Eugenia, get Ivanhoe!

BOB. With pleasure. [*Gets light from piano and is going towards table, R., when Eugenia comes down with book, offers to take it*] Permit me—

EUG. Oh, I can carry it.

BOB. Let me.

EUG. If you insist, but I'll take the light.

BOB. Oh, I can carry both.

LUC. [*At table, R.*] At this rate we shall never begin. [*Bob and Eugenia place light and book hurriedly on table*]

Bob. Now we can commence. [*All sit*]

Caw. [*Aside*] Now for my grand stragetical [*sic*] movement. [*Looks at paper, pretends to have discovered something*] By Jove!

All. [*Look around*] What's the matter?

Caw. Bradish & Company suspended!

Luc. [*Relieved*] Goodness! I thought it was something dreadful. [*Turns back*]

Eug. [*To Bob*] That don't matter to us.

Bob. Let 'em suspend.

Caw. Robert!

Bob. [*Rises, crosses to him*] Yes, sir.

Caw. A word with you.

Bob. [*Coming down*] Shall I send any message, sir?

Caw. [*Crosses to him, aside*] Now for the bombshell! [*Aloud*] No, you must go yourself.

Bob. Where?

Caw. To San Francisco.

Eug. and Luc. [*Rise*] To San Francisco!

Caw. By the Pacific Express tomorrow morning. Attend the meeting of creditors to represent our firm. Bradish & Company owe us $80,000.

Bob. [*Agitated*] If I understand the business sufficiently!

Caw. I have every confidence in you.

Eug. [*At his side*] Oh, Robert! [*Aside, to him*]

Luc. Is it necessary to start tomorrow?

Caw. Imperative. I'll go now and jot down a few instructions. [*Aside, going*] I think that will bring matters to a crisis. [*Exit, L.1.E.*]

Bob. This is thunder from a clear sky.

Eug. Must he go, mamma?

Bob. I dare not refuse.

Luc. He can send someone else.

Bob. No. He means it to be a mark of confidence.

Luc. Pray, don't. A clerk, like a soldier, must obey orders.

Eug. We were getting along so well.

Luc. And Ivanhoe just commenced.

Bob. We'll have to postpone it.

Eug. Mamma, tell papa we'll be through in about a fortnight.

Luc. What would he care? He has no appreciation for such things.

Bob. What troubles me most is, I'm afraid I'll not be able to help him in San Francisco.

Eug. I'm afraid so, too; you are a great deal more useful here, you understand the business better.

Bob. [*Smiling*] Yes. But I'm afraid your father intends to increase my sphere of usefulness.

Eug. It's real mean of pa.

Bob. [*Earnestly*] No. Nothing is mean that he does; I owe him everything—more than I can tell—and if he were to send me to the North Pole, I'd go.

Luc. [*Crosses to L.C.*] Very well. Go and get your things ready for departure. Return in an hour, and then we'll see whether he changes his mind or not.

Bob. In an hour I'll be back. [*Aside, going*] I understand it all. He likes me, but I have presumed too much. This is intended to separate us. But I'll obey. [*Exit, C.R.*]

Eug. Mamma, you must see papa at once. Talk to him in a decided manner. Tell him he must send someone else, or he can go himself.

Luc. No, no, my dear, that would never do; we can't take the bull by the horns in that way.

Eug. Take the bull by the horns! What bull?

Luc. Tut, child! It's merely a practical expression; I mean we must not oppose your father point-blank.

Eug. He's coming back—now is our chance. [*Going off, R.*] Don't let him go, whatever you do. [*Exit*]

Luc. I know he likes the young man, but if he believed I did, he'd do anything to spite me. I shall have to adopt the old method—indifference. [*Walks up C. Cawallader enters, L.I.E.*]

Caw. Where's that boy?

Luc. Ahem! [*Clearing her throat*]

Caw. Did you hear? Where's Robert?

Luc. I'm sure I don't know.

Caw. He was here a minute ago.

Luc. Oh, don't bother me with your business. It's nothing but hurry, worry, go here, go there, start tomorrow, break up an evening, spoil my enjoyment, business, business, business, from year's end to year's end. [*Crosses to L., R. of C. table*]

Caw. Now what's all this grumbling about?

Luc. Grumbling? I wish, my dear, you'd choose your expressions, when talking to your wife.

Caw. I forgot, my angel. I did not mean grumbling. What's my angel flapping her wings about now? [*Sits, C.*]

Luc. [*Aside, R., shaking her finger behind his back*] Oh, you hardheaded block.

Caw. [*Detects gesture*] Are you trying to mesmerize me?

Luc. Mesmerize you! I'd like to put you to sleep once.

Caw. You could, dear, if you'd keep still for fifteen minutes, at any time.

Luc. I'm really worried out of my life; everything goes wrong.

Caw. What goes wrong?

Luc. There are the servants.

Caw. Crumpets?

Luc. Yes—Crumpets and Eliza both.

Caw. What have Crumpets and Eliza been doing?

Luc. Their impertinence is intolerable; one or the other must go.

Caw. Send away Eliza. Crumpets has been with us twenty years.

Luc. Oh, he's the most to blame—gray as a badger, and running after a young girl like Eliza.

Caw. Crumpets running after Eliza—nonsense, he's too old!

Luc. The old ones are the worst, you ought to know that. I can't get any work out of them.

Caw. Oh, come, it's not so bad as that. It's your poetic imaginations. Send them here—I'll prove it. [Rings bell] Crumpets never fell in love in his life.

Luc. What are you going to do?

Caw. To make an experiment. I've observed that when two people in love are sent to light a candle in a dark room, they usually require a quarter of an hour to do it. [Crumpets and Eliza enter, C.R.]

Eliza. Please, ma'am, did you want me?

Caw. No, I want you. Crumpets, light the candles in the back parlor.

Crum. The candles, sir? The gas is lit!

Caw. The gas is not sufficient; light the candles, and bring them here. Eliza, go help him. [Eliza and Crumpets look at each other, then at Mrs. Cawallader, and exeunt, C.L.]

Luc. Well?

Caw. [Takes out his watch] If they are in love—a quarter of an hour— if they are not in love, a quarter of a minute. Five seconds gone—ten—fif- teen—twen—[Crumpets enters with a lighted candelabra, C., followed by Eliza]

Crum. Here they are, sir.

Caw. [Shuts his watch and looks at Lucretia] Very good. [To Crumpets] Now blow them out.

Crum. Blow them out, sir?

Caw. Blow them out. Eliza, help him. [They blow out the candles] No[w] go. Eliza, help him.

Crum. [Aside, going R.] The governor's gone clean out of his head.

Eliza. Missus, too, for she don't never say a word. [Exeunt, R.]

CAW. [*To Lucretia*] You see—you are mistaken! There is some love-making going on in the house, but it is not between Crumpets and Eliza. It is a little more dangerous—and that is why I have sent Mr. Ruggles to San Francisco. [*Pretending sternness*]

LUC. You surely do not mean—

CAW. I surely do.

LUC. Mr. Ruggles and Eugenia?

CAW. Yes.

LUC. And I, with my eyes wide open, looking at every movement? I see nothing.

CAW. Lovers are sly.

LUC. That young man—so quiet, so well-behaved, and our innocent child? It is impossible!

CAW. Come, now, you are very fond of poetical similes. Suppose a donkey —a quiet, well-behaved donkey—were to see a thistle right under his nose, what would he do?

LUC. Eat it, I suppose.

CAW. Imagine a frog coming to the edge of a pond, what would he do?

LUC. Jump in!

CAW. Jump in, of course. Now fancy Mr. Robert Ruggles coming here every evening, meeting Eugenia, playing the piano, singing, reading with her, looking into her eyes, which are constantly seeking his own, what's the result?

LUC. Well!

CAW. He'll fall in love, so will she; it's human nature, it's the doctrine of selection, it's cause and effect, and, if you were as philosophical as you are poetical—

LUC. [*Interrupting*] But I'm always with them.

CAW. Oh, that makes no difference; you only constitute the shadows of the picture; everything has two sides, a bright one and a dark one.

LUC. You are insulting, Mr. Cawallader, and you are impugning my maternal solicitude and care; you charge me with neglecting my duty to Eugenia. But I will protect her, and what is more, I will not rest until I have refuted your calumnies. I will prove that nothing exists between Mr. Ruggles and her, and for that purpose, I insist that Mr. Ruggles shall not leave New York.

CAW. He must!

LUC. You send him away on a mere suspicion?

CAW. I do!

LUC. He shall not be sacrificed. [*Crosses to L.*]

CAW. You appear to be extremely fond of him, all of a sudden!

Luc. His cause is mine. Our interests are the same now, and he must remain to vindicate me.

Caw. What a temper you are in!

Luc. Shall he stay or not?

Caw. What a way you have of putting things!

Luc. Your answer!

Caw. Do as you like. [*Crosses to L.*] But remember, if I discover that my suspicions are well founded, you shall all suffer for it. [*In pretended rage, as he is going*] The plot thickens! That's the poetical way, I believe, of expressing the situation. [*Exit, L.*]

Luc. [*Solus*] Robert in love with Eugenia! Nonsense! And I am to blame for it? To blame, indeed! What blame can possibly—and they have known each other scarcely a month. But the donkey! The thistle! The frog! [*Eugenia enters with some fashion plates, R.1.E.*]

Eug. Here is the *Journal des Modes*, mamma. [*Listlessly throwing herself in a chair, R.*] I wonder whether they dress very fashionably there now.

Luc. Where?

Eug. In San Francisco. [*Lucretia looks at her intently*] Have you spoken to papa?

Luc. About what?

Eug. Mr. Ruggles going away. [*Looks up*] Why, ma! What are you looking at me so for?

Luc. [*Sitting beside her*] Eugenia!

Eug. [*Uneasy*] Why, mamma—[*Bob enters quickly, L.C.*]

Bob. [*Books in his hands*] Here I am back again.

Eug. [*Jumps up*] Already!

Bob. Packed my trunk in five minutes.

Luc. [*Aside*] He seems very indifferent about going.

Bob. [*Aside to Eugenia*] Did your mother speak to Mr. Cawallader about my going?

Luc. I believe you'd rather stay than go, would you not, Mr. Ruggles?

Bob. A thousand times! [*Checks himself*] If Mr. Cawallader—or you—desired it.

Luc. You prefer to spend your evenings here—[*Eugenia and Bob look at each other*] reading?

Bob. Oh, certainly. I brought some more books, got 'em on my way back here.

Eug. [*Going up C.*] Oh, let me see them! [*They speak together earnestly*]

Luc. [*Watching them and aside*] Are they in love? I can try. Eugenia, my dear child!

Eug. Yes, mamma.

Luc. Light the candles, yonder.

Eug. These, mamma?

Bob. Can I not light them?

Luc. You may assist, if you like.

Bob. [*Puts books down*] With the greatest pleasure!

Luc. Be as quick as you can about it; the professor and Aunt Carrie will soon be here.

Eug. Yes, mamma.

Bob. Where are the matches?

Eug. Here they are!

Luc. [*Aside*] I will give them ten minutes. [*Exit, C.R. Bob and Eugenia proceed to light each a match; they are so agitated and preoccupied, that they do not light the candles, but light and extinguish matches repeatedly*]

Bob. [*Absently*] So, uncle is coming here this evening?

Eug. Yes.

Bob. It's too bad, we can't be alone, our last evening.

Eug. Our last evening? How sadly that sounds! [*Draws match*]

Bob. [*Takes match from her, and clasps her hand*] How your hand trembles! Oh, what is the matter?

Eug. Does it tremble?

Bob. Take care, you'll burn yourself.

Eug. [*Blows out match*] Your hand is trembling, too.

Bob. It is strange that both of us—

Eug. I have been sewing today.

Bob. So have I—I mean I have been packing my trunks in such a hurry. [*Pause, both draw matches*] Tomorrow I shall be whirling off to the prairies.

Eug. The prairies! [*Faints. Bob blows out his match, she drops hers, he puts his foot on it and catches her*]

Bob. You're ill.

Eug. No. But you seem to be glad that you are going away.

Bob. Do you wish me, then, to show you how sorry I am?

Eug. We shall miss you very much.

Bob. Will you?

Eug. Yes.

Bob. A little?

Eug. I did not say a little.

Bob. [*Lighting*] Just think! [*Pause*] It is only four weeks ago, that I met you. [*She lights at his light*]

Eug. At the depot.

Bob. It seems like a dream—a bright gleam—and all is over. [*Blows out match*]

EUG. A dream!

BOB. We were happy that day, even for a few minutes. [*Her match has burnt down and scorches her fingers*]

EUG. Oh! [*Bob brushes it down and kisses her finger*]

BOB. But that night, after I met you, when I slept—may I tell you?—I beheld you! At first your image was dim, as if veiled in a light vapor from my sight, then it became more and more vivid, and, at last, gleamed upon my sight with a radiance from the skies!

EUG. Oh! [*Aside*] Virgie's own words.

BOB. But it is foolish for me to tell you! [*Goes to table, and draws match*]

EUG. No—no! [*Goes to him, lays her hand on his arm, and blows out match quickly*] Continue. I like to hear you speak.

BOB. A feeling crept round my heart I had never known before. I was in love with the whole world. If I had riches, I would have scattered them in the streets, to make everyone happy. Then I saw you—your voice was like the soft music of my dreams, and now I am to leave you!

EUG. Do you know it has been like that with me—all of it.

BOB. [*Taking her hand*] Then you, too, love—

EUG. Mamma is coming! [*They separate, scared*]

BOB. The candles! [*They rush to matches and both light one candle*] She's not coming. Oh, Eugenia! [*Arm around her waist*]

EUG. We must light the candles.

BOB. Never mind the candles. [*Drawing her down C.*] This moment may never return. I have so much to tell you.

EUG. What is it?

BOB. That I love you with all my heart, from my very soul.

EUG. I know it. [*Crosses to L.*]

BOB. But you must tell me that you—that it will not be only a dream—that you will be my wife! [*Eugenia nods her head*] You are silent.

EUG. I nodded my head. That is yes. I'm so full I can't say any more.

BOB. My wife! [*Embraces her*]

EUG. Now, I'm sure someone is coming. [*They run to the table*] Where are the matches?

BOB. I can't find a match. [*Lucretia appears, C.R.*]

LUC. It is true, then!

EUG. Mamma! [*Runs out, R.1E.*]

BOB. Who's there? [*Sees Lucretia, and runs out, L.1E. Cawallader enters, laughing, L.1E.*]

CAW. Ahem! [*Pretending anger on seeing Lucretia*] What is all this?

LUC. Oh, Jonathan!

CAW. What? [*Points after Bob*] The donkey?

Luc. Yes.

Caw. [*Pointing after Eugenia*] The frog?

Luc. Yes! [*Agonizing cry. Cawallader drops in chair, laughing*] You monster! [*Exit, R.D.*]

Caw. The deed is done. [*Crumpets enters, C.L.*] Now what do you want?

Crum. Professor, sir, and Mrs. Cawallader and Miss Virginia, sir!

Caw. Already? [*Looks at his watch*] Yes—Crumpets!

Crum. Yes, sir!

Caw. Show them in.

Crum. Miss Virgie's gone up to Miss Eugenia's room, sir.

Caw. Very good. Tell the professor I'll be with him presently, and ask your mistress to see me at once. [*Crumpets exits, C.R.*] Now for the Big Bonanza! [*Exit, L.1.E. The Professor enters, C.R., his hat on, umbrella under his arm, a picture of woe; Mrs. Cawallader follows him*]

Mrs. C. My dear, you haven't taken off your hat.

Prof. Haven't I?

Mrs. C. Let me have it. [*Puts it away*] Do, for goodness sake, look up and say something.

Prof. What shall I say?

Mrs. C. Be cheerful, when Cousin Jonathan comes in.

Prof. Be cheerful!

Mrs. C. Don't think of your misfortunes—look at me!

Prof. You haven't lost $30,000, nor made a fool of yourself!

Mrs. C. I'm not sure that I haven't done both, my dear. At all events, your loss is my loss. [*Crosses to L., aside*] added to a few troubles of my own.

Prof. Oh! Abominable Bonanza! [*Walks about*]

Mrs. C. Now, don't begin to walk, dear; you walked all last night. What's gone, is gone!

Prof. That isn't the worst of it. I've got to stand up before Cawallader, and hear him laugh! But I'll do it; I'm not crushed yet. I've been fleeced, but I'm not floored! [*Slams book on table, C.*]

Mrs. C. Great heavens! [*In affright*]

Prof. What are you scared at? Don't worry me! [*Takes account-book from his pocket*] There's the result—I went in with $30,000, and came out without a red!

Mrs. C. [*L., aside, taking paper out of her pocket*] "Dear madame: We enclose bill for the two dresses, and beg the favor of an early settlement." $380! This is my part of the trouble! I've got on clothes that haven't been paid for!

Prof. Caroline Amelia Cawallader!

Mrs. C. Yes, dear.

PROF. I have taken a resolution! It's a hard one, but I must do it. You know I owe Cawallader—

MRS. C. $30,000.

PROF. More than that.

MRS. C. More?

PROF. Yes—you must know that for a year or two past, since my chemical experiments brought nothing, Cawallader has been advancing me money, on the strength of my expectations from Uncle Rymple.

MRS. C. Your expectations from Uncle Rymple?

PROF. Yes—I went to borrow from him, and he said, "It isn't borrowing; Uncle Bonanza"—I mean Uncle Rymple—"is going to leave us both something one of these days, so consider this an advance on your share." In all, I've had about $3,000. Now, I've made up my mind to see Uncle Rymple, tell him my trouble, and ask him to give me now, what he intends to leave me in his will. [*Exit, R.1.E.*]

MRS. C. And Uncle Rymple, the old miser, told me with his own lips, that my husband was supporting him! I'm certainly dreaming! [*Exit, R.1.E. Bob enters, C.L., Virgie enters, C.R.*]

BOB. Virgie!

VIR. Bob!

BOB. Hush! Where's Eugenia?

VIR. In her room, crying.

BOB. If I could only see her!

VIR. I'll go and tell her.

BOB. No—I don't want—[*Aside*] I feel like a robber! What would Mr. Cawallader do—what would he think if he found me here again?

VIR. So you're going away?

BOB. Yes—Jack has promised to write me every day how she is, and you must tell him.

VIR. Where is Jack?

BOB. Lucky fellow! He is not packed off to San Francisco for daring to fall in love. What I want you to do, is to introduce him here.

VIR. Here?

BOB. Yes—to Eugenia.

VIR. But I can't. Mamma won't even let him come to see *me*, now that papa is ruined!

BOB. Can't you fall sick? [*Crumpets enters, C.L., going to L.1.E.*]

VIR. Yes—but not here. It wouldn't be polite.

BOB. Get somebody in the house to complain of something! The very man! Crumpets!

CRUM. Yes, sir!

BOB. Here are five dollars, Crumpets!

CRUM. Thank you, sir.

BOB. How are you, Crumpets?

CRUM. Very well, sir.

BOB. You don't look so. Oh, you're far from well, Crumpets. Isn't he, Virgie?

VIR. Couldn't you manage to be sick, Mr. Crumpets?

CRUM. What for, miss? [*Faltering*]

VIR. For my sake, Crumpets.

CRUM. I don't understand, miss.

BOB. [*Gives him a dig in the ribs*] Get a pain directly, Crumpets! [*Another dig*] A severe pain.

CRUM. Where, sir?

BOB. Choose your own place, I'm not particular; double up, gasp for breath, roll up your eyes!

CRUM. Oh, sir! You mean make believe. I can do that, sir. Lor, sir, I'll go into convulsions. Oh! [*Begins to writhe*]

BOB. Not now! Good gracious! Not now!

CRUM. [*Recovering*] When shall I begin, sir?

BOB. Miss Virgie will give you the signal, and, when you fall sick, insist upon having Dr. Lymer—remember, Dr. John Lymer, and no one else.

CRUM. I see, sir; all right, sir. I'll watch for the signal, miss. [*As he is going out, he pretends to writhe and moan*] Oh! Oh, my! Oh, won't somebody go for the doctor—Dr. John Lymer! Oh! Oh! Dr. John Lymer! Oh! Oh! [*Exit, C.R.*]

BOB. That'll do. [*Mrs. Cawallader enters, R.D.*]

MRS. C. [*Upstage*] What's the matter with the poor creature?

BOB. [*Aside to Virgie*] For fear he should not do it successfully, you had better begin with something dangerous.

VIR. [*Aside to him*] I understand. I'll have the toothache. [*Puts handkerchief to face*]

MRS. C. [*Coming down*] Robert here?

BOB. Only waited to bid you good-bye, Aunt Carrie.

MRS. C. [*Aside*] He must be detained; Cousin Jonathan said he must be detained. How can I do it? [*Aloud*] Robert, won't you stop a moment, until I find your Uncle Cornelius? You mustn't think of going without bidding him good-bye.

BOB. Certainly. I'll wait, if he isn't too long coming. [*Aside to her*] You don't know all. I don't dare to meet Mr. Cawallader here.

MRS. C. [*Aside*] Unhappy boy! It must be embezzlement. [*Exit, R.1.E.*]

VIR. I'm afraid it's very wrong, to pretend to be sick.

BOB. Not if you don't do it better than that; nobody would believe you. Tie the handkerchief over your head. Here, let me show you.

VIR. I won't. I should be a perfect fright! [*The Professor is led in by Mrs. Cawallader, R.I.E.*]

MRS. C. There he is.

PROF. How can we do it?

MRS. C. Find some excuse. If he escapes, he will be pursued and arrested.

PROF. And we will be disgraced. [*Both advance*]

VIR. Oh, papa! My tooth!

PROF. Ah! My daughter, what is an aching tooth to an ungrateful nephew? [*Crosses to him*]

MRS. C. [*Crosses to her*] My poor child, come here. [*Takes her upstage*]

PROF. And so, sir, you are off to the Pacific Coast?

BOB. Start for San Francisco tomorrow—8:30 a.m.

PROF. It would have been money in your pocket, sir, if you had never been born. [*Crosses to R.*]

BOB. Oh, come, uncle! I'm not such a bad speculation as that.

MRS. C. You should at least have had some respect for us. [*Crosses down L.*]

BOB. What do you mean?

MRS. C. The infamous manner, in which you have betrayed Mr. Cawallader's confidence.

BOB. Who told you?

PROF. He told us himself.

BOB. [*Aside*] Infamous betrayal of confidence, eh? That's what he calls it, then. [*Sobered*] And there is no hope. [*Aloud*] It is enough. I had better leave New York at once. [*Crossing to go up and off, C.L.*]

MRS. C. [*To Professor*] Detain him.

BOB. [*To Virgie*] Good-bye, Virgie.

PROF. Here! [*Seizes his arm*] No, you don't.

BOB. What do you mean?

PROF. Come with me.

BOB. But I say, uncle!

MRS. C. Go without resistance, Robert, or never speak to me again.

PROF. Submit quietly, sir.

BOB. Submit quietly—if you'd only explain—

PROF. No time for explanations—will you come? [*Tries to drag him, he is immovable*]

BOB. But, aunt—

MRS. C. It is my wish—go!

Bob. Your wish! Oh, very well, come along then! [*Darts off suddenly, pulling Professor off his balance, then dragging him off, R.1.E.*]

Vir. [*R.*] What's the matter, mamma? Why do you keep him? He has to start tomorrow.

Mrs. C. Your Uncle Jonathan wishes him to be detained.

Vir. Detained! [*Aside*] Then there is hope! [*Crosses to L. Professor reenters, puffing*]

Prof. I've shut him up in the dining-room, and he promises to remain until I call him. [*Bob reenters*]

Bob. I say, don't go home and forget me, you know.

Prof. and Mrs. C. Go back, go back! [*Professor pushes him off and falls on his knees in doing so, then sinks into chair, R. Mrs. Cawallader in chair, L.*]

Prof. If I only knew how much he has taken. Oh, my poor head! [*Holds it with both hands*]

Mrs. C. I shall never recover this blow! Oh, my poor nerves! [*Lies back exhausted*]

Caw. [*Outside, L.*] Very well.

Vir. [*Aside, upstage*] Here's uncle. Now for my toothache. Oh, my tooth! [*Crumpets appears cautiously, near her, C.R.*]

Crum. Oh, my convulsions! I say, Miss Virgie, is it time? You know! [*Pantomimes sickness*] Oh, my convulsions!

Vir. [*Whispers*] No—no—not yet. [*Sinks in chair with tooth*]

Crum. All right. [*Disappears. Cawallader enters, L.1.E.*]

Caw. Hullo! What's all this? Everybody prostrated?

Prof. Oh, my head!

Mrs. C. Oh, my nerves!

Vir. Oh, my tooth!

Caw. [*To Professor*] You look very well.

Prof. I'm not—I ought to know. Go away, it's catching.

Caw. [*Goes to Mrs. Cawallader*] Why, Cousin Carrie!

Mrs. C. Oh! [*Groans*]

Caw. [*Aside*] Pretty good voice for a sick woman! [*Goes to Virgie*] Now, how is little rosebud?

Vir. Oh, oh, oh! My tooth! [*Leans her head against his breast; he pats her cheek*]

Caw. Why, why, all so very ill! I think the best thing we can do, is to send for a doctor.

Vir. [*Quickly*] Oh, yes—please.

Caw. We'll send Crumpets.

Vir. [*Whispers*] For Jack?

Caw. Jack, eh? Well, as long as it's not I who am sick—send for Jack. [*Virgie darts up, meets Crumpets, and both go off, C.R.*]

Mrs. C. [*Whispers to Cawallader*] Cornelius is really very ill.

Caw. I'll cure him. Leave us together a moment.

Mrs. C. Pray don't quarrel.

Caw. No fear. [*Conducts her off, C.R., and returns and sits by Professor, and lays hand on his shoulder*] Well! [*Quizzically*] I invited you here this evening—as you evidently intended never again to come and see me of your own accord, or without a special invitation—to talk over business. You got the statement from the office today?

Prof. [*Looks up, groans*] Oh! [*Buries his head in his hands*] Yes, I got it.

Caw. You perceive by this time, I suppose, that speculating is not so easy after all.

Prof. No—I don't.

Caw. Well, well! We won't argue that point. The fact is, when we parted last time, I said to myself, "You have been unjust to the professor. You have treated him unkindly. He is a learned and a talented man."

Prof. [*R.*] Did you say that?

Caw. I did.

Prof. It's the first sensible speech I ever heard you utter.

Caw. During the last few days, I found it true, that in matters of business—

Prof. You shan't lose by me. I'll pay you every cent. [*Crosses to L.*]

Caw. [*Looks at him*] You will!

Prof. I shall begin tomorrow to write a treatise I have been preparing for several years. You shall have every cent of the profits.

Caw. You need not take so much trouble for what can be more easily done. Do you remember your invention for fixing colors in dyeing wool?

Prof. No—yes, that was four years ago. You sent it to France, and you never heard anything more of it.

Caw. Well! Being an obstinate business man, I have tried it everywhere, and lastly at home. I have just sold your patent to a carpet manufacturer in Yonkers. [*Exhibits paper*]

Prof. I'm glad of it—will it help to pay?

Caw. Help to pay, my dear old boy! I received cash down—$20,000.

Prof. What?

Caw. Here's the contract and the check for the amount.

Prof. [*Trembling with delight*] Is it possible? [*Almost weeping as he takes the papers*]

Caw. It is the first [fruit] of your labors. Your brain begins to turn into money.

Prof. $20,000!

Caw. Better than Bonanza.

Prof. But I lost your $30,000 in that.

Caw. Not quite.

Prof. How?

Caw. Why, you see, Izard—you know Izard?

Prof. Your cashier!

Caw. Izard is an obdurate fellow, and when he got your orders to buy Bonanza—

Prof. Yes!

Caw. He disobeyed them. In fact, he has the money safe and sound. It was a serious breach of duty on the part of Izard, and, if you say the word, I'll discharge him on the spot.

Prof. Discharge him! Never! Show me Izard, and I'll fall upon his neck. [*Crosses to R.*] Izard is my savior! [*Recollecting*] But there is another matter.

Caw. What other matter?

Prof. Robert! [*Cawallader looks grave*] Has he—has he taken much from you? [*Very anxiously*]

Caw. Yes, very much.

Prof. [*Pressing check and paper on him*] Take this, and if it will make good your loss—

Caw. No, it will not. [*Rises, goes to door*] Robert! [*Calls. Bob enters timidly, R.1E.*]

Bob. Did you call *me,* sir?

Caw. Yes.

Bob. It's not my fault that I'm here, sir. I wanted to go.

Caw. Well, are you ready to start now?

Bob. Yes, sir.

Caw. Go, then! Take this money. [*Gives check to him*] It is a gift from your uncle. Go to the Pacific, to Europe, or where you will, and forget Eugenia.

Bob. I understand all, perfectly, sir, and I promise to go away, but I will not take money, and I cannot promise to forget your daughter, sir. If I were to promise it, I feel my heart would not help my memory to keep my word.

Caw. [*With fervor*] I believe you, and I won't ask you to make any such promise, either; you are a good fellow, Robert, and I believe—God bless you—that you will make my daughter happy!

Bob. Mr. Cawallader! Is it possible—

PROF. Marry Eugenia! Now I have lost my head!

BOB. Oh, sir, I can't speak. I want to cry and to shout! Hurrah!

PROF. [*Closing his mouth*] Robert, be decent.

CAW. No, let him shout. Hurrah!

BOB. Hurrah! [*Hugs Cawallader*]

CAW. Hurrah!

PROF. Hurrah! [*Jumping up*] Yes, I've lost my head. Hurrah! [*Music.* *Mrs. Cawallader, Lucretia and Eugenia enter, C.*]

MRS. C. I knew it—they have been quarrelling again. [*Seizes Professor, who is jumping about*]

LUC. Jonathan—what is all this?

MRS. C. Agassiz, don't get excited!

PROF. I never do, but I will now. Where is he? Let me get at him!

CAW. Your hand, old fellow!

LUC. No—no! [*Tries to restrain him*]

CAW. My dear, you don't understand.

MRS. C. [*Holding him*] Here's your hat. Let us go.

PROF. Damn the hat. [*Knocks it away*]

CAW. Professor!

PROF. My brother—Hurrah! [*They fly into each other's arms, as Mrs. Cawallader and Lucretia shriek, but seeing the result, they also embrace, Bob and Eugenia also. Virgie enters, dragging in Jack*]

VIR. Here's the doctor, papa.

PROF. [*Not noticing*] Send the doctor to the devil!

JACK. Professor!

PROF. Hollo! Is it you?

JACK. Professor, this is the third time you have ordered me from the house. [*About to go*]

PROF. [*Catching him*] And the last! I beg your pardon! Let me offer you an—[*Hands Virgie's hand to him*] apology.

JACK. Professor, I accept the apology.

VIR. Oh! Jack.

LUC. But explain to me.

CAW. They'll explain it all. [*Points to Bob and Eugenia*]

LUC. You consent?

CAW. I consent. Robert!

BOB. Yes, sir.

CAW. Embrace your mother-in-law.

BOB. With all my heart. [*Hugs her*]

CAW. That's what I call poetry. [*Music*]

CURTAIN

PIQUE

A Play of Today, in Five Acts

PIQUE

A LTHOUGH with *The Big Bonanza* Daly had at last found the German
mine of his good fortune, he did not give up prospecting elsewhere.
His next play, if we disregard *The New Leah,* a rehash of *Leah, the
Forsaken,* which had been made necessary by the threatenings of Kate
Bateman's lawyers, was *Pique.* The first three acts of this "new original
play" were based on Florence Marryat Lean's religious novel, *Her Lord and
Master.* The last two were inspired by the kidnapping of Charley Ross. In
the handling of the scene in the kidnapper's den, Daly leaned rather heavily
on Hugo's description of Jean Valjean's encounter with Thenardier at the
end of Book Eight of "Marius" in *Les Miserables.* The first production of
Pique occurred December 14, 1875, at the new Fifth Avenue Theatre.

The title of the play well describes the state of mind of a number of the
theatrical reporters who commented upon Daly's authorship of the new
play. Though an accusation of plagiarism from a manuscript previously
submitted to him was disproved, ultimately in the courts, critics all over
the country took the occasion to belabor the manager for his lack of originality. A quotation from the *Baltimore Bulletin* of January 5, 1876, will
serve as an example of the hostility manifested in many quarters. "It can
surely be no surprise to Mr. Daly, whom we never yet knew to incur the
accusation of being original, to find that his play of *Pique* should be ascribed
to almost any other source than himself."

Toward the play itself the New York critics were fairly lenient. As Daly
himself summed it up, "The press praise the play—but don't waste many
words on it. Sich is critics!" It was hardly fair to complain of the brevity
of the reviews; the first performance did not conclude until quarter to one.
Winter thought *Pique* was "not of a high order, either in literary attributes
or dramatic construction," but he admitted that it blended "comedy, sentiment, and sensation in a way that will not fail to please the average tastes"
(*New York Tribune,* Dec. 15). The *Daily Graphic* (Dec. 15) gave less grudg-
ing testimony to its excellence.

Mr. Daly has made another great hit. . . . There is in this new play material
enough for a first-class comedy, for a melodrama, and for a spectacle, but it is
so deftly and artistically woven into a whole as to form one of the most interesting and attractive entertainments ever offered to the public. Mr. Daly's
career as a playwright has been a varied one, but certainly the best piece he has

hitherto constructed, as far as popular taste is concerned, is by all odds this last play of "Pique." . . . The acting and "business" of the play were simply superb. . . . Miss Fanny Davenport as the heroine showed most unexpected dramatic power.

The season had been going badly (according to one of the dramatic weeklies, Daly's creditors had given him only until December 20), but with the production of *Pique* all worry was over. The play was an immediate hit with the public, especially the women. After a matinée on January 8 Daly noted that out of one thousand one hundred people attending, not fifty were males. On May 2 Daly's box was occupied by the widow of an alleged kidnapper of Charley Ross. Detectives hoped that the play might induce her to tell where the boy was. Except for a few benefits *Pique* ran uninterruptedly the rest of the season. On July 1 one of Daly's most persistent detractors suggested that the run continued "owing to lack of some other *original* (ye gods!) play of his," but Daly was not accustomed to keeping failures on the boards. The final and, according to Daly, two-hundred-thirty-seventh performance occurred July 29.

Long before the end of the New York run, Daly had assembled a company to take *Pique* on the road. One of the first cities visited was Washington. Critical opinion in the Capitol City was sharply divided. "Of all the dire trash which Daly has given the country under the sugared guise of 'cotemporaneous drama' and 'plays of to-day,' 'Pique' takes the palm. . . . The story is a mixture of the newspaper police reports and the New York *Ledger*" (*National Republican,* Feb. 29). "It is the best American society play ever written" (*Washington Chronicle,* March 2). In Chicago it opened at Hooley's Theatre, May 8, 1876, remaining for three weeks. A bitter notice in the *Chicago Times* of May 14 attested its popularity.

There be grave doubts whether Mr. Augustin Daly ever wrote a play "out of his own head." Envious persons who claim to know say he never did, but that the works which are imputed to him, or rather which he claims for his own, were gotten up by other men and afterward gotten away from them. That makes very little difference. None of those plays have been remarkable for intellectuality or even for coherence and common sense. . . . Daly is the great American Shakespeare. This might be construed into a comment upon the decadence of American taste, and indeed would be such a comment, if there had ever been any American taste to suffer decadence; but such a thing has not, up to this date, existed at all. . . . There is not only "nothing in it," but that nothing is of a sort that is very entertaining to the average citizen. . . . To catch the full measure of "Pique's" absurdity, you must see it for yourself—if you have not already seen it. You probably have. The house has been so crowded at each of the performances that most of those who go to theatres must have attended at least once.

After a few kind words for the company, which included B. T. Ringgold, Owen Fawcett, George Parkes, Jeffrey Lewis, and Alice Grey, the reviewer proceeded with relief to Maggie Mitchell and *Fanchon*.

Notwithstanding critical onslaughts of this nature, *Pique's* popularity continued. It played Boston for three weeks beginning August 28, 1876. In Philadelphia it was so popular that on October 2 Daly noted in an account book that Fanny was playing *Pique* to the largest business ever done in any theater in that city. Fanny Davenport continued to appear in it all over the country for a number of years. It is an interesting fact that Daly first saw Ada Rehan, the actress who was to become the star of his company during his second period of managership, while she was playing "Mary Standish" to Fanny Davenport's "Mabel Renfrew" at the Grand Opera House, New York City, April 14-26, 1879. Under the title *Only a Woman, Pique* was given in the Royal Theatre, Brighton, England, October 16, 1882. The play returned to Chicago boards every year except two until it was so mishandled by Manager John Stetson's Fifth Avenue Theatre Company, during a week's revival at McVicker's Theatre, December 3-8, 1883, that the papers protested. "There is no excuse for the resurrection of this irritating mass of mawkish sentiment and emasculated sensationalism" (*Chicago Tribune,* Dec. 4). The presence of Annie Russell in the cast meant nothing to Chicago critics then.

Pique's career, however, was not yet ended. On March 29, 1884, it was produced in a three-act version entitled *Her Own Enemy,* at the Gaiety Theatre, London, with Rose Osborne. Neither play nor actress aroused English enthusiasm. Boston's Castle Square Theatre revived the play for the week of July 12, 1897, at which time a reviewer testified that "with all its crudities, inconsistencies and improbabilities, it appeals strongly to the sympathies of the public." New York performances as late as October 17, 1900, are recorded by T. Allston Brown.

Daly did not welcome imitations of *Pique*. In February 1876, he sent out letters to various theater managers warning them against producing a play called *Piqued*. The only play by this title that I have been able to find was copyrighted by T. Allston Brown, January 28, 1876. It does not seem to have been produced.

Burlesques were a different matter. One brief skit took the stage at Tony Pastor's within two or three weeks of the play's first performance. More pretentious parodies appeared later. Two opened on March 13—*Peaked: a*

Burlesque of Tomorrow by Kenward Philp at the Eagle Theatre and *The Pique Family* by Sydney Rosenfeld at the Lyceum. The following week the San Francisco Minstrels put on *Peek: a Daily Play*.

Although *Pique* was never published as a play, Daly is said to have written the story for the *Fireside Companion*. The text here used is from the privately printed edition of 1884.

DRAMATIS PERSONAE AND ORIGINAL CAST

MATTHEW STANDISH, *the Massachusetts mill-owner, whose word was law*   MR. CHARLES FISHER

CAPTAIN ARTHUR STANDISH, U.S.N., *his son*   MR. D. H. HARKINS

DOCTOR GOSSITT, *everybody well, but his hands full*   MR. JOHN BROUGHAM

MR. RAYMOND LESSING, *to whom the ways of false love and true love are equally rough*   MR. MAURICE BARRYMORE

SAMMY DYMPLE, *a young millionaire, in search of what money can't buy*   MR. JAMES LEWIS

THORSBY GYLL, *his chum, with an eye, however, for Number One*   MR. JOHN DREW

RAGMONEY JIM, *tramp, victim of emotional insanity with respect to what belongs to other people*   MR. FRANK HARDENBERG

PADDER, *his mate. No insanity at all; knows what he wants and tries to get it*   MR. WILLIAM DAVIDGE

PICKER BOB, *another. Engaged in the little job*   MR. CHARLES ROCKWELL

RATTLIN, *boatswain*   MR. W. BEEKMAN

CAPTAIN SPEERS, *municipal police*   MR. I. DEVEAU

GUESTS, TRAMPS, SAILORS, POLICE

MABEL RENFREW   MISS FANNY DAVENPORT

LUCILLE RENFREW, *the banker's pretty widow; rather young for a stepmother, but the right age for a rival*   MISS EMILY RIGL

MARY STANDISH, *"who was passed by"*   MISS JEFFREYS-LEWIS

AUNT DOROTHY, *"everybody's aunt"*   MRS. G. H. GILBERT

RAITCH, *a waif from the slums*	MISS SYDNEY COWELL
MOTHER THAMES, *the tramps' housekeeper*	MISS KATE HOLLAND
SYLVIE, *the foreign maid*	MISS LIZZIE GRIFFITH
LITTLE ARTHUR	BELL WHARTON

ACT I: PIQUE! THE CONSERVATORY AT GRASSMERE ON A NIGHT IN AUGUST (BY JAMES ROBERTS). THE SOFT PASSION IN EVERY FORM. THE CHOICE OF A HUSBAND FROM MANY LOVERS.

ACT II: THE TWILIGHT BEFORE THE NIGHT. THE OLD PURITAN HOME AT DEERFIELD (BY CHAS. W. WITHAM, FROM A STUDY ON THE SPOT). HOW THE BRIDE WAS BROUGHT HOME, BUT SOMETHING WAS LEFT BEHIND.

ACT III: THE PRISONER AND HER CHILD. THE SAME. A MAD RESOLVE— AND ITS CONSEQUENCES.

ACT IV, SCENE I: SEARCHING FOR THE LOST. THE DOCTOR'S STUDY (BY LOUIS DUFLOCQ). DYMPLE UNRAVELS A SECRET DEEPER THAN THE SPHINX.

SCENE 2: BEHIND TRINITY CHURCHYARD (BY JAMES ROBERTS). THE UNDER SIDE OF A GREAT CITY. SCENE 3: LURED TO THE DEN. BEGGARS' PARADISE, THAMES STREET (BY LOUIS DUFLOCQ). THE GREAT WEB SPUN BY CRIME, AND A STRUGGLE IN ITS MESHES. A HAT WANTED.

ACT V: NIGHT AND MORNING. PARLORS AT THE RENFREW CITY RESIDENCE (BY JAMES ROBERTS). LOVE ENDS WHERE LOVE BEGAN.

AFTER THE FIRST ACT, ONE YEAR IS SUPPOSED TO ELAPSE. AFTER THE SECOND ACT, TWO YEARS. AFTER THE THIRD ACT, ONE MONTH. AFTER THE FOURTH ACT, ONE DAY.

ACT I.

SCENE: *The conservatory at Grassmere, a country seat on the Hudson. A night in August. Music heard off, as if from parlors beyond. Padder, a waiter, enters, R.1.E., carrying a tray, with ices, etc. At back, company dancing.*

PAD. I wouldn't be paid to dance on such a night. Hot enough carrying these ices and iced sherries. [*Looks around*] Glass o' wine, Padder? [*Same business*] Thank'ee, if nobody's looking, I will! [*Same business*] He, he. [*Empties one of the glasses*] If I've took one of them, tonight, I've smouched a dozen. [*Dr. Gossitt enters, C., type of old family physician; Padder sees him and is embarrassed, with glass in his hand, which he finally puts in his pocket*]

DOC. [*As if heated, from ballroom*] Whew! Thermometer eighty-eight, and rising! Ah! My good man, you come very seasonably. [*Takes an ice and begins to eat, sitting on seat*]

PAD. I wouldn't like to take a contract to cool him off. [*Exit, C., passing Lucille, who enters C.R.*]

DOC. [*L., seated*] Not a bad place, this, for a quiet reverie.

LUC. [*R.C.*] No, my dear doctor, not a bit of it. [*She comes forward; a fashionable young widow*]

DOC. [*L. Rising quickly*] Eh! Oh! Not a bit of what, Mrs. Renfrew?

LUC. Of seclusion from me or my guests, hermit that you are.

DOC. At least let me have the evening to myself. Tomorrow there will be work enough. First, there will be your headache—then Mabel's headache—and then the usual colics in the servants' hall, after a night of unlimited heel-taps and ice cream slops.

LUC. First, then, my dear doctor, I shall have no headache tomorrow, because I must look after Mabel, and secondly, Mabel will be as sprightly as a lark, because—[*Pauses*]

DOC. Because?

LUC. She is too much in love.

DOC. [*L.*] In love? Are you certain? Are there symptoms of the malady?

LUC. My diagnosis is perfect. She blushes at the sound of a certain voice —starts at a certain footstep—and affects the damp night air on the piazza, with a certain gentleman. [*Crosses to L. Looks off as if watching*]

DOC. From whom I suppose she caught the infection.

LUC. Instantly. [*Crosses to L.*]

DOC. And his name?

Luc. Look behind you! [*Raymond Lessing crosses at back, with Mary Standish on his arm. They chat in a friendly manner, as if mere acquaintances. Both seem to be occupied with other things—both looking off to the R. constantly. They stop before a flower*]

Doc. What? Mr. Raymond Lessing? [*She nods and smiles*] A notorious flirt.

Luc. Oh, doctor! [*Crosses to R. at back, looking into ballroom*]

Doc. A dawdler! A dandy! A fellow who spends most of his time at clubs and in drawing-rooms—the rest of it on the road—and all of it in mischief.

Luc. Hush, he'll hear you!

Ray. [*To Mary*] Fond of flowers, I perceive! [*Yawns slightly*]

Mary. I was bred among them. And when I see them here, [I] feel the same pity that I do for birds in a cage.

Ray. [*Listlessly*] Ah! [*Looking off, L.U.E.*]

Mary. Look at these. They are natives of Mexico, brought here to languish in a hothouse and die for one breath of fresh, spring air.

Ray. 'Pon my word, I think they ought to be very grateful for the trouble they give. [*They stroll off*]

Doc. Idiot!

Luc. On the contrary, I think him a most entertaining person. He has the reputation of being irresistible among the fair sex.

Doc. [*L.*] I have heard that he is as dishonorable and double-faced a fellow as ever made love to two women at once.

Luc. So much the worse for those foolish girls who mistake his well-bred gallantry for sincerity.

Doc. [*R.*] And the young lady with him is one of that sort, I suppose?

Luc. She, oh dear, no! Quite a stranger. This is her first visit to Grassmere. A country lass—cousin of Captain Standish, whom you know.

Doc. Standish's cousin? How comes it that she is leaning on that fellow's arm?

Luc. Ignoramus! Because her cousin, the gallant captain, is at this moment deeply engrossed with—

Doc. With whom?

Luc. Mabel.

Doc. Standish in love with Mabel, and she in love with—?

Luc. Mr. Lessing! Exactly! You have the whole plot at your fingers' ends.

Doc. Where have my eyes been!

Luc. In your bottles and pill boxes, of course.

Doc. Poor Standish. [*Crosses to L.*]

Luc. Poor Mabel.

Doc. Mrs. Renfrew, you know your stepdaughter better than I do, of course. But if she throws her love away on such a creature as Lessing, why—sympathy is thrown away upon her, that's all.

Luc. There are excuses for her—left without a mother—

Doc. And without a father now—two years.

Luc. When I married Mr. Renfrew, Mabel was already a young lady—her ideas formed, her will his law. I did my best.

Doc. To win her?

Luc. No. To govern her!

Doc. Humph!

Luc. It was useless. And since my widowhood—

Doc. There has been war.

Luc. Not open. A slumbering rebellion.

Doc. You must save the girl.

Luc. I wish I could. I know that Raymond—I mean Mr. Lessing—is infatuated—

Doc. Never! The cold-blooded rascal—

Luc. With her money.

Doc. Ah!

Luc. And if he knew that she is penniless—that her father died embarrassed—and that all I possessed when I married him was settled on me, why—

Doc. He would jilt her and pay all his court to you.

Luc. [*Angrily*] Dr. Gossitt!

Doc. [*Hastily*] Pardon me, my dear madam—I mean that he would be base enough to do it.

Luc. But Mabel would be saved.

Doc. So she would. [*Looks around*] Excuse me—he's coming this way. [*Aside, as he is going*] Standish in love with Mabel! A wilful, wayward beauty; proud, vain, but he couldn't help it! Such men as Standish love such girls as Mabel. The truest love the vainest. Even I feel her fascinations in the marrow of my old bones. Nothing but my rheumatism protects me. [*Exit, L.1E., Raymond coming forward from R.*]

Luc. [*Sits R.C., with a slight laugh*] I think I can safely leave the case in the hands of that sagacious old surgeon. He'll cut to the quick.

Ray. [*R.*] Alone?

Luc. [*Gaily*] Unusual, is it not?

Ray. Where are your hosts of admirers? The whole drawing-room was at your feet half an hour ago.

Luc. I have dismissed the court and retreated here for repose.

Ray. No—to plan how you may rule the world.

Luc. I have my moments of thought—as once, three years ago, when you met me at Geneva. Have you forgotten the little garden over the lake, the book that fell from my lap, and the cavalier who restored it?

Ray. And was rewarded by [*Lucille leans forward eagerly*] an invitation to your marriage two months after.

Luc. Capital memory! If you and I had not agreed to laugh over your disappointment, I should think you still felt revengeful, Raymond.

Ray. [*Coolly*] In your presence, my dear Mrs. Renfrew, one can only feel the power of youth **and loveliness.**

Luc. [*L.*] And out of my presence you can feel a very tender regard for my stepdaughter.

Ray. [*Biting his lip*] Do you really imagine—

Luc. Do I imagine? Are you not my protégé? Have I not promised to watch over you with maternal solicitude? Do I not call you Raymond—as I would a son—and do you not address me with filial respect as—

Ray. [*Angrily*] Lucille! [*Crosses to L.*]

Luc. [*Laughing heartily*] Oh, fie! We agreed to forget all that little romance. I've been a widow two years. Two years is an age for a woman.

Ray. You know I have been abroad.

Luc. So have I—utterly.

Ray. And when I returned I hastened to your house.

Luc. [*Turning her face away, laughing*] To fall in love with Mabel.

Ray. But listen to me!

Luc. [*L.*] No, I won't listen, you foolish fellow—I mean to make you happy. But let me whisper one word—you have a rival—

Ray. [*Superciliously*] I know it. He follows her everywhere, and gets snubbed for his pains. There he is now [*Looks off, L.*] standing behind her chair. A sort of sentinel over his own hopeless attachment.

Luc. You feel so confident, then? [*Raymond crosses to R., smiles*] Take a friend's advice—lose no time.

Ray. [*Looks at her intently*] And you actually aid me? What riddles women are. [*Taking her hand*]

Luc. [*Giving him her hand*] Have I not told you a hundred times that I wish to see you perfectly happy? [*Seriously*]

Ray. [*Suddenly clasping both her hands in his*] Lucille, you—

Luc. Hush! Let me go! [*Sees Thorsby Gyll, who enters at that moment, C.L. He is a fresh university boy*]

Thors. [*C.*] I beg pardon—I was looking for—

Luc. For me I know!

Thors. [*Aside*] Not a bit of it. [*Aloud*] Certainly—oh, yes.

Luc. Then take me to the drawing-room.

THORS. Certainly! Oh, yes! [*Aside*] With the greatest displeasure.

LUC. [*Not looking back at Raymond, but talking volubly to Thorsby as they go off, C.R.*] The air was so close there—but the conservatory is so—I haven't had a waltz for an—

THORS. Certainly—oh, yes! [*Exeunt*]

RAY. [*Looking after them*] If I hadn't met Mabel, I should have loved that woman to distraction. But Mabel's beauty, and the fortune which all these men are pursuing! The prize is too tempting. [*Dymple darts in at the back, C.L., and looks around. He is dressed in irreproachable costume; has red hair standing up straight; young, and with embarrassed manner*]

DYM. [*L., looking round*] He was to meet me here at ten precisely. [*To Raymond*] I say, you haven't seen Mr. Gyll anywhere, have you? [*Familiarly*]

RAY. [*Superciliously*] Mr.—ah—Gyll? No! Don't know him. [*Goes up R.*]

DYM. [*Getting round to R.*] You don't? And you've been introduced to him five times to my certain knowledge. I suppose you don't know me, neither?

RAY. [*Stops and looks back*] What say?

DYM. Nothing! [*Raymond saunters off, C.L.*] Conceited humbug. Now those are the fellows that make a man's blood boil. Always take a girl's attention away from you when you've done your best to get in her good graces. This very night, after I had got *her* all to myself, as I supposed, in a chair *I* had brought her, in a corner to which *I* had strategically manœuvred her, with an orange ice in her lap *I* had procured for her, *he* walks up, elbows me on to the edge of the piano, and whisks her off to *his* corner with *my* orange ice. I gave Thorsby the signal agreed upon for the exchange of fresh communications of the highest importance to our common interests; he telegraphed me back: "Conservatory—at ten!" Here I am—and—[*Looks off*] here he is. [*Thorsby entering, out of breath, C.R.*]

THORS. I came as soon as I could. What's the news?

DYM. [*L.*] The news is, I've discovered another rival for Mabel's affections.

THORS. I know—that navy fellow who gave us the strong cigars after dinner—

DYM. And made us so sick. A plot, I'm convinced. But more of him hereafter! No, my dear boy, another still. That slim chap who don't know you, though you've been introduced to him five times.

THORS. Eight times. I managed three more after dinner to make sure he intended to be personal.

DYM. I tell you our difficulties increase. It is now three days since we came here and fell in love with her.

THORS. [R.] On the spot—both of us.

DYM. Yes, both of us on the same spot, for we were playing an unmanly game of leapfrog under the impression that we were unobserved, and I was just going over your head when she seemed to rise out of the ground behind a clump of fuchsias—

THORS. Dreadfully awkward. But she behaved like a lady.

DYM. Yes; she said she liked manly sports.

THORS. From that moment I fell in love.

DYM. And fell on me, for I was gone already.

THORS. And that afternoon we swore to win her or die.

DYM. Behind the bathhouse. Sacred spot where our friendship was cemented. [Music]

THORS. But the next day—

DYM. The captain turned up.

THORS. And we were turned off.

DYM. And tonight, this other fellow! I never felt so like a born murderer [Crosses to R.] as when I saw his sickening attentions. I tell you what it is, Thorsby, since I was let out—

THORS. Since you were let out! You talk as if you'd just come from jail.

DYM. I came from worse than jail.

THORS. Eh?

DYM. Do you happen to know what a guardian is?

THORS. I know what a father is. One who keeps you at college as if you were a malefactor and school a treadmill.

DYM. That's bad enough! But a guardian! A fellow appointed by will to see that you've no will of your own.

THORS. But ever since I met you that commencement day you've been your own master.

DYM. That's three months ago. I was free that very day.

THORS. [L., sighs] With a million of money to do what you like with.

DYM. [R.] Hang the million! If I hadn't a cent, they'd have let me alone. But I was doomed from infancy. First I'm left an orphan with five hundred thousand dollars, and a guardian with a bald head. At ten years of age, an uncle dies and leaves me another five hundred thousand, with another guardian with another bald head, to rivet the chains of slavery upon my tender limbs.

THORS. [Sarcastically] Poor fellow!

DYM. Just wait. I'm sent to school by order of guardian No. 1, and delivered to a pedagogue like a bale of cloth. Then I'm sent to college and allowanced by order of the surrogate; then I'm taken out and put to board by order of the Supreme Court, after being claimed, reclaimed, pulled about and jerked up before a stiff, old file with spectacles in a mahogany box—on a quarrel between guardian No. 1 and guardian No. 2. Then I'm taken to Europe by a tutor, who drinks all the brandy and smokes all the cigars he can buy out of the savings on the hotel bills. Then after I've been caged, led, driven, chained and walked about like a street bear for twenty-one years, I'm brought home—a lot of books, boxes, accounts, certificates, orders and heaven knows what are stuffed in my hands, and I'm told I'm free with a million of dollars I don't know what to do with. [*Crosses to L.*]

THORS. I'd know what to do with it.

DYM. Would you? Just try it.

THORS. Just try me.

DYM. I never felt what it was to be an orphan till that day. I didn't know how to walk or talk or spend my own money. I went up to Jericho and I fell among thieves directly. I wanted a good Samaritan—I found a dozen, who charged rather steeply for the oil they furnished. I wanted a father, and I found a score of old reprobates who brought me up to cards. I wanted a mother, and had to put up with a landlady. Then by degrees I sold myself into slavery—took a valet: a drunken rascal with a wife and eight children, who stole my shirts, got drunk, got arrested, and gave my name at the station-house, so at least once a week I had the gratification of reading in the morning papers that I had been severely reprimanded by the magistrate and fined ten dollars, which I paid on the spot.

THORS. [*R.*] You mean he paid.

DYM. No—I paid. He always stole enough out of my pockets to keep me out of jail. But at last I discharged him and my fooleries altogether. Then I met you, and we swore eternal friendship.

THORS. Yes; and we have agreed to wait until I graduate, and then to marry.

DYM. I know, but we have met our fate, my boy, before you graduated.

THORS. And a sad fate, if these swells cut us out as they do with Mabel.

DYM. Brains must win. We have brains. We will lay them at her feet.

THORS. [*With a sigh*] You've got money, besides.

DYM. Well, your father's worth millions.

THORS. Yes; but he only allows me fifty dollars a month while I'm at college. I can't offer her that.

DYM. [*L.*] If she loves you, she'll wait. [*Crosses to R.*] Look at the disadvantage I struggle under. The reddest hair in New York.

THORS. That's not your fault. She can't blame you for that. Why don't you curl it?

DYM. I've thought of that.

THORS. Or cut it off close.

Dym. I've thought of that. But I say, old fellow, if you happen to speak to her of me, be as mild as you can on that head, won't you?

Thors. You mean on your head?

Dym. Exactly! When you come to the subject of my hair, just—just smooth it over.

Thors I will.

Dym. Tell her the capillary adornment don't make the man. I'll do as much for you.

Thors. Thank you, Sammy. I'm not nervous on the subject of hair; but you can do me a service, you know—that is, if the subject should happen to come up. Make me out a little older, you know. I'm afraid she looks on me as a boy. I wish I had a pair of whiskers. I think women respect whiskers. You might hint that I have to shave every morning, or I'd be a regular patriarch—eh?

Dym. [*Grasping his hand*] I'll do it! It's a bargain! As we resolved day before yesterday—behind the bathhouse—we'll win her, Thorsby, or we'll die.

Thors. She shall be ours! [*Dr. Gossitt and Standish stroll in. Thorsby and Dymple begin to hum and go R., stop suddenly as they see Mary*]

Dym. Hush! Here's Miss Standish.

Thors. Pretty girl, eh? But rather young. [*Mary enters, L.1.E.*]

Dym. Not to be compared to our Mabel.

Mary. [*Advancing*] Look at the beautiful bouquet Mabel gave me.

Dym. Beautiful.

Thors. Did Mabel—I mean did Miss Renfrew give you those? Why, Captain Standish gave them to her.

Doc. [*To Standish*] You see?

Stan. I gave those flowers to Mabel not half an hour ago.

Doc. And she gives them to your little cousin.

Mary. How I should like a stroll on the piazza. The moon is so bright. [*Strolling up C.*]

Thors. [*Quickly*] I'll take you out.

Dym. [*Aside to Thorsby*] Hem! Mabel might see you—and be jealous. Take my advice—don't spoil your chances. Women are not to be trifled with.

Doc. [*Advancing*] Well, what are you boys plotting here? [*Thorsby and Dymple draw themselves up haughtily*]

Thors. [*Indignant. To Dymple*] Boys!

Dym. [*To Thorsby*] These are the kind of men who drive their fellow-men to violence. Boys! [*Sees Standish*] There's the fellow that gave us the strong cigars.

Thors. Let's cut! He might offer them again, and we'd have to take 'em. [*Turning away they meet the Doctor, who offers cigars. They recoil in alarm*]

Dʏᴍ. We'll both go with you, Miss Mary.

Mᴀʀʏ. Thank you. Let me say one word to Cousin Arthur first. [*Crosses to Standish; the Boys whisper together*]

Sᴛᴀɴ. [*R.*] Mary, did Mabel give you these flowers?

Mᴀʀʏ. Yes. She says she dislikes flowers, except in the conservatory. But she wears two roses that Raymond Lessing gave her.

Sᴛᴀɴ. Why do you tell me that?

Mᴀʀʏ. Are you angry with me? I know I ought not to have spoken of it.

Sᴛᴀɴ. No—not angry. Run away and enjoy yourself.

Mᴀʀʏ. I don't dislike flowers anywhere, Cousin Arthur. May I keep these?

Sᴛᴀɴ. [*Coldly*] Do as you please. Come, doctor. [*Strolls off, R.1.E., with Doctor*]

Mᴀʀʏ. He loves her, I am certain of it. Oh, why did I come here! [*Goes up, and is joined by Thorsby and Dymple each side. Padder enters C. with tray of empty glasses. Very red in face and a trifle unsteady*]

Pᴀᴅ. Beg pardon, sir.

Tʜᴏʀs. A tipsy waiter.

Pᴀᴅ. [*Looks at Thorsby with scorn and turns to Dymple*] Have an ice? [*Hic*]

Dʏᴍ. [*R.*] By all that's beastly, my old valet.

Tʜᴏʀs. [*L.*] The fellow that always paid your fines. Treat him decently for the sake of old times.

Dʏᴍ. How did you come here, you rascal?

Pᴀᴅ. [*C.*] New situation, sir! Got it after you left me, sir!

Dʏᴍ. Without a character?

Pᴀᴅ. I knew you'd give me one, sir, for the sake of the children. So, as I couldn't find you, sir, I wrote out one for myself.

Dʏᴍ. And signed my name to it?

Pᴀᴅ. For the sake of the children, sir.

Dʏᴍ. I'll have you kicked out of the house, if you don't leave it yourself immediately.

Pᴀᴅ. Don't distress yourself, sir. I'll go, sir! I've no doubt the children are crying for me now. I'll go, sir! [*Aside, going R.*] But if I ever have a chance to pay you off, I'll—

Dʏᴍ. Well!

Pᴀᴅ. Don't be harsh with me, sir, for the sake of the children! [*Exit, R.1.E.*]

Dʏᴍ. That's how my misfortunes haunt me. It all comes of my being an unprotected orphan.

Tʜᴏʀs. I tell you what it is, Sammy, you don't want a wife—you want a mother.

MARY. Come, gentlemen!

BOTH. Gentlemen! [*Exeunt, very radiant and smiling, each side of Mary, C.L., Dymple, trying to offer arm, gets to R. of steps as Thorsby goes up L. Doctor, reentering with Standish, R.1.E.*]

DOC. Does your father know of this?

STAN. [*Absently*] My father! No! I have not written to him. I wished to be certain first.

DOC. [*L.*] You have not told me how long this has been going on.

STAN. [*Crosses to L.*] How long? I don't know. It seems to have been always so. She is my life, and I have no memories before my love of her.

DOC. You have known her only two months.

STAN. Perhaps.

DOC. Why, I brought you here.

STAN. I have to thank you for the greatest happiness and the most exquisite pain of my life.

DOC. I don't deserve any thanks. I did nothing but a common social service. You are young, generous and single. I thought you ought to have society. The very first home you stepped into becomes the abode of your destiny. It's the old story. A young fellow, fresh from hard service on the ocean, sees in the first young girl he meets in civilized life the destroying angel of his existence. Bah! Rubbish! There are hundreds more like her. [*Crosses to L.*]

STAN. And like me!

DOC. [*L.*] No—not so foolish. To follow up a girl who turns her back on you and flirts with every handsome puppy.

STAN. [*Turning quickly on him*] I have never seen her do anything of the kind.

DOC. Not seen her turn away from you?

STAN. [*R.*] Yes! but not to—she may not love me, perhaps, but she is worthy of my love—of any man's. If sincere devotion, if unselfish attention can win her, I may try. [*Both sit*]

DOC. [*L.*] Yes, you may try. But she has been bred in a false atmosphere. Her father lived half his life in Paris. She adores foreign life and manners. At the foot of a throne she would shine as highly as the rest of its jewels. But in our land she is a diamond buckle on a leather shoe. Let her have her preferences. Let her dazzle a peer and marry him. We have nothing to do with these women. Your father is a man of sterling worth. He rose from the masses. What would he think of such a fine lady for a daughter?

STAN. [*Impatiently, rises*] My heart is my own! My wife is my own. Besides, you wrong my father. He would not fail to appreciate the prize I had won. Let me say a last word. You have demanded my confidence—take it all. I love Mabel Renfrew. I will suffer all that a man may to obtain her. If I fail I will descend to no lesser plane to fill the void she leaves. From the first moment I beheld her, I consecrated to her all my life. I can love her image, I can be faithful to her memory—no matter on whom she bestows the priceless treasure of her hand. [*Goes upstage*]

Doc. I must do it then. I must help him. If she marries him she is saved! But as for him! Perhaps! [*Music and laughter outside. Mabel enters, C.L., on Raymond's arm. Lucille follows shortly after with a gentleman; and afterwards Mary with Thorsby and Dymple. Mabel and Raymond come forward*]

Mabel. Oh, how delicious! And there is the doctor! [*She releases herself from Raymond, and comes to Doctor*] Deserter! Your post has been vacant all the evening.

Doc. My post? Where is that?

Mabel. [*L. of Doctor*] At my side. To warn me against all my adorers. Come, you have not said a cross word against anybody tonight. I want to sit down and be lectured. [*All the Gentlemen make a movement to bring her a chair. Thorsby and Dymple take the same chair*] Nobody but the doctor. I dismiss everyone. [*Slyly pressing Raymond's hand, and in a tender voice*] For five minutes! Is that too long?

Ray. An age! [*Goes up with Lucille; Thorsby and Dymple scowl at him and retire to Mary's side*]

Mabel. [*Sits C., to Doctor*] Now, you delightfully censorious old friend! Of whom must I be afraid tonight.

Doc. Of Arthur Standish!

Mabel. [*Coldly*] Why of Mr. Standish?

Doc. [*Close to her*] Because he loves you. [*Mabel rises, takes a step or two to R.*]

Dym. [*Aside to Thorsby*] Another enemy! Do you see how that old villain is making up to her. Delay is ruinous. I'll propose tonight.

Thors. So will I.

Dym. Let's get a glass of wine! I feel faint. [*They hurry out, L.1.E.*]

Mabel. [*R., returning to seat*] He loves me. Did he tell you so?

Doc. [*Seated, C.*] Yes.

Mabel. [*R.*] Well, then, your warning is unnecessary. There is no need to fear Captain Standish, because there is not the slightest chance of my loving him.

Ray. [*On C. of steps, aside*] What can they be talking about?

Doc. He has not told me more than you know already, Mabel. His admiration of you is open enough.

MABEL. I know nothing of his admiration and care less. My footman may admire me, and the regard of one is as indifferent to me as the other. I can't avoid the admiration of the herd. It is another thing to encourage it.

Doc. There would be nothing extraordinary in your marrying Captain Standish.

MABEL. You are going too far, doctor. I will not hear a hint of such a thing.

Doc. He is a gentleman. His father is immensely wealthy.

MABEL. [Contemptuously] He began life, I believe, as a factory overseer, or something of that kind.

Doc. And ends it as a benefactor of his kind. He comes of the grand, old Puritan stock, and is almost a king in influence in his native place. Arthur has the means of gratifying every taste—nay, every whim of your fancy. He can buy and sell again every fortune that has been offered you.

MABEL. Buy and sell. The expression, no doubt, is his own.

Doc. No, it is mine. He loves you—and—

MABEL. Proposes to buy me?

Doc. He cannot purchase your love, and is resolved to win it. I spoke of his wealth, because I know that your father left you dependent on your stepmother.

MABEL. [Rises, crosses, in tears] Don't speak of poor papa! I beg of you.

Doc. I am not unkind; I wish to guide you.

MABEL. [Drying her eyes] I thank you very much. Whatever my circumstances may be, they will not compel me to make a marriage for bread and a home. If I must descend, it shall be to earn my own living in some other way than by wedding below my station in life.

Doc. There is no such thing as rank in this country, Mabel. These are the false notions you gained abroad in your childhood. Which would you prefer to live on, the bounty of your stepmother, or—

MABEL. Or on that of the factory overseer! Neither! [Crosses to R.]

Doc. [Aside] I have evidently gone the wrong way to work.

MABEL. I would rather starve as Mabel Renfrew, than owe my life to this man.

Doc. Not if you learned to love him?

MABEL. [Indignant] I love him? You are dreaming.

Doc. Mabel! Be more like your poor mother—who was all gentleness and charity itself. If she were here now, she would give you the advice I offer. Do not despise the honest love of an honest man. [Mabel is moved and takes his hand. Lucille comes forward]

Luc. [L.] This must be a sermon.

Doc. No, it's a prayer, madam.

MABEL. [*Music stops. Laughing and recovering*] Lucille does not appreciate fine distinctions, doctor.

LUC. [*L., crosses to Doctor*] Oh, yes, I do. [*Takes Doctor's arm; they go up, R. Raymond glares furiously at Doctor and comes down to Mabel's side, L. Standish, leaving Mary, goes to her also. Mary joins the Doctor and Lucille*]

RAY. [*L., close to her*] Preaching at an evening party. Did he denounce the vanities of wealth and the sinfulness of beauty? How these ugly men always go in for the virtues. [*Sits at her feet*]

STAN. [*Behind, R. of the seat and unaffectedly*] I rather think it becomes every man to go in a little for the virtues.

MABEL. [*With a sudden start and frown, but not looking round, then to Raymond*] Don't say anything to offend the prejudices of the "Grand old Puritan Stock," I beg of you, Mr. Lessing.

STAN. [*Leaning over her chair and gently*] I forgive you for that, Miss Renfrew.

MABEL. [*Suddenly repenting and to him*] Thank you, Captain Standish! I—I ought not to have said it.

STAN. [*Tenderly*] I knew you did not mean it; your heart is too good, too noble, to wound any one.

MABEL. [*Resenting this attempt at familiarity by giving all her attention to Raymond, who sits at her feet*] My heart! Who pretends to read the heart of a young lady at first sight.

RAY. Man is very presuming, you know. Forgive us. We love.

MABEL. Don't jest about a sacred word.

RAY. Well, I have no presumption. I am content to wait at the portal until the goddess of the temple unfolds the mysteries to my eyes.

MABEL. Are you sure you are content to wait?

RAY. Unless by a sign—a sigh—or a glance I am encouraged to rush in, throw myself before the shrine, and declare my boundless faith.

STAN. [*Smothering his feeling*] True devotion uses no force. The gift of love should be a reward—not a spoil.

MABEL. [*Coolly ignoring him, and still to Raymond*] And if the goddess should remain immovable before your ardor? [*Glancing at Standish*]

RAY. Why—I think! Yes, I think I should station myself behind her back and wait until my silent entreaties turned her head. [*Mabel laughs. Standish moves away a step, evidently pained*] That shot told.

MABEL. Is he gone?

RAY. Not exactly routed. Retired on his wits, to try a fresh attack.

Doc. [*R., coming down to Standish*] No use, Arthur.

STAN. Is it possible that she can be so heartless, so cruel?

Doc. Is it possible you can be such a patient ninny? Leave her to the parrot that amuses her with its chatter.

Stan. Leave her to the hawk, you mean, that has marked her for his prey. That man is a scoundrel. I know his character, and I will save her from him.

Doc. Save yourself. Awake from this dream. She will never love you.

Stan. Perhaps not. Yet at times there is such a softness in her look, a tenderness in her voice that I have dared to believe—! But this night shall decide. I will write to her—and if she refuse me—heaven bless her. She shall have a life-long friend who pities, yet loves her. [*Exit, R.1.E.*]

Doc. Soft! Soft as cotton wool! and quite as inflammable. What a change has come over the world. The women are steel, and the men are putty. [*Exit, R.1.E. Thorsby and Dymple appear at the back, C.L.*]

Dym. Now's your chance. Cut him out boldly. I'll stand by—if victory don't crown your banners, step aside and I'll—

Thors. Don't be far off.

Dym. I'll keep my eye on you.

Thors. How do I look—is my necktie straight?

Dym. Perfection! Don't lead the conversation to hair.

Thors. I'm not thinking of hair. I've no head for hair, just now. [*He comes down boldly, and Dymple darts behind a vase, L. Mabel is whispering and laughing with Raymond. Mary and Lucille have strolled off, C.*] Very pleasant here, Miss Mabel.

Mabel. [*Starting, surprised, then to Raymond*] You foolish fellow! When they all begin to dance.

Ray. I'll meet you here! [*Rises and goes off, C.R. Thorsby sits beside her, on her L.*]

Thors. [*Embarrassed, L. of Mabel*] Danced much this evening?

Mabel. Oh, ever so much.

Thors. I saw you! I wish—may I have the pleasure of dancing with you after supper?

Mabel. Certainly! [*Taking out tablets*] What shall I put you down for?

Thors. [*Very sentimental, sits next to her*] All of them!

Mabel. All of them! Oh, you greedy boy!

Thors. [*Aside*] Boy! [*Aloud*] The fact is, Miss Mabel, when I see you standing up with anybody else, I can't keep still.

Mabel. Then you ought to get another partner, at once.

Thors. [*Same business*] There's nobody like you.

Mabel. What a compliment. Do you have a course of gallantry at Harvard, Mr. Gyll?

Thors. I hate Harvard.

MABEL. And I love it. You know I always go to commencement and to the boat race. Will you be in the crew, sometime?

THORS. [*Starts up to L. and back C.*] I want to leave the old place. I'm tired of boats and books, and of being a bo—I mean a man has something else to think of. Oh, Miss Mabel, how beautiful you are!

MABEL. Why what in the world put that in your head?

DYM. [*Behind plants, L.*] Head! It's getting warm. [*Rubs his hair*]

THORS. You did!

MABEL. Then I'm to blame for making you so naughty. You should be thinking of your books.

THORS. [*Blurting out the compliment*] So I am. The book of beauty!

DYM. [*Aside*] That's mine! He's stealing all my neat points.

MABEL. [*With mock seriousness*] Thorsby!

THORS. Yes, Miss Mabel.

MABEL. [*Playfully*] You wish to make me angry.

THORS. Oh, no, I don't—Indeed I don't.

MABEL. Then be sensible. Tell me all about your studies.

THORS. I can't, I want to tell you something.

MABEL. No, you do not.

THORS. Yes, upon my honor—I'm sincere—I lo—

MABEL. Not another word.

THORS. [*Rises*] Only half a one. Let me finish it. Please do. I love you.

MABEL. [*Crosses to L. Debating with herself how to treat him, then turns*] Of course you do.

THORS. [*With joy*] You believe it. Oh, thank you, Miss Mabel, and now—

MABEL. And now let me speak, as I let you.

THORS. [*Pleased*] Yes!

MABEL. You are ever so good, and I like you very much.

THORS. Thank you, Miss Mabel.

MABEL. And because I like you, I'm going to give you some good advice.

DYM. [*Behind tree, L. Aside*] He's dished.

MABEL. The first thing to remember, is, that you will be desperately in love a dozen times before you know your own mind. Now this is your second or third time, isn't it?

THORS. [*With a groan*] The first.

MABEL. Well, then, there are eleven more occasions to come. The first is over, you see, and no harm done—and—I'll put you down for a waltz after supper. [*Crosses to R.*]

THORS. Farewell, Miss Mabel!

MABEL. Until eleven! [*Lucille enters to her, C.R.*]

DYM. [*Seizing Thorsby, who is going up*] Well!

THORS. All is over!

DYM. No, it is not. My turn next.

THORS. Go away!

DYM. No, I won't, and you shan't go away, neither—I stood by you. You just sit down and wait for me. [*Thorsby drops in chair, and buries his face in his hands*] Not that way. Look up! Smile! We are observed!

LUC. [*To Mabel*] Another conquest! [*Sees Dymple buttoning up his coat and approaching*] And still they come!

DYM. May I crave a moment of your time, Miss Mabel.

MABEL. With pleasure.

LUC. [*Aside to Mabel*] Shall I send you a partner for the valse?

MABEL. No, thank you, this will be too nice to lose! [*Lucille exit laughing, C.R.*]

DYM. [*Aside*] She always laughs at me! [*Aloud to Mabel*] Scorn is hard to bear, Miss Mabel.

MABEL. [*Advancing, C.*] Very, I should judge.

DYM. [*Slight false start*] May I entreat you to walk.

MABEL. Thank you, it's very pleasant here.

DYM. The proximity of the maddening throng is unfavorable to a serious proposition, Miss Mabel.

MABEL. Very. No person of sense would attempt such a thing under such circumstances.

DYM. Sense! Miss Mabel. Sense and I have long been strangers!

MABEL. You alarm me.

DYM. There are conditions in which life persists in asserting itself, while the brain and heart, and other viscera, are consumed by a devouring passion.

MABEL. What a pity.

DYM. [*With effusion*] Miss Mabel, I know you to be one fitted to shine in any sphere. On the throne or in the peasant's cot. I cannot offer you either. But somewhere between the two is a home where you would be queen. I know my own defects—

MABEL. Impossible!

DYM. It is useless to enumerate them. The head and front of my offending—no, no, I don't mean that—my chief drawback [*She looks at his head*] is want of appearance. But I have the confidence—

MABEL. I perceive you have—

DYM. To believe that manners, intellect—in short everything that is not perceptible at first sight [*She looks at him again*]—may atone for personal appearance. I have spent the greater part of the night inditing an epistle which I hope to place in your hands. May I entreat the favor of an early perusal, and hope that in your next Answers to Correspondents I shall find a reply to your ardent and devoted admirer—S.D. [*Produces a very minute billet-doux*]

MABEL. [*Not taking it, and looking saucily at him*] S.D.?

DYM. S.D.

MABEL. Well, then—"S.D. Declined—with thanks!" [*Curtsies and goes up*]

DYM. Declined—with thanks! [*Putting it in his pocket and buttoning up his coat*] Ah! I presume Crowded out for Want of Space.

THORS. [*L., moodily, and coming down*] Well!

DYM. Well! I see it all. She has no heart.

THORS. Yes, she has.

DYM. No, she has not. She may have a patent lever with half a dozen attachments ticking in her bosom, but she has no heart. If she had, my address would have touched her.

THORS. [*Crosses to R.*] You're a fool. You don't want a wife. You want a mother!

DYM. [*Angrily*] I do, do I?

THORS. Yes, and so do I; we're both idiots. Here we've been clasping hands and swearing to win or die, and all that, when one of us would be knocked out if the other succeeded. I just begin to see the idiocy of the whole thing. You see, here's the difference between a boat race and a love race. All the fellows in the same boat win, but only one of the fellows in love comes out ahead. The rest are swamped.

DYM. [*L.*] Well, if you got her, I would have been satisfied.

THORS. Well, if you had got her, I wouldn't. I candidly confess it.

DYM. Look here, Thorsby, you haven't got the stuff for Damon and Pythias, you haven't.

THORS. [*Grasping his hands*] No, I haven't. You are the squarer fellow of the two, Sammy. I despise myself. I'm going back to school again. But I say, old fellow, if you and I ever fall in love with the same girl again—

DYM. Well?

THORS. I'll step out and leave you to walk over. [*Exit, R.1 E.*]

DYM. Something's wrong somewhere! All the fellows who borrow my money tell me that, with my million, I can marry any girl I please. Either she don't know I'm worth a million, or the fellows lie, or she's different from the rest of the girls. No, they all snub me. I'm not intended for a husband. Thorsby's right. I don't want a wife—I want a mother. I must hunt up a good, amiable old soul and pop the novel question. For the situation of son, red hair can't be objectionable. [*Exit, R.1 E. Lucille, C.R., and Mabel, C.L., pass in at back as the music recommences*]

LUC. There's music, dear. A waltz. [*Going*]

Mabel. [*R.*] I'm engaged. I'll wait for my partner here. [*A gentleman enters, offers his arm to Lucille, and she goes off as Mabel strolls down to seat, C., and Raymond enters, L.1.E.*]

Ray. [*Softly, and looking about him*] All alone! What a paradise for a flirtation.

Mabel. [*Plucking a flower idly and not looking up*] If anything so insincere as a flirtation entered here it would be paradise lost.

Ray. Yes, an opportunity lost. It was a cant phrase of society I uttered.

Mabel. [*Low tone*] I am weary of its phrases. I wish I could discover if it have a heart. [*Crosses to L.*]

Ray. [*Aside*] If I stay, I'll have to speak out, and it's too soon for that.

Mabel. How well we play our parts in the comedy of fashionable life. We laugh and chat together, and pretend we are the dearest friends, while—

Ray. While?

Mabel. While we are merely neighbors! And neither of us cares a straw for the other.

Ray. [*R., in tender tone*] Do you think so? If I might speak, I could vouch that there is at least one whose whole heart, whose every hope is centered in—his neighbor. [*After a pause, his hand steals down to hers; he takes it; she looks at it fondly*] Am I very presumptuous? Not a word! [*His other hand steals 'round her waist*] Mabel, is there not one other who cares for the happiness of him that addresses her? Say only that you have seen my love, that you do not despise it, that you sometimes think of me, and that my affection is not unworthy of you.

Mabel. [*Turning to him affectionately*] Oh, Raymond, can you doubt it?

Ray. [*Draws her to him and kisses her cheek; an involuntary tremor shoots through her frame*] My darling.

Mabel. Hush, Raymond! [*Rising*] They will see us.

Ray. No, no, there is no one near. Mabel, let me once hear you say that you return my love.

Mabel. Yes. Yes. [*Struggling to be free*] Let me go. Dear Raymond, there is someone coming. [*She frees herself, and hurries off, L.1.E. Doctor enters, R.1.E.*]

Ray. Perhaps 'tis well. Another moment and—

Doc. [*Assuming a gay air*] Ah! Mr. Lessing, I have just left a very lovely woman, who is anxiously inquiring for you.

Ray. [*L.*] Indeed.

Doc. The beautiful widow! What a hero you must be to conquer our haughty hostess.

Ray. You are extremely flattering.

Doc. My dear fellow, I never dose people with flattery. It is a species of sugar pill which anyone can detect. No. When I contemplated the idea of Lucille Renfrew falling in love with you, my mind was lost in visions of your extreme good fortune in a double sense. You see you acquire at once everything that old Renfrew left behind him—his money, and his lovely widow. What a woman—she managed to get the whole estate.

Ray. [*Interested. Hitherto listless*] The whole estate—and his daughter?

Doc. Absolutely dependent on the stepmother.

Ray. Why, she is said to be an heiress in her own right.

Doc. In her own right she is possessed of a wealth of golden hair, sapphire eyes, ruby lips, brow of pearl, coral cheeks, and, in short, a Golconda of beauty—but as for dimes and dollars!

Ray. Nobody seems to know of this.

Doc. Ask Mrs. Renfrew.

Ray. [*L., half aside*] Impossible!

Doc. Then believe me; or better still—go to the surrogate's office and look at his will. No, no, my dear fellow, you will have no one to divide with when the widow divides with you. It's very kind of all you young fellows to pay Mabel so much attention; but, of course, it's all got under a sort of false pretense, and she couldn't complain if, when the little imposture is discovered—

Ray. Doctor—you—you embarrass me—you agitate me. I mean you grieve me if you suppose I—.

Doc. You—Lord bless you, nobody thinks of you. Your attentions to Lucille have been too marked. The whole world talks of that. As for Mabel, no one could, would or should accuse you of acting any other part than that of an agreeable acquaintance. You have no money—she has no money. People never put that and that together. It's preposterous.

Ray. [*Edging off*] Pray excuse me. I see—

Doc. You see the fair widow beckoning to you. So do I. Go to her, my dear fellow—go and be—[*Raymond nods nervously and exit, C.R.*] punished as you deserve, for a confounded, false butterfly son of a grub. [*Mary Standish enters, dressed to go*]

Mary. Have you seen Arthur, Doctor Gossitt? He told me to prepare for our departure. He had only a little note to write explaining his sudden resolution. We are going home tomorrow. To Deerfield. Something has happened. You are his friend. Do you know what it is?

Doc. [*L., looking off and seeing Mabel enter, L.1E., with an open note*] Yes, it's coming this way. [*Up a little with Mary*]

Mabel. [*L., reading*] "I love you with all the devotion and ardor of which man is capable. I beseech you, give me such an answer as my sincerity deserves.

I cannot return to this house nor see you again unless as your accepted suitor. Arthur Standish."

Doc. [*Aside*] Arthur's letter! It is easy to see what the answer will be.

MABEL. Doctor, look at this. [*Tenders letter*]

Doc. I know what it is.

MABEL. Then you know what folly it is—what madness it is. What right has he to address me in this way?

Doc. A man's true love always gives the right to declare it and to demand an answer.

MABEL. [*Crosses to R. About to tear letter, with flashing eye*] An answer —this is my—reply.

Doc. [*Restraining her*] Wait! Wait until tomorrow.

MABEL. Not an instant.

Doc. I implore you. Something may happen to prevent your treating his honest confession with contempt.

MABEL. What can happen? What miracle do you expect?

Doc. One of those miracles that happen every hour without the stars falling or the earth trembling. Look! [*He draws her behind a vase of flowers at the R. as Raymond and Lucille enter, C.L., arm in arm, and pass down L.*]

LUC. Take care, Raymond, there may be someone here.

RAY. [*L.*] You see the place is empty.

LUC. But Mabel.

RAY. She has just received a letter, and passed out into the library, I think, to read it.

LUC. She will return.

RAY. And if she does—why should I draw back? I must speak. I must tell you how you have mistaken me. I can't bear your continued suggestions that I am in love with her, that I—

MABEL. Ah! [*About to faint*]

Doc. Help! Mabel! [*Thorsby darts in from R., catches her. Dymple follows. Standish enters, L.1.E., with Mary at C.*]

RAY. Mabel!

LUC. [*L., angrily*] Mabel, what are you doing here?

DYM. [*R., beside Thorsby*] I'll give you a thousand dollars if you'll let me take your place.

MABEL. [*By a supreme effort regains her composure and steps back, confronting Raymond and Lucille*] I came to find you. I had something to say. [*Standish is about to go*] Stay, Mr. Standish. This letter of yours—an offer of marriage!

STAN. [*At her haughty tone, feels that all is over*] I understand—and I leave Grassmere tonight and forever.

MABEL. Not so. Please stay. [*Extending her hand to him as she looks at Lucille and Raymond*] I accept your offer. There is my hand.

STAN. Mabel! [*Throwing himself on his knee and seizing her hand. Dymple faints in Thorsby's arms. The Doctor goes to Mary, who turns aside to suppress her tears*]

ACT II.

SCENE: *Old Deerfield. Interior of a large and pleasant sitting room in a New England home. Windows at back open on a piazza which is supposed to descend by a flight of steps into a garden. Fireplace at L., with old-fashioned and bright log fire. Old-fashioned stiff-backed chairs with one or more modern sofas and armchairs, covered with neat chintz. Table near the R., with old-fashioned candlesticks and candles lighted. Sofa above the fire with comfortable pillows. Night. Moonlight outside. Raitch is at the fireplace polishing the brasses. Aunt Dorothy seated, C., watching Raitch. Music.*

DOR. [*A hearty, prim, tidy, old-fashioned dame*] There! I'm sure they look as well and feel as soft as if they were covered with satin. I hope she may think so, too.

RAI. [*On her knees at fire, L., a harum-scarum "help"*] And ain't this here a fire to make a regular lady open her eyes! None of your city fires pinched up in a grate like a prisoner behind the bars. A regular free and independent fire I calls it.

DOR. [*Back of sofa*] A capital fire, Rachel, and when Captain Standish's wife warms her pretty feet, she'll surely ask who made it!

RAI. [*Squatting*] Will she so, Miss Dorry! And I can put on my best calico to come in when she sends for me, can't I? I'm to wait on her my own self, ain't I?

DOR. Of course.

RAI. It'll be like Sunday all the week through with my new frock on. [*Rocking herself on the rug, her hands round her knees*] I say, Miss Dorry.

DOR. [*Seated, C.*] Well, Rachel?

RAI. She'll be mighty happy here! It's nuttin' time and cider time, and quiltin' parties in a'most every house.

DOR. Old Deerfield never looked so beautiful. If she loves the country she will enjoy this.

RAI. Lor', Miss Dority, what do city gals know about country! But I can show her everything. How to milk the cows, churn butter and make cheese.

DOR. Yes, if she would like to learn such things.

RAI. And I can show her where the turkeys' eggs is! I know. And then the hens. You know how our hens do hide! I found out two new nests way under the barn! Crept in a'most flat. I'll take her there. I wonder if she's afraid of weasels.

Dor. I'm afraid Arthur's wife wouldn't like to creep under the barn, a'most flat, so it doesn't matter.

Rai. Lor', she can put on one of her common frocks! I dessay she's got lots of frocks made to tumble around in.

Dor. Don't be too sure of that.

Rai. Well, all the city gals has trussos, six dozen o' these and six dozen o' those. And there'll be half a dozen or so of common clothes to muss in. I'll bet my hair.

Dor. 'Sh! Rachel. How often have I told you—

Rai. Yes, Miss Dorry! I forgot! I wasn't to bet anything, for nothing. I'm growing too big, ain't I?

Dor. Yes, and you're growing too big to sit on the floor, too. Come, jump up—there's a good girl. [*Matthew Standish enters upstairs, L.C., with a telegram, lays his hat on the rack near door*] Back from the post office so soon, brother? And a letter?

Mat. Telegram. Boyce brought it over. They will be here at once. [*Stage, R.*]

Rai. [*Crosses to him, jumping up and clapping her hands*] O—oh! They're coming. I'll run and put on my—[*Matthew looks at her*] Miss Dority said I could!

Dor. Yes, run away with you. [*Raitch runs up with Matthew's coat, tripping over it as she goes, and finally hangs it on rack at C. passage, L.C.*]

Rai. I'm so happy I can't walk.

Dor. [*At fire, L.*] Be quick or they'll be here.

Rai. Oh, I'll be quick, you bet!

Dor. Rachel!

Rai. I forgot; but *I* didn't bet, Miss Dority, I said, "*you* bet!" [*Exit up steps, L.*]

Dor. [*As Matthew sits, C., in a reflective mood*] So Arthur is bringing home his wife at last. [*She stands by his chair*]

Mat. [*Seated, C.*] At last! [*Looks at her*] Have you seen Mary this evening? [*Dorothy nods*] It's coming close to her now. How does she bear it?

Dor. Just as she has borne it all along. As if she were going to welcome a sister.

Mat. I haven't been able to look at that girl's face for months past. I see her heart—that is enough. [*Sighs*] To think that you and I planned a match between her and Arthur ever since they were children.

Dor. There's no harm done, brother, we never told either of them our plans.

MAT. That's the harm we have done, sister. If I had spoken to Arthur long ago—

DOR. We thought it over long ago, and made up our minds that old folks' wishes warped young folks' wills. No—no—we did better—we waited—

MAT. And while we waited, Mary began to love him.

DOR. Then it was not for us to speak. If he could not see and understand—

MAT. [*Striking arm of his chair with his hand*] See and understand! Among a lot of flippery women, bedizened in jewels and silks, rustling and dancing in the candlelight like motes in a sunbeam! I tell you I lost him when I let him go into the navy—when I let him enter what he calls fashionable houses—when I—

DOR. [*L.*] When you let him go to college and make friends there—

MAT. No. I would put every laborer on my farm at college if I could. Learning makes a man. It's the company, not the books, that makes the fool!

DOR. You never spoke that way of Arthur before, and now he's coming home. You used to be eager and happy when he came home.

MAT. There's more than Arthur coming home this time.

DOR. His *wife*, Matthew!

MAT. A pretty wife—I'm afraid.

DOR. Very pretty—so Mary says.

MAT. What will you say if she turns up her fashionable nose at us?

DOR. Surely you don't expect that!

MAT. I have my fears. What is she? One of that set who live half their lives abroad—in Paris, I believe—because America is not good enough for them. If they turn up their noses at America, what can *we* expect?

DOR. I am sure Arthur's letters to us—

MAT. I have particularly observed that Arthur's letters never said a word about his lady wife's temper, or her heart, or her sincerity. No. He took delight in filling our ears with her beauty—"regal"—"queenly"—"dazzling." Those were the words. And her family, "the oldest"—"the most aristocratic." And her manners, "the centre of a brilliant circle"—and her wit, and her crowds of adorers. Believe me, sister, a son would not display such a mass of tawdry stuff before his father's eyes, if he had anything more solid to show.

DOR. He supposed, of course, we would take all the rest for granted.

MAT. Depend upon it, we will have to take all the rest for granted, for we'll see none of it.

DOR. But why talk this way now? What is done can't be helped.

MAT. Aye, what *is* done can't be helped. But what is not yet done must be prevented. [*Rises, crosses, puts letter on table, returns to C.*]

DOR. I don't understand.

MAT. If this pretty and witty and queen-like young lady has made a slave of Arthur, we must take care that she makes none of us.

DOR. You are not going to make war upon a poor little girl.

MAT. Do I look as if I would! No. I am going to defend myself when a poor little girl makes war upon us.

DOR. [L.] Well, for the life of me—

MAT. Do you expect this fashionable female tyrant to submit without a struggle? Here are no crowds of adorers, no circle of wits, no throng of flatterers. Only poor you and poor me to be dazzled. We are not to be subdued. In this house for five and forty years a single will has been law.

DOR. [Kindly to him] A good will and a gentle law, brother. She will not dispute what everybody loves.

MAT. [Crosses, L.] Let us hope so. But nothing is to be changed because she comes, you understand. The hours of rising and retiring, the hours of meals, and the family devotions, the order which should reign in every household, are for her as well as for us all.

DOR. Mercy! And is that all you mean?

MAT That is all.

DOR. What a fright for nothing. Arthur's wife will never dream of doing what is not agreeable to her husband's father.

MAT. Don't be too sure—until we see.

DOR. Besides, Arthur would never permit his wife to disobey you.

MAT. Arthur is in love according to the new order of things, sister. The women rule the world in which she was bred, and the men stand in awe of them. Once upon a time the man was head of his house. Now he's a fetcher and carrier for the dainty, selfish tyrant he calls wife.

DOR. But Arthur!

MAT. Mark my words—Arthur never won Miss Mabel Renfrew until she was sure of his conversion to the new social creed. But as for me, I'm a pagan to these society goddesses. The women whom I respect are those who—

DOR. Hush! Here is Mary.

MAT. Mary! She rounds off the sentence. The women I respect are such as Mary. If I had had my will Mary would have been—[Crosses, R.]

DOR. Oh, for goodness sake, brother, spare her! [Mary entering blithely from steps, crosses to C.]

MARY. I have been looking up the road and away over the hill, but there's no carriage in sight yet. And now it's quite dark and growing colder. Why, Aunt Dorothy, how charming you look. That is the wonderful cap, is it? It's the prettiest you ever had. Such a dear, good-natured mother, to welcome

a bride to her home. And Mabel is like me! She just remembers her mother—
and that's all. I'm sure she will love you as one.

DOR. [*L. Clasping her to her bosom*] Oh, Mary! How I wish! [*Wipes away tears*]

MARY. I will tell you what I wish, aunt. That the good folks would come as quickly as possible. I wish they had come before dark. It's a long drive, and she'll be so tired. [*Goes to table, R., and arranges flowers*]

DOR. [*L. To Matthew*] If she has no repinings, why should you?

MAT. [*C.*] Come here, Mary! I have been talking to your aunt.

DOR. Oh, brother! [*Apprehensively*]

MAT. [*C., smiling*] Be quiet! She is terrified at my cruelty—this poor, browbeaten aunt of yours.

MARY. [*R., advancing*] And to whom are you cruel, Uncle Matthew?

MAT. To vanity and frivolity, my dear. I scent their approach from afar, and I have merely said that there is to be no allowance made here for affectation.

MARY. Surely, uncle, you are not going to prejudge Cousin Arthur's wife.

MAT. [*Coolly*] No.

MARY. Nor to seek for grounds of dislike to her.

MAT. [*Mildly*] No.

MARY. [*Her hand on his shoulder*] And above all, uncle, dear uncle! You will not close your heart against the woman your son brings to your threshold?

MAT. [*Moved*] No—a thousand times no. My heart is open to receive her—if she be worthy.

MARY. Your heart must be open to receive her if she were unworthy, uncle. You must shut your eyes and close your ears, and see and hear only your son, who says to you—"Father, this is my wife!" But she is not unworthy. Nay, she is good, or how could she have chosen Arthur from among so many?

DOR. [*L.*] That is true, brother, she—

MAT. Will you be quiet?

MARY. She was worshipped almost, in her sphere, but you see she was sensible and true-hearted, and turned away from them all. She is an angel, uncle.

MAT. [*Kissing her*] *You* are an angel.

MARY. No, you have all been too kind to me. But I saw my own defects. I could never inspire the love she does. There are some girls, uncle, who fill the full measure of man's happiness by their love—and there are other girls—

MAT. [*R.*] Who fill the whole world with love—and you are one of them. Tell me how to welcome Arthur's wife, and I'll do it your way.

MARY. [*Stepping back a pace*] Eyes shut.

MAT. [*Shutting his eyes*] Yes.

MARY. Arms open.

MAT. [*Arms open*] Yes.

MARY. And clasp her to your heart.

MAT. Yes. [*Clasps Mary, who struggles*]

MARY. Oh!

MAT. [*R. Sudden revulsion*] I forgot. You are not Arthur's wife. [*Mary silently turns away and puts handkerchief quickly to her eyes*]

DOR. [*Reproachfully*] Brother! [*Tenderly to Mary*] My own love.

MARY. [*Conquering her emotion and smiling*] Uncle squeezed me so hard. [*Goes to mantel. Music. Carriage wheels heard. Voices of workmen outside: "Hurrah! Hurrah!" "Welcome! Welcome home!" Raitch bounces in in a new frock, partially unbuttoned behind. Hair wild, one shoe off*]

RAI. Hurrah! They're a'coming. The men are all in the road hurraying, and I didn't have time to hook my frock all up—and I forgot they were a'coming and not a'going, and I heaved my shoe at 'em, and it hit Dandy in the off eye, and he reared up on his hind legs. But they're a'coming! Hurrah! Hurrah! [*Gets R.*]

DOR. [*At door, looking off*] Poor thing, she looks blue with cold. There she sits in the carriage, all muffled up. And here's—Arthur! Oh, my dear— dear Arthur! [*Standish hurriedly bounding up the steps*]

STAN. Ah! Aunt Dorothy! [*Hurriedly kissing her*] Father! [*Shakes his hand*] Is there a fire in here? Yes, that's right. I couldn't hand Mabel out of the carriage till I knew just where to take her. She's half frozen; the road was wretched. [*Dorothy runs down and exit. Raitch after her downstairs*]

MAT. [*Kindly*] Have you found the journey very tedious, my son? [*Crossing and going towards door*]

STAN. Yes, indeed! Oh, Mary! How are you? [*To Matthew*] We were jolted over the ground fearfully—my wife is nearly shaken to pieces. This place is altogether too much out of the way. [*Runs down the steps at back. Mary wheels sofa to fire*]

MARY. She will soon be comfortable here. [*Goes to back of sofa and pushes it forward a little*]

STAN. [*Outside*] Come, Mabel dearest, we are really here at last. [*Standish reenters, supporting Mabel, who is enveloped in elegant wraps. Mabel entering impatiently and withdrawing from his aid, passing Matthew at door without recognition*]

MABEL. Thank goodness. Is this the place?

STAN. [*Behind*] Mabel! This is my father!

MABEL. [*Turns and looks at Matthew in surprise*] I beg your pardon. I did not see you. I was only thinking of the fire. [*Gives him her hand*]

MAT. I am glad to welcome—

STAN. [*Interrupting and taking her hand*] The fire! Yes, my poor darling. You must be nearly frozen. This way, Mabel. [*Installs her at fire. Dorothy enters with more wraps and Raitch follows with bundles, etc.*]

DOR. [*To Mabel*] I'll take these to your room at once, dear. [*Exit, R.U.D.*]

RAI. Shall I take these, too, mum?

MABEL. [*Not heeding her*] I should like to go to my room. Is there a fire there?

RAI. Better stay here, mum. The chimbley smokes in there for a good while arter the fire's lit. This is the comfortablest.

MABEL. [*Resigned*] Then I'll stay here. Where is Sylvie?

RAI. Sylvie! Is it the little dog, mum? He's a barkin' like all possessed, out on the box.

STAN. No, no—it's my wife's maid.

RAI. If you please, mum, I'm to be your maid. Miss Dority said so, and I want to be. [*Commencing to blubber*]

MABEL. Oh, dear, dear!

STAN. Leave the room instantly, girl.

RAI. Yes, sir. [*Drops bundles and begins to wipe her eyes. Mary runs to pick bundles up. Dorothy enters, R.U.D. Sylvie enters, C., upstairs, and both begin to pick up things*]

SYL. [*Loftily*] I'll attend to it, please.

RAI. Please, may I do something? I'll go for the little dog.

SYL. [*Shocked*] You? Don't attempt to touch Prince.

RAI. Does he bite?

MABEL. Sylvie, take my things to the room directly. [*Sylvie sweeps off haughtily and goes to the door Dorothy points out to her, R.U.D. Dorothy then leads Raitch off L., by the arm*]

RAI. I ain't done nothing, I ain't.

STAN. [*Still by Mabel's side*] Oh, Aunt Dorothy, for goodness sake, send that girl away. My wife's nerves are—[*Raitch is ejected by Dorothy*]

MABEL. There, never mind. I dare say I shall soon be used to it.

DOR. [*Advancing, C. Kneels by her side*] I hope she hasn't disturbed you. She has been almost wild all day. Perfectly useless. How do you feel, my darling, after your journey?

MABEL. [*Turning to her, kindly*] Somewhat fatigued. Thank you.

DOR. Let me take off your things.

STAN. No, let me do it, aunt. I—

MABEL. Please wait till Sylvie comes; I won't trouble you. [*To Dorothy*] Thanks, very much, for your kindness; it is so delightful to meet with such goodness after traveling so far, and all that.

DOR. You must have been frozen. [*Kneels by her*] Is the fire warm?

MABEL. Very. It's all very nice. When will the smoke be out of my room, please?

DOR. That's Rachel's nonsense. I believe she wanted to keep you here to look at. [*Rises*]

MABEL. Goodness me—is she a lunatic?

STAN. [*Back of sofa*] Don't let her come near the house again, aunt, if you please.

MABEL. [*Rising*] I'll go to my room at once. [*Mary is going, R.C.*]

STAN. Somebody call Sylvie. Oh, Mary! Stop! Mabel, my darling, let me present you to my cousin Mary.

MABEL. [*Looks at her inquiringly*] Your cousin—

STAN. [*C.*] Yes—little Mary. She's been like a sister to me—and she's the pet of the house.

MABEL. [*Kindly*] How sorry I am not to have known you before.

MARY. [*Crosses to C.*] Oh, yes, you did—[*Checks herself*]

MABEL. [*Politely*] Did I? Where?

MARY. I was at Grassmere the very night—

STAN. [*To Mabel*] The very night we were—

MABEL. [*Repressing an emotion*] What a memory I have. But we'll begin our acquaintance now. There's no need to go back so far. [*Tenders her hand, Mary takes it*] I've quite forgotten that evening.

MARY. [*R.C.*] Will you let me show you to your room—it's just off this.

DOR. [*Back of sofa*] And you can have this for your sitting room, if you like.

MABEL. [*L.C.*] Thank you, it will be delightful. [*To Mary*] Is it this way?

MARY. [*At door*] Through this passage.

STAN. [*As Mabel passes out*] Dark as Erebus! Take care, my darling. [*Exit after Mabel. Mary follows*]

DOR. I'll go and hurry the girls. [*She crosses towards L. Meets Matthew, who has been promenading the piazza, with occasional glance inside. He looks at her. She is scared, and makes a slight detour round him, watching his eye. He smiles grimly and comes down. As she goes off*] I hope he won't wait to talk to me tonight. [*Standish reentering, looking off*]

STAN. Ah, father! [*Troubled and anxious*]

MAT. [*Kindly*] Well, Arthur!

STAN. [*Suppressing a sigh*] Married at last, you see, father.

MAT. I see.

STAN. [*Watching his father and trying to appear at ease*] You mustn't observe things too closely this evening. Mabel is somewhat annoyed at her journey—and she's far from well. I'm afraid she's not very strong.

MAT. [*Softly*] Ah!

STAN. Yes. We have been all over Europe—to all the famous watering places. Spent two months at Baden and four in Italy. But nothing seemed to brighten her up.

MAT. It is a great pity. She was exceedingly lively and well—before you were married—was she not?

STAN. But these constitutional weaknesses sometimes develop themselves—

MAT. Very unexpectedly! [*Pause. Standish looks round*] Come, come; let us hope that your care and devotion will effect a cure. You seem quite devoted to her.

STAN. [*With a sigh*] Yes. I owe her the devotion of my life.

MAT. Well. You are paying the debt bravely. I shall be glad to see that she appreciates it.

STAN. [*Quickly*] I am satisfied.

MAT. I'm glad of that.

STAN. I said before, you must not observe her too closely this evening.

MAT. [*Kindly tone, and laying his hand on his son's shoulder*] I shall observe no more than you wish me to observe, my son.

STAN. Oh, there's nothing to hide.

MAT. Exactly. And as there's nothing to conceal, we'll not trouble ourselves to look for it. [*Crosses to R.*]

STAN. How oddly you say that. Why, what were you thinking of?

MAT. Nothing.

STAN. [*Tremulously*] I don't understand you, father. You seem strange. Did your father speak to you like this when you brought your wife home?

MAT. [*R.*] I did not observe his manner. I was so full of joy that I threw my arms around his neck, and never noticed his look or his word.

STAN. [*Hurt*] Is this a reproach to me?

MAT. A reproach to you, my son? No! If you were happy enough to embrace anybody, I should be sure of being the one.

STAN. [*Stage, L.*] You don't mean that you believe me unhappy? [*Laughs constrainedly*] This is nonsense, you know. The fact is, my wife's state of health disturbs me. I can't help showing that. [*With a burst*] Please don't look at me as if you thought me an object of commiseration. [*Getting back to C.*]

MAT. The fact is, Arthur, I am not to observe *you* too closely, neither, is it so? Well, well! Come, take a walk with me. I'm going my usual rounds before evening prayer. You remember our old habits. [*Crosses up to R.*]

STAN. [*Heartily*]   Yes, and I'm glad to get back to them. [*Takes his father's hand*]

MAT. [*Laying both hands on his son's shoulder*]   That's hearty! That's worth hearing from you, my son, come—if you and your wife love each other—

STAN. Certainly, father. I assure you! But come, it's getting late. [*Goes to door, L.C., and down steps, taking his hat*]

MAT. [*Solus*]   I thought as much. This is a marriage that brings no love, nay—kills what love there was. But there's more in it than the common blindness of the young. Well, well. Time will heal the wound or show its depth. [*Exeunt. Dorothy peeps in from L., looks after Matthew. Then comes down, and meets Mary, who enters from Mabel's room*]

DOR. They have gone for a walk. How is she?

MARY. [*R.*]   Ah, aunty, how fair she is—but so pale. I looked at her once, and the tears came into my eyes.

DOR. Mary, how could you?

MARY. She stared at me. She must have thought me a little fool. [*Sinks into chair, C.*]

DOR. Control yourself better, Mary. [*Mary looks down*] Don't think I've seen nothing, Mary. I know your heart. [*Mary sinks in chair and covers her face with her hands*] Oh, dear, dear, don't Mary. What would become of us if this young lady were to think such feelings existed here—in her own house that is to be—

MARY. [*Starting*]   Do you think I would be so base?

DOR. No, but I know your secret.

MARY. [*Rises quickly and proudly*]   I have no secret! [*Softer and laying her hand on Dorothy's arm*] Not now. [*Slowly*] That is all over. And if it had not been for her calm and searching look, I would not have remembered even. But there are some women whom you cannot deceive, and she is one of them. So I looked back into her eyes and she gave me her hand. We are friends.

DOR. Thank heaven for that.

MARY. [*Crosses to L.*]   I will make her happy, if the help I get from There can give peace to other hearts as well as mine.

DOR. She is coming. [*After closing windows and doors, she exits, R. Mabel enters in evening dress, soft and flowing*]

MARY. [*Running to Mabel*]   Will you take your seat by the fire?

MABEL. [*Sitting, C.*]   It is warm enough here.

MARY. [*Sitting on stool at her side*] You look pale and tired, are you sure you are not ill? Perhaps you ought to have gone to bed at once.

MABEL. Thank you, I'm very well as I am. You must not be surprised to see me pale. I am not ill. It seems as if I could not be.

MARY. You say that as if it were a misfortune to enjoy good health.

MABEL. People's ideas differ as to what is misfortune. But don't let us speak of myself—it is the one topic that interests me less than anything in the world.

MARY. I see you are low-spirited. Are you fond of the country?

MABEL. I can't say that I am.

MARY. Oh! Isn't Cousin Arthur sorry for that?

MABEL. I don't know—I never asked him.

MARY. Because this is to be his home, you know.

MABEL. Indeed!

MARY. Of course, that is, of course—if you like it.

MABEL. I am satisfied with anything.

MARY. How strangely you say that!

MABEL. [*Peevishly, changing position*] What do you do with yourselves here all day long? Is there no other house near—no neighbors?

MARY. Down in the village, there are a great many nice people. This is the richest manufacturing district in the State.

MABEL. [*Leans back as if overcome*] How pleasant.

MARY. Cousin Arthur will take care of the factory now, I suppose. Uncle always said he should give it to him when he married.

MABEL. [*Quickly*] Does he intend to resign from his ship?

MARY. [*Surprised*] Why, haven't you and he talked over his future plans?

MABEL. No. [*Looks at her, then smiles*] I'm afraid I begin to tire you. Do you sit up very late here?

MARY. Why it's not ten yet.

MABEL. No.

MARY. And we never go to bed till after prayers. We have our family devotions in the good old way. Uncle has made it a rule, as his father did before him. All the household gather in the parlor at ten o'clock.

MABEL. [*With a slight yawn*] Indeed.

MARY. Didn't Cousin Arthur tell you all about his home?

MABEL. I don't recollect. I think Captain Standish never spoke much about it. [*Arises, R.*]

MARY. [*Rises, aside*] Captain Standish! How strange that she calls him by that name. And she takes no interest in anything. Perhaps she doesn't like me.

MABEL. [*Who has calmly watched her*] Yes, I do.

MARY. [*Confused*] Yes, you do—what?

MABEL. I take great interest in all you tell me—because *you* tell it.

MARY. [*Laughing*] You are a witch! I was afraid that poor little I—who wish so much to love you and be loved by you—will not succeed in either.

MABEL. [*Leans over and kisses her forehead*] You wish me to love you?

MARY. Oh, yes!

MABEL. And that will make up for—

MARY. [*Uneasily*] For what?

MABEL. For what your woman's nature needs! Don't start. Listen to me. There is a void in our hearts which we try to fill with friendships—resignations—duty—and all the rest! It is impossible! They sink in it as in a gulf. It is still empty—cold—and dark. There is but one way—cover it—with indifference and contempt.

MARY. [*Terrified*] Oh, Mabel, you are mistaken—you do not know me.

MABEL. [*Withdrawing her clasp*] I know myself!

MARY. [*Alarmed*] Are you speaking of yourself?

MABEL. [*Calmly*] Hark! There are footsteps. They are coming back. I don't wish to keep you any longer. [*Crosses to fire*]

MARY. [*Crossing, R., aside*] What a dreadful suspicion her words create in my mind. What is coming to this house in place of the happiness I dreamed of? [*Raitch, putting her head in the door, L.*]

RAI. Pst! [*Both Women turn. Raitch makes signs to Mary*] I say—

MABEL. What does she want?

RAI. [*Entering*] I want to wait on you, mum—please.

MABEL. [*At fire*] I don't need you, my good girl.

RAI. I see how it is. They've been telling you I wasn't fit for nothing. Now I know you'll find me handy, mum!

MABEL. Yes, yes—tomorrow.

RAI. Don't never pile anything on tomorrow what you can square off today. That's the copy book and its prime sense, too; you bet. I've got to make a beginnin'. I want to unhook you tonight—then you can see how handy I am.

MARY. [*R.*] Rachel you must not intrude.

RAI. Who ever heerd of a waitin' maid intruding. Other folks intrudes where a waitin' maid is by rights. [*Coaxingly*] Ah, do take me on tonight, mum. I'm ambitious, I am—besides I was promised.

MABEL. But, my good girl, I have Sylvie, who is my maid.

RAI. Be you agoin' to keep *her* on, the whole time?

MABEL. Certainly.

RAI. [*Slapping her hands*] Then it's a do! That's what it is. It's a regular do. You was promised to me. Miss Dorrity promised me. I don't blame you, mum—nor you, Miss Mary! I blames them as promised.

MARY. Go to bed, Rachel.

RAI. I won't. [*Stamping*]

MARY. You shall wait on me.

RAI. You ain't a bride. I was promised the bride. I made the fire for the bride today on my knees and I blew it till I thought I should a busted. Kin your gal make a fire like that? No, sir-ee.

MABEL. Did you really make the fire?

RAI. Yes, mum, I did.

MABEL. It's a glorious fire. You shall come in every morning and make my fire.

MARY. [*Relieved*] Thank goodness.

RAI. Shall I, mum? That'll do, mum. The fires is mine, is they? That's something. Don't let that city gal dare to touch my fires.

MABEL. Are you satisfied?

RAI. Yes, mum—because [*Cunningly*] fires must be kept up, and I'm to come right in to you any time to keep up the fires, ain't I? Of course. Thankee, mum. Oh, I'll keep the fires red hot, and if that city gal meddles, I'll make it red hot for her. [*Exit, L., upstairs*]

MABEL. [*Rises, to Mary*] She looked so distressed I had to use a little diplomacy.

MARY. [*Going to her*] You have a kind heart, Mabel. Let me call you Mabel?

MABEL. Certainly. [*They kiss*] Good night.

MARY. Good night. [*Going*] If I could do good to her and him. [*Exit at R.1.E.*]

MABEL. [*Getting to fire*] It is easy to read her secret. Why did this man pass her by to come to me? [*Sylvie entering with books*]

SYL. [*R.*] Will you sit here, madam?

MABEL. Yes. [*Sylvie lays the books on table, R.*]

SYL. Shall I put out the lights beside you?

MABEL. Yes—all but one. Lock the doors.

SYL. [*At back*] These don't fasten, madam.

MABEL. Never mind. Is that the door which leads to the parlor? [*Pointing where Mary went off, R.1.E.*]

SYL. Yes, madam.

MABEL. Go. I'll call you when I want you. [*Sylvie exit, R.1.E.*] So this is my home. [*All is dark, only the solitary candle burning. Fire bright inside. Moonlight outside*] Here my part is to be played to the end, with all these eyes upon me. His father—and the others. Jealousy and love watching every gesture and weighing every word. It was easy enough among strangers. But these people know what I should be. There has been an honest, homely, loving wife in this house. She is not forgotten. How long will it be before they detect the counterfeit? Why did I come back? There were means enough abroad, heaven knows, to end the wretched comedy and drop the curtain forever on my pitiful story. But I have been looking for what is impossible: some power to undo the fatal mistake I have made. Tied hand and foot! Bound to slavery! Linked with my own self-contempt! Oh, God, if I could die —could die! [*Drops her head on her arms on arm of chair, C. Music. The window opens and Ragmoney Jim with Padder look in*]

JIM.　No one here!

PAD.　Gone to bed!

JIM.　No; we saw the old 'un and the young 'un go up by the creek.

PAD.　The women folks are all in the parlor.

JIM.　And nobody to look arter the trunks. How careless. That's the way places get robbed. Yonder's the way to her room—and nobody's there, neither.

PAD.　I seed her jewels laying on the bureau as I looked through the window.

JIM.　That's all we want. Step softly. Old boards creak.

PAD.　I'm gossamer! [*They come forward. As they approach her chair, Mabel starts, looks up, they look at her, she starts up. Pause. Padder and Jim look at each other; they take off their hats and adopt humble manner*]

JIM.　We didn't think anyone was here, miss, or we would a' knocked.

MABEL.　Who are you?

JIM.　A couple of miserable, starving creeters.

MABEL. [*L.*]　What do you want?

JIM.　Only a little assistance, miss—charity—miss—that's all.

MABEL. [*Looks around, sees window open*]　You entered by the window —you are robbers!

JIM. [*Fiercely*]　Robbers?

MABEL. [*Crosses to R. Suddenly running to parlor door*]　Help! Help!

JIM.　Hush! Hush! The devil! [*Enter from upstairs Matthew and Standish. From parlor, Mary, Aunt Dorothy and Sylvie, R.1 E.*]

MAT. [*L.*]　What is this?

STAN. [*To Padder and Jim*]　Who are you? [*Mary and Dorothy go to Mabel, who is angry and agitated*]

JIM.　Only poor, starving wretches, sir, begging for bread.

MABEL. [*Faintly*]　They are thieves!

MAT. [*Calmly*]　Did they try to rob you?

MABEL.　They entered by the window.

JIM. [*R.C., advancing to Matthew*] All the windows is doors on the piazzy, sir. Ask the lady if we didn't tell her we came to beg. Ask her if we didn't take off our hats and say we was starving.

MAT. [*To Mabel*] You were a little nervous, my dear. There are many poor creatures like these wandering through the country. If we treated them like robbers, it would be punishing the distress we ought to relieve.

JIM. [*Wheedling tone*] That's it, sir! Oh, if there was only more like you, sir, the jails would soon be empty, they would.

MABEL. But these creatures' manner—their stealthy entrance—their— [*Crosses to L.*]

MAT. Pray be calm, my dear. Your nerves are a little more sensitive than ours. We are not quick to impute crime to rags. Arthur, speak to your wife, while I deal with these men.

MABEL. [*To Standish, low and haughtily*] Does your father assume this tone because he wishes to display his indifference to my feelings?

STAN. [*L.*] Do not judge him harshly. He is a just man—a magistrate—and a merciful one.

MAT. [*To Tramps*] You are starving, you say?

JIM. Haven't tasted a morsel since yesterday, sir. Traveled all the way from Hamden on foot.

DOR. And good feet they are to travel on. What whoppers!

MAT. You shall be fed and lodged, tonight. No one leaves my house hungry or footsore. And if you need work—

JIM. Been out o' work for six months, sir.

MAT. The times are hard, I know. [*Calling*] Rachel! I'll find you employment, tomorrow. Rachel! [*She enters, L.D.*] Rachel, take these men to the kitchen.

RAI. All right, sir. [*At the sound of her voice, Jim and Padder look at her, seem to recognize her*]

PAD. [*Aside to Jim*] What luck! Sally!

JIM. Fools' luck! Dropped right on to us.

MAT. Follow that girl.

PAD. and JIM. [*Crossing up to Raitch*] Thankee, sir.

PAD. I say, he'll find us work tomorrow.

JIM. Yes, if he finds us tomorrow.

PAD. Mizzle's the word. [*Turns to go*]

JIM. The blessing of the hungry upon you, sir. [*Exit with Padder, looking searchingly at Raitch as they pass; she exits, L.D., after them*]

MAT. It is late! Come, my children. Arthur, will you bring your wife? [*Goes into parlor, R.1.E.*]

MABEL. Where?

MARY. [*To her, softly*] For prayers. You remember I told you, every evening at ten; but they won't take long.

MABEL. [*Calmly*] It is a matter of perfect indifference to me whether they take one hour or ten, for I am going to bed. Good night.

MARY. Oh, do stay. Uncle will be so vexed.

STAN. [*L.*] Mabel, my dear.

MABEL. Am I not to do as I please in such a matter? What tyranny is this? Captain Standish, will you give me a candle, if I must go alone? [*He gives her one. Matthew reenters, R.1.E.*]

MAT. Where are you going, daughter?

MABEL. To my room. [*Turning away, upstage*]

MAT. But we are about going to prayers.

MABEL. I know it, thank you; but I have no desire to be present. Good night.

MAT. [*Gently, but firmly takes the candlestick from her hand*] My dear, I don't think the rules of this house are very hard rules—but such as they are, they must be complied with. Nothing but sickness can justify absence from family devotions. I cannot compel you to serve Heaven from your heart, but while you are here, you must keep up the appearance of doing so. Stay with your husband, like a good girl. We shall not detain you long. [*Exit, R., with Dorothy, Mary and Raitch, R.1.E.*]

MABEL. Did you understand what treatment I was to receive at the hands of your father, when you brought me here?

STAN. I did not. I will have an explanation with him, tomorrow.

MABEL. You need have no explanation. I leave this house in the morning.

STAN. [*Goes to parlor door quickly and closes it*] I beg you not to make a rash resolution. I cannot devise a pretext that will satisfy those who will be hurt and astonished at our sudden departure.

MABEL. Our departure! I can go alone! Let the blame rest on me.

STAN. There is no blame which I shall not have to share. In *that* we are one indeed—if in all else, Heaven help us, we must be divided. But our compact was that in all things we should keep up an appearance of concord before the world.

MABEL. I release you—indeed, it was always a matter of indifference to me. Stay with your people; they are not mine, and I shall not regard their opinion. [*Stage, L.*]

STAN. I beseech you, Mabel—for the sake of what I have suffered already —to think better of this!

MABEL. You suffered? You?

STAN. I—I was guilty of no crime except that of blindly loving you. I have endured every slight which the coldness of an unloving heart could put upon me. In this instance it is not my affection, but my honor you treat with contempt. You will not dare do that.

MABEL. Not dare?

STAN. Not dare! Mabel—I thought better of you. [*Crosses to R.*]

MABEL. Who told you to think better of me? What in my conduct has led you to think that for your sake I will suffer the tyranny of this house? [*Up*]

STAN. Nothing—Heaven knows. From the day we were wed till now, you have tortured me by an indifference no man ever endured from a wife. But your duty—

MABEL. Duty! Is it not enough that I married you as I promised? That I kept my pledge given in a moment of wounded pride and girlish resentment, that I have lived with you—gone where you led me—worn the mask of deceit you shaped for me—without you forcing on me the duty of obeying the whims of this old man?

STAN. Have a care, Mabel. I am in no mood to trifle. Your actions tonight have told the miserable truth to him and to all who love me.

MABEL. To all who love you, indeed—and hate me. [*Up L.*]

STAN. It is false.

MABEL. It is true—for I deserve their hatred! Do you suppose I cannot understand that they wonder at a marriage to which no love was brought on my side?

STAN. I will not believe it.

MABEL. You will not? Recall the history of that night. But a moment before you knelt at my feet an accepted suitor, I had avoided you. Yes—shunned you! But a moment before I had laughed in your face—and yet in that one moment I mastered this aversion—this contempt—and said to you: I will be your wife. And you tell me that you believed I loved you!

STAN. I was mad enough then—to believe anything. [*Crosses to L.*]

MABEL. [*R.*] When we stood side by side to be married, you saw that I neither smiled—nor wept—nor spoke. Already I contemned—I hated myself! Then you began to understand—

STAN. [*L.*] That you did not love me! But I asked for no reason—I spared you—

MABEL. *You* spared me! You led me to this living death, exulting in the miserable chance that satisfied your pride and your passion! You spared me! You! [*Turns from him up, round C.*]

STAN. What should I have done?

MABEL. The duty of a man who loves without selfishness: exacted the truth and saved me!

STAN. The truth! What truth?

MABEL. That truth which all the world saw—that I gave myself to you because I had lost all in the world I had to live for—love! [*L.*]

STAN. Love! Whose love? Mabel, have you waited till now to tell me that you loved another?

MABEL. Have you waited till now to ask me? Yes—I did love another. I thought that he deceived me. My heart was broken. [*Turns away. He catches her hand*]

STAN. Mabel, who was this man?

MABEL. I will not answer you.

STAN. His name! You have but to speak his name, and you are free.

MABEL. You know him.

STAN. His name!

MABEL. Raymond Lessing!

STAN. You loved him! You love him still! [*Mabel flings herself sobbing on the chair*] And because you could not marry him, you married me!

MABEL. [*Stung and rising*] Yes! If you will have the truth—that is the truth. [*Matthew appears at the door, R.*]

STAN. [*Casting her from him*] Miserable woman! You have no need to leave this house—I give you your freedom and your self-contempt. What we have been to each other, let Heaven, in its mercy, keep an eternal secret. What we shall be henceforth, let the world know and mock at. Farewell, forever! [*Rushes out, downstairs. Music*]

MABEL. Arthur! [*Makes a step, sees Matthew, who advances after Standish, and draws herself up, leaning against back of sofa for support in her pride. Matthew bars her progress, thinking she intended to follow Standish*]

ACT III.

SCENE: *Same as last. Dr. Gossitt enters with Dymple, upstairs, L.C. Music.*

DOC. Unannounced and unheralded so far—but, I hope not unseen.

DYM. [*Looks off, L.*] Evidently not. For yonder stands a maiden of a particularly curious, not to say gimletty, eye, who watches our movements.

DOC. Call her.

DYM. [*Raises his finger and crooks it*] She smiles and rolls down her sleeves preparatory to leaving her dishes and waiting on us.

DOC. What's become of Thorsby?

DYM. [*Looking off, C.R.*] He's at the gate, and apparently rooted to the spot.

DOC. Bashful as ever.

DYM. His eyes are fixed with a steadfast gaze on vacancy. By jove! No! I beg her pardon—on another young woman—over there by the maples.

Doc. Also possessed of a gimletty eye?

DYM. She looks up! Gimletty! The softest—largest—darkest—loveliest eye—I ever saw. No wonder he can't come in. Who can she be? I say—you don't want me here.

Doc. [*Catching his coat*] Combustible and inflammatory youth, I forbid you to stir. We are going to see a pair of eyes as dark and soft and lovely as any in the world.

DYM. [*Still looking off*] Who can she be?

Doc. [*Coming down*] Who? Why, Mrs. Captain Standish! The lovely Mabel Renfrew. Have you forgotten your old flame so soon? Yours and Thorsby's?

DYM. He's making up to her.

Doc. [*Astonished*] The deuce he is. She's married.

DYM. [*Coming down to Doctor*] Is she? What's her name?

Doc. Eh? What is Mabel Standish's name?

DYM. Oh! I beg your pardon. It's a mistake. I was thinking—

Doc. Where are your wits?

DYM. As usual—hunting in couples with Thorsby's—after a pretty face. [*Raitch enters, L., wiping her arms with her apron*]

RAI. [*C.*] Please, sir, who was yer wantin'?

Doc. Mrs. Standish, my good girl; is she at home?

RAI. Yes, sir.

Doc. Give her my card. [*Gives card*]

RAI. Can't, she's gone out.

Doc. Then she's not at home?

RAI. Yes, she is! I guess I know. But her and the baby and old Miss Dorothy's out for a walk.

Doc. Exactly so. I should like to see her.

RAI. Kin you wait?

Doc. Certainly, with pleasure.

RAI. Well, then, she'll be along before much. They don't go fur. Old master won't allow that.

Doc. [*Aside*] So, so. [*Stage, R.*]

RAI. [*After looking at Dymple—to Doctor*] Son? [*Jerks her head to indicate Dymple*]

Doc. Eh?

RAI. [*Same play*] Son? [*Arms akimbo*]

Doc. No, my child; he's not my son.

RAI. Nevvy?

Doc. Nor my nephew.

Rai. He don't look like you! What's he looking at? [*To Dymple*] I say, mister, is it a woodchuck? Lots o' them here.

Dym. A woodchuck? No, a wood nymph.

Rai. Shall I fetch the gun? Old master is down on all them animiles. He'll thank you for poppin' it over.

Dym. Thorsby's talking to her.

Rai. [*At fire*] Talking's no use. Them critters won't come down for soft words.

Dym. I hope not in this case. Look there! Would you go gunning for such a lovely specimen of the animal creation as that?

Rai. Why it's Miss Mary!

Dym. Miss Mary? Who? What! Miss—the captain's cousin. What a fool I am! Excuse me, doctor, just a moment. Thorsby's walking off with her. Hol-lo! I can't stand that. [*Runs out*]

Doc. Here, I say. Stop! You combustible institution.

Rai. No use, mister. He's off. I say, do all your city gents carry on like that? You're from the city, ain't you?

Doc. [*Sitting, R.*] The expression city and country are merely relative terms, my child. Do you ask for information?

Rai. [*Reflectively*] I ain't got no relatives there as I want information about. Be you a friend of Miss Mabel's?

Doc. She is such a general favorite that the question must on second thoughts seem to you wholly superfluous.

Rai. [*Suspiciously*] I don't understand.

Doc. Then your comprehension does not equal your curiosity, my child.

Rai. [*Keenly*] I begin to see it—I does.

Doc. Do you!

Rai. [*Drawing herself up with firmness*] We don't want no books, mister —nor maps—nor sewing machines—nor fly traps—nor patent churns—nor guns! we don't—

Doc. What does the girl mean?

Rai. We takes the *Weekly Tribune,* and that's enough for the whole family. We don't want the *Ledger,* nor the *Weekly,* and we don't subscribe to nothin'. You're wastin' your time.

Doc. Does she take me for a book peddler?

Rai. You're wastin' your time, I tell you. We ain't in want of horse liniment, nor hairpins—

Doc. My good girl, I'm a doctor.

Rai. A doctor! Wuss and wuss! If master catches you here he'll break your nasty bottles over your head—

Doc. But, my dear—

RAI. [*Sits on arm of chair*] Are we out o' spirits o' hartshorn and Blood Purifier and Instant Relief and Sand's Sassyparilly and Mrs. Winslow's snoozing syrup? Yes, we are, and we mean to stay out of 'em. Take my advice and git.

Doc. Allow me!—

RAI. What, you won't go? You will wait and see old master! Very well! But if he calls the dog on ye, don't blame me. [*Aside*] I guess I'm square with him now! Curiosity, indeed. [*Exit, L., door, 1.E.*]

Doc. Confound the minx! [*Calling after her*] Do I look like a patent medicine peddler? [*Matthew entering at R. door*]

MAT. I don't know, my dear sir. Those invaders of domestic peace assume all sorts of shapes.

Doc. [*L., confused*] I beg your pardon. I was addressing that impertinent little baggage.

MAT. Rachel! Yes, she assumes the duty of receiving and dismissing all itinerant vendors!

Doc. Allow me to introduce myself—Doctor Gossitt, of New York.

MAT. I am Matthew Standish. Pray be seated.

Doc. Mabel's father-in-law! This is fortunate. [*Shakes hands with him*]

MAT. [*Dryly*] Perhaps! We don't discuss it.

Doc. [*They sit*] I've heard of you very often, Mr. Standish—from your son.

MAT. [*L.C., quickly*] Do you know where he is?

Doc. [*R.C.*] No. Don't you?

MAT. I do not.

Doc. He has not written to you?

MAT. Yes—once! Soon after he went away—

Doc. A sad case, this, Mr. Standish!

MAT. It is only what might have been expected.

Doc. I can't dispute it. I had my apprehensions long ago.

MAT. You were acquainted with my son's wife, then, before her marriage?

Doc. Yes, and with your son. The blame is not altogether on one side. His excuse was his blind infatuation.

MAT. I believe she cannot pretend to any such apology.

Doc. Well, well. It's over. The inevitable has occurred. They have separated. Let us wait for time to reunite them.

MAT. You are exceedingly hopeful, doctor.

Doc. Good heavens, sir! They have a child. I hope everything from that. He cannot desert the mother of his child.

MAT. If you had heard her talk to the father of her child as I did—

Doc. Pish! [*Rises*] A girl's temper and a girl's tongue. Two ungovernable things.

MAT. Very. [*Rises*]

Doc. Let misfortune threaten her, and his love will revive.

MAT. Exactly. But what is there to revive her love? Which, as an Irishman would say, never existed.

Doc. This is no jesting matter, Mr. Standish.

MAT. Excuse me—it is a very excellent jest. To deceive an honest man into the belief that she loved him. To marry him—from pique! And then drive him from her when his society becomes distasteful. A capital jest, sir, in the cultivated circles from which my son chose to take a wife.

Doc. [*Impatiently*] My dear sir. I beg you won't fall into the vulgar error of believing that people of superior station hold common virtues in no esteem.

MAT. Oh, no. I only conform to the aristocratic view, which holds love, marriage and duty subordinate to pride.

Doc. You misjudge this young lady.

MAT. I do not—and I never did!

Doc. Yes, you do! Excuse my warmth. I knew her from a baby. I knew her father—a man who would not hurt the feelings of a beggar. I knew her mother—an angel on earth, and long since one in Heaven.

MAT. Do not excuse yourself, doctor. I recognize your right to take this young lady's part. You will never offend me by that; she is very well able to take her own—and she does not offend me by doing so, neither.

Doc. [*R.*] Then, why in the name of all that's irritating, is she treated as she is?

MAT. Treated as she is? What, in the name of all that's wonderful, is the treatment you speak of?

Doc. I have received a letter from her. Here it is. She asks me to come here—to see her. I have the good fortune to see you first, and I'm glad of the opportunity of asking you why she is compelled to call on her friends for assistance.

MAT. For assistance?

Doc. For aid—to escape from this place.

MAT. To escape from this place? Pardon me for echoing your words. This is not a prison.

Doc. But she wishes to leave it—to return to her own home and friends.

MAT. She is at liberty to do so.

Doc. She and her child?

MAT. That is a different matter.

Doc. What is a different matter?

MAT. [*Rising*] Listen to me, doctor. I am the father of her husband. She drove my son from this house—his home. When he left it—in the dead of night—without a word to me, his father—despair in his face and in his heart —he left me a duty to perform: to watch over his wife while she remained here.

Doc. Well?

MAT. And to watch over his child whether his wife remained here or not. I cannot surrender this child to any other care. My son lives—he is the guardian of his boy—*he* may dispose of him as he pleases—until he does so, I will keep him. [*Enter Mary at door*]

MARY. Come in. Let me introduce you to uncle. [*Comes forward, followed by Dymple and Thorsby, who are very distant to each other*] Uncle, let me! Ah, doctor, do you remember me?

Doc. With the greatest pleasure, Miss Standish.

MARY. Uncle—Mr. Dymple! Mr. Gyll.

Doc. Friends of mine who accompanied me. They are going to shoot in the neighborhood.

MAT. [*Keenly*] And to fish? There is capital sport in the streams. Glad to see you both. [*Aside*] The bodyguard of the doctor, I suppose. Knight-errants sworn to rescue the lady from that ogre, her father-in-law! [*To Mary*] Where is Mrs. Standish?

MARY. I saw her return from her walk a moment ago. She went through the garden. And uncle—those tramps I spoke to you about last week—I saw them in the road again today. Watching the house too, I thought.

MAT. Go. I'll find out what they want. Doctor, if you will follow Mary [*Crosses to R.*] she will show you where my daughter-in-law is to be seen.

MARY. [*Bringing Matthew down*] Oh, uncle! Mabel is looking more and more unhappy every day.

MAT. [*Sarcastically*] Her husband's absence is so protracted.

MARY. You are cruel.

MAT. I am.

MARY. [*C.*] Think how many weeks she has been ill and nearly dying.

MAT. [*To Doctor*] Here is another, doctor, who does not offend me by taking the part of my son's wife. [*Crosses to Boys*] Will you excuse me for a few moments? I have to see my farmer. [*Boys bow. He exits, L.C., downstairs*]

Doc. [*To Mary*] I thank you. [*Takes her hand*]

MARY. Make her happy, and I will thank you with all my heart. [*Doctor and Mary exit, R.U.D.*]

DYM. Now we're alone, perhaps you'll be good enough to explain your behavior to this young lady. I can't see any difference between the way you go on and regular spooning, I can't. I thought you said your heart was broken and the world was a desert.

THORS. [*C., horseback on chair*] That's pretty good for you. You agreed with me that your hopes were blighted, and you were soured with the world.

DYM. Well!

THORS. Well! You've been doing your best for the past ten minutes to cut me out.

DYM. Cut you out! You admit it. And we swore to go hand in hand for the rest of our existence, cherishing one image and forswearing the rest of the sex.

THORS. [*Rises*] I know I did. But this one's an old acquaintance.

DYM. [*Rises*] Look here, Thorsby! I have such regard for you that I don't mean to let you become a perjured villain. *I'll* take charge of this young lady while we stay here.

THORS. Much obliged.

DYM. I'll keep you out of temptation. I'll remain constantly by her side.

THORS. Very well! Go on!

DYM. What do you mean by go on?

THORS. I'll be there.

DYM. You'll be where?

THORS. On the other side.

DYM. I'll inform her that you've sworn never to marry, and show you to be a perjured villain.

THORS. If you dare! Mind! Everyone for himself! She don't like red hair!

DYM. [*Disturbed*] You don't mean to say—

THORS. [*Crosses to R., to back of chair. Waving him off*] Everyone for himself. She'll prefer a perjured villain to a red-headed one.

DYM. Thorsby! [*Going to him. Ragmoney Jim, at window*]

JIM. Pst!

DYM. Who are you, my effervescing friend?

JIM. [*Very hoarse*] Governor about?

DYM. [*Same tone*] Do you mean the old gentleman?

JIM. [*Nods*] Yes, the tall old file.

DYM. Off there! [*Points L.*]

JIM. [*Enters*] Good! Where's the young lady? Her as came in a while ago.

THORS. [*To Dymple*] What does he want with Mary?

DYM. [*Stiffly*] Miss Standish, if you please. [*To Jim*] What's your business?

JIM. [*Hands him old yellow envelope*] Give her that. Mum's the word. You look like a downy cove, you do.

DYM. [*Pleased*] I look like a downy cove!

THORS. He alludes to your head. [*Dymple annoyed*] Everybody notices it.

JIM. Not a word! Only give her that! [*Exit, downstairs*]

THORS. Give her that? Let's see it! [*After watching him off*]

DYM. Perjured villain! What have you to do with it?

THORS. I've as much to do with it as you have.

DYM. I've always observed that when a man deliberately becomes a perjured villain, he seldom hesitates at minor indiscretions. Would you violate the seal of a confidential communication? [*Mary enters, R.U.D.*] Miss Mary, [*With bow*] a letter just delivered.

MARY. [*C., takes it*] What a dirty letter.

DYM. The messenger was fully as dirty as the letter.

MARY. [*Reads*] "I've talked it over with my pal, and we agree"—why, what a curious letter: a lot of printed words seemingly cut from a newspaper, and pasted together. [*Looking on the envelope*] No name! Are you sure it is for me?

DYM. Oh, yes. The man described you, I'm certain.

MARY. [*Reads again*] "I've talked it over with my pal, and we agree that the job ought to be done at once. If you're willing, there's no time like the present. Wait till night, and when the governor calls the servants to prayers leave your window open, and leave the rest to us!" What does it mean? No address! No signature!

DYM. [*L.*] Job! What's the job?

MARY. [*C., to Thorsby*] A messenger brought this?

THORS. [*R.*] Looked like a tramp.

MARY. A rough man! My mind misgives me. I must show it to uncle. [*Crosses to R.*]

DYM. Do.

THORS. I'll go with you.

DYM. So will I. [*Crowding on Thorsby, pushes him away*]

MARY. What horrible plot does it disclose?

DYM. [*To Mary*] Some scheme worthy of a perjured villain. [*Glances at Thorsby, stage, L.*]

THORS. [*Same business*] The base emanation of a red-headed intellect.

MARY. Please come with me, Mr. Gyll. Uncle will want to know more of this messenger. [*Exit with Thorsby, who casts a triumphant glance at Dymple, R.1E.*]

DYM. [*Solus*] She deliberately selected Thorsby! He's got her! That ten minutes' start of me did the business. I have tried to save him. But he won't be saved. What's left for me? [*Dorothy enters, L.C., up the stairs at back with the child Arthur*]

Dor. No, my darling, mamma will want you now. You are too tired to run about any more. [*Sees Dymple*] I beg your pardon. [*Aside*] One of Doctor Gossitt's young friends. [*To Dymple*] Mr. Gyll or Mr. Dymple?

Dym. [*R.*] Dymple, ma'am. Gyll has plunged into the vortex of passion! If you wish to see him inquire of the first lovely woman you meet!

Dor. Dear me! [*To Arthur*] Stay by aunty!

Dym. Hem! A lovely child, ma'am. Hem! Yours?

Dor. Mine, sir? It is Mrs. Standish's son.

Dym. Come to Uncle Sammy! [*The Child extends his hands. Dymple sits and takes him on his knee*] As an old friend of the family, in fact, a rejected suitor of his mother, I think I may claim a sort of relationship.

Dor. Dear me! You seem to take it very coolly, sir.

Dym. [*Gives Child his watch to play with*] Madam—I beg pardon, are you Madam or Miss?

Dor. Miss—Miss Dorothy.

Dym. My prevailing characteristic, Miss Dorothy, is my shy and retiring disposition.

Dor. Indeed!

Dym. If I had been as bold as some people—who knows, this boy might have been mine.

Dor. Bless me!

Dym. But I took "no" for an answer, Miss Dorothy, and ever since have carried a crushed heart in my bosom.

Dor. It certainly does not show.

Dym. What I lacked was knowledge of the world. Miss Dorothy, I am an orphan. If I had had a mother I should probably never have taken "no" for an answer. I want a mother or a wife. Perhaps both. But I am convinced that I shall never get a wife until I have found a mother.

Dor. Really! You are a very odd creature, Mr. Dymple. I don't know whether to be amused by your frankness or not!

Dym. Thorsby Gyll, who, although a perjured villain, has no lack of judgment, advises me to get a mother. What do you think of it?

Dor. I think you certainly need somebody to advise, to look after you.

Dym. [*Quickly*] Do you! Somebody to advise, to guide, to direct, to protect me.

Dor. Exactly!

Dym. Someone into whose bosom I could confide my hopes and disappointments. Miss Dorothy—*you* have a motherly air. [*She half rises*] You have! Don't be startled! I am about to make you an offer! Be a mother to me. [*Rises, Child goes to Dorothy*]

Dor. [*Smiling*] My dear Mr. Dymple, you are evidently out of your senses. [*Stage, L.*]

Dym. [*R.*] All for want of a mother! I want a good, kind, motherly, but firm and decided, creature to bring me to my senses.

Dor. Then I recommend you to get—

Dym. What?

Dor. A mother-in-law! Marry the daughter of one of those ladies who are accustomed to govern their families. I think that, after a short experience, you will be tolerably well satisfied. [*Takes the Child, crosses up R.*]

Dym. I never thought of that. It's capital advice. But in the meantime, if you would only think over what I've said.

Dor. I must respectfully decline to adopt you myself. I really have too much to do now. All the poultry is under my charge, and I really can't look after any strange chickens.

Dym. Ha, ha! Very good! Capital. [*Aside*] I'm glad she didn't say calf. It appears to be as hard to get a mother as it is to get a wife. The entire range of female relationship seems to be denied me. [*Exit, R.1.E.*]

Dor. Come, darling, and see if we can't find some pretty books to look at, and wait till mamma is done talking to the naughty old doctor. [*Going, and pauses to look after Dymple*] I must really ask Mary if all the young gentlemen nowadays are cracked. [*Exit into parlor. Ragmoney Jim and Padder look in cautiously and then enter*]

Jim. [*R.*] It's too late—the wrong one's got it and gone.

Pad. Well, you are a precious soft one! Give the paper to the wrong 'un. Where's our fifty thousand dollars gone to? Up in a balloon, I suppose—for now they'll find us out and stow away the babby.

Jim. Oh, shut up. Trust me! I must see the gal.

Pad. Why, what can Sally do?

Jim. Never you mind. If that babby don't come into our hands by mild means—why—the game's not spoiled yet. Why the very heartstrings of that old file is bound round the child—and as for its mother! Fifty thousand dollars would be only a drop in a bucket to them.

Pad. I could sit down and cry. All our little game knocked. [*Someone stumbles outside*]

Jim. You babbling fool. Hush! get out! [*Padder darts out and Jim crouches up the stage as Raitch enters*]

Rai. [*C.*] Well, only to think. Miss Mary as never had no beau all her life—got two to onct. Oh, give me them sly gals for making a scoop when they gets a chance.

Jim. [*At back*] Sis!

Rai. [*Starts, then looks around hurriedly and anxiously*]   Oh, go back—
go back. You'll be ketched if you're seen.

Jim. [*L.*]   You fool, I tell you I've made a mistake, given a message to
one of them chaps and he's given it to—

Rai.   To Miss Mary?

Jim.   Yes.

Rai.   Then it's all over. Oh, do go back! Hide! I'll see what can be done.

Jim.   Something must be done at once. Tell the lady.

Rai.   I'll tell her, but do go away! Go! [*In fright closes the window on
him, he disappears*] Oh, what shall I do? [*Mabel and Doctor enter from
her room, R.U.D.*]

Mabel. [*As she enters*]   I have thought of all that and I have made up
my mind.

Rai. [*Trying to catch her attention*]   Miss Mabel.

Mabel.   Another time, I'm busy now.

Rai.   But Miss Mabel, I can't wait.

Mabel.   Go to my room, then. I'll come presently.

Rai. [*Goes up wringing her hand*]   If I only knowed what to do. [*Exit,
L.U.D.*]

Doc. [*R.*]   To what have you made up your mind?

Mabel.   To return to Grassmere, to my home, and to take my child
with me.

Doc.   Against the wish of your husband's father.

Mabel.   Yes, in spite of it. In spite of the precautions he takes. Do you
know that his servants follow me wherever I go with my own child, as if I
meditated the theft of what did not belong to me?

Doc.   How will you elude this watch?

Mabel.   By a means as desperate as his tyranny is vile. Chance threw in
my way two men who will hesitate at nothing. I have made use of these
people for my purpose. I have arranged with them to—

Doc.   To steal your child away!

Mabel.   To assist his escape and mine from this prison house. [*Crosses
to R.*]

Doc.   Mabel, my dear girl, pause before you commit this act. There must
be some other way.

Mabel.   There is no other way. I have tried to soften this father.

Doc.   That was right.

Mabel.   But I have committed the unpardonable sin in a father's eye. I
have driven away his son.

Doc. [*L.*]   Let me speak to him. Besides I have not come alone. I consulted with your stepmother. [*Mabel looks up*] I had to consult someone.

She has followed me down—she would not be denied. We will all have authority with this stern old man. He must yield. [*Lucille, upstairs, appears at doorway, C.*]

LUC. May I come in?

DOC. [*Goes to her, C.*] Do, my dear madam.

LUC. [*Aside to Doctor*] Raymond is outside.

DOC. Why couldn't he stay at home?

LUC. [*L.*] He wanted to come. He wouldn't lose sight of me for a whole day.

DOC. [*Sarcastically, crosses to L.*] Devoted fellow!

LUC. Isn't he! You see we are not married yet. [*Comes down as the Doctor goes up C.*] My dear Mabel! [*Takes both her hands*] I could not stay away. I felt that you needed my sympathy. What is this extraordinary story? Have you married into a family of lunatics? First your husband runs away from you, and then his father keeps you under lock and key. What a pity, dear, they couldn't change dispositions. Why didn't the old man run away and the young one show such a desire for your society?

MABEL. Your sympathy is truly consoling, madam.

LUC. I knew it would be, my love. But come, tell me the whole of the dreadful thing from beginning to end. What a scandal!

MABEL. Scandal?

LUC. Why, my dear! Your husband deserting you so shortly after your marriage.

MABEL. He had to join his vessel. His orders were imperative.

LUC. Indeed. Why didn't he resign?

MABEL. That was his own business. You will surely allow him to judge for himself in such a matter.

LUC. But to leave you here alone—away from New York.

MABEL. From your tone one would suppose he had gone without consulting me.

LUC. Oh! He did consult you then?

MABEL. Yes.

LUC. Then there has been no misunderstanding? No quarrel?

MABEL. Certainly not.

LUC. [*Leaning back*] And he loves you just as much as he always did?

MABEL. [*Biting her lip and trying to master emotion*] Yes.

LUC. [*Looks at her sharply*] Well! No one will believe it.

MABEL. Do people always put the worst construction on the absence of a husband who happens to be an officer in the service of his country?

Luc. Don't talk nonsense, Mabel! Everybody knows that Captain Standish is rich enough to give up the service. He would have done so if he had been fond of his wife.

Mabel. [*Quickly*] But I dissuaded him from sending in his resignation.

Luc. You wouldn't have done so if you had been fonder of your husband.

Mabel. [*Rises and crosses to L.*] Enough! My husband's affairs are no subject for your interference, or for the gossip of the world. [*Crosses to L.*]

Doc. Good! We'll have it all right yet. [*Strolls off, R.U.E.*]

Luc. Well, there is one matter in which you have asked outside interference, my dear. You wish to leave this place, with your child! And this father-in-law of yours objects.

Mabel. [*Coolly*] A mere difference of opinion as to what is best for little Arthur's health.

Luc. [*Keenly*] But you wrote a letter to the doctor!

Mabel. [*Smiling triumphantly*] Certainly, to ask his advice on the subject.

Luc. [*R.*] Ah! You are as clever as ever, my dear. And pray what does the doctor advise?

Mabel. That I should remain.

Luc. [*Rises*] Well, I'm glad of that. All things considered, you are better here among the set of people you have married into. Honest people, I dare say; but it was a dreadful descent, Mabel.

Mabel. [*Turning passionately*] And who drove me to it?

Luc. [*Scornfully*] Who, indeed!

Mabel. [*L.*] You! You who schemed to get from me the man whom I loved.

Luc. [*Flushing*] I schemed!

Mabel. There are no secrets between us, although till now never by word or sign have we referred to this subject. You schemed, you planned to ensnare him. [*Raymond appears at back and listens*]

Luc. You are mad, I believe. I will not stay here to be insulted. [*Crosses up L.*]

Mabel. [*Stage, R.*] Yes, perhaps I am growing to madness. And that will be my excuse for any want of politeness, when I tell you that—

Luc. [*Trembling with anger*] You wish me to go.

Mabel. At once!

Luc. Thank you, my dear! I forgive you. You may think better of this some day, and want my sympathy. Send for me when you do. [*Exit down steps. Raymond comes forward*]

Mabel. Raymond! [*Breathlessly, as she retreats a step*]

RAY. [*L., in tone of deep sympathy*] Forgive me, Mabel. I came here with her because there was no other way to see you in this home. But I came on my own mission, not hers, to offer you the protection and help that is due even from a stranger to a woman who needs it.

MABEL. *You*—have come to seek *me*?

RAY. I know that you hate me, that you despise me. But you have no cause—on my life, you have no cause.

MABEL. Not after what I heard and saw!

RAY. The night that I clasped you in my arms, that I wrung from you a confession of love! [*She makes a quick gesture for him to be silent, and suddenly closes her ears with her hands, then buries her face in them*] Yes, what you heard and saw that night would have stamped me as the veriest traitor breathing—but for one thing. It was that same night you gave your hand to Arthur Standish.

MABEL. [*Proudly*] Well, sir.

RAY. But I do not blame you.

MABEL. [*Crosses to R. chair*] Indeed! [*Rises, bitterly*] Perhaps, too, you have forgiven me.

RAY. [*Warmly*] Yes—for all the misery you caused me by taking that step before listening to my explanation. But now that I see you again—

MABEL. [*Starts up*] You will hear me say that the past is forgotten. There is no need to revert to it. [*Goes to chair, R.*]

RAY. But the past has left its sting!

MABEL. What sting? Remorse? Pray cease to feel any, since you have done no harm.

RAY. You cannot deceive me, Mabel! You know that you are not happy. You cannot conceal the truth from me, for I, too—

MABEL. [*Clasping her hands on her knee*] I have no wish to conceal the truth. God help me, it is stamped in my face and burned into my heart.

RAY. And that I am the cause—

MABEL. [*Same*] No. No. The fault is mine!

RAY. [*Eagerly*] But from the consequences of this fault, I will rescue you at the peril of my life. Oh, Mabel, let there be no further misunderstanding between us. For your sake, and to retrieve my folly, I would brave everything and dare everyone. Only say that you will accept the protection that I offer against the horrors of the pit into which my blindness has plunged you. [*Kneels*]

MABEL. [*Rising*] Mr. Raymond Lessing, have you not slightly mistaken me?

RAY. I did mistake you until the day you married Arthur Standish. Then I saw what I had lost. What a wealth of love she could offer whose hate could drive her to the sacrifice of a whole life! But I do not mistake you now, when you tell me that you are wretched, and that your pride and anger are alone to blame for it, for I see that you would spare me and not yourself.

MABEL. Yes, I would spare you and not myself.

RAY. You will let me sue for your pardon on my knees. You will let me read the secret of that heart I lost in my hour of triumph, to find again in my hour of despair! You will let me tell you of the love that has followed you to another's arms, ready when that sacred refuge was denied you, to save you from utter and hopeless misery.

MABEL. Yes, I have let you tell me all this, that my cup of shame might be filled to the brim, and not lack the bitterest ingredient of all—the knowledge that my crime has subjected me to the last insult a woman can bear. [Rises, stage, L.]

RAY. [Rising] No, not a crime, Mabel. A fault, to revenge yourself on me by marrying another—but not a crime!

MABEL. Am I speaking of you! Miserable one! My crime was to revenge upon an innocent man the treachery I suffered from you!

RAY. You loved me then?

MABEL. No! I despised you. But the store of hate you heaped in my heart I have scattered broadcast among the guiltless. Yes, I have tortured this man who deserved it only by loving me—by trusting me! I have driven him from his home—from his child!

RAY. [Crosses] I know it, and I have come to make what reparation lays in my power.

MABEL. [Turning short on him] Your reparation! If you had a hundred lives to live, and each were offered me, I would hold them lighter than the least breath of the man I have injured. I brought him scorn and hate—he gave me tenderness and love. I brought him falsehood—he gave me constancy and truth. I can speak of him before you, because I am humbled to the dust, and in my wretchedness I can do him no dishonor. [Crosses R.]

RAY. Charming! Then you love your husband?

MABEL. I love him? Yes! Heaven is my witness that I love him now, as he loved me. From the moment he left me I knelt and prayed that some judgment might fall upon me, for my wicked blindness. I have begun to suffer what I merit, since I am forced to listen to you.

RAY. [After a pause] I am delighted that your husband is destined to be a happy man. Delighted! I wish he were here to receive the same assurance. As he cannot be, and I will not be permitted to witness your reconciliation, I have no alternative but to bid you good day. [Aside, as he is going] For the

second time in my life I have been a fool—and about the same woman!
[*Exit down steps*]

MABEL. This, then, is what it is to suffer. God forgive me what I have
caused the father of my child to bear! [*Sinks in chair, R. Matthew enters,
L.U.E., and watching Lessing, then comes down to Mabel*]

MAT. Is that man your accomplice? [*He has the letter of the Tramps in
his hand, open*]

MABEL. Sir! [*Mildly, not understanding*]

MAT. I ask you the name of that man?

MABEL. Raymond Lessing.

MAT. The person for whose sake you insulted your husband in his own
house?

MABEL. Yes! [*Breaks down again*]

MAT. And now your accomplice, who is to assist you in your plot?

MABEL. [*Rises*] I do not understand.

MAT. Look at this paper. It has fallen into my hands by accident. By
some inspiration I comprehend its meaning. You are about to remove your
child by stealth. Is it not enough that you cast yourself at the feet of yonder
wretch—that you brought him here—here, beneath an honest man's roof,
to complete your infamous bargain with him—but you must drag your
child with you to this new career of shame?

MABEL. [*Appealing*] Oh, sir, do not drive me back to the madness I have
been trying to escape! Have pity on me, I beseech!

MAT. [*Crosses R., behind*] Beseech me not. I am no dupe of your tardy
repentance.

MABEL. [*L. Frenzied*] On your life I warn you not to drive me, by new
insults, to the desperate step I had resolved upon!

MAT. Your threats are as weak as your repentance. Go! Leave this home
polluted by the presence of that wretch! Begone—join him—when and
where you please! As for your child, I will keep him safely, never fear. I
have been warned in time! [*Exit into room, R.1.E.*]

MABEL. Be it so! Hard and implacable old man. It is you who drive
me forth. [*Mary entering from R.1.E.*]

MARY. Mabel, what are you about to do? Take little Arthur from us?
You cannot mean it. You shall not do it.

MABEL. Shall not! [*Passionately*]

MARY. No, no! I should not have said that. I mean only to show you the
folly you contemplate.

MABEL. What have you to do with me or my folly? I leave this house
free to you and to the man you love—when he comes back. You should be
thankful for that. [*Going up*]

MARY. Oh, you cannot mean—

MABEL. Deny it not! Did I not read your secret the very night he brought me here?

MARY. Mabel! If you have ever known what it is to feel the sting of an insult that spared neither your sex nor your weakness, you can understand what a bitter wrong you have done me by this suspicion. [*Turns away weeping*]

MABEL. Fool! Wretch that I am! How can I hope for pity that shows none. Mary—sister, I was mad! I wished to revenge my own outraged feelings on someone, and like a coward I struck the defenseless. Mary, see I am on my knees to you. Forgive me, poor heart, that has suffered so silently. I am more wretched than you, for I deserve no pity.

MARY. [*Clasps and raises her*] No, no, no. I love you with my whole heart. I love your dear little child. I wish you to be happy again, and I came to beg you not to place an eternal bar between you and that happiness. [*Dorothy enters with Child asleep, very softly, R.1.E. Music*]

MABEL. [*Darts forward, C.*] My child!

DOR. Hush! He's asleep. [*Goes to sofa near fire and lays him down*] I'll go and see that his bed is prepared. [*Exit, R.U.E.*]

MARY. Oh, sister, for you have called me so! Will you not stay with us and with him? He is your guardian angel. [*Mabel kisses her silently and drops on her knees by the sleeping Child. Mary, after lingering a moment, goes out, R.U.E.*]

MABEL. [*To Mary*] Yes, he is my guardian angel! [*After Mary goes out*] From what sin, what despair, does he not keep me! Oh, Thou! Who has given him to me so helpless and yet so strong to save, make me worthy of this precious gift. These tiny hands about my neck shall draw me to a better life; this innocent head resting upon my bosom shall cast out my hate and pride. And I will watch over thee, my baby—lest in my hour of guilt, my punishment should come through thee. Oh, dreadful thought! [*Clasping her hands on high*] No, no, no, not through him! Not through him! Spare my child. [*Pause. Music. Ragmoney Jim appears at the window, opens it and leaps in lightly. Padder appears after him*]

JIM. Pst!

MABEL. [*Gets R. of C., in terror*] No, no, go, leave me!

JIM. Now's your time lady! All's clear.

MABEL. I have changed my mind. Here is money. Go! With what you have already it will pay you well.

JIM. [*Eagerly watching Child and glancing around the room*] The horse and wagon are outside, mistress! Let them catch us if they can! We'll give 'em our dust for forty mile. [*Stretches out his arms for the Child, who is on sofa, L.*]

MABEL. No, no, do I not tell you I have changed my mind!

JIM. [*Fiercely*] What of that! I've not changed mine! A bargain's a bargain. [*Dashes her aside, seizes Child and flies to window, handing it to Padder, who disappears*]

MABEL. Help! Help! My child! [*Clutches Jim, who strikes her*]

JIM. Off! [*Mabel screams, Jim leaps through window, as all enter from various doors: Matthew, Dorothy, Mary, Doctor, Dymple and Thorsby*]

MABEL. There! Gone! Gone! Ah! [*Falls senseless as Raitch rushes off, C. Matthew and Doctor go to window, the Boys after Raitch, C.*]

ACT IV.

SCENE 1: *Dr. Gossitt's study in New York. The Doctor is discovered at desk, C., finishing some writing. A handbill and a mass of opened letters are before him. Music.*

DOC. There! That's for the morning papers. Twenty thousand dollars reward! Double the offer we have made in our posters and advertisements so far. [*Folding up handbill and writing as he speaks*] And perhaps we shall have something more satisfactory than these! [*Taps letters. Dorothy enters, R.*] Well, how is our patient?

DOR. The fever seems to abate! Was it prudent, doctor, do you think, to bring her here?

DOC. My dear madam, she would have gone raving mad if we did not let her share in our efforts to recover her child. It was a choice between a fever and a coffin, and I preferred the fever.

DOR. [*R.*] No news yet?

DOC. None!

DOR. And so many searching. Matthew, Mr. Dymple, Mr. Gyll—

DOC. And the whole police force.

DOR. What are those? [*Points to letters in his hand*]

DOC. Answers to our last advertisement.

DOR. [*Delighted*] Then he is found? They will bring him to us?

DOC. Not quite! These are the jackals who follow the scent with the hunters. The customary city swindlers trying to rob grief and mulct misfortune. [*Shows one letter*] From a person boldly avowing himself a professional thief, who says he knows where the child is concealed, and will tell for five hundred dollars down mailed to his address! [*Shows another*] From a "Private Detective Agency," hinting at certain mysterious information we can have for five hundred dollars down! [*Shows another*] From a clairvoyant, who has had extraordinary visions, which she will reveal for five hundred dollars down! [*Folds them up hastily, rises*] By Jove! I believe all the rascality of the city has fixed its price at five hundred dollars down!

Dor. [*Mysteriously*] Doctor! [*Looking around*] I'd try her.

Doc. Try whom?

Dor. You know! [*He looks at her; she looks around again; he follows her action*] The clairvoyant. [*Mysteriously*]

Doc. [*Laughs*] My dear woman, are you mad?

Dor. It can't do any harm, and I've heard of a person—quite a lady—who lost a watch and went to one of these persons—unknown to her husband, of course.

Doc. Well, did she get the watch?

Dor. No, you see she hadn't any proof except what the clairvoyant said; but she had her suspicions confirmed about a cook she had discharged for drunkenness! It's a fact, I assure you.

Doc. [*Pretending solemnity*] My dear Miss Dorothy! Would you—a Christian woman—invoke the assistance of the powers of darkness in this case?

Dor. Oh, dear no! But if it would lead to the discovery of poor little Arthur—

Doc. You wouldn't mind giving the devil the job.

Dor. [*Shocked*] Doctor!

Doc. Trust me, my dear lady—if we must have mystery and witchcraft—let's buy our own brimstone and raise the devil ourselves. It's much cheaper.

Dor. Now you're laughing at me.

Doc. No. Not at you. At the clairvoyants. We shall find the villains yet without their help. They have been traced to New York. They are only waiting for the temptation of a large reward, and tomorrow we offer twenty thousand dollars. [*Enter Dymple and Thorsby, as if from street, tired*] Well, young gentlemen, what success?

Dym. Same as ever! Miles of walking and no results.

Thors. [*L.*] Done half the city in three days.

Dor. [*Taking his hand*] Ah, Mr. Dymple, what a self-sacrificing, unselfish heart you have.

Dym. You see what you lost when you wouldn't have me for a son.

Dor. Never mind! I'm everybody's Aunt Dorothy. I'll be yours.

Dym. That's something. It isn't everybody that has an aunt.

Doc. [*R., to Thorsby*] A useless search. I told you so.

Thors. [*Crosses to Doctor*] We must do something! We can't sit down patiently and wait for answers to advertisements. I begin to see what a fraud the census is! Why, there's at least a million girls and babies in New York, let alone men, women and children.

Doc. Have you been to police headquarters, today?

Dym. [*Crosses to Doctor*] Yes, and they begin to treat us in an extremely snappish way. We annoy them, I suppose. Nothing annoys police headquarters so much as inquiries after what they ought to find out and can't.

Thors. [*Aside to Dorothy*] Any news from—from Deerfield—Miss Dorothy? [*Dymple watches Thorsby while Doctor continues to address him in dumb show*]

Dor. From Mary? Only a letter she sent us today.

Thors. Is—is she—well?

Dor. Yes, poor child! I suppose so, at least, for she doesn't speak of herself.

Thors. I think if I were to go up there, and make inquiries in the neighborhood, I might get some clew.

Dor. Oh, no, we have exhausted all means of information there. [*Goes to Doctor*]

Dym. [*Close to Thorsby*] I heard you. You want to get a clew, do you? Haven't we sworn to share all our clews together?

Thors. [*Impatiently*] Oh, you are always suspecting. [*Going to door*]

Dym. No clews to yourself, old fellow—especially in that quarter—without first consulting me. [*They exeunt*]

Doc. Did you show Mabel Mary's letter? Does she know that her husband is coming?

Dor. I'm afraid to speak to her till she asks me.

Doc. And she has not mentioned his name?

Dor. No.

Doc. I can't understand it.

Dor. I can.

Doc. Perhaps so. You women comprehend all the turnings and twistings of that maze you call a woman's heart. Thank goodness, I'm a bachelor. But one thing I know: if this punishment don't soften her—[*Matthew enters, L.C., wearily, as from the street*] never was one more justly—

Mat. We have no business with that now, doctor.

Dor. [*Running to him, taking his hat and stick as he sinks wearily on chair*] Oh, brother!

Doc. My good friend.

Mat. [*Crosses to C.*] I heard your words as I came in. Let us speak of this poor girl's faults no more, doctor. Heaven has made her its own by a sovereign affliction. She has passed from our censure to the chastisement of One that loves whom He chasteneth.

Doc. You are right.

Dor. [*L.*] Ah, brother, it is good to hear you speak so.

Mat. I have been to blame that I added to this young girl's sorrow.

Dor. You?

Doc. [*R.*] I do not understand.

Mat. You need not, for the present. Doctor, I shall want to consult you by and by. [*To Dorothy*] Any news from my son?

Dor. Mary has sent us a telegram from him. It came to Deerfield yesterday. He is on his way from Hampton Roads.

Mat. And Mary?

Dor. [*L.*] She is still on the watch.

Doc. For whom?

Dor. That poor creature, Rachel.

Doc. [*Angrily*] The hussy! I'm certain now she was in league with the thieves.

Mat. No! I won't believe that.

Doc. Hark ye, Mr. Standish. Your sister has given me that girl's history. Rescued from the very gutters of this metropolis, when a mere infant, by the officers of the mission, she was sent into your part of the country, as hundreds of young vagrants like her, for adoption.

Dor. [*L.*] But that was nine years ago.

Doc. [*R.*] Well, her friends or relations have reclaimed her. She has gravitated back to the depths from which she sprang. These kidnappers are her people. Perhaps her parents. That's the whole story.

Dor. What? Go back willingly to them—after the way I brought her up?

Doc. [*R.*] Why haven't we heard from her?

Dor. Like enough they keep her under lock and key.

Doc. She was seen in the wagon when they drove off—she wasn't under lock and key then. If she turns out to be anything better than the thieves she ran off with, I'll take my own physic, that's all.

Mat. I'll trust the girl. If these wretches have not killed her, we shall hear from her in good time. [*To Dorothy, bringing her down; Doctor sits at desk*] Mabel—is she better—does she speak of me—of him, her husband, of anyone but her child?

Dor. Of little Arthur—no one but little Arthur. But, brother, I was sitting in the chair near the sofa where she lay—she thought me asleep, for I had been dozing—when I saw her take a letter from her bosom and read it with streaming eyes. I recognized it. It was the one she got from Arthur when he went away. It is the only bit of his writing that she possesses. I watched her read it when she could hardly see a word in it for the tears in her eyes! Oh, brother! There is a Providence in affliction. [*Street door bell heard*]

Doc. [*Starts up*] Visitors! Perhaps some news!

Mat. [*Wiping his eyes*] Yes, good news!

Doc. Eh? How do you know?

Mat. I know. [*Smiling*] For my heart tells me so.

Doc. My heart never tells me anything when the street door bell rings.

Mat. It's Dorothy's news—news for a father to hear. I can only repeat her words, doctor, there's a Providence in affliction. [*Dymple, L., outside*]

Dym. Come right in. [*Enters with a parcel open in his hand*] News! We have something at last. [*Mary and Thorsby follow in, L.1.D.*]

Mat. Mary.

Mary. [*Kissing Matthew and Dorothy, and taking Doctor's hand*] I came as soon as I got it.

Doc. Got what?

Mary. A parcel by express—this morning. Look, uncle! It is Rachel's frock. The one she wore when they took her away.

Dor. Her frock?

Mary. Wrapped up! Here it is! I couldn't stay there and write to you. I had to come.

Doc. [*Dymple crosses to him*] Let me see it. [*Takes frock from Dymple*] Did you search the pockets? [*Does so*] Nothing! What does it mean? [*Looks over it*] Is there no paper pinned to it? Where's the wrapper it came in?

Dym. Not a word here but the direction. [*Gives the paper to Doctor and takes frock, and he and Thorsby examine it together*]

Mat. I think I understand what it means.

Mary. What is that, uncle?

Mat. The villains wish us to understand by this that any recognition of the girl by her clothes is useless. It was one mark by which the detectives were to know her.

Mary. I had a terrible suspicion, uncle, that they had killed her and sent this dumb message to tell the dreadful story.

Dor. No, no! They would not dare do that.

Thors. [*Aside to Mary*] Don't fret, Miss Mary.

Dym. I say, doctor—I think, if, instead of sending us a dress they had sent us an address, it would have been more to the purpose.

Mary. [*To Dorothy*] Is Mabel awake? [*Dorothy nods and points off*] May I go to her? Is she well enough to see me?

Dor. Certainly.

Thors. This way, Miss Mary.

Mary. Thank you. [*She passes out with Dorothy, R.*]

Dym. [*Who has been cut out by Thorsby in showing Mary out, following and slapping Thorsby on the back*] Serpent!

THORS. [*Gaily, returning and taking hold of the dress*] Let's have another look at the frock, Sammy.

DYM. [*Tears it from him*] No, sir! You follow your clew. I'll have this one to myself. [*Off, L., Thorsby R.*]

MAT. [*L., to Doctor*] Now quick, my friend—while we are alone together. As I came in just now, a messenger, near the door, gave me an envelope—here it is—and immediately disappeared. A shabby-looking old man—see, a sheet on which are pasted words cut from a book or paper. [*The Doctor takes the paper*] He did not wait for me to open it, as you may suppose.

DOC. [*Finishes reading and turns paper over*] Humph!

MAT. What do you think of it?

DOC. A trap.

MAT. [*L.*] You believe it?

DOC. Plain as day. An appointment at night—behind a churchyard—a desperate and deserted neighborhood—a mere plan to rob you.

MAT. But the letter itself—exactly similar to the one left by the tramps at Deerfield. The sender offers to give the child into my own hands, if I will come to his terms.

DOC. He couldn't offer a better bait. And you are to go there alone. *Alone,* understand, with the money—a likely story.

MAT. The sender warns me expressly to seek no aid from the police.

DOC. And very properly, if he wishes to get you in his power.

MAT. But we dare not neglect any means—even the most dangerous or the least promising—to find my grandson. I am not afraid. I will go.

DOC. You will?

MAT. Yes.

DOC. Then what the devil did you ask my advice for?

MAT. I merely wished to let you know where I proposed going tonight.

DOC. Very well. Now I know, I shall have Captain Speers and half a dozen of his best officers there to look after you.

MAT. I beg you will do nothing of the kind. I need no protection. I have seen the vagabonds your police pointed out to me as the thieves and burglars of the metropolis. I believe I am a match for half a dozen of them.

DOC. [*R.*] My dear sir, this is the usual New England estimate of its own ability. Don't disparage our burglars, I beg. They are the only things we New Yorkers take a just pride in.

MAT. [*Seriously*] I value my life as nothing, doctor, compared to the reparation I owe Mabel. I have wronged her deeply—if I am to atone for it by this sacrifice, I am ready. But something tells me that I have this mystery now in my grasp. [*As he is about to go, Matthew looks off, R., and then detains the Doctor. Doctor advances, R., with outstretched arms, and Matthew shyly draws back*]

Doc. Mabel! It is the first time she has been out of her room. [*Mabel enters, R., supported on Mary's arm*] My dear, this is imprudent; you are not well enough yet. [*Gently*]

MABEL. [*Nervously*] But I cannot sit there all alone. I must help you—go somewhere—do something to aid your search. [*Matthew sinks in chair*]

Doc. [*Gently*] You can help us all and give us aid by your patience—by brave and courageous patience.

MABEL. Have I not been patient? But you tell me nothing. Rachel has sent to us. What does it mean? What do you intend doing?

Doc. We must think about it, dear. This dress is as great a mystery as any we have had to deal with.

MABEL. It is all clear to me. It means that someone is thinking of us—that the broken link is reuniting and a hand is stretched out to us through the darkness. It is a message of hope, doctor, sent by that poor girl, but it is also a call to us for help. Can we not help her? Where she is, my child is.

Doc. If we could help her we would do it instantly; but there is no word—no suggestion how to reach her. Trace the parcel back step by step to her we may—but that requires time and the exercise of judgment.

MABEL. This is what is so hard to bear. You want time, time, time! You always say so. Is it possible my child can be taken from me—carried through villages and towns in broad day—and no one question? How are the people found who flee with no burden save the guilt they carry in their bosoms? Why did no one stop these ruffians bearing a delicate child! Or if they hide, has the law no net to drag the depths which conceal them? [*Crosses to L.*]

Doc. The law is doing its best—but we don't rely on that—we are all searching.

MABEL. [*Back to him*] And can I do nothing? I have heard of mothers in other times who went through the streets calling aloud at every door, so that at sound of their voices their little ones might cry out and so discover themselves. The rudest people respected their grief—kind but hardy friends sprang up at every step and helped them in the search.

Doc. We can do much better in these days, my dear. A hundred mighty agencies are at work for us. The avarice and greed of men search more diligently than even a mother's love! We have doubled the reward we offered: cupidity or treachery must soon disclose him.

MABEL. [*Crosses to Mary*] Who then is searching?

MARY. [*R.*] All of our friends—Thorsby, I mean Mr. Gyll, Mr. Dymple—and, above all, one whose feet never weary pacing the streets to bring back little Arthur.

MABEL. [*Doctor gets L.*] Of whom do you speak? [*The Doctor and Mary stand aside so as to reveal Matthew*] He? [*A struggle of resentment and emotion*] Mr. Standish.

MARY. [*To Mabel*] You may call him by another name now, Mabel! He could not do more were he indeed your father. [*Matthew advances with hesitancy and timidity*]

MAT. There is no merit in any sacrifice I or mine make you, my child. I—an old man—stern in my fancied integrity and sense of right—humble myself before you, whom I wronged by my cruel and unjust suspicions that day. I ask your pardon, my daughter. [*She holds out her hand, he takes it, then as she, giving way to her feelings, begins to sob, he draws her softly to his bosom*] There, there! My poor child. [*Wipes his own eyes*] It is I who have brought this misfortune on you. Gentle words, kindness from me—might have averted it. I owe you reparation and I promise it. You shall have your child again, I promise it. I—there—there. [*Resigns her to Mary, and as he is going L., aside to Doctor*] Do you wonder that I risk my life? It belongs to her! [*Exit, L.1 E.*]

DOC. [*Aside*] What a wonderful deal of good a little trouble does for us. This baby will be a blessing yet. [*Exit after Matthew, L.*]

MARY. Do not despair, my darling. For Arthur loved you—and he is returning.

MABEL. Yes, and by so much as he loved me he will not forgive me.

MARY. Put away the thought. The heart that can feel so much will soften.

MABEL. There is only One who forgives, who embraces, who feeds and who spares them that trample on His love. And even that forgiveness I dare not invoke. [*Exeunt, R. Dymple, L.1 E., reenters with frock in his hand*]

DYM. There they go! The only two women whom I ever loved. One I couldn't get, and the other I can't. I watched her with Thorsby. When I talk to her she looks me straight in the eye; when he talks to her she looks at his boots. I've noticed the peculiarity in the female sex before. They won't meet your eye if they love you for fear you'll discover the fact too soon. Well, they've both gone from me forever, and I'm left with this gingham! This gown, like everything else pertaining to womankind, eludes, avoids and baffles me. I have literally turned it inside out and upside down—explored the tucks, verified the seams and inspected the gathers, and yet it is a wrinkle beyond me. [*As he is feeling about the waistband he touches something and stops*] There is a peculiar lumpiness about this particular portion of the anatomy! I wish I was a dressmaker! I wonder if it's natural. [*Takes *out penknife*] I've been tempted half a dozen times to rip it open! [*Cuts the dress*] If it's nothing—By jove, it is something! It's a piece of paper. A piece of brown paper. There's nothing on it! A substitute I suppose for buckram. A piece of paper—full of pinholes. Evidently a pincushion before its incarceration in its late place of interment. [*Holds it up suddenly, then calls*] Thorsby! Thorsby! [*Thorsby enters, R.1.E.*]

THORS. Well?

DYM. Come here! Look! Take this! Look at it! Do you see anything? Hold it up to the light.

THORS. Full of holes. Pinholes.

DYM. Then I'm not blind! Pinholes that make letters and words!

THORS. Letters and words?

DYM. Look here! This is a word! P-R-O-M-I-S-E—promise written as clear as pen and ink could make it.

THORS. So it is. "Promise!"

DYM. Give me air! Don't go away! Oh, if it should be something.

THORS. [*Reads over Dymple's shoulders*] "Promise made to me!"

DYM. What's that next line?—"at"—what's this? "Beggar's Paradise." "Promise made to me at Beggar's Paradise!" Where's that?

THORS. I never heard of a beggar's paradise. Perhaps the paper will explain.

DYM. It does. "Promise made to me at Beggar's Paradise—Thames Street." Where's that? Ever been there?

THORS. [*Continuing*] "Thames Street—near the river!"

DYM. [*Continuing*] "I am to share in the reward!" It's all as clear as day.

THORS. Is it?

DYM. I see it all.

THORS. So do I—all there is to see—and that's not much.

DYM. Isn't there? It's a clew. Beggar's Paradise. Thames Street near the river! We'll go there!

THORS. You're a lunatic.

DYM. Am I? This paper is either a hint to us, or a telltale record of a partner in the stealing. There's no accident about it, Thorsby. Pins never did this by themselves.

THORS. [*Crosses, L.*] Let's ask the doctor.

DYM. Not for worlds. It may be nothing—it may be something. Let's find out first. Will you go with me?

THORS. Won't I!

DYM. Beggar's Paradise! Let's be a couple of peris and knock at the gate of paradise. Thorsby you can have the other clew—I mean the other girl, all to yourself. This clew and this girl with her new-fashioned pinpointed handwriting belongs to me. Patent applied for! [*Exeunt, L.*]

SCENE 2: *The wall behind Trinity Churchyard. Snow. Old posters cover it. Among them one or two as follows:*

"*$10,000 Reward! Child Stolen. This sum will be paid to any person restoring to his parents Arthur Standish, a child, 2½ years of age. Light complexion. Blue eyes. Mole on the ear. Had on when stolen from his home, at Old Deerfield, Mass., a white frock, white socks, blue kid boots. Apply to Matthew Standish at Old Deerfield; or to Henry Gossitt, M.D., 14 Washington Square; or to the Chief of Police!*"

Another handbill reads: "*$1000 Reward! Will be paid by the Trustees of the Town of Deerfield, Mass., for the return of Arthur Standish, a child, stolen on the 13th of November. Description: 2½ years old, etc, etc.,*" ⸺⸺ *as above.*

Arthur Standish enters, R., in naval uniform, cloak; followed by a Sailor carrying a valise.

STAN. You only have to go with me to the park, Rattlin. There I'll get a carriage. Then you may wait ashore with the boys.

RAT. Thank your honor for the leave. They'll be glad enough to get a whiff of land air.

STAN. But keep them together, and wait at the ferry house for me till one o'clock. I may return on board tonight. And no drinking, mind! You see that group yonder? Policemen! Land marines, as you call them! Don't fall into their hands.

RAT. Never fear, your honor! We hates a policeman as we hates the devil! [*Retires up*]

STAN. Called back again, but not by her. Other voices summon me. Not a word—not a line from Mabel. Even the loss of her child does not soften her hard and icy heart. But what of that? Let me lay her infant once more in her arms and my duty is done. [*Exit, L., followed by Rattlin. Music. After a pause Matthew Standish strolls on, R.*]

MAT. This is the place. No one in sight save the two yonder; and now they turn the corner and are gone. It's a quiet spot, indeed. Just the place for an ambush. Ugh! In the heart of this populous city I wait and watch as my ancestors did two hundred years ago in the woods of Deerfield, when the stealthy savage lurked in the darkness. [*Picker Bob has entered, L., during above, with sack on back and basket on arm, pick in hand. He watches Matthew, and when latter turns, Bob pretends to be groping for rags*]

P. B. [*Nearing Matthew*] Cold night, sir! [*Crosses to R.*]

MAT. [*Suspiciously*] Very.

P. B. Too cold to be out alone!

MAT. I need no company for what I have to do.

P. B. Are you sure?

MAT. Quite sure.

P. B. So much the better! [*Exit, R.*]

MAT. Who can he be? A picket thrown out to reconnoitre? [*Padder enters, smoking a pipe, L. Dog under his arm. Dressed like a dog fancier*]

PAD. Evenin', friend.

MAT. Good evening.

PAD. Want to buy a dog?

MAT. No, I thank you.

PAD. Perhaps you haven't got the money handy to pay for him.

MAT. Perhaps not.

PAD. Or p'raps yer a savin' up yer soap for another kind o' commodity.

MAT. You've hit it, my man.

PAD. Well, you won't get it. [*Crosses to R.*]

MAT. Why not?

PAD. [*Indicating police, off L.H.*] Too many bidders at the sale, that's all. [*Exit, R.*]

MAT. These gentlemen speak in parables. He comes back. Can it be the rascal I'm to deal with? [*Reenter Padder, R.*]

PAD. I say.

MAT. What do you say?

PAD. [*Meaningly*] Do you know the way to the nearest police station?

MAT. No!

PAD. Then where did you get the crowd of cops at the crossing yonder?

MAT. I did not get them.

PAD. Look ye, governor! Don't waste your time here. It's a dangerous place—and particularly for a cove what can't move through the streets without a peeler at his heels. Take my advice. Go home. I'm going, understand! It's late! Shops shut up! No business to be done tonight. Go home! Understand? [*Exit, after laying his finger on his nose several times, R.*]

MAT. I understand! These rascals have taken alarm at the doctor's police. I must get rid of them. [*Makes a step towards L. Ragmoney Jim, disguised as a beggar cripple, enters*]

JIM. Send me, your honor!

MAT. Who are you? Send you where?

JIM. [*L.*] You want to call the police up there, or you want to pack them off about their business. I'm a poor fellow in want of a job. I'll run for you—

MAT. [*Aside*] Another! Why it's a hornet's nest. [*Aloud*] Yes, go tell the officers I shall not need them and that I request them to watch me no further.

JIM. Oh, they wouldn't take my word, your honor.

MAT. Ask the captain to come here, then.

JIM. Aye, that's the business. [*Gives low, soft cry like a bird. It's answered by another in the distance*] That'll do it. You'll excuse my not waiting till he comes. [*Crosses to R.*]

MAT. But—

JIM. You want to know what to do with yourself when the cops are gone? Why, come on an errand of charity. My poor old wife will show you the way. I'll send her. You'll see our poor little children, especially the Youngest! And you'll take such a sudden benevolent interest in us as never was. Follow the old woman. I'll send her—[*Meaningly*] when you're alone! Mind—alone! [*Exit, R., as Padder enters, L., followed by Captain of Police*]

PAD. There's the genelman as sent me! [*Steps behind house, L., and listens*]

CAPT. We are on hand, sir! Eight of us—some in the churchyard looking over at us now, some up by Trinity building—all within call.

MAT. My dear captain! There are just eight too many of you. You must leave me to myself—unattended—unwatched—or, I shall discover nothing.

PAD. [*L., aside*] That's gospel.

CAPT. Well, sir, as you please. But it's a dangerous game you're playing.

MAT. Have no fear. I can play it.

CAPT. As you please, sir. I'll draw off my men. [*Aside*] It's lucky his son has just turned up and met us, too. I'll consult him. The old gentleman will have his own way, but there's no help for it. [*Padder watches him off, L., Captain pokes him in stomach with club as he passes. Padder doubles up*]

PAD. He will have his joke, the dear, funny—old, infernal cop! But it's done. Now, to be sure that they hoist sail and sheer off. There's old mother witch now, prompt as a dinner bell. [*Exit, L.*]

MAT. It's a desperate game! A shrewd gang of rascals. But if there are so many out in the streets upon the watch, I shall have fewer to deal with in whatever den they lead me to. [*Mother Thames enters and stands by entrance, R. She is an old crooning hag, dressed much like a ragpicker, with her head half enveloped in an old shawl*] You come for me? [*She nods and *points off, then beckons him*] Go on. Show me the way. I'll follow you. [*Exeunt, R. Padder reentering from L.*]

PAD. Yes. She'll show him the way—the long way—up the streets and down the streets: for it's a hard road to paradise! [*Looks back*] The cops don't follow. All's well! [*Gives a crow, off, like that of a cock. It is answered by another*] Good enough! Now for a short cut and in at the brush. Fifty thousand dollars! It's too good to be true! Much too lovely to be realized! But we'll have it if Ragmoney can make it. [*Exit, R.*]

SCENE 3: *"Beggar's Paradise." Interior of a decayed house, showing the attic and the room beneath it. A door and window in attic. Window, C. Door, R. Trapdoor in floor of attic, and ladder reaching from it to the stage. In room beneath, a door, L.C., window, C. Door at R. of same room and window, L. The attic is furnished with a small stool and a pallet bed on floor. The room beneath is furnished with a stove, in a sandbox. Table, C. Two stools and a long bench, L., a straw mattress, and old blanket. Night. No light in the rooms. Snow falling. Over the roof are seen the tops of surrounding houses, the telegraph poles, etc. A stairway leading up from a lower floor at L.C. Music. Dymple and Thorsby creep up the stairs, L.C., cautiously. Both very much wrapped up and variously armed.*

DYM. Nobody here, either.

THORS. [*C.*] No wonder—who would stay in such a hole?

DYM. [*L.*] We have the solemn word of the policeman on the beat, that this was Beggar's Paradise.

THORS. Yes, but he also informed us that no one lived in the old trap, now—that it had been deserted since the murder of a thief by his companion—six months ago.

DYM. Well, nobody may live here. But if our pinpoint memorandum is not a delusion, somebody has been here within a week, and the very people we want, too.

THORS. [*At stove*] The stove's warm—and the remnants of a fire in it. That's not bad for a deserted house.

DYM. Stove, eh! [*Groping for it, knocks his head against the ladder*] What the deuce is this? A ladder!

THORS. A ladder!

DYM. [*Rubs his head*] Yes, a hard ladder. It's an invitation to mount higher.

THORS. To the roof, I suppose.

DYM. Or the top story of paradise. [*Goes up*]

Thors. [*At stove, trying to warm his hand*] Look out for your head and the scuttle.

Dym. [*Pushes up trap*] I've got it.

Thors. [*Flapping his arms*] Hold on to your hat, the wind blows hard in high latitudes.

Dym. No wind here! And no roof! Dark as pitch! It's another room. [*Enters attic*]

Thors. [*Listening below, over stairs*] That sounds like a footstep. Someone's coming up. [*Calling up ladder*] Sammy!

Dym. [*Who has been groping about, stops*] Well?

Thors. [*Alarmed and in whisper*] Somebody's coming!

Dym. Come up here then, quick.

Thors. There's more than one. [*Runs up ladder; when at top*] Do you hear them?

Dym. Quick! Shut the trap! [*They close it gently. Then kneel breathlessly and peep through holes in floor. Ragmoney Jim enters up the stairs with a candle, L.*]

Jim. [*To Person below*] What the devil are you waiting for? Come up! [*Raitch enters, dressed in rags, her face dirty; she wears a wicked and scowling expression*]

Rai. [*L.*] I was a listening.

Jim. What for?

Rai. Voices, I thought.

Jim. Couldn't be. [*Looks around*] You're getting squeamish.

Rai. [*Indignantly*] No, I'm not. But what wonder, after the scare we had an hour ago, that drove us all kiting out of this trap.

Jim. I thought the cops were on us sure enough—curse 'em.

Rai. Then this is a ticklish moment, Jim. It's win or lose everything tonight.

Jim. So it is, gal. You're right. Nothing like caution. You're your father's daughter, you are, and I'm proud of such a niece. The psalm-singing duffers haven't spoiled you, Sally—for all the years they had you.

Rai. Can you spoil the real stuff, Jim? Ain't true grit like true gold? Won't it shine as bright and feel as hard and ring as sharply after all its hoarding?

Jim. So it will.

Rai. I've only been saved up for the old trade, I have, Jim. Saved up to make our fortunes.

Jim. So you have.

Rai. And yet you doubted me at first. You wanted to put me out of the way, you did, Jim.

Jim. I axes your pardon, Sally. I didn't know you was the old sort at heart. Oh, you're a prize, Sally.

Rai. [*Savagely*] And yet you keep me like a prisoner.

Jim. We're so fond of you, Sally. Besides, you've got a soft spot in you yet. You would send back that frock of yours. My mind ain't easy about it yet. It may get us into trouble.

Dym. So it may.

Rai. I didn't want their charity frock, Jim. We're in for bigger game than frocks. And what harm can come of it? Didn't you search it? [*Laughs boisterously*] I tell you, Jim, it will take a smart feller to spell anything out of that frock. [*Crosses to R.*]

Dym. So it did. Eh! Thorsby.

Jim. [*L.*] Well, p'raps it's all right. But where's Mother Thames? She's to go for the old 'un, where's she?

Rai. [*Points off L.*] In there. Mad as ever. I say, Jim, how long has she been cracked? She wasn't so when I was a young 'un here before.

Jim. Ever since her husband was hanged, and the babby she was nursing died that same day in her arms. Go get her. [*Raitch exit, L.*]

Dym. It's Raitch, sure enough.

Thors. They call her Sally. She's evidently one of the gang.

Dym. I can't make it out.

Thors. We'll have a healthy time getting out. [*Mother Thames enters with Arthur in rags, sleeping, following Raitch*]

Jim. Now then, old woman.

Mother T. Hush! You'll wake him.

Jim. No we won't. [*Takes the Child*]

Mother T. Is he dead?

Jim. No, you fool.

Mother T. What did they kill my baby for! He was not sentenced. Wasn't poor Bill enough! Stiff and cold! Cold and dead! He had done no harm. Give me my baby.

Jim. By and by. By and by. I'll keep him safe till then. Hark ye! An old man is waiting by the churchyard wall. Go bring him here.

Mother T. Was he one of them that hanged my man?

Jim. Yes.

Mother. T. And you mean to kill him—you mean to kill him!

Jim. Yes. To squeeze the money from him first, and the life from him afterwards.

Mother T. I'll go! I'll go! [*Draws shawl round her, goes up*]

Rai. I'll show you the way.

Jim. [*Rudely shoving her back*] No, you stay here!

MOTHER T. I know the way! I know! With the crook of my finger I'll bring him here. Trust me. When the death is on them they come. My boy went. Trust me. He'll come. [*Exit, L., staggering. Jim puts the Child roughly on the pallet*]

RAI. Shall I take him?

JIM. No! [*Savagely*] Haven't I told you so a thousand times? I'll trust him to no one, out of my arms, but to that mad woman. I defy the devil himself to get the brat from her, while she holds him in her arms and thinks in her crazy way that it's her dead child. He's safe there. He sleeps soundly. That last dose I gave him—

ARTH. [*Waking*] Mamma!

JIM. The devil! He's up again; light that fire! Ah, my precious kid, you want your mamma, do you?

ARTH. Mamma!

JIM. Your mamma's coming, my dear! I'm the new nurse, I am.

THORS. [*Astonished*] It's the baby. We've got 'em.

DYM. More likely they've got us.

THORS. What shall we do?

DYM. Wait and see.

JIM. Baby must go to sleep again. Sally, dear, where's the lovely sweet syrup of sugar plums.

RAI. [*Gets phial and spoon*] More drugs. Be careful, Jim.

JIM. Oh, I'll be careful. Baby must have a sweet sleep and dream of mamma. Baby must sleep, or mamma won't come.

ARTH. [*Putting the spoon away*] No.

JIM. You don't like it, eh! Not when its own Jim gives it to its pretty baby.

ARTH. No. [*Pushes it away again*]

JIM. What, you won't! [*Gets whip from under mattress*]

RAI. Don't beat him again, Jim. I won't have it.

DYM. I would like to give Mr. Jim some of that medicine for himself!

JIM. Then make him take the dose, you sniveling fool. [*She gives dose to Child. Jim throws whip down*] There! Hollo! Who the devil left this ladder here?

RAI. [*Watching the Child, who sleeps*] You did.

JIM. I must have forgot. [*Takes it away*]

DYM. [*Aghast with terror*] He's taken away the ladder.

THORS. Now we are gone.

DYM. [*Rising*] There's a window!

THORS. [*Goes to it*] Three stories from the ground.

Dym. But the telegraph pole is not five feet from it. I could jump it if I had to.

Thors. [*Tries door, R.*] Here's a door.

Dym. A door?

Thors. But it's locked!

Dym. Oh! [*Padder entering up the stairs below*]

Pad. He's coming.

Jim. The child?

Rai. Fast asleep! The drug's done it again.

Jim. Hide him! Under the pallet!

Rai. Under the pallet? You forget what's under the pallet!

Jim. I know what I'm about. Under the pallet! [*Raitch raises the pallet and conceals Arthur in a space below*]

Pad. Look ye, Jim! I think I ought to have the kid for safe keeping.

Jim. [*R.*] You do—do you?

Pad. Yes, I do. While you've got him, you hold all the cards. What sort of a game is that for half a dozen to play?

Jim. Now see here, Padder—

Dym. Thorsby!

Thors. What?

Dym. That's my rascally valet. Oh, why did I ever part with him! But I won't after tonight.

Jim. No more words now! Go to the room below. You've no business to come up. Go below with the others.

Pad. There's enough there.

Jim. And there's enough here! Go, I tell you!

Pad. All right! All right! So long as you leave him under the pallet I'm satisfied. I can have him if I want him.

Dym. Yes, and I'm satisfied. I'll have you when you don't want me.

Jim. Away! They're coming. [*Padder hurries down stairs, L.C. Raitch into room, R. Music. Mother Thames enters by door in back, L.C., followed by Matthew. She points to Jim and goes back and off by same door. Matthew looks at Jim, and then looks around suspiciously*] No fear, governor! We are alone here, you and me.

Mat. [*L.C.*] I wish to be sure of that.

Jim. You shall be. [*Goes to each door and bolts it*] There! Take a seat. We can talk at our ease.

Mat. [*Sits by table*] You are the writer of this letter?

Jim. Yes.

Mat. You can restore my grandchild to me?

Jim. I can.

MAT. Where is he?

JIM. Safe enough! Pay for him and he's yours.

MAT. Are you the man that took him from my home?

JIM. [R.] Don't you remember me?

MAT. [Looks at him] Yes, I remember you! I fed you when you were starving, and instead of sending you to jail for a vagrant, I gave you shelter in my house.

JIM. Why, as for that, governor, I was no more starving than you are! And as for not sending me to jail—the more fool you—

MAT. Where is the child? Here?

JIM. Oh, no! we don't keep such precious jewels here. We have a safe deposit vault of our own. Pay our price and you can have him.

MAT. What is your price?

JIM. [Impressively] Fifty thousand dollars, down.

MAT. You are mad.

JIM. Oh, no, I'm not. You're rich! You'd give half a million rather than know this boy was lost to you forever. But I'm not extortionate. Fifty thousand!

MAT. You don't expect me to carry such a sum.

JIM. Oh, no! I'm not unreasonable. You've got twenty, perhaps, with you—or ten—even five! I'll take that and give you time for the rest.

MAT. How much time?

JIM. Half an hour.

MAT. And suppose I have no money with me?

JIM. You shall have half an hour to get it.

MAT. [Rising] Very well! I'll be back in half an hour. [Jim rises quickly and lays his hand on Matthew's arm]

JIM. [Catching his arm] Oh, no! We'll send. We couldn't trouble you to go yourself.

MAT. [Coolly] And that means—?

JIM. That you must stay here.

MAT. [Sitting again] My good fellow, you have locked all the doors. That is to say, you have put yourself in my power. I have only to stretch out my hand and you will be completely at my mercy.

JIM. [Leaning over the table and slowly eyeing him] You'll try your strength with me?

MAT. Certainly. [Suddenly grasping his wrist] So think better of it. Give me the child or tell me where it is! [Forces Jim, after a struggle, to his knees. Meanwhile the door on the L. opens, and a Man masked, dressed like a laborer, enters, carrying a pick. He stands by the window. This is Picker Bob]

JIM. Well played, governor! Give me time to think. Five seconds will do. Give me five seconds and you shall have my answer. [*On his knees. Another masked man enters, it is Padder, from door, C., flat, carrying an axe. He stands down by L. door*]

MAT. You have your five seconds.

JIM. And you have your answer. [*Two Men, also masked and disguised as laborers, enter at R.; they carry a spade and an iron bar, and confront Matthew. He sees them, releases Jim and turns slowly. As he does so, another Ruffian enters from door, C., and stands by it*] Would you like to try your strength with me now, eh? [*Down R.C., baring his arms*]

MAT. What do you wish, gentlemen?

JIM. Write a letter to the mother of this child. Tell her to come here—alone—and with the money we demand. With her jewels, too—do you hear? We know she has them and what they are worth. [*Puts pen, ink and paper on table, which he gets from shelf before window*] Write, and quickly.

MAT. I'll write! [*Aside*] It may gain time. [*He advances to the table and writes. The Men around the room are as immovable as statues*] There!

JIM. [*Picks it up and reads*] What? So near? At a hotel, eh? They all followed you down so's to be handy, did they? So much the better. We won't have long to wait. Here, mother! [*Mother Thames enters, followed by Raitch*] Take this! [*Whispers in her ear*] You understand?

MOTHER T. I understand. [*Shows knife*]

JIM. That's handy, if they try any of their tricks on you. Quick. [*She exits at back*]

MAT. One bold push, and I'll be before her.

JIM. [*Bolts, L.C.*] There.

DYM. Why can't we shoot him at once. [*Pulls out very large horse pistol*]

THORS. There are six of 'em. Wait.

DYM. Wait! While we wait they'll bring Mabel here.

THORS. Hush! Look at the old man.

MAT. [*Who had passed down, R.C., near a stool or broken chair*] The window can't be far from the ground. I've leaped many a time further than that.

JIM. Come, governor, sit down and be patient. The old gal won't be long. She's a little flighty in the head, but she goes an errand like a bullet to its mark. These are all good fellows. Owing to the very strong light of the candle they have to wear shades, but that rather improves their appearance.

MAT. Aye, they look like agreeable fellows, and so, if you don't object, I'll —[*Suddenly fells Jim with the chair*] I'll say good night to you all. [*Darts to the window, places foot on bench and tries to get out*]

JIM. [*On floor*] Seize him! Stop him! [*All lay hold of Matthew. A scuffle between him and the Men, and Jim, who seizes a rope from the pallet. Dymple and Thorsby, in their excitement, run up and down the attic. Matthew is finally brought to his knees*] Hark! [*A dead silence ensues. Dymple and Thorsby stand petrified*] I heard a noise up there! In the attic.

DYM. We are gone!

JIM. [*To Raitch*] You, there! Up and see what it is! [*Raitch goes to door, R., and exit*]

DYM. She's coming up here.

THORS. Shall we shoot her?

DYM. No use. Shooting her won't kill the others. [*Raitch enters attic by door, R., looks at them. They gaze at her, transfixed. She goes to the trap and opens it*]

JIM. [*Looking up*] Well?

RAI. [*Peeping through scuttle*] There's nobody here!

JIM. Are you sure?

RAI. Yes. [*She exits, looking back at Thorsby and Dymple without uttering word or sign*]

JIM. Secure him. [*They pinion the old man noiselessly and wait*]

THORS. Thank heaven!

DYM. She's a trump!

THORS. Do you know if her face was washed she'd be rather a pretty girl.

DYM. [*Peremptorily*] None of that! She belongs to me. She's my clew. I've got her frock, and damme, I will have her. [*Raitch reenters below*]

JIM. What was it?

RAI. Rats. [*Thorsby looks at Dymple and bursts into a suppressed laugh. Dymple punches him in side indignantly*]

THORS. I say, Dymple, you're a rat!

DYM. A live rat! That's some comfort.

JIM. [*To Men*] Tie him to the rail yonder. [*They fasten him, kneeling, to the bannister at C.*] It was a bold stroke, governor. A risky thing, though, for one of your years. But I admire your pluck.

MAT. Well, I'm in your power.

JIM. Of course you are. You're a rich man, governor! Owner of ten mills and factories, worth four or five millions, but just now you're in the hands of the laboring class, the hard-fisted men of toil.

MAT. Thieves, you mean.

JIM. That's right, call us thieves—that's all you can do. We call you rich men thieves—that's all we can do. But now we'll have no hard names. We'll adjust the differences between capital and labor in a quiet way. You hire eight hundred men to work for you. You've made your millions out of them. It isn't fair. Share your profits with them as earned 'em.

MAT.   Did any of you wretches ever work for me? No! I won't believe it.

JIM.   No. We're simply a committee of the whole. We can't bring the eight hundred here. I'm chairman! My name's Ragmoney Jim.

MAT.   Humph—you're Ragmoney Jim!

JIM.   Yes. Don't sneer! I'm Ragmoney by name, but I'm hard money by principle. But they call me Ragmoney because I haven't got any money at all. And as I read in the papers that rag money's no money, why the name suits me exactly.

MAT.   Well!

JIM.   [Sits, R.C.]   Padder, the chair appoints you a committee to search the capitalist and find out how much of our money he's got about him.

PAD.   All right! [Searches him] Not a red!

JIM.   [Throwing chair away, angrily]   What! Nothing? A regular plant. You never meant honest and fair then, did you, when you came after the child? Damme if I ever trusts a Massachusetts Yankee again.

PAD.   He came here to nose out our secret. He's a spy.

ALL.   Yes, a spy!

JIM.   What shall we do with the spy, lads?

ALL.   [Intensely, but not loud]   Kill him!

JIM.   You hear these gentlemen. They actually feel that you're too mean to live. And I'm of their opinion.

P. B.   Here's my axe handy.

JIM.   [Crosses to Matthew]   Come, what do you say? [Padder whispers to him as if dissuading him]

DYM.   Now or never, Thorsby! It's to save his life we must risk ours. Is the window open?

THORS.   [Holds it open]   Yes.

DYM.   Take my pistol. If the worst comes to the worst before I come back, give it to them hot and heavy. As for me, I'll go for the police. Here's the pole and here goes, by telegraph. [Gets out]

THORS.   Look out, old fellow! There! He's on it. He slides down. The deuce, he's torn his trousers to ribbons. He's on the ground! He's off! [Closes window and returns to watch]

JIM.   [Nodding and putting Padder off]   All right! [To Matthew] Well, are you dumb?

RAI.   [Coming down, R.C.]   Speak out, governor, don't be shy.

MAT.   [To her]   You belong to this wretched life in earnest then. Blood will tell after all.

RAI. Aye. Blood will tell. Did you think you had turned it to water by your Sunday schools and primer books?

MAT. Rachel, think of the poor mother whose heart bleeds for her stolen child tonight. I don't care for my own life, but if all the innocent years you spent under my roof have left one good impulse in your heart, make that mother happy again.

JIM. Stuff! Let's have no more of that. Come, boys, let's finish the sermon. [*They advance, Raitch stays them*]

THORS. [*Cocking the pistol*] One shot at the first man that touches him.

RAI. [*To Jim and Padder*] Don't be a fool! Nor you neither. Let's have no blood for them to track us by. Take him below. That's the way to settle him.

JIM. [*To men, who murmur*] She's right! [*To Padder*] Who's in the room below?

PAD. All the rest, armed and ready, watching the signal and ready for the police, with the kid.

JIM. Then the room below won't do. It's no use, Sally. We must give him a dose.

RAI. You shan't kill him.

JIM. Out of the way.

RAI. Jim, he was good to me.

PAD. Out of the way! [*They hurl Raitch aside. Door opens and Mabel enters, disguised as Mother Thames. All stop*]

JIM. What! Old Flighty! Back so soon? The woman?

MABEL. Coming.

JIM. Alone?

MABEL. Aye, my precious.

JIM. She's a plucky one. But I knew the bait would bring her. Now get into your room. We've accounts to settle, and you're in the way.

MABEL. [*Crosses to C.*] Yes, I'll go! Give me the baby!

JIM. Never you mind the baby! Get into your den!

MABEL. Oh, my poor baby! He isn't dead. I've had him in my arms all day—he isn't dead.

PAD. [*Seizing her and flinging her to R.H. corner*] Stop your raving!

JIM. Curse me if mother hasn't lost her voice and her wits together. Get to your room.

RAI. [*Aside to her, on her L.*] Oh, what brought you here?

JIM. What's this? [*Roughly seizing Raitch and flinging her aside*] Get up! [*To Mabel, whom he flings downstage to L.C., near Matthew*] Where's the woman I sent you for?

MABEL. On the stairs, below! [*Commences to untie Matthew's bonds and aside to him*] Father! 'Tis I—Mabel!

JIM. [*To Padder*] Bring her here. [*Padder goes towards door at back*] Now, boys—who'll finish this old fraud? What shall it be? Axe, or knife, or rope? [*They hold back. Tears paper at table, and writes on one*] Here! We'll do the job by lot. The one that draws this wins the prize. Where's a hat? Give me a hat. [*Padder by this time opens the door, and Captain Standish steps in*]

STAN. Scoundrels! You want a hat? [*Takes off cap*] Take mine.

JIM. Betrayed! [*Padder and Raitch exeunt precipitately at L.*]

STAN. Stir hand or foot and you are dead men. [*Dymple and Police appear behind him; Jim and the Ruffians with Picker Bob make a dash for the stairs. Sailors, led by the Doctor, appear there*]

THORS. Hurrah!

MABEL. [*Throws off disguise*] My child! [*Cuts Matthew's bonds and he springs up*]

DYM. Beneath the pallet.

MABEL. The bed! [*Jim falls on his knees and raps on floor, as Thorsby seizes him. Mabel runs to bed, which Dymple removes. They discover an open trap and no child*] He's gone!

JIM. Now find him if you can! The first that puts a foot to follow gets a bullet through his heart. [*All fall back*]

MABEL. If no man dares go, let me!

MAT. No! No! [*Holds her back*]

STAN. Scoundrel! [*Hurls him to L.*] Farewell! Mabel! My life for our child's! [*Darts down trap. Pistols heard*]

ACT V.

SCENE: *Parlors at the Renfrew city residence. Night. Twenty-four hours have elapsed since the last act. Chandelier lighted. Mabel is discovered lying on sofa, C., propped with cushions, her face buried in the pillow. Doctor Gossitt walks up and down at back, in thought, his hands behind him. Mary is at table near the sofa, pouring from a vial into a small wineglass a potion. Thorsby looks in at door, R.1E. Music.*

THORS. [*In whisper to Mary, still on threshold*] Can I come in? [*Mary puts up her finger in caution; puts vial on table, goes to Mabel, finds her apparently asleep, then comes down to Thorsby*]

MARY. [*L.*] Have you just got back?

THORS. Yes.

MARY. [*Crosses to C.*] We have been waiting so anxiously. [*The conversation that ensues is carried on down C., so as not to disturb Mabel*]

THORS. The information we got was correct. The villains carried him across the river.

DOC. [*L., coming down*] Arthur and his father have gone there! [*Dorothy enters from L.1.E.*]

DOR. Ah, Mr. Gyll—what have you discovered?

THORS. [*R.*] They will soon know the worst.

DOR. The worst?

THORS. I'm afraid the report sent us this afternoon was true. Poor little Arthur!

MARY. Poor Mabel! [*Goes up to her*]

DOC. I was afraid of it. Cold, exposure to the wintry night, brutal treatment, all have done their cruel work.

DOR. It is impossible. I won't believe it! [*To Thorsby*] Have you seen your friend?

THORS. Sammy? Yes—for a moment! He just got a message from that girl—

DOC. Rachel! Humph! [*Turns off impatiently and goes up, stopping a moment to look at Mabel*]

THORS. Yes—and he went off in search of her, expecting to bring her and the baby back together. [*Dorothy shakes her head doubtfully and goes up to the Doctor, as Mary returns to Thorsby's side*] Does Mabel know—

MARY. She suspects the worst.

THORS. It will kill her.

MARY. I never was so miserable in all my life.

THORS. And to think that if it had only ended happily—you and I, Mary, would have been so happy, too. [*Takes her hand*] But I can wait. For your sake I'd wait twenty years.

MARY. Don't let's speak of ourselves now.

THORS. [*Going towards R.*] And perhaps it's all my fault. I could have shot that villain a dozen times over.

MARY. But that would not have saved little Arthur. Their plans were too well taken.

THORS. All our trouble came to nothing.

MARY. You all did the best you could.

THORS. We did nothing at all, if all we did comes to nothing. [*They go off, R.1.E., looking back at Mabel*]

DOR. [*At back, to Doctor*] That's Arthur's step! [*Standish enters, R.1.E., hat and coat; quite dejected. Dorothy runs to him as if to question; he sadly shakes his head. She goes off, L., handkerchief to her eyes. Standish lays his hat and coat off*]

STAN. [*To Doctor*] Has she slept any? [*Very low*]

DOC. I hope so. She has not moved!

MABEL. [*Half raises her head*] Who's there? Is that Arthur? [*Standish presses the Doctor's hand. Doctor goes off, R. door. Standish comes down*]

STAN. [*R.*] Mabel?

MABEL. You have come back—alone! [*He is about to speak*] Don't speak. I understand! There is no hope! Arthur is dead. [*Sinks on sofa*] My child is dead! [*Standish approaches her*]

STAN. My wife!

MABEL. [*Starting up in tears*] It is I have done it—I have killed him.

STAN. [*Taking her hand*] Mabel, an hour ago you were calm. You were prepared for the worst. Do you forget that I knelt by your side, and in our doubt and suspense we promised each other that if this new sorrow must be borne, we would bear it together?

MABEL. [*L. of him*] Oh, my little one! I shall never—never see you again! [*Sinks onto seat*]

STAN. [*Sinks on knee, gently*] Mabel!

MABEL. It is pitiful, is it not—to have my baby suffer for me! I would have borne death—I did confront it in that den last night, with unfaltering courage—because I hoped to give him back to you. It is denied me. But they will bring him here—they will let me see my baby.

STAN. If you are able to bear this grief.

MABEL. Don't let them keep him from me. I have been punished enough. [*Rises*]

STAN. Who speaks of punishment, my darling, my wife? Am I not here? Is not the past forever buried out of sight? Are we not reunited, never to part?

MABEL. [*Crosses to R.*] I dare not listen to your love and kindness. I dare not meet your glance, for it will ask me for what I have not to give. His life would be pardon—would be mercy—would be love—what have I to live for since I deserve neither pardon nor mercy?

STAN. We will live for each other, Mabel. Not despairing! Not hopeless! The remembrance of our child shall not be a gloom, but a joy to us. We will think of little Arthur as he used to be. At night the glimmer of a little face in the darkness will greet us. In sleep the soft fingers of your baby will press your bosom, and you will smile in your dream of happiness. And when we walk forth the flowers opening their blossoms to the sky, will point to his true resting place, and teach us what happiness may spring from grief.

MABEL. Oh! My little one! My little one! [*In a flood of tears she buries her head on his shoulder. Dorothy entering, L.U.E.*]

Dor. Tears! Blessed tears! They will soon wash away her sorrow. Let me take her to her room, Arthur! Come, my darling! [*All exeunt, L. door. Dymple entering cautiously, R.1.E.*]

Dym. No one here! [*Looks around cautiously*] I'm glad of that. I wouldn't have Thorsby see me for the world. Came in by the basement way to avoid him. Here! [*Turns to door and speaks off*] Come in! [*Impatient*] Come in! [*Raitch appears dressed neatly in the frock of third act, new boots, etc., hair very tidy. Dymple grasps her hand*]

Rai. [*As he pulls her*] Oh!

Dym. Don't mind my holding on to you. You're our best bower anchor now—and I'm afraid of your slipping the cable and drifting away.

Rai. If you please, I won't drift away.

Dym. Perhaps not. But luck has taken so many turns lately that I can't trust even myself. You're an important person now, Rachel. Principal witness for the prosecution. You can identify every one of the rascals, and you can prove they dosed the baby with drugs.

Rai. Yes. I couldn't even prevent that.

Dym. Perhaps it's as well—for you made Padder and his mates believe he was dead when he slept so long, and so Padder and the rest deserted you in a fright—and you sent word to the police and me—and so the baby is found.

Rai. Mayn't I see Miss Dorothy now?

Dym. In a moment. I say, you're not in a hurry to get rid of *me,* are you?

Rai. Oh, no indeed, Mr. Dymple. You are so good and so clever. You found out the paper I put in the frock—and you came and found out me!

Dym. Yes, I did—I found you out—you see I've been thinking of you.

Rai. Of me?

Dym. Don't you know you saved my life up there in the attic—last night —when you called me a rat?

Rai. You know why, now!

Dym. I began to think of you then. And when the wretches in the room below carried off the baby—you followed them—in the cold and snow—with nothing on worth thinking about! Do you know what you are, Rachel? [*Puts his arm around her waist*]

Rai. No, sir!

Dym. A heroine! If you were in a book everybody would fall in love with you. As it is—I love you! [*Kisses her*]

Rai. Please, sir.

Dym. Please? What, *more?*

Rai. That's very wrong.

Dym. What's very wrong?

RAI. To kiss me!

DYM. How old are you?

RAI. Sixteen!

DYM. [*All right, kisses her again*] Then it'll not be wrong for a couple of years yet.

RAI. Please let me go!

DYM. Rachel, I want to ask you something! Don't be frightened—I want you to promise me something. When you are eighteen years old, Rachel, I want you to marry me.

RAI. [*Swinging hands to and fro*] Oh, sir—I couldn't.

DYM. You don't know what you can do when you're eighteen.

RAI. [*Turning away*] No, no—I couldn't if I was eighty.

DYM. Why not?

RAI. I am only a poor girl and very ignorant.

DYM. I'll put you to school, and if in two years you are not as accomplished, as intelligent, and as good as any young lady in the land, I won't marry you—I'll eat you!

RAI. Oh, I couldn't—Miss Dorothy'd be angry.

DYM. Miss Dorothy shall be your aunt by marriage. She's mine now. I adopted her yesterday.

RAI. No—it's impossible. I'd do anything in the world to make you happy, but it's impossible.

DYM. Impossible?

RAI. Yes, sir, please.

DYM. [*Angrily*] I believe there ain't a woman in the world, high or low, will have me. It's a conspiracy among the sex! Look here, Rachel—

RAI. I can't, sir, it's impossible!

DYM. Rachel, in the adjoining apartment there is a perjured villain, who is at this moment sitting with his arm around the waist of a young and beautiful creature. He's going to marry her. He's happy! You wouldn't see a perjured villain happy, and me miserable, would you?

RAI. Oh, no, indeed!

DYM. Then I tell you what I'll do. Promise me, and I'll speak to Aunt Dorothy. She'll take charge of you, and in two years—[*Hugs her*]

RAI. There's somebody coming!

DYM. Let 'em come! [*Kisses her as Raymond and Lucille enter, R.U.E., and stop, seeing the kiss*]

RAY. Hollo! [*Raitch screams and runs out, R.1.E.*] I say—it's young Pimple, kissing the girl.

DYM. Dymple, sir—not Pimple!

Luc. [*Crosses to C.*] My dear Mr. Dymple, what news have you got for us? These weddings are such a bother, and I've been out all the afternoon shopping for mine. Mabel was asleep when I went out, and everybody was so sad and quiet, I felt more like preparing for a funeral than a marriage. But, of course, Mabel is welcome to every comfort my house affords—and her dear little baby—any further news of dear, little Arthur?

Dym. Oh, you'll see him, soon, Mrs. Renfrew; his grandfather is bringing him.

Luc. He's found, then? That's so nice!

Dym. Yes, he's found, safe and sound, too—after a good, long sleep. [*Aside, going out*] They are going to be married, are they? I wish 'em joy. [*Exit, R.1.E.*]

Luc. [*L., to Raymond*] You must be good to everybody, now, you naughty boy, that we're going to be married.

Ray. [*Quizzically*] Yes, the long agony is over.

Luc. What long agony? Do you refer to our courtship?

Ray. No, dear, to the doubt and suspense in which I have been kept for these years, by your fickleness.

Luc. You mean by your own procrastination, my love. It's only within a week or two that you've actually urged me to name the day. It's well you did, you naughty fellow—for I actually began to think you were waiting for *me* to ask you.

Ray. Why didn't you? It would have been so deliciously original and novel. As it is, there's nothing original about our marriage—not even the bride, for she's a widow.

Luc. And I'm sure you're as bad. You can't deny you've made love to a dozen.

Ray. No, I can't deny it. Nobody would believe me. [*Strokes his moustache. Crosses, L.*]

Luc. Oh! If you were not so vain.

Ray. Can't help being vain. You've accepted me as your future husband.

Luc. [*Tartly*] There, there! A truce! You always get the best of me when you begin your compliments. But mind! [*Tapping him sweetly on cheek with her fan*] I don't believe one of them. [*Dorothy enters, R.1.E., agitated and breathless, followed by Raitch*]

Dor. [*Crosses to C.*] Oh, sir, where is Arthur?

Ray. Captain Standish? Can't say.

Dor. I have such news for him.

Luc. What news?

Dor. His child alive, and well.

Luc. Mr. Dymple just told us.

Dor. But Arthur believes—they told him—

Luc. What?

Dor. That his child was found, but dead. [*Doctor Gossitt enters quickly, followed by Dymple, R.1.E.*]

Doc. [*To Dorothy*] Have you seen him?

Ray. [*To Dorothy*] Captain Standish believes his child dead? And Mabel, too? [*Standish appears at L.U.E.*]

Stan. What is the matter? What has happened? [*In low, anxious voice*] Have they brought him back?

Doc. [*Crosses to L., advancing*] Arthur, are you able to bear good news?

Stan. [*Looks from one to the other*] Good news?

Ray. [*Frankly advancing and restraining Doctor*] Doctor, I have a favor to ask of you. Captain Standish has reason to think bitterly enough of me. I wish to be remembered by him in connection with the happiest moment of his life, and I beg you to let me be the first to tell him—[*As he turns to Standish*] that his child is alive and well.

Stan. [*L.C., supporting himself against sofa, and in a hoarse whisper*] My child is alive?

Doc. The report of his death was false, founded on a natural mistake.

Stan. Do you believe this? [*Looking from one to the other*] All of you?

Rai. [*Coming forward*] I *know* it!

Stan. Rachel! Then it is true! [*Thorsby and Mary enter, R.1.E., in excitement*]

Mary. Arthur, have you heard!

Thors. The good news?

Mary. They are coming!

Stan. [*Runs to L.U.D. and calls, agitatedly*] Mabel.

Doc. [*Stops him*] For heaven's sake!

Stan. I must tell her.

Doc. In that fashion? No, no, come back. The news must be broken gently. She has suffered too much. Sudden joy sometimes kills.

Dor. But Matthew is coming. He may be even now at the door. [*Runs up to window, C.*]

Doc. Run and keep him back. [*Thorsby and Mary dart out, R.*] Who will tell her? Not you. [*To Standish*] I have it. Rachel! The sight of her is half the glad tidings told. Stay here, Rachel. And all of you go. Go with me, Arthur. [*Exit Standish into door, R.U.E.*] Come, my boy. [*Ring heard at door*]

Dor. It is Matthew.

Doc. Go to him. [*Dorothy exit, R.1.E.*] Now all of you. [*Dymple, who has been whispering to Raitch, kisses her, exits with a wink at her, L.1.E., followed by Lucille and Raymond. Doctor goes off, R.U.E., as Mabel appears, L.U.E. Music*]

MABEL. Arthur! Did you call? [*Comes down*] No one here? I thought I heard his voice calling to me, and in a tone so strange and loud. Is it fancy—am I then becoming crazed with this great sorrow? [*Raitch has crept forward and kneels softly at her side, and takes her dress in her hand*] Who is this? Rachel!

RAI. [*R., kneels*] Yes, it is I—it is I, Miss Mabel. Don't look at me so sorrowfully. I have come back to you.

MABEL. [*Looks around eagerly*] Alone!

RAI. No—no—no! Not alone! You don't believe I would come back without little Arthur! I was with him every day—every minute. I wouldn't let them touch him when I could help it—for I had promised the little angels in Heaven to protect him—so he is coming.

MABEL. They are bringing him to me.

RAI. He is coming. Oh, Miss Mabel, don't you understand—would anybody hurt a little child?

MABEL. [*In a frenzy of agitation*] Rachel! Do you know what you are telling my heart? You are telling me of hope—to expect—

RAI. Yes, Miss Mabel—to hope for joy! To expect your greatest happiness. Oh, Miss Mabel, they are at the door. Don't start back—don't cry out—he may be asleep.

MABEL. Arthur, where are you? [*Standish enters, R.1.D.*]

STAN. My darling!

MABEL. My child? [*Matthew appears at R.U.D., holding little Arthur aloft in his arms. The child's arms are outstretched. All enter. Thorsby and Mary, R.1.E. Dorothy and Doctor, R.U.E. Dymple, Lessing and Lucille, L.1.E.*]

CHILD. Mamma!

MABEL. My baby! [*With a cry of joy she rushes towards it. Matthew meets her halfway and places the Child in her arms. She sinks on her knees to clasp it and cover it with kisses*]

STAN. Father! [*Matthew and Standish embrace*]

MAT. Joy—joy, my son. No happier day can my old eyes ever see. There! Poor mother, clasp your child. Safe and sound. Thanks to Providence, and under Providence to her.

MABEL. Rachel! [*Raitch kneels by the Baby and kisses him and Mabel's hand*] Father! [*Taking his hand*] Arthur! [*Standish raises her, she sits on sofa, C., with the Child, and a group forms about her*]

MAT. If there's an enemy in the world, I forgive him. I could take by the hand the veriest scamp in the universe. [*Sees Raymond, and suddenly comes forward and grasps his hand*] Ah! Mr. Lessing!

RAY. Thanks! I'm sure you're very good. But I've reformed. I'm going to be married. Retribution has overtaken me. [*Takes Lucille's hand in his arm*]

MAT. I wish you joy. Everybody ought to be married, now. We couldn't celebrate our happiness better than by a wedding.

THORS. [*Advancing, stepping forward with Mary*] Do you think so, sir? Then of course you'll consent to—

MAT. What you? With all my heart. Take her. She's a good girl! And —who else?

DYM. [*Takes Raitch's hand*] Who else? We.

MAT. You will marry Rachel!

DYM. This day two years. I'll order the cards tomorrow. [*Padder enters at R.I.E., and beckons on Ragmoney Jim*]

MABEL. [*Seeing them*] Those men! [*Clasps her child*] Arthur!

DOC. Those scoundrels here?

PAD. Don't forget us in the general joy. Don't forget I was the means of restoring the precious babby. I cleared out so as Sally could send word where he was this morning—

JIM. And I would have done it myself if I could.

PAD. Any little remuneration you feels like giving us for our good intentions will be werry acceptable.

JIM. The winter's on us—and—

STAN. [*C.*] Why, you scoundrels, did I not see you both lodged in prison?

JIM. We was bailed out this arternoon!

MAT. You shall not escape.

JIM. Oh, yes we will. We has a good lawyer and a good defense.

DOC. Defense?

JIM. Yes, sir! Emotional insanity. I lost a babby myself some years ago, and ever since I've had a hankering arter other peoples—

DYM. [*Advancing to him*] Get out.

PAD. Sir, think of our former relations.

DYM. Get out! Thorsby! [*Thorsby goes to him*]

PAD. Oh, very well, if you treats us that way.

JIM. We wishes you good evening!

PAD. Ditto! Ditto! [*An Officer appears at R.I.E. and beckons them off*]

MAT. Can they escape?

DOC. Don't be afraid of that. I see twenty years apiece written on both their faces. No. Let us now think only of the happiness we have here.

MABEL.   Yes. A happiness that begins tonight for me—[*Takes Standish's hand*] and that will endure while heart can beat, or life can last. Father! [*To Matthew*] Tomorrow you will take us home.

CURTAIN

MABEL

MATTHEW CHILD STANDISH

DOCTOR   LESSING

DOROTHY   LUCILLE

THORSBY   DYMPLE

MARY   RAITCH

NEEDLES AND PINS

A Comedy of the Present, in Four Acts

From the German of Rosen

NEEDLES AND PINS

THE season following the production of *Pique* was the worst of Daly's first eight years of management, and the ninth began with the complete failure of *The Dark City,* a melodrama with local scenes upon which Daly had been counting heavily. On September 15, 1877, Daly closed his theater and retired for a year and a half from the New York stage. His return came with the production on April 30, 1879, of *L'Assommoir,* a dramatization, perhaps his own, of Zola's famous novel. The play failed, but it is, nevertheless, significant for it brought together for the first time Augustin Daly and Ada Rehan. With the opening of Daly's (formerly the Broadway) Theatre in the fall, Miss Rehan joined Daly's company serving under him continuously until his death June 7, 1899.

Early in the second season of his occupancy of Daly's Theatre, the manager produced *Needles and Pins*, the sixth of his adaptations of German farce-comedy. When Daly's version of Rosen's *Starke Mitteln* was presented for the first time on November 9, 1880, the famous quartet, Ada Rehan, Mrs. Gilbert, John Drew, and James Lewis, appeared together for the first time in the type of rôles with which they delighted theatergoers for a dozen years. Describing the rôles and the actors, the next day's *Herald* reported:

Mr. Lewis as an antiquated bachelor is extremely funny; his old ways are as amusing as ever, and he has some comical new business. Mr. Drew plays a lawyer who is terribly infatuated by his only client, which does not prevent his falling desperately in love with Miss Van Dusen, a very youthful feminine character, which Miss Rehan dresses and plays admirably. . . . Mrs. Gilbert's part is an improvement upon the usual gushing maiden of uncertain age; it is almost entirely without exaggeration, yet none the less amusing for that reason.

The play itself was "far better in construction than most pieces made only to provoke laughter." However, "some indelicate and not at all necessary lines about a child, the parentage of which is uncertain, might be omitted without the slightest harm to the piece." Both the *Herald* and the *Tribune* were pleased by the masquerade scene, and they praised Mrs. Gilbert's dancing of the hornpipe, as did the papers in other cities later.

Needles and Pins was acted at Daly's from November 9 through January 15, when it was succeeded by *Zanina,* an Oriental musical comedy featuring a troupe of nautch dancers for whose use at this time Daly had previously contracted. On February 14 *Needles and Pins* resumed, continuing through

March 4. Concurrently with the New York run, some of Daly's company seem to have been playing the piece on tour, for on March 1 the *Philadelphia North American* complained of the poor cast in spite of the fact that it contained John Drew. By the time of the Chicago engagement at Hooley's, June 20-July 2, the company was reunited, the famous quartet being supported by Digby Bell, Laura Joyce, May Fielding, and others. The play and the acting were "a decided hit." Boston agreed that the play was "thoroughly enjoyable" when it appeared at the Park, September 11, 1882. A critic on the *Transcript* even went so far as to praise the dialogue. "Brilliant and witty" were not terms frequently used to describe Daly's lines. In August of 1883 *Needles and Pins* was presented in San Francisco where it secured a better reception than had *The Big Bonanza* eight years before. The following year *Needles and Pins* was given at the Crystal Palace, London, during the company's first English visit. The play did not find great favor but the acting was so well liked that, as one reviewer wrote, it "would have made a worse comedy enjoyable" (*London Era,* Aug. 16, 1884).

In the years which followed *Needles and Pins,* Daly and his company repeated their earlier successes again and again with *Seven-Twenty-Eight, A Night Off, Nancy and Company,* and many other productions of his industrious pen. Because of previous publication or copyright restrictions these later plays are not represented here. This is not as great a loss as it might seem, however, because, with the exception of the many productions of refurbished classics, Daly's later hits, usually adaptations or mere translations from the German, were more or less only repetitions of *The Big Bonanza* and *Needles and Pins.*

The privately printed edition of 1884 is the basis of the present text of *Needles and Pins.*

DRAMATIS PERSONAE AND ORIGINAL CAST

MR. NICHOLAS GEAGLE, *an elderly party in search
of the antique and curious in art, comes
across a bit of Nature's own bric-a-brac,
and learns the true reading of an old
nursery riddle*   MR. JAMES LEWIS

MR. CHRISTOPHER VANDUSEN, *a retired merchant,
formerly in "corks," now in anything but
lavender, who cherishes a youthful memory
and finds he has been nursing a poetic
serpent with an unpoetic sting*   MR. CHARLES FISHER

KIT VANDUSEN, *the dutiful son of the before-
mentioned Christopher, with his own little
secret romance and its corresponding
consequences*   MR. JOHN BRAND

TOM VERSUS, *a spry young attorney who, not
unlike some of his elder brethren of the
bar, makes a muddle for his solitary client,
while he feathers his own nest*   MR. JOHN DREW

SERGEANT MACDONALD, *of the 99th Precinct,
temporarily assigned for duty at the
Triton Masquerade*   MR. ROBERTS

JONAH, *the superannuated clerk and copyist
at Versus's*   MR. E. P. WILKS

BLOT, *waiter at the Triton Masquerade*   MR. BEEKMAN

BOX, *the porter*   MR. LAWRENCE

MRS. VANDUSEN, *the home partner of the retired
cork merchant, full of business in her own
sphere and in fact an entire paper of
needles and pins in her own person*   MISS FANNY MORANT

MISS DOSIE HEFFRON, *a giddy young thing of
——(date missing), who proves to be an*

unexpected heartbreaker and an unsus-
pected siren in unexplored spheres   MRS. G. H. GILBERT

SILENA VANDUSEN, *her niece, a thorn in her*
aunt's side, though a rosebud in every-
body else's sight   MISS ADA REHAN

MISS MARY FORREST, *her first appearance this*
season. A young lady recently come into
a fortune; with highly romantic ideas as to
its disposal   MISS MAY FIELDING

CAROLINE, *a maidservant of the period, and a*
solemn warning to all future eras   MISS MAGGIE HAROLD

HANNAH, *another*   MISS LEVERE

CHARACTERS IN THE MASQUE AND NURSERY COTILLON

Lahdedah	Miss Evesson	Gypsy	Miss Shandley
Captainjenks	Miss Kirkland	The Frog	Mr. Sterling
Fanchette	Miss McNeil	Januario	Mr. Bennett
Gretchen	Miss Donaldson	Tommydodd	Miss Vinton
Red Riding Hood	Miss Flagg	The Royal Middy	Miss Weaver
Humpty Dumpty	Mr. Wilks	Aladdin	Miss Trevalyan
Robinson Crusoe	Mr. Lawrence	Little Bopeep	Miss Hinckley
Champagnecharly		Mother Goose	Miss Brooks
	Miss Maxwell	Puss in Boots	Mr. Macdonough
The Four Dominoes in Black,		Bluebeard	Mr. Hewitt
by Miss Vaughan, Miss Wil-			
liams, Miss Howard, Miss			
Featherstone			

MEPHISTOPHELES   MLLE. MALVINA

(Under whose directions the dances are given)

SYNOPSIS OF SCENES

ACT I: THE HOME OF THE VANDUSENS! (BY ROBERTS).—A SUBURBAN HOUSE
TO WHICH THE RETIRED CORK MERCHANT HAS FLOWN FOR A QUIET WHICH HE DOES
NOT FIND. TWENTY-FIVE YEARS OF THE NEEDLES AND PINS OF WEDLOCK DO NOT
DETER TWO OR THREE MORE COUPLES FROM VENTURING. THREE SILENAS MAKE THEIR
APPEARANCE TO DISTURB THE CALM—AND THE FATE OF THE WHISPERER IS SETTLED.

ACT II: THE LAW OFFICE OF MR. TOM VERSUS IN THIS CITY.—IN WHICH THE ROMANTIC YOUNG MILLION-HEIRESS ENGAGES HER HEART, LOSES HER HEAD, AND PUTS HER FOOT IN IT. THE THREE SILENAS TURN UP IN UNEXPECTED FORCE TO THE CONFUSION OF SEVERAL PEOPLE. A LESSON IN DANCING.

ACT III: THE HIPPODROME SUMMER GARDEN DECORATED FOR THE TRITON MASQUERADE (BY MR. JAMES ROBERTS).—NEEDLES AND PINS MAKE THEMSELVES FELT IN MORE BOSOMS THAN ONE, AND A DOMINO RIDDLE WHICH PUZZLES THE PLAYERS, PLACES ONE OF THEM AT THE MERCY OF THE POLICE. THE DISASTROUS RESULTS OF AN EXCHANGE OF ROSES AND OF A SIP OF SPICED JAMAICA. ONE OF THE SILENAS IS UNMASKED AND ANOTHER OF THEM UNMASKS HERSELF, WHILE THE BRIC-A-BRAC HUNTER IS BEREFT OF HIS PRIZE. LOOK UP!

(INCIDENTAL TO THIS ACT WILL BE A DUET BY MISS FIELDING AND MR. BRAND AND A CHORUS AND COTILLON OF NURSERY RHYMES BY ALL THE CHARACTERS.)

ACT IV: RETURNS TO THE VANDUSEN MANSION AND DEVELOPS SUNDRY HEADACHES AND HEARTACHES, AFTER THE DISSIPATION AND DISAPPOINTMENTS OF THE PREVIOUS EVENING. A HONEYMOON TO THE UBJIBBELOOLA! A NEW CHINESE PUZZLE IS PUT TOGETHER, AND THE FINAL SILENA IS QUIETED AT LAST, WHILE THE FABLE COMES TO END WITH A NOVEL RENDERING OF AN OLD RHYME.

ACT I.

SCENE: *Parlor in pleasant country house near New York. Substantial furniture. Door of entrance, C. Door, R., to Mrs. Vandusen's room, and door, L., to Mr. Vandusen's. Mantel and fireplace, R.2.E. Armchairs and sofa, L. Window, L.2.E. Small table, with vase, books, etc. Time, winter. Morning. Winter landscape. Music. Caroline enters, L.C., with a broom and a bundle of newspapers. Puts newspapers on table.*

CAROL. Lor'! How is it one can be up all night dancing and never feel a bit tired, while a day's work does fatigue one so? What a goloptious time I did have at that ball last night. It was the most genteel ball of the season, it was. I just remember one of 'em: *Him.* "I don't know you to talk to, miss, but I guess you're Caroline Smith, aren't you?" *Me.* "I guess I am." *Him.* "My sister knew a girl named Caroline. May I dance the next raquette with you?" *Me.* "I guess you may." Oh, it was like a dream! One, two, three and a kick, two and a kick, etc. [*Dances raquette waltz with broom for partner and off C. Silena Vandusen enters, L.D., cautiously*]

SIL. I wonder if my letter's there yet. [*Steals to table and takes a letter from vase*] Yes, ma didn't discover it. [*Looks at it*] It's from Gussie at school. She's a happy girl. No mother to find fault and no horrid old aunt to worry. And yet ma don't want me to correspond with her! Because it will make me dissatisfied! So she hunts for letters everywhere. Last night, when I was in bed, she came in to change my pillow, just to see if I had anything hidden under it. What *will* happen when I *do* have a *real* correspondence which she mustn't see? For she thinks I'm nothing but a child, and keeps me four hours a day at the piano, and aunt says I'm a mere chit and ought to wear short skirts. It's just because she's an old maid and wants to keep young herself. Now I know I am *not* a child. I am a young person who ought by rights to dress, go out, shop, make calls and receive attentions. [*About to open letter, goes to L., looks off. Conceals it and goes to poke fire, R. Mrs. Vandusen enters, L.D., in morning costume. A woman of forty-five, resolute and prompt*]

MRS. V. What are you doing there? [*To Silena*]

SIL. [*Embarrassed, and rattling the poker between the bars*] Fixing the fire, ma.

MRS. V. It's quite warm enough—look at the thermometer.

SIL. [*Goes to wall, R.C.*] Why, it's only seventy.

Mrs. V. [*Scrutinizing her*] Only seventy! That's hardly high enough to account for the color of your face. Your cheeks are as red as if you had been found out in something wrong.

Sil. Well, ma, if only a pale face is consistent with a clear conscience, that accounts for Aunt Dosie powdering so much. She'd be turkey-red if she didn't.

Mrs. V. Children shouldn't observe so much, especially what their elders happen to be doing. Go and call your father. [*Crosses to R.*]

Sil. I don't believe pa's up yet.

Mrs. V. I saw him in the garden at the flowers. Go and do as I tell you. [*Haughtily*]

Sil. [*Affected meekness*] Yes, ma, I will go and bring him to your feet. [*Exit, laughing, C.R.*]

Mrs. V. That girl is going to give me a great deal of trouble. [*Turning*] She's growing too fast, and begins to understand that she's no longer an infant. [*Goes about, and looking deliberately at and into everything*] If I could only get my sister off my hands and Kit married to a fortune, I could devote myself to securing a good *partie* for the child. [*Silena enters, C.R., bringing on Mr. Vandusen, who enters in morning gown, C.R., with watering pot. He is a pleasant, easy-going man of fifty-five*]

Van. You want me, my dear?

Mrs. V. [*R.*] Yes. Perhaps you are not aware that our new girl Caroline went to a ball, or a party, or something last night.

Sil. [*Aside*] A ball or a party! Happy creature!

Van. [*C.*] I hope she enjoyed herself.

Mrs. V. No doubt she did, as it was five in the morning when she came home.

Van. Then she really must have liked it.

Mrs. V. I gave her permission to stay out till twelve at the latest. We must stop this sort of thing at the commencement, or she'll be spoiled completely. You will therefore send for her and give her a good talking to.

Van. Who—I, my dear?

Mrs. V. Yes, you. I don't wish to be always scolding the servants. It gets one the reputation of a faultfinder and termagant, and then one cannot get or keep a decent girl. A few words from a man, on the other hand, will keep the creatures in order without giving the house a bad name.

Van. [*Putting watering pot off, R.C. door*] But, my dear, I don't exactly like to.

Mrs. V. Come! Be a man of inflexible determination for a few minutes. Silena, go and call Caroline. [*Crosses to C.*]

SIL. [*Laughing, and aside, going*] Papa a person of inflexible determination! I should like to see that. [*Aloud*] Yes, ma. [*Exit, C.R.*]

VAN. I believe it will spoil my whole day.

MRS. V. [*L.*] I have laid out my plans, and expect your cooperation. We must live in the country for the sake of economy, and it requires peculiar management to retain good servants.

VAN. Well, if you and I are to change places, I think we'd better go back to the city.

MRS. V. On the means we have?

VAN. Oh, business is sure to improve now the election is over.

MRS. V. At all events we secured a good education for our children.

VAN. My dear, you talk as if we were reduced to a final crust.

MRS. V. It's little better. All my money gone in the fall of coal.

VAN. What a pity you didn't put it in ice.

MRS. V. And now I'm dependent.

VAN. On me and Kit. That's only right.

MRS. V. Hush, here comes the girl. Now be firm. [*Crosses to R. Caroline appears, C.R. Silena follows her and comes down R.*]

CAROL. [*L.C.*] You want me, ma'am?

MRS. V. Mr. Vandusen has something to say to you.

CAROL. [*Frightened*] Mr. Vandusen, ma'am?

VAN. [*After sighing deeply, affects a stern air, looks at Caroline, advances a few steps, and slaps the table fiercely*] Attend to me. [*Folds his arms*]

CAROL. [*To Mrs. Vandusen*] Oh, ma'am! What have I done?

MRS. V. [*Crosses to C., and sweetly*] My child, you had permission to stay out till twelve last night. You exceeded the time by five hours.

CAROL. It was only three o'clock, ma'am.

MRS. V. It was five. Was it not, Mr. Vandusen?

VAN. [*Thumping table, R.*] Five o'clock!

MRS. V. [*To Caroline*] Mr. Vandusen is dreadfully angry. I have interceded all I can, and if you promise *never* to do it again he will forgive you in the end, I'm sure. [*Going, looks at Vandusen, coughs to brace him up, and exit, R. door*]

CAROL. Please, sir, it shan't happen again.

VAN. Silence! [*Pause*] Explain yourself! [*She attempts to speak*] Not a word! [*Looks over his shoulder, R., to assure himself that Mrs. Vandusen has gone, then pleasantly*] Did you have a nice time?

CAROL. Nice time, sir? Oh, at the ball, sir? Oh, it was splendid. I couldn't get away sooner. I was engaged for four quadrilles yet, and three polkas and a schottische—and all with the best dancers, too—and then I thought as you were all in bed, and I wasn't wanted—

Van. [*Reflectively*] That's a very good point. In fact she was *not* wanted. I don't believe my wife gave that consideration due weight.

Carol. Yes, sir!

Van. So you enjoyed yourself, very much?

Carol. Oh! Very much, sir. They were all young people, sir.

Van. [*Sighs*] Yes; that is so.

Carol. I guess the best way to avoid any trouble in the future, sir, is not to expect me till five o'clock—when I go to a ball.

Van. [*Looks at her*] Yes, I guess that's the best way. I don't believe my wife thought of that simple solution of the difficulty. You may go, Caroline.

Carol. Thank'ee, sir; is that all, sir?

Van. [*Crossing, R., sits on sofa*] Yes; I don't think of anything else, at present.

Carol. You are very kind, indeed, sir. I'll always come to you instead of to missus, when I want anything. [*Exit, C.R.*]

Van. I don't believe my wife thought of that. [*Turns and sees Silena laughing*] Oh! You were there!

Sil. [*R.*] Yes, I heard every word. [*Slaps table in imitation*] Silence! Go on! Not a word! Explain yourself! [*Laughs, advancing*]

Van. [*Dubiously*] Was I too rough with her?

Sil. Too rough! I wish mamma had been here; it would have done her good. [*Crosses to L., laughing*]

Van. Well, if she forces me into the housekeeping department, I shall certainly make a mess of it. [*Mrs. Vandusen enters R. door*]

Mrs. V. Is she gone? [*To Vandusen*] The next time you needn't hammer the furniture to pieces. It's no use to overdo a thing. You have probably frightened the girl.

Sil. [*Laughing*] I'm afraid he has not.

Mrs. V. [*Crosses to C.*] Is that you, my child? I have a word or two to say to you. [*Vandusen sits and takes up paper*]

Sil. [*L.*] To me, ma? Have I done anything?

Mrs. V. Your aunt has complained of you.

Sil. Aunt Dosie?

Van. [*R., looking up from his paper*] You are a continual source of irritation to your aunt, my dear, because you are young and she is not.

Mrs. V. She is not too old to have offers, although she has remained single so long.

Sil. I'm sure that's not her fault.

Mrs. V. I see an opportunity now for her to settle—before her chance is altogether gone.

Sil. Pa, how old is aunty?

VAN. That is something known only to Heaven and your mother.

MRS. V. Your aunt, child, is about thirty-five.

VAN. [*Reading*] Reverse the figures.

MRS. V. [*To Silena*] Before you came from school, she was the young lady of the family.

SIL. Why didn't you leave me at school?

MRS. V. Because we could not afford the expense any longer.

SIL. [*Gravely*] I did not know that. [*To Vandusen*] What must I do so as not to vex aunty?

VAN. [*Reading*] Grow old and ugly.

MRS. V. Well, show yourself as little as possible in company till she is married.

VAN. [*Same*] Then good-bye to company forever.

MRS. V. Keep your very bad jokes for yourself. [*To Silena*] You ought to keep out of the way of Mr. Geagle, especially. He seems to take a great interest in your aunt. I think she can get him.

VAN. What, old Geagle? Ha, ha!

MRS. V. [*Confidentially to both*] I have observed him closely. He loves her.

VAN. Nonsense. He's merely a bric-a-brac hunter, and runs after anything old and curious.

MRS. V. For shame, Christopher! [*To Silena*] Your aunt is a little displeased at his whispering to *you* in corners.

SIL. Yes, but ma, he does so to everybody. Whenever he comes in he sidles up, puts his mouth to your ear, and whispers "Good morning."

VAN. The same with me. Took me outside, last Saturday, to remark confidentially that it was going to rain.

MRS. V. [*To Silena*] Well, try to keep out of his way until your father has sounded him with respect to his intentions regarding Dosie. [*Vandusen jumps up horrified*]

SIL. Certainly, ma. You may assure Aunt Dosie that I have no designs on Mr. Geagle.

VAN. [*Advancing*] Did I understand you to speak about my sounding Geagle as to his intentions?

MRS. V. Insinuate to him gently that he's in love.

VAN. I suppose he knows his own business best.

MRS. V. He'll believe whatever you tell him.

VAN. My dear, consider. I never did such a thing in my life.

MRS. V. It's time you learned, then. [*Vandusen about to speak*] Now don't argue the point. I have maturely considered it and it must be done. [*He settles back to his paper*] Silena, I wish you would call your brother.

Sil. Yes, mamma. [*Going*] She is full of business this morning. What is Kit to do, I wonder. [*Exit, C.R.*]

Van. [*R., rising and laying aside his paper*] You must excuse me, this time. Leave me out of the matchmaking business.

Mrs. V. Now, for Dosie's sake.

Van. Do you want me to make that man wretched for life?

Mrs. V. Dosie hasn't a single bad trait.

Van. With the exception of being a flippant, flirting, finical, foolish woman. If she'd been sober and sensible, she'd have been married long ago.

Mrs. V. Time has softened every fault.

Van. I'll swear it has removed every charm.

Mrs. V. If Mr. Geagle don't see it, there's no harm in encouraging his attentions. He comes up every week, dawdles about her, makes a fool of himself, and her too, and so far it all amounts to nothing. Besides, I must get her out of the way, so I can attend to our own family.

Van. Our own family will get along. Kit has got a capital opening.

Mrs. V. Twelve hundred a year. Just enough to pay for his clothes and cigars. We must find a good match for *him* while he's young and impressionable.

Van. Now, you are not going to shove that poor boy into matrimony by the neck and shoulders.

Mrs. V. I certainly shall not let him miss the chance of a rich wife.

Van. Suppose he won't fall in love with her.

Mrs. V. Nonsense! Everybody falls in love with a rich girl.

Van. I differ. All the money in the world will not buy an honest boy's heart.

Mrs. V. Don't talk that way. You are to follow my instructions without question. These are matters peculiarly within the province of a woman.

Van. Exactly, that's why—

Mrs. V. That's why you are to obey implicitly. [*He drops in chair and rubs his head*] Dosie married, Kit provided for, we shall then be able to settle Silena.

Van. You'll settle them all, I expect.

Mrs. V. Marriage is woman's destiny.

Van. I say, if you get rid of them all, you and I will be left alone. That'll be very lonesome.

Mrs. V. [*Haughtily*] Thank you for the compliment. [*Silena enters, C.R.*]

Sil. He's coming. [*Comes L. Kit enters, C.R., young man of twenty-three*]

Kit. What is it, mother?

VAN. What is it, my son? A mere trifle. Your mother wishes to prepare you for immolation on the altar of mammon or matrimony, which, in this case, is the same thing.

KIT. [*R.C.*] Matrimony? I?

MRS. V. [*Severely to Vandusen*] Mr. Vandusen! [*To Silena*] Go to your room.

SIL. [*Pettishly*] What for?

MRS. V. [*Crosses to her*] Go this instant. [*Sits down to sew. Sofa, L.*]

SIL. [*Going up L.*] But I like to hear secrets. [*Goes up, making a face of discontent, which suddenly clears off. Aside*] I'll go to papa's room and read my letter. [*Exit gaily, L.D.*]

KIT. [*Sitting on sofa, L.*] Now, mother. Give us a few points about this matrimonial speculation.

VAN. [*Seriously*] Nonsense. It is a mere whim of your mother's.

MRS. V. Kit, listen to me attentively. You have a position with a moderate income. We sent you to college and to a foreign university at considerable sacrifice. We have led you to the threshold of fortune. You must enter by your own exertions.

KIT. [*Surprised*] At considerable sacrifice? I thought—

MRS. V. Don't interrupt me.

KIT. I beg pardon.

MRS. V. Your father is not in a position to support you and all of us for the balance of his life.

VAN. [*Warmly*] My love, I can sustain him until he works into a position of his own. He is under no necessity of selling himself.

MRS. V. Your generosity goes a little too far, my dear. You are beginning to grow old, and yet you have given up many of your accustomed luxuries. Your club—horses—wines—house in the city—and much more. I hardly think Kit will consent to further sacrifices of the kind for his sake.

KIT. [*Rises energetically*] Why, mother—father—I'd sooner work at a wheelbarrow—I'd no idea—

VAN. [*Rising, takes Kit's hand*] My dear son, this is a little fiction of mamma's. [*To Mrs. Vandusen*] You are a very shrewd woman. You know the boy's weak point—his love for us both—and you would use me as a weight to mould him. [*To Kit*] Don't be concerned, my boy. I gave up luxuries that were really hurtful to a man at my time of life—that's all—

KIT. [*Takes his hand*] Father, the thought of such a possibility would drive me instantly to obey mother in anything she proposes, even if it were repulsive to my sense of honor and independence.

VAN. [*Crosses to Mrs. Vandusen*] Do you hear what he says? Your plans are repulsive to his sense of honor and independence. For all we know, he may be in love already. I should be rejoiced to hear that he is. [*To Kit*] Tell me, isn't it so? You *are* in love.

KIT. [*Laughing, R.*] Not exactly. Although I may say I have been thinking of one young lady a great deal.

VAN. [*C.*] Who is she? What is her name? Where does she live? Is she good? Does she love you in return. But, of course she does. Well, she must wait for you. And you will both be unspeakably happy. [*Mrs. Vandusen makes a gesture of despair*]

KIT. [*R.*] It's impossible for me to answer all the questions. I saw the young lady a year ago, at Silena's school—or rather in that place—at the church. She played the organ and sang. We looked at each other—our looks, that is, I can assure you—my looks spoke what I could not utter in words.

VAN. She was one of the scholars? [*Rapturously*] A sweet, innocent schoolgirl?

KIT. [*Hesitating*] No—o—

VAN. Oh, a visitor—a sister of one of the pupils?

KIT. No. I think she was a piano teacher—taken on trial without a salary. [*Mrs. Vandusen makes a gesture of horror*]

VAN. [*Crosses to R., less enthusiastic*] Hem! Hem! Ah!—well, Silena knows her, of course.

MRS. V. [*Satirically to Vandusen*] Well, what do you think of it? Does it meet your approval?

VAN. [*Crosses to C., stoutly*] I always believe in first love.

MRS. V. [*Seriously*] Perhaps you believe a person must necessarily be unhappy who cannot marry his first love. [*With meaning*] Are you unhappy?

VAN. [*Crosses to R., uneasy*] I? What do—why do you ask? What have I to do with it? [*Sitting, R.*]

MRS. V. [*On sofa, L.*] Very well, you can assure Kit confidently that time will heal every wound of that character.

KIT. [*Sitting, L.C., next to her*] Well, mother, have you any particular person in view for me?

MRS. V. All in good time.

VAN. [*Gruffly*] You had better insert a matrimonial advertisement, or look up a matrimonial bureau—

MRS. V. [*Dryly*] I have no doubt it would be an extremely expeditious way of arranging it.

VAN. [*To Kit, solemnly*] Then look out, my son, for the appearance of a marriage broker—a connubial agent—who will introduce you to a customer for one per cent of the purchase money. There's no telling to what lengths your mother proposes to go.

Mrs. V. [*To Kit*]   It will be time enough for you to know what I propose, when I understand your views of principle in the matter, my son.

Kit.   Dispose of me as you please, mother. [*Rises, kisses her forehead*] My view of principle in the matter is—that I should no longer be a burden here. [*Exit, C.*]

Van. [*Walks up and down in rage*]   A burden! My darling son a burden here! [*To Mrs. Vandusen*] Your cold, calculating, selfish barter and sale of your children is detestable—is wicked—I could—Heaven forgive me—I could leave you at this moment and forever.

Mrs. V. [*Lays aside her work*]   I do not doubt it, for you never loved me.

Van. [*Astounded, stops*]   How can you say such a thing!

Mrs. V.   Your mother was not very good at keeping a secret. [*Rises*] She wished me to look upon you as a hero—and so she told me everything before she died. Everything. [*With meaning*]

Van.   And what was everything?

Mrs. V.   That you had been in love with a young girl—a governess—by the name of Silena Summers. You were both young and poor, but full of hope—for you were just attaining a position in life as your son is now, and you were engaged to be married.

Van. [*In low tone*]   Well. [*Sitting near fire, R.*]

Mrs. V.   Suddenly your father died, leaving you greatly embarrassed—leaving your mother to your care. You made a proposition to Silena to postpone the wedding, but she insisted on releasing you fully. She said to you, "We dare not wait till your mother's death leaves you free, for as your love for me grew stronger, you might come to look upon that sacred life as a burden. From that hour my love for you would die."

Van. [*Looks up*]   Well, was this girl not worthy any man's affection?

Mrs. V.   I have not finished. You parted. After a little while you met me. It was your mother's wish that you should marry me—and you did.

Van. [*Quickly*]   Because I loved you.

Mrs. V.   Is it true? Tell me then—why did you call your daughter Silena, if you desired to forget Silena Summers?

Van. [*Rises*]   Have I not been a good husband?

Mrs. V.   To be sure you have, and I should have been perfectly happy if your mother had only kept her secret to herself.

Van. [*Embarrassed*]   But you don't suppose for a moment that I still think of Sil—of my youthful nonsense?

Mrs. V.   Memories are dangerous things. They are the only ones that grow more beautiful with age.

Van.   My dear. I have no longer any eye for beauty. The tooth of time—ah! [*Sits at fire*]

Mrs. V. Gnaws away our defenses and lets in the enemy. But don't be uneasy, I'm a practical woman, and know I've no cause for jealousy.

Van. Jealousy at our age!

Mrs. V. Where there is love there is always jealousy. Age has nothing to do with it. *You,* I dare say, are *not* jealous.

Van. Now, my dear, do you want me to make you a declaration of love?

Mrs. V. Not at all. I only wish you to study the happiness of yourself and your children. Do you really believe Kit will be unhappy because he marries a wife of his mother's choice? Didn't you? And are you unhappy?

Van. [*Rising, gallantly*] Nonsense. Why should I be unhappy? Just the reverse. I am happy. [*Gives her his hand*]

Mrs. V. Thank you! I was sure you would be sensible. [*Exit, R.D.*]

Van. [*Looks after her*] She's a good woman. If she didn't have such a genius for managing everybody. [*Thoughtfully*] So she knew the story of my youth—and never spoke of it till today—when I opposed her plans about Kit. But I've done nothing wrong, perhaps. Yet the recollection of Silena was always a pleasant memory. A shrine to which I fled for repose, after a connubial storm. Yes, it was right to expose it, to tear away the veil, to shatter the idol, to close the shrine, and I'm glad she did it. But I would like to get in a devil of a rage with somebody. [*Walks up and down; sees Silena, off L.*] Silena! What letter is that you are concealing?

Sil. [*Behind scene, L.D.*] What letter, papa?

Van. Come out here. [*Silena enters, L., embarrassed*]

Sil. Here I am, papa.

Van. I saw quite plainly, that you put a letter in your pocket.

Sil. [*Takes out letter*] I wouldn't have hidden it from you. I was only afraid of mamma. It's only from Gussie Archer at school—and it makes the tears come into my eyes to read it.

Van. Indeed, what does she say?

Sil. Sit down and I'll read it to you. [*Sits at his side, he C.*]

Van. Yes, read it, it will divert my thoughts.

Sil. [*Reads*] "Dear Silena: You remember our piano teacher, Miss Forrest, whom everybody liked so much? She has inherited an immense fortune from a very distant relative—half a million they say. She gave a dinner before she left to all the teachers and to six of the biggest girls. It was delicious. She is very romantic and is going to do ever so much good with her money; to help the struggling and to unite those who are victims of disappointed hopes. She spoke particularly of a pair of young lovers she had heard of—a real true story. It seems there was a lovely young girl of eighteen named Silena—just like you—and who taught music. She was beloved by a splendid young fellow named Christopher, just making his way in the world. While they were anticipating with the deepest happiness the day of their marriage, his father died and left him and his mother in the deepest poverty." [*Feeling a tear drop on her hand she looks up and sees him weeping, his head resting on his hand, which is pressed to his eyes; he had listened attentively at first, then becomes deeply moved*] Papa, what is the matter, are you ill? [*Puts letter on desk behind her*]

VAN. [*Pressing her head to his breast*] My dear child.

SIL. Shall I call mamma?

VAN. [*Holding her to him*] No! Don't call anybody. I am perfectly well. There! It's all right. [*Kisses her, puts her off his knee, rises*] I'll take a walk in the garden, that will do me good. [*Exit, C.R., after kissing her forehead*]

SIL. [*L.*] What is the matter with papa? I never saw him that way. I hadn't got to the sentimental part of the story, and yet it was too much for him. [*C. Caroline enters, C.L., with card*]

CAROL. This gentleman wants to see a member of the family, miss.

SIL. [*Takes card, reads*] "Thomas Versus, Attorney and Counsellor-at-Law." Whom does he wish to see?

CAROL. Guess anybody'll do, miss; he said he wasn't particular so long as they was *composentus* and could testify ineligibly.

SIL. [*Puts card and letter on table*] Ask him in, Caroline.

CAROL. Yes, miss. [*Exit, C.*]

SIL. I don't believe papa wants to see anybody and mamma's upstairs. I wonder if he's a country lawyer. [*Looks off, C., and returns*] Oh, no; he's city. [*Stage, L. Tom Versus enters, C.L., hat in hand, is young, lively, well-dressed young fellow*]

TOM. [*R.*] Good morning—Miss—Miss—

SIL. [*Looks at him intently*] What do you wish?

TOM. [*R., aside*] By Jove! She's handsome. [*Aloud*] I should like to know if a Mr. Kit Vandusen lives here. Miss—Miss—

SIL. Kit? That's my brother.

TOM. Your brother? [*Aside*] I didn't know he had a sister, and yet I thought I knew all about him. [*Aloud*] But 'twas ever thus. We imagine we are thoroughly posted about a man and yet his greatest recommendation [*Bows*] remains unknown.

SIL. [*L., curtsies*] Oh, thank you.

TOM. For what?

SIL. [*Disconcerted*] I thought you were paying me a compliment.

TOM. My dear Miss Vandusen, if your perfections were targets and my praises were arrows, they would fall far short of the mark.

SIL. Oh, thank you. Don't do it any more, please. That one hit. [*Crosses to R.*] I am quite unaccustomed to such flattery.

Том. [*L.*] Indeed. Then they must keep you away from the gaze of impressionable man.

Sil. Well, I'm not secluded exactly; but I have to keep out of the way, till my aunt gets married.

Том. [*Smiles*] How old is your aunt?

Sil. Well, both of us together are fifty.

Том. I see. Aunt old—disappointed, lean, lank, sour and savage. You young—fresh, beautiful, beloved by everybody. Tyrannical persecution. Immured from the world, but not forever. Look up; hope. *He* will come. Radiant with love and hope. His bright eye flashing, his dark hair flowing. [*Running hand through his hair*] His hair will be dark. Chestnut brown.

Sil. [*Laughing*] Allow me to call my brother and tell him you are here. [*Exit, C.R.*]

Том. [*Looks after her*] She's charming. Now that I begin to find Mr. Kit Vandusen the possessor of such a sister, I begin to take renewed interest in my mission. Let us prepare for the interview. My notes [*Takes out notebook and opens it*] are full and explicit. I am first to touch lightly on the history of the heroic music teacher and the exemplary son. Then unfold the purpose of a mysterious benefactor—my friend and client, Miss Mary Forrest, who has heard their story and intends to make them happy. The lover shall not despair, the maiden shall not pine, the mother shall not die. A competence will be settled upon them—conditioned upon their immediate marriage. All complete. [*Shuts book and ruminates*] I have found the exemplary son, the despairing lover, Mr. Kit Vandusen. I am to send him to Miss Mary Forrest. She will do the rest; reunite him to the music teacher, who has pined so long. I should do very little credit to my own penetration if I doubted for one moment it was Mary herself. She was a teacher of the pianoforte, which is the same as music, if you know how to play. Happy Kit. He will get half a million and his long-lost love. [*Silena reenters, C.R.*]

Sil. My brother will be here immediately. Please take a seat. [*Points to sofa, C.*]

Том. [*C.*] Will you? [*She sits, L., then he does, C.*] I hope you told him there was no hurry. An hour or two makes no difference, if you can stay. [*Rises and bows*]

Sil. [*L., rises and bows*] Oh, thank you. Kit can't imagine what you want with him.

Том. I bring him some very agreeable and unlooked-for intelligence.

Sil. Oh! Is it a great secret?

Том. It is.

Sil. Oh! Are you a government official, or something?

Том. No, I'm only a lawyer.

SIL. Oh! Do you dance?

TOM. Dance? It's not exacted by the rules of the Supreme Court as a qualification for the bar, but individually I do dance, and personally I like to.

SIL. [*Sitting on sofa, moves nearer to him*] I'm so glad. I love dancing so much, and young dancing men are so scarce nowadays.

TOM. Do you go to balls? Are you going to the Triton Masquerade, next week? They give it at the Hippodrome this year, you know.

SIL. Oh, I should love a masquerade. But till aunt's engaged I have to stay at home.

TOM. That's a poor prospect, to wait for the engagement of a maiden aunt of fifty.

SIL. [*Quickly*] You forget that *I* am counted in the fifty.

TOM. [*Rises and bows*] I could not forget you.

SIL. Thank you. [*Rises*] But here's my brother. I must go. [*Seriously and bowing*] I have been very much entertained.

TOM. The pleasure on my side has been tenfold.

SIL. Oh, thank you. [*Going, aside*] He's just splendid. [*Exit, R.D.*]

TOM. What an ingenuous little thing; says "Thank you" for every compliment. [*Kit enters, C.R.*]

KIT. [*L.*] You wish to see me?

TOM. [*R., aside*] Fine looking fellow. Mary has taste. [*Aloud*] I come on a delicate errand—very delicate. Affairs of the heart, the domain of the affections, the uniting of kindred souls, are a little out of the common, as professional employment, but it's got to be done and I'm here to do it.

KIT. [*Crosses to R., looks at him, aside*] It can't be possible. Has mother actually set a matrimonial agent at work? [*To Tom*] It's too absurd. My dear sir, my mother—

TOM. Don't say a word, sir! Not necessary—it's all right. Your devotion to your mother, your unselfish sacrifice—I know all. I sympathize with you deeply.

KIT. [*Looks at him*] Do you? [*Turns and aside*] It's astounding—

TOM. [*Sits, C.*] But to the point. I represent a young lady who has just come into a large fortune, which enables her to give full sway to the dictates of an emotional nature.

KIT. [*Sits R. of sofa*] Well, sir—you represent this young lady?

TOM. Who requests the pleasure of a visit from you this afternoon at four o'clock.

KIT. And the address.

TOM. [*Giving card*] She is stopping at present at my house with my mother, being herself an orphan.

KIT. An orphan?

Tom. Yes—the young lady—and a friend of our family from infancy. I am not permitted at present, for obvious reasons, to disclose her name. You will discover it from her own lips.

Kit. [*After considering card*] I'm a little green in these matters. Am I required to say anything in particular when I see her, or wait for her to begin the conversation?

Tom. If you've got anything to say, I suppose you'll say it. I always do. [*Crosses to R.*]

Kit. [*Rises*] Well, I'll come. And take the greatest pains to act the amiable, and secure *you* your commission. Good morning! [*Going up C.*] It's wonderful. [*Exit, C.R.*]

Tom. [*Watches him off turns*] I like the sister better. [*Mrs. Vandusen enters, R.D.*]

Mrs. V. Caroline said a person had called. [*Sees Tom*] Ah! You wish—

Tom. [*L.*] My mission is ended, my dear madam. I have spoken to Mr. Vandusen.

Mrs. V. I am Mrs. Vandusen.

Tom. [*In admiration*] The mother! [*Advances with outstretched hands, takes hers*] Madam! I am most happy to make your acquaintance.

Mrs. V. [*Trying to free her hands*] What do you say, sir?

Tom. [*Releasing her, folding his arms, exhorting her*] Courage, poor mother. Courage, noble creature! [*Mrs. Vandusen comes down, looking at him*] It's a long lane that has no turning; even misfortune must have an end.

Mrs. V. My dear sir—

Tom. You have suffered. You have lost your husband. You will never get another.

Mrs. V. Sir!

Tom. I mean you will never want another. But you have a son—an heroic son, and a lovely daughter. [*Catches her hands*] Cherish that daughter. She was the first to receive the dove bearing the olive branch in its beak. I was the dove, the olive branch is peace. Peace after all your sufferings. [*Hurriedly*] I represent a wealthy heiress—Miss Mary Forrest. Now you can guess all. Courage, poor mother, courage! [*Shakes her hands, and at door*] Courage! [*Exit, C.*]

Mrs. V. The man must be crazy. Miss Mary Forrest? I never even heard the name before, and he referred to my husband. I'll just call Christopher and ask him what it's all about. [*Takes Silena's letter from table*] What's this? A letter to my daughter! Is it possible that innocent child corresponds behind my back? [*Runs over it*] Piano teacher—Mary Forrest—the very name. [*Reads further*] Why, here is my husband's own story related in this boarding school. Let me see about this. [*Reads*] "Miss Forrest heard all the particulars from one of the chief actors in the drama, Silena Summers herself. She now declares it her resolution to bring the unhappy couple together. I have money, she says, it shall be the means of uniting those noble hearts. I will search for the devoted lover and son. I will—" [*Drops the letter*] Everything is turning round in my head. This person going to find my husband and unite him to Silena Summers! Where is this wealthy lunatic? She must have sent the other insane person who was here just now. And he has seen Vandusen and spoken to him. Good heavens! His mysterious language, "You have lost your husband." Can it be possible they were secretly married? Oh, pshaw! [*Sits and holds her head*] It's nonsense! There's some mistake, of course. But whatever it is, there's a mystery I must solve. [*Puts letter in her pocket and rises. Silena running in, C.L.*]

SIL. He's coming!

MRS. V. [*Starting*] Who's coming?

SIL. [*Mysteriously*] Mr. Geagle!

MRS. V. I can't see him. You stay here till I send your aunt down.

SIL. But suppose he commences to whisper?

MRS. V. Don't hear anything he says. [*Sternly*] You and I, miss, have a little account to settle afterward.

SIL. [*Aside, and frightened, feeling in pocket*] I left my letter on the desk.

MRS. V. Deceitful girl!

SIL. [*Crying*] Don't say that, mamma. Upon my honor, I would not conceal from you anything important.

MRS. V. [*In tremulous tones, drawing her toward her*] You ought to be a comfort to me. [*About to push her away, recalls the purpose and kisses her*] Be a good, dear, little child! [*Exit, R.D., hurriedly, handkerchief to eyes*]

SIL. [*Surprised*] Mamma kissed me, like papa did. What *is* the matter with my parents today? I know they're out of humor on aunt's account. Why don't Mr. Geagle say what he wants—whether he wants to marry her or not. Suppose I ask him. I've a great mind to. He'd have to give *me* an answer one way or the other. [*Determined*] I'll do it. I'll secure a husband for aunty, liberty for myself and a waltz with the dancing lawyer. [*Gets L. Geagle enters, C.L.; a man about fifty, neatly dressed, quite bald, save a narrow fringe of hair around the sides of his head. Extremely smiling and confidential in his address. Looks at Silena, smiles, lays his hat on chair, R., looks again and smiles. Unbuttons a long ulster, takes it off, folds it. Looks for a chair to put it on, L. Looks at her, smiles again, deposits coat, R., then comes down, hat in hand, softly. Keeps hat behind him*]

GEAG. [*Whispers in her ear, R.*] Good morning! [*Nods, winks and smiles*]

SIL. [*Takes his hand, leads him to L. corner, and in his ear*] How do you find yourself today?

GEAG. [*Looks at her beamingly*] Pretty well, but I don't sleep.

SIL. [*Leads him to R. corner, and as before*] Why?

GEAG. [*Tapping his head*] Buzzing in my head.

SIL. Lor'! what is it?

GEAG. I don't know. Perhaps it's because I have of late taken to deep philosophical inquiries. I discuss with myself: Who are you? Why are you here? What for? Why do you exist?

SIL. Well, what do you make of it?

GEAG. [*Looking around*] Nothing—really nothing. Of course, I didn't come on the planet to collect curiosities. That affords employment for about one-eighth of one per cent of my intellectual and physical faculties. Then what is the rest of me for? In the evening [*Mysteriously*], when it grows dark and I'm all alone, and everybody is sitting at home with wives and children, I become depressed. I feel a want—a void—a vacuum—

SIL. [*Same to R.*] You want a wife.

GEAG. My dear, it is only a short time since I have been able to accumulate capital enough to support a wife.

SIL. [*L.*] Then why don't you marry now?

GEAG. I would, but I've been having a race with Time. I've been piling up dollars and he's been piling up years.

SIL. That's nothing. All you have to do is to look out for someone who is not too young. Haven't you had your eye on somebody already?

GEAG. [*Seizing her hand*] I wouldn't breathe it for the world.

SIL. But I've seen and I know.

GEAG. [*Same*] I hope no one else noticed it.

SIL. No! No one but I.

GEAG. [*Stage, R., and back*] How clever the children are nowadays.

SIL. So you do love Aunt Dosie? Eh?

GEAG. I don't know if it's love, not having had any experience.

SIL. Aunt Dosie is a mighty fine-looking woman.

GEAG. Is she? [*Crosses to L.*] I'm so nearsighted. At all events, she'd suit me better than a young girl. But I'm afraid of being refused. [*Close to her*]

SIL. [*R.*] Why should she refuse you?

GEAG. [*Looking around cautiously*] Because—I wear a wig!

SIL. [*Regarding his bald head*] You wear a wig? [*Astonished, walks round him*]

GEAG. I don't wonder you look astonished. It's made to imitate nature so perfectly that no one would suspect with the naked eye.

Sıl. [*Getting R. of him*] You amaze me. Do sit down. [*Takes his hat to put on the table, looks in it and draws the wig out of it; aside*] He pulled it off with his hat. [*Replaces it and lays hat on table, then sits beside him*] But why should your wig interfere with your success?

Geag. [*R.*] Because it's a deception she doesn't dream of. How could I tell her, and yet there should be no secrets between man and wife.

Sıl. Then you'd marry her if she'd have you? [*He hesitates. Firmly*] Yes or no?

Geag. [*Determinedly*] Yes! [*Rising, goes L.*] Well, what these children don't know nowadays!

Sıl. [*Calls, L.D.*] Aunt Dosie!

Geag. [*Aside, R.*] I'm frightfully nervous. [*Feels pulse*] I can't feel any pulse. And I've got a hot flush with a chill. I ought to have taken a pill before coming out, but I couldn't foresee the crisis coming so suddenly. If she says yes, I wonder if I must hug her or kiss her. I never did. I never could. I'll do it wrong. But she isn't a widow. She can't make any odious comparisons.

Sıl. [*At door, L.*] Here she is. [*Clasps her hands*] She looks beautiful.

Geag. [*R.*] Now for it. [*Blows his nose and tries to get up an attitude. Dosie enters, L.D. A maiden lady of fifty. Much overdressed and too youthfully painted. Hair in long braids with ribbons, but not too much of a caricature; quick, active and effusive*]

Dosie. [*To Silena, as she runs in*] Did you call me, darling? [*Stops, bashfully, on seeing Geagle, then, placing her arm around Silena, à la schoolgirl, comes down with her*] How do you do, Mr. Geagle? [*Giggles with Silena, hides her blushes in the latter's shoulder*]

Geag. [*Gasping for breath*] Gug—gug—good morning. [*Aside*] How dry my larynx is.

Sıl. Aunt, dear, Mr. Geagle has something important to say to you.

Dosie. Me, darling? It's some little foolish, foolish thing, only fit for giddy girls. [*Smiles sweetly at Geagle*]

Sıl. You'll be giddy in a minute. Just sit down here. [*Places her in chair, C. Crosses to R.*]

Dosie. What does the child mean?

Sıl. [*To Geagle, whom she takes by the hand and seats beside Dosie in another chair*] And you sit just there.

Geag. [*Aside to Silena*] Don't go away.

Sıl. [*Stands off to view them; to Geagle*] Speak up, like a man.

Dosie. What is all this preparation for?

Geag. My dear Miss Heffron—Theodosia, I believe we have both arrived at an age—

Dosie. At a what?

GEAG. At a—period—a period when we ought to think of—of—you know.

DOSIE. [*Aside*] It's come at last. [*Aloud*] I don't know what you mean.

GEAG. I'm only fifty.

DOSIE. Oh, years make no difference.

GEAG. Oh, yes, they do. I consider that, particularly in your case—[*Catches a warning gesture from Silena*] I mean, in my case. Let us say *our* case.

DOSIE. [*Decidedly*] Never mind pursuing that subject. [*Simpering*] What did you want with me?

GEAG. [*With a burst*] To marry you. [*Jumps up*] It's out. It's out. [*Blows his nose as he crosses, and takes stage, R.*]

DOSIE. [*With a cry*] Oh, catch me! [*He props her up with one hand and fans her with a newspaper with the other, which he takes from his pocket. Recovering*] You have so taken me by surprise. I never even thought of marriage.

SIL. [*Upstage, R.*] Oh, aunty! [*Geagle waves her off. She goes off, C., and afterwards peeps in, C.R.*]

DOSIE. I had no idea of changing my mode of life. There is everything here to make a young thing like me happy. I was like a bird, joyous all the day long.

GEAG. Well, we'll be a pair of birds, and go off and flock together.

DOSIE. [*Both sit*] I can't decide upon the instant. I don't know you, Mr. Geagle.

GEAG. [*R., on seat*] You've known me fifteen years.

DOSIE. [*Sentimentally*] It seems as if I had seen you but yesterday.

GEAG. Well, it *was* only last Saturday. Now to business. What am I to do, hope? Is it a bargain, or shall we call it off?

DOSIE. I must consult my sister.

GEAG. Then I needn't go right off and drown myself, eh?

DOSIE. Would I sit here if you were indifferent to me, dear Nicholas. [*Titters and drops her head on his shoulder*]

GEAG. Dear Dosie. [*Takes her hand, then suddenly stops and draws back with a sigh, looking fixedly at her*] I think it proper to call your attention to a little defect. [*Dosie looks at herself and feels her toilette in alarm*] Oh, on my part. [*Dosie relieved*] A—a—fault—a deficiency.

DOSIE. A fault, a deficiency?

GEAG. A big one.

DOSIE. [*Soothingly*] Can't you get rid of it?

GEAG. I do take it off sometimes, but I can't get rid of it altogether.

DOSIE. How singular.

GEAG. Look at me, don't you observe something singular?

DOSIE. You alarm me.

GEAG. The fact is, then—[*Places her on seat*] I—I—wear—I wear—

SIL. [*C., who has been watching, holds up the wig*] The fact is, aunty, he wears a wig.

GEAG. [*Starting away, L.*] What's that? [*Feels head*] Why I didn't have it on at all. [*To Dosie*] And you didn't refuse me, even though I went for you bald-headed. I am a happy man. Victory! [*Seizes Dosie's hands, and both go skipping over to sofa, L., and sit*]

DOSIE. Did you think I would have loved you the less on account of a wig?

GEAG. The danger is past. Now I can speak. We'll celebrate the festivity by a little wild dissipation. We'll go to the Triton Masquerade, eh?

SIL. Me, too!

GEAG. You! Of course. [*Motions her to retire*]

SIL. [*Aside*] They'll do. Won't pa be glad I've taken the business off his hands. [*Runs off, C.R. Music. Instantly reappears, and runs to L. and off, C.R. Geagle whispers in Dosie's ear. She puts her hands before her face, then whispers to him. He hides his face in his hands. She runs over to chair, R.H. He misses her, and looks under the sofa and behind it, then sees her sitting, R., with handkerchief over her head. Steals over, lifts corner of handkerchief and says "Peek-a-boo"*]

DOSIE. [*Running back to L.*] Nicky can't catch me. [*Geagle follows her. Both on sofa, L. He whispers in her ear. She shakes her head. He whispers again, holding up finger, as if asking for one kiss. She hesitates, finally throws her handkerchief around his neck, he getting on his knees before her, back to audience. She pulls his head forward to her and kisses him twice on top of the bald spot. Mr. and Mrs. Vandusen enter, C., with Silena. They all exclaim "Bravo! Bravissimo"*]

GEAG. [*Leading Dosie to Mrs. Vandusen's feet, and kneeling*] Mother, your blessing! [*Back to audience*]

ACT II.

SCENE: *Handsome library, bookcase of miscellaneous books, L.C., and bookcase of law books, R.C. Door of entrance, C. Doors L. and R., table R., sofa behind it, chairs, etc. Music. Jonah, an old clerk, in rusty black, is discovered arranging papers on table, has on white tie, pen behind ear, has habit of taking snuff. Mary Forrest enters, C.L.; she is a young girl of twenty-one, elegantly dressed.*

MARY. [*L.*] Is Mr. Versus in his office, Jonah?

JONAH. Yes, miss. He's drawing some pleadings.

MARY. Ask him if he will come to me as soon as he is disengaged.

JONAH. [*Going. Crosses to L.*]   Yes, miss.

MARY.   And, Jonah, I believe the callers for Mr. Versus are usually shown in here. Will you attend particularly, this morning, to showing them to the outer room.

JONAH.   Yes, miss.

MARY. [*Going to table, R.*]   That is all, thank you.

JONAH. [*Aside, going*]   When a body comes into half a million, other bodies go to the outer room. [*Exit, L.D., snuffling and shuffling*]

MARY.   By this time my letters and telegram must have reached the school, and Silena is reading them with more than surprise. She will hear that I have found her Kit. Poor heart! She had given up all hope of happiness, and it was reserved for me to fill her with joy. [*Rising*] What better use to make of riches! When I feel her sobbing on my breast—when I see him clasp her hand—when they are married, and they shall be married—I shall have my reward.

JONAH. [*Shuffles in, L.D.*]   Mr. Versus coming, miss. He's in a hurry. [*Tom Versus enters, L.D.*]

TOM. [*To Jonah*]   Run off and post those letters, Jonah, and try to serve Boggs on your way back. We must catch Boggs. [*Jonah nods and exit*] Came as soon as I could. [*Crosses to Mary*] Very busy this morning. Most important divorce case. Lady in a great hurry. [*Sits*] I sent you word I'd found your man.

MARY. [*Sits, C.*]   I want to ask you all about him. You have really found Christopher Vandusen?

TOM. [*Sighs*]   Yes, alas!

MARY.   What's the matter?

TOM. [*Sits next to her*]   What's the matter? I've found a rival, of course.

MARY.   A rival? Do you love Selina Summers?

TOM.   Why not? I presume that Selina Summers and you are one and the same person?

MARY.   Don't talk nonsense. You are my lawyer, and a good one—extremely conscientious for a lawyer, and I want your advice.

TOM. [*Profoundly*]   State your case.

MARY.   There is a young man, good-looking, clever, full of life, a little unsteady and flighty, yet brave and good, whom I have known since childhood. [*Tom looks at her*] He never cared a snap for me all my life, until I came into a fortune, when he announces himself deeply attached to me. [*He rises, takes stage, R.H.*] What do you advise? Shall I trust him? Come, answer like a sagacious and conscientious lawyer, consulted on a matter of business. [*Tom scratches his ear*] Well?

TOM. [*Advancing to her*]   Well, my advice is, take him, if you don't find anyone better.

MARY. [*Extending her hand to him*] That is exactly what I think. So we'll let the matter rest there for the present.

TOM. [*Holding her hand*] So you *are* Silena Summers?

MARY. [*Rising*] You are mistaken. The proof is this telegram I have sent two hours ago, to the true Silena Summers. [*Takes paper from pocket and hands it to Tom*] Read it please.

TOM. [*Reads, R., crosses to L.*] "To Miss Silena Summers, Music Teacher. Miss Bunker's Seminary for Young Ladies, Middleburg, Montgomery County, New York." It's a good thing they don't charge for the address. [*Reads*] "Have found your Christopher. Come on by next train. He will be at my house. All is well. Remember the story you told me. Mary Forrest."

MARY. [*Rises*] You believe in her existence now?

TOM. Well, I have a resource against the disappointment—the remembrance [*Enthusiastic*] of a charming creature—by the way, the sister of your friend, Christopher—a delicious little innocent, who always says "thank you," when I pay her a compliment.

MARY. [*Surprised*] Christopher has a sister?

TOM. A rosebud. Voice like a bell. Eyes like a gazelle. Altogether bright, and fresh, and beaming, like a May morning.

MARY. Did you intimate to Mr. Vandusen why he was requested to call here?

TOM. Oh, yes! I explained.

MARY. How did he take it?

TOM. Well, he didn't appear overjoyed.

MARY. He controlled his feelings?

TOM. [*L.*] Admirably, if he had any. Now, his mother, the widow, she was much more excited. But it struck me she was not altogether the helpless creature we supposed.

MARY. She is a most deserving person.

TOM. I don't think you'll find her a very thankful one. Do you know it occurred to me that these people may have got over the old fit—I mean the original affection. It must be a couple of years, at least, since it all happened. Christopher may have braced up and got another girl. [*Crosses to R.*]

MARY. Are men so fickle?

TOM. [*R.*] If I may judge by myself, there isn't the slightest dependence to be placed on any of them.

MARY. If they are all as honest, there is some hope. [*Hannah, servant maid, appears, C.L.*]

HAN. A gentleman, by the name of Mr. Vandusen, has called to see Mr. Versus.

Tom. [*Rising*] I'll be there in a moment. [*Hannah exit, C.L.; he looks at watch*] I told him four o'clock. He's punctual.

Mary. [*Crosses to R.*] Please send him to me.

Tom. [*Going up*] Don't forget you're to have me, if you don't find a better.

Mary. [*R.*] Suppose the "May morning" were to hear you?

Tom. Ah! The "May morning," what a pity most of them turn out November afternoons. I'll go and rattle off that divorce. [*Exit, L.D.*]

Mary. [*Sits on sofa, C.*] I am really curious to see Silena's lover. [*Kit Vandusen enters, C., shown in by Hannah, who exits. He is carefully dressed. Does not perceive Mary at first*]

Kit. The lamb is led to the slaughter. I trust the victim is becomingly decorated for the sacrifice. [*Sees Mary*] Madam!

Mary. [*Turns, recognizing him*] He! Who is this? [*Crosses to L.*]

Kit. [*Recognizing*] You! [*Aside*] It must be the same! That Sunday at the church. How is it possible?

Mary. [*Aside*] It is he, and he belongs to another. I have brought them together. What a destiny is mine? [*Leans against table for support*]

Kit. [*Hastens to her*] You are ill; can I assist you? [*She drops in seat*]

Mary. [*Motions him away coldly*] Pray be seated.

Kit. I thought you were about to fall.

Mary. No—I—only sat down—energetically, that's all.

Kit. [*Aside*] I'll marry her, of course that's all right. But how fortunate; mother might have proposed somebody else and then—[*Shudders*]

Mary. Please take a seat.

Kit. [*Sits, C.*] I am at your service.

Mary. You are aware, I suppose, why you were sent for.

Kit. Certainly. I had a conversation with my mother, this morning.

Mary. Your mother seems to take more interest in the matter than you.

Kit. I confess I was indifferent, but now that I find you are the person—who—or the person which—

Mary. [*L.*] Let us talk of your affairs. You are willing to be married?

Kit. If *you* wish it—with the greatest pleasure.

Mary. How much of a dowry do you think a bride ought to bring?

Kit. [*Entreating*] Don't let us talk of money. Let us speak of the time when we first met—when our souls, stirred by the solemn tones of the organ —sought expression for their feelings and spoke to each other through our glances.

Mary. [*Rising, excited*] How can you talk in this strain to me! Do you forget that you are going to be married?

KIT. [*Rising and ardently seizes her hand*] Yes; and I felt I ought, for that reason most of all, to show you that from the first moment our eyes met—

MARY. [*Crosses to C.*] Not a word more. Tell me what sum of money a bride ought—

KIT. Do you—can you—believe me capable of entertaining one sordid thought in your presence?

MARY. [*Agitated*] The sum! The sum!

KIT. I refuse to discuss the topic. With me marriage is too sacred for the intrusion of a selfish thought. [*Hannah appears, C.*]

MARY. [*To her*] What is it?

HAN. Lady, miss. Says she is Mrs. Vandusen.

KIT. Mother! [*Aside*] Come to see how I'm getting on.

MARY. [*To Kit*] I'm exceedingly glad. She, at least, will discuss this matter in a practical way. [*To Hannah*] Ask her to come in.

KIT. [*To Hannah*] Wait a moment. [*To Mary*] Allow me to withdraw. I don't wish to meet mother here. I'm not anxious to hear a practical discussion of the topic between you. I have some sense of shame in the matter.

MARY. [*Points, R.; he crosses*] You can step into that room, but do not leave until I speak with you again.

KIT. I will wait. [*Aside, going*] Heavens, is there no youth—no love— even in her! [*Exit, R.1.E.*]

MARY. [*To Hannah*] Ask Mrs. Vandusen to enter. [*Hannah exit, C.*] Will Silena ever know the sacrifice I am making for her sake? [*Mrs. Vandusen enters, C.L., shown in by Hannah, who exits, C.L.*]

MRS. V. Have I the honor of addressing Miss Forrest?

MARY. [*Graciously*] Mrs. Vandusen? I am delighted to see you. You are exceedingly welcome. [*They sit*]

MRS. V. You are extremely kind.

MARY. I should find it hard to be otherwise to one who had suffered so much—one who has the misfortune to be left a widow—

MRS. V. [*Rising suddenly*] Widow again!

MARY. [*Slightly amazed, R.*] I beg your pardon, but let us come to the point. I expect Silena Summers today.

MRS. V. [*Smothered excitement*] Do you, indeed.

MARY. I telegraphed for her this morning.

MRS. V. [*C., aside*] This is dreadful. [*Sits*]

MARY. You don't appear to believe that I can effect the arrangement I propose.

MRS. V. [*With burst*] But what arrangement in heaven's name *do* you propose?

MARY. Well, to be practical, I intend to advance the necessary funds to remove all obstacles to her happiness. How much do you require?

MRS. V. [*Controlling her voice with an effort*] My dear young lady, will you first do me the favor to explain by what right you meddle in my affairs?

MARY. Silena is my friend.

MRS. V. [*More forcible*] By what authority do you dare imperil my legal and lawful claims upon Mr. Vandusen?

MARY. Why, don't you understand, I propose to put her in a position to claim him as her own.

MRS. V. [*Rising, excitedly*] And do you think, madam, that because you have come into a fortune, you have the right or the power to take away a woman's husband and the father of her children? Pray, don't forget, my dear young lady, that we have the police [*Mary rises in alarm*], and the laws and the courts to stop any such proceedings. [*Crosses to R.*]

MARY. Do you mean to say that he is married and has children? Christopher married!

MRS. V. Don't you presume to call my husband by his Christian name.

MARY. Your husband? But he's dead, isn't he?

MRS. V. This is too much. [*Shrieks and falls in chair*]

MARY. [*Bewildered*] There must be some mistake.

MRS. V. [*Rising*] There's no mistake. My husband was in love with Silena Summers—he gave her up for reasons that were sufficient and commendable—and this was twenty-five years ago.

MARY. Twenty-five years ago? Why, the Silena I mean is not twenty-five years old. [*Jonah enters, C., with envelope*]

JONAH. Telegram, miss. Just come. [*Hands it to Mary, who opens it; he goes, and aside*] The fellow's proposing by telegraph. Lord, what draft there is in half a million! [*Exit, C.*]

MARY. From Silena herself. Now we shall see. [*Reads*] "Your message is quite a puzzle. I do not know any Christopher. The story I related to you was that of my mother.—Silena." [*Aside*] What have I been doing? How can I explain or apologize. [*To Mrs. Vandusen*] You see, madam, it was an error, and all on my part.

MRS. V. [*Preoccupied with another idea*] Yes—yes—I understand. But what is the name of this daughter—this—[*Points to telegram*]

MARY. Silena Summers.

MRS. V. Why, that was her mother's. How can it be hers! [*Crosses to L.*] *Who* was her father? [*In thrilling tone*]

MARY. I don't know.

MRS. V. She does not bear his name, because—because she has no father.

MARY. But she must—

Mrs. V. No *legal* father. It is shocking. [*Crosses to R.*]

Mary. Who can he be?

Mrs. V. [*Seizing her arm*] I know him. I know him too well—and he shall know I know him. [*Up and downstage*]

Mary. I hope that you will forgive *me,* that in following the promptings of a generous impulse, I have committed this folly. I regret having caused you unnecessary excitement. It will be a good lesson to me. I needed one. [*Crosses to R.*]

Mrs. V. [*Advancing to her*] Don't apologize, my child, you have done me a great service. I am not angry with you. Dark deeds will come to light. My duty now is to sift this mystery to the depths. [*Wrings Mary's hand and going up, C., aside*] Oh, Christopher! Christopher! What have you done? [*Exit, C.L.*]

Mary. [*Solus*] I do believe it's all Tom's fault. Hunting for a son he's found the father—or rather looking for the father he's brought me the son. [*Her face begins to brighten*] But Christopher here—and *not* Silena's lover. I believe it's all for the best. He is free—and seemed to take a great interest in everything relating to me. Gracious me! How much better I feel now that I'm not doing anything benevolent. [*Pushes door open*] Mr. Vandusen, we are alone. [*Comes down. Kit enters nervously, R.D.*]

Kit. I suppose my mother entered into your views very promptly and thoroughly. I heard her talking quite forcibly.

Mary. [*Laughing*] There was a misunderstanding on both sides.

Kit. Yes, I thought so from her tone.

Mary. But never mind, it has made us acquainted—oddly enough—but let's be thankful all the same.

Kit. Then we do not refer to the financial topic again.

Mary. [*Confused*] Spare me. I deserve your ridicule. [*Sits down and indicates sofa to him*] Won't you be seated? I believe there is nothing more to detain you.

Kit. [*Sitting*] I'll go immediately. [*Pause*] Do you mean to send me away now? [*Rises*]

Mary. No—not at all. [*Rises embarrassed*] Unless you wish [*Sits, he sits*] to chat about—

Kit. [*Drawing a little nearer to her*] I should dearly love to chat about—

Mary. You left the school and the village very suddenly.

Kit. [*Quickly*] Before I could manage to procure an introduction to you, I was summoned home to take a position that was offered—

Mary. I left suddenly, too, to take a new position for me—that of an heiress.

KIT. [*Advances, sits next to her*] I congratulate you with all my heart, you are so good.

MARY. How do you know I am so good?

KIT. [*Moves closer*] You remember the first time I saw you, it was in church—after all had gone—you knelt and prayed. I don't believe anyone could be guilty of wearing a mask in such a place.

MARY. [*Coquettishly*] Don't be too sure. I knew you were watching me.

KIT. You knew it—you felt it. [*Embarrassed*] You have no family—no friends?

MARY. I am an orphan. [*Pause, both look at the floor*]

KIT. [*Sighs*] I suppose it is time for me to go.

MARY. If you have business.

KIT. Oh, no! It's after four—the office is closed. Besides, I took a half holiday today, and I'm spending it with you.

MARY. [*Gives him her hand*] I should like you to spend a *whole* holiday now and then with me. [*Mr. Vandusen and Silena appear, C., but seeing Kit and Mary, retreat, C.L.*]

KIT. [*Overjoyed*] All—if you'll let me. [*Knock outside*] Did you hear a knock? [*Rises*]

MARY. [*Rises*] It's strange! Come in! [*Mr. Vandusen and Silena appear at door, C., and look in*]

VAN. I beg your pardon. We found the front door open. Somebody must have gone out in a hurry. We came to see Mr. Versus, the lawyer. [*Recognizes Kit*] Why, my son, you here?

SIL. [*Crosses to R.C., recognizes Mary*] Good gracious! There's Mary Forrest [*Running to her and embrace*], the "Beautiful." You know that's what we always called you. Our last teacher was the "Griffin," and the one before her was the "Cat."

MARY. [*R., embraces her heartily*] Little Silena! I never knew your other name. [*They chat together vivaciously*]

VAN. [*Coming down to Kit*] What are you doing here—with this young lady?

KIT. [*Drawing Vandusen down, L.*] Sh! Don't you remember mother's plans for my settlement in life?

VAN. [*Vigorously*] Which I detest.

KIT. I intend to meet her wishes fully.

VAN. [*Sarcastically*] What a good boy you are. But I won't have any such sacrifice. I'll set this matter right at once. [*Turning to Mary*] My dear young lady. [*She comes down*]

KIT. [*Pulling his coat*] Father, let me explain—

Van. [*Trying to release his coat tails*] My dear young lady—Let me alone. [*To Kit*]

Kit. [*Same business*] But I tell you—

Van. [*Releasing himself*] I do not wish to be told—I understand everything. [*To Mary*] My dear—

Mary. [*Crosses to R.C.*] If you are looking for Mr. Versus, his office is the next room. He has kindly surrendered his library to me.

Van. [*Loftily*] I was in search of that gentleman, but at present my business is with you.

Mary. With me?

Van. And I beg a private interview for a few moments.

Mary. With the greatest pleasure.

Kit. Father, you will certainly do me a very great injury.

Van. No, my boy. I'll prevent you doing yourself an injury.

Mary. [*To Kit*] Will you consent to be banished to that little room again? [*Pointing, R.*]

Kit. [*Crosses to her*] I—

Mary. Are you afraid of what your father has to tell me?

Kit. [*Going to R.*] I am afraid of nothing. [*Aside*] All's lost. [*Exit, R.D.*]

Van. [*Perceiving Silena, who has been watching with interest*] Have you got another room we can put this child into?

Mary. If you like she can take your message to Mr. Versus.

Sil. [*Alarmed*] Oh, I couldn't.

Van. The very thing. We have come to get a little marriage settlement drawn up. She knows all about the names, ages, and other particulars of the delinquents, and can give the lawyer all the points. The delinquents will follow within half an hour to sign.

Sil. [*Solemnly, C.*] Papa, do you really intend to send me to the lawyer?

Van. Certainly—he won't eat you.

Mary. [*Touching bell*] We can call him.

Sil. But, papa, I don't know anything about marriage settlements.

Van. You made the match and you had better see it through. [*Silena crosses to C. and up. Tom enters gaily, L.D., crosses to R.C.*]

Tom. Once more unto the breach, dear friends. [*Stops, seeing Silena, aside*] The pretty sister!

Mary. [*Whispers to Tom*] The May morning?

Tom. [*Same*] You are an angel!

Sil. [*Who has been remonstrating with her father*] Oh! [*Vexed*]

Van. You will have to, and that's an end of it.

Sil. I'll muddle it all up.

VAN. [*Laughingly to Tom*] My daughter seems to have taken an extraordinary aversion to you.

TOM. [*Surprised*] Indeed?

SIL. [*Pulling his sleeve*] Papa!

VAN. Now go, and don't be foolish.

TOM. [*Offering his arm*] I should be terrified and reluctant, my dear Miss Vandusen, for you are exceedingly dangerous to my peace of mind.

SIL. Thank you! [*Exeunt, L.D.*]

MARY. Now we are alone. Mr. Vandusen, will you not be seated?

VAN. [*Loftily, L.*] Thank you! I shall be brief. What I have to say may not be very agreeable, and will be much more appropriately delivered standing.

MARY. [*Surprised*] Indeed, sir. [*Walks away a few steps*]

VAN. Is it possible you do not blush to find yourself in this situation? [*She turns, astounded*] You are young—rich—and, I suppose, respectable. Cannot you wait until your destiny crowns your brow with the diadem of chaste and honorable matrimony? What reason is there for you to anticipate it by a resort to disreputable and speculative means—

MARY. [*Almost speechless*] Sir! This is monstrous! You are out of your senses!

VAN. My son is a good boy, but energy is not his characteristic. He has my disposition—heroic at the bottom; but the heroism only rises at the strongest provocation.

MARY. Well, sir?

VAN. His mother is differently constituted. She has ordered him to provide for himself by a marriage with some wealthy young person. I must do him the justice to say that at first he resisted—because he loved another. But in the end I find him here, ready to immolate himself in obedience to the maternal wishes. If I had not taken this opportunity to interfere, he would have married you and sealed his misery.

MARY. [*Amazed and mastering her emotion, which has been perceptible during the whole of the foregoing*] Let me understand you. You say that your son came here in obedience to his mother's wishes. [*Crosses to L.*]

VAN. To marry you, or rather your money. Ah! The crime of such a union. Those who wed should give heart for heart, not buy and sell them! To convince you let me tell you a story of real life.

MARY. [*Impatient*] I beg you'll spare me that old story about Silena Summers. [*Crosses to R.*]

VAN. [*Dazed*] Eh?

MARY. [*Recrosses to L. during speech, excitedly to herself*] It was detestable to deceive me in that manner. Talking to me about the solemn tones of the organ—and the language of the soul—and all the while loving someone else and thinking of my money. [*Sits L., leans her head on her arms and sobs*]

VAN. [*Aside*] I've been too abrupt. It was cruel. [*Aloud*] Pray, don't grieve so, my dear. I was too severe. I beg your pardon. My only excuse is, I am a father who loves his children.

MARY. [*Rising and looking at him fiercely*] All your children, sir?

VAN. All? Of course, all! I've only got two.

MARY. [*Hysterical bitterness*] Two? Ha, ha, ha,! Two! Two!

VAN. [*Nonplussed*] Ha, ha, ha! [*Leans brow on finger in severe effort to remember if there were more*]

MARY. [*At door, R.*] You are as false as the rest. With regard to your son, however, I will soon set your paternal mind at rest. [*Pushes door open and calls*] Mr. Vandusen! [*Enter Kit*]

KIT. [*Aside*] That tone bodes me no good.

MARY. Take your son. I have nothing more to do with him. [*Up to C.*]

VAN. [*Aside to Kit, C.*] Come, my boy, and remain true to your secret affection.

KIT. [*Excited, aside*] Father, you would not hear my explanations. This is the lady of whom I spoke.

VAN. [*Amazed*] The organ? The church? [*Turns and looks at Mary*]

MARY. [*Suppressing her tears forcibly*] Farewell, sir! We shall never see each other again. [*Exit, C.R.*]

KIT. [*Follows her to door, C.*] Mary! Miss Forrest! All is over. [*Comes down*] And I was so happy! [*Crosses, agitated, by his father, on whom he turns suddenly*] You have done very well. An excellent piece of business. [*Down, L.*]

VAN. [*Soothingly*] It's all for the best.

KIT. [*Indignant, crosses to R.*] All for the best?

VAN. [*Taking his arm*] You may be happy yet.

KIT. [*Softer*] You believe it?

VAN. I'm sure of it. There are dozens of girls every bit as nice.

KIT. [*Disengaging himself, paces to and fro; gets R.*] You are trifling with me.

VAN. [*Soothing and detaining him, with both arms clasped around him*] Very well, very well! You shall have this one. Don't despair. If you're true to her, you're sure of her. Explain and she'll forgive. Come, let's talk it over soberly on our way home. [*Gets Kit's hat and his own*] There is one thing, however, we ought to agree upon. [*Nervously*]

KIT. What is that?

VAN. To not mention what has taken place here to your mother. She always contends that when I undertake to rouse for action, I'm sure to do something foolish. We needn't furnish her with such convincing proof of the correctness of her opinion. [*Exeunt, C.L. Silena, after slight pause, opens door, L., and peeps in*]

SIL. Why, where is papa? This is the room where I left him. I never saw such a lawyer. He doesn't understand the least bit about law. Never asked me the names of aunt and her intended. Was very anxious to know mine. And he was so nervous. Kept continually mistaking my fingers for the pens, and grabbed them—so. If I could find papa. [*Going up. Tom enters, L.D., carrying several sheets of paper and pencil in mouth*]

TOM. Oh! There you are.

SIL. [*Retreating up and getting L.*] I'm looking for papa.

TOM. [*At table*] My notes of the contract are not finished. Will you be kind enough to proceed with your statement. [*Sits at table and spreads papers*]

SIL. I will if you'll call in your clerk. For I won't stay with you alone. Not for anything.

TOM. And why, if you please?

SIL. Because you're so very nervous and make *grabs* for me.

TOM. [*Steps forward*] You are so beautiful that you confuse me.

SIL. [*Starting from him*] If you don't go about your business immediately, I shall leave the room.

TOM. It's all right. I am going about my business. Here's pencil and paper. Sit down. [*Makes room for her on the sofa beside himself*]

SIL. [*Aside, deliberating*] I won't sit opposite him. I tried that, and he looked right through my eyes. If I sit away off, he'll move right up to me. [*Looks round and sees law books in case*] I know what I'll do. [*Goes to case, R., twice, each time gets a pile of law books and piles them in the middle of the sofa*]

TOM. What are you doing with my law books?

SIL. Are they law books? So much the better. The law shall protect me. [*Sits down on the other side of books from him*] Do you see? I am under the protection of the law. Now, go on with your questions.

TOM. [*Bending toward her*] First! Have you ever thought of love?

SIL. [*Rising, decided*] I am *going*.

TOM. [*Changing to business tone*] Why, that's all right. How do you suppose you can instruct me to draw up a marriage contract, unless you know what you're about?

SIL. I *do* know what I'm about.

TOM. And *I* am trying to ascertain the fact.

SIL. [*Sitting timidly*] What do you want to know?

TOM. [*Ardently*] Tell me, I implore you, have you ever loved?

SIL. [*Rising*] Again?

TOM. [*Changing tone, and rapidly*] I merely wished to show what questions are unnecessary. As [a] matter of strict law you are not bound to answer. You understand? I see you do.

SIL. I don't!

TOM. Ah! Well, it's of no consequence. What's the name of the bride? [*Writing*]

SIL. Miss Theodosia Heffron.

TOM. Bridegroom?

SIL. Mr. Nicholas Geagle.

TOM. [*Writing*] The vast and varied experiences of human life furnish no more sublime spectacle than the union of two beings who love each other fervently. [*Silena involuntarily takes one of the law books, opens it, shuts it without reading it, transfers it to her L. hand, with which she places it on her L. side; this she does, alternating with Tom several times. Tom, as if preoccupied, lays his pencil down and leans back; goes through the same operation with the books, alternating with Silena, both very slowly, he laying them aside on his R., and talking all the while as if to himself*]

TOM. His soul yearns for her presence, her heart throbs at his approach.

SIL. [*To herself, looking at him*] What a remarkable document he's getting up.

TOM. [*Same business*] Love is the sunshine of human existence. It warms the heart, beautifies the world, and makes the universe teem with joy. It is the key to the mystic language of the soul, which we must possess in order to fitly communicate with the kindred being destined to share our lot.

SIL. [*Who has listened intently*] How well he expresses himself. I can understand every word.

TOM. How wretched must that creature be who has never learned to love. Alone—uncomprehended, tortured by the dull round of petty cares, ignorant of a blessed recompense—living without knowing the true principle of existence, an uncultured flower, an unsought gem, an unrhymed line in the fragment we call life. Oh, how I should have mourned to have lived without loving—without having found an echo for the voice of my heart. [*Turns to her and in low tone*] Silena! Do you understand me? When you pictured the man you felt you could love, and saw him in your dreams, was he so different from me, Silena?

SIL. [*Jumps up as if from a spell*] The books are gone!

TOM. [*Seizing her hand*] Silena! Answer me.

SIL. [*Wringing her hands*] Oh, that contract, will it never be finished?
[*Mary enters, C.*]

MARY. You here yet, Silena? [*Tom begins to work furiously*]

SIL. [*Running to her*] I was waiting for papa. Please stay with me till he comes.

MARY. Why, you look frightened. [*To Tom*] What does it mean?

TOM. [*Covering his head with papers*] I can't possibly imagine.

SIL. He draws up such strange contracts—it makes me grow hot and cold to listen.

MARY. That's it, is it? A poor child's heart fluttering near one of the traps set by the designing creature called man. Silena, believe nothing they tell you—they lie and deceive—all of them—this one not an hour ago proposed to my half million!

TOM. [*Angrily, rising*] This is too bad of you.

SIL. [*Half pouting*] I am mistaken in him. I never met him before this morning, when he gave me his card, and I took him for a talented, conscientious and accomplished young man who wanted clients, and I intended to make papa give him all his business. I would have done the same for any young lawyer, or baker, or shoemaker. [*Half sobbing*] But I am deceived. I believe he's an old hand. I am sorry I took any interest in him. [*Severely to Tom*] For he's got nothing attractive about him. Not a single recommendation. [*Exit sobbing, C.L.*]

TOM. [*Enraged, to Mary*] That was exceedingly kind of you.

MARY. You are like all your sex, perfectly heartless without apparently being conscious of the fact. From this time forth I shall make it my duty to warn every girl I meet—to tear the mask from their deceivers—to save them. [*Exit, R.D.*]

TOM. [*Calling after her*] They don't want to be saved! [*Comes down*] I must say I feel exceedingly cheap. It's too bad, just as I was beginning to feel that I was sincere—to mean every word I was saying—honestly. I see how it will be. Back to my old resolutions—shun the sex, fly marriage—rail at the fool that yields. Just look at those books. All I've gained is the job of putting them up again. [*Buttons his coat*] I'll take hold of that divorce now, and if I don't have the parties a thousand miles apart in less than a week, I'm a Dutchman! [*Exit, L.D., in passion. Jonah appears, C.*]

JONAH. This way, mum; he brought his papers in here a little while ago. [*Dosie enters, C., elaborate street toilette*]

DOSIE. We want Mr. Versus.

JONAH. [*Looks around*] Why, he isn't here!

DOSIE. We can wait, thank you. [*Goes back to C. and calls off*] Nicholas, darling—this way! Come along!

GEAG. [*Outside*] It's all very well to say come along, but these confounded bundles—

DOSIE. [*To Jonah*] Would you have any objection to assist Mr. Geagle in with his bundles? We've been shopping and he would bring everything himself. Ah! He's all right. [*Comes down*]

JONAH. Yes, ma'am! He's doing famously. [*Geagle enters, C., arms full of bundles, carrying fancy parasol over his head, open*]

GEAG. Where do we go now?

DOSIE. [*R.*] Are you sure you haven't dropped anything?

GEAG. Just count 'em, will you? They kept slipping one after another, as if they were all alive. [*They slide off on floor. Dosie flutters around him counting*] Is the lawyer in?

DOSIE. [*Continuing her count*] Thirteen, fourteen, fifteen. They're all right. What did you say? [*Sweetly*]

GEAG. [*Sulkily*] I asked if the lawyer was in.

DOSIE. Oh! Goodness knows. Sit down, darling—you look tired.

GEAG. Do I? That's remarkable! I *am* tired. [*Sits*] Phew! [*Takes off his hat and polishes his head with his handkerchief*] Do you know it's an awful relief not to have to wear that wig any more? I always felt like a perambulating tarradiddle while I had it on. But when you insisted I should wear it no longer—since I had won you without it—I felt as though I could do anything you asked me in return.

DOSIE. It was a duck to go shopping with its lovey-dovey. What a heavenly day we've had. A girl needs so many things when she's going to get married. I believe I look a perfect fright. Am I too red, dear?

GEAG. [*Back towards her*] I guess not.

DOSIE. Oh, yes I am! [*Takes out pocketglass and powder-puff, looks around at Jonah*] You can tell Mr. Versus we are here.

JONAH. Yes, ma'am! [*Exit, shuffling*]

GEAG. I'm rather glad the lawyer isn't in.

DOSIE. [*Patting his chin*] It was an old goosey, and now you must tell me what you've been worried about all day. Don't deny it. I saw you looking very, very serious several times. It wasn't the lobster salad, darling, was it?

GEAG. [*Gravely*] No-o-o!

DOSIE. Tell its sweetheart. I know it *is* something.

GEAG. Well, the fact is we're going to that ball—

DOSIE. Oh, Geagle! I've got my domino and my mask. We'll have a lovely time.

GEAG. Got your disguise?

DOSIE. Yes! You've got yours?

GEAG. Yes—do you want to see it? [*Takes a false nose from his pocket*] There, do you think anyone will know me with that on?

DOSIE. Is that all you are going to wear? [*He looks at her indignantly and then turns away*] Well, now put it on, and let me see how it looks.

GEAG. No, I can't put it on now—somebody might come in.

DOSIE. Oh, now. I want to see you in it.

GEAG. There! [*Puts nose on*]

DOSIE. You shall dance the first quadrille with me.

GEAG. I don't know the first quadrille. I never danced a quadrille in all my life.

DOSIE. I can teach you in one lesson. We'll try it now. Nobody will see us.

GEAG. Oh, I'm afraid! The lawyer might look in.

DOSIE. Just look at me. [*Lifts skirts to show steps*] One, two, three—one, two, three—one, two, three. [*Dances*]

GEAG. That seems easy enough. [*Hitches up his trousers and tries it*] One, two, three—one, two, three—[*Kicks his corn*] Oh! It's no use, I can't manage anything but a hornpipe, such as I used to see the sailors dance on the stage when I was a boy.

DOSIE. Well, let's try one now.

GEAG. What, you can't dance a hornpipe? [*Dosie nods*] What here?

DOSIE. Yes, nobody will see us.

GEAG. No! I'll stand around with the rest of the boys in a dress suit and look pretty. I'll be a wallflower.

DOSIE. But just a little hornpipe now. [*Geagle, after some persuasion, yields; they dance. Jonah enters at beginning and finally does some steps of his own upstage. After the dance, they drop on sofa exhausted. Jonah has picked up all the books. Tom enters, L.D., at end of dance, L.*]

TOM. Well, sir. What do you want? [*Jonah runs off, L.D.*]

GEAG. [*Crosses to him*] We want to see the lawyer.

TOM. [*Walks around him in amazement*] I'm the lawyer, I suppose.

GEAG. [*Goes to him and whispers in his ear*] We came for the papers.

TOM. [*Getting away from him*] What papers?

GEAG. The contract! The marriage settlement! [*Tom looks him hard in the face, then pulls his false nose down and leaves it sticking on his chin*]

TOM. Are you the culprits that are going to be married?

GEAG. [*With dignity crosses to C.*] Yes, sir. I am one, and this is the bride.

TOM. I draw no more marriage settlements. I make no more creatures wretched—you a gray-headed man—

GEAG. Sir!

TOM. [*Snatching his hat off*] Well, then a no-headed—I mean a bald-headed man—

Dosie. Oh!

Tom. Whose placid countenance has been petrified by the blessings of a bachelor life. You—[*Steps forward. Geagle retreats behind Dosie*] You give into the hands of one of those creatures called woman—[*Crosses to C.*]

Dosie. Who do you call woman?

Tom. The legal power to disturb your holy quietude of life, to distort the serene outlines of your face with anger, fright and fear; to rob you of means— money, friends, freedom—everything. You are standing on the brink of an abyss. Draw back before the fatal plunge. [*Crosses to L.*]

Dosie. He calls me an abyss. Help! Oh! [*Gives a shriek and drops in a heap, supported by Geagle, whose clasp has slipped up to her armpits*]

Geag. [*Indignantly*] Look here—I say—see what you've done. [*To Dosie*] Look up, my darling! Look up. [*Tries to lift her*] This is a nice situation. [*Gives her a sudden jerk*] It's no go. I can't lift her. [*To Dosie, with a shade less tenderness*] Look up! [*To Tom*] Young man, you've got this lady on your conscience. I wish you had her on your back. [*Jerks at Dosie savagely and with vigor*] Look up! [*Gazes over into her face*] I believe she's dead. Look up!

Tom. Dead? No fear of that. She won't die before she's married, nor afterwards.

Geag. Look up! [*Jerks at Dosie*] Look up! Heavens and earth! What shall I do with her? Look up? [*Jonah enters, L.D., and gets around to table, R. Dosie at his next jerk suddenly straightens up with a shriek and Geagle throws her into Tom's arms and falls back exhausted against Jonah. Tom throws Dosie back and Jonah throws Geagle back. Dosie totters to and falls in chair, Geagle same*]

ACT III.

Scene: *Garden, decorated for the masquerade ball. Flags, banners, armorial insignia, exotics in tubs, etc. A centerpiece of plants with rustic seat around it. Music distant; loud when no one on scene speaking. Scene opens with procession of maskers, R. to L. and off. Mr. Vandusen discovered in evening dress, seated C., eating ice cream. When all are off speaks.*

Van. If I were not so apprehensive as to what is coming, I'd enjoy myself exceedingly in this place. It's just twenty-five years since I've been out alone. How jolly it is—only I have an occasional hot and cold change when I remember my mysterious appointment for this evening. I'm trying to keep cool on a third plate of cream. I believe I'll try another. [*Waiter appears, L.*] Ah, waiter! Bring me another cream.

WAIT. [*Surprised, Dutch dialect*] That's three.

VAN. I suppose you have got another?

WAIT. Oh, yes, sir! But it's lucky you're taking yours now. When the rush commences—if every gent orders four plates—

VAN. That's why I get all I can at present. I anticipate the rush.

WAIT. [*Takes dish*] All right, sir! [*Exit L.*]

VAN. [*Looks around uneasily*] What can be the matter? [*Takes billet-doux cautiously from his pocket and reads*] "Dear Christopher:—I must see you once more before I die. I have something of the utmost importance to tell you. If you attach any value to the memories of the past, meet me at the masquerade tonight between eleven and twelve near the supper room. Your *Silena*." [*Puts billet-doux away*] The poor thing must be very much changed. She forgets that we never were so intimate as to write each other as "Dear Christopher" or "Dear Silena." Well, it's twenty-five years ago and that explains. In my thoughts she was always "Dear Silena." [*Looks around*] It's extremely fortunate that my wife refused positively to come. I will take the occasion to talk seriously to Silena and insist on my family's account that she shall not address me in the future. She may think of me as much as she pleases—I have nothing to say against that. I think of her, but somewhat as I think of my youth, as something that I can never return to. [*Waiter enters, L., with cream*]

WAIT. Here you are, sir.

VAN. [*Paying*] And here's your money. [*Waiter about to exit. Tom Versus enters, R.U.E., in evening dress and stops waiter*]

TOM. Two orange ices in box five—

WAIT. Box five, sir? Yes, sir. [*Exit, L.*]

TOM. [*R.*] Ah! Mr. Vandusen. How do you do?

VAN. [*Eating*] Mr. Versus, I believe. You are an extraordinary attorney and counsellor-at-law to refuse to draw up marriage settlements.

TOM. Principle, my dear sir. As far as my experience goes, marriage is a short lane, with a wedding at one end and a divorce at the other. I cannot conscientiously assist people to pay so heavily for such a short excursion. [*Crosses to L.*] By the way, I suppose the happy pair are here this evening?

VAN. Oh, certainly! With my daughter. They are in black dominoes.

TOM. Like everybody else—there are fifty black dominoes here tonight. [*Waiter crosses, L. to R., with ice*] How do you recognize your party?

VAN. By the color of the bouquets in their collars, white and yellow roses. Miss Silena's is white and Miss Heffron's is yellow. [*Laughs and winks*] Got yellow by lying so long on the shelf. [*Waiter enters, R., and crosses to L.; Vandusen speaks to him*] I think I'll take another cream, waiter!

WAIT. What another! All right, sir!

VAN. [*Imitating him*] Yes, another! I feel a flush in the back yet. [*Exit after waiter, L.*]

TOM. Black domino with white roses. I shall find it. I'm a changed man since I met that girl. Can't rest, can't sleep—see her everywhere. Provoking, refusing, denying, delightful May morning. I'll have to give in; have no defense against her charms, can't demur, don't object, and she takes me in execution—body, soul and senses. [*Exit, R.U.E. Geagle without, L.*]

GEAG. I give you my word of honor. [*Enters, L.U.E., followed by Sergeant of Police, an extremely gentlemanly official*] You are utterly mistaken; I did not intend the slightest impropriety, I assure you.

SERG. [*L., looking at him steadily*] Several ladies in masks have complained about it. You go up to them as if you were about to whisper something and then kiss them on the ear.

GEAG. [*Indignantly*] Kiss them on the ear? I assure you, sergeant, I have not nursed the ruthless passion that would lead to violence of that description for a great number of years. My intentions were wholly mistaken. The facts are that the lady I came with forgot her fan and sent me home for it. I'm looking for her, that's all. It's exceedingly hard to pick one black domino out of a thousand. I thought I had her several times, but on attempting to whisper the signal agreed on, "Your Nicholas is here," I found I had caught the wrong pig by the ear.

SERG. It sounds exceedingly flimsy, Nicholas, and I warn you for the last time, that if I hear another complaint your name will be taken and you will be ejected from the building—and don't you forget it. [*Exit, R.1.E.*]

GEAG. [*Wiping his forehead*] This is the first time I ever incurred the censure of the police. But I don't care—somehow I grow desperate. As the happy day approaches I feel miserable. For two days I've been dragged around the city like a—like—a—Well, the only creature who seemed to suffer in a like manner was a poodle—on a string—led by just such another foolish old— [*Checks himself, blows his nose*] Well, a man can't make a supreme ass of himself but once in his lifetime, and I've done it. Haven't been near the club since I was engaged—am worked like a district messenger boy. We hardly got here when I was sent back for a fan she forgot. Walked all the way and I'm used up. [*Sits*] It's a most extraordinary thing that a woman of her age should try to imitate the airs of a kitten. I don't like it—I don't want it. If I wanted a kitten I'd have gone in my back yard and looked on the fence for one. I selected a middle-aged person and she's playing *fifteen* on me. [*Tom strolls in again, R.U.E.*]

TOM. How are you, Mr. Geagle?

GEAG. [*Aside, R.*] Here's that monkey grinning at me again. [*Aloud*] I'm pretty well!

Tom. Your bride is not dead yet, I suppose?

Geag. No, sir! She got over it finely.

Tom. [*Looking off, L.*] I should say so—she's coming this way in uncommon spirits. [*Strolls R. in arbor*]

Geag. [*Aside*] If she comes the kitten over me again, I'll try the *cat*—
and we'll come to the scratch in no time. [*Dosie enters with Silena, L.U.E.,
each masked and with black dominoes. As they enter the Cat and Frog jump
up and frighten them, then strut off arm in arm, L. Dosie wears a bunch of
yellow roses and Silena white. They unmask as soon as they enter. Silena
stays at back and looks L. and R. as if in search of someone*]

Dosie. [*Perceiving Geagle, comes down vexed*] Where have you been
all the time, Nicholas?

Geag. [*Sulkily, L.*] I've been looking for you half an hour.

Dosie. Did you get my fan?

Geag. [*Draws it out of his pocket, done up in brown paper*] Here it is.

Dosie. [*Unrolls it and throws paper away with disgust*] I wish I had
told you to bring my bottle of salts. I declare, I don't know what's coming to
me, I forget so—but you can go for it now.

Geag. [*R.*] Do you mean to say I'm to go back to the house for your
salts again?

Dosie. [*Loftily*] You hesitate?

Geag. [*Pause*] I'm tired to death. You are driving me like a cart horse.
[*Sinks on seat, C.*]

Dosie. [*Instantly beginning to wheedle and patting his cheek*] Excuse its
ducky darling—she's so excited. The happiness of being your wife makes her
forget everything and everybody but you. You drive me into wandering,
you naughty man. [*Geagle evidently begins to relent*] You will go for your
deary—deary—poor little bridy—pidy—and get the botty of salts—won't oo?

Geag. [*Rising*] If you talk like that, I don't mind going anywhere. Where
is it? What's it like? Big bottle?

Dosie. No, little. You'll know it by the smell, darling—sweet.

Geag. [*Going, L.*] I'll know it by the smell—all right. I'll be back as soon
as I can. [*Aside, buttons coat*] On my way back, I'll stop in at the club and
have a little hot spiced Jamaica, I really need something to brace me up.
[*Exit, L.I.E. Tom enters rapidly, having perceived Silena, who puts on her
mask and comes down; he hovers about trying to speak to her*]

Dosie. Where can your father be, Silena?

Sil. [*R.*] I don't know, aunty.

Tom. [*Coming down*] He's in the supper room—I—if you'll allow—

Dosie. [*Measures Tom with a withering look, and moves to L.*] Come,
child. [*As she is about to exit, the Frog, Cat and Clown run on and frighten*

her. Sergeant enters and arrests Clown and Frog. Cat has gone R. He marches Prisoners, crosses to R. Clown escapes, he seizes Cat by the tail and lugs Cat and Frog off R. Clown takes his hat and club and marches off, L.1.E. Dosie off]

TOM. [*Stopping Silena*] Beautiful lady, let me entreat a word with you.

SIL. [*Assuming a false voice and angry tone*] Don't be so familiar with me, sir.

TOM. Familiar? Why, this is a masquerade—everything's fair.

SIL. I forbid you to use such freedom with me.

TOM. Why do you treat me co coolly?

SIL. [*Sits, C.*] The millionaire young lady you proposed to set me the example.

TOM. [*Sits R. of Silena*] You are unjust. Miss Forrest had some excuse. I renounced her half million for your sake. And this is how you appreciate the sacrifice.

SIL. What assurance! There never was such a brazen lawyer before.

TOM. Do you always speak the truth?

SIL. Always.

TOM. Then tell me—didn't you come to this ball solely on my account?

SIL. I never thought of you. [*Hangs her head as he looks at her*]

TOM. You are indeed a miracle of truthfulness. Such a candid—honest— and frank girl is hard to find.

SIL. [*Tormented*] You are unbearable. [*Rises*] I wish you would go.

TOM. So you really want to have nothing to do with me?

SIL. I don't ever want to know you.

TOM. All right. We shall see which sticks to his colors longest. For my part, from this moment, I intend to do all in my power for you. I will go to your father and mother—to your father, then your mother—no—first to your mother and afterwards to your father [*Silena gets impatient*] and ask them for your hand.

SIL. [*Angrily*] Do you call that doing something for me! [*Crosses to R.*] I wish you would leave off jesting.

TOM. You surprise me. Call marriage a jesting matter? But never mind, my programme is laid out. First your brother shall be made happy.

SIL. My brother?

TOM. Yes. I have a little plan that I intend to put in operation immediately. Then you—

SIL. [*Mock seriousness*] Do think of yourself a little.

TOM. I only covet the satisfaction of doing good. [*Laughs*] *Au revoir!* We shall meet—at the altar. [*Exit, R.*]

Sil. His defects are a certain obtrusiveness and persistence; but apart from them I can't deny he is clever and funny—and you can't get angry with him. Just as you begin to, he gets you so interested that you want to know what he's got to say, and then he comes out with more impudence and makes you mad, and then begins to talk again; and so it goes on and on in such a whirl that when he's gone it's quite dull and stupid. Heigh-ho! He manages to have his own way, so that if he insists on marrying me, I think he will. [*The Cat, close behind her, R., meows in her ear. She turns in fright, L., the Frog jumps at her. Clown drives them both off, R. Dosie enters unmasked, L.*]

Dosie. Why didn't you come? I've had an ice. It was so refreshing.

Sil. I wanted to rest here. [*Rises*] You know, aunt, that in spite of our masks, a great many people know us.

Dosie. Why, did you mean to remain unknown? I don't think that's the object of a masquerade, at all.

Sil. But where's the mystification and the fun, then?

Dosie. Do you want to mystify anybody?

Sil. Certainly. And if you'll make an exchange with me, I think I can.

Dosie. What exchange, my dear?

Sil. [*Takes off her roses*] Take my white roses and give me your yellow ones.

Dosie. With the greatest pleasure. [*In affected tone*] The perfume of this yellow rose is rather strong for my poor nerves. [*Exchanges bouquets with Silena*]

Sil. [*Fastening hers on*] Mr. Geagle will know you, anyway.

Dosie. Oh, I don't care for that. I shall enjoy myself flitting from flower to flower. He can have his fun flitting after me.

Sil. He will be very happy when you're married.

Dosie. He? Oh, certainly. But shall I be happy? I begin to fear he's too old for me. [*Sighs, crosses to L.*]

Sil. Somebody is coming. [*Both mask. Tom enters, R., running, crosses to C., stops, looks at both dresses, and then to Dosie, offering arm*]

Tom. I've found your brother, and I've found Mary. He's all right. And I've put my little plan in motion. Let's go and watch them make up. [*Dosie throws an indignant glance at him and goes up, is met by Mephistofeles. She takes his arm and exit, R.U.E.*]

Sil. [*Putting her hand through his arm and holding him tightly while he looks after Dosie, and in assumed voice*] Won't you stay with me? I've no one to talk to.

Tom. [*Aside*] The aunt! Bah! [*Aloud*] You must excuse me. I have something particular to say to your companion.

SIL. Do you know her?

TOM. I am happy to say I do.

SIL. You are in love with her?

TOM. It's natural I should be.

SIL. Why, she is a mere child!

TOM. Old age is no especial recommendation.

SIL. Do you mean that as a fling at me?

TOM. Geagle's looking for you. He'll be jealous. [*Crosses to R.*]

SIL. Never mind, I want to keep you away from my little niece. You'll be turning her head.

TOM. I wish I could.

SIL. Answer me—do you intend to marry her?

TOM. I suppose it'll have to come to that. As I would go through fire and water for your niece, I don't see why I shouldn't go through matrimony for her. [*Runs off, R.1 E.*]

SIL. [*Clapping her hands*] He loves me. [*Suddenly*] But I'll tease him a little. He's very easily spoiled, and must be managed with great care, if I expect to train him for a husband. [*Exit in arbor, L.1 E. Music, and Masquers enter for quadrille and nursery-rhymes, after which, when all are off, Mary Forrest enters, R.U.E., letter in hand, removes mask, looks hurriedly about, replaces mask as Kit Vandusen enters as if following her, with a letter in his hand. He looks at his letter, then at her. She same. She wears a black domino. Duet from Boccaccio*]

> Strange request indeed, and unexpected,
> Yet methinks the author I've detected,
> Something tells my beating heart
> We are not far apart,
> I know we are
> On this—the spot selected.
> If I rudely shun the proffered meeting,
> She'll (He'll) mistake my reasons for retreating;
> When in truth my only fear
> Is that the writer is not here.
> What can it be
> He (She) wants with me?
> Here he (she) adjures me
> To come—and assures me
> Something of weight
> He (She) has to state.
> This puzzles me—what can it be?

'Tis he (she) what delight,
I knew I was right,
I'm in such a fright.
Yes, 'tis he (she),
Oh, yes, it is she (he).
What delight your kindness tonight,
How can I requite.
I'm here as you see,
What can he (she) have to say, etc.

[*After the duet they sit back, C.*]

KIT. [*R.*] First, let me thank you for this opportunity of speaking with you alone.

MARY. I am perfectly willing to hear all you have to say.

KIT. A last interview was indispensable to us, whose friendship began so happily and ended so abruptly.

MARY. I am glad to hear you admit that it's at an end. It saves us much trouble.

KIT. Yes, it's at an end. All we have to do now is to look back. I was weak to yield to my mother's wishes. I sinned against my affections and my convictions. But I have the right to show you that a majority of the world would have approved my act. How many women have married so!

MARY. This is the difference in the cases. Women have often nothing but marriage to depend on. Men have themselves. [*Mask on. Geagle enters, L.U.E., coat collar turned up, pants turned up, rubber overshoes, too large for him, very smiling*]

GEAG. Back again! [*Smacks his lips*] That hot spiced Jamaica really did me good. I took three of 'em. It was freezing cold, and now it's glowing. [*Sees Mary*] There she is. I'll whisper the signal in her ear. [*Manœuvers around behind her. While doing so the Sergeant of Police enters, L., evidently following Geagle, watches him, his hands behind him. Geagle bending down, whispers*] Nicholas is here.

MARY. [*Starting up*] What?

KIT. [*Rising and down C.*] What do you want?

GEAG. [*Alarmed*] It's not Dosie!

KIT. What do you mean, sir? [*He and Mary go to seat, C.*]

GEAG. This is simply devilish. This makes half a dozen mistakes since I came in.

SERG. [*Advancing, R.*] Now I guess I'll stop your little game. [*Geagle turns, horrified*] It won't work any longer. I spotted you myself, and I see what you're up to.

GEAG. [*R.C., after looking at him in a dazed manner, draws the flacon of salts from his pocket, removes stopper and mechanically takes a whiff. It staggers him*] Ach! Ugh! Oh! [*Holds bottle out at arm's length toward Sergeant*]

SERG. [*Looks at bottle*] What's all this? [*Takes a sniff that nearly lifts his head off*] Ugh! Ach! Oh! Cork it! Cork it! [*Geagle corks it at arm's length*] That's a healthy drug to carry concealed on your person. Why it would blow the door off an iron safe. [*Stage, R., draws club*]

GEAG. She said I'd know it by the smell. It's only smelling salts. The lady I'm engaged to forgot 'em, and sent me back.

SERG. [*Collars him*] The old game again. It's T.T., old man, you'll just come with me to the office.

GEAG. [*Frightened*] Are you going to run me in? [*To Kit*] Kit, tell him I'm a respectable person.

SERG. [*To Kit*] Do you know this party?

KIT. [*Advancing*] Yes, he intends to become my uncle.

SERG. Then you must both come with me, if you want to get him out tonight.

GEAG. It's the first time I was ever collared by a policeman. I deserve it. A man of my age to get married. "Needles and pins, needles and pins, when a man marries his trouble begins." Needles and pins! Egad! Handcuffs and jails. [*To Sergeant*] You needn't hold me up by the collarband. [*Sergeant releases*] I'll go anywhere. [*Turns down his collar and pants, and sees rubbers*] These are not my rubbers. I must have changed with somebody by mistake. [*Hands them to Sergeant*] Sergeant, these are not my rubbers, take them to the club, will you? [*The Sergeant threatens*]

KIT. [*To Mary, aside*] Wait for me, I entreat you. I shall be back immediately. Come, uncle. [*Takes his arm and hurries him off, L.U.E., impetuously; Sergeant following rapidly. Music*]

MARY. [*Unmasking*] No. I will not remain. It will end by my yielding against my own convictions. [*Looks round*] This is my opportunity. I can regain the box. [*Exit, R. Dosie enters, R., nervously, unmasked*]

DOSIE. Nicholas does not return, and Mr. Versus pursues me like my shadow. He pours the most ardent proposals into my ear with a passion, an impulse, an eloquence that carry all before them. Oh, Geagle, Geagle, why did you leave your Dosie so long? There is danger, Geagle. [*Sits*] I would like to find out if he knows who I am. It seems as if he did, though I refused to answer his entreaties. [*Sighs*] If I had not accepted Geagle so precipitately. But I'm not married yet. It's not too late. [*Puts on mask. Kit reenters, L.U.E., sees Dosie, mistakes her for Mary*]

KIT. Still here, my darling? [*Sits beside her*] Thanks, a thousand thanks. This is a token that you forgive me. I so accept it. [*Seizes her hand*]

DOSIE. [*Aside*] My nephew. [*Pulls her hand away*]

KIT. Don't rob me of all hope. [*Mr. Vandusen enters, L.1 E. Kit rising.*] Father, join your prayers to mine. You were the innocent cause of my distress, help me to regain this angel.

VAN. [*Sitting on R. of her*] My dear, it is your duty to pardon. My son loves you. Don't throw away an honest heart, or you may fare like my old sister-in-law, who got so ancient and was so afraid of dying an old maid, that she took up at last with a bald-headed bachelor. [*Dosie bounces on seat. Kit and Vandusen each take one of her hands*]

KIT. Oh, speak, dearest.

VAN. Say you forgive.

DOSIE. [*Jumping up and tearing off her mask*] Yes, I'll speak! I'll forgive you! Whom do you take me for?

KIT. [*Rising quickly*] Aunt Dosie! I beg pardon. I thought it was Mary. [*Runs to R.*] Where has she gone? [*Exit, R.2.E.*]

DOSIE. [*Turns to Vandusen, who looks at her puzzled*] Your "old sister-in-law." Thank you. You will please to remember that I am the younger sister of your wife, and that in a few days I shall be a young bride. [*Replaces mask and exit skipping, L.1 E.*]

VAN. [*Solus*] If she could poison me now, she'd do it. These confounded black dominoes look so like one another. [*Rising and looking at watch*] The hour of the rendezvous, twelve o'clock, is past and Silena has not come. She has thought better of it. Concluded to stay at home and go to bed. Sensible woman. I think I'll try a piece of cake. If she's not here by the time I finish it, I'll go home and go to bed, too. [*Exit, L.1.E. Geagle and Sergeant enter, L.U.E.*]

SERG. I hope this warning will do you good. Don't try that manœuver on me again. We have strict orders to stamp out the least impropriety.

GEAG. I'm actually afraid now to stir a step in search of my future bride. The first time I think I've got her there'll be an impropriety, and you'll want to stamp me out.

SERG. You'd better come with me, then. I'll help you to look her up. [*Crosses to R.*]

GEAG. [*Takes his arm*] You're an angel. A blue-coated and brass-buttoned angel. You ought to be superintendent. Honest, now. Haven't you often thought so yourself?

SERG. Well, yes.

GEAG. [*Aside*] I knew it! They all do.

Serg. But, I say, aren't you afraid of your friends seeing you walking with me?

Geag. No. You are much superior to the average of the force. Besides, you haven't got me, I've got you. That makes all the difference. [*Exeunt, R.2.E. Music. Mrs. Vandusen enters in black domino, mask in hand. Looks around cautiously*]

Mrs. V. It's dreadfully warm, and I'm so frightened. Will he keep the appointment I made in the letter? He received it. I know that, for I searched his pockets last night. The serpent, to sleep with that letter and never tell me. So far my suspicions are correct. He is capable of deceiving me. I shall not force his secret. I'll discover who that daughter is. Then let him beware. Someone is coming. [*Masks. Mr. Vandusen enters, L.1.E., in good humor, watch in hand*]

Van. Time's up, and she won't come. Notwithstanding that last cake, I feel as light and happy—

Mrs. V. [*Lays her hand on his shoulder*] Hist!

Van. [*Startled*] Who's that? [*Turns*] Here she is! [*Crosses to R.*]

Mrs. V. [*Assumed voice*] Christopher! Dear Christopher!

Van. [*Aside*] How her voice has changed! [*Aloud*] Madam, permit me to correct you. I am not your "Dear Christopher," and I am willing to believe you are laboring under an hallucination.

Mrs. V. [*Aside*] He seems very cool. [*Aloud*] Oh! How you have changed, Christopher.

Van. Yes, I have grown old, and I hope you have learned how to do so. If not, I pity you from my heart.

Mrs. V. Have you forgotten the past?

Van. By no means. Let us sit down and talk about it. [*They sit, C.*] How have you been all the while?

Mrs. V. Well and ill—as fate used me. Often ill, very ill.

Van. I'm sorry for that.

Mrs. V. And these twenty-five years, in which we have not met, how have they passed with you?

Van. Better than I could have hoped. I did my duty; a reflection that consoled me when I thought once my heart would break.

Mrs. V. But you married?

Van. Yes.

Mrs. V. Have you been happy?

Van. Much more than I deserved.

Mrs. V. Indeed!

Van. Yes, I learned to respect and honor my wife, who was worthy of the most devoted love. Our children were born. I doted on them. I confess that you would have been forgotten, Silena, utterly forgotten, but that sometimes, in spite of myself, the—the—temper of my wife—her habit of command—forced me to recall your patient gentleness. [*Sighs*] Ah, well! No one is perfect.

Mrs. V. [*Aside*] What do I hear!

Van. [*Brightening*] I hope you are not hurt at the frank avowal of my contentment?

Mrs. V. And you could be contented, knowing of the burden you left me to bear?

Van. [*Astonished*] Burden! Our separation was your wish.

Mrs. V. But the consequences.

Van. What consequences?

Mrs. V. You forget our daughter.

Van. [*Jumping up*] Our daughter?

Mrs. V. [*Wringing her hands*] Oh, Christopher! Christopher! [*Buries her head in her hands*]

Van. [*Aside at L., keenly*] This is some impostor, trying to blackmail. [*Aloud*] Give me your arm, Silena.

Mrs. V. [*Rises and puts her arm in his. He draws it through and holds it securely*] Where do you want to take me? Oh, you are squeezing me.

Van. I am afraid of losing you—come. [*Moves, L.*]

Mrs. V. But where to?

Van. To that little office just over there, where you see several police officers. They will be most happy to make your acquaintance, you impostor!

Mrs. V. Impostor!

Van. Yes! You are not Silena Summers—a woman as spotless, as stainless as snow, who joined the purity of womanhood to the talents of a man, and the courage of a hero. No—no, so just come with me.

Mrs. V. [*Struggling*] Oh, sir! Please let me go!

Van. [*Stopping*] I will let you go on one condition. Take off your mask.

Mrs. V. Never!

Van. I intend to know with whom I have the pleasure of conversing, here or at the office.

Mrs. V. [*Threateningly*] Don't pull me, sir, or I will cry fire. Do you want to create a disturbance?

Van. No, I only wish to know who you are.

Mrs. V. [*In frenzy*] Let me go, or I'll do something dreadful!

Van. [*Struggling with her*] You've done all the dreadful you're likely to do for a long time. If someone would come! [*Tom enters, R.*] My dear sir, come here.

Tom. [*R.*] What is it? What! Trying to detain a lady against her will? You are going too far, even for a masquerade.

Mrs. V. [*C.*] Yes, that's what he's doing.

Van. This is no masquerade affair, my friend. [*Laughs*] It's a masked battery I've taken by assault.

Tom. I don't understand.

Van. Will you get me an officer?

Tom. Is it possible!

Van. Or will you do me the favor to hold this person till I get one? The peace of my future life depends on my seeing her face. Hold her till I get back, and I'll do anything you ask.

Tom. Anything I ask?

Van. Yes. You have my word.

Tom. Hand her over.

Van. Take hold—so—so—[*Transfers the imprisoned arm to Tom*] But hold tight, or she'll get away. Now, my interesting domino, we'll invoke the aid of the authorities to investigate you and your "daughter." [*Exit, L.*]

Mrs. V. [*To Tom*] O sir, I pray—I entreat you, let me go before he gets back.

Tom. Didn't you just hear me promise to do nothing of the kind?

Mrs. V. The peace of my future life depends upon it.

Tom. So does his. The peace of one future life is as good as the peace of another future life. So I think that I'd better leave things in *statu quo.*

Mrs. V. I'll scream. I'll faint.

Tom. Faint by all means. We'll see your face, then.

Mrs. V. You are a monster.

Tom. [*Struck*] Your voice sounds very familiar. Have I ever done business for you?

Mrs. V. Oh! You know me very well.

Tom. Do I—what was it—shoplifting—blackmailing—perjury?

Mrs. V. What in heaven's name do you take me for?

Tom. Not guilty, of course. Do you know that I begin to feel quite an interest—

Mrs. V. Give me some proof of it. Release me.

Tom. Show me your face—tell me everything, then, perhaps, I can do something.

Mrs. V. I consent, but in the strictest confidence. [*Unmasks*]

Tom. [*Starts, and aside*] The alleged widow! And engaged in an altercation with her alleged deceased husband.

Mrs. V. Well!

Том. [*Aside*] If I let her go, he'll be furious. If I don't, she'll be furious. Either way I make an enemy. And I want that alleged daughter. [*Aloud*] What was the disturbance about? Perhaps—

Mrs. V. I cannot explain. But if my husband discovers me I am lost. He will never forgive my suspicion and my attempt to impose on him. Let me go and you may rely on my lifelong gratitude. [*Music*]

Том. Madam, I'll venture my happiness on a single word. I love your daughter.

Mrs. V. Let me go—and we'll see.

Том. May I count on your assistance?

Mrs. V. You may—

Том. [*Rapidly, and looking off, C.*] She is coming now. Will you leave me here with her—alone?

Mrs. V. [*Joyfully*] With the greatest pleasure.

Том. You are free.

Mrs. V. [*Masking*] Was ever anything so fortunate? [*Hurries off, R.1.E. Dosie enters, mask in hand, L.*]

Dosie. I cannot find Nicholas. Once I thought I saw him in a secluded corner drinking from a champagne bottle in company with a person in blue clothes; but it must have been fancy. [*Sees Tom and masks*] That young man again.

Том. [*Goes to her, clasps her waist and hand*] My own! [*Brings her down*] Don't avoid me. [*Overcomes her faint struggles*] We must talk together earnestly and seriously, for our union is no longer a matter of doubt if you but consent.

Dosie. Heavens!

Том. [*Leads her to seat, C., sit*] Listen to me.

Dosie. [*Aside*] Oh, Nicholas! Where are you?

Том. You must be mine.

Dosie. No! No!

Том. Don't be frightened. I am not so bad. To offset the few faults we share in common, I have a good nature, good temper, sincerity, devotion, tenderness, a loving heart and a thoroughly good disposition. These are little; but add passion, the adoration I feel for you, and it is no unworthy homage I lay at your feet.

Dosie. [*Aside*] He loves me. I am sure of it.

Том. I have the best reasons for believing your family will not oppose our union. It is for you to whisper—to breathe—to look that *yes* I long for.

Dosie. Oh, spare me!

Том. Your answer, dearest!

Dosie. Impossible.

Tom. You cannot speak. Then give me a token, a sign that you feel for me, that you pity me.

Dosie. [*Gives him her white rose*] Here!

Tom. Emblem of your freshness and innocence!

Dosie. [*Suddenly, throws her arms around him*] Oh!

Tom. My own—forever! [*Clasps her in his arms. Vandusen, Geagle and Sergeant of Police enter, L.U.E.*]

Van. Just look how he has to hold her.

Geag. [*Pretty tight*] That's right, Blackstone, hold her tight. You don't get such a prize every day. What a thoroughly wicked-looking person she is even under that disguise.

Dosie. [*Aside and steps forward*] Geagle here! What will he say? [*Falls back on seat*]

Van. [*Alarmed*] Hold her!

Geag. [*Springs at her*] Would you? [*Turns up his cuffs*]

Tom. [*To Vandusen*] Don't be alarmed. *This* lady will not run away.

Serg. [*L., to Vandusen*] What do you want me to do?

Van. I wish the lady to unmask. I must know who she is, because she has ventured to make an accusation as false as it is insulting.

Dosie. [*Astonished*] I?

Tom. [*To Vandusen*] It was all a joke.

Van. [*Crosses to C.*] I don't take such jokes.

Geag. [*Slaps Vandusen's shoulder*] I approve my friend Vandusen's course. We want the facts.

Van. [*Testily*] Yes—yes—

Geag. [*Irrepressible*] If our friend, Vandusen, has been doing anything, we shall be glad to know it. If the lady—

Van. [*Same, trying to stop him*] I've said all that.

Geag. [*Same*] We want the truth—the whole truth—that is to say, not too much truth—but just enough.

Tom. The lady is known to us all. I beg you to desist from your demand.

Van. [*Firmly*] Let her take off her mask. [*Kit enters, R., and Silena, mask in hand, appears, L., and listens*]

Tom. She shall not take it off. This lady is my affianced wife.

Sil. [*Aside*] His affianced? Good heavens!

Van. A subterfuge to shield her. You are not going to marry a person of that description?

Geag. I don't know, he might.

Tom. Well, then, I declare solemnly in the presence of these witnesses [*Pointing to Geagle and Kit*] that I intend to marry this lady. And I ask you to treat her with becoming respect.

GEAG. Show us her face and we'll show her respect.

TOM. You shall all see it. But I must beg you to dispense with the presence of this gentleman [*Indicates Sergeant*], as I don't perceive the necessity of announcing my engagement to the police department.

VAN. I am satisfied. [*To Sergeant*] You see I have gained my point without the need of troubling you.

SERG. [*L.*] So much the better. [*Bows to Dosie and exit, L.U.E.*]

TOM. [*Leads Dosie to Vandusen*] Show this gentleman your face. [*Aside to her*] Fear nothing! [*Dosie takes off her mask, so as to show only Vandusen her face, then replaces it*]

VAN. [*Nearly speechless*] Good gracious! And you say you propose to marry this lady?

TOM. I do, sir. And if you have any objections to make, I would remind you—

VAN. Not the slightest. [*Grasping Tom's hand*] I congratulate you. [*Shakes hands and goes up, L.*]

TOM. Thank you. [*To Dosie*] Now show the witnesses, my darling. [*Dosie, same business with Kit, R.*]

KIT. [*Astonished*] What? Impossible! [*Goes up to Silena*]

TOM. No, sir! Quite possible!

DOSIE. [*Same business with Geagle, L.*] Forgive me! [*Aside to him*] I can't marry you—I love him. You are free. [*Remasks*]

GEAG. [*Thunderstruck*] It can't be! [*Growing joyful, and to Tom*] You don't mean it? Let me embrace you. [*Dosie half turns to him*] No, no! Not you. You, Blackstone, you—my benefactor. [*Throws himself on Tom, who turns and flings him against Kit, who turns and throws him sitting on stairs, R.*]

TOM. I do not exactly comprehend your raptures, sir. But I accept your felicitations. [*Takes Dosie by the hand*]

SIL. [*Approaching, indignantly*] Accept mine also.

TOM. [*Staring at her, open-mouthed*] Wha—what—

SIL. [*Tears yellow roses off and flings them at his feet*] Base! False! Heartless! I hate—I despise you. [*Crosses to Vandusen, L.*]

TOM. Silena! [*Turns to Dosie*] What have I got here? [*Dosie tears off her mask*]

TOM. [*With a cry*] Ah!

DOSIE. Thine forever! [*Throws herself on Tom. He struggles free, totters, and falls in Geagle's arms*]

GEAG. [*With a shout of joy*] Look up!

ACT IV.

SCENE: *Same as Act I. The morning after the ball. Music. Mr. Vandusen discovered walking up and down.*

VAN. My wife, who stayed at home last night, has got a headache this morning. Her sister, who went to the ball, is as fresh as a daisy. That's very odd. As for myself, I'm all at sea. Mr. Thomas Versus, attorney-at-law, has played me false, that's certain. Dosie was not the female I gave into his custody. I've questioned her adroitly and she's perfectly innocent. All she thinks about is that young scamp. Now, what on earth possessed him— with an aged mother at home—to steal Geagle's bride. He must be mad. There is one bright spot in the whole dark picture, though. Nicholas is happy. Ah! He's had a narrow escape. [*Front doorbell*] Callers so early? [*Caroline enters, R.I.E., crosses to exit C., sees Vandusen, stops, and familiarly*]

CAROL. Lor', sir! Is that you?

VAN. [*Surprised*] Yes, Caroline.

CAROL. Did you have a nice time at the ball, sir?

VAN. I cannot complain.

CAROL. I guess they bothered you some, them ladies in masks. They always goes for an old gentleman as looks as if he was green.

VAN. Indeed!

CAROL. [*R.*] Did you have any mysterious adventures?

VAN. [*Stopping her as she is about to cross*] What do you know about mysterious adventures?

CAROL. [*Confused, crosses to L.*] Oh, I know what they do at masquerades. [*Aside*] I almost let out on missus.

VAN. Just explain a little more definitely what you mean.

CAROL. [*Going*] Someone at the door, sir. I must be going. [*Aside, going*] I'll keep out of his way the rest of the day. [*Exit, C., on a run*]

VAN. What did she say about mysterious adventures? Can she be an accomplice of the unknown criminal? [*Caroline reenters, C.L.*]

CAROL. Please walk in, miss. [*Mary Forrest enters, C.L.*] I'll see if Mrs. Vandusen can receive you. She's got a dreadful headache. [*To Vandusen*] Young lady to see missus. [*Rapidly, and going, R.*]

VAN. Caroline—

CAROL. [*Going*] Yes, sir—directly! [*Aside*] Not if I knows it. [*Exit, R.*]

VAN. [*Taking out his glasses*] Pray, be seated, madam.

MARY. [*Sits, L.*] Thank you.

VAN. [*Looks at her*] Why, bless my heart, Miss Forrest! [*Goes to her and insists on shaking hands with her*] It does me good to see you. I was going to call on you this very day. Now, say that you forgive me, that you forgive my son, and that you are going to marry him, like an angel. [*She is about to speak*] Now don't say a word if it isn't yes. But of course it's yes. You came to tell him—of course. That's why you are here. Why didn't I think of that?

MARY. If you thought a little more, Mr. Vandusen, you might remember that the girl has gone for your wife. I came to see her.

VAN. She's in bed with a headache. Let me send for Kit; he'll do every bit as well.

MARY. [*Rising*] In that case I can leave this letter for Mrs. Vandusen. Will you be kind enough to give it to her?

VAN. [*Takes unsealed letter and turns it over*] A letter. What's it about?

MARY. [*Smiles*] No doubt Mrs. Vandusen will tell you. It refers to a subject we discussed when she called on me.

VAN. Called on you?

MARY. A short time ago.

VAN. What for?

MARY. About Silena Summers. [*Crosses to R.*]

VAN. [*Slowly dropping in chair and looking at her*] I beg you'll sit down and discuss it with me for a few moments. I'm exceedingly interested in the topic.

MARY. [*Smiling, sits*] As much so as your wife?

VAN. [*Preoccupied*] As much so as my wife. There is a faint glimmering of light on the mystery of last night. [*To Mary*] Did she talk about Silena's—

MARY. Silena's mother? Yes.

VAN. No! Silena's daughter.

MARY. Silena is the daughter.

VAN. [*Puzzled*] Then who is the mother?

MARY. Oh, we know *that* well enough. The only question was who was her father.

VAN. Ah!

MARY. You see there were two—

VAN. Two fathers.

MARY. No, mothers. Silena, the daughter, and Silena, the mother. Both named Summers. That, of course, was mysterious.

VAN. Of course, Silena's daughter ought to be Silena something else.

MARY. This gave Mrs. Vandusen a most uncomfortable idea. She began to fancy she knew the mysterious parent and that her own happiness was at stake.

VAN. [*Smiles*] It begins to dawn.

MARY. Her suspicions were so hurtful to Silena and her mother—and you—that I took the liberty of writing to my friend on the subject.

VAN. Very proper.

MARY. There is her answer.

VAN. From Silena?

MARY. The daughter.

VAN. [*Rising, reads*] "Your question was very natural. My real name is Silena Howard. Poor papa was stricken down in health and in fortune at the same moment, and when I saw myself forced to teach in order to support us all, it was at mother's suggestion I adopted her maiden name to spare papa, who is as proud as he is helpless, all the pain we could. That is my little romance."

MARY. You see?

VAN. [*Folds letter, crosses to R.*] So, Silena married? That spoils my little romance. I wasn't constant to her image, exactly. But I—liked to fancy she was constant to mine.

MARY. [*L.*] The selfishness of the sex.

VAN. Ah! We're a bad lot, Miss Forrest—all of us.

MARY. Not even excepting your son.

VAN. [*Warmly*] Now let me explain. He—

MARY. Give the letter to your wife as soon as possible. I'm quite sure it will cure her headache.

VAN. So am I. [*Mysteriously*] You don't know the extremities to which her jealousy led her. It's broad daylight now. The mysterious mask—the blackmailer! Who would have believed a woman of her years would have played such a prank. [*Changes his tone*] Poor thing! How she must have suffered, though. [*Seizing Mary's hands*] This news will make her happy. [*Pleading*] Oh! If you'd only make Kit happy.

MARY. [*Disengaging*] This is happiness enough for one day.

VAN. I will call on you tomorrow with my wife. We will—

MARY. I leave the city today. [*Crosses to R.*]

VAN. We'll call this afternoon. Where are you going?

MARY. I have not settled.

VAN. Give me some message for Kit. What shall I say to him?

MARY. [*Moved*] Tell him—that I said—good-bye! [*Hurries off, C.*]

VAN. Obstinate little thing. The whole race of young people of today are like little pigs, with kinks in their heads as well as in their tails. [*Looks at letter and smiles*] O Georgiana! Georgiana! Was it you? Have I got you? Won't I be revenged! Won't I! We have been married twenty-five years, and today I am for the first time master of the situation. [*Rubs his hands and crosses. Caroline looks in, R., and, seeing him, darts across to C. to go out. She carries a bundle. Vandusen, calling sternly]* Here, girl!

CAROL. [*Turning at C.*] Sir!

VAN. Humph! What have you got in that bundle?

CAROL. This, sir? This—this is the Vienna bread the baker has just left for breakfast.

VAN. By the way—what is your name?

CAROL. [*Flippantly*] My name? My name is Caroline.

VAN. [*Solemnly*] Well, then, Caroline, I want you to tell me the truth—as master of this house. Did anything extraordinary happen last night?

CAROL. [*Comes down*] Last night? No, sir. Nothing at all.

VAN. When did my wife go to bed?

CAROL. Eleven o'clock, sir.

VAN. Was she sick then?

CAROL. Yes, sir. She had a headache.

VAN. Is that the truth?

CAROL. I never tells nothing but the truth.

VAN. Humph! And what have you in that bundle?

CAROL. This—this, sir—this is the Vienna bread that the baker—

VAN. Humph! Yes. That will do.

CAROL. [*Flippantly*] Can I go? [*Crosses to C.*]

VAN. Yes! When your month is up.

CAROL. What do you mean, sir?

VAN. That you leave in a month. I don't tolerate untruthful persons in my family.

CAROL. [*Excited, in loud tone*] Sir! [*Drops bundle, domino rolls out*] Oh, sir! Please, sir!

VAN. Behave yourself! I have finished. In a month you go.

CAROL. I'll tell Mrs. Vandusen this very minute. [*Crosses to R.*]

VAN. You may if you wish.

CAROL. This minute. I'll tell her everything. [*Going R.*]

VAN. Hurry up, then! Hurry! Here! You'd better pick up your Vienna bread. [*She picks up domino, and exit, R. door*] My wife will be astonished! Well, it will do her good. [*Geagle enters, exceedingly gay in dress and manner, boisterously rushing to Vandusen and grasping his hand*]

GEAG. Ah! Old boy, how are you? [*R.*]

VAN. [*Surprised*] Geagle, is that you?

GEAG. No! It's not I. It's somebody else. It's a transmogrification. Slept last night for the first time in twelve months. Woke up this morning twenty years younger. Look at me.

VAN. New clothes?

GEAG. My wedding suit. Wear 'em today because it's the happiest day of my life.

VAN. My dear fellow, you ought to wear weeds. A jilted bridegroom—

GEAG. I find it my natural element. Life has been a mystery to me for years. My eyes are opened. Nature smiles. Why? I have passed through great grief to great joy. I shall never be able to repay that young man! Never! [*Crosses to L.*]

VAN. The lawyer?

GEAG. He has saved me. He is an exceedingly promising young fellow, isn't he?

VAN. I'm afraid he has promised too much, this time.

GEAG. He got me out of *my* promise.

VAN. You had better go and thank him.

GEAG. Oh! I shall, warmly! I want as a particular favor to stand up with him, only I'm afraid when I hear her give herself to somebody else for good, I'll swoon with joy. But I've sent him a token of my regard already.

VAN. Indeed!

GEAG. A cartload of tokens, in fact. He, he, he! All the things I bought for *her*. I don't want 'em. He may have 'em. Good idea, eh?

VAN. Excellent! I say, Nicholas. [*Takes his arm*] What do you think will be the upshot of it all?

GEAG. Oh! He'll go on.

VAN. No, no! He'll back out, somehow.

GEAG. I don't think so. They say he's wild with delight. Runs about singing and dancing. House upset—things upset. Says he wants to get married as soon as possible. [*Crosses to R.*]

VAN. It's incredible!

GEAG. It is! But it's providential—for me. I've had my lesson. I'm done. I intend to find a nice young couple with a family, and adopt them.

VAN. That's an idea. Sensible and generous. Have you got a family in view?

GEAG. Well, I've got the pieces—they're like a Chinese puzzle. I must get them together, and then I'll be all right. I'm after one of the pieces, now.

VAN. Which one?

GEAG. The young man. Where's Kit?

VAN. What do you want with Kit?

GEAG. To adopt him. I intend to make him a proposition: Business is business. I've got sixty thousand dollars. They shall be yours. You are to marry somebody you love, and let me bring up the children.

VAN. Wonderful!

GEAG. [*R.*] Feasible, eh?

VAN. Feasible and plausible. I've got the other piece of the puzzle.

GEAG. The girl?

VAN. If you can put them together, you are the benefactor of two young hearts.

GEAG. I'll do it. When a man starts out to benefact his fellow creatures, he frequently fails in the attempt, but when he starts out to benefit himself, it's wonderful how he succeeds. This is *my* happiness at stake. [*Buttons up his coat*] I am going to do good to Geagle—and I guess I'll do it. [*Exit, C.*]

VAN. He may manage. He's so happy, he'll infect everyone. Nobody can stand such determined efforts to make them do what they want to. [*Strikes his forehead*] But he don't know who she is, and I forgot to tell him. Of course he'll be back as soon as he remembers that he don't know. [*Caroline enters, R., impudently*]

CAROL. Missus was very much surprised when I told her what you said. She's getting up now. And she'll be right down to interview you.

VAN. Don't forget—when your month is up.

CAROL. I don't care for what you say. [*Crosses to L.*] I'll go, if Mrs. Vandusen says so, and she says I'm to stay. [*Exit, C.*]

VAN. That's the extent of authority I've exercised for twenty-five years. The country demands a change. [*Silena enters, L. door, her forehead tied up with handkerchief, groaning and leaning against wall. Bringing her down*] Why, my darling!

SIL. [*Piteous tone*]   Good morning, pa.

VAN. Are you ill?

SIL. I feel miserable. I didn't sleep all night, and my head is so dizzy, and my heart so heavy. [*She speaks very feebly, her hand often wandering to her head*]

VAN. You've got the blues!

SIL. Perhaps. But that isn't what I came for.

VAN. What do you want, my love?

SIL. You must go to Mr. Versus, right away.

VAN. To Mr. Versus?

SIL. [*Nestling to him*]   Certainly—I'd go if I could, but I'm not able. The poor fellow is in a fearful state of embarrassment, on account of getting hold of the wrong one, last night. [*Hand to head*]

VAN. What wrong one?

SIL. He knew I was wearing a white rose in my black domino. So, to fool him, I changed flowers with aunt, and that's the way he came to get hold of her.

VAN. So he intended to get hold of you?

SIL. Certainly—he's in love with me.

VAN. Very good, upon my word—a nice piece of news! Suppose your aunt won't let him off?

SIL. Oh, she must! [*Crosses to R.*]

VAN. Yes, yes! But suppose he's in love with her.

SIL. Don't talk nonsense, papa.

VAN. But I hear he's making preparations for his wedding.

SIL. [*Insisting*] With me!

VAN. [*Positively*] No! With her.

SIL. You don't know anything, papa. Oh, how my head aches! [*Throws herself on sofa, L.*]

VAN. I know that you played him a very bad trick—made him look very foolish, besides leading him into what may prove a trap; and if he don't get even, somehow, he's not—[*Caroline at C.*]

CAROL. Mr. Versus wants to see you, sir. [*Exit, C.*]

VAN. [*To Silena*] I'll have him up now. Be reserved in your manner until we ascertain whether he wants you or your aunt. [*She sits down, L.*]

SIL. Oh, dear! [*Tom Versus enters, C.L., and down, R.*]

TOM. Ah! Good morning, brother-in-law. How do you do this morning? [*Vandusen, speechless, turns a glance of commiseration on Silena. Tom crosses to C., looks at Silena and approaches her*] Ah! Did our little niece sleep well after the ball? [*Silena bursts into tears and turns her back to him. Tom, after looking at her, turns to Vandusen and in declamatory tone*] And she—the goddess of my dreams—has she risen from her slumbers?

VAN. [*Looks at him open-mouthed, aside*] He's a fool. [*Aloud to Tom*] If you mean my sister-in-law—she's been up this two hours.

TOM. Oh, lead me to her.

VAN. You want to see her?

TOM. I grudge every second that separates me from my love. [*Silena cries loudly*]

VAN. [*Pats him on shoulder*] Don't you cry, sonny. I'll have her here right away for you. [*Goes L. and aside*] He's having his revenge. [*Exit, L.D. Silena looks after her father, then goes to C. seat and sits, back to Tom*]

TOM. [*Leaning against mantel, looks at her a moment*] Well, Cupid!

SIL. Whom do you call Cupid, sir?

TOM. What are you doing with that band over your eyes?

SIL. [*Tearing it off*] I've got a headache.

TOM. [*To himself aloud*] Oh, that she were here!

SIL. [*Goes to him*] You must not quite take me for a fool, Mr. Versus.

TOM. [*Astonished*] What do you mean?

SIL. A person can be in love and not act as silly as you do.

TOM. As I do?

SIL. Yes—and I tell you—you don't love Aunt Dosie one bit.

TOM. Not love my bride?

SIL. Ugh! She's your bride because you thought she was somebody else.

TOM. You astonish me.

SIL. [*L.*] I know everything. I'm sure I ought to if anybody does, for I got up the foolish trick to change the roses. [*Beginning to cry*] And I never would in this world if I'd known what would happen. Oh! Mr. Versus! Oh! Tom! What *are* we going to do about it?

TOM. So you arranged the plan by which I gained Miss Dosie. Accept my warmest thanks. [*Crosses to R.*]

SIL. [*In a rage*] You are a detestable man—but one thing I vow: no matter who asks me, never, never, to go to a masked ball again! [*Goes up L., crying. Mr. Vandusen enters, R., leading Dosie by the hand*]

TOM. [*Opens his arms à la Claude Melnotte*] My love! My sun! My star! My Dosie. [*Dosie, with a shriek, rushes to his embrace, and is folded in his arms. Tableau*] My own!

VAN. [*Stepping up and tapping Tom on shoulder*] I guess I'd better go, as I'm only in the way. If you want me I'll be in there. [*Points to R., and exit, C. door*]

SIL. [*Comes in front of them and savagely*] And I guess I'd better go, since Aunt Dosie doesn't know any better than to go on with such actions before a child. If anybody wants *me*, I'm in here. [*Exit, R.D.*]

DOSIE. How they envy me! [*About to throw her arms around his neck, he catches both*]

TOM. Now let's sit down and talk sensibly.

DOSIE. [*A little taken aback*] Yes! [*Tom pushes sofa forward; they sit*]

TOM. [*R.*] Now listen to me.

DOSIE. Speak! Do with me as you please. Mould me to your will.

TOM. First we'll get married.

DOSIE. Yes!

TOM. Then we leave the city.

DOSIE. For a wedding tour?

TOM. No, for good. I've disposed of everything belonging to me.

DOSIE. What for?

TOM. Above all, because the world will talk. This is no place for us. You were the betrothed of Geagle. Now you are mine.

DOSIE. I don't care what people say. [*Rises*]

TOM. I will defend you with my life, for I love you. [*She is about to embrace him, he catches her hands and prevents her*] I am jealous of that love. My angel, let them utter one breath of slander and they die. [*Crosses to L.*] Do you want me to fill the city with tombstones?

Dosie. [*Crosses to R., aside*] How he loves me. [*Aloud*] Be it as you will, we will go hand in hand.

Tom. [*L.*] To the end of the world—literally—for I have chosen my destination. We sail Saturday. I write for passports today. Give me your figures.

Dosie. [*R.*] My figures?

Tom. Your dates—born so and so—

Dosie. [*Rising*] Nonsense!

Tom. [*Rising*] Nonsense?

Dosie. I'll look in the book—it's down, of course. I don't know who put it, and I doubt if they knew.

Tom. [*With ardor*] Send it to me—and I'll send thee—

Dosie. [*Same*] What, darling?

Tom. [*Changing tone*] A few necessary articles for our journey. [*Changing back*] You'll not refuse them?

Dosie. I cannot!

Tom. [*Changing*] With full instructions. [*Changing*] For we must wander far, my love. [*Changing*] And you must know what's before you. [*Changing*] And now farewell, my sweet. [*Draws her to him*] One kiss— [*Pushes her slowly back*] No—no—it is too much. I must not take advantage of your youth and weakness. [*Sighs and rushes off, C.R. Meets Vandusen at door, takes his arm and hurries him off, C.R.*]

Dosie. How he controls himself. What character, what firmness—and he loves me to delirium. [*Sinks in chair*] What could have possessed him to go where we have to get passports? It's ridiculous to ask it [*Rising*], and I promised him to send the book. [*Goes to desk, unlocks it and takes out small 12mo volume, thick, and in old binding, opens it carefully*] There it is. I never saw such ink for getting blacker and blacker every year. [*Looks around, whispers*] There's a fatality about it. First of June, eighteen hundred and thirty—[*Shuts book suddenly and gasps, looks around, reopens it and looks again*] Eighteen hundred and thirty. I could make that three a five, but the whole date is written out in letters, too. [*Angrily*] But I won't have such a thing in existence. I won't. [*Sees inkstand in desk, suddenly seizes it and pours it on page*] Now it's all gone—accidentally, of course. [*Calling*] Caroline! Caroline! Come here, I've spilled the ink! Bring something to wipe it up! Caroline! Quick! [*Caroline enters, C., Mr. Vandusen, R., Silena, L.*]

Together { Carol. What is it, ma'am?
           Van. Who cried out?
           Sil. [*Looks over her shoulder*] Oh, aunt! What is it?

Dosie. Look what I've done. Spilled the ink bottle all over the book.

CAROL. [*On her L.*] Is it fresh? Oh, we'll soon have that all right! [*Seizes the book and darts out, C., holding it at arm's length*]

SIL. How came you to have it open at the family register, aunty?

DOSIE. I had just opened the book.

SIL. [*Mischievously*] And the ink bottle flew over and blotted out all the dates, your birth among the rest.

VAN. Very curious coincidence.

DOSIE. What do you wish to insinuate, brother-in-law?

VAN. That you were the accomplice of the ink bottle.

DOSIE. [*Crosses to L.*] Wait until I have a strong arm to defend me.

CAROL. [*Brings back page clean*] Here you are, miss, clean as a whistle. The bleaching powder does it while the ink's fresh. You can read it like print now. Born the first of June, eighteen hundred and thirty—

DOSIE. [*Tearing book from her*] Girl! Go about your business. [*Exit, R. door, Caroline gets L. corner, pretending to cry. Vandusen laughs*]

SIL. [*Wringing her hands*] Eighteen hundred and thirty—that's old enough to be his mother. [*Exit, R.*]

CAROL. [*Weeping*] I did all for the best.

VAN. [*Kindly*] You did very well—I am very pleased. You can remain when your month is up.

CAROL. [*Softened and low, after looking at him*] Thank you, sir. [*Exit, C., with her apron to her eyes*]

VAN. [*Goes to table*] A great waste of ink, but enough left to write a note to Kit's sweetheart. That idiot, Geagle, won't find her. [*Writes*] "My dear Miss Forrest. I am sorry to say that I cannot deliver your farewell message to my son for the reason that—" [*Continues to write a line more and addresses the envelope, after he is interrupted by Geagle, outside, shouting, C.L.*]

GEAG. In yet—I'll find him. [*He bounces in, in a great heat, looks around, sees Vandusen, rushes to him, drags him out of his chair, and stands on tiptoe to whisper in his ear*]

VAN. [*Having heard him*] My very thought. Look here. [*Hands letter. Geagle opens it, reads, cries aloud for joy*]

GEAG. What! Glorious!

VAN. It'll do.

GEAG. I'll bring her—whoop! [*Seizes Vandusen and both waltz around to a lively air which they shout. Mrs. Vandusen appears, R.1.E., and stops astonished. Geagle releases Vandusen, seizes his hat and rushes out, C.L., with letter. Vandusen leans against sofa, laughing quietly*]

MRS. V. [*A little faltering, but trying to assume her former command*] You are exceedingly gay, Mr. Vandusen!

VAN. [*Quite self-possessed. Fanning himself*] Oh, no—glad to see you up, my dear.

MRS. V. Caroline has a very curious story to tell me.

VAN. It's nothing to the story she told me. I discharged her for it on the spot. I cannot tolerate lying.

MRS. V. [*Amazed*] Mr. Vandusen!

VAN. Lying, my dear. She tried to deceive me about your absence last evening. She said you had not been out of the house.

MRS. V. [*Frightened and half inarticulate*] I was—I w—was—

VAN. Of course you were out, and the unprincipled creature thought I knew nothing about it. Had the audacity, in fact, to suppose that you kept any secrets from me. It was an insult to me and a worse one to you. I acted on the impulse I felt as your husband and the father of your children, and I dismissed her.

MRS. V. [*Stammering*] Perhaps she thought—

VAN. [*Interrupting*] She thought you went to the masquerade to watch me—to play a part and to surprise the unworthy secret *I* was supposed to cherish.

MRS. V. [*Going to him with clasped hands*] Christopher!

VAN. [*Still going on*] She didn't know that I would have been the first to reveal everything to my wife, as well as the last to deceive her. She did not know that I carried [*Taking Mary's letter out*] a proof that I longed for an opportunity to show you. [*Gives her the letter, which she opens and reads, crosses to R.*]

MRS. V. [*Having read*] What must you think of *me?*

VAN. So, of course, I had to punish her promptly and severely. But she has since given unmistakable proof that she is sorry for her fault, and if you ask me to forgive her, I shall do it gladly. For we will have but one thought and one will.

MRS. V. [*Overpowered*] I have done wrong, and you are heaping coals of fire on my head. Pardon me, my dear husband! [*Puts her arms round his neck*]

VAN. Do you forgive her, too? [*Caroline enters, C.*]

CAROL. If you please—[*Stops. Mrs. Vandusen about to withdraw from Vandusen's arms, he detains her*]

VAN. [*To Mrs. Vandusen*] Stay a moment, I want her to see there is no quarrel—no scandal—in this house. [*Releases her*] There, she has seen enough. [*To Caroline*] What is it?

CAROL. If you please, sir, here's a big box come for Miss Dosie from Mr. Versus.

VAN. Bring it in, and then go and tell the lady.

CAROL.   This way! My sakes, it's a whopper! [*Two Porters enter with big chest*]

PORT.   See here, how much further have we got to take this?

CAROL.   Put it right down there.

PORT.   This is extry. Ain't included in the express charges.

CAROL.   Oh, ain't it? Well, you'd better go and get yer extry outer them as sent yer. [*Shows Porters off, C., and exit, R.1.E.*]

MRS. V.   A box from Mr. Versus—for Dosie. Why, I thought that he and Silena—

VAN.   Never mind; let him do as he likes—he knows what he's about. [*Dosie enters, R.*]

DOSIE.   Where is it? [*Sees Mrs. Vandusen, runs and kisses her*] Oh, sister, you don't know how happy I am!

MRS. V. [*Coldly*]   I don't know anything at all, it seems. What has become of Mr. Geagle?

DOSIE. [*Unfastening chest*]   Mr. Geagle is too sensible, at his time of life, to take a young wife.

MRS. V.   I should have thought *you* were too sensible, at your time of life, to let a young man make a fool of you.

DOSIE.   We'll see who's made a fool of. [*Opens chest*] Why it's full of all sorts of things. [*Takes out a box*] What's this—a revolver? [*Takes it out*]

VAN.   A very sensible present.

DOSIE.   For a bride?

VAN.   For a bride who has to shoot tigers in self-defense.

DOSIE.   Shoot tigers—where?

VAN.   Where you are going.

DOSIE. [*Takes a bottle and read label*]   Poison!

VAN.   Poison. To take in order to escape a more painful death.

DOSIE.   I wish you would explain and not joke. Do you know anything about all this?

VAN.   I know everything about it.

DOSIE. [*Draws out hammock*]   A hammock! [*Spreads it out*]

VAN.   Your bed.

DOSIE.   And this?

VAN.   Your blanket. You won't need any warmer bedclothes. [*Dosie draws out a pair of Turkish trousers, holds them up and shrieks*] Your travelling suit. You are especially desired to begin wearing them immediately to get used to the sensation.

DOSIE.   What is the meaning of all this nonsense?

VAN.   My dear sister-in-law, you are going to Africa on an exploring expedition to extend the discoveries of Stanley. Mr. Versus not only intends to explore the vicinity of Ubjibbeloola, but to settle among the natives and convert them. He will probably be made king. You, of course, will be queen.

Dosie. [*Irritated*] It's a very poor joke.

Van. It would be if it were a joke. But his plans, although spiced with the adventurous, are exceedingly practical. You will conform to the customs of the country. As queen, you will be at the head of an extensive harem, or seraglio. You will find thirty-five female dresses of all sizes in the bottom of the chest.

Dosie. [*Slapping the things back into the trunk*] I begin to think you have taken leave of your senses.

Van. [*Sighs*] Poor Versus has taken leave of his—his love has turned his brain.

Dosie. [*Decisively*] Where is he?

Van. In my room writing farewell letters to a few friends.

Dosie. [*Goes to door, L., and pushes it open, calls*] Mr. Versus, will you step here a moment? [*Tom enters, L., an Indian crown of feathers on his head and a few in his hand*]

Tom. My goddess calls me.

Dosie. Just drop all those fancy names, and tell me plainly what all this means. [*Points to chest*]

Tom. Only a few necessary articles to begin with. By Jove! I forgot, we shall require some canned tomatoes and some preserved peaches, and we want a bowstring and a sack. [*Hurries to L.*] I must order them at once.

Dosie. Stop. [*He turns*] You need not have taken these absurd means of letting me know that our union is distasteful.

Tom. My angel—

Dosie. Do you expect me to believe all this stuff about Ubjibbeloola, or whatever it is?

Tom. You said you'd follow me to the end of the earth, and I'm only going to the middle of it.

Dosie. I said as many foolish things as you did. I ought to have known that your making love to me was meant for someone else. I know it now. But you need not have resorted to such very strong measures to undeceive me. If you had said it was a mistake, I'd have said well and good, we'll say no more about it. But you acted like—well, no matter. You are free. You are free. [*Bursts into tears and exit, R.*]

Van. I knew she had sense, and it's coming out at last.

Tom. [*Takes off his crown, looks at it, and pitches it away*] She ought to have boxed my ears.

GEAG. [*Outside*] Run, I hear him. This way. [*Mary Forrest enters, followed by Geagle, who winks at everybody in delight. Points to Vandusen*] There he is!

MARY. [*In great agitation*] For heaven's sake, tell me what has happened?

MRS. V. Happened, child? Happened to whom?

MARY. To your son. Where is he?

MRS. V. My son?

MARY. Don't you know? Hasn't Mr. Vandusen told you yet?

MRS. V. [*Frightened, crosses to Vandusen*] What has become of Kit? I have not seen him today.

MARY. [*Gives her letter*] Look! Your husband's message to me. [*Geagle enters at C. with Kit, restraining him*]

MRS. V. [*Reads*] "My dear Miss Forrest: I am sorry to say that I cannot deliver your farewell message to my son, for the reason that I have a son no longer. Yours, C. Vandusen." [*To Vandusen*] What does it mean? You have a son no longer!

VAN. No, because Geagle has adopted him. [*Geagle releases Kit, rushes down and dances a jig on box*] Hurrah!

KIT. [*Rushes to Mary. She is so overcome that her head sinks on his shoulder, and he has to put his arm around her waist*] You cannot deny it. You do love me. I may speak now. [*Draws her to L.*]

MARY. I'm so glad you are not dead. [*They go up*]

TOM. I suppose I'd better go.

GEAG. No, you don't. [*Runs to R., and calls*] Silena. [*Comes down*] She made a match for me on this very spot, and I mean to give her tit for tat. [*Crosses to R.*]

SIL. [*Outside, R.1.E.*] Papa!

GEAG. [*Goes to R.*] There she is. [*Silena appears, led by Dosie, who is radiant. Geagle retreats in alarm to L. corner. Silena goes over to Tom*]

DOSIE. Let me present Mr. Versus with the bride he really wanted.

TOM. [*C.*] Is it possible? [*Takes Silena in his arms*]

SIL. You won't go to Africa now.

TOM. [*Holding her*] No. It's quite warm enough here.

DOSIE. [*R.1.E., peeps across roguishly to Geagle. He glances timidly. She smiles. He is alarmed*] Ahem!

GEAG. [*Aside*] I don't like that. She can't mean to go for me again.

DOSIE. Are you very much blighted, Mr. Geagle?

GEAG. Frostbitten to the core.

DOSIE. [*Beckons to him*] He, he! [*Geagle shakes his head. She whispers*] I want to speak to you.

GEAG. Say it right out.

Dosie. [*Advancing a few steps*] Come over. [*He advances a step, then stops*] I won't hurt you.

Geag. Honor bright?

Dosie. [*Coming to C., Geagle also. Confidentially*] We've been a couple of geese.

Geag. Yes!

Dosie. But we've come to our senses at last.

Geag. [*Doubtfully*] You are sure about yourself?

Dosie. For a time I felt as if I were a girl again. Heigh-ho! It had all the freshness of May and the balminess of June.

Geag. I know. It was our Indian summer—a sort of warm spell late in the fall.

Dosie. Poetic thought! Ah! [*Sighs and casts loving eyes at him*]

Geag. Ah!

Sil. [*Mischievously interrupting*] Needles and pins! [*Dosie and Geagle retreat to their respective corners. Silena laughs. All laugh*] I didn't mean to frighten—only to warn you.

Tom. Oh, hang it, darling! Remember, I'm just about to get married. Don't sing that old song.

Van. No. Give us something a little more cheerful.

Mrs. V. Let Mr. Geagle express his feelings.

Mary. And Miss Dosie.

Dosie. Not before everybody.

Geag. Oh, yes! I don't mind. [*Steps forward*]

Sil. Something poetical!

Mrs. V. Practical!

Van. Historical!

Mary. Æsthetical!

Kit. Musical!

Tom. Autobiographical!

Geag.   Hey diddle, diddle, the cat and the fiddle—
          We wanted a late honeymoon!
          But the merry dogs laughed to see such sport,
          And the Miss ran away with the Spoon!
                    [*Indicates Silena and Tom*]

CURTAIN

AMERICA'S LOST PLAYS

I. *Forbidden Fruit & Other Plays,* by DION BOUCICAULT. Forbidden Fruit. Louis XI. Dot. Flying Scud. Mercy Dodd. Robert Emmet. Edited by ALLARDYCE NICOLL and F. THEODORE CLOAK.

II. *False Shame and Thirty Years,* by WILLIAM DUNLAP. False Shame; or, The American Orphan in Germany. Thirty Years; or, The Gambler's Fate. Edited by ORAL SUMNER COAD.

III. *Glaucus & Other Plays,* by GEORGE HENRY BOKER. The World a Mask. The Bankrupt. Glaucus. Edited with introduction and notes by SCULLEY BRADLEY.

IV. *Davy Crockett & Other Plays.* Rosedale; or, The Rifle Ball, by LESTER WALLACK. Across the Continent; or, Scenes from New York Life and the Pacific Railroad, by JAMES J. McCLOSKEY. Davy Crockett; or, Be Sure You're Right, Then Go Ahead, by FRANK MURDOCH. Sam'l of Posen; or, The Commercial Drummer, by GEORGE H. JESSOP. Our Boarding House, by LEONARD GROVER. Edited by ISAAC GOLDBERG and HUBERT HEFFNER.

V. *Trial Without Jury & Other Plays,* by JOHN HOWARD PAYNE. Trial Without Jury; or, The Magpie and the Maid. Mount Savage. The Boarding Schools; or, Life Among the Little Folks. The Two Sons-in-Law. Mazeppa; or, The Wild Horse of Tartary. The Spanish Husband; or, First and Last Love. Edited by CODMAN HISLOP and W. R. RICHARDSON.

VI. *The Last Duel in Spain & Other Plays,* by JOHN HOWARD PAYNE. The Last Duel in Spain. Woman's Revenge. The Italian Bride. Romulus, the Shepherd King. The Black Man; or, The Spleen. Edited by CODMAN HISLOP and W. R. RICHARDSON.

VII. *The Early Plays of James A. Herne.* Within an Inch of His Life. "The Minute Men" of 1774-1775. Drifting Apart. The Reverend Griffith Davenport, Act IV. Edited with an introduction by ARTHUR HOBSON QUINN.

VIII. *The Great Diamond Robbery & Other Recent Melodramas.* A Royal Slave, by CLARENCE BENNETT. The Great Diamond Robbery, by EDWARD M. ALFRIEND and A. C. WHEELER. From Rags to Riches, by CHARLES A. TAYLOR. No Mother to Guide Her, by LILLIAN MORTIMER. Billy the Kid, by WALTER WOODS. Edited by GARRETT H. LEVERTON.

IX. *Five Plays* by CHARLES H. HOYT. A Bunch of Keys. A Midnight Bell. A Trip to Chinatown. A Temperance Town. A Milk White Flag. Edited by DOUGLAS L. HUNT.

X. *The Banker's Daughter & Other Plays,* by BRONSON HOWARD. Hurricanes. Old Love Letters. The Banker's Daughter. Baron Rudolph. Knave and Queen. One of Our Girls. Edited by ALLAN G. HALLINE.

XI. *An Arrant Knave & Other Plays,* by STEELE MACKAYE. Rose Michel. Won At Last. In Spite of All. An Arrant Knave. Edited, with introduction, by his son PERCY MACKAYE.

XII. *The Cowled Lover & Other Plays,* by ROBERT MONTGOMERY BIRD. The Cowled Lover. Caridorf; or, The Avenger. News of the Night; or, A Trip to Niagara. 'Twas All for the Best; or, 'Tis All a Notion. Edited by EDWARD H. O'NEILL.

XIII. *The Sentinels & Other Plays,* by RICHARD PENN SMITH. The Sentinels; or, The Two Sergeants. The Bombardment of Algiers. William Penn (Incomplete). Shakspeare in Love. A Wife at a Venture. The Last Man; or, The Cock of the Village. Edited by RALPH H. WARE and H. W. SCHOENBERGER.

XIV. *Metamora & Other Plays.* Metamora; or, The Last of the Wampanoags, by JOHN AUGUSTUS STONE. Tancred, King of Sicily; or, The Archives of Palermo (Fragment), by JOHN AUGUSTUS STONE. The Spy, a Tale of the Neutral Ground, by CHARLES POWELL CLINCH. The Battle of Stillwater; or, The Maniac, by H. J. CONWAY (?). The Usurper; or, Americans in Tripoli, by JOSEPH STEVENS JONES. The Crock of Gold; or, The Toiler's Trials, by SILAS S. STEELE. Job and His Children, by J. M. FIELD. Signor Marc, by JOHN H. WILKINS. The Duke's Motto; or, I Am Here! by JOHN BROUGHAM. Edited by EUGENE R. PAGE.

XV. *Four Plays* by ROYALL TYLER. The Island of Barrataria. The Origin of the Feast of Purim; or, The Destinies of Haman & Mordecai. Joseph and His Brethren. The Judgement of Solomon. Edited by ARTHUR WALLACE PEACH and GEORGE FLOYD NEWBROUGH.

XVI. *Monte Cristo & Other Plays.* Monte Cristo (JAMES O'NEILL's version), by CHARLES FECHTER. Hippolytus, by JULIA WARD HOWE. Mistress Nell, by GEORGE C. HAZELTON. Becky Sharp, by LANGDON MITCHELL. The Warrens of Virginia, by WILLIAM C. DE MILLE. Edited by J. B. RUSSAK.

XVII. *The Plays of Henry C. De Mille,* written in collaboration with DAVID BELASCO. The Main Line, by HENRY C. DE MILLE and CHARLES BARNARD. The Wife, by DAVID BELASCO and HENRY C. DE MILLE. Lord Chumley, by HENRY C. DE MILLE and DAVID BELASCO. The Charity Ball, by DAVID BELASCO and HENRY C. DE MILLE. Men and Women, by HENRY C. DE MILLE and DAVID BELASCO. Edited with an introductory essay by ROBERT HAMILTON BALL.

XVIII. *The Heart of Maryland & Other Plays,* by DAVID BELASCO. La Belle Russe. The Stranglers of Paris. The Girl I Left Behind Me, by DAVID BELASCO and FRANKLIN FYLES. The Heart of Maryland. Naughty Anthony. Edited with an introduction and notes by GLENN HUGHES and GEORGE SAVAGE.

XIX. *The White Slave & Other Plays*, by BARTLEY CAMPBELL. The Virginian. My Partner. The Galley Slave. Fairfax. The White Slave. Edited by NAPIER WILT.

XX. *Man and Wife & Other Plays*, by AUGUSTIN DALY. Man and Wife. Divorce. The Big Bonanza. Pique. Needles and Pins. Edited with Introductory Notes and a Play List by CATHERINE STURTEVANT.